PRINCIPLES OF BUSINESS AND MANAGEMENT

Second Edition

David Spurling, James Gachihi, Simon Cruickshank & John Spurling

First Published 2006 by arima publishing

www.arimapublishing.com

ISBN 978-1-84549-624-1

Printed and bound in the United Kingdom

Typeset in Palatino Linotype

Abramis is an imprint of arima publishing.

arima publishing
ASK House Northgate Avenue
Bury St Edmunds, Suffolk IP32 6BB
T: (+44) 01284 700321
www.arimapublishing.com

This book will be helpful for people studying for A-Level business studies or for business courses at universities for example the University of London international degree examinations. It will also be helpful to people working in business.

Learning Through Cooperation Ltd can provide distance learning using this book to cover such business courses. Details can be found on their website: www.learningthroughcooperation.com

ABOUT THE AUTHORS

David Spurling BSc, PGCE, DGA, FCILT:
He is a founder of 'Learning Through Cooperation Ltd' and its subsidiary 'LTC Kenya'.

He was Senior Lecturer in Transport Economics at City of Birmingham Polytechnic now (University of Central England). At Centre for Business Studies, he was head of a department of Transport and Shipping with about 250 students.

He was the statistics examiner for 3 exams for the intermediate level of the then Chartered Institute of Transport. He has been an assistant examiner with Edexcel for Labour Economics. He has been an examiner for the Association of Business Managers and Administrators (ABMA).

He has had textbooks on economics, accounts, business and transport published by major publishers. He has also had a joke book published. He was a councillor in both Southend on Sea and Swale Borough council. He was a parliamentary candidate in Meriden.

James Gachihi MSc CPA: James is the Business Development Manager of Learning Through Cooperation. He has authored books in accounting and statistics and has vast business experience ranging from human resource management, financial analysis, business planning and management. He is also a fellow of the Royal Statistical Society in London.

Simon Cruickshank MSc With Distinction (University of Kent): He obtained a first class honours degree in Management Science and Business Administration at the University of Kent and later became an Assistant Accountant at the University.

John Spurling BSc (Hons), DipTP, PGDip (Law), PGDip (CMI), MRTPI, MCMI:
John Spurling is a successful Town Planning Manager with over 15 years experience working at various local authorities in a variety of roles. He has recently been a prominent figure in defending a local authority in a public examination.

He is currently working as part of a project group that is responsible in helping set out career pathways for planners.

He is also a mentor; helping colleagues throughout the authority develop their skills.

He enjoys studying and his latest qualification is a Post Graduate Diploma in Strategic Management and Leadership.

In his spare time he enjoys cycling, walking and spending time with his family.

ACKNOWLEDGEMENTS

We would like to thank the following individuals for their contributions to the preparation of this book:

- Manjit Benning and Margaret Gichuki for their editing skills.

- Tammy Maines and Tatiana Perez-Campillo for their tireless typing.

- Anna Berrisford and Jonathan Fronteras for the editing, updating and proof reading of this new edition.

- Anthea Spurling for her moral support in this endeavour.

We would also like to acknowledge the following organisations for allowing us to refer to their operations for our examples:

Triodos Bank
BMW Group
Honda Motors
Traidcraft – additional thanks to Peter Collins.
Good Energy – particular thanks to Hugo House.
Ethical Property
UNCTAD

Many thanks to all the people not mentioned here but who offered their help and support in the completion of this book.

PREFACE

We have included case studies such as the Traidcraft one below, since it is important for anyone studying business studies to apply ideas to real life problems. In particular they can be applied to two of the key issues facing the world, those of poverty and the environment. The Stern report, in November 2006, highlighted the importance of the environment and stated that without action being taken, future economic growth would be jeopardised.

David Spurling, one of the authors, believes that Organisations such as Traidcraft can help solve such dilemmas. For this reason, he has formed Learning Through Cooperation Ltd and LTC Kenya whose aims include providing educational provision for everyone at a reasonable price. He would welcome any constructive suggestions about this book and how to achieve these aims.

This article was written by Mr Peter Collins and first appeared in PSI Magazine on 2005.

Traidcraft – fighting poverty through trade

Twenty-five years ago, in the heart of urban Tyneside, a pioneering mail-order business was launched with a hand-drawn catalogue featuring a small selection of jute products from Bangladesh.

Today, the Traidcraft trading company has a turnover of around £15 million, carries hundreds of fair trade food, beverage, craft and textile products from tens of thousands of producers in almost 30 developing countries, and lists most of Britain's leading supermarkets among its customers.

At the same time, its associated charity, Traidcraft Exchange, has won prestigious contracts from the British Government, the Community Fund and the EU, enjoys an international reputation for delivering practical help to small businesses across the developing world, and was recently voted one of the most innovative charities in the UK.

With awards for its development work and social accounting, as well as its mail order business, Traidcraft is working in many areas to fulfil its mission statement – fighting poverty through trade.

It has three primary weapons in that fight: its own trading activity, the developmental assistance it offers, and, increasingly, its advocacy work both in the UK and the EU.

"Helping small business to be more successful may be a long way from what many people think of as "aid" but it is sustainable development at its best," says Paul Chandler, Traidcraft's chief executive.

It is also in the long-term interest of British business, he argues. "Sustained development leads to economic growth and stable government. That's an environment in which responsible business can operate and which attracts inward investment."

At the heart of Traidcraft's activity is a firm – even passionate – belief that justice in trade requires a commitment to partnership that goes beyond the merely commercial.

Inevitably, given the nature of the small businesses with which it works and the principles informing its mission, that sort of approach can involve levels of intimacy, transparency and mutual understanding uncommon in more conventional partnership agreements.

"The partnership we make of trade, support and influence is helping people find their own solutions to their poverty," says Paul Chandler.

"For Traidcraft, partnership is about relationship. It's about experiencing the ups and downs together, about learning from one another, growing and changing together, encouraging and picking each other up, valuing one another's contribution. Crucially, it's about equity not exploitation."

And the real impact of Traidcraft's work is best seen through the lives of the producers and their communities who are benefiting from its inputs.

"Many have social programmes associated with their business and their relationship with their communities is far more positive than many UK businesses with theirs," says Paul Chandler.

"We hear regularly of their community developments …a herd of goats, a piped water supply to the village, schools, health centres… all made possible by our fair trade purchases and the other assistance we've been able to offer."

Traidcraft's trading provides an important route to the UK export market for producers in Africa, Asia and Latin America. But there is a limit to the number of producers the trading company can work with – and that's where the charity plays a vital role in helping producers develop beyond the fair trade market.

Paul Chandler explains: "Sometimes producers just can't find ways to access markets. So, in addition to our own trading activity, Traidcraft Exchange has been involved in setting up trading companies in country, and facilitating trade links between poor producers and international buyers, like UK supermarkets and High Street businesses.

"Producers often lack the knowledge or skills to access markets. We build the capacity of local organisations to offer the practical support that they need through, for example, the provision of market information, product development assistance, or training in quality assurance. And to do this, we also draw upon the experience and expertise of the trading company.

"And even when they have knowledge and skill, sometimes producers face other barriers to trade, not least the complex and demanding rules and regulations that govern world trade, or high import tariffs or import quotas.

"We try to understand the barriers that poor producers face in the countries where we work and build the capacity of local organisations to speak for the poor and to lobby and advocate for change on their behalf. And we talk to governments and big business in the developed world about the need for change and how it can be achieved.

"Trade, support and influence: these are the three emphases which both our trading company and our charity share. They are reflected in the activity of our thousands of supporters who buy our goods, donate to the charity and campaign with us to change the way the world trades.

"And it's working. We're making a difference to the lives of thousands of people in the South, we're making a difference to the way business operates in the North, and we're making a difference to the way people exercise their spending power when they shop.

"As an example of practical, effective partnership, it's hard to beat," adds Paul Chandler.

To find out more about Traidcraft and its work go to www.traidcraft.co.uk

Q1. Why might it appeal to consumers to buy items on a fair trade basis? What might this say about consumer behaviour? Does it prove that the concept of the rational consumer is wrong?

Q2. What are the advantage and disadvantages of starting a business in such a small ways?

Q3. What are the barriers mentioned in the article that poor producers face? Have they changed since the article was written?

CONTENTS

Chapter 1: BUSINESS AND MANAGEMENT

1.1: Introduction

The relationship between business and management is clear insofar as one is the result of the other and vice versa. Business is the occupation of a human being; the activity that occupies his or her time. Nowadays, the meaning of the word *business* has been narrowed to economic occupation, one that is deemed to produce some commercial benefit. We are aware of businesses around us; these businesses provide both a source of employment where we can earn a wage or salary and produce the goods and services that we need to survive. Businesses have therefore taken the centre stage in our lives and lifestyles.

Businesses have become so important in our everyday lives that political systems and even social structures are heavily influenced or even controlled by businesses. Karl Marx, the famous social scientist first documented the importance of businesses in society through his theories of 'economic determinism'. Marx proposed that society was built around the prevalent economic conditions and the class system was maintained through the unequal distribution of productive resources. Today the importance of economic development is indisputable the world over. Businesses are manifestly the most important tools of acquiring, developing and maintaining the productive means on which societal and political systems are set.

In this book, we will begin by defining the principles of business and management in their application today. We will go on to show the relationship between business and management and describe key concepts that make the two inseparable. In further chapters, we will explore these key concepts in detail beginning with setting up a business. By the end of the book, we hope that the reader will firmly appreciate and understand the cardinal role that businesses play in everyday life.

1.2: Definitions of Business

In our context, a business refers to a commercial entity whose purpose is to generate wealth. A business can be defined as the allocation of productive resources to the creation of wealth. It is the combination of different productive resources to create more value than can be assigned to the productive resources prior to the business activity. This can sound like a highly technical definition yet it is not. Individuals who go into business aim to produce more than they input in terms of capital, labour, land, technology or even entrepreneurial know how. This applies to businesses the world over, be they a successful international motorcar manufacturing company or the small and humble grocery shop located at the corner of your street. The grocer situated at the corner of the street uses his or her money to buy groceries, which they then transport to sell in their shop. Sometimes the groceries have to be pre-washed and the bulk-purchase broken down to create smaller packages that we can buy. The grocer aims to earn more than he or she spent in purchasing the groceries. Therefore, if the grocer spends £200 on buying in groceries then he or she would hope to earn a further £80 through onward sale to customers in their shop. The same principle applies for large multinational car-makers such as Toyota. By using skill, a lot of capital, land, labour and entrepreneurial savvy they are able to produce cars that will make a profit.

Profit is the difference between the cost of a product or service and the revenue gained from sales in a business activity. This brings us to an important point; a business may be formed for the purpose of making a profit; the profit in turn may be saved for future investment or immediately reinvested to create more wealth. Therefore, one of the reasons why businesses are formed is to produce wealth. However, defining businesses as entities that are simply geared toward generating wealth would leave out a significant amount of human occupation. There are other entities that are not profit orientated in nature, yet they use up productive resources. They must therefore serve a business purpose as they take up productive resources and time. As an example, voluntary and charitable organisations as well as government departments confer a benefit different from profit.

Business therefore does not just refer to organisations created for the sole purpose of turning a profit, but also to organisations that create value and benefit to humanity. A broader, more inclusive definition would therefore be that business refers to all activity that confers benefits to human beings. We can further define benefit as increased wealth, better living conditions, alleviation of poverty, better medicine, freedom from oppressive rule, lowering of carbon dioxide emissions, maintenance of law and order in a society. All these activities can be referred to as business since their successful completion is dependent on the use of productive resources. Another undeniable fact about businesses is the clear organisation and predetermination in the activities that use productive resources. The outcome is often anticipated and the benefits of using the resources in that manner are foreseeable. This means that the waste of productive resources in unclear pursuits is not business. A lot of thought and planning goes into successful businesses, as we shall see later in this book. We can therefore define business as:

'Any human occupation that uses productive resources in an organised and predetermined manner to confer benefit to humankind.'

	Exercise
	Look around your locality; how many local, national and international businesses can you identify? Make a list of these businesses and the benefits they confer to humankind in that area, nationally or internationally.

1.3: Definitions of Management

Management is a word that connotes people who are high ranking in an organisation and who make decisions on the direction of the business. In lay parlance management is the ability to keep things on an even keel, or the ability to cope. What relevance do these definitions have to the management of businesses? To answer this question we need to understand what we mean by management.

Management involves the activity of managing the ongoing prudent direction and allocation of productive resources. Through management, we expect to make the most appropriate decisions in allocating resources. This is important as productive resources are scarce and therefore need to be applied to the most productive activity. This obviously does not happen most of the time. The difference between successful and unsuccessful businesses is in the management. This is a moot point; other factors can affect the success of a business, but the most important of these is management. For example, a business based on coal mining may be unsuccessful if an alternative and more efficient fuel is discovered. However, many companies have survived changes in the industry through well thought out management plans. One very successful strategy in management is leading the change and development. A television set (TV) manufacturer may find that black and white TVs are no longer in demand, and therefore switch to producing colour TVs. He or she then finds that coloured cathode-ray tube TVs are going out of fashion, in the face of increased demand for a higher-quality picture and the move to digital TVs, and therefore invests in producing plasma screen or Liquid Crystal Display (LCD) TVs. Further digital technology development has lead to the demand for High Definition (HD) televisions. Management therefore seems to be the most important function in business.

So what is management? Management can be defined as:

'The process of planning, organising, staffing, directing, and controlling business organisations'

This means that management is actually five distinctive processes that are used to prudently allocate scarce resources. Later in this book, we will discuss each of these functions individually. Briefly, we can define each of the terms:

1. **Planning** is the process of anticipating the future and making provisions for anticipated events. It is the development of a conscious course of action in the event of anticipated occurrences. For example, if we planned to buy a house in the next six months, we would develop a logical series of actions that would enable us to buy the house in the time we have anticipated. We would make an appointment with a mortgage advisor at our local bank, contact estate agents or housing agencies, and view as many properties as possible. Without a plan, we would not know what action would follow the other and we most likely would waste resources.

2. **Organising** is ordering (arranging) productive resources. We need to create a system or framework within which we will allocate productive resources. One key element of organising is creating an efficient and appropriate system through which the allocation of productive resources can be achieved. To run a business, for example, we would need to appoint managers who will be accountable for the resources that we allocate the business. We may also hire staff members, premises, transportation and so on.

3. **Staffing,** which is sometimes thought of as part of organising, is recruiting, training, developing, and retaining the best possible human resources and skills to meet the needs of a business. Staffing involves the arrangement of human resources to meet the goals of the business.

4. **Directing** is the process of leading, motivating and communicating within the business organisation. Human beings are the most important productive resources in a business, unlike other resources such as land or capital. The productivity of human beings depends on these three functions of directing. Human beings need to be inspired through leadership and motivation. Successful business empires are usually built around extraordinary individuals who inspire other people to produce more than they would normally do. Proper communication also ensures that businesses do not waste resources through misunderstanding.

5. **Controlling** is the process of ensuring that the business organisation operates along the plan devised. This function ensures that negative outcomes are minimised and the positive ones are enhanced. Without this process, business entities might find that they have wasted many productive resources and have attained no tangible outcome or are heading in a direction that they had not intended.

1.4: Business Management

So far, we have seen that management is the process of planning, organising, staffing, directing and controlling business organisations. We have also seen that businesses are human occupations that use productive resources in an organised and predetermined manner to confer benefit to humankind. Therefore, business management is the prudent allocation of scarce resources in occupations that have been predetermined to confer benefit to human beings. This definition need not be daunting, if you observe businesses around you and if you think of what they do on a daily basis then you will appreciate this definition. The following are two examples:

BMW: as a leading car manufacturer, BMW produces high quality cars that are fast, safe and comfortable (confer benefits), by employing highly skilled engineers, in a factory in the town of Bavaria in Germany, using high quality material and spending millions of Euros (allocation of productive resources). BMW announced in 2012 a first-quarter profit of 2.13 billion Euros[1] (profit objective). BMW also has a corporate strategy; this statement summarises its plans. The strategy can be seen in the plans and ideas that they are implementing. The strategies are managed and organised by the management team.

'With the three brands, BMW, MINI and Rolls-Royce Motor Cars, the BMW Group has its sights set *firmly on the premium sector of the international automobile market. To achieve its aims, the company knows how to* deploy its strengths with an efficiency *that is unmatched in the automotive industry. From research and development to sales and marketing, BMW Group is committed to the very highest in quality for all its products and services. The company's phenomenal success is proof of this strategy's correctness.'*

BMW has clearly decided the market niche, which they want to dominate in and the popularity of the three brands is evidence that they are succeeding in this pursuit. A business without an aim or vision wastes its resources. BMW has the aim as well as the ability to 'deploy its strengths with an efficiency that is unmatched in the automotive industry'. Proper management is therefore key to the success of this business.

---

[1] http://www.bmwgroup.com/e/0_0_www_bmwgroup_com/investor_relations/corporate_news/news/2012/news_q1_2012.html

The Department for Business, Innovation and Skills (BIS), United Kingdom (UK) government: *The Department for Business, Innovation & Skills is the department for economic growth. The department invests in skills and education to promote trade, boost innovation and help people to start and grow a business. BIS also protects consumers and reduces the impact of regulation.*[2]

	Exercise
	Using this information about the Department for Business, Innovation and Skills, discuss the various facets of management that are evident within the BIS, the productive resources that they may employ in reaching their stated aims and the measurements they may employ in ensuring that these objectives are met.

Self-examination Questions:

1. Define, with examples, the terms 'Business' and 'Management'.

2. 'Management is the vital organ of a business; poor management inevitably leads to failure.' Discuss with examples.

3. Large multinational corporations and businesses control most aspects of human life and should be disbanded. Discuss this statement using examples.

4. Some management scientists believe that good management arises when businesses are competent; others argue that businesses, as we know them today, are a result of improved management. Giving examples argue each case.

5. Discuss what would happen if one of the five processes of management failed. Pick any one of the five at a time and discuss its role to the overall management function.

---

[2] https://www.gov.uk/government/organisations/department-for-business-innovation-skills/about

Chapter 2: TYPES OF BUSINESS OWNERSHIP

2.1: Private Sector Organisations

2.1.1: The Sole Trader

Many people decide to become self-employed rather than joining an existing organisation. In some cases, such as farming, there may be relatively little choice. Self-employment may be perceived by many as a chance for independent decision making as well as freedom of implementing ones ideas in the way that they would wish to implement them. The sole trader is the most basic form of self-employment. A sole trader is a person who owns the whole business. This should not be confused with a business that is run by one person. A sole trader can employ other people to work for him or her, but he or she enjoys all the profit. There are various advantages and disadvantages to sole trading, which include:

Advantages

1. A sole trader can start a business with minimum legal formalities. In most countries, there is minimal regulation on the operations of sole trader. Generally, sole traders are bound by the normal law of the country, such as it is illegal to trade in banned substances, and every person and business must disclose his or her income for tax purposes.

2. Small firms and, in particular, sole traders have the ability to make business decisions quickly. This is useful where there are frequent changes in prices or activities, e.g. in greengrocery and in road haulage. However, quick decision-making can be disadvantageous if it leads to impulsive decisions. In larger firms, with some degree of bureaucracy, decision-making may be slightly improved though much slower.

3. There is often a better relationship between workers and customers since there is a much greater element of personal service. The owner is usually at the front-line, continually interacting with the customers.

4. All the profits of a sole trader business belong to the owner. This is advantageous so long as the business is making profits; if it starts making losses then the owner has to foot all the losses.

Disadvantages

1. One of the problems for the sole trader, as for many small businesses, is that there is a considerable degree of legislation to be complied with when employing other people. This may be more of a perceived problem rather than actually being restrictive. Small businesses can receive information and advice about such legislation from Small Firms' Advice Centres. Commercial bankers and local authorities, wary of losing income and taxes raised from small firms

in the event they fail, often produce helpful booklets. They can also offer advice on finance, premises and, in some cases, give grants.

2. Another problem for the sole trader is marketing and costing. For example, they may have limited knowledge of marketing themselves to their market. A sole trader may be very good at carpentry but may not know what prices to charge in order to cover their costs. In many cases, sole traders have not considered whether they can actually sell enough goods or services to make the business viable. There can also be problems if illness occurs or if they wish to take holidays since goodwill may be lost during this period of inactivity.

3. A sole trader's business depends entirely on his or her input, whether it is decisions, capital or man-hours employed. In case of illness or incapacitation, the business can cease to exist. Sole traders can obtain advice from banks, accountants or solicitors before setting up a business. There has been some criticism in industry press suggesting some bank managers may have limited knowledge of business areas.

4. Whilst most traditional economists assume profit maximization, the Bolton Committee of 1971 (which carried out one of the few thorough appraisals of the small business sector) suggested that one of the major objectives of many small businesses (including sole traders) is independence rather than profit maximization. Some surveys seem to suggest that, in view of sole traders' opportunity costs (i.e. what they could earn elsewhere), they would be better off if they were employed by someone else, rather than trying to set up their own firm. However, during a recession many sole traders set up partly because of being made redundant by traditional large employers.

5. In the retail trade, assistance about pricing may be given by manufacturers or wholesalers who give a series of recommended retail prices (RRP). It is also often possible to observe the prices of competitors. However, in other industries, where prices are not necessarily published and information is less readily available, pricing may present more of a problem. Many small firms use the mark-up principle, i.e. looking at average costs and adding on a percentage. Whilst some economists have condemned the practice of marking up, they ignore the problems which many small firms have in obtaining adequate data about the price elasticity of demand of their goods and services. As far as costing is concerned, not all small businesses make allowances, for example, for the replacement of equipment. This is a growing criticism of small road haulage firms.

6. Many sole traders use their own premises as offices. One possible limitation to this practice is the need to obtain planning permission, but this may not present any problems if the business does not create a nuisance for other

people. The problem of obtaining suitable premises for setting up small businesses has not been helped by the increasing tendency towards larger shopping precincts (where the initial cost of rent is high) and the demolition of many older inner city areas.

7.   Another problem involved in setting up business is the possible difficulty in obtaining finance. Sole traders may be reliant on personal finances, such as second mortgages. However, many financial institutions, including the commercial banks, are now more willing to help the small firms. However, a sole trader still puts more of his or her savings at risk in a business when compared to firms involving partners or shareholders.

8.   A major disadvantage is that the sole trader has unlimited liability. If the business makes a loss the sole trader is liable for the entire loss, which means that he or she not only risks business' assets but also personal assets. If a limited liability business makes a loss then the liability to pay those it owes is limited up to the value of the assets within the organisation.

2.1.2: Partnerships

The Partnership Act of 1890 governs the operation of partnerships in the UK. The legislation lays down a model partnership agreement, which can be used unless the partners agree otherwise. Generally, there must be a minimum of two and a maximum of 20 partners. There is however, greater scope for individual partners to specialise in different areas of the business; this is an advantage over a sole trader where all the ideas and expertise may come from one person. An important advantage of a partnership is that there will be more access to finance because there are more partners. The risk associated with the initial capital is also reduced. However, more owners reduce the share of profit. Unlimited liability still exists and unanimity regarding decisions on important problems may be difficult to obtain when there are several partners. Responsibility and trust may also cause problems. Partly for these reasons, many partnerships are nowhere near the legal maximum of 20. Partnerships with between 2 and 5 partners are more common.

(a) Advantage of a partnership over a sole trader

1.   The partners may have more skills and capital than a sole trader. For example, if several people get together they may be able to carry out a building job much more effectively by using their own specialist skills such as planning, carpentry and plastering. One of them may have some commercial skill as well as a craft skill and this will be advantageous. There is more possibility of scope for skilled, professional management and in some cases it is possible for

people without the necessary capital, but with skills, to join with those who have capital and create a partnership – actually, this is often the case.

(b) Disadvantages

1. Decision-making may take longer than with a sole trader and, though the legal maximum is generally 20 partners, if there is any great overlap of functions, decision-making may well be very time consuming.

2. One of the major disadvantages of partnerships (as of sole traders) is that the owners have unlimited liability. They are completely liable for all the losses incurred in the business. However, in a partnership unlike in a sole trader the loss is spread amongst the partners reducing the liability accruing to any one individual.

3. A partnership will be affected by the death of a partner, as part of the capital may have to be returned. It may be advisable for partners to take out life insurance policies on each other to overcome this problem. By law, a partnership ceases to exist if one of the partners dies; this is because all partners are viewed as general agents of a partnership. Therefore, once a partner dies then other partners cannot be deemed to operate on his or her behalf. In some cases, the heirs' of the partner's share may wish to withdraw from the partnership forcing its cessation. Partners may however include in their partnership agreement what they think should happen in case of their deaths.

(c) Why form a partnership rather than a limited company?

1. It is generally cheaper to set up a partnership than a limited company. The formation of a company requires that the promoters (people who intend to be formed into a company) meet certain legal requirements as well as prepare legal documents, which mean the hiring of lawyers. A partnership on the other hand can be easily formed by writing a partnership agreement, which may not require legal guidance.

2. In some professions, such as lawyers' practices and doctors' surgeries, there are rules forbidding the formation of limited companies, partnerships are founded in such professions. The reason for this as we shall see later is that these professions depend on the personal integrity of all the lawyers or doctors who work in the firm. This responsibility may be avoided through limited liability.

3. Depending on current legislation, partnerships may have less documentation (such as less detailed accounts) and tax advantages (this was often the case in

former West Germany). Thus, there is also a tendency for less disclosure of information and reduced administration costs, which could lead to poor accounting. The advantage of having to disclose less information is that your competitors cannot obtain sensitive information about you. If a firm obtains another's accounts, they may indicate their intentions in the future. For example, if a firm is building up a cash reserve they are more than likely planning to make a large investment. With this information, a rival firm can prepare for the effects this will have on their own operations.

(d) Other features of partnerships

1. Once people become partners, they cannot be removed unless there is prior agreement to the contrary. Depending on the partnership agreement, partners can only be removed by dissolving the partnership altogether.

2. Partners share equally in capital and profits (or losses) unless there is an alternative agreement made at the organisation's inception. In other cases, a partner's share is dependent on their capital contribution.

3   All partners are entitled to be a part of the management. However, partners may choose to contribute to the initial capital, but stay out of the day-to-day management of the business. Such partners are known as *sleeping* or *silent* partners.

(e) Sleeping partners

Sleeping partners are those who join a partnership by contributing to the capital of the partnership, but they do not participate in the day-to-day running of the business and are therefore not liable to third parties nor do they face unlimited liability. In case of a loss, their liability is limited to their contribution only. A partnership with a sleeping partner is known as a *limited partnership*. Sleeping partners are paid a dividend for their investment depending on the provisions of the partnership agreement.

2.1.3: Limited Companies

A limited company is a business owned by shareholders through equal portions of the total capital known as shares. People who own a company own it through these portions. The more shares you hold of a company the more of that company you own. Limited companies enjoy limited liability; this means that shareholders can only lose what they have invested; this is unlike a partnership or sole trader where creditors can recover their debts from the private property of the owners.

A limited company is formed by promoters. Promoters are people who intend to be formed into a company and they apply to the Registrar of Companies (Companies House in the UK) for registration. Before a company is registered, the proposed company name is searched against the list of existing companies in order to prevent two companies being registered with the same name. This search also avoids misleading third parties. For example, the use of the name 'Her Majesty's' is prohibited as it gives the impression that the activities of the company have been sanctioned by Her Majesty, the Queen of the UK and Commonwealth. The promoters of a company must submit Articles of Association (AoA) to the Registrar of Companies which lists the rules and regulations governing the internal operations of a limited company. The Memorandum of Association (MoA) is another mandatory document which gives details of the liability of company members, the amount of share capital, and the aims and objectives of the business.

Limited Liability

The main advantage of forming a limited company is limited liability. This means that the owners of the company are only liable for losses of the business up to their total investment and no more. The limited liability clause was introduced in the 19th century to encourage people to go into business without risking all their property or life savings. Indeed, limited companies are very popular in the UK; according to Companies House in July 2013 there were 2,836,875 active companies registered[3].

There are two types of limited company; *private* and *public*. In a private limited company, shareholders are restricted to the people and numbers stated in the MoA. Any new shareholders must be approved by the existing shareholders. Private companies are not obliged to make their operating information public. Public companies are those listed on the stock market; anyone can become a shareholder and their financial information and other specified information has to be reported in a public place. Public disclosure is important as it safeguards the interests of the shareholders. Shareholders of both types of companies enjoy limited liability. In the case of very small private limited companies, the advantage of limited liability may not be as great as many textbooks suggest. For example, when seeking premises, the directors may have to give personal guarantees, since property, owners will tend to be wary of potential problems and risks should a small firm go bankrupt. Nonetheless, limited liability is important for company members, since it means that, in the event of bankruptcy, the most that the shareholders will lose is the value of their shares.

---

[3] http://www.companieshouse.gov.uk/about/statisticsAndSuurveys.shtml

Differences between private and public companies

1. Under the Companies Act of 1980, both private and public companies must have a minimum of two members and public companies have to have a minimum of £50,000 in capital.

2. The most important difference is that in a private limited company there are restrictions on the sale of shares which in general can only be sold without advertisement. In public companies, however, as the name implies, shares can be sold publicly, with the company quoted on the Stock Exchange. The Stock Exchange can be used as a source of finance; the public will subscribe for shares after they have seen a prospectus, which gives an idea of the history of the company and its profit record. Some public companies go far beyond the minimum legislation and give a great deal of information which is helpful to prospective shareholders and, possibly, also to employees and other stakeholders. Firms may also organise rights issues. These are shares sold to existing shareholders. One of the advantages of these is that the administration costs of issuing these shares are likely to be lower than with other shares since the firm can contact its existing shareholders more cheaply than the public and the proportion of take-up is likely to be higher. However, the disadvantage is that it probably limits the total capital available.

The divorce of ownership from control

In both private and public limited companies, directors are in control. Theoretically, members of the company (the shareholders) could elect a new Board at Annual General Meetings (AGMs). However, in the very large public companies, for example British Telecom (BT), which was privatised in 1984 creating over two million company shareholders, it seems unlikely that shareholders could really have effective control over the business affairs. Members may exercise some control through voting at AGMs or specially convened meetings if, for example, profits are too low or another firm wishes to make a takeover bid or propose a merger. In large public companies, there is likely to be a divorce between management of the company and ownership. This has had a number of important consequences:

1. It has led to management becoming more specialised; people without capital have become part of the management structure. The directors who are also shareholders may not have the expertise required to run the company. They therefore appoint managers who are trained and experienced in management to run the affairs of the company on their behalf.

2. According to some economists, such as Baumol and Marris, it has led to management pursuing its own objectives, subject to minimum profit levels

being made. This is dangerous as managers may pursue objectives that the owners did not endorse or are unaware of.

The majority of shareholders usually do not attend AGMs. It is only in the event of major catastrophes, takeover bids or the possibility of mergers, that shareholders are likely to exercise their voting right. Therefore, in the day-to-day running of a company, the managers may be accountable to no-one. One problem with the separation of ownership and management is that the employees of a company may feel alienated and fear that they have very little control over their working lives. They may feel that management decisions are taken solely in the interest of shareholders.

The main distinction between a public and private limited company is that private companies cannot offer shares or debentures to the public. However, under the Companies Act existing members of a private company and its employees can be offered shares. The minimum number of shareholders for both private and public companies is two. Private companies can have no more than fifty shareholders; there is no limit on the number of shareholders in public companies.

From the owners' point of view, the choice between whether to form a partnership (with unlimited liability) or a private company (with limited liability) may largely depend upon current legislation, which may require greater disclosure of information, involving higher administration costs for limited companies than for unlimited firms.

2.1.4: Holding Companies

A holding or parent company is the largest shareholder in a subsidiary company and, therefore, is the major owner of a subsidiary company. As a result, a holding company will have significant (if not total) control of the running of a subsidiary company if it so desires. This can lead to possible economies of scale, which we will discuss further in later chapters, and integration with subsidiaries may lower the costs of the holding company as it acquires raw material for its production or seeks to distribute its products. However, such integration can be abused if a holding company builds up a pyramid of control. With relatively little capital, the smaller subsidiary company will have to do what the holding company dictates. The Companies Act, however, has largely prevented this in the UK.

2.1.5: Joint Stock Company

One of the main characteristics of a joint stock company is that of unlimited liability. If you buy shares in a joint stock company, you would be liable to lose everything you possess if the company were to go bankrupt. One of the advantages of a joint stock company is that it can tap a greater variety of sources of finance than sole traders or partnerships. Unlimited companies (the other name for a joint stock company) would be able to issue shares, preference shares and debentures. It also offers continuity in that even the death of a main shareholder will not affect the business. However, there are some disadvantages since legislation creates more formalities than for a sole trader or for a partnership. In practice, in the very largest companies, shareholders cannot really have effective control over business affairs unless a small number of shareholders own a large percentage of the shares.

2.1.6: Multinationals

Multinationals are companies that operate in more than one country. Unilever and Nestlé are good examples of multinational companies. The advantages of multinationals, from the shareholders' viewpoint, are greater economies of scale and a wider spread (and thereby lower level) of risk. Several economists, however, (notably the late J.K. Galbraith) have expressed reservations about their lack of accountability either to shareholders or to the countries in which they operate. Developing countries may welcome multinationals as long as they are not too dominant, since they provide training for workers and managers, and provide employment, but they may be worried about the outflow of dividends to overseas shareholders. They will, however, take account of the opportunity costs if, for example, a multinationals' product had previously been imported; the balance of payments would be worse without the multinational producing the product in the developing country in question. The effect of multinationals are undeniable worldwide and their positive effects can be seen especially in developed countries where there are adequate legislative controls to reign in negative operations. In 2013 the multinationals came under considerable scrutiny because of tax avoidance by some of the major ones.

2.1.7: Workers' Co-operatives

In large public companies, management and ownership are separate. By contrast, in workers' co-operatives employees will have contributed towards the capital of the organisation and may elect managers at annual meetings. The advantage of workers' co-operatives is that all workers can take part in discussions regarding their firm. Therefore, there is a strong incentive for workers to perform well and increase profitability if they anticipate receiving higher dividends from their shares. Another advantage is that taking part in the decision-making process helps to motivate workers. However, if the co-operative becomes bankrupt then workers will risk losing both their jobs and the value of their shares. It may then be difficult to persuade employees to put more capital into the business. The objectives of co-operatives are usually to provide goods and services to consumers at reasonable prices and to pay fair wages to the workers.

Whilst workers' co-operatives have been in existence for a considerable length of time, there has been a noticeable increase in numbers. By 1984 there were around 700 co-operatives affiliated to the Industrial Co-ownership Movement (a federal body aiming to represent workers' co-operatives and to give advice to its members). Some co-ownership firms have been founded when the firm for which the employees were working went bankrupt. The Meriden Co-operative, which took over a motorcycle factory, is a case in example. There are immense difficulties in such circumstances, since the morale of existing staff may already be low and the fact that the previous firm went bankrupt indicates that there are probably many unresolved problems. Other co-operatives have been formed partially through the altruism of the previous owners. This is where previous owners offer the business to the workers at a lower than market price. One of the largest co-operatives is Scott Bader, formed by a Quaker. The largest and commercially successful workers' co-operative is the John Lewis Partnership, which controls, among other organisations, the chain of Waitrose supermarkets.

Whereas public companies increasingly show a divorce between management and ownership, workers' co-operatives are increasingly marrying ownership to management. Workers will generally elect managers at an annual meeting and will have contributed towards the capital of the organisation. Managers are often appointed on a fixed-term, usually a five-year period, in order to ensure that there is some continuity of management, but to avoid the problem of having managers appointed for life, which would partially defeat one of the objectives of the co-operative; i.e. that all workers should be able to participate in decision-making for the firm.

In many workers' co-operatives, there are fewer differences between the re-numeration of the lowest and the highest paid workers than in most firms. The co-operatives claim that this reduces the problems of morale that are caused by large wage differentials, but some economists have claimed that this makes it difficult to attract the appropriate level of top management. Workers' co-operatives, like other companies, are registered under the relevant partnership legislation and there has to be a minimum of two members. Like limited companies, there is no maximum number, though some managers within worker co-operatives would suggest that too large a number of workers would tend to make the firms more bureaucratic and would make it more difficult to conform to the original objectives as well as make quick decisions.

2.1.8: Consumers' Co-operatives

The best-known consumers' co-operatives in the UK are the Co-operative Retail Societies and the Co-operative Wholesale Society. These organisations can be found in the high streets of most major towns and cities and in many smaller towns and villages. They grew from the first co-operative store in Rochdale in 1844 when the aim was to buy food at wholesale prices and sell to their members.

The objective of these organisations is not profit maximisation but to provide goods and services to the consumers at reasonable prices and to pay fair wages to their workers. The Co-operative Retail Societies historically redistributed any profits, often in the form of dividends, but this practice had declined, it has however returned in line with competition from loyalty cards.

The Co-operative Retail Societies have, among themselves, set up the Co-operative Wholesale Society, which, in some ways, is like other wholesalers. Profits from the Co-operative Wholesale Society are shared between retail societies. The Co-operative Wholesale Society is itself a large manufacturer of many goods.

2.1.9: Non-profit Making Private Sector Organisations

In the UK, these include building societies and mutual insurance companies, where there are no shareholders. Mutual insurance companies can be very large. There have been many changes to building societies since the Building Society Act of 1986. For example, in 1995 the Halifax and the Leeds decided to merge following an overwhelming endorsing vote from their members. A large number of building societies have converted to banks following favourable voting on the proposals by their members. In many cases, these have led to cash windfalls for members when they opted to sell shares acquired through demutualisation. The building societies apart from Northern Rock were much more stable than the banks during the credit crunch.

2.1.10: Franchises

A franchise is not in itself a type of business. It is a licence to use the name and sell the products of another business. Small franchisees may decide to be sole traders or form a partnership, while franchisees with complex or large businesses may choose a private limited company for the reasons discussed previously. Franchises are found in all realms of business but most predominantly in restaurants and retail environments.

The franchising industry was one of the most rapidly growing sectors during the 1980s. By 1997, it was estimated that it employed about 270,000 people (out of a total workforce of 30,000,000). The sales volume was in the region of £7 billion out of a total of £270 billion for all consumption in the UK. In the 21st century, this sector has continued to flourish. Franchises are often found in the rapidly growing fast food sector, for example, Burger King, Wimpy, some Pizza Hut outlets and even McDonald's. There are also franchises in environmental shops such as Body Shop. PC World operates franchises in the computer sales industry, similar to Prontaprint in the printing industry. Even milk rounds have been offered to franchisees.

The British Franchise Association suggests that only 10 per cent of franchisees fail within the first 10 years and this percentage is even smaller within longer established franchise businesses. It is claimed that franchises are better because applicants are vetted for suitability and they are given advice on location and marketing. Vetting of suitable applicants may help if the franchiser is scrupulous. Many people enter with only a vague idea of their talents and all too often underestimate the amount of cash that they will require. This must include living expenses in the first few years when business revenue may not be enough to pay them a normal income. The advice on location may help since large firms will have a much clearer idea of the total population that will be needed for certain types of business. They may also have economies of scale that they can pass on to their franchisee. For the individual franchisee, this might well be more than he/she might afford but, because the cost is spread, the amount paid by each franchisee will be quite small. In cases such as Body Shop, where the firm is well known, the general publicity will be much more helpful than any advertising the franchisee could do on his or her own. Franchises combine the motivation of the entrepreneurial shopkeeper with the economies of scale of the large firm.

Problems with franchises

Franchisees are dependent on the franchiser. They generally sell the franchiser's goods and replicate the business model. Some franchisers may not offer adequate support to the franchisees. This usually leads to failure; since failure of a franchisee has no direct monetary impact to the franchiser, then it may not be a priority.

2.1.11: National Enterprise Board

One of the main roles of the former National Enterprise Board (NEB) was to encourage mergers of companies where it was thought there were potential economies of scale. It was set up to encourage industrial efficiency. NEB no longer exists; this is because today most businesses understand the importance of merging and the resultant economies of scale. In fact, in some cases governments and international bodies such as the European Union (EU) may discourage or even break apart huge corporations that compromise consumer choice.

2.1.12: Management Buyouts

A management buyout (MBO) occurs when a company's managers buy or acquire a large part of the company. An MBO is a unique case of acquisition in which the goal may be to strengthen the managers' interest in the success of the company. In most cases, the management will move the company toward private status. MBOs have assumed an important role in corporate restructuring, sitting alongside mergers and acquisitions. Key consideration through MBO includes fairness to shareholders, the price of products or services, the future business plan and legal and tax issues[4].

In recent years, there has been an increase in the occurrences of MBOs. One of the causes of this popularity is privatisation. Examples include Travellers Fare, which was formed from part of the catering division of British Rail; National Freight Consortia, which had been the National Freight Company; and the Maidstone and District Bus Company, which had been part of the National Bus Company. At one time, the Union of Democratic Miners (UDM) and the Electricity Boards were aiming to buy some of the coal pits in the UK. All these MBOs were followed by a rapid change into private companies.

Another cause for an MBO is high unemployment or recession. Where the company is in danger of going under, the managers may choose to buy it out instead of filing for bankruptcy and incur loss of jobs for the managers. In other cases different divisions of the firm may have been halved off if they were either unsuccessful or if they were peripheral. In other cases the firms have been faced with a takeover which may have threatened jobs e.g. in the paper industry. The management will probably think it has the expertise through its knowledge of the market and the internal organisation of the company instead of letting that portion of the business be sold off to third parties. They may opt to buy it and use their expertise to build a successful business while making an investment and saving their jobs.

The availability of credit during the 1980s encouraged MBOs. Up until 1989 house prices were rising so the equity on the house was useful as collateral when borrowing money. However, in the early 1990s, when house prices fell, it was more difficult to obtain credit in this way so financing buyouts was more difficult. However, since 1998, house prices have increased and the interest rates on loans have fallen; thereby managers have been able to put in bids in support of MBOs. Houses prices increased till about 2008 and have fallen since then.

---

[4] Investor Dictionary

> Exercise
>
> *You are a partner of Quick Drive, a road haulage organisation. Trade is currently expanding. Explain to your fellow partner, in the form of a memo, why you feel it would be favourable to form a private company. Outline any disadvantages.*

Suggested approach to the exercise:

MEMORANDUM

From: David Jones   Ref: D2A0001
To: Andrew Farland   Date: 27/06/XX

Dear Andrew,

I would like to suggest that we consider forming a private company. Whilst business is currently expanding and our personal assets are not currently under threat, the formation of a private company would ensure that our personal assets are not seized should our business go bankrupt. In fact, I feel that as trade is currently expanding, this is a good time to form a private company because we are in need of new vehicles in order that our fleet may be expanded. Neither of us, individually or collectively, have enough capital to buy these vehicles.

The formation of a private company would not entitle us to approach the public for capital; both Mr Brown and Mr Smith have shown interest in our business recently and would be willing and able to provide us with the necessary capital as long as they do not have to face unlimited liability.

A further advantage to be gained in forming a company is that if trade continues to expand we may wish to have more than 20 members, which would necessarily involve forming a company anyway. On the assumption that trade will continue to grow, it would seem sensible to form a private company than continue as a partnership and have perhaps one or two sleeping partners.

Before we take any final decision on the matter of whether to form a company or to remain as a partnership we must also consider any tax advantages a partnership has over a private company and just how many formalities would be involved in forming a company.

Regards,

David Jones.

Question: Why does separation of ownership from control often occur in modern companies? What are the economic consequences of this?

Feedback to the exercise

One of the reasons for the separation of ownership is that in larger joint stock companies, for example, BT, there were, at the time of privatisation, over two million owners. Whilst some of the workers and managers own shares, it is obvious that not all the owners are also managers or workers. Often, especially with multinational companies, the owners may live in different countries to those of both workers and managers. In the public sector, ownership is in the hands of the public, though in practice more decisions are likely to be made by government ministers. It is uncommon for nationalised industries to issue shares but even where they do, the owners will not generally be the managers.

There are some advantages of this separation. For example, it has enabled people without capital to become managers if they are seen to have the necessary ability. Equally, companies do not have to depend upon people with both money and managerial ability since the managerial ability can be brought in. From the firms' viewpoint, finance, especially in joint stock companies, becomes easier to access because there are a wide variety of methods of obtaining large-scale funds including the issue of shares, preference shares and debentures as well as overdrafts, loans and government finance. In turn, these different types of finance will appeal to different types of investors and thus money will be available to optimise production.

There are, however, a number of disadvantages. For example, shareholders may have a very narrow time horizon and be only interested in capital gains in which case prospects for long-term research and development and future growth of the company may well be sacrificed for these aims. Shareholders as well may take little interest in the conditions of employees. There have been criticisms of a number of companies, especially firms operating in developing countries that subject the workers there to terrible work conditions to turn a profit and high dividends for their shareholders in the developed countries. In other cases there is the possibility that managers will pursue their own interests, for example, increasing their own salaries over and above that which would be necessary to keep them in their present occupation. There is evidence to show that in some companies there is little correlation between profitability and managers' salaries. Firms may indulge in prestige projects or take on extra staff and equipment, which adds to the prestige of managers but which may not be in shareholders' interest. Managers may wish to expand the firm because this would give them both status and salary far beyond what shareholders might wish. A case in point is Enron, which maintained a façade of well-being while hiding mounting debts at the expense of shareholders. When this company collapsed, unaware of the operations by the management and complicit directors, investors lost most of their money through stock market losses and employees lost their livelihoods.

The divorce may also lead to considerable economic power being in the hands of relatively few people. This is one of the criticisms which has been made particularly of some of the very large financial institutions. Some of the largest multinationals may well have a turnover that exceeds the Gross National Product of some small developing countries. This gives them immense power, which may be abused. J.K. Galbraith in particular has criticised practices of some multinational companies. Whilst in theory shareholders can control the company, in practice the large numbers of shareholders and the inability to obtain information or to understand the relevant information can lead to problems. Shareholders, in many cases, have only the option of disposing of their shares if the company performs badly. However, even in the case where shareholders do seem to play a part in management, for example in football league clubs, there is no guarantee that they will exercise control in a sensible manner.

Case study 1

Your elder brother and sister decide to set up a local shop. They ask you for advice on what they could sell. Explain how they would determine their pricing. For example, do they have to match competitor's prices?

They are not sure about what type of business organisation they should choose. They are aware of the position of sole traders but are not aware of the implications of forming a partnership or a limited company. What advice can you give them? They have heard the term 'limited liability' but do not know exactly what it means. Explain this to them.

Case study 2

About twenty years ago, two brothers set up a partnership in engineering. One had the financial expertise whilst the other had more expertise in engineering. Since then they have developed the business so that it currently employs 200 people. They are wondering whether they could form a public limited company but are worried about the problems of losing control, not only for financial reasons but because they want to ensure that their workers are well looked after. They fear that if they become a public limited company shareholders may be interested in only profit and will not care enough about the environment or the workers. In the light of your knowledge, can you advise them what would be the advantages of becoming a public limited company and whether there are any disadvantages? What other options are available to them, if any?

Self-examination Questions

1. The following are some of the major forms of private sector business organisations:

    - Workers' co-operatives

    - Consumers' co-operatives

    - Public limited companies

    - Private limited companies

    - Partnerships

    To which of the above forms of organisation do the following apply?

    a. Each member has one vote.

    b. The organisation will generally cease upon the death of one of its members.

    c. There are limits on the number of members, and at least one member has unlimited liability.

    d. The workers will generally elect the managers.

    e. Shares are issued but are not freely transferable.

    f. There is no limit to the number of shareholders and voting is based on the number of shares held.

2. What is meant by the term 'sole trader'? Why are sole traders more frequently found in some trades than in others?

3. What are the advantages of partnerships compared with sole traders? Are there any disadvantages?

4. Why might a sole trader who wishes to expand his or her business want to form a private limited company rather than a partnership? What legal requirements will they have to satisfy to achieve this change?

5. Why do people become self-employed? Are there any major disadvantages in being a sole trader?

6. It is sometimes said that a partnership offers a greater scope for specialisation than being a sole trader. What would this mean when, for example, setting up a construction business?

7. 'The sole trader has too many roles to play to be really efficient'. Discuss.

8. Why might it be difficult to find evidence of profit maximisation, as defined by the economist, when looking at sole traders' accounts?

9. Why might it be difficult to obtain an agreement between twenty partners in a partnership?

10. It is sometimes said that small traders have a problem if there is illness. Why is this problem not found in a large company?

11. Explain the differences between the various types of organisation found in the private sector. In particular, refer to ownership and control.

12. What is limited liability? Explain the importance of limited liability to - (i) a shareholder; and (ii) a potential creditor.

13. What is a holding company?

14. It is said that in a joint stock company there is unlimited liability. What are the advantages and disadvantages of a joint stock company?

15. How has limited liability led to the separation of ownership and control in some large companies? What is the economic significance of this?

16. What is meant by a 'workers' co-operative'? What would be the advantages and disadvantages of setting up such an organisation?

17. What are multinationals? Should developing countries welcome or try to refuse the growth of multinationals in their countries?

18. What are the advantages of multinationals from the point of view of – (i) the shareholders; and (ii) the workers?

19. Some economists have suggested that multinationals are neither accountable to shareholders, or to the countries in which they operate. To what extent is this valid criticism?

20. Multinationals should be welcomed by developing countries since they will pay higher wages than local firms and train more workers, but should be discouraged when profits do not go back to the country in which they are made. Discuss.

21. In what ways do consumers' co-operatives differ from other organisations? How far in practice, do their pricing and output policies differ from other organisations?

22. Why has there been increasing interest in workers' co-operatives in recent years? What are the disadvantages to workers in such organisations?

23. The Bolton Committee, 1971, suggested that independence more than profit might be a major factor for setting up small businesses. Discuss.

24. The Co-operative Societies generally charge the same prices for goods irrespective of the location of their shops. What are the economic consequences of this? Explain your answer with reference to a small Co-operative Society located in a village with limited demand and to another Co-operative located in a high demand area.

25. The National Enterprise Board was set up to encourage mergers of companies if there are potential economies of scale. Why might the price mechanism not be used to secure the same effects?

Chapter 3: PRODUCTION

3.1: Introduction

Basic human needs include food, shelter, warmth and good health. However, this is an over simplification since whilst babies can live entirely on milk, adults need a variety of protein, vitamins and calories in order to stay healthy. It is not just a question of diet as health also depends upon fresh water supplies and personal hygiene. However, in modern society our wants go much further than this. As people become richer, they often require a wider variety of food for enjoyment as well as nutrition. People also want entertainment; if you live in one of the larger towns or cities, you will undoubtedly find cinemas, and perhaps theatres. Increasingly people have their own forms of entertainment such as radio, television, CD players and so on. Similarly, people demand clothes, not just for warmth in colder countries, but also as a form of display (fashion statement) and social tools of interaction and identification.

In today's world, production is elaborate and more businesses are being formed daily to meet a wide diversity of needs. The word *production* is derived from the word product. A product is anything that can be offered to a market that might satisfy a want or need. However, it is much more than just a physical object. It is the complete bundle of benefits or satisfactions that buyers perceive they will obtain if they purchase the product. It is the sum of all physical, psychological, symbolic, and service attributes. Production is therefore the process of creating products.

3.2: Categorisation of Production

In order to achieve both wants and needs, production has to take place. Economists divide this into three categories: primary, secondary and tertiary production.

- Primary production is the production of raw materials. It can be subdivided into extractive industries such as coal mining, and agricultural and fishing industries.

- Secondary production includes manufacturing and construction.

- Tertiary means services such as banking and transport.

3.2.1: Primary Production

Primary production refers to extractive activities such as mining, agriculture, fishing and forestry. In some countries, agriculture is still a predominant production category. Production in agriculture can be improved through growing high yielding crops and by having crops that are disease-free or disease resistant. Fertilisers may also help to improve yields. There are statistical techniques available, which are beyond the scope of this book that can help agricultural scientists to determine the best type and combination of crops to grow in any particular environment. Enhanced knowledge of soil management and agricultural techniques will help farmers to improve their productivity.

3.2.2: Secondary Production

The secondary sector includes construction and manufacturing. In the construction industry, we see the advantages of specialisation. If you watch a major building undergoing construction you will almost certainly observe different people doing a wide variety of different jobs. Management techniques such as linear programming and network analysis will almost certainly be used in planning the construction process. Computers, as we will see in Chapter 15, can also help to speed up processes. The need for trained people in this, as in most industries, is increasingly apparent. Without training, most people will not be competent at carpentry, plumbing or other building tasks. In the manufacturing sector, the UK textile industry has faced problems from imports of textiles from overseas, notably from countries with lower labour costs. Here again, newer, more efficient machinery and specialised staff could help remedy the situation.

One of the most important occupations in the secondary sector is that of engineering. Engineering itself can be subdivided into a number of different categories. For example, civil engineering is very important since it involves the building of highways, bridges, railways, airports, as well as other infrastructure that is necessary for a country to develop. Civil engineers will not only be able to make the best use of materials but will also work out the stresses and strains on structures so that risk can be assessed. Civil engineers are trained to look at the most cost effective way of building as well as knowing the qualities of different materials. Electrical engineers form another category. These specialists can calculate the electrical resistances encountered and are able to advise firms on the best methods of wiring. Unqualified workers often cause electrical accidents. Mechanical engineering is another type of engineering. As the name implies it is concerned with machines and the way, in which they work. Mechanical engineers, like other branches of engineering, are also concerned with ergonomics, which is the science studying the interrelationship between people and machines. They will look at the most effective ways of using both human and mechanical energy.

3.2.3: Tertiary Production

The tertiary sector, often referred to as the 'service' sector, has been the fastest growing sector in the UK for the past two decades. This sector has witnessed significant improvements during the last quarter of the 20th century. First we had the use of electric and electronic typewriters, which helped to improve typing speeds and, though more expensive, were easier to use than manual typewriters. Word processors allowed similar letters to be personalised from a standard base document. In the commercial sector the use of computers, which will be discussed in more detail in Chapter 15, has helped the sector develop considerably. The use of advanced filing systems, whether geographical, chronological or subject based, have helped people find the information they need much more quickly and give a better service to customers. Computer software has provided organisations with electronic systems enabling multi-level, integrated, information filing and retrieval capabilities. The introduction of such systems has necessarily required training of staff and end-users.

In the tertiary sector, as well as in other sectors, computer programmers play an important part in making the best use of existing programmes and adapting them to the specific needs of firms, in addition to creating new or custom-built software packages. This may be important, since in many cases, the programmes themselves are devised in countries such as the UK, the United States of America (USA) and Japan and users in countries other than these may need their software regionalised. For example, accountancy software would have to be changed to take into consideration the difference in tax laws in different parts of the world. The use of specialised accountancy software has increased as the price of Information Technology hardware and software has fallen. Perhaps even more important than computer programmers is the need for system analysts who look at systems as a whole. System Analysts are widely used by large organisations in most countries since they will not only have knowledge of computer languages, but more importantly, they will be able to apply the computer to the specific needs of companies and the public sector. As more and more software is devised for general business purposes such as accounts, stock control and so on, there is an increasing need for system analysts who can apply both the hardware and software to help individual firms.

In the transport sector, services can also be improved. For example, bus services can be improved if people have specialist knowledge of the types of buses that will be suitable for an area, as well as using commercial criteria to judge how long buses should be kept in service and to ensure that they are well maintained. The use of adequate supervisory systems should help them to run punctually on long distance routes. Within towns, it will be helpful if some priority can be given to public transport. In the transport and aviation sector, the use of computers has helped. They can be used for studying reservations for the assessment of future needs or can be used to calculate prioritised landing orders for aircraft in busy airports. The industry drive is for modern aircraft to be more fuel-efficient and environmentally friendly. Therefore, airline companies will have to be able to calculate the trade-offs between the savings made on fuel, the impact on the environment and the cost of upgrading their aircraft. Similarly, in other parts of the transport industry, new fuel and space efficient lorries, forklift trucks and other handling equipment may help to improve productivity.

3.3: Methods of Production

There are many different ways that a firm can produce its goods or services. Organisations must choose their method of production carefully. The three broad categories of production are set out below.

3.3.1: Job Production

Job production is also known as 'one-off' production and is often used for specialised products and services. A single product is completed before the next is started. Examples of one-off production include personal stock brokering and bespoke house construction. This form of production is usually very labour intensive as a high level of skill and artisanship is often required. As a consequence, the unit cost of job production items or services is usually very high since the economies of scale provided by other approaches are not available with this approach. An advantage to this form of production is that firms need not keep large inventories as work is done as and when needed. It is also the cheapest form of production to set up, which is due to the use of labour as opposed to expensive to purchase machinery.

3.3.2: Batch Production

This involves producing a set number of goods or service encounters by taking them through a variety of operations together. The prime example of batch production is bread in a village bakery where a number of loaves of bread are made at once. However, the stages of production, from converting the raw materials into the final loaf of bread, are distinct and performed separately; for instance, first the weighing of ingredients, then the mixing, followed by kneading of the dough and so on until the loaves are taken out of their tins and put on display. Other examples could include construction of housing estates, sheds and production of set menu meals in restaurants. In contrast to job production, batch production techniques take advantage of the division of labour. In the bakery example, there may be one person for each major stage of the process. If this is the case then the workers may not need to be highly skilled or trained in order to produce the product to the standards required. Increased use of machinery and mechanisation will mean that unit costs are lower than job production but set up costs for the production system are much higher. This is offset slightly by a reduced need for labour. Higher inventories are needed in order to keep the process running smoothly. It is usual to keep enough stock for a few batches but this depends on product or service throughput. In order to increase production volume more batches need to be produced. Due to the use of fixed capacity systems, it is often not possible to increase the batch sizes themselves.

3.3.3: Flow Production

Flow production is also referred to as *mass production*. This is very expensive to set up. It requires heavy investment in planning and machinery that is used in the production process. Examples of flow-produced goods and services include the majority of cars, telecommunications, light bulbs and most canned soft drinks and foods. Stages of production are divided up into their most simple operation and products flow from one stage to the next continuously. There is nearly always an extensive amount of automated machinery and relatively low amounts of labour involved in this form of production. Only products that are demanded in large volume are economically viable to construct in this manner. Significant economies of scale are achieved through high volume production, but the set up costs of such operations are enormous.

There are a number of factors to consider when choosing a production method but the most influential one is the variety-volume trade-off shown in Figure 3.1.

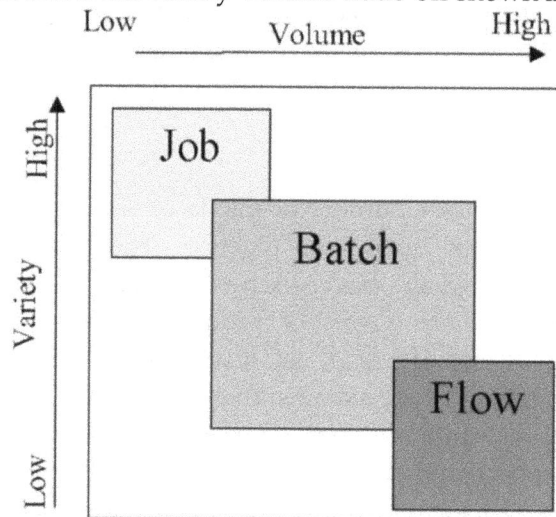

Figure 3.1

When a firm wishes to produce a high variety of products at low volume, job production is deployed. Conversely, if they wish to specialise in one design of good or service and produce it in large volumes then flow production is the approach that should be considered. For example, flow production would be used by a car manufacturer producing a large number of a specific model of car.

3.4: Stock Purchasing and Control

One area of production that has been focused on in recent years is stock control. Firms have begun to realise the potential for cost savings and increased efficiency in this often-neglected area of operation. All businesses need stocks or inventories to function but there have been many different theories as to how to best organise them and their use. In organisations that produce goods, especially in the primary sector, stocks can be extremely expensive and tie up the majority of working capital available to the firm. If stocks are controlled more efficiently then more of this capital is available for other, possibly more profitable uses.

3.4.1: Just-in-Case Production

It was traditionally the case that stocks were purchased in bulk and then worked through until another batch was required. This took advantage of the economies of scale often offered by suppliers to purchasers of large volumes of products. There are a number of advantages related to this method of stock control, commonly known as Just-in-Case (JIC). See Figure 3.2.

Raw materials or components are held in stock to prevent a firm from running out. These buffer stocks allow some flexibility if new deliveries arrive late or incomplete. Production lines can continue if sections of the line break down due to buffers of 'work in progress' stocks. Stocks of completed goods are held to reduce the possibility of 'stock outs'. If a customer places an order, and there have been production problems, stocks of finished items can cover this up and allow the orders to be fulfilled

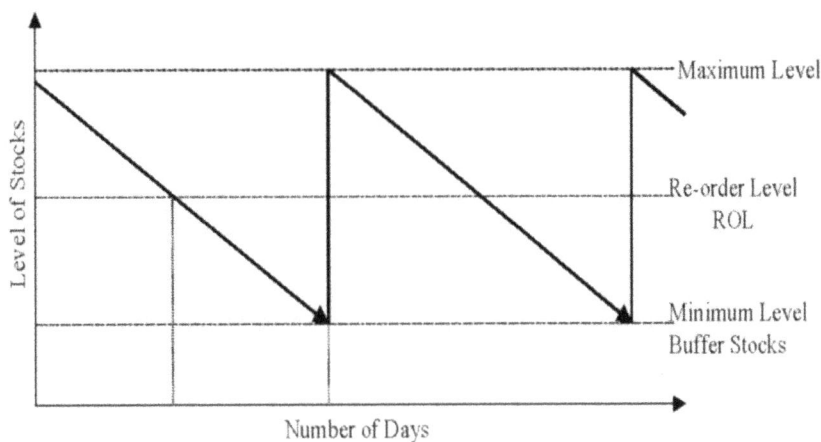

Figure 3.2

3.4.2: Just-in-Time Production

The disadvantages to the JIC system, as discussed above, are the costs that are tied up in the holding of often unneeded and unused buffers of stock. In an attempt to reduce these inefficiencies, the Western firms that typically used this approach looked to the Japanese to see how they reduced these financial burdens. The Just-in-Time (JIT) system of stock control and component ordering aims to reduce the amount of stock held by a firm to a minimum. According to J. Bicheno in his article *Implementing Just-in-time* published in 1991: 'JIT aims to meet demand instantaneously, with perfect quality and no waste'

The main idea behind this definition is that stock arrives at the instant it is needed for production. This means that there are no stocks kept to buffer problems in production. If there were broken or unsatisfactory stocks delivered then this would cause production to slow or stop. This is obviously not what the organisation wants and so it is imperative that all of the items delivered are fit for use. The buffers used in JIC cover up bottlenecks or poorly performing sections of production and the implementation of a JIT system will reveal these. It is important that once these problem areas are located, that they are solved to smooth the flow of production through the entire process.

In order to have components and raw materials arrive on time there needs to be reduced lead times. These are the times between an order being placed and it arriving. Some firms have solved this problem by allocating their suppliers floor space in their factories. The suppliers only pay for the supplies when they cross over the company borders to occupy more than the allocated space. Such involvement of suppliers means that prices may increase slightly as the supporting firm has to do more work. The storage savings and the increased efficiency of the JIT production line is usually more than the allocated floor space costs.

The JIT graph below, Figure 3.3, shows the effect of a JIT system of stock control and purchasing on the lead times and levels of stock of a typical production company when compared to Figure 3.2. It can be seen that there is a lower maximum stock level and there is no safety buffer in place. The lead-time is reduced so smaller, more frequent, orders are made to fulfil demand in the production process.

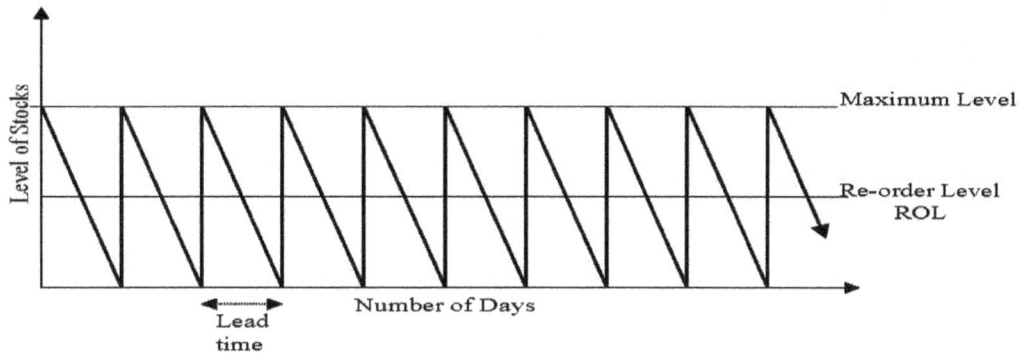

Figure 3.3

JIT requires that:

- Production is market led.

- Supplies are delivered only when needed.

- There is no store of work-in progress.

- Goods are only produced if they have been ordered.

- Reliable and flexible production process.

- Reliable and flexible workforce.

Advantages of JIT:

- Reduces waste, damage to stock and obsolescence by quick stock turnover.

- Reduces the use of factory space attributed to stock this can be used for more profitable activities.

- Cost of holding stock itself is reduced significantly.

- Improved relationships with customers and suppliers.

- Improved motivation of workers, they are involved more in the production process and teamwork is encouraged.

Disadvantages of JIT:

- Reliability and flexibility of workers and machinery is needed to keep the system going and orders fulfilled.

- Suppliers have to be reliable and on time with their deliveries for the production process to be continuous.

- Economies of scale are lost and prices are likely to be higher as more supplier effort is needed.

- Difficult to cope with large unexpected increases in demand.

3.5: Factors Affecting Productivity

Total production in any nation is obviously enhanced through greater productivity. If the same quantities of factors of production can create a greater amount of product then this creates an increased number of goods that can be purchased in the market place by consumers. This increase in productivity usually means that the products themselves will become relatively cheaper. The consumers will demand more. Demand may also increase in foreign markets as the products become more favourably priced. More overall demand leads to increased production levels and hence higher wages, which in turn increase the demand for products further. This will lead to a positive effect known as a 'virtuous circle' whereby greater demand for a country's products leads to a greater level of production.

Perhaps the main factor, which may help improve productivity, is that of specialisation. The specialisation of workers in a production process does have its advantages; these were clearly documented by Adam Smith in 1776. The division of labour not only enables workers to become more skilled in their respective jobs and hence lead to a corresponding increase in the speed of the workers production, but time is also saved by workers not having to switch from one job to another. There are many examples where such specialisation techniques can be put into practise. In hospitals, different staff may specialise in different diseases and treatment, while in the transport industry workers may specialise in using different types of vehicles.

Other factors, which might be adopted to improve productivity, include policies, which reinforce or improve workers morale, and programmes that attempt to 'breed' loyalty and respect between the workers and the company as a whole, which is something the Japanese have excelled in achieving.

In most countries, savings need to be obtained so investment can take place. An adequate financial system may help to channel these savings into intelligent investment whether it is more machines for factories, farming and mining or merely updating existing machines, which again will increase productivity. If a country can harness these savings, it may result in a lower standard of living now, but will result in a higher standard of living at a later stage. Obviously to set up an adequate financial system, to help encourage useful investment, will require the expertise of the developed world together with large amounts of money to help set up such systems. One such source for countries lacking these systems may be to borrow from other countries or seek aid via the International Monetary Fund (IMF).

Labour needs to be adequately trained. Some countries have tried to develop long term planning in order to determine what labour will be needed in the future and consequently to try to provide appropriate training in schools and universities. Unless a country knows what people it requires in the future it is difficult to provide adequate education and training.

The ways in which the factors of production are utilised in a country is vital for its future living standards. Without an adequate volume of production, a country will not meet its material needs. It needs to produce enough products, at competitive and efficient prices, so that they will not only help to satisfy domestic needs, but also through exporting, can earn valuable foreign currency. This will then enable the population to buy a greater variety of imports that leads to an increased standard of living.

In most Western style, economies including the UK, the proportion of workers in the primary sector have declined rapidly. This is also true to a lesser extent of the secondary sector whilst the tertiary sector has grown rapidly. In the rest of this chapter, we consider factors that affect changes in the production sectors and the consequences of these changes. Below is a list of groups that can both contribute towards these changes as well as be influenced by the results.

1. Consumers

2. Producers

3. Government

4. Shareholders

5. The media

6. The public

7. Workers

8. Trade Unions

9. Pressure Groups

1. **Consumers**, whether individually or collectively through WHICH? (a consumer body), affect production. As consumers get richer, they spend more on consumption of most goods and services. There are exceptions called inferior goods which defy economic theory that states that a rise in price will reduce the quantity

of a good demanded. When the price of inferior goods, or 'Giffen' goods, rises people tend to buy more of it. If the population is becoming richer then they buy less of the Giffen goods. This is true for goods that are bought out of necessity such as staple foods. The richer people become the less they buy a commodity that they consider inferior and the greater the preference to buy expensive goods instead. Richer people will buy luxurious cars not because they are different from less-expensive or standard models, but rather because they convey a message, a status symbol.

Consumer tastes change continually. For example, in the UK more people have become vegetarian and more health conscious. This has had important consequences for the agricultural sector and for the food processing and retailing industries. In recent years, there has also been a movement towards organic foodstuffs in a reaction to the uncertainty surrounding Genetically Modified (GM) crops. As another example, clothing retailers are holding sales more frequently since fashion trends change quickly within the year requiring organisations to find ways of selling their newly outdated stock rapidly so as not to risk being left behind in the market place and incurring a loss on unsold items.

2. **Producers**, particularly in a recession, have often looked to reduce costs, which in the past has led to mass redundancy. The overall effect of redundancy is lower demand for products and services. This is the so-called 'feel bad' factor as opposed to the 'feel good' factor and it tends to deepen the recession as people demand less, therefore requiring less production and fewer jobs or lower wages. This pattern is known as the 'vicious cycle' and is often witnessed in the poorer countries of the world. The introduction of technology and particularly computer products has affected not only the number of workers but also the type of workers. The availability of information at the fingertips of the consumer is both a blessing and a curse for the producers as consumers today go shopping after having a 'virtual walk' on the Internet and deciding on the best offers for the goods they need. Using the Internet most producers can now reach millions of would be buyers considerably reducing advertising costs.

Producers have also become more interested in management science techniques, which we explore further in Chapter 18. The use of computers has helped in terms of operational research. There is still however a great deal of criticism of the inefficiency of management in many UK firms.

3. **The government** has introduced a large volume of Health and measures at work provisions that affect the way in which firms can carry out their activities. Consumer protection may affect the way in which organisations sell their products.

Land use and planning legislation may affect the design and operation of buildings. For example, there will often be measures to prevent environmental nuisances. The role of government is explored in detail in Chapter 27.

The European Union (EU) has issued a considerable amount of legislation and ideas such as the Social Chapter that affect industry. In many cases, local government has tried to attract investment into their areas. This has not just been confined to British industry but also overseas investment. One example of this is Nissan which chose to locate in South Wales. Other local authorities have 'pedestrianised' their High Streets (making them exclusive for walking shoppers only) not only to make it more pleasant but also to attract more shoppers.

4. **Shareholders**. In the UK, institutional shareholders have become increasingly more important and private shareholders less so. The divorce of management and control of companies is almost complete in most large firms. Whilst the government in the 1980s talked about a share owning democracy, in practise few small investors have much effect on industry. This in turn means that managers can often set their own objectives. Due to the investment muscle of institutional shareholders, management is likely to be more heavily influenced by institutional investors than private shareholders.

5. **The media** may influence public opinion. Today the impact of the media is very significant; not only does it influence the course of government and politics, but also the private sector. In other cases such as through travel programmes or even wildlife programmes, tourism is likely to increase in an area, as more people are aware of a much wider range of destinations. In some cases, as with the Thalidomide affair, the media will put pressure on firms. Thalidomide was a drug prescribed to pregnant women to combat the symptoms of morning sickness. It was introduced in West Germany in October 1957. However, it was found to cause horrific birth defects in thousands of children around the world if taken by women during early pregnancy. The media aided the spread of this news and Thalidomide was no longer prescribed as a morning sickness treatment worldwide by 1962.

6. **The public** not only have a role as consumers but also as householders and tenants. This has particular importance for the transport industry where new roads, the Channel Tunnel link or the 5th terminal at Heathrow airport may be welcome.

7. **Workers** become more educated as a country moves towards a more tertiary production based economy. This shift will affect the skills available within the population. This will often lead to employees having different expectations about working practises. Legislation has recently been introduced to bring equality

between the rights of full time and part-time employees. In the past, part-time employees have not been offered the benefits that full time employees have enjoyed. This is likely to change the composition of the UK workforce as the number of part-time workers increases far more rapidly than the number of jobs created within the economy.

8. **Trade Unions**, while less strong than in the 1970s, may affect working practises, pay and redundancy. Unions are typically pressure groups acting for employees. They are also usually for employees who work in the same trade although multi-disciplinary organisations are in existence. The increase in the Health and Safety legislation by government and the EU and the increase in the 'lawsuit' culture have once again justified the need for strong trade unions to protect employees from the actions of their big business employers.

9. **Pressure Groups** may modify the type of products or working practises. For example, many firms now advertise that their products have not been tested on animals. Pressure groups are considered in more detail in Chapter 28.

Case study 1: Computer Essentials

A computer organisation, *Computer Essentials*, which has its base on the continent, has recently moved into the British market. It makes a limited range of computers for small businesses and home users. The main selling point has been that it has undercut its rivals for similar specification machines by about 5 to 10 per cent. However, with rapidly changing technology the firm recognises that it would be difficult to keep this margin ahead of its rivals.

Until recently, it has sold through about 20 shops, which it owns, and which deal exclusively with its products. However, an opportunity has arisen to purchase 100 sites since a major chain of electrical stores has withdrawn from the market because of intense competition. Computer Essentials is inclined to take over the shops partly because it avoids lengthy negotiations with many different retailers and agents throughout the UK. It also avoids the uncertainty of these negotiations. Commercial properties have gained demand along with the housing market. The price asked for the shops is higher than it would have been in the 1990s.

If it takes over these shops, it estimates that it will need 15 per cent of the market segment compared with the 7 per cent that it currently has. It is also considering the possibility of diversifying into other segments. The most obvious segment would be to move into networks for small to medium sized firms where the demand is typically for 10 to 100 computers, which are linked. The advantage of this is that a higher price is paid for a single order. Whilst the mark up is lower than those on individual purchases the total profit can still be higher. Firms may require more sophisticated machines and network solutions which the Computer Essentials, cannot at present, supply at a reasonable price.

Whilst the firm has the ability to produce machines, mainly for games, it is reluctant to do so since one of the best-known firms in the market has recently run into financial difficulties. Therefore, it considers one option would be to buy out this firm. The advantages of this are that the name is already well known. It also has the advantage that there are magazines, which already bear the name of the product. They only advertise the computers from this firm.

Integrated Business Package

In the business market, a possibility is to combine facsimile, photocopying, document scanning, a modem and a telephone answering machine in one package. This would have the advantage of being easy to use by the self-employed and other small businesses. Such businesses often have limited office space and combining all of these functions in one machine would be very space efficient. This has actually been the trend, with powerful machines being made that combine all the functions and some processing capability.

Internet

The Internet has become very important, particularly for businesses and educational establishments. By using Email, it is possible for businesses to communicate electronically worldwide providing the computers are fitted with a modem and they have access to the Internet. Computer Essentials wonders if this is an area that it could explore as a venture.

Laptops

Some business people, who have bought from Computer Essentials in the past, have suggested that the firm should consider moving into the laptop business. There are two different suggestions that this approach could follow. The first is that the firm should have a machine with all the speed, storage and memory of the best machines that Computer Essentials currently provides. This could be used to replace the desktop computers in offices and could then be taken out of company offices if workers needed to be mobile. The second suggestion, coming mainly from small firms and also firms with several sales representatives, is that a more inexpensive machine with limited memory and other resources is quite acceptable provided that the machine is compatible with Computer Essentials' existing machines.

Renting and Leasing

In order to encourage firms to purchase networks Computer Essentials is considering allowing firms to rent a network. If the firms decide to purchase, the network Computer Essentials will refund 50 per cent of the rent. Computer Essentials is also considering leasing networks if the cost is over £10,000. This avoids the capital outlay for firms and makes it easy for them to cost computers. An extension of this is that Computer Essentials will allow the firm to upgrade to a better network at a relatively low cost. However, the disadvantage of this is that Computer Essentials will have to enter the second hand market, which it has no experience of.

Upgrading

In the business sector, the ability to upgrade is important since software packages for word processing and accounts, etc. are being introduced all the time. A firm that is locked in to a computer, which cannot use the new packages, will find it difficult to get repeat orders. The ability to upgrade will therefore encourage firms to buy now. With computers, prices are constantly falling and perhaps more importantly computer specifications are improving, firms find it easy to defer decisions about computer buying. It is difficult to tell at what stage of the production life cycle the computer market is at for small businesses. However, the proportion of replacement machines has grown rapidly over the years. Upgrading may also be important for computer whiz kids who enjoy using computers at home for their own sake.

Distribution

It is also considering other options. One would be to try to distribute its products in different ways. There are four main ways of doing this. The first is to try to persuade high street electrical chains to sell its products. However, these firms, because of their purchasing power, will only be willing to buy its computers at a low price. Unless Computer Essentials is better known it is not even certain that the high street chains will be interested. The second option is to approach individual specialist retailers. These tend to locate on the outskirts of the high street. It would be very time consuming for Computer Essentials to approach these and its existing products are probably slightly more expensive than most independent retailers wish to stock in any quantity. The third option is to approach the large specialist computer retailers. The fourth option is to sell directly through mail order. This would mean high publicity costs compared to the firm taking out full-page advertisements in high quality press. Many people wish to try the products before buying. This is perhaps even truer of monitors, scanners and other peripherals than of the systems themselves.

The firm could try to expand its market share through better after sales service. Like most computer companies, it now offers two options. The first is a return to base option for repairs for five years to include both parts and labour. This is offered at 15 per cent of the purchase cost. The second option is to offer an on site guarantee which guarantees that they will come out within 24 hours. Although this costs 25 per cent of the purchase cost, it has been more popular especially with small firms where one computer going wrong can make it difficult for the administration to function.

There is also scope for training purchasers. One possibility here is for the firm to charge a relatively low price (utilising a market penetration policy). The advantage is that many prospective purchasers have limited knowledge of technology and do not use the machines to their full potential. A cheaper solution would be to have more comprehensive manuals and/or disks, which were written assuming no knowledge of computers. An alternative would be to have a technical hotline, where faults could be discussed and any enquiries into how best to use the machine. A maximum limit on the time taken could be allowed.

Questions

1. What are the advantages and disadvantages of vertical integration, i.e. manufacturing computers and owning shops?

2. Are there any disadvantages of buying a chain of shops rather than buying individual shops?

3. Why might the firm find it difficult to establish itself as a supplier to very large firms such as insurance companies, banks and the major retailers?

4. If the firm does take over the existing maker of computers mentioned above, what advantages and disadvantages, are there of keeping the existing name rather than having all the computers bearing the new name?

5. How far is brand loyalty important in:

    a. The computer games market.

    b. The small business market.

    c. The large business market.

6. In relation to question five, is brand loyalty transferable between these segments?

7.   What would be the advantage of an integrated leisure package including a computer?

8.   What are the possible risks in following the integrated leisure package option? What are the benefits of being the first firm to enter the market?

9.   What are the advantages to Computer Essentials of selling an integrated business package including Internet access?

10. It has been suggested to Computer Essentials that at the present time laptops are an example of conspicuous consumption, i.e. that they are not really used for essential business purposes but to impress other people. Is this true and if so what are the marketing implications?

11. What are the advantages in the short and long term of Computer Essentials entering the leasing and renting markets?

Case study 2: Cars

The car industry, since Henry Ford, has been regarded as the supreme example of mass production. Unlike coal mining, it is not generally regarded as a dangerous industry. However, the car industry has been prone to industrial disputes and strikes in many countries. The work is considered by many to be very boring and conditions are often unpleasant partly because of the noise levels. The management style has often been authoritarian. The work is repetitive and so it is comparatively easy to automate. Robots have been increasingly used by the industry particularly for unpleasant jobs such as spraying. They can also be used in awkward locations where human beings could not reasonably work. Robots are very expensive and it is difficult to give them a sense of touch, e.g. a human being would soon realise if too much paint were being used or an item was fragile, robots do not unless they are given very specific instructions. However, robots do not get bored and therefore their production rate is constant. They can also operate 24 hours a day.

Some firms, such as Volvo, have moved away from ever-greater specialisation to task teams. This means that the teams can decide themselves how to allocate tasks. The tendency has been towards ever-larger firms that dominate markets rather than many small ones. The UK now has no major domestic manufacturer since British Aerospace sold the Rover group to Volkswagen. Rover then collapsed after being sold off by BMW, which retained the highly profitable Mini Rover brand.

It is often suggested that there are economies of scale partly because of the high cost of research and development and because of the high costs of tooling up. There are suggestions that some customers are very brand loyal, e.g. the Mini has been in existence since the early 1960s. The VW Beetle, with its distinctive shape, has also been a long-lived name. On the other hand, the industry itself seems to assume that customers wish to have changes since new cars are brought out regularly. The customers themselves can be subdivided into two groups: private buyers and corporate buyers. The percentage of company cars was about 70% of total new cars in 1985 according to a report by Southampton University. This percentage has been decreased with tax changes. For a long while, there was an incentive because in the UK there were significant tax advantages for people having a company car rather than an equivalent rise in salary. Companies typically only use company cars for 3 years. Critics say that this had unfavourable consequences for car design. Whilst as Sweden shows it is possible to build cars to last for about 18 years with significant depreciation advantages, there is little point in doing this for company cars.

The government could have considerable influence on the car industry by trying to encourage hybrid and electric vehicles.

The government has also had an effect though taxation. The Vehicle Excise Duty (VED, the correct name for what is usually called car tax) is imposed on cars in one of two different ways. Cars registered before 1 March 2001, were registered under two price bands; one for cars with engine capacities below 1549cc and a higher one for engines that exceed this limit. If the car was registered after 1 March 2001 then there are a number of pricing bands based on the level of carbon dioxide (CO_2) emissions, which depends partly on whether the car uses diesel, petrol or alternative fuels. There were suggestions from time to time that it should be scrapped in favour of higher duties on fuel. There have been calls for this tax to be increased to ease the burden on the UK Road networks; the congestion charge introduced in London in February 2003 may have more of an effect. Due to the problems caused to the environment when old vehicles are left to rust, etc. people have suggested that there should be a partial refund on the initial tax if the vehicle is handed in to a responsible firm.

One previous minor concession was that in 1981 VED was scrapped on battery-operated vehicles. These are mainly used in the milk delivery business.

Tax is also imposed on fuel. In order to improve the environment there has been a differential rate between diesel and unleaded petrol.

Pressure groups have also influenced the industry. The industry, through its association 'Society of Motor Manufacturers and Traders,' persuaded the government to alter the date of registration from once a year in August to twice a year in March and September. Many customers have waited until the new registration dates to buy new cars. The car industry, like any other production industry, would like to have a constant demand for its product. By having two new registration codes per year this spreads the previously concentrated demand away from the busy month of August and avoids problems of having to employ different numbers of people at different times of the year and the associated high storage costs, insurance of cars etc.

Questions

1. Why is the car industry associated with low motivation? Discuss the likely solutions to this lack of motivation.

2. Some firms in the car industry traditionally lay off a large proportion of its work force during the year. Why do you think that this happened?

3. What problems occur if a region is very heavily reliant on one industry? Why do firms in the car industry and its suppliers tend to be located in one area? What are the implications for the Government if it is concerned about location of industry?

4. Do the different psychological groupings such as conservatives, reformers, aspirers etc. have any effects on the car market? What different types of cars would you expect them to have? What effects would a tax on cars that was solely based on fuel have on the manufacturers when designing future cars?

5. What effect would it have on the car market if one manufacturer were to announce a much longer car life of its vehicles? What effect would it have if all manufacturers did the same?

Case study 3: Coal

Coal mining has nearly always suffered from poor industrial relations whether in the UK or in other countries. This may reflect the close-knit nature of the industry. Coal miners, partly because of the shift system and also the geographical nature of the pits, tend to live very near the coal mines so will know each other much better than workers on an industrial estate. The influence of the peer group is therefore even stronger than Mayo would have found in the famous Hawthorne experiment.

The work is almost by definition carried out in unpleasant conditions. This has sometimes led to the seeming paradoxical conclusion that more pay may, in conditions of full employment, lead to less hours being worked. Whilst coal mining was traditionally a major employer in areas such as South Wales, Scotland and Yorkshire, the numbers of workers has fallen drastically from its peak of about 700,000 in the 1950s. Whilst strikes are often thought to be about pay, redundancy has been more of a problem for the Trade Unions. The mining dispute, which lasted a year in the mid 1980s, was mainly about possible redundancy. The NUM (National Union of Miners) has always wanted to be an industrial union, i.e. representing all the workers in the industry. In practise, overseers often belonged to a different trade union and partly for political reasons the Union of Democratic Miners was formed in the mid-1980s.

In recent years, productivity per week in British mines has increased dramatically. The demand for coal has been affected by a number of different considerations. Immediately after and during the Second World War, the maximum amount of coal was needed almost irrespective of cost. However, consumption by firms and households fell partly because of the Clean Air Act 1957. This in turn was a reaction to the smog of the early 1950s. Smog is fog mixed with smoke and heavily pollutes the air. It was estimated that one of these incidences of smog killed about 4,000 people in England. The railways were a large coal consumer but steam engines were phased out, especially in the 1960s. There has been increased competition from other countries' coal. German coal has been cheaper because of subsidies paid by the German government. Colombian coal has been cheap, partly because of the very poor working conditions. Some concern has been expressed about closures since if demand was to pick up in the future it would be difficult to re-establish pits especially if the mines had been flooded. If Carbon Capture and Storage (CCS) were to be feasible this would have a major influence.

The nuclear industry in the UK was subsidised in spite of the original claims that when Bradwell power station in Essex was built that nuclear energy would be so cheap that metering would be unnecessary. In 2013 the government announced an expansion of the nuclear industry in the UK.

In 1993, the electricity industry was accused of being over hasty in using gas as the major fuel in the industry rather than using coal. In the past, the electricity industry often subsidised the coal industry. Some environmentalists were also concerned about using gas since the total reserves of gas measured in terms of years used is much smaller than that of the coal industry.

Oil had been regarded as a very cheap fuel during the 1950s. In 1973 however, the OPEC cartel increased the price of oil considerably. In 1979, following the Iranian revolution the price was again increased but not to the same extent. Because the price elasticity of demand is much greater in the long term rather than the short term it was difficult to judge effectively the impact of price changes.

Questions

1. What effect does the close-knit nature of the mining community have on the industrial relations in the industry?

2. How far is there a trade off for the Government between environmental concerns and the desire for more employment?

3. Is there any logic in subsidising the nuclear industry?

4. What effect would the closure of a local coal mine have on the housing market? Would it have a different effect if it were a closure of a nuclear power station?

5. By the mid 1990s, about 80 per cent for the demand for British coal came from the electricity industry. What are the advantages and disadvantages of having one large customer from the coal industry's point of view?

6. Why have commentators often looked at fuel in terms of current years use and how long it would last at this level? Is this the best measure that can be used?

7. Why might other countries, particularly Scandinavia, be interested in the type of fuels that the UK uses?

8. What is meant by an industrial union? Why might different grades of workers not always wish to belong to the same union?

9. In 1995, the coal industry was effectively privatised. Why is the coal industry in many countries a nationalised concern?

10. The EU has suggested that there should be a tax on fossil fuels. What is the logic of this?

11. It has been suggested that the principle of the 'polluter should pay' should be adopted. What would be the effects of this on the fuel industry including coal?

Case study 4: Bikes

Mark 1 Cycles is a small cycle manufacturer. They deal in small quantities of custom built racing and touring bikes. They have never tried to sell mountain bikes although they have had the occasional order from existing customers. Custom-built bikes are made for individual customers according to size and other individual specifications. These could include the material from which the frame is made, number of gears, etc. The typical prices of custom-built bikes may range from £600-£1,500 although some are much more expensive than this. They have advertised mainly in the enthusiast's press and in the local free newspaper. Demand tends to rise in the summer and to a lesser extent at Christmas. The total number of bikes that they sell is about 20 a month though this fluctuates. Now John helps produce the bikes and doubles up as the marketing manager. His Father started the business

10 years ago and is willing to put in an additional £50,000 into the business but he is unwilling to work for more than one day a week on administration unless there is an emergency. This is because he values job satisfaction, which he obtains from having a tangible product.

They employ one person from time to time on one of the government schemes to help young unemployed people. They find that the quality of people on the schemes varies tremendously. If the person is enthusiastic then this helps the other workers but in other cases, they have found that the lack of morale has spread to the other two employees. These two employees are in their 30's. The site on which they work is about 100 yards from the family's home and has been bought outright by John's father. It is unlikely that planning permission would be given for anything apart from a shop if the site were sold. The local authority is however willing to accept a slight expansion for existing uses since no complaints have been received from neighbouring households. As existing small retailers are having difficulties in surviving, the chances of them selling the site seem small.

Mark 1 Cycles is concerned that its existing marketing is unsatisfactory. However, neither John nor his father has much expertise or interest in this. They have considered the use of a marketing consultant but have concluded that the consultant would be expensive and they have been unable to find anyone who specialises in their market.

One of the problems in custom built work, as with any other JIT production, is that of continuity of work. They are considering a range of options. One would be to have a shop selling their cycles. The rent for this would be about £50 a week. John is in favour of this as the recent pedestrianised High Street has a cycle lane, which makes it attractive not only for local residents, but also many other people who come to the area as tourists. His father, on the other hand, feels that it would be necessary to employ another full time person to do this and that this would not be commercially worthwhile. He thinks that there are a number of other possibilities. His preferred option would be to have a cycle shop, which would sell a range of cycles including cheap mountain bikes in the £150 to £400 range. They could also sell children's bikes and carry out repairs. If a person is to be employed it would seem to make sense to offer cycle hire. This is very popular in the region. John, however, is concerned about damage to the bikes and the possibility of bikes not being returned.

The other possibility would be to share facilities with an existing company, which is currently located in another market town 20 miles away. This could make a wider range of bikes and whilst at this stage they would not enter mass production, they could produce mountain bikes in the £300 to £600 range, as well as their existing types of bikes. There would also be some economies of scale since they could buy in items more cheaply. The existing company, David's cycles, whilst newer, has been more marketing orientated and has succeeded in selling on average, 50 cycles a month.

A third option, which the two employees have suggested, is to produce a standard frame, which could be sold in its own right. The standard frame could have other accessories added to it such as different forks and tyres. The advantage of this is that it would overcome the problems of continuity of production, which has concerned them. This is particularly important since there are few other jobs and most of them are seasonal. They also have high job satisfaction.

Questions

1. Which of the options about expansion would seem to be preferable? What further information would you recommend the firm to have before making a final decision?

2. They are therefore considering advertising more widely including local radio. They have also considered the use of vouchers in the cycle press, which could be used within a specified period, particularly within the winter months. Would these options seem to be suitable or are there any alternatives that they should consider?

3. They could try to develop their own site but the capacity would be limited to about 80 cycles a month with existing equipment since there is only limited space available. They are reluctant to move to David's Cycles location since about 20 per cent of Mark 1 Cycles demand is from their local town and they feel that this would be lost if they moved even 20 miles away. An alternative would be to move to the industrial estate on the edge of the town. This has the advantage that sites are available of almost any size or shape. The disadvantage is that leases are only granted for a minimum of 10 years. What factors should they take into account when deciding where to locate?

4. If they change the types of bikes they sell, how will this affect their target market?

5. If Mark 1 Cycles changed to mass production as opposed to unit production, what effect would this have on the organisation?

6. They are considering having one more full time employee in the short term rather than relying on people from government schemes. What problems might there may be in recruiting a suitable person?

Self-examination Questions

1. What is meant by 'basic human needs?' How far is it true that in a modern society our wants go much further than this?

2. What is meant by the phrases primary, secondary and tertiary production? Discuss the trends in each of these areas.

3. How far can agricultural production be improved without risk to future production through loss of soil?

4. What factors can influence the construction industry in a country? How far have different management methods affected the industry?

5. Why would you expect to find more tertiary sector workers in a developed rather than a developing country?

6. Explain how computers and word processors might help to improve productivity in the secondary and tertiary sector.

7. Why is it important for a country to have an increased proportion of savings?

8. What are the advantages and disadvantages of JIT production? How does JIT production differ from JIC production?

9. In what circumstances can JIT cause problems with production? Hint: Think of natural disasters/ terrorism.

10. Can organisations in all industries benefit from JIT techniques or is it just those in secondary production?

11. Why is it important to have a good relationship with your suppliers if you wish to change from a JIC to a JIT system? Is it best to have a number of suppliers for each component or just the one?

Chapter 4: BUSINESS OBJECTIVES

4.1: Introduction

What are the objectives of an organisation? They can vary enormously between firms, ranging from profit maximisation and customer satisfaction to just simply surviving in the market place. Many factors influence the achievement of business objectives. Throughout this topic, we will be looking at the presence and actions of different groups that affect business objectives. These groups are often referred to as *stakeholders* because they have an interest in some part of an organisation. Stakeholders usually include business owners, managers, staff, suppliers, customers, governments, pressure groups, trade unions, the media and the public. We will examine the interaction of stakeholders and how their actions might lead to problems and tensions in business. We will also explore how, if at all, such issues can be addressed and overcome in business.

4.2: Multinationals and Society

A frequently asked question is, 'to *whom* do multinationals owe allegiance?' For example, Lonrho has a variety of interests and immense power. It was the largest commercial landowner in Africa; it has owned regional newspapers and a car distribution network. For a long while, Lonrho was associated with the late Tiny Rowlands as the leadership of the company seemed to be very much in the hands of one man. The late Sir Edward Heath, the former Conservative Prime Minister, at one stage described it as the unacceptable face of capitalism. Lonrho was founded in 1909, and owned land in the sensitive parts of Africa that offended many sensibilities. Takeover battles for ownership of Harrods and the resulting media reports portrayed the image of Lonrho as a cold and calculating multinational in the eyes of the British politicians and public.

In the USA, the State of Alaska, which has relatively few opportunities for economic growth, has to weigh up the risks of a potential environmental disaster, such as an oil spill, against the opportunities for employment and wealth creation by allowing large multinationals to access to the States valuable natural resources.

Do multinationals owe allegiance to the governments of the countries in which they are operating? Do they only owe allegiance to shareholders, or should they have a wider responsibility? In 1996, these questions were asked of Shell on the anniversary of the execution of some Nigerian 'dissidents'. These people were peacefully protesting about the devastation caused to their land by the large multinational oil companies. The government, which was aware that 80 per cent of the country's income was oil-related, arrested nine men of the Ogoni people. A number of environmental and human rights organisations pressed Shell to condemn the arrests but to no avail. On the 10 November 1995 all nine men were executed. There is no doubt that there are economies of scale within multinationals. We can quantify the technical economies of scale, such as the lower unit costs of a large oil refinery rather than a smaller one. The diseconomies of management when a firm gets too large are more difficult to assess. In many cases, management does not recognise these diseconomies of scale.

Should we take more account of the environment? Firms can look at effects at different stages of production. At the input stage, some substances might be harmful to the environment, while alternative options might be less harmful. In the processing stage it may be possible to use renewable energy sources that eject zero emissions compared to low-grade coal which generates considerable pollution. In recent years, there has been growing criticism about the excessive amount of packaging used for goods. Apart from being a waste of resources in the first place, it forces local authorities to spend large sums of money on its collection. Once the goods have been produced, the distribution process may further add to environmental pollution and congestion. For example, badly sited factories tend to require lengthy transportation of goods by road using large lorries that consume fuel and produce carbon emissions, in addition to increasing the volume of traffic on roads across the country.

The government can influence a number of these stages. In 1995, the government proposed a landfill tax, which was based on the tonnage of waste sent for disposal. The principle behind the tax was to encourage firms to use fewer raw materials, improve efficiency in production and reduce the amount of packaging used in the distribution and retail of the goods. The landfill tax is in operation across the UK, although it is nowhere near as high as in Germany. Another way in which the government can influence the use of resources is to subsidise or tax certain types of fuel. This brings together financial incentives for businesses and the benefits of more environmentally sound energy options.

Businesses also need to take account of the environment. Uncontrolled businesses can lead to wide scale pollution, noise and accidents. This is very easy to see with some road haulage businesses. Some lorries are not well maintained and so may cause excessive pollution and will often be very noisy. The safety record of some road haulage businesses has not always been very good. Government intervention in these matters is often needed as well as regular checks to ensure firms are complying with the various rules and regulations that have been put in place to eliminate these problems.

4.3: The Objectives of Firms and their Effects on Society

How do the objectives of a firm affect its internal and external environment? If a firm wishes to maximise profit it must look at both its costs and revenue. The tendency is for different firms to look at either one or the other. For example, firms that have managers with a background in accountancy will tend to be cost-orientated, whereas a firm controlled by managers with marketing or promotional backgrounds will often seek to increase revenue.

When examining operating costs, firms may be inclined to reduce expenditure on staffing, since labour often represents the single largest expenditure area in an organisation, especially in the tertiary sector. In 2011, there were relatively high levels of unemployment in the UK which resulted in approximately 2.7 million people claiming social security benefit with a cost to society (through government provision) of between £5,000 to £10,000 per person per year. The effect of this was not only that individuals cut back on their expenditure, but the government also had to reduce public spending in certain areas to balance the budget. Long periods of economic downturn and unemployment can lead to the phenomenon known as a 'downward spiral' of depression.

If managers are mainly looking at revenue then they may spend more on marketing and the sales effort. This may have a positive or negative effect on society. For example, managers of companies that include tobacco products may try to expand production and sales growth. This would be difficult in many developed nations due to the tight advertising regulations surrounding tobacco products. However, they may choose to promote their product in Third World countries that have less stringent regulation against tobacco advertising. Organisational growth may be particularly important for senior management since their salaries and prestige will most likely depend upon success in the market place. The sheer size of some firms, especially multinationals may pose problems for even the largest of governments. Multinationals have the potential to rapidly move production from one country to another to minimise costs, which may adversely affect the policies of a government in pursuit of full employment and economic growth.

How can firms achieve economic growth? One method is by moving into the production of different goods or services. This is known as diversification. In 1995, there was controversy about takeovers of electricity firms by outsiders to the market. In 2013 there were concerns about the complexity of charging by the six major companies, some commentators felt that if an outside firm took over the electricity companies then it would be difficult to compare the companies' costs.

One of the arguments for privatisation of the electricity industry was that consumers could compare costs between providers. The growth of firms is one of the reasons why an organisation may choose to pursue a takeover or a merger. If planned thoroughly the resultant firm will be able to use the resources and capabilities of the two separate firms more efficiently than if they were still independent organisations. This is a concept known as *synergy*, commonly referred to by the phrase 'more than the sum of their parts'. In some cases, firms have not been able to diversify successfully because of their lack of knowledge of other products.

Many people have suggested that we need to look more at social objectives such as the need for employment, control of pollution, etc. Should the difference in private and social costs be reflected in the price system? The government has used the constraints of law about health and safety of workers to control pollution and to put social pressures on firms. Whether enough pressure has been put on firms was a matter of debate in 1994/1995 and again in 2005/2006 when there were many comments about the inadequacy of water supply after the very dry winter, followed by a hot summer, in the UK. This pressure can come from appointed independent regulators or through government legal frameworks. In 2012 there was a concern about water supply.

4.4: The Need for a Legal Framework

Why do we have a legal framework? Is it to look after the interests of different groups such as shareholders, consumers and the public? Whilst the legal framework is not the only way in which conflicts can be resolved, it has become increasingly important. For example, we can see how the growth of consumer protection has risen in the UK. There are also other reasons for having such consumer protection, like the growth of consumer durable goods, particularly electrical goods where the usual principles of *caveat emptor* (let the buyer beware) does not apply so easily. During the last 15 to 20 years, there has been more concern about environmental issues; many people feel water pollution should be rigorously controlled. Part of the problem here is that it is very difficult to detect what is happening.

In addition to chemical pollution, there has been increasing concern about noise pollution generated by industry, firms and individuals. More recently, the issue of light pollution has come to a head. There has been need for extra legislation in the housing market where consumers cannot easily check on the condition of houses. There have often been conflicts in the use of land and planning applications where younger people would like to see new housing built for them while older people do not wish to see encroachments into the countryside. There have also been conflicts between the desire for more employment and visual pollution as well as the desire to conserve good agricultural land.

4.5: Firms and the Greening Effect

Should we take more account of the environment? If government and society are serious about trying to reduce pollution they have to look at the effect of pollution at the input stage. For example, a firm might use hydroelectric power rather than fossil fuels. At the processing stage, it might consider the effect of smoke from chimney stacks on the local environment. This is often important for steel producers. There has been considerable controversy over the amount of packaging that is not just used for protection purposes but also as part of marketing products. At the output stage, manufacturers need to consider the efficiency of their machines, particularly in terms of energy consumption. For example, some computers use far more electricity than others. Governments might influence this using tax, subsidies or legislation. There are problems of ownership and control where negative environmental factor from one country to another; e.g. pollution in the Mediterranean Sea. It might be concluded that international as well as national action is therefore needed. The Kyoto Agreement may have altered the behaviour and operations of many national and international firms.

4.6: The European Union and other International Trading Blocs

The changing nature of the EU, from 15 members in 1995 to 27 members in 2007 and again to 28 in 2013, will have affected all of the states in different ways. Countries with the largest economies, Germany, UK and France, have had to support smaller and economically-weaker members, such as Greece and the newer Eastern European nations. Presently the effect of the introduction of the Euro is hard to judge on the separate countries. Firms raise several questions in relation to the EU which include:

- What will be the effect of the free movement of labour?

- What is the effect of harmonisation of regulations?

- What effect would the single currency have on outside investment?

- How will tax harmonisation affect the goods and services markets between member states and countries outside the European market?

- How stable will the single currency and a unified interest rate be if implemented throughout all member states?

- What will be the effect of further expansion of the EU?

Many academic and business commentators the world-over have put forward different views on all of these questions. One of the few things that they agree on is that only time will truly tell. This means that firms need to find ways of minimising their exposure to possible risks while not missing the positive opportunities the uncertainty provides.

4.7: Demographic and Social Changes

A demographic change is where there is a change in the population statistics of a community, whereas a social change is where the people organise themselves differently within that community. An example of a demographic change in the UK in recent years has been the increase in population in England and the projected decreases in Scotland. There has been an increase in the population of England of around 1.6 million every ten years between 1951 and 2001. This growth is predicted to increase to a rate of 1.75 million every ten years until 2025. The reverse is true for Scotland's population. This has been relatively stable over the last 50 years but is predicted to decline in the next 24 years. These changes have consequences for many groups, including private sector businesses – their market will either grow or recede over time; public sector bodies – local authorities and health organisations – responsible for community services; and national government which needs to ensure economic and social stability.

Estimated and projected population of the United Kingdom and constituent countries, 2010 to 2035

	2010	2015	2020	2025	2030	2035 millions
United Kingdom[1]	62.3	64.8	67.2	69.4	71.4	73.2
England	52.2	54.5	56.6	58.6	60.4	62.1
Wales	3.0	3.1	3.2	3.2	3.3	3.4
Scotland	5.2	5.4	5.5	5.6	5.7	5.8
Northern Ireland	1.8	1.9	1.9	2.0	2.0	2.0

Table notes:
1.   Figures may not sum due to rounding.

Source: Office of National Statisitcs; Summary: UK Population Projected to Reach 70 Milllion by Mid-2027 26-Oct-2011

Figure 4.1

Demographic changes on a national level are mostly influenced by births, deaths and immigration. These three factors themselves can be influenced by changes in society.

Sociology can be defined as the study of human social behaviour including the origins, organisation, institutions and development of human society. Therefore, for example, an increase in migration to the UK may be caused by political problems in another country or that there is simply a more attractive job market available in the UK. The influx of foreign nationals to another country will affect its ethnic and cultural diversity. It may change the demand for certain goods and services. For example, the large number of British people going to live in Spain may have an effect on the local demand for tea.

Another example where a social factor affects the population of a country would be the continual improvement in medicine and the standard of living in the developed world. This has caused the death rate in these countries to decrease, both by prolonging life expectancy through healthy living and curing diseases that may otherwise be fatal. While good for the inhabitants, this has caused countries many problems as they find themselves having to deal with an ageing population. This has many consequences for organisations as a lower percentage of working age people will have to support a growing number of elderly.

The changing nature of the family will affect what firms sell and whom they sell to and thus their ways of fulfilling their objectives. The average size of a household in the UK has reduced from 2.9 people in 1971 to 2.4 in 2002 according to *Social Trends*, an annual publication by the Office for National Statistics (ONS). This has consequences not only for house building and education but also for the holiday industry and car manufacturers. In fact, any firm whose product or service design depends on the number of people involved is likely to be affected.

Over the last 50 years or so there has been a change in the aspirations of women. While in previous times the woman would generally stay at home and look after the house and children, this is no longer the case. Figures showing university entrance for 2008-09, show that 51% of young women entered higher education, up from 49% the previous year[5]. The overall figures also show an all-time high of 45% going to university, including 40% of young men. This has not yet had its full effect on the greater employment market where most of the highly paid managerial jobs still go to men. It is only a matter of time however until greater equality is achieved in the UK job market. This will have a profound effect on many industries. With

[5] http://www.theguardian.com/commentisfree/210/apr/02/female-students-majority-women-university

parents spending more time at work, and so less time at home, the childcare industry will need to expand. The increase in hours worked by the country's population may lead to an increase in the money people spend on leisure. This is because it has been observed that the less time someone has to relax, the more they are likely to pay for the activities they choose to do to 'make the most of it'. These outcomes will also be contributed to by the rapid growth of higher education in many countries. Although this may mean it is harder for graduates to find jobs in a more competitive marketplace, it should mean that firms get to pick from a wider range of individuals when recruiting.

4.8: Types of Groups

The above factors influence and change the objectives of a firm. The following section deals with the influences of different groups, also known as stakeholders, on the objectives of organisations.

4.8.1: Employers

Businesses will have to deal with employees, customers and suppliers as well as people who may be indirectly influenced by their decisions. Employers are likely to be subject to rules concerning health and safety. Even if there were no legislation, one would expect firms to take account of these issues for ethical reasons. For example, the best firms will be aware that excessive hours worked by employees might cause deterioration in their health. Other, less scrupulous firms may ignore these concerns all together. Again, the best firms will be aware that unsafe practices may have a very damaging effect on employees and in some cases, may cause fatalities. A good road freight firm will try to ensure that its lorries are well maintained to reduce risk to employees or the public through excessive pollution from exhaust fumes or the possibility of an accident caused by a poorly maintained lorry. Apart from pay and working conditions, employers may feel a moral obligation to pay a satisfactory pension to past employees. Some firms, including the Co-operatives mentioned in Chapter 2, share their profits with the workers.

4.8.2: Managers

Managers may have a variety of objectives such as prestige, job security, wages and professional benefits. How can we measure these objectives? Do managers achieve these objectives or are they constrained by shareholders wishes? What happens if managers' objectives conflict with that of society? For example, a manager may want to choose the cheapest form of waste disposal, which could harm the environment.

There is a concept of expense preference by managers; this means that they may spend more money on a prestige building for their departments than is warranted on profit grounds. There has been considerable comment about both the gas and water industries where more was spent on the salaries of top management than on providing a good service. Managers may also spend more on prestige items such as computers than more useful non-prestige items such as training. They may also take advantage of 'perks' like bigger offices and company cars.

The objectives of managers may influence their management style. In 1961, Robert Blake and Jane Mouton developed a classification of managerial styles called *Blake's Grid* often referred to as the *Management Grid*. This rating system is based on two dimensions, 'concern for production' and 'concern for people'. The nine by nine grids can be used to classify management styles and the two organisational psychologists suggested a few characteristics of common positions. An example of the grid can be seen in Chapter 7.

It is also useful to note the three extremes of leadership. *Autocratic*, which comes from the Greek for 'ruling by oneself'; *Democratic*, which promotes consultation; and *Laissez Faire* derived from the French language meaning 'leave us alone', actually advocates minimal regulation and interference in the affairs of individuals.

Autocratic managers are most likely to allocate tasks to employees and demand their compliance. The advantages gained from this type of leadership are quick responses from staff and a clear chain of command. This means that if there is a problem that needs to be solved it will be obvious who to ask. Autocrats tend to make the majority of important decisions themselves. There are a number of obvious drawbacks to this approach of employee management. As the sole focus of the group, without the manager the group may have no direction, they may not be able to function without their input. The authoritarian nature of the organisation will require constant supervision to continue to operate. In situations where people are expressly instructed there tends to be an element of rebellion against the system if staff are not kept in line. The other disadvantage is that many people respond negatively to this style of management. They may see the approach as an affront to their expectations of their working environment.

Democratic leaders seek consultation with their subordinates. They also tend to encourage employees to offer suggestions to issues and often go to great lengths to explain why they take certain approaches to issues. The benefits of a democratic working environment are the increase in support, the motivational effects of employees contributing to decisions and the increased sense of commitment to the team cause. The disadvantages to this style may include a lack of respect for the leadership of the organisation and decisions may not be made so quickly or decisively.

The third approach to management and leadership is Laissez Faire. The philosophy behind this approach is that workers get on better without supervision. This is an increasingly popular management approach in the design industry, but has been prevalent for longer to an extent in the higher education system. Advantage to this approach is a freethinking environment. A good idea should be implemented regardless of who comes up with it. A major disadvantage to this is lack of control and if self-regulation mechanisms do not work then organisations cannot be sure of making any progress

There is no lone best style of management or leadership. The appropriate kind can only be found by looking at a number of factors. These include what the business does, its cultural and ethical views, the size of group to be managed, the type of group members and the personalities of not only the leader but also those that are to be led. Therefore, a firm's objectives have a major impact on the type of management that is most effective.

4.8.3: Pressure Groups

In most countries, there are various groups concerned with business. These will be subject not only to legislation but also to social pressures to conform in such a way that they do not adversely affect other groups. Different pressure groups will have different objectives. They may be environmentally concerned, related to employment or involved in any other form of lobbying governments and large firms to change their policies. The influence and power of pressure groups is discussed further in Chapter 28.

4.8.4: Businesses and Customers

Businesses also have to take account of their customers. At the very least, they will try to ensure that they do not harm them. For example, a food company would make sure that strict hygiene is always adhered to when dealing with food. It would aim to ensure food is kept in good condition and that meat or fish that can carry disease is properly handled and processed. In all countries, there have nearly always been regulations about weights and measures. It is extremely difficult especially when some foods are pre-packed, for the customer to make sure that they are getting what they have paid for.

Electrical appliances can be dangerous if they are faulty. This is not something that a customer can judge easily for him or herself. Customers also cannot usually judge whether a product has been properly made until they take it home. Good firms will wish to earn a good reputation and so they ensure their products meet required standards since dissatisfied customers will return poorly assembled goods and demand their money back, thereby reducing profitability and tarnishing the reputation of the firm. It is often quoted in the business world that it costs ten times the expenditure to get a new customer than it takes to keep an existing one. Repeat custom will only be obtained if the purchasers are impressed by what they receive the first time. If consumers are content, not only will they buy from the same firm again, but they are also likely to tell their family and friends about their good experience with a product or service, thereby building a good reputation for a firm that is very difficult to achieve otherwise.

However, not all firms have a good reputation. There have been many complaints about firms that sell milk powder claiming that it is better than breast milk, although most medical evidence contradicts this claim. This is compounded when the same firms sell the milk to developing countries where the water supply is often contaminated. This encourages mothers to feed their children with milk powder mixed using diseased water instead of their own breast milk. Similarly, there have been complaints that the tobacco industry has tried to increase sales to these countries because sales in the developed world have fallen. Some businesses have been extremely bad with customers who buy items on credit. Complaints about excessive rates of interest are common. A good firm, on the other hand, will try to ensure that it does not give credit to people who cannot afford it and will also try to ensure that interest rates are reasonable.

In general, however, businesses are more powerful than customers and so the obligations are often the other way around. As a result, there has often been pressure upon governments to modify the underlying principle of caveat emptor ('let the buyer beware'). In particular, since businesses are likely to have greater knowledge of the law than their customers, the principle sometimes seems somewhat unfair.

4.9: Employee Obligations

Employees have social obligations in the course of working for organisations. Employees are supposed to act in good faith on their employer's behalf. They should not, for example, charge less or give goods away to their family or friends. Working in the public sector, they should not accept undeclared gifts, hospitality or bribes. Employees are expected to work conscientiously even when their employer is away and not to take advantage of their employer, for example, by using the office telephone for lengthy social calls. Employees should also ensure that they do not undermine health and safety measures set up by a firm. Even in the absence of clearly defined health and safety regulations, employees would be expected to use their common sense when using machinery or other heavy equipment in a factory. Employees are expected to treat customers in a pleasant and efficient manner, irrespective of their social background. While there is no legal obligation for employees to suggest improvements to their organisation, there may well be a moral obligation, especially if employees can see that some current practices waste resources.

4.10: Customer Obligations

Customers have obligations too. For example, they should not apply for credit if they know that they are not creditworthy. If they were buying on credit, one would expect them to maintain payments. In some cases, as with insurance, they are under an obligation of utmost good faith. Someone should not take out a life assurance policy and declare that he is in good health if the contrary is the case. Similarly, it would be a breach of the conditions of good faith if someone insured one of their vehicles and not declare that it was likely to be driven by someone with a poor safety record. In some cases, customers may be much more powerful than their suppliers. This situation is found in the cocoa industry where some of the customers represent the large chocolate manufacturers. These firms have more power and wealth than those supplying the cocoa and so can dictate what prices they will pay.

4.11: Supplier Obligations

Suppliers have some obligations. Even if it is not written in a contract that they will supply goods or services within a particular time, they may still have a moral obligation to do so. For example, if a supplier has always supplied items within a week, the business may well feel entitled to expect this in the future. A supplier also has legal obligations to its customers. It must supply goods or services that are said to be of merchantable quality. Firms will be expected to ensure that the items reasonably conform to what has been requested. For example, in the textile industry, it would be irresponsible for the supplier to supply cloth of the wrong colour or size.

Self-examination Questions

1. Do people's expectations differ between Western society and the Far East?

2. In what ways can greater emphasis on green issues lead to changes in the inputs of an organisation? Consider also their outputs and their distribution processes.

3. Why might poorer countries both fear and want multinationals?

4. How do the aspirations of women change employment patterns, the size of families and the demand for different goods and services?

5. In what way does the EU affect firms operating within it? Hint: think of Nissan threatening to stop production of Nissan Micra's in Sunderland UK because of the strength of the Sterling pound against the Euro.

6. What effect has the single currency had on firms outside of the EU?

7. What have been the effects on UK firms of the restrictions on the maximum number of hours in the working week and the introduction of the minimum wage regulations?

8. What effect will an ageing population have on a country's economy? How will the government cope with the extra burden on health, social security and social services?

9. What are the main objectives of managers? Hint: what would you look for in a job? Does this vary much between different country's cultures or the age of managers?

10. Does the management grid affect the underlying personality of managers or their beliefs? Where would your most recent manager appear in the grid?

11. How may managerial aspirations conflict with those of the shareholders?

12. What factors affect the supply of labour? Will the quality and quantity be different in the future?

13. Is the movement towards temporary contracts inevitable?

14. Can we ever return to an era of full employment?

15. What do we notice about geographical mobility within and between countries?

16. What are the main social responsibilities of a large factory that pollutes heavily, but is situated in an area where there is large-scale unemployment?

17. What obligations does a firm have to its employees? Does it differ as to whether these are long serving or short serving employees?

18. Does a firm have any obligation to its suppliers? Hint: should they try to keep them informed of any major developments?

19. Are there any differences between the legal and moral obligations a firm has to its creditors?

20. What obligations might a multinational company have to its community?

21. Is a firm's only obligation to make as much money as possible for its investors irrespective of what effects this may have on other groups?

22. Will we ever get to the work from home concept being a major part of the employment market? What would be the consequences?

23. Why would different styles of management be more appropriate in different organisations and departments? Hint: compare production and marketing.

Chapter 5: INTERNAL ORGANISATION

5.1: Delegation

The term delegation means the handing over of certain tasks or responsibilities to others. It is a very important part of a manager's job but many are incapable of delegating properly. This may be because they regard themselves as indispensable or are so proud that they do not realise that if they try to get involved in everything they will not achieve very much. Sometimes the problems of delegation arise due to a lack of trust between managers and their subordinates and sometimes they occur because people delegate tasks for the wrong reasons. These include the manager's inability to do the task themselves and delegation of tedious or unpleasant tasks such as disciplinary action. It is important to realise that the manager who delegates still retains ultimate responsibility. When managers delegate tasks, they may need to check occasionally that the work is being completed or provide guidance to ensure it is done correctly. Constant checking-up, however, can lead to feelings of resentment.

5.1.1: Accountability

Accountability can be defined as ultimate responsibility and is an important concept in all organisations. It may mean that one person is responsible to the person immediately above him or her and no one else. For example, in a small school the teacher may be directly accountable to the headteacher. Looking at it from the top down, it can be seen that the headteacher, therefore, has ultimate responsibility for all the staff in the school and the results that each of them produces. In a factory, the operatives who work the machines may be responsible to supervisors. The supervisor in turn may be accountable to the head of section. In turn, the head of section may be accountable to the head of department who is, again, accountable to the appropriate director, probably the production director. Company directors are accountable to their shareholders. In some organisations, however, accountability is less clear-cut. For example, in a college a teacher may teach students in more than one department and will therefore be responsible to more than one head of department. Management writers often distinguish between line management, which is, as indicated, where employees are directly accountable to a superior staff manager. The term 'staff management' refers to specialists who may not have direct responsibility. For example, in some firms personnel management will advise managers on recruitment issues but will not make the final decision on hiring a new employee.

5.1.2: Decentralisation

As firms get larger they may become multinationals (the head office is in one country but there may be branches in one or more other countries) or transnationals (senior management operates in more than one country). Firms like these, and companies that are widely scattered across a country, have to decide on the degree of decentralization that they are willing to establish. Making major, company-wide, decisions centrally has its advantages and disadvantages. Advantages usually centre on economic and administrative considerations and include easier implementation of a common policy and consistency across the company as a whole. Having one head-office can also lead to reduced overheads and the increased feasibility of specialisation, this in turn can lead to more effective decision-making. Advantages of decentralisation, that is allowing local offices to make their own decisions, include the ability to make decisions based on what is happening locally. This follows on from the idea that one common policy may not be suitable for everybody especially in the case of a multinational company. Decentralisation also provides local offices with a sense of responsibility that enables them to make the decisions that will affect them and their customers, thus providing a positive effect on the motivation and morale of staff.

5.1.3: Division of Work

Many modern firms deal with more than one product. For example, Lonrho had interests in several areas including farming, and gold and platinum mining. Sometimes such firms will set up divisions which deal with each of area of specialisation. This involves grouping employees by their expertise and providing them with resources they need to carry out their work in a particular division.

5.1.4: Profit Centres

Profit centres are set targets for profit which are considered reasonable given their investment, degree of competition, wage rates, etc. If all the activities are reasonably independent of each other, it becomes relatively easy for a branch manager to make decisions, as he or she should know the objectives of the profit centre and therefore those of each activity. Past and current decisions such as investment can also affect the profitability of an organisation. For example, a factory that invested in modern equipment may be more efficient and therefore more profitable than a firm with obsolete equipment.

5.1.5: Organisation

Organisations that grow quickly may do so without much regard to the management structure. What works well for a small firm may not work at all for a larger company. For example, having a small group of people in charge of the finance for a small firm would be adequate, but a larger firm will need a much larger finance department. This is true regardless of the type of organisation, whether it is a school, textile factory or an airport. In an organisation such as a small school, the headteacher will not only know all the staff but all the pupils too.

Similarly, regular customers become familiar to a small shopkeeper or market stallholder. In large organisations, this is not usually the case, and therefore there is a need to try to identify people, notably customers. In any large organisation, the managing director will not appoint all members of staff, instead there will be identifiable procedures for the relevant departments to organise tasks such as recruitment and promotion. It can therefore be said that a large business needs organisation in order to determine priorities. Generally, top management look at long-term priorities, middle management look at the middle term and supervisors are concerned with immediate tasks.

5.1.6: *Unity of Purpose*

One of the problems of any large organisation is that different people and departments within the organisation may hold distorted views of others. For example, the production department may think that production is by far the most important component in a firm and may regard the marketing department as a luxury. On the other hand, the marketing department will be concerned with trying to win orders and consider that without these orders the firm cannot exist. If each department works independently there is a danger that they will work in silos, (separate from other departments), thereby not recognising and working to the common purpose and objective of an organisation. One of the purposes of organisation, therefore, is to ensure that everybody is aware of the organisations objectives. Unity of purpose can be equally applied within non-commercial organisations such as schools or colleges. The business studies department in a college or university may feel that it provides the best possible tuition and that all students should join its courses. Similarly, the engineering department may feel that without their subject a developing country cannot thrive. There is a need for unity of purpose to ensure that the educational facilities are the most appropriate for the country. This can be achieved by involving department managers in decision making with the aim of reaching a consensus by understanding the views of all concerned.

5.1.7: *Operational Efficiency*

Part of the purpose of organisation is to ensure that the company works efficiently. In a factory, efficiency can be measured by the profitability or by the cost of each unit produced. This can apply equally to service industries such as road freight where it is possible to calculate operating costs and to judge them against other firms in the same business. However, care has to be taken to measure like with like. For example, the airline industry in more remote countries has to provide more long-distance flights and therefore prices will be higher. Profitability is also affected by decisions made in the past. A firm, which has always invested sensibly and recruited suitable staff, will find it easier to make a profit than firms that have not.

5.1.8: Work Planning

An important aspect of organisation is to plan the work to be done. Work may be subdivided into routine, peak, priority and emergency jobs. The demand for routine jobs such as the payment of employees' wages is known in advance. Being routine does not make the job any less important but it does make it easier to plan. In some organisations, there are peaks in demand items at certain times. For example, farms will have to cope with peak demands at harvest time and shops may increase sales near religious festival times, like Christmas. Similarly, factories may receive peak demands at certain times of the year or even at certain times of the week. These peaks have to be considered when planning the production schedule.

Organisations may also plan to allow for emergencies. For example, if deliveries of essential items do not arrive, then substitutes or other work must be found, as firms cannot afford to be idle. Similarly, if a member of staff is ill then someone else must cover his or her work. One of the methods used to help cope with peaks and emergencies is to use a wall-chart or computer package to create a timetable showing when work has to be completed. If two jobs have the same completion date, it may also be relevant to consider the priorities of each to decide which to do first. It is common in many offices to see that almost everything is marked 'urgent' as a matter of course, leaving the secretary to decide which work is genuinely urgent. The risk here is that the secretary's opinion of urgent work may not be the firm's priorities. It is also important to distinguish between jobs that are urgent, and those, which are important. For example, students going to university or college may have a career planned, which is important to them. If they are in the first year of a three-year course, the career plan may be important but it is unlikely to be urgent. Going to a dentist for toothache may be comparatively unimportant over a lifetime but it is obviously urgent. Similarly, firms have the same problems in determining what is urgent and what is important. A managing director of a large factory may well find it important to have a long-term plan but a disruption in the power supply may be an immediate and therefore urgent problem for him to deal with.

It is important that priorities be established in accordance with the overall needs of the firm. For example, if the marketing department asked the production department how long it would take to carry out a particular order. The production department may neglect it in favour of getting on with its own job, which it regards as more important. However, in the long term, without marketing the factory is unlikely to function.

5.2: Organisation and Methods

All industries need to have some idea of organisation and methods. The organisation and methods department is sometimes regarded as being part of an internal consultancy procedure. This phrase is very helpful. The organisation and methods department looks at the way the firm currently does things and works out if there is a better, more efficient procedure they could follow instead. For example, it may look into how a factory carries out its ordering process. Does the order originate from the production department or the purchasing department? Does the firm gather several quotes to ensure they are getting the best deal? Another activity to investigate could be how a firm decides upon the number of people who will operate a particular machine and looking into the consequences of changing that number. One of the problems with an organisation and methods department is the choice of suitable staff. If staff are permanently employed, there is a danger that they become part of the elite and lose touch with the reality of working in one of the departments they are trying to optimise. However, if they are likely to be transferred back to their original departments there is a danger that they may not suggest bold decisions in case it makes them unpopular with their colleagues.

Organisation and methods is not confined to factories, it can similarly be applied to building organisations. For example, the workers who built the large hotel in Accra, over a very efficient eleven months, would almost certainly have used organisation and methods. One technique they may have used is network analysis. This involves identifying those activities that can be carried out simultaneously (independent activities) and which have to take place in sequence. It is then possible to estimate the shortest timescale possible for each job and work out the effects of any changes on that timescale.

Self-examination Questions

1. What is meant by delegation? Why do some managers find it difficult to delegate?

2. What is meant by decentralisation? Why might it be common in multinational firms?

3. What do we mean by centralisation? What activities if any might we want a local authority or the Department of Education to centralise?

4. What is meant by divisionalisation? Why might it be common in multi-product firms?

5. What is meant by accountability? Is it true that in all firms everyone is accountable to one person only?

6. What is meant by profit centres? Why are they used?

7. What does saying that 'one of the objectives of organisation is to achieve unity of purpose' mean?

8. What is meant by the term operational efficiency? Why might it be more difficult to measure this in a school than in a business organisation?

9. What does the phrase 'work planning' mean? Why might it be difficult to plan for emergencies?

10. What is meant by planning? Does planning have to take place in all businesses?

11. What is organising? Which resources have to be organised?

12. What are natural resources? What is the difference between renewable and non-renewable resources?

13. What is meant by co-ordination? Why do different departments need to co-ordinate activities? Illustrate your answer with reference to the typical production and marketing departments in a manufacturing firm.

14. What does the 'division of work' mean? Why might it be common in multi-product firms?

Chapter 6: ORGANISATIONAL DEVELOPMENT

6.1: Why do Organisations Develop?

There are many different reasons for the development of different organisations. They may be due to internal or external changes, which are discussed in more detail in Chapter 26.

6.1.1: Selling More Goods and Services

The changes may occur because there are opportunities to sell more products or services to customers. As an example, the development of UK airports where the British Airports Authority (BAA), the owner until recently of Heathrow, Gatwick and Stansted airports amongst others, makes as much revenue from duty free shopping as it does from the airline fees. Another example is the diversification strategy pursued by two of the big UK supermarkets into non-food sectors. Both Tesco and Sainsbury's have moved into music and film sales and financial services. The reason for these expansions can be attributed to the gap in these markets for a low-cost entrant. The cost of adding these types of goods to their stores is marginal, as they take up little display and storage space, and so can be achieved on a trial basis with limited risk. The main reason that these supermarkets entered the banking industry was that through their food sales they had an extremely good daily cash flow. Customers pay for their shopping when they leave the store but the supermarkets often do not pay their suppliers until much later, by monthly account or quarterly invoicing. This meant that they had an opportunity to lend money over the short term. With access to this kind of money, they sought out profitable ways of using it.

6.1.2: Growth

Firms may wish to expand for a number of reasons. The most obvious is to increase profits. Other reasons include cost savings, the power gained through an increased market share, to avoid being taken over by a larger firm and so on. In fact, it may be the case that growth is the only option to ensure survival for some firms. If all major players in a market are expanding faster than your firm is then you must grow just to stay competitive. There are many different ways of expanding but these can broadly be categorised into either internal or external growth.

6.1.3: Internal Growth

Firms may opt to grow internally, this is also often known as 'natural' or 'organic' growth. The idea behind these analogies is that there is a form of organisational evolution as opposed to the revolution which is often linked with external growth strategies that are discussed later. To achieve organic growth a firm may open more branches or attempt to sell more products through their existing stores. The advantage of internal growth is that it can be done slowly with small incremental steps spreading the risk over a longer period of expansion. In terms of staffing, it may give opportunities for existing staff to gain promotion. The advantage to the firm in this respect is that they will know what an employee is capable of before they are promoted. This may not be so clear when assessing a potential newcomer to the firm during an interview process.

In many cases, internal growth may be slow since managers already have their own range of responsibilities and may find it difficult to find time to develop new services or outlets. This is why it is important that the correct amount of management time be devoted to the project. Many firms in a period of continuous growth have dedicated managers that travel around the country overseeing the setting up and development of new branches and ventures. If this is not the case then it can often be a slow form of growth since existing managers already have their own work to do. It should be noted here that just because a manager has the skills to run a successful branch does not mean that they have the abilities to organise the creation and integration of a new one. It may be difficult for them to develop the skills necessary for the expansion of activities.

6.1.4: External Growth

External growth can take many forms. These include a takeover, a merger, a joint venture or a franchising agreement.

A takeover is defined as when one firm gains a controlling interest in another. The pharmaceutical and entertainment industries in recent years have provided some of the largest takeovers in the world. There are two forms of takeover and these can be classified as being either 'hostile' or 'friendly'. A friendly takeover occurs where both firms agree to the takeover. An agreement is usually made as to how the two will integrate and all sorts of decisions are made prior to the deals' finalisation. These could include factors such as sorting out which top management will remain, whether their roles will change, and who reports to whom in the new consolidated organisation. A hostile takeover is likely to be, as it sounds, a bit messier. A firm that wishes to acquire another but, for whatever reasons, cannot or will not do so in a friendly manner and hence may attempt a hostile takeover where it makes a bid for the shares of a company in order to purchase a controlling interest. This is only possible in public limited companies where there are a large number of shares issued for public ownership. The aim of the purchasing firm is to gain control of its target against the agreement of the other firm's board. This aggressive tactic can cause many problems, the most obvious being the unwillingness of the management and staff to work in an environment that they would ordinarily have rejected. This leads to many motivational issues that are discussed in further chapters.

A merger can be thought of as a marriage of firms. Usually two (or more) firms agree to merge for mutual benefit. The reasons for such a decision are the same as for takeovers. Firms seek out resources and capabilities that they want or need to improve and they find partners who have them. The most successful mergers are those where both parties have an equal gain to make from joining forces. An example of a successful merger in the past is that between Disney and Pixar, the consequence being that Pixar can now create more movies with the support of Disney to help in the marketing of the products.

Joint ventures are typically projects that a number of firms enter into together to achieve their collective aims. They are a special form of the joint stock company mentioned in Chapter 2. This kind of organisation is often found in high technology markets where companies that would usually be competing commit to working together towards advances. This allows the firms involved to spread the cost of research and development and the associated risk of failure. By forming a joint venture, the firms' owners may be able to research projects that the individual members may not be able to afford to on their own. The opportunities for growth using this strategy are reduced, as all of the firms involved will be able to expand as they have access to the same research. However, if key players are not involved in the joint venture then a number of smaller firms may be able to steal market share away from the leaders.

We have already explored the aspects of franchising in Chapter 2. The major advantages to the franchisee are that they have a guaranteed number of customers, market share and they only have to concern themselves with the delivery of services and goods directly to the customer.

6.2: Definitions of Vertical and Horizontal Integration

In Chapter 3, we developed the ideas of primary, secondary, and tertiary production. In general, firms will buy raw materials (primary production), develop them (secondary production) and transport them (tertiary production). This is often referred to as the production process or supply chain. If a firm, wishes to expand there are a number of different directions that it can pursue as seen in Figure 6.1 below.

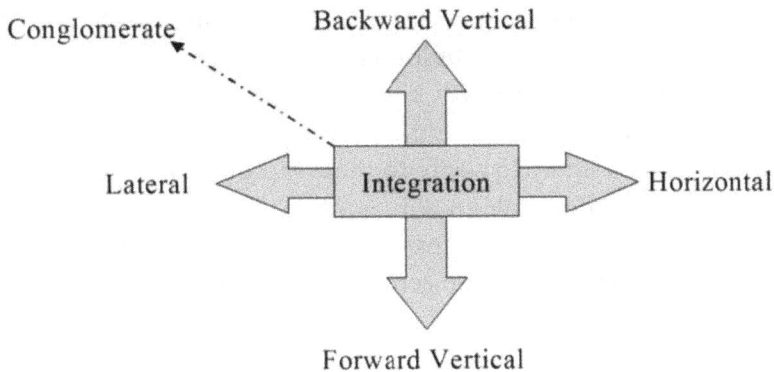

Figure 6.1

A company can go back-up or down the supply chain on the vertical axis or it can choose to move sideways into related markets or expand their existing operations. Alternatively, a firm may choose to enter a completely unrelated market and become a conglomerate organisation.

6.2.1: Vertical Integration

Vertical integration is defined as a firm moving backwards or forwards through the production process. This means that a firm takes over production of its raw materials or sale of its products. In many cases, this is achieved to ensure that an organisation has a continuous supply of raw materials or component parts and to secure outlets to sell its products to end-consumers. Backward vertical integration may help to ensure supplies to create or provide a good or service; for example, an oil company may take control over an oil refinery or untapped oil reserves. However, the expertise required for these associated stages may well be different. This would apply for example to the ownership of farms by the Co-operative Wholesale Society. There may be problems with backward vertical integration if the firm has to supply the raw materials or components to rival firms. For example, when the car manufacturer Ford took over Pressed Steel, Jaguar, which was then an independent company, was reluctant to buy steel from Pressed Steel once the takeover had occurred since it objected to buying from a rival car firm and felt that Pressed Steel might not give them necessary priority as their loyalty would be to Ford. Firms such as Cadbury, for example, owned their own cocoa plantations (backward vertical integration) for this reason. Breweries such as Whitbread have acquired their own hop fields.

Forward vertical integration often aims to ensure that there are customers for the goods or services produced. In the late 1980s, building societies bought estate agents. The reason for doing this was to increase the take up of their mortgages by gaining direct access to potential customers and offering them special rates for using both the estate agency and building society mortgage services. However, building societies did not necessarily have the capabilities to run estate agencies because the skills required are quite different. Independent estate agents would probably have been less likely to apply to these building societies for their clients' mortgages. Forward vertical integration is often pursued to ensure outlets are available to increase control over distribution. For example, many breweries own their own public houses and many oil companies own their own petrol stations.

6.2.2: Horizontal Integration

Horizontal integration refers to where a firm develops similar goods or services, for example, horizontal expansion could mean a firm opening more shops or having more factories producing more components at the same level in the production process. In some cases, organisations wish to have more outlets for their goods or services. The horizontal integration caused by the merger of banks Lloyds and TSB between 1995 and 1998 allowed the combined organisation (Lloyds TSB) to take advantage of an increased presence on High Streets across the UK. The advantage of standard horizontal integration is that management already have expertise in the particular good or service. For example, a building society will be able to use the expertise of existing managers and staff to run new branches. There are also economies of scale of infrastructure and equipment for the building society. It will be able to use the same computer system, offices and company vehicles. If, however, there is a merger, the same economies of scale may not arise, at least in the short term. For example, the former Halifax and Leeds building societies did not have the same computer system and so there were problems of compatibility in combining them. The banking sector has suffered from managers assuming they have more ability than they have and also from the bonus culture which encouraged reckless lending.

A special form of horizontal integration is lateral integration. This can occur if a firm buys or moves into production of products that are complimentary or substitutes to ones that it already produces. These goods must be at the same production level as the existing products. For example, if a toothpaste manufacturer enters the toothbrush market, while this is different from the original market, it is likely that the firm's brand name can be transferred across to create an instant market share if promotional activities are effective. This move also has a number of associated advantages. When Colgate started to produce their own brushes, they designed a product with a very large brushing head. The main reason for this was that it was a more effective shape for cleaning; it also had the advantage that people would use more toothpaste on it. This obviously had a positive effect on the sales of the brand's range of toothpastes.

6.2.3: Conglomerates

A conglomerate is a firm that has a stake in various unrelated markets, producing goods or providing services that seem to be wildly different from each other. A good example of this is the Virgin Group. This organisation operates in the airline, rail, music, cosmetics, finance and soft drinks markets. There are often few economies of scale gained by such diversification but the main advantage can be found in branding. By cross branding their products Virgin can benefit from positive consumer attitudes to other branches of its organisation when launching new lines and subsidiaries.

Conglomerates expand through diversifying into activities that seem appropriate at the time. This may mean that an opportunity to exploit presents itself and the firm enters the market with the backing of its financial muscle. For example, Unilever has control of the detergents Surf and Persil, Walls ice creams, Stork margarines, and frozen products from Birdseye. The advantage of conglomerates is that if one activity fails, the firm is not solely reliant on it so there is less risk than with a firm that is tied to just one activity. The disadvantage of such a company is that the span of control or chain of command may become too large.

6.2.4: Divesting

Divesting refers to where a firm sells off some of its operations. Firms often want to divest themselves of non-core activities that are not profitable or are consuming too much management effort. Unilever dispensed with SPD, which was the transport organisation for the company, and more recently Walls meat products because it was not essential to the firms core strategy.

6.3: Factors Leading to Organisational Change

Changes in legislation

Changes in legislation may affect businesses operations, for example, the Building Society Act of 1986 meant that the Abbey National Building Society could become a bank.

Changes in demand

Changes in demand may alter the nature of a firms business. For example, Halfords was originally a bicycle shop, but developed into selling mainly car components.

Increased Competition

For many years, IBM (International Business Machines) was the major manufacturer of mainframe computers. This special form of computer was used solely by medium to large firms due to their large cost and size. Increased competition from other smaller manufacturers forced it to enter the small business and personal computer markets to ensure a consistent level of turnover.

Changes in land use

This has particularly affected the retailing industry. In many cases, the inner cities have had declining populations. Firms have therefore had to change location in order to keep up demand for their products. The transport industry has been even more affected. For example, city railways have often had to extend their services to new suburbs. In some cases, as with the Metropolitan Line in London, the firm assisted with the sale of houses along the line.

Research and development

If a firm can use an existing product or material in a new product or market segment then the marginal cost of development and production is reduced as they will often have access to the staff and machinery needed to produce the new product. Dunlop has developed more uses for rubber; i.e. for tyres, footwear and conveyor belts. The oil industry has now produced about 2000 derivatives that are oil based, such as plastics. The Shell Research Centre, while not confined to research in oil, has been helpful in this area.

Fashions in management

It can be argued that the tendency for 'big is beautiful' in the 1960s led to mergers such as that between the British Motor Corporation, which produced Austin and Morris cars, and Leyland, which produced road haulage vehicles and buses. The logic was that there would be marketing economies of scale. In contrast, in his book *Small is Beautiful* (1973), Schumacher suggested the need for small organisations and less capital-intensive production. Whilst his ideas about less capital-intensive production have been ignored in the industrialised West, the concept of smaller organisations has become much more fashionable.

Personality of the owner

In some cases, as with Rupert Murdoch and News International, the late Tiny Rowlands and Lonrho, and Richard Branson and the Virgin Group, the firm has been identified with the person. In these cases, the growth of the business has often been a major objective. There have sometimes been opposite trends, for example, Lord Hanson who had built up a huge commercial empire including Imperial

Tobacco suddenly announced in January 1996 plans to divest the company. Such businesses are built around the leadership and motivational skills of the dominant owner.

Use of waste materials or spare capacity

Firms can try to use waste materials, or spare labour, machinery or capital capacity. In the oil industry, petrol and natural gas were originally waste products and so were consequently burnt off. Nowadays, petrol and gas are major products in themselves. Tate and Lyle, the well-known sugar firm, historically sent vehicles full in one direction only, creating the problem of empty return journeys. This was a waste of resource and so ways to fill-up lorries on return journeys were investigated. In the 1930's the shipbuilding industry had great problems, partly because of protectionism. In some cases, shipbuilding yards used part of their capacity to produce prefabricated buildings.

Additionally, in the 1990s, it was suggested that Railtrack could use its track to carry new telephone lines for competitors who were setting up in the same market as British Telecom (BT). The docklands railway, in East London, used old railway viaducts and old track bed to reduce costs. Similarly, in 2005, British Waterways announced high profits because it was using its towpaths and land for a variety of other purposes. Firms sometimes find new uses for existing products; e.g., the successful Range Rover vehicle had its origins in the Jeep. Jeeps were used in the Second World War to transport troops and light equipment. Colditz, which was used in the Second World War as a prisoner-of-war camp is now being used as a holiday centre. Beamish, an old coalmine in the north east of England is now a major industrial museum. Computers, originally used for industrial simulation, were widely developed for all sorts of uses after the 1980's.

Case Study: British Rail

Much of the UKs railway network was built during the 1840s due to the railway boom when George Hudson, a well-known businessperson, encouraged massive investment. In the 19th century, the railways developed so that they were within reach of almost all villages with a population of over 3,000. They competed vigorously and in some cases, they had problems with finding suitable routes. In order to extend the competition and their service, the firms developed shipping services. For example, the Gravesend to Tilbury Ferry was developed so that services from London, north of the River Thames, could compete with services south of the Thames. The ferry services to the continent from Dover, Harwich, and Folkestone were made so that the railways could also serve the people travelling to

Europe. In some cases, the trains were actually carried on the ships so that passengers and freight were not disturbed.

Originally, the railways were competing vigorously with the canals. There were allegations that the railways took over the canals in order to close them down, though this has not necessarily been proved to be the case. Competition tended to arise from road transport of both passengers and freight, partly in order to give a better service to its passengers and partly to reduce the risk of competition. The railways took over many of the road passenger services so that by the time of the nationalisation of British Rail in 1947, the railways were amongst the biggest road passenger operators. In order to give door-to-door service for freight the railways also bought up large number of well-known road haulage companies such as Pickfords. In some cases the railways could not give a satisfactory service by surface transport; for example the Devon to South Wales' shipping services was not applicable. Consequently, the Great Western Railways developed an air service, Railway Air Services (RAS) with the other large railway operators in 1933.

To give a service to passengers who might arrive at awkward times in large cities a number of hotels were built so that passengers arriving at inconvenient times could find accommodation, for example at Kings Cross and Liverpool Street stations in London. On longer journeys, passengers would often require catering so there were two possibilities; either catering could be done enroute or passengers could have meals at stations. The railways developed both of these types of services.

Nationalisation in 1947 prevented the logical diversification of the railways. During the Conservative Government from 1979 many of the services which British Railways owned, were privatised. For example, Sealink was sold originally to a British owner who in turn later sold it to Stena, a Scandinavian shipping line owner. Some of the residual road freight services were sold to the National Freight Company (later called the National Freight Consortia). The road passenger services were set up as a separate company under the Transport Act of 1968 and subsequently were privatised during the 1980's. The hotels were sold generally as separate entities while management bought out the station catering services.

British Rail and the previous private companies ran the engineering services because safety is paramount and in many cases, there would be few other sources of obtaining locomotives and rolling stock or wagons. Many towns such as Swindon and Derby became railways towns, not so much in terms of passenger or freight traffic, but because of their engineering importance. British Rail Engineering Limited was privatised during the 1980s. During 1993, it faced yet another crisis partly because of lack of continuity of ordering from British Rail. The uncertainty about privatisation did not help it either.

During the mid-1990s, the government announced that railway operations would be privatised. In early 1996, some of the first franchises were announced. This included the routes to the South West of England, which were bought by Stagecoach, one of the largest bus operators in the country. It could be argued that for Stagecoach it was a logical diversification from bus services to rail, which in some cases could be complementary. Railtrack the organisation that controlled the track and signalling was privatised in 1996. This organisation went into administration after failure in the early 2000's. A new, non-profit organisation, Network Rail, was established in Railtrack's place to run network railtracks and safety systems. In 2013 there has been considerable criticism of the franchising system

6.4: Organisational Development

At times, there is a straightforward desire for vertical integration, such as Allied Breweries taking over Victoria Wine, which would have been a large-scale customer. In the 1990s, Volkswagen took over Skoda. It invested considerable sums of money in Skoda, possibly because Skoda, in spite of jokes about its performance, was a source of cheap labour and its cars would complement Volkswagen's own range. News International, the Murdoch Empire, took over Fox, a well-known USA film and television organisation.

Other times, firms try to take over others so that they can survive as separate entities. For example, Cadbury, Kraft took over Cadbury in 2010. However, it should not be thought that such moves were necessarily successful. In 2010 there was controversy as Kraft laid-off workers at the plant near Keynsham near Bath having previously given reassurances about employment. The controversy also arose partly because of the different management style where Cadbury originally founded by a Quaker had continued with a paternalistic management style which was in contrast to Kraft. Cadbury is now owned by Mondelēz International. The take-over of Allied Carpets and MFI were widely perceived as being disastrous. One of the problems with such moves is the difficulty in financing. In some cases the transaction could be financed through the running down of working capital; for example, Nestlé had two and a half billion pounds cash which it has used to finance the buying of Rowntrees. On the other hand, Metropolitan Hotels sold their hotel chain in order to finance the buying of Burger King. Whilst this was widely regarded as going down market at the time, it subsequently seemed to be a successful strategy. This was because the hotel trade, being what an economist would call a normal good, tended to suffer very considerably during a recession (a normal good is one that consumers will spend more money on as incomes rise). Burger King will tend to maintain sales whatever the level of income. In some cases, as people trade down, it may actually gain during a recession. Therefore, in the longer term it seems to make sense to have both a rapidly growing business such as Burger King and to have industries which would flourish whatever the level of the economy.

Firms have sometimes used what are called 'tactical sales' in business. For example, a business may sell a property to a property developer and then lease it back. While this reduces the possibility of any capital gain from property, it does release cash. If the cash can be invested at a higher rate of return than can be obtained from the property then it will be worthwhile. If such a move at selling the property takes place immediately before a downturn in property prices, as in the early 1990s, it would have made more commercial sense. Firms alternatively can borrow money but this may lead to problems of capital gearing which is discussed fully in Chapter 13. The alternative is to borrow money from existing shareholders using rights issues.

6.5: Takeovers and Mergers

Takeovers and mergers take place for a number of different reasons. In many cases, the idea of a takeover or merger is that economies of scale will result. There are numerous economies of scale, for example in terms of marketing, finance, specialisation of labour or equipment, and technical economies of scale. While these economies of scale are often recognised, unfortunately many takeovers and mergers occur without recognising the main diseconomies of scale, which are essentially those of management and communication.

While economies of scale may be important, many firms do not distinguish between economies of scale and the minimum efficient size of the firm. For example, there are economies of scale in terms in using computerisation. In some cases, however, these economies of scale can be obtained at a relatively low level as computer and software prices fall rapidly in real terms.

In some cases, firms may merge in order to gain a dominant position. Fears were expressed in the 1960's that if certain bank mergers had gone through the resultant organisations would be too dominant. The credit crunch 2008 onwards has confirmed these fears. In the 1990's, there were reservations about the extension of power of some of the independent television firms and also other parts of the media. In other cases firms will merge or takeover in order to gain the advantages of vertical integration. For example, breweries may take over public houses or petrol firms may take over garages. This is called vertical integration forward. In other cases firms may wish to have vertical integration backwards; for example at one stage it was suggested that the electricity regions might be interested in taking over coalfields.

Firms can merge or take over for defensive reasons. For example, Sinclair was taken over by Amstrad in the 1980's because Sinclair was otherwise likely to have become bankrupt. Similarly, BBC computers were taken over by Olivetti for much the same reason. In other cases, the advantages may be that plant or scarce resources are more easily acquired by a takeover or merger than by other capital outlay. This may be one of the reasons why BMW took over the Rover Group in 1994. Apart from this, it also gained access to a ready-trained workforce. In some cases, it may be helpful to gain outlets in different areas. For example, building societies may well merge, not merely for technical reasons but also because some building societies will be stronger in some areas of the country than others. This may also occur at the international level.

The number and type of mergers may vary according to whether it is a boom or a recession. In a boom period, firms may well merge or takeover because of the ease of obtaining finance. They may also merge or takeover because it is easier than trying to find new sites in already overcrowded areas. In a recession, on the other hand firms are much more likely to merge or to be taken over for defensive reasons. Some management writers have put forward the concept of mergers and takeovers as a fashion trend - so called merger or takeover waves. One of the reasons for this may be if one firm is taken over, other firms react accordingly. The external events may alter the pattern. For example, at the time of British entry into the European Market in 1973 firms such as Dunlop and Pirelli merged to be a more effective competitor in the European Common Market.

There is a move towards global mergers and takeovers. In many cases, it is easier to buy an established firm in a foreign market place than risk entering from scratch. This is most often the case when the market is served by a select few large organisations and there is no room for entry from a start-up firm. This was the case when Wal-Mart wanted to enter the ultra-competitive UK grocery market. Instead of setting up their own chain of stores and investing in their own distribution networks, they took over ASDA. In doing this, they obtained all of the resources they needed to trade and an established market brand name and share. This also meant that they had one less firm to compete with.

Legislation may also influence the number of takeovers or mergers. If there are restrictions on takeovers, then mergers will not take place, whereas in 1994 when the government announced that there were no longer such stringent rules there were immediate repercussions. In some cases firms may merge or takeover rivals to get around problems of government clamp downs on areas like price fixing. Sometimes, firms may merge or takeover because an established firm already has a considerable degree of goodwill. For example, Nestlé took over Rowntree partly because many of the Rowntree brands such as Kit-Kat were extremely well known in the chocolate market. It would have been difficult for a new brand to get itself so well-known without a massive investment in product development and advertising campaigns, and even then success is not always guaranteed.

Self-examination Questions

1. Why might a firm wish to develop horizontally?

2. Why might a firm wish to develop vertically?

3. What are the advantages of internal growth?

4. What are the advantages of takeovers?

5. What are the advantages of mergers?

6. Why do firms sometimes divest themselves of certain operations?

7. Why might a firm develop using established materials in new ways?

8. In what ways might research and development affect the organisation of the company?

9. It is sometimes stated that firms have the desire for growth as their major objective. Why might this be true where managers rather than shareholders control the organisation?

10. It is sometimes stated that firm's managers over estimate their ability and therefore firms grow larger than would be warranted. Why might this be true and what would be the consequences?

11. It is sometimes suggested that takeovers occur because of fashions. Under what circumstances might a firm wish to merge for defensive reasons? Illustrate your answer with reference to the computer industry.

12. Why might the introduction of the Euro in 2002 have affected the organisational development of some firms? Illustrate your answer with reference to the financial industry.

13. Why might a firm such as Lonrho wish to divest itself of the Observer?

14. Why might management limit the rate at which a firm can grow?

15. Would the use of consultants help to overcome the problems of existing managers having too many tasks?

16. Why might finance in the short term affect the ability of a firm to grow? Would this affect the faster growing or slower growing organisations?

17. Why might lack of skilled people affect some high technical firms such as those in the aircraft industry?

18. Will land limits affect firms in primary, secondary or tertiary industries most?

19. How far will government legislation affect the growth rate of firms? Would it affect firms more within one industry or under what circumstances, if any, would it affect diversification?

20. Why might a building society wish to take over another building society?

21. What would be the advantages of a building society taking over an estate agency? Are there any disadvantages?

22. What has been the failure rate of the building societies compared with the banks since the credit crunch in the UK?

23. What would be the advantages of building societies obtaining investments from wholesale deposits rather than from individuals?

24. Why might building societies wish to carry out conveyancing?

25. Why has the government not allowed building societies to carry out conveyancing for their own customers?

26. Why did Walls produce both sausages and ice cream?

27. What link if any is there between Birds Eye, Bachelors and Walls? Why are they all part of Unilever?

28. What is the link between Dunlop's choice in producing footwear and tyres?

29. Why did Dunlop and Pirelli merge?

30. Why have newspapers moved into online versions?

31. Why are Boots and Halfords part of the same organisation?

32. Why have airports sometimes moved into the property business?

33. Why did British Aerospace take over Rover Group? Why was the EU concerned about this?

34. Why did Shell move into the chemical business when other petrol giants had not done so?

35. What is meant by (a) horizontal integration; and (b) vertical integration? What are the advantages and disadvantages of expansion in this way?

36. Why might management fashions affect the ways in which firms develop?

Chapter 7: MANAGEMENT

7.1: What is Management?

There is no universal definition of management. Management involves:

a.   Managing people

b.   Managing items such as factories, plant and equipment

c.   A mixture of (a) and (b)

Generally, management at the higher level will be concerned with the long term while lower level management will be concerned with the short term. Managing people is interesting but it poses difficulties because people are different and they react in different ways to similar circumstances. However, there are some general principles, which are discussed in more detail in the topic on personnel. Apart from the individual characteristics of people, management also want to ensure that the best people are appointed for the appropriate posts. They need to ensure that people have the right amount of work. While too much work leads to stress, many people may feel that having too little work is less challenging and boring. People who have too little work are likely to become frustrated and will find it difficult to work if more work has to be done. At a national level, the government has to consider the need for an adequate workforce to maintain the economy.

Managing plant and machinery tends to be subject to techniques that are less susceptible to change. There are well known techniques of investment appraisal. There is also a variety of mathematical techniques to ensure that projects are completed in the shortest time and to show the effects of more equipment on time taken queuing. Managers also need to select the most appropriate equipment and to ensure that it is kept in good condition. Too often, there are examples of machines and vehicles which have been bought but have been abandoned when repairs were necessary because of poor maintenance.

Good financial management and adequate data about production will help management to carry out its tasks. However, data, while helpful, does not prevent management from its key task of decision-making. Good management will, when making choices, consider feedback from staff, customers and other key groups.

Management also has to consider land availability. One problem with land use is that decisions made may be irreversible. For example, if an area of land is used for a factory, it cannot then be used for timber even if the loss of tropical forests poses many problems for the community and the government.

7.1.1: Administration

There is no clear-cut distinction between administration and management. However, administration covers the processes used to achieve the goals and objectives of a firm and the people carrying out the tasks. For example, it is common in some countries such as the UK to refer to the current government as the present administration. One definition of administration is the organisation (of people) required to run a firm. This in turn might involve drawing up an organisation chart. An organisation chart shows the titles of the jobs within a company, and who reports to whom in the form of a tree. From this, a job description can be derived which describes the duties the person is expected perform. The job description normally outlines the terms and conditions of employment; for example, the hours of work, where the job holder would be located and to whom he or she would report. It may also give information of an organisation's promotional, health and safety and grievance procedures.

7.1.2: Definition of Management Principles and Administration

People have different views about the important principles of business management. We shall see, however, that though different people may use slightly different terms the main principles of business management will apply to a wide variety of different organisations whether these are in the agricultural, manufacturing or education sectors.

7.2: Organisation

Organisation is another underlying principle of business management. Within any business, organisation managers will have to carry out tasks, which have been allocated to them. In the business sector, for example, a head of a large financial department will try to get the best possible accountants and will organise the tasks which have been set for them. Within the production department, there will be a need to organise the operatives. In some business organisations, there may be a legal department which require suitably trained staff.

7.3: Management Aims

Management is sometimes defined as getting other people to work. This is perhaps slightly over simplified but it does highlight the point that managers have to get the best from their staff. This implies that there must be two-way communication between the manager and his or her subordinate. There are a maximum number of people over whom one can exercise control effectively.

7.4: Span of Control

This refers to the number of people reporting to one person, which should generally be limited. Examining the education sector, one can observe that if too many people report directly to one headteacher then he or she is likely to be overwhelmed and will not be able to carry out basic management tasks. Generally when organising, it is better if people report only to one person to reduce the risk of conflict. However, in practice this can be difficult to achieve. For example, within a school a mathematics teacher might need to report to the head of year and to the head of the mathematics department.

7.5: Styles of Management

The Managerial Grid, created by Blake and Mouton, gives two principal dimensions of management from which different styles can be ascertained. The two principles are (a) concern for production; and (b) concern for people. The point to note is how the manager acts on his concern for production and people. The grid and its dimensions is shown in Figure 7.1 below.

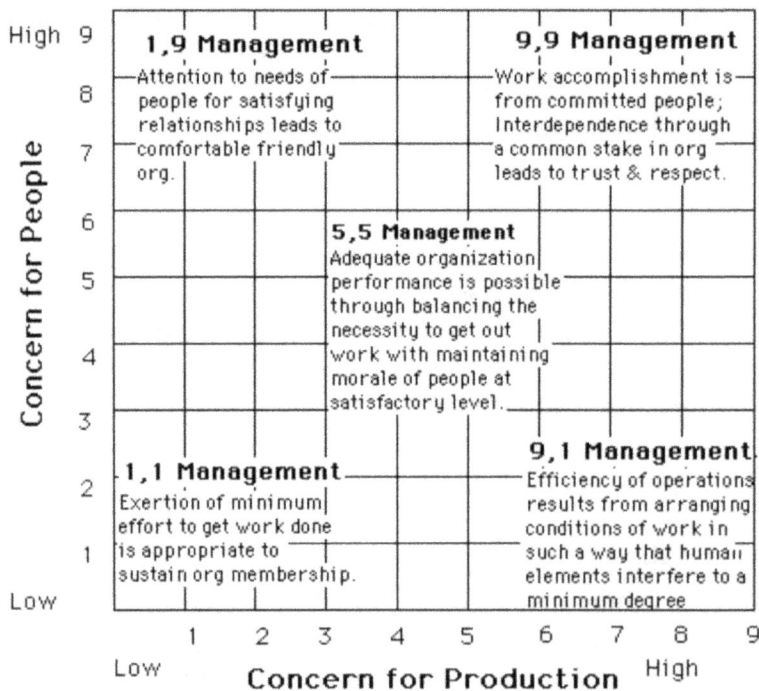

Managerial Grid from R. Blake and J. Mouton, "Managerial Facades", Advanced Management Journal, July 1966, 31.

figure 7.1

The grid has scales from one to nine, one being the lowest score and nine the highest. Five basic combinations can be derived from the four corners and the centre point of the grid as described by the following:

- **The Impoverished Manager** - (1, 1 rating): This manager has low concern for both production and people. He or she does just enough to maintain group membership.

- **The Authority-Compliance Manager** - (9, 1 rating). This manager has high concern for production but low concern for people. He or she considers human resources as tools for getting the job done and does not believe in their creativity.

- **The Country Club Manager** - (1, 9 rating). This manager has a low concern for production and a high concern for people. He concentrates on being liked and considers interpersonal relations more important than the task in hand. This can be described as 'soft Theory X' and is not considered a good human resources method.

- **The Middle of the Road Manager** - (5, 5 rating). This manager has moderate concern for both production and people. He relies on tried and tested techniques and avoids taking risks. In a conflict situation, he looks for compromise over sound resolution.

- **The Team Manager** - (9, 9 rating). This manager has very high concern for both production and people. He motivates people to get them to work hard to get the job done and is flexible and open to change. This style of management is considered ideal.

One of the basic philosophies regarding people management is that of involvement. This encourages an open flow of communication between the manager and his or her subordinates. The aim is for the manager to understand the issues and desires of people reporting to him or her, and for the subordinates to understand the issues and desires of their manager. This can be achieved by the practice of 'Management by Walking About'. This involves the manager taking an active interest in the work of subordinates and spending more time with them. This has to be handled carefully, however, as it may lead to feelings of suspicion about the manager's motives. Another factor associated with participation in management is that objectives and targets are established through participation between subordinates and their managers. This means that the subordinates are allowed to decide how best to get the job done and therefore set their own rules to a certain extent.

Different styles of management are appropriate to different departments and types of workers. Compare, for example, the marketing and the production departments.

The practice of management by participation may work well for the marketing department but not so well for the production department. This is because marketing involves a lot of teamwork and brainstorming to come up with new ideas. This calls for a democratic style of managing allowing managers and subordinates to work together to produce better results. The production department may find that an authoritarian approach to management may work best where managers set the targets and manage the people to ensure that these are met. This does not necessarily mean treating people as tools to get the job done since motivation is an important factor in working with people to achieve the desired results.

7.5.1: Maslow's Hierarchy of Needs and Management Styles

In 1943, Abraham Maslow published his Hierarchy of Needs which identified eight innate human needs, divided into five categories. The idea is that once one set of needs has been met it no longer acts as a motivator and people move to the next level in the hierarchy. Maslow suggested that most people's needs follow this order, but he stressed that it is not the case for everyone. For example, a very creative person may be driven by the need for creativity and self-actualisation without satisfaction of lower-level needs. Differences in what motivates people affect the style of management needed.

Maslow's Pyramid of Needs

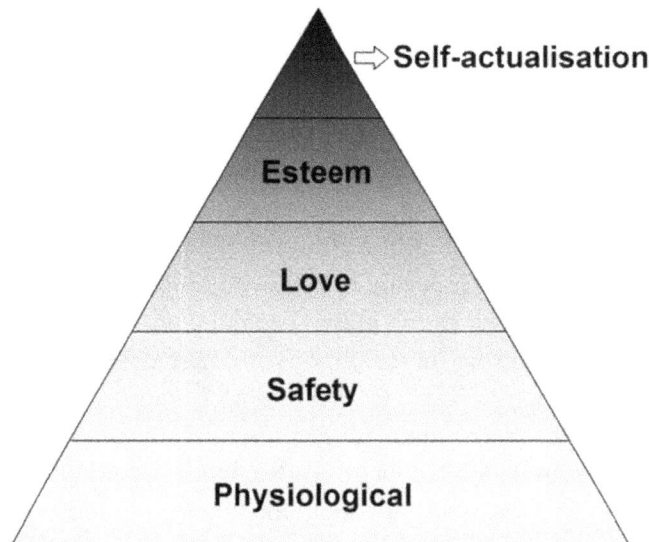

figure 7.2

- **Physiological** needs include basic needs such as food, water, warmth and sleep.

- **Safety** needs include safety from attack, pain and danger and the need for orderliness and predictability.

- **Love** needs include social desires such as friendship and a sense of belonging as well as the giving and receiving of love.

- **Esteem** needs are made up of self-respect and the esteem of others. These include a desire for confidence, independence and freedom as well as status, appreciation and recognition.

- **Self-actualisation** needs describe the development and realisation of ones full potential. This varies considerably from one individual to another.

7.5.2: Culture

Management style can differ between companies and the countries in which they operate. There are large cultural differences between countries such as Japan and America which affects the style and approach management. Deal and Kennedy carried out a study of hundreds of organisations and the environment in which they operated and derived four generic types of culture which are explained below.

- **Tough-guy, macho culture**. This is found in organisations made up of individuals who frequently take high risks and receive fast feedback on the results of their actions. This includes people such as surgeons and police officers. The financial implications are usually high and the emphasis is placed on speed. The danger with this culture is that it leads to early 'burn out' which in turn leads to a high staff turnover and associated difficulties when trying to create a strong culture.

- **Work-hard/Play-hard cultures** are found in organisations whose employees rarely take high risks and responses on their actions are still fast. Examples of organisations in this category include estate agents, mass retail stores and fast food restaurants. These organisations tend to be very dynamic with their primary focus on the needs of customers. The culture encourages games, meetings and promotions to increase volume and maintain motivation. The only danger is that there is a trade-off between volume and quality.

- **Bet-your-company culture**. This is found in organisations that make high stake decisions but do not find out the results for a long time. This includes organisations such as the military and investment banks. These organisations tend to make decisions from the top-down and move very slowly.

Consequently, they produce high quality inventions and scientific breakthroughs but are susceptible to short-term changes.

- **Process culture** is found in organisations which take low risk decisions and do not find out the results for a very long time. This is useful when there is a need for order and predictability; for example, in organisations such as banks and the civil service. The lack of feedback forces workers to concentrate more on how they do a task instead of what they do.

7.5.3: Conflict

In his book, *Management and Organisational Behaviour*, Mullins defines organisational conflict as, 'behaviour intended to obstruct the achievement of some other person's goals'. It can be caused by different people, departments or organisations having different or conflicting objectives. Conflict can be negative or positive, depending on how it is managed. Negative results include people feeling defeated and an atmosphere of mistrust and suspicion, which in turn can lead to a high employee turnover. Positive outcomes can include new, fresh and better ideas to business issues, the stimulation of interest and the resolution of previously hidden problems. There are a number of strategies designed to resolve conflict or turn it into a positive experience. They are based around sharing information to reduce misunderstanding and teaching people to work as a team – listening and considering the ideas of other people.

7.6: Business Plan

Organisations may need a business plan for a variety of different reasons. A business plan will give a firm direction and enable an organisation to anticipate changes rather than reacting to them after the event. Firms seeking finance such as an overdraft facility will need to have a business plan to demonstrate how it intends to develop and deliver on objectives and the expected monetary rewards in order to secure funds from investors such as banks or shareholders.

7.7: Market Research

The first stage in creating a business plan is likely to be elementary market research. When conducting research, it is desirable to use existing data, at least as a basis for further work. For example, to plan for a retirement home it would be beneficial to know the likely proportion of elderly people within a constituent area. In planning for the expansion of a college, an age profile of the local population would be useful. For these two examples, census data or information from the electoral roll would be very useful. In order to plan a new freightliner network (the container load trains), as in the mid 1960's, it would be useful to know the level of traffic throughput in any given town or city location.

Information contained on invoice documents can be used to establish where the majority of customers originate from. Additional information can be gained from product guarantees and store card schemes; the latter have proved to be particularly beneficial to large supermarkets in determining the pattern, habits and general profile of consumers shipping in their local stores. Sales representatives and other workers can also provide valuable information; for example, sales assistants may know of products that people frequently request but are currently unavailable in the particular retail outlet. Large firms can often use trade association data to estimate necessary production figures and can get import/ export data from the government.

Customer data can also be gathered from other sources such as questionnaires. Unfortunately, these are often complicated to construct and may produce biased results due to a certain type of person being more likely to complete them than others; for example, older (retired) people may have more time and the inclination to complete and return a product or service questionnaire. Telephone-sales or surveying might be helpful in rural areas, particularly for selling products like agricultural equipment. However, telephone sales (particularly 'cold-calling') tends to be treated with suspicion and resentment in the UK, placing even greater emphasis on the need for a company to carefully identify its target audience before launching a campaign.

Market research should necessarily include analysis and research on potential competition. Information such as the pricing and additional products or promotions offered by rivals can help a company identify a niche area in a market. The practice of comparing oneself to the competition through market research is known as 'benchmarking'.

7.8: Location

Once a company has established a market for a product or service, it needs to find a suitable location from which to operate. The decision of where to locate may come down to a trade-off between locating near the customer and the cost of the area. For example, the town centre would be the most desirable location for a restaurant, but it may also be the most costly. A restaurant on the edge of town might not attract as many customers, especially in the short term, but the costs would be less.

7.9: Finance

One of the most important factors in creating a business plan is finance; the amount of capital and investment required, and where it can be sourced. The basis of business finance depends upon the type of organisation; for example, whether a sole trader or partnership. If a decision is made to go seek an external source of finance, the lender or investor will require a business plan that shows expected cash flow – that is the regular payments being received by the organisation for goods or services rendered. In order to get an idea of cash flow, the organisation needs to work out its total costs and the price that it can realistically charge for its product or service. Total costs are made up of fixed and variable costs and these may change with the quantity of goods or services produced. For example, the rent for a factory is going to be the same regardless of the number of units it produces. Therefore, the more units produced, the lower the per-unit costs in terms of rent. Similarly, it may be cheaper to buy materials in bulk, although there may be oncosts in bulk purchase, like keeping an inventory and paying overtime or hiring temporary workers to increase production in order to avoid inventory costs.

7.10: Prices and Revenue

In order to get an idea of cash flow, a company must establish a realistic pricing strategy. Taking the example of a restaurant, pricing may be determined partly by the prices charged by close competitors. The likely volume of sales also needs to be estimated. This is often hard to determine so firms sometimes produce a pessimistic, expected and optimistic set of estimates.

7.11: Formulation and Implementation of Objectives

Peter Drucker introduced the phrase 'Management by Objectives' in 1954. It refers to a participative approach to management that includes planning, organisation and directing. Its aim is to relate organisational goals to individual performance. The roots of a management by objectives system are:

- Setting goals.

- Participation of individual managers in deciding their unit targets and how they will be measured.

- Continuous review of results.

For example, the top level of the firm may wish to lay down targets for employee turnover and market share. These targets then need to be translated for individual departments or branches, which may lead to the need for independent departmental or cost centre budgets. By involving local managers in this process, the firm is reconciling the goals of the individual units with those of the organisation as a whole.

7.11.1: Planning

One of the first principles of business management is that of planning. People at the top of the organisation generally undertake planning for the long term. For example, in the education sector, the Minister of Education will decide how many schools or colleges will be opened over the course of five years. Long term planning usually takes place over a period of five or more years. Medium term planning is defined as the period from one to five years. Short term planning would encompass an annual (one year) period. Middle management tends to be responsible for the medium term planning while more junior managers deal more with day-to-day planning. Before managers can begin to plan, the organisation needs to come up with an overall policy. For example, in the education sector someone has to decide how to cater for the rapidly growing number of young people in a particular country. Decisions can then be made regarding the action to be taken, for example, is it better to expand existing schools or to build new ones? Once these decisions have been made, it may be important to carry out an appraisal of the underlying reasons. For example, changes in population or employment prospects may alter the demand. In addition, the introduction of new technology may affect the demand for vocational education as well as how information is presented in class.

7.11.2: Directing

Another important business concept is that of directing. Too many people think the term directing means simply giving orders which will be obeyed without question. In reality, directing involves telling people what to do and how to use their talents to their best ability while doing it. People (human) resources are usually an organisation's greatest asset so it is important to get the most out of them. One way of maximising people resources is to consider their motivation. For example, a headteacher who gives orders without any underlying reasons may cause the staff and students in a school to become disillusioned. On the other hand, a headteacher who helps to motivate his staff through constructive discussions is likely to do well. Motivation, and thereby productivity, is highest if people understand why tasks need to be undertaken and are given help when necessary.

7.11.3: Co-ordination

In a large organisation it can often be difficult to make contact with the right person. This may well be due to insufficient co-ordination within the business. Sometimes departments overlap and therefore business tasks and responsibilities span across traditional department divides. There is a danger that some tasks fall in between the divide and may not be dealt with satisfactorily or they may even be ignored altogether. Co-ordination can help solve such problems and can take a number of different forms. For example, the marketing and production managers will have regular meetings to ensure that production is neither too large nor too small for the likely volume of sales. Committees are another form of co-ordination. However, they have to be organised sufficiently in order to achieve satisfactory results, otherwise they become unruly, hard to direct and chair, and ultimately pointless.

7.11.4: Staffing

As mentioned before, human resources are likely to be the most important resource for an organisation regardless of type or location. As a consequence, staffing normally accounts for the largest percentage of the total costs incurred by a company. In the long term, employing the right type of people will aide the successful development of a firm and help ensure low staff turnover. The recruitment of satisfactory staff, training and motivation, therefore are some of the most important tasks of management. Indeed, it is often suggested in the business world that the most important thing is to have the right number of people, in the right place, at the right time. Although this is an over simplification, it is a helpful phrase.

7.11.5: Budgeting

Every department of every organisation will have a budget; even a single farmer running a small farm will need a budget although it may be kept in his head rather than stored on paper or in a spreadsheet. In the case of a school, the budget may be determined at different levels either by central government through the Department of Education or, in some countries, directly by the school. A school may be given a budget dependent on criteria such as the number of students and expected maintenance costs. How the money is spent is almost entirely in the hands of the school management. Discretion may be limited, however, since a large percentage of money is spent on teachers' salaries, in accordance with national pay scales. In all schools, governors have been given increased powers when it comes to tasks such as budgeting and staff appointments. For this reason, it is sometimes said that the governors have a role in schools which is comparable to that of a director appointed to the board of company. Regardless of how the budget is determined and whoever is responsible for spending the money, the idea of efficiency and value for money is very important in both education and business. Knowing what income is likely in the ensuing year and therefore what expenditure is possible is very important.

7.11.6: Control

The common phrase 'things have got out of control' can apply to any industry or sector. There are various types of control, one of the most important being stock control. A large inventory ties up a lot of capital and, in the case of perishable items, can lead to unnecessary waste. Too little stock can lead to the inability to satisfy customer needs or production demand. Stock is divided into three categories: raw materials, work in progress and final products. Other types of control that concern managers include budgetary control and behaviour control.

7.11.7: Reporting

Another important aspect of business is that of reporting. In a school, students and their parents receive feedback on academic performance. As well as providing feedback, these reports may be used when applying for work or further study. The same idea is also prevalent in businesses. A business manager may need a report about past sales, in order to ensure that current production levels are adequate. The business may also need to send reports containing finance and other data to shareholders. The principle of management by exception means that managers only receive reports about exceptional items. The idea is that reports about exceptional items are shorter or less frequent than reports containing information on normal activities. For example, many organisations now have computers to assist in working out current stock levels and stock requirements. It can be set so that a warning will be automatically sent to management if the stock level is too high or low. In this case, the management would not receive unnecessary reports telling him that everything is all right. This is comparable to the idea within a school whereby a teacher may ask for a list of absent students, which are the exceptions, rather than a list of those present.

7.12: Resources

The Collins Dictionary defines the term *resource* as 'a source of economic wealth especially that of a country or business enterprise'. Economists tend to classify the term resource under four main headings:

1. Land

2. Labour

3. Capital

4. Entrepreneurial ability (this category is sometimes omitted)

7.12.1: Capital

In this case, 'capital' means resources that are used in the production of other goods or services. For example, factories, machines, and road haulage vehicles are all examples of private capital since they are used to provide more goods and services. Other examples of capital, include shops, market stalls, warehouses, agricultural machinery, lorries, buses, trains and aircraft. All countries decide whether they want to consume now or try to build up their capital. They also have to decide whether to encourage private capital such as factories and agricultural machinery or to try to invest more in social infrastructure, like schools, universities, hospitals, libraries, and power stations.

7.12.2: Population

The most important resource of any country is likely to be its population. Some countries, notably Hong Kong had almost nothing in the way of raw materials, but still managed to achieve a very high standard of living. Increasing population can be regarded in two ways; either it means more mouths to feed or it can mean extra people to work and produce more goods and services. If the population of a country increases rapidly, the additional mouths to feed and clothe are, at least in the short term, more important than having more workers. Many countries suffer from both unemployment and under-employment. The latter includes people working as part of an extended family business who are not really being fully utilised; rather they represent the underutilisation of human resource.

7.12.3: Entrepreneurs

The word 'entrepreneur' means someone who takes risks in business. All countries require people who can assess the likely risks and are willing to take a chance, often with their own money, in order to develop such businesses. However, it is a matter of political debate whether these people should be the predominant form of business.

Case Study: Decision Making Processes within the Education Sector
Setting up a small college

People

One of the first tasks involved in setting up a small college is to create a team of people to act as decision-makers. These people must share the same objectives and maybe temperament too. There is no point in having four people who want to make every decision or who let someone else make all the decisions.

There is always the problem of money and finding investors. A situation may arise where a person has the money but no great skill coexisting with people who have skills. At the start different skills are needed, for example, one will need to know about equipment required and the type of space needed; while another will need to know the type of person the college wishes to attract and how to do so. Someone else will need to be able to look after the finances though this could be contracted out, if necessary.

Type of market

There are several possibilities open to the college, when trying to identify the target market:

- **The Crammer Market**: These colleges charge high fees and will attract those who have just failed the exams, those who want unusual subjects or possibly those who want to get through the subject quickly. The name crammer market is derived from 'cramming' which is the memorisation of facts without necessarily digesting and understanding their meanings. Most crammers do so to pass an examination in a subject they do not like or cannot understand.

- **The English as a Foreign Language (EFL) Market**: This can be subdivided into the young person market and the executive market. It will attract young people who come to improve their English and to be entertained as well. These colleges, therefore, are often situated at the seaside during the summer months. The executive market is getting more and more popular as improvements in travel and communications continue. Courses that are attractive to this market are likely to be part-time and online or short, intensive, residential courses.

Accommodation and Equipment

A key question here is whether it better to rent or buy and if so how much? To answer this effectively, the team need to consider factors such as the likely number of students that will attend and how many and which subjects the college will offer. As far as property is concerned, a lease of about 3 to 5 years is preferable as it allows for a change in circumstances affecting student numbers. In the case of EFL colleges, location is an important issue. The accommodation may only be utilised for a few weeks a year but it needs to be in a nice place to attract the students. Many universities rent their accommodation out to run EFL courses in the summer months, when their own students do not occupy them.

Equipment, in this case, includes items such as computers, printers, office equipment and suitable chairs and tables for staff and students. Because prices and specifications of computers are constantly changing, an approximate idea of price is more important than a detailed breakdown.

Fees charged

Another important consideration is how much to charge. Benchmarking may be a useful practice for this. In large towns and cities there may be a wide range of fees reflecting factors such as the different facilities available and size and variation of courses.

Questions

1. Why might personal characteristics be more important in setting up a college than in some other businesses?

2. What limits might there be on specialisation of labour in such an enterprise?

3. What is meant by market segmentation? Why is it important in this type of business?

4. What are the advantages and disadvantages of leasing property rather than buying it outright?

Self-examination Questions

1. What is an executive director?

2. What is the advantage of non-executive directors? Think about the analogy of the governors of the school.

3. What would be the advantage in a college for example if the heads of department became the directors? Why might they neglect the following issues, use of fuel, use of land and new courses? In what ways is this similar to a firm?

4. Whom would non-executive directors logically consult with?

5. What do we mean by the chain of command? How does this apply in a school or college? What problems may arise?

6. What is the problem with too long a chain of command?

7. What is meant by the span of control? How many people can one person look after? Why might it vary? Think of the types of people responsible for catering, word processing, and teaching.

8. What rules do we have in a school or college? Are all of them written down? Can we apply the same ideas to a firm?

9. Are there rules about expenditure? Who will determine them? Does observing the rules necessarily lead to a good organisation? Think of working to rule.

10. Are there limits on what decisions we can make? Are there similar controls in firms? For example, are there limits on the number of people that we can employ or the amount of money that head teachers can spend?

11. Are there limits on the type of items that they can buy? Why is there nearly always some discretion on some items but not others? What are the problems with computers? There is a link with centralisation and decentralisation here.

12. What is meant by democratic rules about expenditure? Who determines them?

13. What is meant by the term operational efficiency? Why might it be more difficult to measure this in a school than in a business organisation?

14. What is meant by planning? Does planning have to take place in all businesses?

15. What is organising? Which resources have to be organised?

16. What are natural resources? What does saying that some resources are renewable and other is non-renewable mean?

17. Why does poor management lead to waste? (Think of what happens to perishable products if they are not used; what happens to staff if they are not used properly?)

18. What is meant by co-ordination? Why do different departments need to co-ordinate activities? Illustrate your answer with reference to the production and marketing departments.

19. What are the main objectives of managers? (Hint: What would you look for in a job e.g. security etc?) Does it vary much between countries? Does it vary according to age of managers?

20. Why does conflict arise within organisations? Is it inevitable?

21. What is meant by expense preference? Why in a recession might it be less important?

22. How may departmental budgets help firms to reconcile corporate and individual department objectives?

23. What types of firms are likely to be production orientated? What are the effects of this?

24. Does the management grid reflect the underlying personality of managers or their beliefs?

25. What is meant by the term 'management'?

26. What is meant by the term 'administration'?

27. Why are management and administration important for developing world countries?

28. Can you think of examples of waste of scarce resources in your area? What are the main causes of the waste?

29. Which level of management is responsible for long range planning?

30. Which level of management should be responsible for tactical planning?

Chapter 8: DEPARTMENTS

8.1: Introduction

Most medium and large firms are divided into departments. The names of these departments can vary slightly between one firm and another; for example, Personnel departments are equivalent to Human Resource departments. We can broadly assume that firms in a manufacturing industry usually have a Production department, an Accounts department, a Personnel department and sometimes a Transport or Distribution department. Sometimes the Purchasing department is a separate unit or it may be part of the Accounts department. Service based firms may not have a Production department at all, although possibly a sales or administration department provides much of these firms' revenue.

8.1.1: The 'General' Office

Firms too small to have separate administration, personnel and sales departments often have a general office. One of the functions of the general office is to appoint staff and ensure welfare is maintained. The general office will update staff records, making sure that confidentiality is maintained and Data Protection legislation adhered to. The general office is also often responsible for office stationery and supplies. It is likely that in such a small firm, members of staff will oversee more than one different area. For example, sales staff may also work on producing company accounts.

8.1.2: The Personnel or Human Resource Department

In most commercial firms, the cost of staffing accounts for a large proportion of total operating costs. The same is also true of non-profit or public organisations, such as local authorities and central government. The personnel department is responsible for the hiring, training, appraisal, promoting, welfare and discipline of all staff within an organisation. The personnel department will try to ensure that they obtain staff of the right calibre for the firm, as well as draw up an overall workforce plan to ensure the organisation has the right number of staff, doing the right jobs, at the right time. The plan will need to take account of any future employment needs to enable expansion of an organisation's workforce. If expansion is planned the personnel department will need to be engaged in decisions on new staffing levels, including assessment of skill and expertise sought in the creation of new posts; their location and timetable for induction into the organisation.

The department will also need to consider internal and external training to decide which is most cost effective for the firm in different areas. For example, some training can be conducted in-house at a much lower cost than buying knowledge and expertise externally. In other cases, there may be no one within the firm who can train people on required skills, in which instance the personnel department would consider cost-effective opportunities to hire an individual consultant or organisation to undertake training. The personnel team will also be responsible for promotions and redundancies. The original function of the personnel department was staff welfare and it is still the case now. Human resource departments need to work closely with employee trade unions organisations to ensure the firm is meeting the needs of its employees. Increasingly, firms employ personnel managers, belonging to the relevant professional bodies such as the Chartered Institute of Personnel and Development. We shall explore employment and motivation further in Chapters 17, 18 and 20.

8.1.3: The Accounts Department

Up until the mid-1960's, the typical accounts department, in a medium to large organisation, comprised a large number of employees carrying out basic bookkeeping tasks. Since the 1960's, there has been a move away from this set-up for two primary reasons. The first is the introduction of computers to carry out most of the bookkeeping calculations; thereby reducing the number of staff required in the department. The second is that, increasingly, the accounts department is responsible for management accounting. The days of the accounts department working purely on financial accounting matters are widely over. Management accounting, as a branch of accounting, has become more important over the years. Techniques used in this branch include calculating Net Present Value, Payback Periods and Internal Rates of Return for current and future investments. These techniques are discussed in detail in Chapter 9.

The accounts department is traditionally charged with ensuring that the firm has an adequate cash flow. Too large a cash balance may mean that the firm is not acquiring enough capital goods to carry out work efficiently. Too small a cash flow will lead to bankruptcy through inability to pay off creditors. The accounts department may also carry out internal audits and budget checks to ensure that money has been spent wisely within other departments. The audit will also ensure that legal provisions have been complied with, although external auditors will also carry out this role.

There has been an increasing volume of legislation, including the Companies Acts, which the accounts department will need to comply with. Inadequate and poorly controlled accounting procedures have been blamed for the downfall of several prominent firms in recent times, like Enron in the USA where there had been manipulation of accounting procedures by the management, leading to understated liabilities and overstated income and profit. The Enron case has become one of the biggest corporate bankruptcies in modern times 2001.

8.1.4: The Production Department

The production department is responsible for producing the goods in a company, meeting the quantity and quality production targets set for the firm. There are different types of production, such as unit production, batch production, mass production and flow production. These have been mentioned in earlier chapters; however, a brief overview is given below.

Unit or Job production

Unit production refers to items produced to an individuals' specification. There are many examples of unit production industries, like custom tailoring. One-off suits, known as bespoke tailored items, are unit or job produced as opposed to off-the-peg manufactured. Each garment is made individually for the customer. There are also examples in the building trade; for instance, a house that has a unique design. Any product or service that is produced uniquely to the specification of a consumer can be viewed as unit produced. Further examples include, wedding cakes, custom, hand-built cars, and main courses in expensive restaurants. Unit production can lead to problems in costing, since each item by definition is different, although these can be avoided where standard component parts are used, but made-up in a different way to form the unique good or service. For example, in the shipbuilding industry, nearly all ships constructed have traditionally had unique features making it more difficult to accurately cost production, particularly when compared to standard processes that use identical components.

There are also other problems with unit production, such as the difficulty to utilise people and equipment to their maximum capacity since, by definition, unit production means that you cannot build or make items and then store them. For example, a firm which manufacturers a large number of identical clothes can have the same production each day using the same materials, the same machines and the same levels of staff carrying out set tasks. A bespoke tailor cannot do this, which makes it more difficult to have an even flow of work. Job or unit production is therefore only successful when making highly variable goods in small quantities.

Batch production

Another type of production is batch production where items are made in batches with a maximum number being produced at any one time. The first item in a batch is likely to be expensive whereas the marginal costs of remaining items in a batch are likely to much lower. For example, if you make 100 bread rolls individually using batch production processes it would cost more, on average, than making 100 rolls using the same production techniques at the same time. The dough has to be made; rested; then kneaded and proved before shaping into rolls; baked; cooled; wrapped and finally sold 100 times to make all of the rolls. If each of these processes were done separately for each roll then it would take a long time to make 100. However, it is obvious that if enough dough is made to make 100 rolls and then passed through all of the stages the rolls would be made much faster. There is a need as far as possible to equate orders with the size of the batch. Examples of this can be found in the bakery trade. If the baker's oven will take 50 cakes, then the baker will not want an order of 51 cakes since this will require two batches rather than one. This will mean that 51 cakes will require a lot more power and time than 50 cakes.

Mass production

Mass production implies continuous production, as in the case of most car manufacturers. One of the foremost advocates of mass production was Henry Ford. Up until his time, much of car production was based on similar principles to the carriages which they had replaced; i.e. they were built individually. Henry Ford found that through simplification and standardisation, the costs of production could be reduced tremendously. His famous comment that customers could have any colour as long as it was black illustrates the point about standardisation. It has been found that mass production can lead to automation of production. Examples of this can be found in the production of white goods, such as refrigerators and washing machines where the capacity of mass production can be easily measured. It may depend upon bottlenecks (production coming to a halt because of hold-ups caused by one machine or person) being overcome. For example, if one machine has a capacity of a hundred units per hour this will influence the capacity of the next machine. Firms may decide how capacity can be altered through changes in machinery or working practices. In many cases, mass production leads toward the introduction of shift work to make the best use of expensive machinery. It is typical in many industries to run machinery for 3 shifts of 8 hours per day so that the large fixed costs of purchasing the highly automated/computerised production lines is spread over as many products as possible to reduce the percentage cost per unit. Mass production is therefore used in situations that are the exact opposite to unit production; i.e. low variation (high standardisation) and high volume.

Firms may decide to use network analysis to improve capacity utilisation and more importantly to determine the shortest time to produce different items. Network analysis is described in more detail in Chapter 16 where we will look at when it will be useful to speed up production and how we can determine the consequential costs. Firms will also decide when they might need this, for example, in just-in-time (JIT) or just-in-case (JIC) production described in earlier chapters. The concept of mass production has often been linked to poor motivation. Jobs on the production line are often rightly regarded as monotonous. People do the same simple tasks day in and day out. The jobs are so specialised that the workers do not feel they have contributed very much skill or effort to the job.

The Japanese have a different style of management. Their managers tend to have the same style of dress as their employees. This helps to overcome the 'us and them' attitude that is very common in the UK and often leads to staff conflicts with management. The managers often assume that they are the only ones who have any ideas that would be useful to the firm. The workers feel that the main objective of management is to keep workers down on the job. It is often the case that the best ideas come from the members of staff that are actually *doing* the work since they are most likely to spot a problem in the course of their everyday work and come up with a solution to overcome it.

Mass production has often been associated with job insecurity. In the 1960's, for example, some car firms on average made one in four workers redundant during a typical year. This contributed to poor motivation and loyalty of staff. In contrast, redundancies in Japan, until recently, have been virtually unknown and both management and workers feel very committed to the firm even at the expense of outside life.

Flow production

The concept of flow production can be found, for example, in the oil industry. In flow production, it is not meaningful to talk of so many discrete units of production, say 10 pieces of oil. Therefore, flow production is measured in capacity per hour or day. Flow production is likely to be found in the case of liquids or gases and in particular may be associated with pipelines. Flow production tends to have economies of scale. For example, an oil pipe where the diameter is doubled will be able to carry four times the capacity. There are problems that occur if demand is larger than existing supply capacity. It may be difficult to replace pipelines while still keeping a continuous service going. There may also problems if demand is smaller than the existing supply capacity.

In flow production, input/ output analysis might be used. For example, if different grades of oil cost different prices at any given time, the firm may decide to alter its outputs to profit maximise. Input/output analysis can take account of changes in input or even changes in demand. This can be used within the firm in both the short term and the longer term to optimise profit by altering production.

Production planning analysis

Where do new ideas for production come from? We could use brainstorming where people come up with new ideas in a short period, however far-fetched they may seem. This is a good way of involving people from different disciplines. Pre-production planning may be seen to have become increasingly important, partly because the timing between concept and launch of a product has become much longer. In the early 20th century, there was a short time lag between these in the car industry. Nowadays, it may take four years from the original concept of a car to its manufacture and launch. The cost of developing a new product may well be considerable and the time lag quite long; take for instance the development process for the European Airbus and the Boeing Dreamliner.

Pre-production planning is not solely the responsibility of the production-planning department. The department must liaise closely with the other departments upon which they rely for information before making decisions about production. The planning may develop along the following lines:

Refer back to any market research conducted concerning the product being investigated, and communication of the results to the sales department. This would have helped to avoid some of the well-known commercial flops of firms. In the 1960's, the Ford Edsel was a large inefficient car, which consumed large amounts of petrol during a time when fuel consumption was becoming more important. The Saunders Roe flying boats (seaplanes) were a commercial flop. More of them could have been sold if they could have coped with the problems of choppy seas. They would have had commercial advantages for many countries since there was no need for runways. However, there were problems in getting people from the sea to dry land.

A sales programme is prepared, and divided into suitable periods to show the estimated sales for each period. This may be very difficult for firms where demand is not known with any accuracy. The production-planning department receives the sales programme and, with the assistance and information obtained from other departments, is able to break it down and prepare a pre-production programme. At this stage, the following points have been decided:

- The product description based upon the specification supplied by the design department.

- Quantity: How many are required?

- Time of delivery: For shipbuilding, this is very important and was one of the reasons why other countries gained at the expense of the British shipbuilding industry in the 1960's. In some cases, part of the orders may be dispatched at different times. For example, a firm ordering a fleet of buses may require them at six-month intervals.

- The firm will need to consider the different processes that will be used to complete the production. In some cases, they may have a choice of both different machines and different grades of people.

- The department will also have to consider what resources are currently available. For example, in some cases they may already have stocks of finished products as well as of raw materials and components. They may also have suitable machine tools but in other cases it may be worthwhile investing in new machinery.

- The production department, having considered the resources may need to liaise with the purchasing department about any new plant machinery and materials that may be necessary.

- The production department, probably in liaison with the accounting department, will need to estimate its costs, at different levels of production. This will take account of the likely times taking to complete different levels of production and the varying types of wage payment.

- The production department will need to consider its controls. This will include quality control to ensure, for example, that dimensions and tolerances are complied with. A firm ordering components may specify the size of components that it wants and within which limits of dimensions it will accept the orders. The production department will also need to control the time taken by workers per unit of production. It can use operational research techniques to achieve this. It will also need to look at utilisation of machines.

8.1.5: Research and Development

In large firms, a separate department may perform the function of research and development. For example, Shell has employed large numbers of people for this purpose. However, in smaller firms, any research and development may be the responsibility of the production department. Research and development may be carried out for specific purposes; e.g. a large pharmaceutical firm may wish to produce an Aids vaccine or to produce a chemical to deal with particular insects. A major challenge in the chemical industry is to produce chemicals without side effects. For example, Thalidomide, a fertility drug, produced many side effects. In the UK and the USA, a large part of research and development tends to be defence orientated and this in turn has implications for the aviation and computer industries. In 1995, a computer for the defence industry was claimed to do one trillion calculations a second. We can have pure research; e.g., at universities into prime numbers. Sometimes pure research develops into commercial products. Sometimes, product and service ideas are conceived purely by chance.

Commercial stages in production planning

- Test concepts. For example, can they produce the goods in the quantities desired? Do they have enough people with the right skills? Do they have enough space? Do they have enough machines? They can ask relevant departments for any obvious bottlenecks.

- Questionnaires or panels can be used to get an indication of what people would like or dislike.

- Use of physical models. For example, models of vehicles or buildings to see what they will be like. An example of this would be using wind tunnels, artificial waves as at Wallsend (near Newcastle) to test stability of ships.

- Test new products. For example, firms can run cars round tracks. They could also use crash test dummies to gauge the safety of a car in different impact situations. They can test drugs for side effects and more importantly monitor them for any symptoms or side effects that may take a long while to detect. Firms can test consumer durables for effective lifetimes; e.g. test cars for many miles on a variety of surfaces and speeds, we can test bulbs for long life and calculate standard deviations. They can also test for 'ease of use'; for example DVD recorders, mobile phones or other machines. Research shows that many people do not know how to programme videos and a firm that can offer one that really is easy to use will gain a competitive advantage over its rival's products.

- Test the market again before going into full-scale production. This should show up possible defects and the popularity of the product without the costs of a full launch. In 1993, The Times did a test market with a reduction in the price in Kent. Both The Independent and The Times have test marketed a 'tabloid' shaped version of their papers in London; as this was successful the broadsheets, except the Financial Times and the Daily Telegraph, have all converted to 'tabloid form'. The Guardian has adopted a Berliner format. Often by analogy, firms do a test market in one area. It is not always that a positive test-marketing launch will translate to a full-scale launch success. There may be local variations that are not present within the national market that help sell certain products. It is for this reason that it is most useful if the test area mirrors the target market.

8.1.6: The Marketing Department

The way in which the marketing department is organised is important. Firms have realised that marketing is not just advertising or selling as we shall explore in Chapters 22 to 24. Firms will also have to consider why market research may be important to them. It is important to stress that small firms may have to concentrate on desk research whilst larger firms may have their own individual department. The marketing department needs to liaise with other departments before arranging for market research. For example, there is no point in looking at the demand for a product if there is no possibility of the production department making it in sufficient quantities at a reasonable price for the market.

The whole firm, as part of its corporate strategy, will also discuss how the department needs to consult with other departments before advertising. For example, there are many instances where the production department fails to meet the demand requested by sales representatives and therefore lose goodwill as a result. The marketing department may need to liaise with the accounting department so that they can determine the range of prices that can be charged. The marketing department may look at the use of price discrimination following these discussions.

8.1.7: Purchasing

There are three main reasons for purchasing:

1. To have materials which are used in the overheads of the business; this would include items such as office stationery and cleaning materials.

2. To purchase raw materials, components and fuel which are used in the production process.

3. To buy items which are then resold.

There are some other purchases. For example, fuel for use in lorries delivering the finished product. This can be regarded as part of the second function.

In general, we find that offices will mainly purchase for the first reason. In a factory, however, raw materials and components are likely to be the main items in terms of value. When buying raw materials the purchasing department may need to consider long and short-term needs, it may need to consult the production department for example, about using glass in place of plastic for packaging. If they need to buy fuel, they will need to consider the current energy cost compared with capital costs. In the short term, there may be little choice since the machines currently used may determine the type of fuel required. In the longer term it may prove economical switching machines to a cheaper source of energy, but only if these energy prices are likely to remain stable. The overall heating and lighting bill also needs to be considered. This can be a problem with many firms as no one is in charge of the energy policy.

Retail outlets will be mainly be concerned with the third category; reselling items. However, they still need to consider category two items, such as packaging, bags and till rolls. In some cases, organisations have a central purchasing department, which may be responsible for all or nearly all purchasing for the whole organisation. In other cases, purchasing may be done by individual departments or locations.

Centralised purchasing

Firms will have to decide whether a central purchasing department is actually necessary. In small businesses, there is often not a separate purchasing department. A centralised purchasing department is likely to employ specialised staff that may well be members of the Chartered Institute of Purchasing and Supply. Centralised purchasing will apply where the range of goods does not vary much across the different branches. For example, Curry's the electrical retailer, tends to have the same electrical equipment in all their stores and this forms part of their national advertising campaigns. Similarly, Marks and Spencer tend to stock the same items and this is helpful to customers who may wish for whatever reason to return items to a different branch. The advantage of a centralised purchasing department is that it may be able to obtain economies of scale through bulk purchasing. It may also be through this specialist knowledge that they know when to buy items. This may be particularly important, for example, where buying is possible on the futures markets. Futures markets are where buyers pay for items now at a fixed price for future supplies. This applies to commodities such as tea and coffee.

Centralised purchasing also has the advantage that general managers have fewer tasks to deal with. A general manager may be capable of ordering suitable stationery but may well resent the time that it takes to look through competing products to get the best value. Where prices are changing rapidly as with computers this may be even more helpful. The disadvantages of centralised purchasing tend to apply when the value of an order is small. In some cases, there may be a lengthy chain of communication so that one person's requisition passes through several hands. This is not only time consuming but also any cost savings on the purchase price may be offset by the administrative costs. Where items are required urgently; e.g. with computer disks or flour in a bakery it is even more of a disadvantage. Partly for this reason, some firms give discretion to local branches or departments to be able to order items themselves providing the total value is not above a specified amount.

Centralised purchasing is also common in supermarkets. This may be helpful for pre-packaged items; e.g. tins of baked beans. It has however been criticised for the purchase of fruit and vegetables and similar items since local products are often ignored if the farmer does not produce enough. Local market stalls may well therefore be able to undercut prices and give better local produce.

The purchasing of computers has often posed problems. Each individual department or location may well feel that the computers, which it can purchase, will be the best for its own needs. If the computers are incompatible however, then data that is available to the accounts department may not be in a suitable format for the marketing department. Schools have also suffered from the same problem. Whilst the County Council can buy more cheaply generally than the local schools this is not always the case. Problems then occur however, since software, which can be run on some computers, will not be available to other schools.

In the road haulage industry if different depots buy different vehicles it will be more difficult for them to have compatible spare parts available. This may cause problems where vehicles serve several depots. It may also cause problems for maintenance. For durable items, the purchasing department should be able to work out the total life cost of items. For example, if computers are bought they can work out the initial cost of the computer as well as the cost of media, servicing and software updates throughout the lifetime of the product. Similarly, in the road haulage industry the purchasing department can estimate the total lifespan, cost of replacement parts and maintenance.

Purchasing and Downtime

Using statistical data the firm should be able to work out the likely downtime (i.e. the time when machines are likely to be out of action for repairs or routine maintenance) and thus the department can order the optimum quantity of machinery. It may also help to determine the capacity of the machines that it orders. For example, a more expensive photocopier will often give cheaper costs per photocopy. The firm may be tempted to buy this. However, if the machine breaks down the office operations may be interrupted, so it may be better to buy two smaller machines.

If the purchasing department can calculate the lifetime costs of a product it can also calculate the best time to replace assets. For example, the firm has a trade off between continuing to use the machine, which means lower depreciation cost per year and higher maintenance and repair costs, and purchasing a replacement. The firm can also use this data to decide whether to buy second hand machines rather than new.

One or Several suppliers

The purchasing department will normally keep lists of potential suppliers. It will not only need to look at price but also at delivery times. It will also keep records of any warranties or guarantees. Some firms will tend to keep to one supplier even if that firm is slightly higher priced for some items. The advantage of this is that the firm supplying may be more likely to give discounts and perhaps more importantly will make an effort to supply items even if there is a current shortage. One supplier may also be more willing to give advice, which may help offset any individual price disadvantages.

Testing the market

Even where firms make products themselves they sometimes wish to ensure that producing the items themselves is the best value. They may therefore tender to outside suppliers in order to have an idea that they are getting the best value.

Asking for tenders

Both local authorities and national government, along with some private firms, frequently use tendering. In some cases, they have no choice but in other cases, purchasing departments may use this if they wish to buy a product in very large quantities. An example of this would be the buying of refuse sacks. Where the purchase is one off tendering may also be used. For example, if a firm wishes to have a building of an unusual type, tenders may be called for. One of the problems of tendering is to ensure that the right specifications are clearly made. For example, there have been complaints that when tenders for school meals have been made that the cheapest quote has been accepted but the meals are totally inadequate. Tenders usually have to be submitted in plain envelopes by a specified date to try to avoid firms being able to apply pressure on the purchaser.

Firms have been known to collude on tenders by submitting exactly the same price. This defeats the object of competition. If firms have to tender for very large contracts, only very large firms will be able to take advantage of this. In the USA, sometimes there have been insistences that when large contracts are given to large firms, then when possible sub-contracts are given to smaller firms. For example, if a large building complex was tendered for; small builders could carry out some of the functions. Where only a few firms, are capable of supplying equipment, the purchaser may not wish any one of them to go bankrupt otherwise they could be faced with a monopoly. For example, there are few suppliers of rail equipment. In 2013 there has been considerable speculation about who would get the contracts for new carriages and trains as a result of electrification of the railway line from London to Cardiff.

Choice between Outright purchase, Leasing and Renting

Outright purchasing means that the firm buys the item and is therefore the owner. The advantage is that if the firm has cash in hand that it is generally cheaper over the lifetime of the asset to take this approach. If the firm wishes to keep the asset for its commercial lifetime this is usually the best method of acquiring the asset.

Hire purchase

Small firms sometimes use this method of acquiring equipment. The costs (APR) of doing so are often quite high. The equipment does not become the property of the purchaser until the last payment is made.

Leasing

Leasing is commonly used for property and for vehicles. The reason why it is used for property is that few firms wish to commit themselves for long periods. If they are successful, they will probably wish to have more space whilst if they are unsuccessful they will wish to move to a cheaper or smaller property. The advantage of leasing is that there is no initial outlay. The contract often includes maintenance, as with photocopiers, where firms do not wish to have a period when such machines are out of action. Leasing often gives the firm flexibility, as with computers and photocopiers, to update the machinery if the firm requires it.

Renting

Renting is in many ways similar to leasing. The major difference in practise is that the firm is generally not committed to a specific period. It may be suitable for a new firm setting up in a small office. In some cases, a minimum period is specified. In other cases, a firm may be able to try out a product on a rented basis but will get back a proportion of this back if it decides to buy the item outright. This has been done occasionally with computers where it is very difficult for a small firm to know whether a computer system is completely suitable before it has tried it.

8.1.8: Stock control

The purchasing department will be responsible for stock control. If an organisation has insufficient stocks, this may lead to loss of production. In retail outlets, insufficient stocks may lead to disgruntled customers. This is important since buying consumer goods is partly a matter of habit. If people cannot buy certain goods from a shop this week, this could mean loss of custom in subsequent periods. Over stocking, on the other hand, means that the cost of warehousing and possibly insurance will be high. Some goods are commercially perishable. For example, if the firm has too many copies of the latest pop CDs it may not be able to sell them later. Other items may be conventionally perishable, such as food items.

The purchasing department will need to keep records to ensure that items, which have been ordered, have been delivered, in both the desired quantity and quality. The purchasing department will need to take account of lead times. This is the time taken between ordering and delivering. For example, if it usually takes two weeks to deliver goods, the firm may have a policy of having two and a half weeks of stocks, in the factory. This is to avoid the possibility of 'stock out'. There are mathematical techniques that will help the firm to decide on the best batch size to order. Sometimes problems with compatibility may arise. For example, when purchasing vehicles, if one is not careful, different departments or different locations will have different types of vehicles. This may mean that spare parts will not be readily available.

The purchasing department may also need to be aware of queuing theory. If one considers the number of checkouts in a supermarket, it is comparatively easy to predict what the length of queues will be, given a variety of numbers of outlets. If they buy in too many tills, the costs will rise but the shorter lengths of queues will annoy fewer customers. On the other hand, if they buy too few, the cost of installation will be much smaller but queuing time will be excessive with a likely subsequent loss of customers. This concept of queuing theory will equally apply, for example, to the number of berths in a port. This is also applicable within an office. More photocopying machines will mean fewer queues but is the expense justified? Similarly, more telephone lines will mean that it is easier to get through to the firm but is it worthwhile?

Some raw materials are in seasonal supply, so the quantity ordered must be sufficient to ensure continuity of production throughout the year. For example, this could apply to a fruit-canning firm. However, in most cases, as the seasonal supply finishes in one part of the world, supplies are obtainable from other markets.

8.1.9: Transport and Distribution Department

The late Peter Drucker, the well-known management expert, once said that distribution was the last frontier of management. By this, he meant that whereas other management tasks, such as accounting and personnel, had been studied, this was frequently not true of the tasks of transport and distribution managers. The average figure for transport and distribution, as a proportion of total costs, is typically about 10 to 15 per cent. In other firms, it may be as high as 40 per cent or more of total costs. Many firms have their own road haulage vehicles whilst the oil firms, in some cases also own ships. Other firms, including paradoxically, car manufacturers are linked to the rail network so that the railways can give a door-to-door service. The running of a road haulage fleet has become increasingly more complex with the growing volume of legislation. The Channel Tunnel opens up new opportunities for long distance freight. Even firms that have their own road haulage vehicles may use some other form of outside transport. For example, some firms will hire in other firms vehicles to cater for their peak demands rather than having their vehicles idle during the year.

Total distribution costs

Surveys, such as the Whitehead survey in 1974, showed that many firms did not have a clear idea of their total distribution costs. Whilst matters may have improved slightly, many firms still do not have a clear idea. Total distribution costs will include the cost of stock holding, warehouse costs, insurance costs, and opportunity costs of stock as well as managers' time.

Self-examination Questions

1. Where do firms get new ideas? Is it solely from their staff?

2. Can you think of any new products that would help the standard of living in your area?

3. Why might the government be wary about some new products?

4. Why might there be a long time between a products conception and it finally being brought into production?

5. Why might the firm try to have basic, middle range and deluxe versions of their products?

6. Why might the marketing department prefer to have a bigger range of products whereas the production department may wish to have a smaller range?

7. Why might the marketing department wish to change the range of products frequently whereas the production department may wish to keep them constant?

8. What is meant by saying 'firms might wish to continue to make goods or provide services providing they contribute to fixed costs?'

9. Why might the marketing department want to know about socio-economic factors at work within their markets?

10. Why might the marketing department wish to use past sales figures including seasonal trends?

11. Why might the marketing department be interested in creating and publicising their own brand names?

12. Why did Esso spend about $50 million on coming up with a new name?

13. Why did Nestlé change the name of most of its products; e.g. Rowntree Kit-Kat to Nestlé Kit-Kat?

14. Why have other firms adopted the other policy of keeping brand names even when the firm has been taken over?

15. Why might the marketing department be interested in different psychological groups?

16. Why might the marketing department and production department need to liaise?

17. Why might the marketing department and purchasing department wish to liaise, particularly in retailing?

18. Why might the marketing department wish to liaise with the personnel department before engaging on a marketing campaign?

19. Why might the marketing department wish to liaise with the legal department, particularly on credit sales?

20. Why might the marketing department wish to co-operate with the accounts department?

Chapter 9: INVESTMENT APPRAISAL

9.1: Types of Investment Appraisal Methods:

Investment is important for firms and there are several different motives for investing capital. Investment relates to the purchasing of capital goods. A capital good is one that is used either directly or indirectly in the production of other goods or services. Examples of these include machinery, plant, tools or equipment. Firms have to replace their capital goods that have become obsolete. This can happen through either advances in technology or just standard wear and tear. Growth also requires investment, as do the refurbishment of buildings and the purchase of other firms.

There are two types of investment: autonomous investment, which is where a firm buys goods to replace existing worn out items, and induced investment, where an organisation buys to expand its operations.

It is important to have a good idea of the possible outcome of each investment option, as well as how this will affect the firm's finances throughout the lifetime of the project. Several methods of appraisal are detailed below. Generally, we will only invest if we think the benefits; however, we quantify them, are greater than costs.

9.1.1: Payback Period

One of the most common is called the payback period. This is where the firm looks to see how quickly the project or investment pays for itself. For example, if a firm was buying a computer and it estimated that it would cost £10,000 but would save £5,000 per year then the payback period would be 2 years using the formula below:

$$\frac{Cost}{Saving\ per\ year} = payback\ period, \quad So\ \frac{10,000}{5,000} = 2\ years$$

	Project 1	Project 2	Project 3
Cost	£10,000	£8,000	£16,000
Return Year 1	£5,000	£1,000	£4,000
Return Year 2	£5,000	£2,000	£4,000
Return Year 3	£5,000	£3,000	£4,000
Return Year 4	£0	£4,000	£4,000
Return Year 5	£0	£5,000	£4,000
Return Year 6	£0	£6,000	£4,000
Payback Period	Year 2	Year 4	Year 4
Total Net Profit*	£5,000	£13,000	£8,000

Figure 9.1 (*Net Profit=Total Returns-Total Cost)

In practice, many small firms use this method but it has many drawbacks. One of these is that the method does not take into account all the benefits that occur from the investment. In particular, it ignores the longer-term benefits. Consequently, a firm would never decide to send someone on a long-term course such as a degree programme since the payback period would be too long. The Channel Tunnel would never have been considered since during the seven years of building there was no revenue and very large costs. The time after the payback period has been calculated is not taken into account so this method does not consider the overall profitability of the project in question. An example of this is shown in Figure 9.1.

The Payback Period method of investment appraisal would suggest that Project 1 is the best, as the break-even point is easier to achieve. Further calculation and closer inspection reveals that both Projects 2 and 3 make a greater overall net profit for the firm.

9.1.2: Average Rate of Return (ARR)

The Average Rate of Return (ARR, sometimes known as the accounting rate of return) method gives the annual net return on the investment as a percentage of the cost. The formula used is shown below:

$$ARR\ (\%) = \frac{\text{Net Return per annum (profit)}}{\text{Initial Cost}}$$

$$\text{Where,}\quad \text{Net Profit per Annum} = \frac{\text{Net Profit}}{\text{Number of years}}$$

It is best explained by referring to the example in Figure 9.2:

		Project A	Project B	Project C	Project D
Cost		£50,000	£75,000	£90,000	£60,000
Return	Year 1	£11,000	£17,000	£32,000	£7,000
	Year 2	£11,000	£18,000	£30,000	£10,000
	Year 3	£11,000	£18,000	£30,000	£12,000
	Year 4	£11,000	£22,000	£10,000	£16,000
	Year 5	£11,000	£17,000	£8,000	£16,000
	Year 6	£11,000			£16,000
Total		£66,000	£92,000	£110,000	£77,000
Net Profit	£16,000	£17,000	£20,000	£17,000	
Net Profit Per Annum*	£2,667	£3,400	£4,000	£2,833	
ARR	=2667/50000	=3400/75000	=4000/90000	=2833/60000	
ARR	5.33%	4.53%	4.44%	4.72%	

Figure 9.2

There are four investment projects (A, B, C and D) each with different initial costs, periods and values of returns. The best project to undertake according to ARR, is Project A. whilst this gives a lower amount of net profit than Project C the percentage return is higher. This means that, on average, for each £1 invested, project A returns just over £1.05 in the first year compared to around £1.04 for the first year of project C.

This technique is useful when comparing projects with different starting costs and return periods. It can also be used to compare between the projects and other options, such as putting the capital into a bank account. In the example, if we could obtain a better interest rate at the bank than 5.33% per year then the firm in question may wish to invest the money with the bank.

These first two techniques do not take into account the time effect on money. If the project horizon is over a large number of years, figures should be adjusted to take into account interest rates. These approaches do not do this and so the actual rate of return may be lower and the costs may take longer than is calculated to be paid back in full.

The Effect of Interest Rates (Test Rate or Discount Rate)

We wish to translate all the monetary figures to the present day values. As a demonstration, we will assume that the rate of discount (*i*) is 10 %. We can adjust future values by *dividing* by (1+*i*). The best way to think about this concept is to consider saving accounts. If you have access to a savings account that pays 10% interest per year and someone offers to give you £100 in a years time or £100 today then which one would you chose?

If the person gives you the money now and you put it into the account, it would be worth £110 next year. Therefore, if you take the £100 in a year's time then you are £10 worse off than if you would have taken the money today. So if you are offered one pound in a year's time it will obviously be worth less at the present time, the real question is exactly how much less?

If 'I', denoting investment, is £1000 then we will find that the discounted amount at 10% is £909.09 one year earlier. Therefore, to obtain £1000 in one year at an interest rate of 10% we must invest £909.09 now. If we wish to get to the target in 2 years time then we have to divide i by (1+i) again, effectively (1+i)2, in this case 1.21, giving a present value of £826.45 If it is in 3 years time it will be (1+i)3 so 1.331 (see figure 9.3)

Year	1995	1996	1997	1998	1999	2000	2001	2002	2003
Discount	2.14	1.95	1.77	1.61	1.46	1.33	1.21	1.10	1.00
Value	£466.50	£513.10	£564.40	£620.90	£683.00	£751.30	£826.40	£909.00	£1,000

Figure 9.3

9.1.3: Discounted Cash Flow

Discounted Cash Flow (DCF) considers this important point. The basic logic of discounted cash flow is that returns in future years do not have the same value as cash now. In most cases people or society, prefer to have money now rather than money later. This is sometimes called 'social time preference'. This is conceptually different from the effects of inflation although the ideas may overlap.

Interest rates are sometimes denoted by the letter *i* and occasionally by *r*.

We can outline the two concepts that are called Net Present Value (NPV) and Internal Rate of Return (IRR). We are used to the idea of going forward i.e. if we put £100 into the bank now it will be worth say £105 in a year's time. We do this calculation by multiplying by $(1 + i)$. If i is 5% we multiply the original amount by 1.05. If i is 10% we multiply the amount by $(1 + i)$, which is 1.10. If it is 15% we multiply it by 1.15 etc.

If we put the money aside for a second year in the bank we multiply it by $(1 + i)$ again or simply $(1+i)^2$. If we put the money aside for a third year we multiply it by $(1+i)^3$.

The interest rate that is to be used will depend upon the circumstances surrounding the decision. For example, if we can borrow from the bank at 20% then the test rate or discount rate needs to exceed 20% otherwise we will not be making any profit when financing the project through bank loans. We wish the rate of return to be more than 20% in this case because in most investments there is an element of uncertainty. This higher value allows us to take into account some of the possible problems and any over estimations of the returns.

If we put £100 into a bank for a year then we are saying that we prefer the money in one year's time to £100 now. If we do not do so then we are saying that we prefer the money now to later. When firms invest in machinery or capital they are making these decisions about preferring money now or later. One of the problems in practice is that there is always an element of uncertainty with investment projects. In the case of the Channel Tunnel, about which there has been a great deal of controversy, there is no certainty that the £10 billion that has been spent on the construction will be recovered. However, this is not always the case. For example, if a householder is offered a remission of ground rent (paid for the privilege of building on another person's land) for a specific sum the calculations are quite straightforward. If the payment was to be £150, in order to save a ground rent payment of £15 per year then the rate of return is 10%.

The Main Formula

The aim, generally, is that the total benefits are greater than the total costs.

In this case, we write that Total Costs 'C' in all years up to the final year (n) is less than Total Benefit 'B' gained in those n years, adjusted by the discount factor i. Therefore, we want:

$$C_0 + (C_1/(1+i)^1) + (C_2/(1+i)^2) + (C^n/(1+i)^n) < B_0 + (B_1/(1+i)^1) + (B_2/(1+i)^2) + (B^n/(1+i)^n)$$

This can be reduced to:

$$\circledcirc (C_n/ (1+i)^n) < \circledcirc (B_n/ (1+i)^n)$$

A demonstration of this formula can be seen in the following example.

Example: A firm wishes to update its distribution vehicles and has been persuaded by an automobile manufacturer that investing in one of its new vans, which costs £20,000, will produce savings of £4,500 each year for 5 years. The company does not have the capital to invest in the van now so they plan to get finance from the manufacturer at a rate of 6% per annum. What is the total discounted cash flow for the next 5 years? Does this seem like a good option to pursue?

Solution: We are spending £20,000 now, say Year 0, and will receive £4,500 in Years 1, 2, 3, 4 and 5. The interest rate is 6%. The table below shows the cash flows and the discounted cash flows using the formula above.

Figure 9.4

Interest rate	6%
Cost	£20,000
Benefit per year	£4,500

Year	Cash flow	Formula	Discounted Cash flow
1	4,500	$4500/(1+0.06)^1$	£4,245.28
2	4,500	$4500/(1+0.06)^2$	£4,004.98
3	4,500	$4500/(1+0.06)^3$	£3,778.29
4	4,500	$4500/(1+0.06)^4$	£3,564.42
5	4,500	$4500/(1+0.06)^5$	£3,362.66
Total	£22,500		£18,955.64

Total Discounted Cash Flow is £18,955.64

Here $\circledcirc (C_n/ (1+i)n) > \circledcirc (B_n/ (1+i)n)$
Or more simply £20,000.00 > £18,955.64

As the total discounted cash flow value is less than total costs of the project it should not be taken up. This would not have shown up had the discounted cash flow method not been used.

Net Present Value

A useful and often used term in investment appraisal is Net Present Value (NPV), which is the value of investment income minus the cost.

NPV = Present value of returns – Costs

    If   NPV = 0 then the project should breakeven.

          NPV > 0 then the project should make money

          NPV < 0 then the project should lose money

In the example above NPV = £18,955.64 - £20,000.00 = -£1,044.36 therefore the project is likely to lose money.

9.1.4: Internal Rate of Return (IRR)

The mathematical formula to work out the rate of return is quite complicated. We can however demonstrate by working backwards with a 2-year example. If we are offered £121 at the end of a 2-year period for a sum of £100 now then the rate of return is 10%.

This is because $100 = \dfrac{121}{(1 + i)^2}$ which rearranges to:

$100 (1 + i)^2 = 121$

$\sqrt{100} (1 + i) = \sqrt{121}$

$10 (1 + i) = 11$

$10 + 10\, i = 11$

$10\, i = 1$

$i = 0.1 = 10\%$

The Internal Rate of Return calculates the percentage return on a project at which Net Present Value equals 0. If the market rate of interest is known then any project that provides an IRR above this value is calculated to be worthy of investment. The main advantage of using this method is that it can be used to compare various different projects more fairly than the other techniques discussed in the chapter. The problem to this technique is that it gets increasingly difficult to calculate the IRR of projects lasting more than 2 years. This is because using a square root is not too difficult to deal with, as shown above, but cube roots (used for 3 years) and above tends to be more difficult to handle without computer software.

9.2: Types of Benefits

Generally, we can subdivide benefits received by investing into 3 categories, although these may overlap. They are:

- Cost Savings: For example, if we install a computer we could save money by reducing the administrative tasks carried out by staff.

- Increases in Capacity: The computer will allow us to do more things such as store larger quantities of information.

- Increases in Revenue: A more powerful computer may allow us to serve more customers.

In many cases we are not certain what benefits will result from the investment. It is generally easier to ascertain savings in costs rather than increases in revenue.

9.3: Sensitivity Analysis

Because it is often so difficult to estimate the cost, and even more difficult to quantify the benefits, we may wish to carry out a form of sensitivity analysis. This means that we test how sensitive the project is to possible changes whether in interest rates, demand or initial costs etc. If the project is very sensitive to changes, we may carry out further work to see if we can make our forecast more accurate in any way. However, if the project were robust, meaning that the range of possibilities does not greatly affect it, we would proceed.

An example of what this means can be demonstrated with energy saving measures. One of the most effective ways of saving energy is through the insulating of a building's hot water tank. Let us suppose we are doing this purely for financial benefits and so any environmental benefits are ignored. Suppose we find that this costs us £20 and that it saves us on average £1 per week. This certainly seems worthwhile since the effect will last for several years. Even if we think that the benefits are overrated and that it will only save us 50p per week then it is still worthwhile. Even if the cost of the project doubles, then at £40 and savings were again reduced to 50 p per week, the project is still worthwhile as we will save money within 80 weeks and therefore we would say that the project is robust. The next most cost effective way of saving energy is loft insulation. This may cost about £80 and the savings will be typically about £1 per week. Again even if our estimates are incorrect it is still reasonably robust.

Cavity wall insulation is more expensive. It may cost about £700 depending upon the number of walls in the house. We might estimate the savings at £120 per year. This gives a rate of return of just over 17%. Is this worthwhile? If we have money, it is almost certainly a better rate of return than we will get from the bank. If however we have to borrow the money it will not be worthwhile. We might need to do further estimates of how much more expensive fuel will become. In other words, the project is not robust.

9.4: Problems of Forecasting

All of the investment appraisal techniques in this chapter are based on predicted values of current assumptions. The return on an investment may be overestimated or the cost underestimated. The interest and inflationary rates may change over the period of the investment and so affect its outcome. These factors mean that there is a need to build in some form of margin of error. Nobody knows exactly how the economy may change over time and so managers must not blindly follow the maths without considering the external influences upon those decisions and their possible changes.

The further into the future a project goes the more likely that there will be changes that affect it. For example, if we were trying to estimate the traffic for a new road bridge, once the project was under way we could use regression and extrapolation methods. If however we were trying to estimate the traffic in 40 years time so many changes could take place that we would be very uncertain indeed. Any number of factors would affect the usage of the bridge including changes in holiday patterns, growth or decline of different types of transport, business communications patterns, population changes or even natural disasters.

9.5: Independent and Interdependent Projects

In some cases, the portfolio of project options may be independent. In other cases the projects may be interdependent. An independent project is one that, if chosen, has no influence on the outcome of any other project. Interdependent projects are those that affect the outcome or otherwise influence each other.

When they are interdependent it is worthwhile considering Project A alone, Project B alone and 'A' and 'B'. For example, if a firm were to invest £40,000 in a new computer system for its head office it may expect to make savings of £4,000 a year.

If the firm kept its existing system but trained its workers to use it more effectively this may cost £8,000 and give savings of say, £1,000 per annum. If however the firm invested in the new system and training then the figures could well be different.

In this case, the benefits of the project as a whole may be greater than the sum of its parts. The total cost may be lower as a deal with the supplier, may be possible. The returns may also be higher than the two individual projects combined. In this case, it may mean that the combined costs are only £45,000 saving £5,500 per annum.

The reverse may also be true. If we wish to improve our existing paper filing system and to install a computer system then either may be worthwhile on their own but not necessarily together.

Self-examination Questions

1. What is meant by the payback period when referring to investment? What are the advantages and disadvantages of using this technique?

2. What does DCF stand for? Why, if it is such a good method, do many small firms not use it?

3. Why is it often easier to quantify costs rather than revenue? What is the importance of this when referring to investment?

4. 'Since we can rarely be certain about the future there is no point in carrying out investment appraisal'. How would you reply to this argument?

5. It is often said that the returns from incremental investment are ignored when forecasting by firms. What is meant by this statement and why is it important?

6. What effect will higher interest rates have on investment? Will the effects be greater on short-term rather than long-term projects?

7. Why in the discounted cash flow technique is it important to have a common unit?

8. What is meant by 'independent' and 'interdependent' projects? Why is the distinction important?

9. Calculate the Payback Periods, ARR and NPV (at 5% discount rate) of the following 4 projects.

		Project A	Project B	Project C	Project D
Cost		£40,000	£27,000	£10,000	£50,000
Return	Year 1	£12,500	£9,000	£1,500	£0
	Year 2	£12,500	£8,000	£1,750	£10,000
	Year 3	£12,500	£7,000	£2,250	£12,000
	Year 4	£12,500	£6,000	£2,500	£14,000
	Year 5		£5,000	£3,000	£16,000
	Year 6			£3,250	£16,000

A) With each of the 3 appraisal methods, which project would you choose to pursue if your firm could only handle one?

B) Why is it difficult to calculate the IRR for this set of projects?

10. Calculate the IRR for the following two project options.

	Project A	Project B	Project C
Cost	£10,000	£20,000	£15,000
Return Year 1	£11,000	£0	£0
Return Year 2	£0	£22,000	£16,500

11. In which project would you choose to invest?

Chapter 10: THE BALANCE SHEET

10.1: Introduction

A balance sheet shows the assets and liabilities of a business at the end of the financial year. In many firms, the financial year does not end on the 31st December but on a convenient date. It sometimes coincides with the tax year-end, which in the UK is April 6th. The balance sheet is said to be a snapshot of the company's wealth. Assets are anything that the firm owns and has monetary value whereas a liability is anything that is owed by the firm.

10.1.1: Comments about the Balance Sheet

Fixed assets are shown in order of permanence. For example, land, then property and then machines. There may be problems in determining what fixed assets constitute. Cars that are held by a car dealer are not fixed assets but considered stock. Similarly, property that is owned by a property dealer would not be fixed assets. For most other businesses, however they would be fixed assets. The question is, are the assets being held as capital to produce other goods or services, or for resale? Most assets, apart from land, depreciate over time and therefore lose value. Therefore, in the balance sheet, the net value of the asset is shown along with the historic cost.

Capital goods are shown as fixed assets whilst goods for resale are current assets. There are sometimes problems in the evaluation of tangible assets. For example, a factory might have been built in the 1930s at a cost of £10,000. In 1990, it might have been valued at £500,000 but because of the collapse in property, prices would not be worth as much in the mid-1990s, in 2013 people were unsure about house prices. Accountants should always try to be prudent, i.e. it is better to err on the side of caution rather than to overstate values. There are also problems of evaluation of intangible assets. For example, during a take-over a price may be paid for the goodwill given by a brand name. For example, the Guardian newspaper group took over the Observer newspaper, even though the Observer was making a loss, whilst in the Lonrho group. The Observer name (a Sunday newspaper with roots in the 18th Century) will add more value to the Guardian than if it had tried to set up its own Sunday newspaper.

Balance sheets can be shown either in a vertical form or in the more traditional horizontal form. An example of the later is shown below in Figure 10.1. This particular balance sheet is for a small sole trader firm called K. Marshall.

K. Marshall

Balance Sheet as at 31 December 2XX2

Capital	£	£	Fixed Assets		£
At start		107990	Land and		
Add net profit	21 007		Buildings		34500
Less Drawings	(9500)	11507	Plant and		
		119497	Machinery		14800
			Furniture and		
			Fittings		8650
			Motor Vehicles		12420
Long-term					70370
Liabilities Mortgage		10 000	Current Assets		
			Stock at close	£	
			Sundry Debtors	9762	
Current			Bank	17250	
Liabilities:			Cash	38 640	
Sundry Creditors		8265		1 740	
					67392
		£137762			£137762

Figure 10.1

Notes

1. Fixed assets are assets that last a long time (certainly longer than one year) and therefore serve the business during their lifetime.

2. The longest lasting is Land and Buildings, while motor vehicles have a relatively short life and are therefore shown last in the order of permanence.

3. Current assets are assets that are to be used within one year. For example stock will be sold in the next few weeks and replaced by further supplies. Debtors should normally pay within one month, and cash, and bank monies are the most liquid assets. This means that they are easily convertible to cash.

4. On the liabilities side we may look on the liabilities as debts that we must pay sooner or later. Starting at the bottom we have the creditors - who are due to be paid within the year. 'Long-term Liabilities' are liabilities that are not due to be paid for more than a year. The best examples are mortgages and bank loans. In this case we have a mortgage of £10000, which may be repayable over many years.

5. The Capital Account is of course the longest term liability of all, for the business only repays the proprietor on the day he/she ceases to trade, usually because of retirement. In the event of the proprietor's death the business becomes part of the estate and the capital is repaid to the beneficiaries under the will.

6. Note that the indented section of the Capital shows how the proprietor drew £9,500 of the profits during the year, leaving £11,507 to be added to the capital. This

is called 'ploughing back' profits into the business. Suppose the proprietor had enjoyed a richer lifestyle and had drawn out £30000 drawings, when the firm only made profits of £21,007. This would have meant a negative figure of £8,993, which would have reduced the capital to £98,997. Such a trader is said to be 'living off his capital' - never a wise thing to do.

10.2: Depreciation

Depreciation computation can take one of many different forms. These include straight line, reducing balance, sum of digits and revaluation methods. For example, revaluation can apply to antiques, livestock, or goods where there are no general trends e.g. classic cars or art, which can go up or down in value. In each case, the idea is to charge for the benefits.

10.2.1: Depreciation and Revenue Expenditure

We should note that all the expenses of running a business are known as 'revenue expenditure' and as such can be deducted from the receipts of the business at the end of the financial year when we are trying to work out the profits for the year. There is one type of expense that is rather different from ordinary expenses like rent, rates, light, heat, etc., but which must still be taken into account when we work out the net profit of the business; depreciation. Depreciation is the loss in value by the assets of a business because of their use during the course of the year. It is often called 'fair wear and tear'. For example, if we buy a new van on 1 January for £14,000 and use it for a year it will not be worth £14,000 at the end of the year. Everyone knows how quickly motor vehicles depreciate and by the end of the year it is quite likely that if we traded the van in and purchased a new one we would not get much more than £10,500 as the trade-in value, possibly even less.

Where has the missing £3,500 gone? It has obviously been 'fair wear and tear' during the year, one of the expenses of the business during the current year. We should really treat this as a revenue expense, and write it off the profits when we work them out at the end of the financial year.

There is another point here which is very important, and which we can adjust at the same time as we deal with the depreciation of the motor vehicle. When we purchase an asset such as the motor vehicle referred to, we bring the asset onto the books by debiting the asset account. Thus, the double entry for the purchase of a van for £14,000 by cheque would

A.   Debit Motor Vehicles Account with £14,000.00 (it has received value)

B.   Credit Bank Account (in the Cash Book) with £14,000.00 (it has given value)

Now, by the end of the year, the value of this vehicle has fallen because of depreciation, to £10,500.00. Therefore, unless we do something about it, we have the asset on the books at an out-of-date value; it has ceased to be worth £14000.00 and is now only worth £10,500. Fortunately, as we shall see, we can write down the value of the vehicle on the books at the same time as we take notice of the depreciation. Before we do the depreciation entry we must just say a word about the depreciation account.

10.2.2: *The Depreciation Account*

The depreciation account is an account where we collect together all the various losses suffered by a business as a result of fair wear and tear of assets. Of course the eventual aim is to write off these losses against the profits at the end of the year, but until the end of the financial year arrives it is convenient to have an account where we can collect the various losses together. Therefore the rule in depreciating any item is to compute the fall in value and reduce the asset book value, by this amount, taking the loss to the Depreciation Account. Later, when all the depreciation has been pooled together we shall make a single entry, transferring all the losses to the Profit and Loss Account, which is one of the final accounts of the business where final profit for the year is computed.

As mentioned earlier there are many ways of calculating depreciation. Three such ways are described below.

10.2.3: *The Straight-Line (Equal Instalment) Method*

In the simple example used earlier, we know how much the motor van has depreciated because we asked a garage for a trade-in value for the vehicle. This is easy enough to do for a motor vehicle, but with most other assets there is no ready market for second hand items. The first method is called the straight-line method; sometimes called the equal instalment method because it results in the same amount of depreciation being written off the asset each year. There is a simple formula for working out what amount should be written off each year.

$$\text{Annual Depreciation} = \frac{\text{Original Cost - Residual Value}}{\text{Lifetime of Asset}}$$

Suppose we expect a machine, which cost £14,000 to last ten years and then to be worth £2000 when sold at the end of its useful life. This is called its residual value. The calculation is therefore:

$$\frac{£14,000 - £2,000}{10 \text{ years}} = £12,000 \text{ per annum}$$

Each year we shall debit the Depreciation Account with £1,200, which will be written off the profits for the year, and we shall credit the Machinery Account with £1200.

The Machinery Account will be as shown on the next page. This shows how an asset account declines in value over the years.

Machinery Account:

Year 1
Jan. 1 Bank b/d	£14000.00
Dec. 31 Depreciation	£1200.00
Dec. 31 Balance C/D	£12800.00

Year 2
Jan. 1 Balance b/d	£12800.00
Dec. 31 Depreciation	£1200.00
Dec. 31 Balance C/D	£11600.00

Year 3
Jan 1 Balance b/d	£11600.00
Dec. 31 Depreciation	£1200.00
Dec. 31 Balance C/D	£10400.00

And so on until Year 10

Year 10
Jan 1 Balance b/d	£3200.00
Dec. 31 Depreciation	£1200.00
Dec. 31 Balance C/D	£2000.00

Year 11
Jan 1 Balance b/d	£2000.00

Figure 10.2

148

Notes

1. The amount written off each year is the same hence the name 'equal instalment method'.

2. By the end of the lifetime, in this case ten years, the asset is reduced on the books to its residual value (sometimes called the scrap value). If the asset continues to be used it will stay on the books at this value, until finally disposed of.

10.2.4: *The Diminishing Balance Method*

There is one disadvantage about the straight-line method of depreciation described above. Some assets require maintenance and repairs from time to time, and these become more necessary as the item gets older. Thus a motor vehicle requires few repairs in its first two years, but after these breakdowns become more common and repair bills rise. It follows that equal instalment for depreciation and larger repair bills mean that year-by-year the charge for the asset increases. For example:

	Year 1	Year 2	Year 3	Year 4	Year 5
Depreciation	£1,200	£1,200	£1,200	£1,200	£1,200
Repairs	£160	£240	£386	£540	£ 540
Total	£1,360	£1,440	£1,586	£1,740	£1,740

If we can devise a system that charges more for depreciation in the early years, when repair bills are low and less in later years when repair bills rise, we shall even out the charges. This is what the diminishing balance method tries to achieve. It charges a fixed percentage rate (say 25%) on the diminishing balance year by year. In the following example, Cruickshank Logistics buys one van at a total cost of £34,000, which it decides to depreciate at an annual rate of 25%. The useful lifetime of the van for the firm is four years, at which point Cruickshank Logistics will seek to sell it.

The asset would therefore decrease in value as shown below (calculations to the nearest £1).

Heavy Motor Vehicles Account:

Year 1	£
Jan. 1 Bank b/d	34 000.00
Dec. 31 Depreciation	8500.00
Dec. 31 Balance C/D	25500.00

Year 2	£
Jan. 1 Balance b/d	25 500.00
Dec. 31 Depreciation	6375.00
Dec. 31 Balance C/D	19125.00

Year 3	£
Jan. 1 Balance b/d	19125.00
Dec. 31 Depreciation	4781.00
Dec. 31 Balance C/D	14344.00

Year 4	£
Jan. 1 Balance b/d	14344.00
Dec. 31 Depreciation	3586.00
Dec. 31 Balance C/D	10758.00

Year 5	£
Jan. 1 Balance b/d	10758.00

Figure 10.3

Notes

1. The amount charged for depreciation is falling year by year as the balance diminishes.

2. However, as the repair bills will be increasing the total cost of the vehicle charged to Profit and Loss Account will be steady year by year.

10.2.5: The Revaluation Method

Some assets do not depreciate steadily over a lifetime but vary in value from year to year. Thus, a farmer's herds or flocks cannot be said to suffer from fair wear and tear. They might fall in value if disease hits the herd, but in most years, they would increase in value as more animals are born. When an asset increases in value this is called appreciation. Another asset, which varies in this way, is the Loose Tools

Account. These are the kind of tools made by toolmakers (a skilled engineering trade) in which, for example, steel press plates are made to stamp out plastic or soft metal articles. Some of these tools cost thousands of pounds, the surfaces being polished to a mirror finish so that when pressed out the plastic article is perfectly smooth and shiny. Since such tools might be kept for many years and new ones are made every year the stock of such tools is liable to rise and the value of the asset in total may increase. Outside valuers usually revalue such assets each year (rather than by someone within the firm or company). If the value is found to have increased over the year the extra value will be taken on to the books as a profit for the year, while if the value has fallen the decrease will be taken on to the books as a loss. Because of the difficulty of treating such losses as depreciation, it will often be best to take the gain or loss direct to the Profit and Loss Account.

10.2.6: 'Provision for Depreciation' Accounts

Company legislation in the UK calls for assets to be shown on the Balance Sheet at cost price, less the total depreciation to date, and this has led to a new way of keeping track of depreciation, not only by companies but by sole traders and partnerships as well. This is understood easily if you consider the earlier example (see Figure 10.2). In this figure, we have the original cost of the machinery and the depreciation deducted from it. The balance carried down at the end of the year shows the reduced value of the asset on the books at the start of Year 2. Over the years, we might lose track of what the original cost of the machinery was, and therefore find it difficult to comply with the Companies Act, 1985. We can overcome the difficulty if we leave the asset account alone on the books. To account for the loss in value we open Provisions for Depreciation Account.

10.3: Short and Long-term Liabilities

Liabilities are those items listed on the balance sheet that the organisation owes or is *liable* to pay other organisations or individuals. They can be split up into two different categories dependant on the time in which they must be paid back. Short-term Liabilities e.g. trade creditors, dividends owed, taxes or overdrafts have to be paid within 12 months whereas the Long-term Liabilities have to be paid outside of this period. Long-term liabilities often include loans, mortgages or debentures.

10.4: Factors affecting Cash Flow

The firm needs to look at its cash flow diagram. Some of the factors affecting cash flow can readily be seen from the balance sheet. Cash, which will come into the business, includes retained profits. Any cash raised through the issue of shares, including rights issues, will also add to the cash flow. Other sources of finance such as the issue of debentures and preference shares will add to the firm's cash whereas payments to preference shareholders, debentures and dividends to shareholders will reduce the cash to which the firm has access. Payments for corporation tax will also reduce the amount of cash held.

10.5: Break-even Charts

We should note that total costs include both fixed and variable costs. The total cost curve will start from the total of fixed costs. Why is this? This is because when there is zero production, there are no variable costs. Since fixed costs remain constant, by definition, the total cost curve is parallel to the variable costs curve.

The higher the fixed costs the higher the break-even points other things being equal. We can note that total revenue will start from the origin since with zero sales we get zero revenue. The break-even point is where the total revenue equals the total costs.

However, there are some limitations of the conventional simple break-even charts. The straight line for revenue assumes that we can sell all stock at the going price. In practice, we may have price discrimination, e.g. selling at different prices or we may need to reduce the selling price to sell more bulk sales e.g. selling large quantities of paper.

It assumes that variable costs are constant. We may find that average variable costs reduce, e.g. with bulk purchase of materials. Alternatively, they may increase since the firm may have to put staff on overtime or hire more staff. Both of these methods, of increasing output, will lead to higher costs of labour per unit produced.

10.6: Valuation of Assets

We have already mentioned the idea of straight-line depreciation. The Company's Act specifies that the profit and loss account and the balance sheet must show directly attributable costs as well as valuation of fixed and current assets.

10.7: Profit and Loss

The simple definition of profit is income minus payments is unsatisfactory since for example, farmers and authors may receive incomes at different times from their expenditure. Similarly, expenditure may well be indivisible, e.g. a taxi firm may buy a taxi in one period therefore there are payments in that period. However, these payments will contribute to the organisation earning revenue in several periods. A taxi driver cannot charge passengers in the first year enough to cover the purchase price of the taxi. Similarly, the taxi driver will wish to charge passengers an amount towards the cost of the taxi in subsequent periods.

A firm may buy assembly machines in a particular period and this will lead to cash outflows in that period. Conversely, there may be share issues, which will lead to cash inflows in that period. Other factors leading to cash inflows could be debentures, overdrafts, etc.

10.8: Cost of Sales

If we look at cost of sales on the left-hand side (LHS), of the account for a DVD manufacturer, we have opening stock, e.g. completed DVDs. We add purchases such as raw materials; then deduct closing stock, i.e. number of DVDs still left. This gives the cost of sales. Refer to Figure 10.4.

10.8.1: Calculation of Overheads

The firm also has to do a calculation of overheads. This will include rent and uniform business rate, insurance, HQ (headquarters), staff, etc. There is no easy way in a multi-product firm of allocating overheads. A firm may allocate on a unit basis. However, would this be sensible in a firm making musical instruments and vehicles? In this case would it seem reasonable to allocate an overhead charge of £50 to both a £200 saxophone and a £18,000 van?

The firm could allocate on a floor basis, e.g. if the musical instruments take up one tenth of the floor space then charge them one tenth. Or we can allocate on a personnel basis, e.g. if the people making musical instruments account for one third of the workforce then charge this department one third.

How can the firm allocate rent? One way of doing this would be to look at floor space, e.g. if factory is divided 40% for one item and 60% for another item then allocate rent in a similar ratio. However, in a shop this may be arbitrary since the ground floor may be much more worthwhile than other floors. Therefore, if we paid £100,000 for rent for a 4-floor shop and let the bottom floor for £25,000 to a boutique we would probably be losing money. If we allocate on a per employee basis on the other hand in department store than a labour intensive part like a sweet section would get much bigger costs than a capital-intensive one like the furniture department.

Lighting and heating can largely be directly attributed especially in a multi-sited firm. In other cases where power is concerned, we can carry out sampling to look at direct costs of particular products. For example, if the firm makes several different types of machine in the same factory it will look to see how many of them are made in a particular period.

For carriage (the term used to denote the money paid for the transport of goods.), we can allocate directly except where the same vehicle is used for several different items e.g. carriage of computers and cash tills in the same lorry.

Postage can sometimes be allocated directly but for brochures etc. will be more difficult as well as for general enquiries. This is because brochures will often show details for more than one product. A firm selling computer printers may well send out details of a number of printers in the product range at the same time. A travel agent's holiday brochure may give details of a number of resorts. If will be difficult to specify which resorts or holidays will produce the most profits. Paper and photocopying can again be allocated directly to the different departments or sections. Some printing can be allocated directly as can stationery but some will be allocated per sales total or sales volume e.g. for brochures.

Cars for company sales people could be allocated as a percentage of sales though the sales people may take much longer on small sales proportionately than large sales items. Where the company car is a perk it can be allocated directly as part of wages. For travelling, the same allocation can be made as with cars. Cleaning can be allocated on the amount of space used, though some items such as dirty machinery may require more work. Repairs and renewals of vehicles and most machines can be allocated per department although this may be more difficult for computers and word processors that could be allocated on a time basis.

Trading Account for Queenborough Videos Ltd
For Year Ending 31st December 2XX1

	£	£
Sales		196,384
Opening Stock of Finished Goods	232,528	
Cost of Manufactured Goods	122,657	
	146,185	
Less: Closing Stock	(18,764)	
Cost of Goods Sold	127,421	
Warehouse Wages	17,268	
Warehouse Expenses	3,568	
Less: Cost of Sales		(148,357)
Gross Profit		48,127

Figure 10.4

154

Insurance on property can be allocated on a floor basis. Insurance on other items can be allocated to department or to the particular machines covered.

10.8.2: Stock Movements

Valuing stock is often problematic for many firms. Raw materials should be valued at the lower of original cost or net realisable value. Note that this may depend upon circumstances e.g. bricks in a bankrupt builders store may be easy to value whereas specialist materials in a defunct factory may not.

Work in progress is extremely important to value in a shipbuilding yard since they only sell a few ships each year. We add administration costs and distribution costs to date. Think of the implications for Euro tunnel whilst the Channel Tunnel was being built.

10.9: Appropriations of Profit

Note that expenses are not the same as appropriation. Profits can be divided in several ways. Part will go for taxation, part will go for dividends and part will be retained in the company.

10.9.1: Gross Profit Margin

If we buy goods for 30p and sell for 45p we will have a gross profit of approximately 33%. The formula for this calculation is as follows:

$$\text{Gross Profit Margin} = \frac{\text{Turnover - Cost of Sales}}{\text{Turnover}}$$

$$\text{In this case:} \quad = \frac{45p-30p}{45p} = 33\%$$

Is this good or bad? It will depend upon the circumstances. For example, in a prestige shop like Harrods it might be low whereas on a market stall it might be high and for small goods like groceries it might also be high. It might alter in a recession. There may be many reasons why gross profit margins change.

- Stolen takings: We can check on different tills.

- Stock taken: Computerised stock keeping will help to keep stock records and movements.

- Stock breakages and double handling. This is where stock is damaged; double handling is specifically when stock is moved unnecessarily by the organisation.

- Bad purchases: Many firms, particularly in a recession like 2007, may have been over optimistic and therefore have to sell at a lower price than anticipated.

- Inflation and changes in exchange rates: This can reduce profits if, for example, there is an OPEC price rise and higher prices cannot be passed down the supply chain. This is often the case if the exchange rate changes and the firms are tied to a fixed contract.

- Competition: The development known as 'Lakeside', a very large purpose built shopping centre in the countryside in Essex, gives much competition to shops in nearby areas. Lakeside itself has experienced increased competition in recent years from 'Bluewater' a similar centre in neighbouring Kent.

10.10: Cash Budgets

Many firms now draw up cash budgets that show all the regular items of expenditure. Some of these will be known with precision. For example, rent and unified business rates as well as the telephone rental. For other items reasonable estimates can often be made, such as for the lighting bill. For others more imprecise estimates will have to be made. The cash budget will not only show costs but also revenue. The importance of the cash budget is that firms need to be aware when they are likely to become overdrawn. A negotiated overdraft will be much cheaper than one which has not been prearranged.

In order to improve cash flow, firms may take a number of actions. These may include the restriction of trade credit. They may include trying to improve the rate at which bills are paid to the firm whilst delaying payments to other firms. In some cases, expenditure on capital goods may be deferred. However, a problem here is that some of these methods may lead to problems at a later stage. For example, cutting down on preventive maintenance may reduce cash flow problems now, but will lead to higher costs in a later period. One way to ease cash flow problems can be to use Hire Purchase agreements in order to finance the purchase of new machinery or vehicles. This is a form of credit whereby the business does not own the item until it has made the last payment on it. Hire Purchase allows firms to obtain the equipment they need without a large single cash outlay, however, interest is charged on the life of the loan.

Figure 10.5 shows a cash flow forecast for a mail order stationery company. The forecast shows seven months from the start up of the firm in January.

	Jan	Feb	Mar	Apr	May	Jun
Receipts						
Total Receipts	£0.00	£20,000.00	£35,000.00	£30,000.00	£35,000.00	£40,000.00
Payments						
Courier Company	£0.00	£1,000.00	£1,750.00	£1,500.00	£1,750.00	£2,000.00
Rent office	£534.00	£534.00	£534.00	£534.00	£534.00	£534.00
Rent warehouse	£1,440.00	£1,440.00	£1,440.00	£1,440.00	£1,440.00	£1,440.00
Insurance	£100.00	£100.00	£100.00	£100.00	£100.00	£100.00
Wages						
Packers	£2,000.00	£2,000.00	£2,000.00	£2,000.00	£2,000.00	£2,000.00
Operators	£2,045.30	£2,045.30	£2,045.30	£2,045.30	£2,045.30	£2,045.30
Management	£2,000.00	£2,000.00	£2,000.00	£2,000.00	£2,000.00	£2,000.00
Computers						
Server	£2,000.00					
Workstations	£2,400.00					
Internet Access	£50.00	£50.00	£50.00	£50.00	£50.00	£50.00
Advertising	£8,000.00	£5,500.00	£500.00	£500.00	£500.00	£500.00
Stationery/Postage	£40.00	£40.00	£40.00	£40.00	£40.00	£40.00
Electricity	£170.00	£170.00	£170.00	£170.00	£170.00	£170.00
Telephones	£50.00	£0.00	£200.00	£0.00	£0.00	£200.00
Water	£0.00	£0.00	£90.00	£0.00	£0.00	£90.00
Gas	£0.00	£150.00	£0.00	£0.00	£150.00	£0.00
Stock	£75,000.00	£0.00	£10,000	£0.00	£50,000.00	£8,000.00
Loan repayments	£2,000.00	£2,000.00	£2,875.00	£2,000.00	£2,000.00	£2,875.00
Total Costs	£97,829.30	£17,029.30	£23,794.30	£12,379.30	£62,779.30	£22,044.30
NetCash flow	-£97,829.30	£2,970.70	£11205.70	£17,620.70	-£27,779.30	£17,955.70
Balance b/f	£90,000.00	-£7,829.30	-£4,858.60	£6,347.10	£23,967.80	-£3,811.50
Balance c/f	-£7,829.30	-£4,858.60	£6,347.10	£23,967.80	-£3,811.50	£14,144.20

Figure 10.5

It can be seen that in January, February and May that the company will be overdrawn on its bank account. There are a number of ways to remedy this situation. The first is to reduce stock orders in the first month or delay paying them if possible until February. Organising to delay payment is an effective choice but sometimes not possible for many firms. Another option is to arrange credit agreements with the suppliers of the computer systems that the firm will buy in January. The negative closing balance at the end of the first month is quite substantial and if the owners cannot invest more money in this period then a negotiated overdraft facility may be the option to pursue. This can still be an expensive solution so all other routes to increasing cash inflow or reducing cash outflow should be considered before this option is chosen.

Case Study

You are appointed as a finance assistant to an engineering firm which is competent in technology but whose manager confesses that he knows little about modern sources of finance. He asks you why not all modern businesses can use retained profits as they did in the past. How would you answer this?

One of the points you might make is that whilst retained profits are useful and lacks commitment to pay, like preference shares or debentures, the rate of growth of the firm might well be limited. You might explain that modern machinery such as computers and office equipment is very expensive but is necessary in many cases if the firm is to have an adequate system of control and productivity is to improve. Therefore, retained profits are one source but it cannot be wholly relied upon.

The manager has also heard about some firms that have sold their assets. He asks why firms do this. You explain that fast growing firms sometimes do this because, for example, they need machinery that is more modern and will sell their outdated machinery to other firms. This can also apply not just to production machinery but also to computers. In other cases however, selling assets is often a sign of failure since the firm does this in order to improve cash flow or to avoid bankruptcy. One of the reasons behind this is that quite a number of firms do not have a satisfactory concept of cash flow.

In other cases, you could explain that the very large firms, such as conglomerates, often sell some of their assets if the management of the assets is too complex or if one branch or division is making losses. The manager also asks you why interest rates on loans offered seem to differ for one firm to another even from the same commercial bank. You explain that partly interest rates depend upon the length of the loan, for example to borrow overnight might be cheap but generally, longer-term loans cost more. It would also depend upon the purpose, as most banks are more willing to lend money if they think it is for investment in machinery rather than being used solely to pay off existing debts. It would also depend upon the security offered, for example, banks might well be more willing to lend at a cheaper rate to a well-established firm, which they assume will be able to pay it back rather than a new firm. The size of the loan may also help to determine the interest rate because the administration costs will be similar whether the loan is large or small.

Financial Case Study

One of your friends is thinking of setting up a shop and knows that you are studying business. He therefore approaches you to obtain your advice. What would be the advantages of renting a shop rather than buying it outright? Why might it be expensive to alter a shop?

He is concerned about how much stock he needs to buy. He knows that it will be expensive to buy a large amount of stock and some of it may deteriorate. However, if he has insufficient stock he will not be able to satisfy customers and may lose goodwill. He is concerned about how he can estimate the optimal demand.

He is also concerned about the number of staff he needs to employ and the wages he needs to pay. Why would both of these have to be included in a cash flow forecast, which a banker might require?

He is also concerned about what type of security, if any, could be offered to the financier. For example, would the bank consider the shop as security? He is also concerned about how much money he should put into the venture. He is aware that if too little is put into the business then banks may be reluctant to grant him a loan whereas if he puts in too much he may have liquidity problems.
What advice or suggestions would you give to this friend regarding the issues brought up in the previous paragraphs?

Task 1

Try to find out the rates of interest offered to different firms. Try to see if there is any reason behind the different rates. Does it, as the case study suggests, vary according to the purpose and size of the loan and the security, which is offered? Do some banks seem less expensive than others do?

Task 2

For a business of your choice explain what information you expect to give if you were applying for credit. You should give, as far as possible, an idea of the product, the amount of money that you are willing to put into the business, and the amount of money that you would need.

Self-examination Questions

1.   It is often suggested that many firms do not consider how much capital they require in the first place. What happens if firms do not have sufficient finance?

2.   What happens to firms if they withdraw too much money in the form of living expenses in the first few years of their existence?

3.   What are bank loans and overdrafts? What information do you expect to give to the bank before they will lend you money?

4.   What is meant by a financial plan? Why is this important both to the individual setting up a firm and to people lending it money?

5.   What is meant by the term 'security'? What type of security would satisfy a bank?

6.   What are the advantages of issuing shares from a company's viewpoint?

7.   What are debentures? Why might firms not wish to issue these if interest rates are high?

8.   What is meant by Hire Purchase? Why might some firms use this?

9.   Johnspur Engineering Ltd purchase a machine for £74,000 on 1 January 2011 Its estimated life is five years and its residual value is estimated at £14,000. Show the Journal entry for depreciation in Year 1 by the straight-line method and the postings to the ledger on 31 December of Year 1.

10. On 1 January 2013, Anthea purchases 12 sewing machines for her fashion workshop at a total cost of £3,600. They are expected to last four years at the end of which period the second hand value will be £1,400. Show the calculation for the annual depreciation charge by the straight-line method.

11. A new electrical retailer, Smiths & Co Ltd, purchase their first three high street outlets in January 2013. The accounts department is trying to decide how best to calculate the depreciation on the assets. Advise them of the different options and give your opinion on the best to choose.

12. A local haulage firm has bought two new trailers for its lorries. The total purchase price was £40,000 and the firm has decided to use the diminishing balance method of depreciation with a rate of 20% per annum. What is the combined value of the two trailers after 5 years? Once the value of the trailers drops below £2500 each the firm will seek to sell them, how long will it take at 20% to reach this point? What happens if we use 25% instead?

Chapter 11: COSTING

11.1: The Purpose of Costing

There are many reasons and benefits involved by a company carrying out thorough and accurate costing exercises. The main ones are listed below:

a)   Firms publish balance sheets every year but, due to commercial confidentiality, they only contain a limited amount of information on costs. A balance sheet can be described as a snapshot, produced after an event. This means they are not of much use to many managers, who need current information on costs to give an internal check on individual departments.

b)   Costing can be used for benchmarking. Cost information for other firms can be obtained from trade associations. This information can be compared to the company's own and if it shows that its costs are much higher, the management can then work on finding out why. Some reasons as to why costs can be significantly higher than those of comparable firms include having bought the wrong type of machinery in the past and paying higher rent for a factory or office. In other cases, it could be that productivity per head is higher than in other firms.

c)   In some cases, costing is needed to check the benefits of outsourcing a particular service. Care has to be taken in making this decision since a recession leads to other firms quoting very low rates just to get the business. If the firm closes down its own department, in order to take advantage of these low rates, it may not be able to provide its own goods or services later. Tendering and producing a quote for a potential customer involves costing.

d)   Costing is used to establish prices as all firms in the private sector aim to make a profit. A profit will only be made if all costs are covered. Therefore, the firm needs to know its average costs at different levels of output. This may sound simple but in multi-site firms, costing can be very difficult.

e)   Cost information is required by management to compare what is happening currently against what should be happening. Accountants use the word 'variance' to describe the difference between the expected costs and actual costs.

f)   Costing may be important in order to achieve a satisfactory cash flow. With suitable costing, firms are able to use the best sources of finance to ensure that they do not take unnecessary risks and go out of business as a result.

11.2: Methods of carrying out Costing

In order to cost goods and services, accountants and economists will usually classify costs in a variety of different ways. The distinction between overheads, direct and indirect costs may be important. The problems of allocating overheads and methods by which this can be done will have to be analysed. Examples of how overheads may be allocated are per employee, per unit of production or per square metre of floor space etc. The effects of the different methods of allocation of costs will affect the firm's perception of costs.

As mentioned before, firms have to cover costs in order to make a profit. Yet, in some cases, it is sensible for the firm to produce items that do not cover average costs, providing that they contribute to the fixed costs. The use of average and marginal costing and especially the problem of costing for one-off contracts are important and not always understood.

The problems of costing stock, especially during periods of inflation, are also important. One of the underlying hypotheses is that in business, firms aim at profit maximisation. To achieve this, they will supply additional items until the marginal revenue equals marginal cost. Factors of production, that is land, labour and capital, are required by firms in order to be able to supply goods and services. As a firm employs more factors of production, its total costs, namely the rewards to those factors: rent, wages and profit rise. This means the firm must produce more units of its product or service in order to cover these inflated costs.

11.3: Definitions of Costs

11.3.1: Fixed Costs

Fixed costs are those that occur independently of the level of output, even if it were nil. Fixed costs include management and administration costs, which in some service industries can be very high while in others they are relatively insignificant. Rents and rates are also fixed costs. They form a significant part of total costs as well, especially in the centre of a large city such as London. To some extent, depreciation of assets can be regarded as a fixed cost. Depreciation can also be regarded as a variable cost depending upon usage. For example machinery should be depreciated faster the more it is used due to increased 'wear and tear'. Interest payments are another example of fixed costs and may well be very substantial particularly if interest rates are high.

11.3.2: Direct Costs (Accountants), Variable Costs (Economists)

These costs vary according to the volume of output. For many firms, a large variable cost is that of fuel. Variable costs also include the costs of raw materials as well as semi-manufactured goods. Although labour costs are often considered as variable costs, it is possible to lay off workers or to reduce wages at times when demand for a firm's products is low. Even so, overtime payments might be regarded as variable costs.

The relationship between variable costs and fixed costs is partly one of timing. For example, if we consider the running of a railway service, in the short term we would see that almost all costs are fixed. Even if the demand for train travel in a particular area were falling, we would not expect trains to be cut (and staff to be made redundant) until a new timetable had been organised.

11.3.3: Indirect Costs

Those costs not directly attributable to the manufacturing of a product or provision of a service are known as indirect costs. Examples of indirect costs include lighting, heating and some forms of taxation. If a firm produces more than one item then it is difficult to allocate these costs to a particular good. It is often the case that the percentage floor space taken up by the production of a good indicates how much of the indirect cost is attributed to each product. Therefore, if a firm devotes 25% of its floor space to one product then it may decide to apportion it 25% of indirect costs to that product.

11.3.4: Labour Costs

As has already been suggested, it is difficult to classify labour costs as being either fixed or variable, partly because much depends upon the terms of contract. For example, casual labour, which was common in the 1960s in the docks, can be hired or laid off according to demand and therefore casual-labour costs are variable costs. However, following legislation in the 1970s, most workers can only be laid off at the expense of relatively high redundancy payments (though the government usually meets part of this expense) and therefore most labour costs can be regarded as fixed. In the 1990s, casual labour became more important again. Today many temporary-work agencies supply staff for short contracts. The most popular are those for teachers, nurses and office workers. The importance of high fixed labour costs is that any disruption, whether caused by strikes, accidents or poor management will tend to lead to difficulties for the firm. This is because the costs still have to be paid irrespective of whether there is output or not.

11.3.5: Total Costs

Total costs equal the sum of the fixed and variable costs. In the case of high capital cost projects such as the construction of a new airport, the importance of estimating demand accurately cannot be overlooked. This is especially true in cases of projects such as the construction of the Channel Tunnel, as the opportunity cost of it is very high given the capital outlay and the human hours needed to complete it. Since the project could not be used for anything else other than a train link to France, then the resources used in its construction cannot be recovered using alternative uses, hence the low opportunity cost. This is something the potential investors for the project would have considered carefully. In many industries, fixed costs tend to increase as a proportion of the total as firms become more capital- intensive. This can be seen in the increased mechanisation of industries where labour hours are reduced and more money is invested in production lines and the machines needed to perform production tasks. Where this is the case, it becomes even more important to carry out a sensible investment appraisal.

11.3.6: Marginal Costs

Another important cost for firms to consider is marginal cost. Marginal cost is defined as the change in cost resulting from a change in the number of factor inputs. It is the extra cost incurred by producing one more item of product. The marginal cost curve, above the point where average variable costs equal marginal costs, is the supply curve. It is often convenient to divide marginal costs into short-run marginal costs and long-run marginal costs.

11.3.7: Average Costs

These are defined as total costs divided by the total number of units produced. Average costs tend to decrease as production increases due to economies of scales. This is because the fixed costs are being spread over a larger volume of production. However, average costs will increase again if more investment is needed in fixed costs in order to increase production further.

11.3.8: The Relationship between Average Costs and Marginal Costs

The marginal-cost curve will cross the average-cost curve at its lowest point. For example, if a firm had total costs of £1,000 and produced ten units the average cost is £100. If the marginal cost of the eleventh unit were greater than £100, then the average cost would rise, while if the marginal cost were less than £100, the average cost would fall.

11.3.9: Covering Average Variable Costs

For it to be worthwhile for any profit- maximising firm to start producing any output or employing any workers, it must be able to cover its costs.

Given a cost schedule, a profit-maximising firm will not produce an output at which it does not cover at least its average variable costs. For example, if a firm's average variable costs are the labour costs per unit of output and the level of demand is such that the price it is able to charge is less than these costs, then there is no point in the firm being in business. To look at it another way, if a firm has direct labour costs of producing a radio of £7 and the material costs are £5 then it would not produce radios unless it can achieve a price of £12. If its average overheads per unit were £10 then, in the long term it would need to charge at least £22 to stay in business. However, in the short term, if it can only obtain £15 then it is achieving a £3 contribution per radio to fixed costs. This means it is worthwhile continuing production assuming that the materials and labour cannot be used more profitably for any other business.

11.3.10: *Covering Average Costs*

Even if the selling price is greater than the average variable cost (£22), it may not be breaking even, that is total costs may still be greater than total revenue and average costs are greater than average revenue. The 'break-even price' is the point where price is equal to average costs, which is equal to marginal costs. It may still be worthwhile for a profit-maximising firm to supply an output when the price is below the 'break-even' point, as long as the price is covering the average variable cost. This is because the loss to the firm will be smaller than the costs of producing nothing, since the firm has fixed costs, for example, rent. As mentioned before, fixed costs have to be paid by the firm whether or not it is producing anything.

11.4: What is the Significance of the Terms 'Fixed Costs' and 'Variable Costs'?

Fixed costs do not vary with output. When setting up any project a firm will have to consider the cost of land, the rent payable or the interest payable on a loan for premises. Variable costs vary with the amount of output and include labour and material costs. Before commencing production, the firm must carry out market research to ensure that both fixed and variable costs will be more than covered by revenue, if it wishes to make a profit. Once the firm is in operation, the minimum that it can charge and still stay in operation will be its variable costs and, in this respect, the fixed costs are irrelevant. The saying 'bygones are forever bygones' is an important one here. For example, since the Channel Tunnel has been built the original costs will be irrelevant to any pricing decisions. Of course, it is unlikely that a decision to build the Channel Tunnel would have been taken unless it was expected to be profitable.

In practice, the difference between fixed and variable costs differs according to the period being considered. In the short-term, almost all costs except material costs tend to be fixed. For example, it is not generally possible to reduce the labour force without some minimum notice being given; other costs, such as rent, rates, heating and lighting, exist whatever the level of output. However, in a slightly longer term, firms might be able to move from their premises and more easily control the size of the work force.

Self-examination Questions

1. Which of the following would be fixed costs to a firm?

    a) A mortgage on premises at a fixed interest rate.

    b) A mortgage on premises, which fluctuates according to the general trends in interest rates.

    c) Contract, which allows the firm to hire a fluctuating number of vehicles at a fixed cost per vehicle.

    d) Number of freelance workers, working for a firm whose hours may fluctuate, but which has an arrangement that their wages per hour are fixed for a period of two years.

    A. a only.

    B. a and b only.

    C. a, b and c only.

    D. d only.

    E. All.

Study the table below, detailing a firm's costs and answer questions 2-4.

Output	Direct costs	Total costs
0	0	100
1	20	120
2	35	135
3	45	145
4	55	155
5	70	170
6	90	190
7	120	220
8	170	270

2. What are the firm's fixed costs?

    a) 0.

    b) 100.

    c) 270.

    d) It is impossible to tell from the given information.

3. At what level of output are direct costs minimised?

    a) 0.

    b) 1.

    c) 2.

    d) 3.

    e) 4.

    f) 5.

    g) 6.

    h) 7.

    i) 8.

4. At what level of output are average costs minimised?

    a) 0.

    b) 1.

    c) 2.

    d) 3.

    e) 4.

    f) 5.

    g) 6.

    h) 7.

    i) 8.

Study the table below showing the amount produced per worker.

Workers	Output
1	150
2	280
3	350
4	400
5	420
6	430

5.   Given that fixed costs total £2,500 and wages (the only variable costs) are £5,000 per worker:

a)   At what quantity of labour is average cost at its lowest?

b)   At what quantity of labour is marginal cost at its lowest?

6.   What is the difference between fixed and variable costs? Explain how, in a manufacturing industry, these affect the prices at which the firm will supply goods or services.

7.   Usually, it assumed that the more units supplied the higher the costs. Under what circumstances might this not be true?

8.   What are fixed costs? Give examples of fixed costs for: -

(a)   A typical supermarket

(b)   A petrol garage

(c)   A road haulage company

(d)   A computer manufacturer

(e)   A car manufacturer

9.   In what ways, if any do your answers to question 8 differ and in what ways are they similar.

10. What happens to average fixed costs as production rises? What is the significance of this for: -

(a)   A car manufacturer

(b)   An oil refinery

(c)   The Channel Tunnel

11. What happens to average fixed costs if demand falls unexpectedly? Using examples in question 10, explain the significance of this.

12. What are examples of variable costs for: -

(a)   A typical supermarket

(b)   A petrol garage

(c)   A road haulage company

(d)   A computer manufacturer

(e)   A car manufacturer

13. Why is it difficult to classify depreciation as a fixed or variable cost? Explain in relation to a firm's car fleet with several different company cars.

14. What is meant by saying that firms might wish to continue to make goods or provide services providing they contribute to fixed costs?

Chapter 12: ACCOUNTING CONVENTIONS

12.1: The Nature, Purpose and Limitations of Accounting Conventions

Accounting conventions refer to the established "codes" of basic principles and procedures that apply in recording and reporting financial information. These conventions are important because financial information is used by stakeholders who should be able to understand and use financial information.

Academic writers on accountancy, and others, have identified many accounting concepts, which could be regarded as forming part of the accounting conceptual framework. However, the fundamental accounting conventions are defined in SSAP 2.

These include:

1. **Realisation:** that a transaction and any profits arising from such a transaction is recognised when the good is delivered to the buyer rather than when they pay for it. This means that a good delivered to a buyer is deemed sold and the profits made at the time of delivery rather than at the time when it is paid for. The same applies for the provision of services.

2. **Materiality:** In accounting, it is important to decide which items are both relevant and consequential; as we can see from the application of accounting standards and accounting policies, the preparation of accounts involves a high degree of judgement. Where decisions are required about the appropriateness of a particular accounting judgement, the "materiality" convention suggests that this should only be an issue if the judgement is "significant" or "material" to a user of the accounts. This convention might be used to overrule a strict interpretation of other conventions. It is used to determine the appropriateness of conventions.

For example, the repainting of machinery worth £5,000,000 might cost £20, this will increase the value of the machinery to £5,000,020, however this amount is immaterial compared to the value of the machinery and it is not appropriate to include it in the depreciation account. Instead, it will be included as part of the revenue expenditure. The same would apply to items of office stationery that would be included as capital and accounted for as stock, but their value may be so immaterial that it is only sensible to include such items as revenue expenditure. This convention thus lends flexibility to accounting.

3. **Going concern:** while preparing accounts for a business, accountants assume that the business will continue. This has an important implication in the valuation of resources of the business. If we assume that the business is being

closed down then we value the assets at cost or at the going market price. Certain highly specific assets might not even fetch the cost price. However if we assume that the business is a going concern then assets are valued at the going concern rate which might be either the depreciated value or the market price.

4. **Consistency:** where there is a subjective judgement made in the preparation of account then that subjective decision must be consistently applied year after year so that users of accounts can make meaningful comparisons from period to period. For example, the depreciated values of assets must be determined in the same way period after period. Accountants have to be consistent. For example in accounting for the depreciation of assets, they cannot use straight-line depreciation one year and the reducing balance method the next. They will have to use the same method of valuation of stocks from one year to the next; that is, not use LIFO (last in, first out) one year and FIFO (first in, first out) in the next.

5. **Prudence:** simply stated is that accountants recognise an anticipated loss as soon as they become aware of it and make provisions for such a loss even before it is realised. On the other hand, they never recognise a profit until it is realised. Prudence however dictates that accountants anticipate a loss but never a profit; this would have the effect of having the business always prepared for adverse outcomes. Prudence might seem to be the opposite of realisation where a profit is recognised at the point of sale. However, these two conventions can be reconciled if the accountant will recognise a sale at the time it occurs, rather than when it is paid for. The accountant, using his/her judgement will decide whether the sale will be realised. Thus, an accountant can recognise a sale and the profits thereof if there is a reasonable certainty that it will be paid for.

If accountants have a choice, they will choose the methods that understate rather than overstate profits. For example, assets should be valued at a lower, rather than a higher, price. This might be particularly important in the case of structures, which could only be used for a specific purpose, such as a swimming pool. Similarly, it is sensible to overstate the likely future taxation rather than underestimating it.

6. **Matching:** Incomes should be correctly matched to the expenses of a given period. This means that all expenses of a given period should be matched to the incomes they generate. This agrees with the principal of accrual, which states that all goods and services are recognised at the point of sale rather than at the point of payment. Adhering to this convention ensures that profits or losses of a given period are assigned to that period rather than a previous or future period.

7. **Capital and Revenue expenditure:** A capital expenditure is one where there is residual value after the accounting period during which the expenditure was incurred. As such, an expenditure that remains of value to the business for more than one accounting period is taken as a capital expenditure. Revenue expenditure is one which is spent by the end of the accounting period and has no residual value.

8. **Depreciation:** a capital expenditure is apportioned to the profit and loss account during each accounting period. This is meant to capture the gradual wear and tear of such an asset. It also ensures that the period during which such an asset is bought is not overcharged with the value of the asset since the usefulness of the asset does not end with the end of that period.

Following are the basic accounting conventions; these have not been included in the legislation however, they are widely agreed upon by accountants.

9. **Historical Cost Convention:** The most commonly encountered convention is the "historical cost convention". This requires transactions to be recorded at the price ruling at the time, and for assets to be valued at their original cost.

Under the "historical cost convention", therefore, no account is taken of changing prices in the economy. This might present an incorrect picture because the value of currencies changes over time due to inflation and other economic factors. However, this method of accounting especially for assets' value recorded at cost, is deemed objective and generally accepted.

10. **Separate entity:** this convention holds that the affairs of a business should be held separate from those of any other business or individual even if such individuals own the business. This enables accountants to measure the performance of each business accurately.

11. **Monetary terms:** accountants only account for those items that can be measured in terms of money. All accounting items must thus be quantified in monetary terms. Other items may be quantified if someone is willing to pay money for them for example workforce skill, morale, market leadership, brand recognition, quality of management etc.

12. **Double Entry:** refers to the convention of recognising the dual effect of financial transactions. This is where each transaction affects two different accounts in a business. This convention shows how resources flow from one part of the business to another part.

13. **Objectivity:** this implies that accounting information should be prepared in an unbiased, neutral manner and should not be seen to serve the purposes of any one party.

14. **Accruals:** This means that expenditure and income have to be matched. This can cause problems in some cases. For example, work on ships may last for 18 months from the date of order to the time of launching. If in this case, the ship is finally launched on April 15th and wages for March have not been paid, the wages should be recorded in the period in which they were earned. They would appear in the previous year's accounts if the firm's financial year ended on April 6th. If the work were carried out over a long period, it would be unreasonable, if the total price were paid on April 15th, to allocate all the revenue to that month. Therefore, a method has to be used to allocate the revenue during the period in which the ship was being built.

There is general agreement that, before it can be regarded as useful in satisfying the needs of various user groups, accounting information should satisfy the following criteria:

Other conventions that have not been codified are those of:

Relevance; this implies that, to be useful, accounting information must assist a user to form, confirm or maybe revise a view - usually in the context of making a decision.

Consistency; implies consistent treatment of similar items and application of accounting policies.

Comparability; users of accounts should be to compare different businesses using the financial information provided by the accountants.

Reliability; accounts should be presented in a truthful, accurate and complete manner. Such accounts should be verifiable and nothing significant should be left out of the accounts.

A regular time interval; which implies that accounts will be after a specific period. This ensures that accounts for different periods are comparable.

Separate valuations; this means that each asset is valued separately. The value of one asset cannot be attributed wholly or in part to another asset. Each asset has its value and a provision of depreciation applicable to it.

12.2: Cash Flow Statements

It has become more common for firms to issue cash flow statements even though, until recently, they were not legally obliged to do so. Cash flow is important since a firm could be profitable in the long term but still go bankrupt in the short term. For a large retailer the information would include some of the following:

- The amount of cash that collected through the sale of goods to customers. The term, net cash inflow is used since this is of the greatest significance e.g. if a tin of baked beans is sold, the important thing from the point of view of people reading the report is the difference between the price paid to the shop and the amount which the company has paid.

- What influence the investments have had on cash flow. For example, a large supermarket chain might have sold smaller sites in the centre of town and purchased comparatively cheaper ones in an out of town developments, sometimes jointly with other stores. It may also have made shorter-term investments, for example, in treasury bills if it is sitting on a 'Cash Mountain'. This term refers to when an organisation has surplus cash balances. It is often wasteful to leave this money in a bank account, as business accounts do not attract large rates of interest. Spare capital is therefore invested in the short term to make use of the so-called 'Cash Mountain'.

- Any interest that has been paid, for example, on mortgages and how much interest it has received for example, on its bank accounts including deposit accounts.

- It will also show what dividends, if any, have been paid to shareholders.

- Under financing it will show how much has been paid through the sales of equities (ordinary shares) as well as the expense of issuing any new shares.

- It will show the proceeds and repayments of any long-term borrowing.

Self-examination Questions

1. What are the main accounting conventions?

2. Why might it be difficult in the shipbuilding industry to get an idea of profits from the balance sheet whilst ships are being built?

3. In the mid-1990s Lloyds of London, the well-known insurance organisation produced its accounts showing losses 3 years after the financial year in question. Why does such an organisation always produce its accounts so late?

4. Which will give the highest rate of deprecation in the earliest years the straight line or the reducing balances method discussed in Chapter 10? If the principle of prudence was always to be strictly applied, which should the accountant apply in the case above? Why therefore do accountants use both methods?

5. How would it be possible for a firm to be potentially viable in the long term but to go bankrupt in the short term? Why might this influence the ways in which it tries to raise money?

6. Why is taxation paid to the home government and taxation paid to other governments shown separately?

7. What effect would a large outlay on out of town shops have in this year's cash flow and that of future years?

8. Why have some firms sat on Cash Mountains rather than investing the money in developing new sites or products?

9. Why might firms issue a cash flow statement even if they are not legally obliged to do so? For whom might cash flow statements be of interest?

10. Why is net cash inflow from customers of importance? How far does it help to compare one year's results with the previous years? What external factors could affect this?

11. Why is the total amount raised through the issue of shares compared to other sources of finance?

12. What other sources of information would shareholders want to have if they wished to forecast the cash flow for the next year?

Chapter 13: RATIOS

13.1: Types of Ratios

Accounting ratios are widely used when analysing annual company accounts but are also a useful management tool at any time of the year. It should be noted that balance sheets are a snapshot of the organisation at a particular date. Shareholders, managers and other stakeholders may want to look at the firm and its performance over a longer period. Ratios are one way of doing this.

The most important thing to remember about the group of accounting ratios below is that they can be misleading on their own. For example, is a Gross Profit Margin of 35% good? There is no way of knowing this without other background information. Previous years ratios are a good place to start when looking at comparisons. If the same firm had a Gross Profit Margin of 24% in the previous year then this may be seen as a positive movement towards increased profitability. However, it is not just within a firm and its history that we must look. If the industry in which this firm is operating has an average of 50% then the firm is underperforming quite badly. It is important to consider these factors and ensure that you look at a ratio with perspective before making a decision as to what it may mean.

Accounting ratios can be broadly divided into four different categories; these are Performance, Liquidity, Gearing and Shareholders' ratios.

13.1.1: Performance

These ratios investigate the profitability and efficiency of a firm.

$$\text{Gross Profit Margin} = \frac{\text{Profit before interest and tax (Gross)}}{\text{Sales}} \times 100$$

$$\text{Net Profit Margin} = \frac{\text{Net Profit}}{\text{Sales}} \times 100$$

Profit margins may vary according to the economic prosperity of the country or the market that the firm is operating in. For example, since the 2007 'Credit Crunch' customers, whether individuals or firms are less willing to purchase goods and services for non-essential items and the profit margins of firms offering these products suffer as a result. Some firms rely on the slogan "Pile them high, sell them cheap" and therefore their profit margins will be low. Other organisations sell products less often and so the margin on the goods has to be higher in order to make reasonable profits. Think of the different levels of profit margins between a car dealer and a grocery supermarket. The car dealer will need to sell products at a higher margin compared to the owners of the supermarket just to stay in business.

The difference between the two ratios above is the inclusion of overhead expenses. As Net Profit = Gross profit – Expenses, the Net Profit Margin shows the firms ability to control the indirect costs that it incurs in the running of the business. A firm's Net Profit is always lower than its Gross Profit and so should be the associated ratios.

The efficiency of a firm can be measured in several ways. The ratios below attempt to quantify the effectiveness of the business to operate in its environment.

$$\text{Return on Capital Employed (ROCE)} = \frac{\text{Net Profit before interest and tax}}{\text{Capital Employed}} \times 100$$

This ratio shows what the organisation has managed to achieve with each £1 invested in it. Care has to be taken when looking at this ratio. For example, some modern shops located on an out of town site may use very little capital since the property value is lower compared with a department store in a high street.

$$\text{Sales to Capital Employed} = \frac{\text{Sales}}{\text{Capital Employed}}$$

This figure will also give an indication of efficiency. It is possible to find someone having several market stalls that would require very little capital and to assume that a small shop on the high street with more capital employed is less efficient would obviously not be true. On the other hand, if an electrical goods firm were expanding by buying similar shops in different parts of the country we would expect to find that sales grew as more capital was employed and this would be a reasonable comparison.

$$\text{Overheads to Sales Ratio} = \frac{\text{Overheads}}{\text{Sales}}$$

This is a useful measure of efficiency. Some insurance companies have used it to show, for example, that less of their money is used up in administration and commissions to agents. Therefore, more money is available for the main purposes of endowment policies, to provide life cover and a good return on the money that has been placed with the insurance company. It is also a ratio that charities find useful to show how much of the donations received go to helping those it is intended for instead of those running the organisation.

Productivity can also be measured by average sales per employee. The higher the sales value per employee the better the firm is utilising its inputs to the production process. This simple ratio is calculated as follows:

$$\text{Sales per Employee} = \frac{\text{Sales Revenue}}{\text{Number of Employees}}$$

This ratio is most useful in a labour intensive organisation such as a cleaning business. It is less relevant in industries that utilise high levels of mechanisation or computerisation, as the number of employees will be less significant in comparison to the level of investment in plant, robots or computer systems. Asset usage ratios are also useful in determining the efficiency of a firm. The Stock turnover of a firm shows how many days of stock cover the firm has.

$$\text{Stock Turnover} = \frac{\text{Stock Held}}{\text{Cost of Sales}} \times 365$$

There must always be a number and a period specified. In this case the Cost of Sales for the year is used and the number of days of stock currently held by the firm is shown. This shows, on aggregate, if the firm ordered no more stocks or raw materials, how long they can operate for without running out of supplies. Different industries will require different levels of stock and work in progress to operate. For example, if we take a newsagent who is open Monday to Saturday then daily newspapers will be sold every day and the rates of stock turn will be about 312 per year. If the newsagent sells £1,000 of newspapers per day at cost price he sells £312,000 of newspapers per year the cost of the stock sold will be £312,000 and the average stock at cost price will be £1,000 meaning he has enough stock to supply 1 day (assuming 312 trading days per year). However, a manufacturer of Christmas Crackers will need to hold enough stock for the entire season. This may mean that they need to build up stocks during the year and store them to ensure that they have enough to supply during December. This will show as a very low, but quite expected and acceptable, level of stock turnover in the months approaching the festive season.

Another useful asset utilisation ratio is the Debt Collection Period. This shows the number of days, on average, that the firm takes to recover monies owing to it. The equation below can be used to work this out.

$$\text{Debt Collection Period} = \frac{\text{Debtors}}{\text{Sales Revenue}} \times 365$$

It should be noted here that a firm that only sells to a few customers on credit terms and takes payment in cash for the rest might have a misleadingly low Debt Collection Period using this equation. In these cases, it is more reliable to use the Credit Sales figure from the balance sheet as apposed to the larger Sales Revenue value.

13.1.2: Liquidity

The liquidity of a firm is important in ensuring that they have access to enough cash to pay for all of the operating expenses incurred by the firm in a given period of operation. Two main ratios are used for this purpose; they are the Current Ratio and the Acid Test.

$$\text{Current Ratio} = \frac{\text{Current Assets}}{\text{Current Liabilities}}$$

The widely accepted rule of thumb is that a Current Ratio value of 1.5 to 2 is acceptable and seen as a healthy position for a firm to be in. Any lower and a firm may have trouble repaying its liabilities, any higher and the firm is not using its assets to their full potential as discussed in Chapter 10, current assets can include raw materials, stocks, cash and debtors. Which of these can be used to pay off debts? If we take the example of a builder, cash obviously can, raw materials such as bricks can, and debtors usually can, assuming you have not lent to an unreliable firm or person. All of these sources are said generally to be liquid. However, cash is more liquid than debtors balances and these are usually more liquid than stock.

In some cases, stock is not seen as being particularly liquid. Sometimes fashions can change and leave a firm with stock that is hard to dispose of, other times it may be hard for a firm to find a buyer for its products in certain market conditions. The BSE crisis in the UK in the 1990s left many cattle farmers with no one to purchase their herds. The Acid Test ratio considers this questionable liquidity. The formula is the same as the Current ratio but excludes stocks form the Current Assets valuation.

$$\text{Acid Test Ratio} = \frac{\text{Current Assets - Stocks}}{\text{Current Liabilities}}$$

This ratio is also often referred to as the Quick Ratio and firms are often said to have a good Quick Ratio at around the 1:1 mark.

13.1.3: *Gearing*

Gearing ratios, sometimes also referred to as leverage ratios, attempt to show the firms reliance on capital obtained from different sources. These ratios are of interest to most stakeholders but particularly organisations that lend to the organisation. It is important to know how likely it is that they will receive their money back.

The Gearing Ratio shown below shows the relationship between a firms' total capital and that which is subject to fixed interest payments or dividends.

$$\text{Gearing Ratio} = \frac{\text{Loan Capital} + \text{Preference Share Capital}}{\text{Total Capital}} \times 100\%$$

Preference share capital is that which is raised through the issue of special shares that have an agreed percentage dividend. Preference shareholders have a fixed interest given to them after creditors have been paid. They can be cumulative in which case interest not paid in one year is paid in the next. For example, if the preference shareholders have an agreed rate of interest of 12% but only 8% is paid one year then the shortfall can be paid next year if profit levels permit. Preference shareholders receive their dividend before ordinary shareholders so there is less risk in holding such investments.

Total Capital includes all of the sources of capital involved within the firm. This could include Loans, Preference, Equity or any other source of financing such as Debentures. These are loans to the company at a fixed rate of interest for a fixed period. If debenture holders are not paid in time, the firm can be declared bankrupt. This is not true of preference shareholders or ordinary shareholders. Because of the slightly greater risk for preference shareholders, the rate of interest will usually be higher.

A 'low geared' company will have a gearing ratio of less than 100%, whereas a 'high geared' firm will have a ratio exceeding this mark. This indicates that the majority of finance comes from external loans. This company may find it hard to grow in the future as it already relies on risky capital and so financers are less likely to want lend more to such a firm. This is in contrast to a lower geared organisation where the owners predominantly finance activities in the long term.

The Interest Cover ratio calculates the ability of a company to pay the interest it has accumulated in the year on its loans.

$$\text{Interest Cover} = \frac{\text{Profit before interest and tax}}{\text{Interest Payment}}$$

An interest ratio below '1' means that the firm did not make enough money to cover its interest payments for the year. Therefore, 1 means that the firm must use all of its profit to make the payment. It is generally agreed that a figure of 1-2 may cause the firm problems.

13.1.4: Shareholders' Ratios

Potential shareholders of a firm can request a set of accounts for the firm that they are interested in investing in. The following ratios are useful guides as to the returns that they may expect to receive for their input. The first ratio that an investor might look at is the organisations **Return on Equity**. This is calculated with the equation below.

$$\text{Return on Equity} = \frac{\text{Profit after Tax, Interest and Preference Dividends}}{\text{Ordinary Share Capital} + \text{Reserves}} \times 100\%$$

The higher this figure is the better. It should be noted that this is not the percentage that the shareholder will receive as a dividend but the rate that the firm could afford to give if it did not keep any of the profits for reinvestment.

It is also worth observing that a firm that has capital mainly from shares would find, other things being equal, that this ratio went in line with its gross profits. On the other hand, a firm that was mainly financed through debentures could well find that this ratio changed quite dramatically with relatively small changes in gross profits.

Another useful ratio for potential and current shareholders is the **Earnings per Share (EPS)**. This shows the amount of applicable profit that is made for each share.

$$\text{EPS} = \frac{\text{Profit after Tax, Interest and Preference Dividends}}{\text{Number of Ordinary Shares}}$$

It is useful to compare this value to the actual dividend issued to see how generous the firm is in distributing the profits made back to the owners.

The EPS is most useful if compared to the actual market value of the firms' shares. It shows the market's view of the potential of the organisation to make profits in the future. This figure is called the Price/Earnings Ratio or P/E ratio.

$$\text{Price/Earnings Ratio} = \frac{\text{Shares Market Price}}{\text{Earnings Per Share}}$$

A value of 10 is often common for firms in most industries so a number much higher than this indicates belief in future profit growth and so increases in EPS or, conversely, that the share price is currently undervalued.

Dividend cover is similar to the interest cover discussed in the gearing ratio section. It provides information of the ability of the firm to pay its dividend. The formula is:

$$\text{Dividend Cover} = \frac{\text{Profit after Tax, Interest and Preference Dividends}}{\text{Total Dividend Payment}}$$

If this value is too low, the firm may struggle to meet the promised payout. If the value is too high without good explanation, shareholders may question why the firm did not give a higher dividend payment if it could so easily afford it.

Perhaps the most telling ratio for a small investor is the **Dividend Yield**. This shows the actual return on the investment that the current shareholders have received. This is found using the following equation.

$$\text{Dividend Yield} = \frac{\text{Dividend amount per share}}{\text{Share's Market Price}} \times 100$$

The resultant figure should be compared to other share's values to see if the return is acceptable. It may also be used as a comparison to other types of investment such as savings accounts. The problem with doing this is that the market price of a share may rise and, if sold for a higher price, will increase the return on investment but the above equation will not consider this.

13.2: Limitations of Ratio Analysis

As mentioned at the start of this chapter it is important to compare ratios between similar firms. Care must be taken when choosing the organisation to compare. Two firms operating at the same levels of efficiency may have different ratios because of other factors. For example, it would not be wise to compare the supermarket Tesco to Marks and Spencer for a number of reasons. The first is that the accounts available will not often distinguish between departments in a firm. While they both sell groceries, they also sell other products and so it will be difficult to compare the accounts. Tesco sells a range of music, DVD and books while Marks and Spencer does not. Its range of clothing is far more important to it than Tesco, where it is more of a supporting range of products. A better comparison for the supermarket would be Sainsbury as it operates in more of Tesco's markets at around the same volume of sales.

When using ratios to compare performance over time the user must take into account a number of possible changes that may have taken place between the comparative periods, these may be:

Inflation may have affected the market. It would therefore not be sensible to compare a number of the ratios without considering this.

Firms may have entered into or divested out from different markets between the two periods. The supermarkets Tesco and Sainsbury's have both entered the banking markets in recent years. It would not be very sensible to compare the performance of the companies before and after the move into this market without taking account of this major shift and expansion. Similarly it would not have been representative to compare the ratios based on the accounts either side of British Airways sale of Go in 2000. The disposal of BA's low cost carrier would have had such a dramatic effect on the company's accounts that without noting this change the differences in the ratios may have seemed very unusual.

Accounting procedures may have been altered. Sometimes it is necessary to change the way that items such as depreciation and stock is calculated and so entered into the company accounts. It is unfair to compare years that have used different procedures as these can alter the profit that the firm states at the end of the financial year. The best solution to this situation is to recalculate the changed values for the previous year using the new conventions (or vice-versa) to make sure that the ratios are based on comparable figures. This factor should also be considered when comparing ratios and any other accounting information between different firms. Care should be taken to ensure that different accounting procedures do not bias the ratio analysis within markets.

Economic changes in the wider business environment will have an effect on the performance of companies. In periods of depression, demand is likely to be reduced for most goods and so revenues will decline. In years where there is growth, the firm may benefit from the associated increase in demand. The normal vicissitudes of markets should be considered when looking at different year's accounts information it is useful to compare results of similar firms. This way if the industry as a whole is not doing well a firm will be able to tell how well they have responded to the changes in comparison to their peers.

The final consideration when using ratios is to understand that they are only based on historical financial data. This presents us with two limitations. The first is the popular phrase used in the investment industry that *'the past is not necessarily a guide to performance in the future'*. There is no guarantee that if a firm has performed well in the past that it will perform well in the coming years. The second is that it is just based on numerical data. There is a wealth of other information to look at concerning a company's performance and future aims. Chair's reports, independent analysts' findings and mission statements amongst others provide different sources of information often just as useful. These should be considered when analysing a firm whether as a potential or current investor, supplier, customer, employee, manager or other interested party. With this in mind, ratios can provide a simple way of judging a company's accounts and trying to estimate their future performance.

Self-examination Questions

The following accounts are for DemiJohn PLC. This firm operates in the international wine merchant industry. As an external consultant to the firm, you are to calculate and comment on a selection of ratios studied throughout this chapter.

DemiJohn PLC
Profit and Loss Account for year ended 31st December 20x2

	20x2 £'000s	20x1 £'000s
Turnover	50,045	47,064
Cost of Sales	25,806	27,050
Gross Profit	24,239	20,014
Operating Expenses	17,054	15,768
	7,185	4,246
Income from Investments	564	503
Interest received	0	432
Net Profit before Interest and Tax	7,749	5,181
Interest Payable	2,507	2,300
Profit on Ordinary Activities before Taxation	5,242	2,881
Taxation	1,940	1,066
Profit on Ordinary Activities after Taxation	3,302	1,815
Extraordinary Items	550	0
Profit for Financial Year	2,752	1,815
Dividends	1,080	1,000
Retained Profit	1,672	815

Demijohn PLC
Balance Sheet as at 31st December 20x2

	20x2		20x1	
	£'000s	£'000s	£'000s	£'000s
Fixed Assets				
Tangible Assets		15,140		14,986
Investments		3,560		2,980
		18,700		17,966
Current Assets				
Stocks	9,340		9,500	
Debtors	8,804		10,700	
Cash at Bank	7,680		3,400	
Cash in Hand	6		8	
	25,830		23,608	
Current Liabilities				
Amounts falling due within one year	5,670		5,043	
Net Current Assets		20,160		18,565
Total Assets less Current Liabilities		38,860		36,531
Long-term Liabilities				
Amounts falling due after more than one year	5,000		4,800	
Provisions for Charges and Liabilities	780		750	
		5,780		5,550
		33,080		30,981
Capital and Reserves				
Share Capital		10,000		10,000
Other Reserves		1,008		581
Profit and Loss Account		22,072		20,400
		33,080		30,981

1. Using the data available for the years 2XX2 and 2XX1 plus the additional information above calculate and comment on any changes in the following ratios.

    a) Gross Profit Margin   i) Gearing Ratio

    b) Net Profit Margin   j) Interest Cover

    c) Return on Capital   k) Return on Equity

    d) Sales to Capital   l) Earnings per Share

    e) Stock Turnover   m) Price/ Earnings Ratio

    f) Debt Collection Period   n) Dividend Per Share

    g) Current Ratio   o) Dividend Yield

    h) Acid Test

2. Using the following table and your answers from Question 1, comment on the performance of DemiJohn PLC in regards to the industry averages.

Industry Averages

Ratio	Industry
Gross Profit Margin	50%
Net Profit Margin	13%
Return on Capital Employed	15%
Sales to Capital Employed	1.14
Stock Turnover	140.00
Debt Collection Period	75.00
Current Ratio	3.50
Acid Test	3.00
Gearing Ratio	14%
Interest Cover	2.40
Return on Equity	7%
Earnings per Share	£0.2590
Price/ Earnings Ratio	40.00
Dividend Per Share	£0.0940
Dividend Yield	1.00%

3.   Which of the following stakeholders would be most interested in each of the ratios listed below and why?

Choose from one or more of the following: Suppliers, Customers, Government, Employees, Management, Owners (Shareholders), The Public, Creditors or Competitors.

a)   Current Ratio

b)   Earnings Per Share

c)   Net Profit Margin

d)   Sales per Employee

e)   Dividend Cover

f)   Interest Cover

g)   Gearing

4.   Why is it useful to look at inter-firm comparisons? Why must you be careful in choosing which firm to use as a comparison?

5.   Why does inflation have to be taken into account when comparing figures and ratios from different years?

6.   Will the location of a business need to be taken into account when comparing their accounting ratios? Consider a PLC operating mainly in the south of England to one in Scotland.

7.   Try to obtain a set of accounts for another Public Limited Company and perform your own ratio analysis. Use any of the ratios discussed in the chapter to judge the performance of the firm. Would you invest in this company?

8.   Read the Chairman's and Director's reports. Would you still like to invest in the firm?

Chapter 14: EFFICIENCY

14.1: Measures of Efficiency

Efficiency can be defined as the ratio of useful or effective output per unit of input. Most people assume they could recognise an efficient firm when they see it and nearly everyone who has been shopping or worked for an organisation will have experienced inefficiency. However, the majority of organisations are in between; they are neither completely inefficient nor completely efficient. All firms would prefer to be more efficient, but before they can, they need to set objectives and establish a way of measuring it. The measure of efficiency is unique for each organisation and each department within each organisation. The technical efficiency measure produces the following formula to measure efficiency:

$$\text{Efficiency} = \frac{\text{Input}}{\text{Output}}$$

This equation may not give accurate results in every situation. For example, if one bank clerk carries out 6 transactions in an hour and another 12, the above formula would suggest that the second bank clerk was more efficient than the first. The equation has not taken into consideration however, the complexity of each of the transactions. If the transactions completed by the first clerk were, significantly more complex than the second then it may not be correct to say that clerk two is more efficient than clerk one.

14.1.1: Comparing Full Time and Part Time Workers

The above example demonstrates the importance of comparing like with like as well as taking all factors into consideration. The same is true when comparing the efficiencies of full and part time workers. Some people argue that part time workers are more efficient because they work shorter shifts and so stay motivated for the entire duration, whereas full time workers, working a long shift will have times when they are less efficient. Others argue that full time workers are more productive because they know the job better and can work more efficiently. It therefore can be seen that comparing the productivity of shops in France and the UK as output per head may not be feasible. This is because the comparison does not take into consideration the amount of hours worked by each employee, as well as the fact that the UK retailers employ a greater number of part time staff than the French do.

14.1.2: Comparing Vertically Integrated Firms with Non-Vertically Integrated Firms

Vertical integration is the extent to which a company owns other parts of its supply chain. For example, a car manufacturer may own retail branches or manufacture component parts as well. A firm, which just assembles cars, will need fewer people and a smaller plant than if it was to make tyres and batteries as well. Many firms find it cheaper to subcontract many of their non-primary activities, for example, many car manufacturers sub-contract out carrying out repairs. This means they need fewer staff themselves but the staff are still employed elsewhere and the firm is paying for their services. Therefore, slimming down is not necessarily always more efficient.

14.1.3: Comparing Skilled and Unskilled Workers

Firms may have to make a decision between hiring highly skilled workers for large sums of money and hiring less skilled workers for lower wages. Therefore, another measure of efficiency may be the wage bill as compared to the output. This is a reasonable measure within a country, but it is more difficult to compare across countries than production per head is. This is because a fluctuation in currency can suddenly make one country appear to be more efficient than other countries. Multinational firms may however wish to use the measure to indicate where costs are cheapest, for example, many companies today are transferring their call centres to cheaper countries such as India. Other factors such as the amount of capital invested may also affect wage rates. For example, a firm that has invested large sums of money in technology would be expected to have relatively lower wage bills than one that had not.

14.1.4: Comparing Tertiary and Primary Production Efficiency

Firms that produce and sell a final product sometimes appear bigger than the ones that supply them. For example, a loaf of bread costs 50p, the farmer might charge 5p, the miller 12p, the baker 30p and the supermarket 50p. However, the supermarket charging 50p will appear as a larger production figure than the baker because this is whom the end customer has contact with. In a supply chain, each link will add value to the item that they bought from the supplier. This is done by improving or changing the item in order to be able to charge more for it. In this case, the farmer adds 5p, the miller 7p; the baker adds 18p, and the supermarket 20p. This gives a more accurate idea of what the firms or organisations are doing and more accurately reflects their production.

14.1.5: Productivity and the Workforce

It is not always fair to assume that productivity depends solely on the workforce. A port that is heavily automated with large containers will be able to have a much greater productivity per head than an old-fashioned port that has little handling equipment. Until the 1950s or 1960s, dockers did a great deal of handling in the ports, each carrying a heavy load. Nowadays machines do the hard work, for example, bulk silos deal very quickly with grain and packaged timber is taken ashore by crane. Similarly, if we look at offices, secretaries with the latest equipment will generally have a greater output than those using old-fashioned equipment.

14.1.6: Productivity and Profit

Efficiency cannot be viewed entirely in terms of profit. Just because the Mirror Group makes larger profits than a smaller newspaper does not mean that it is more efficient. It might be helpful therefore, to compare profit with something else, for example turnover or profit per person employed.

Profit depends partially on the type of business and the amount of competition facing the company. A firm that has no competition can easily increase its profit by raising its prices; this is one of the biggest complaints against privatised firms in the UK. If a firm produces large-scale fluctuations in its profits, it does not necessarily mean it has become less efficient. In a recession, for example, companies often have to lower their prices significantly, leading to a decrease in profits. The Government can control price increases of nationalised industries and some private companies. In many cases these firms would charge much more and make larger profits if they were not subject to these constraints. The lower profits that they make because of the restrictions they have borne are no reflection on their efficiency.

14.1.7: Efficiency and Costs

Efficiency can be measured in terms of cost. Fixed costs include set up costs; in some industries such as the motor industry, these are considerable. The average fixed costs curve is a constant shape, as demand for products increases towards the later stages of the production life cycle; we would expect costs to decrease. This is partly why firms become more efficient, as the fixed costs are spread across a greater number of units of demand. For example, the initial cost of setting up a factory and filling it with equipment is very high. If the factory runs for one month, the fixed costs associated with each unit produced will still be high. If the factory runs for 2 years, the fixed costs per unit will be less. There are many costs associated with a product during its production life cycle. At the beginning, there will be significant costs involved with marketing the new product and introducing it to potential customers. As more people become aware of the product, these costs will fall. Firms can alter average fixed costs by producing more units, for example, by adding an extra shift. A paper mill that has three shifts a day will find that its costs such as those of depreciation of the expensive machinery will fall the more the machinery is used. This is assuming the machinery has the same life span, irrespective of how much it is used. Firms may be able to get grants from local authorities or central government to help with these initial start-up costs. Such subsidies reduce the fixed cost to the firm, and encourage investment. Many firms avoid committing themselves to high fixed costs, for example renting rather than buying a factory and giving short-term labour contracts that may be based on commission.

14.1.8: Productivity and Management

Productivity depends on the style of management used and the efficiency of that style. Many people claim that Japanese styles of management are more efficient than authoritarian ones. However, two Japanese style management teams will not necessarily be equally efficient.

14.2: Economies of Scale

The term 'economies of scale' refers to the fact that a large company will be able to spread the costs of its expensive equipment out over more units than a small company would be able to. For example, the price of a 500,000-ton tanker will by no means be the same as 5 times that of a 100,000-ton tanker. Likewise, it would be expected that a larger firm in the oil industry would be more efficient, that is having lower costs, than a smaller one.

The uptake of technology has altered this conclusion. In the early 1970s, it was claimed that large firms would be more efficient than smaller ones because they could afford to invest in technology such as computers. Today even the smallest companies can afford computers and the cheapest computers that are available today are much more powerful than the most expensive ones in the 1970s.

Larger firms can lower their unit costs and become more efficient by taking advantage of bulk purchase. A large firm will also be able to borrow at just above base rate (the rate of interest which the Bank of England alters from time to time) whereas a small firm will pay much more. Similarly, large firms are able to issue preference shares and debentures that may well be cheaper than raising money through other methods such as bank loans or overdrafts. Large firms have more staff so can employ specialists instead of having a few people whom multi-task. For example, in a large insurance company, different people will specialise in different types of claim, which is more efficient than having people going from one task to another.

14.3: Work Study

Work-study involves managers studying their employees to set goals and monitor progress. The data collected can be used with techniques such as linear programming, network analysis or queuing theory to see whether tasks are being carried out in an efficient way. Taking a sample of observations can test time taken to complete a task. If people know they are being watched, they may alter the time it takes them so the results may not always be accurate. For example, people being watched may be less slack than they would be normally. Alternatively, if they think the study is going to be used to work out piece rates, they may work slower. Another way of establishing efficiency goals is to use simulation. This is especially useful before introducing new practices. For example before St Pancras was opened for Eurostar traffic in 2007, the different staff undertook different roles so that the changeover from Waterloo International to St Pancras ran very smoothly. Similarly, before the Olympics in 2012, some simulation also took place.

Activity sampling involves breaking down a process into a series of activities. For example, using a machine may involve a series of movements and checks. The time of each activity can then be estimated and added together in order to estimate the total time needed to complete the process. Note that because of the learning curve these times are likely to change as the employee becomes more experienced. This causes problems when firms pay people on a piece rate basis because it may lead to people being paid less while they are learning.

14.4: Problems of Allotting Times in Multi-Product Firms

In multi-product firms, there are often problems in determining how efficient people are because they are working on more than one product. Some firms use job cards to identify how long a worker spends in each section. Job cards can be useful, even within a section, to give an indication of how long tasks should take. For example, if one person takes twice as long as another does to achieve similar results then management will have to decide what actions should be taken. This might be reallocation of tasks or giving the slower worker more thorough training.

Work-study may help to identify bottlenecks. Bottlenecks are processes where there may be too few machines or people and this holds up other processes. In offices, it is common to find many people waiting to use the photocopier. Once bottlenecks are identified, the management may look into ways of overcoming them. For example, in the 1970s when most computers used punched cards, the computer often held up tasks such as surveys, but it would not have been cost effective to speed up the process by buying a more expensive machine. In other cases however, it may be possible through training or the acquisition of another machine to eliminate the bottleneck. In other cases, the bottleneck may be eliminated by employing more staff or using overtime. In most cases however, the use of regular overtime is a sign of inefficiency, except in industries such as transport where there are special circumstances relating to demand.

14.5: Quality Control

Quality of a product is harder to measure than quantity produced but it is just as important. Quality control in a factory may involve testing the typical life of a light bulb or measuring the weights of items produced. However, it is often harder to measure the quality of a service because it can be heavily based on opinion. For example, each pupil in a class may perceive the quality of a lesson differently. Despite these difficulties, there are more people involved in quality control in the service industries than in the manufacturing industries.

14.6: What Techniques can a Production Manager use to Improve Efficiency?

The techniques used can be subdivided into those that can occur at any stage during production and those that occur in the pre-production phase. During the pre-production stage, one of the first things to consider is where the production is to take place. Factors to consider when choosing this location are the ease of access to suppliers bringing in raw materials and, if the location is close enough to the suppliers to ensure minimum delivery costs. For example, if large amounts of raw materials are to be used, a coastal or river based plant may be convenient since bulk shipping is the cheapest form of transport. Therefore, consideration needs to be given to the ease and cost of distributing the final product. In some cases, the costs of transporting the finished product are significantly higher than being supplied with the raw materials. In such cases, the firm may try to locate near the customers, which is why originally the car firms often located in or near the Midlands, as did the component manufacturers. Another factor that needs to be considered is any incentives the local authorities or the Central government are giving to companies who choose to locate in a particular area. For this reason, Nissan chose to locate its plants in the north of England.

Once the location has been chosen, the design and layout of the factory need to be decided. The main considerations here are to minimise the movement of workers and materials around the factory. Conflicts of movement are not only time-consuming but can also lead to accidents. If the firm is producing the goods for the first time, a mock-up of the layout may be helpful. This mock-up can also be used with a simulator to predict where bottlenecks or conflicts may occur. Another factor to consider is the comfort of the workers, apart from any legislation; most people do not work well in extreme temperatures although in a few cases this is unavoidable. Likewise, the lighting and ventilation should be good and there should be adequate floor space. Other considerations depend on what the factory is to be used for; for example, a food factory must be easy to clean. In other cases, it may be necessary for people to interact with each other. If the factory has been expanded by adding new buildings to it, a problem may arise.

Before production starts, the production manager needs to consider what inputs and outputs are required. The manager may be able to use a technique called input/output for this. This technique has been used in the oil industry and is appropriate where the product is clearly defined, for example, the need to produce a chemical, which is 99% pure. The technique will allow the manager to test whether a change in prices of one input or output will make it worthwhile to alter the production technique. For example, if oil prices change drastically is it worthwhile to substitute glass for plastic?

If the firm is engaged in a new or even a modified product, it will need to consider which types of workers it requires. Even for existing products, the numbers of workers will need to be considered. Many questions need to be answered; for example, will the firm try to use some of its existing workforce and if so is any retraining necessary? Will there be a good system of induction training for new workers? The number of workers that are needed can be partly determined by network analysis. This sets out the minimum times for activities. The activities are then subdivided into those that are dependent and must run in sequence and those that are independent and can run simultaneously. A minimum duration time for the project can then be determined. Once this has been established, the manager can test the effects of making alterations, for example, using more staff or a delay in the supply of a part.

The manager may also choose to use the queuing technique to identify and solve any bottlenecks. In many cases, bottlenecks arise because the capacity of one machine is insufficient for the load placed upon it. This is not necessarily confined to the shop floor, for example, delays may occur if there are insufficient telephones for messages to get through. Firms always face a dilemma. More machines will reduce the time wasted in queues but add to costs. The analogy of the photocopier may be used here; a photocopier for every member of staff would reduce queues to zero but would be expensive. To have only one photocopier would be cheap but queues would add to waiting time considerably. There needs to be a little slack in the system to avoid delays in the event of a machine or worker being out of action.

Once production is being considered and even before it, the views of workers can be considered. This can be achieved by use of a quality circle, where a small group of workers (6-8) meet to discuss how productivity can be improved. Whilst it is probably most applicable to skilled work, it can be applied elsewhere. For example, workers may be able to identify bottlenecks and production difficulties from experience. A new firm taking over or a new manager is unlikely to be aware of all the problems. In other cases, workers may be able to identify new methods or adapting existing methods to improve productivity.

Self-examination Questions

1. What does the term work-planning mean?

2. When planning routine tasks, is it necessary to try to ensure that all workers and machines are used one hundred per cent.

3. What is meant by the terms urgent and important? Are they interchangeable?

4. How can we allow for unscheduled events, for example, breakdown of machines?

5. How can we ensure that people are carrying out routine tasks?

6. Do most people have a single task to carry out in an organisation?

7. In many firms, 70% of work for word processing is marked urgent. What might this imply about the organisation?

8. How can a firm allow for scheduled peaks?

9. When are the scheduled peaks likely to apply for accountants?

10. What are the problems of comparing costs per unit of output in the UK and the USA?

11. The labour costs in Harrods would be much higher than in many shops with a similar turnover. Does this imply that Harrods is inefficient?

12. How far are monthly or yearly charts helpful in carrying out work planning?

13. What stages are involved in using work planning for building a house?

14. How far might network analysis help the shipbuilding or housing industry?

15. How can the firm be sure it allocates the right amount of time for tasks?

16. Why do many firms fail to allocate sufficient time when considering computerisation of the system?

17. What does activity-scheduling mean?

18. What does time scheduling mean?

19. Some firms produce job cards or action sheets. Why might this be helpful?

20. Under what circumstances might it be helpful to try to re-distribute staff to cover peaks? What problems might occur if this is done?

21. How far does a rigid hierarchy hinder moves towards efficiency?

22. How far should work planning take account of individual abilities and temperaments?

23. How far is a checklist helpful for people? Would some people resent it because they might think it is paternalistic?

24. What problems exist in offices that lead to correspondence not being done on time?

25. How far would use of a computer help to ensure that items are not overlooked?

26. What is meant by work-study?

27. Is it always possible to set standards for quantity of work produced by a person or group of persons? How can the amount of work done by a personnel officer be tested?

28. Why might it be more difficult to measure quality than quantity of the work?

29. Why in many firms is it worth identifying bottlenecks or surpluses?

30. Why, when carrying out work-study management, is it helpful to prepare present and future expected results?

31. What is meant by quality control?

32. Why might personal observation help when considering quality?

33. Why might employees' estimates be helpful when considering quality control?

34. What problems might arise with the use of time sheets and diaries?

Chapter 15: THE COMPUTER

15.1: Overview of Computers

Computers are widely used throughout the world; they are considered an essential part of modern life. They are constantly evolving and changing the world in which we live.

A computer is a programmable electronic device that can store, search, and process data. A computer is also a device capable of executing a pre-recorded set of instructions known as a program. Computers today take many forms from the familiar desktop computer set-up to the Smartphones that fit into the palm of your hand. Computers are also found embedded into many everyday devices such as cars, washing machines and digital cameras. Computers have had a large effect on the way organisations do business. They have helped automate repetitive tasks such as typing letters, creating spreadsheets and formulating sums. Along the same lines, the ability to save a document means that it can be printed off numerous times. Advances in communication such as the introduction of the Internet and Email have changed the way companies deal with each other and their customers. This has led to many businesses encouraging practices such as working remotely and a 'paperless office', which can lower costs. Companies have now started to go 'Green' by having their employees working at home to cut down on the emissions made by traveling.

15.2: How Computer Size is Measured

Computer size is often measured in megabytes, which is approximately one million bytes (units) of information, or gigabytes, which are approximately one billion bytes of information. Some computers have memories that are measured in terabytes, which are approximately one trillion bytes.

15.3: Network of Computers

A desktop computer can be a stand-alone computer performing all of its functions or a client linked to a server. A server is a powerful computer or processor that manages files or devices to be used by numerous clients simultaneously. The client accesses programs files and devices managed by the server; it may even use the server for some of its processing power. This means lower costs because devices such as printers and commonly used programs can be shared. Computers connected to one another are said to be in a network.

In the example below, there are five clients connected to the server.

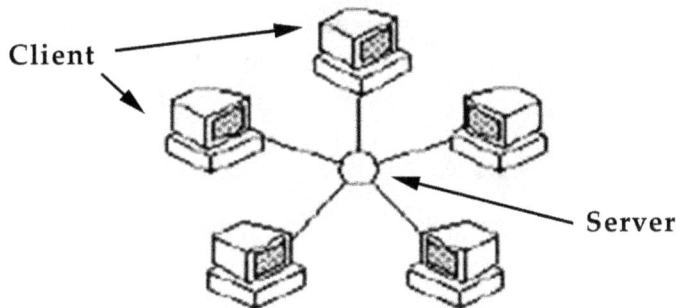

Figure 15.1: **A Star Topology**

15.4: Computer Programming

A computer is not an intelligent device; it needs programs (sets of instructions) to tell it what to do. Every tool or application used on a computer is a program. The operating system that manages the computer's resources is also a program as is the set of instructions that allows a washing machine to check that the water is at the correct temperature. Many programming languages have been created to enable programmers to write different types of program. One of the most popular, all-purpose, programming languages today is Java. Java was created by James Gosling in 1995 to write programs that would run on any device regardless of software or hardware. Other examples of common programming languages include SQL for creating and maintaining databases and HTML for creating Web pages.

Computer programmes open in what is called a 'Window'. Several different 'windows' can be open at the same time and which can be easily switched between. For example, in doing accounts one could have the balance sheet on one part of the screen whilst having part of the profit and loss account underneath. This is logical because items from the profit and loss account will appear on the balance sheet.

15.5: Types of Documents

15.5.1 Spreadsheets .xls

A spreadsheet contains numerical data displayed in columns and rows. Calculations can then be performed on these rows and columns. Spreadsheet packages make the process of creating a spreadsheet and performing calculations on it much more accurate and efficient. It enables the effects of a slight change in one or more pieces of data to be seen immediately. One of the most common uses of spreadsheets by organisations is to construct models of businesses. For example when an overdraft is requested, the business plan may be entered into the computer. Then calculations, such as making certain assumptions about inflation in a country's economy, can be performed. Information may then be obtained as to what the figures would be if the inflation rate rose higher than the government predicts. Similarly, the effects can be gauged if there is a downfall in sales. A bank can then use this information to work out whether the overdraft should be awarded.

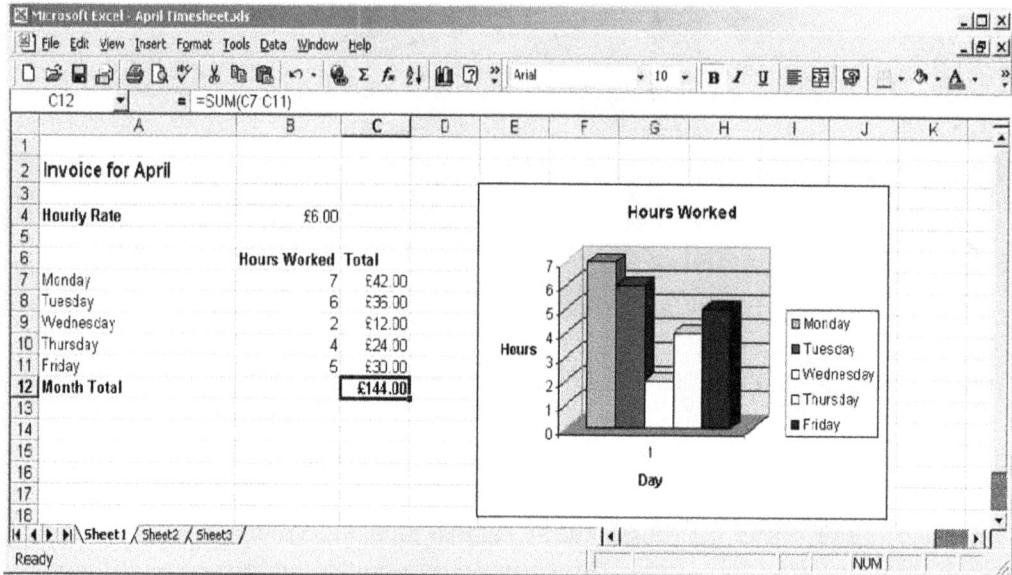

Figure15. 2: **An example of a Spreadsheet with a Chart**

A big advantage of spreadsheet packages is the size of the worksheets it allows; many work sheets have 256 columns and 8192 rows. This is obviously far more than can be shown easily on conventional paper.

Spreadsheet packages can be used for stock control. The term 'stock control' refers to the rate at which stock is consumed and replaced. This may vary from one month to another. Stock control also needs to take account of delivery time, the advantages and disadvantages of bulk purchase and ensuring that items are re-ordered so that they are always available.

Spreadsheet packages can display numerical data in a variety of ways including graphs and charts. This means that the user can choose to display the data in a way that its intended reader can best understand.

15.5.2: Documents .doc

For small firms, which need to have written contact with their customers, the main use of the computer is probably word processing. It is very easy to create master documents, for example an invoice template where the user just has to enter the customer name and the amount. The mail merge facility contained in most word processing applications can personalise a standard letter by including the name and address of customers from an address book. Modern packages such as Microsoft Office and OpenOffice, allow integration between spreadsheets and word processing packages. This means information from the accounts spreadsheet can be automatically copied into a text document. Firms can go further than this and automatically customise letters so they are relevant to the intended recipient. This helps to avoid the problems of standardised letters, which start Dear Sir/Madam and contains information which is of no use or interest to the recipient.

For example, people in their nineties have complained about being sent details of long-term savings plans of 20 years or more, which are not likely to appeal to them. Legal firms such as solicitors involved in contract work and wills, may have standard paragraphs or legal terms that can then be added in as and when needed, thus avoiding duplication of work.

15.6: Uses of the Computer

15.6.1: Accounting

Accounting departments use computers especially for spreadsheet packages. The advantage of a computer is that it can work through calculations extremely quickly and, providing the programme and the data entered is correct, there is no possibility of error. Spreadsheet packages can be used to produce information about actual and budgeted costs and be set to highlight any differences. They are also widely used in order to predict cash flow, which can be a considerable advantage when considering tasks such as the negotiation of overdrafts.

Computer programs can be written to facilitate invoicing and billing. The program can also be set to classify the information in a number of different ways, for example it can indicate when an invoice is unpaid and a reminder needs to be sent. It can also add the invoice to any other amounts owing by the same person or trader very quickly. The program could also classify invoices by the type of items sold, which would help the sales manager and stock control. Details of any available discounts can be entered and the program calculates these automatically, for example a discount for early payment or buying in bulk. A discount for early payment is a good idea as it encourages customers to pay early, which reduces charges from the bank and improves cash flow. A program can be written to issue statements of account, which detail the amount of money that is outstanding at the end of every month.

Personnel records are often computerised. This is partly because it is much easier to calculate wages and piece-rate payments by using computers. A big advantage of a computer is that data is saved so more than one copy of it can be produced. This also means that the information can be sent to more than one department. For example, salary information would need to be processed by payroll but may also be used by the individual departments to calculate their budgets.

15.6.2: Aviation

Computers are widely used in the aviation industry for both general business and research.

It is extremely expensive to develop new aircraft; therefore aircraft manufacturers want to test the possible consequences of using different materials and systems, and consequently the aircraft's air-worthiness, without going to the risk and expense of testing the aircraft in practice. To do this, they use computer simulation by which the computer shows the potential effect of factors such as weather and stress on aircraft and aircraft systems. This removes the need to risk human life and high costs because a prototype will not be built until many developments mean that the aircraft can be reasonably thought to be safe.

Computer simulation is also used to train pilots and for them and test pilots to experience a simulation of what is it like to fly the aircraft under a variety of conditions. The 'autopilot' function of a plane is run entirely by a system of on-board computers and 'blind landing' systems can land an aircraft in fog, when the pilot may not be able to see the ground. The computer is also used to check the fuel consumption of aircraft and check that all features, such as the engines are working correctly.

Air traffic control makes great use of computers. Air traffic control is responsible for the safe landing and taking off of all aircraft in a certain area. Computers are used to show where each plane is on the radar and to assume contact with the pilot when necessary.

The aviation and travel industries use computers for the booking of airline seats. A computer can search through and, if necessary, update a large amount of data very quickly. This enables it update records and to check for alternative flights very efficiently. Travel agencies have access to many airline companies and the information on available seats and prices is constantly updated through the Internet. This enables companies such as STA Travel to search the available seats on many airlines to find the customer the cheapest fare possible. The concept of 'e-tickets' is now becoming increasingly more popular within the airline industry.

With e-tickets, the customer's flight and details are stored in a computer system and a paper ticket is not issued. This saves the airline money and eliminates the problem of a customer losing his ticket. The customer simply inserts his credit card into a machine at the airport to receive a boarding card. The passenger can even bypass check-ins if he/she has no luggage to put into the hold.

15.6.3: Manufacturing

Computers are also used in the manufacturing businesses. For example, sales representatives can now use e-mail or the Internet instead of mail or telephone to send details of their orders back to the main office. If the company has an e-Commerce site, the customer can fill out an online order form and even enter their payment details. This information is then transferred to the company's order system at the touch of a button. The introduction of an e-Commerce site may well mean that the role of a sales representative changes from dealing with current customers to attracting new ones.

Within the production business itself, computers have been widely used in network analysis. This means that activities can be identified as being either independent or dependent upon each other, that is, they can run simultaneously or must run sequentially. The computer can then estimate, for example, how long a building would take to build and calculate the costs and results of speeding up or delaying certain processes. A computer program can also be set to test and calculate functions such as queuing theory. Queuing theory is used to help managers understand and make better decisions about queues. For example, what would the effects be if more machines were used in a factory where a so-called 'bottleneck' normally occurred and would these benefits outweigh the cost implications? SIMUL8 is a computer package that specialises in simulating queues and showing the long-term effects of changes such as these.

As mentioned earlier, computers are widely used in stock control. Electronic Point of Sale (EPOS) systems can be linked to the supplier and show the exact sales of items. The supplier can then construct an order to replenish the stock that has been sold or used. For example, a textile manufacturer who owns shops can transfer sales information from the shop to the production manager who can arrange to alter the production levels of different items accordingly.

15.6.4: Medicine

Computers have been widely used in medical activities. For example, details of diet or medicines can enable doctors and others to study and test the probabilities of certain factors causing disease or illness. For example the relationship between certain foods and heart disease can be studied by using figures stored by the computer. Computers can be used for the smooth running of hospitals by storing appointments and records and making the most efficient use of doctor's time.

Computers can also be used; for example, giving routine checks of the body/mass ratio to check if patients are under or over weight. Computer tablets are now becoming a more common sight in hospitals as they are replacing the standard patient chart which normally consisted of sheets of paper.

15.6.5: Insurance

As mentioned before, computers have the ability to search through vast quantities of data and perform complex calculations very quickly. This makes them very useful in the field of insurance. A life insurance company can use a computer to work out a policy's premium taking into account several factors such as smoking, drinking habits, employment and where they live. Car insurance companies use computer programs to work out quotes based on the age and type of the car, occupation and age of the owner and where the car is parked. House insurance companies use computers to check a customer's postcode because research has shown that some areas in the country are more prone to crime than others are.

15.6.6: Data Checking and Quality Control

Computer packages can be used to verify data, for example, they can readily be used in conjunction with confidence limits to look at unlikely items. If 99% of sales lie within a particular range then, the program can be set to trigger an alarm for those that are outside this range. This is even more important when used in conjunction with quality control. For example if a firm knows that on average it has 1% defects the computer can be programmed to tell the manager when the quality of the product is falling. This could be done manually but there would usually be a time lag between receiving the information and being able to act upon it.

Computers can be used to test whether items produced are of the correct size. For example, it can check that a particular component is within the limits of 10 centimetres plus or minus 0.001 centimetres. It would be impossible for human quality control staff to deal with measurements as slight as these. The Computer can also check weight, as in food processing items, to satisfy the various Weights and Measures Acts.

Another use for computers in data checking is for bills that are usually within the £10,000 to £15,000 range. The computer can be programmed to inform all heads of department if a bill is received for an amount outside this range. Banks use computers for data checking in a similar way. They program computers to pick up anomalies and duplications in the transactions on peoples' accounts. For example, the same amount of money leaves an account on two consecutive days or an unusually large amount of money is drawn out over the counter, when all other withdrawals have been made at a cash machine.

15.6.7: Architecture

Computers are frequently used in architecture, especially to simulate the stresses and strains, which would be imposed on certain materials. For example, to check how a floor will take the strain of heavy furniture and people.

Increasingly architects can use computers to show how a building or other structure might look when it is built and how it will be affected by certain conditions such as high winds. This may be achieved by using virtual reality, that is, pictures displayed in 3D that gives a more accurate representation of space. In some simulators, the user can 'walk through' the design, making it seem even more realistic.

15.6.8: Education

Nowadays schools all have 'Information Technology' rooms and the ability to teach computing skills to pupils. Charles Clarke, the then Education Secretary and later Home Secretary suggested the idea of making Information Communication Technology (ICT) compulsory for all pupils up to the age of 16.

Universities are increasing their use of computers to enable students to participate in virtual seminars and even virtual courses. Most universities also store information on their staff and module guides on computers and allow students to access them.

Schools keep a database of all their students and staff information. Different departments may have access to different parts of this information. For example, the school nurse may have access to details of any allergies or illnesses, a person may have. The records department would have access to student information such as the dates they attended the school and the grades they received.

15.6.9: Marketing

Computers are frequently used in the marketing department. They can analyse past invoices to identify a potential market for a new product. A good example of this is Amazon, an online retailer. When a user purchases an item the screen displays the message: "people who bought this also bought this and this". Word processing packages such as Microsoft Word can use the data from invoices to create mailing lists by type of sales, regions, income or other information. The company can then 'push' relevant marketing material at these customers; the idea being that they only receive adverts that are applicable to them. This can be done via either e-mail or the traditional postal system. Personal details are not just collected from invoices. They are also collected every time a user fills out a form online, for example, to enter a competition or to sign up for a website account. If the user agrees, the company can then sell this information to other advertising companies. This, combined with the popularity of e-mail has led to the term 'Spam' becoming commonplace. Spam is the name given to junk mail received via e-mail, some of it is specially targeted to the user, based on information they have given in the past and some is not. The use of popular e-mail providers such as Outlook and Yahoo have led to millions and millions of people, world-wide, having very similar e-mail addresses, for example, something@outlook.com. This means organisations can create a program that can send an e-mail to millions of combinations of Outlook addresses at once. If a user replies to, or in some cases opens the e-mail, the organisation that sent it would know that it is a valid address and simply send more. As well as being incredibly annoying, many of the e-mails sent contain explicit content such as pornography or fraudulent money schemes such as, fake lottery winnings. As these e-mails are not targeted at anyone in particular, these messages can be received by anyone including children.

15.6.10: Banking

As mentioned before, computers have large memories and a rapid speed of calculation, meaning they can deal with credits and debits on accounts very easily. At the same time, they can also submit items to be paid to another bank. For example, if HSBC has a number of cheques drawn on it which are payable to Barclays' customers and vice versa. At the end of the day, the banks know how much money they owe each other and can then settle the net indebtedness very quickly. This is known as bank reconciliation.

Computers can also calculate the amount of interest owing, for example on a loan or an overdraft, and can calculate charges that might be made for special items. They can also supply instant information regarding customer accounts, for example businesses or individuals may wish to know how much they have in their account or how much they owe the bank. Having the computers of a bank linked together in a network means that this information can be accessed from anywhere within the banks system. This has enabled the introduction of national and international call centres, which deal with enquiries such as these. Manual account keeping meant some delay, as the accounts could only be done from one location.

15.6.11: Personnel

Nearly all personnel records, today, are held on computers. The basic requirements of anyone will probably be their name, address, where they work, their age, grade and scale of payment. However many other items may also be added, for example what training they have received whilst in the firm, whether they have been promoted and whether they have been absent for unspecified reasons. The computer can collate information in a number of different ways. For example, if it were suspected that Mr X is a better manager than Mr Y, it would be easy to obtain figures regarding absenteeism, which may confirm that this is increased when Mr Y is in charge. Computer packages can also produce details about labour turnover, which means the percentage of employees who have left as a percentage of the total work force. This information may need to be sub-divided into reasons for resignation, for example, promotion, dissatisfaction, illness or pregnancy. Dissatisfaction is important because it may indicate a lack of morale within the particular firm or department. The processes of recruitment and training are very costly so identifying and resolving the factors that lead to high turnover is very beneficial to an organisation. The personnel data can also help the organisation to assess how workers are deployed within the organisation. For example, thirty people may be employed within an accounts department whilst another accounts department has only twenty employees. Providing that the factory sizes are comparable then it would be interesting to investigate why one department needs ten more employees than the other. Similarly, the package can give details of production levels to enable comparisons to be made.

Computers are widely used for payroll records, enabling over-time or other additions to pay such as bonuses to be quickly calculated for large numbers of people. This is very important in large firms where, previously, large numbers of clerks had to be employed. Computer packages can cross classify information, meaning the amounts payable to individuals can be allocated to particular items. For example, if Mr. X has been working an eight-hour day of which three have been on a particular assignment the package will supply this information from time sheets. This is particularly useful if the rate of pay differs, such as an increased hourly rate for work of a hazardous nature.

15.6.12: Retailing

A popular business practice now is that of e-Commerce. This involves a company setting up a web site that allows customers to browse their products and place an order. Some e-Commerce sites allow customers to submit their payment details online, making the process even more efficient. The major advantages of e-Commerce are that customers can shop 24 hours a day, seven days a week and that customers from all over the world can browse and buy from the shop. The practice of e-Commerce can also reduce a company's overheads by reducing or eliminating the need to keep stock. A company may also be able to replace its expensive high street shop with a cheaper warehouse.

Electronic Point of Sale terminals (EPOS) are now commonplace in UK shops. They allow the user to scan or enter information about the items being purchased. This information is then saved, printed out on a customer receipt and used to aid stock checking and stock replacement. The information can also be used to improve forecasting of sales, which in turn helps the shopkeeper to make better purchasing decisions.

As mentioned before, many EPOS systems have a scanner, which uses a laser beam to read the barcode on the item. This barcode contains the price and type of the item being bought as well as any discounts associated with it.

Many large stores and supermarket chains have introduced loyalty card schemes. This enables the customer to collect points for every pound they spend. These points can then be exchanged for vouchers or other products and services. The advantages for the store are that customers may be more likely to shop there to build up their points bank and that the store can collect information on the customer. To apply for the card, the customer has to provide personal details such as name, age, occupation and address. Then, every time the card is used a record of the items they buy and how much they spend can be collected and used to create a personal shopping profile. This profile is then used to identify feasible promotions and to send relevant vouchers and advertisements to the customer. If the customer agrees, the store is able to sell their information to other companies for use with their promotional material.

15.7: Computer Input

All computers need some form of input equipment; these are commonly known as peripherals.

Keyboard

The most common form of input into a computer is still the standard QWERTY keyboard. These keyboards contain alphanumeric, punctuation and special keys. Special keys include function keys that perform special functions inside certain applications, arrow keys, which help the user scroll through a page, and others such as the caps lock key. The main advantage of the keyboard is that it is fast, especially for a competent typist. There have been some concerns about the need to avoid repetitive strain injuries (RSI). These occur in people who use a keyboard for extended periods. For this reason keyboard, manufacturers have carried out a lot of research into making their keyboards more comfortable to reduce this risk.

Figure 15.3: **Examples of Ergonomic Keyboards**

Mouse

The mouse is a hand-held device, usually with two or three buttons, which is usually sited on a foam mat. It moves a pointer on the screen to the place where an adjustment is to be made. Another type of mouse is the trackball mouse that differs from standard mice, as they are not moved over a mouse mat; rather a ball is moved with the fingers to position the pointer on screen. Laptop computers have a version of a trackball mouse incorporated into them.

Figure15. 4: **Examples of a Standard Mouse and a Trackball Mouse**

Handwriting Recognition

If a document is handwritten, it may be desirable to display it in a typed format. This can be achieved by using a piece of Optical Character Recognition (OCR) equipment, which reads documents line by line and converts the handwritten words into text. More popular, however, are devices that allow the user to write on a pad and have their writing displayed as text on the screen. Many PDAs (Personal Digital Assistants) have this feature; they ask for a sample of the user's handwriting and then use that sample to compare the characters as the user writes them. A recent introduction in this field is that of the Microsoft's Tablet PC. This smart screen is the size of a notepad, with built in handwriting recognition software. Initially it has been aimed at niche markets such as health care workers.

Voice Recognition

Prices of voice recognition software have fallen drastically but the idea of using them for dictation has not really caught on. One factor affecting the uptake of voice recognition systems is that many words in the English language sound the same, for example, "there" and "their". To combat these problems, statistical techniques have been used to test these homonyms. Using these techniques, it is usually possible to distinguish between two, too and to with surprising accuracy.

One use for voice recognition, today, is with mobile phones, many of which have a voice-dialling feature. The user sets this feature up by verbally inputting the names of the people in his or her address book. The user can then speak the name into the phone and it will automatically dial the number associated with them. They have become very cheap and many business executives use them.

Touch Screens

Another form of input is that of touch screens. As the name implies the person merely has to touch the screen to indicate what they want. They are sometimes used to enable people, who do not regularly use computers, to press pictures or icons to get information. A wide use of touch screens is at exhibitions, where people can use them to find out more information about the item on display. PDAs also use touch screens. Depending on the device, the user may have a tool called a 'stylus'; this is similar to a pencil which they can use to touch the screen. This tool works in a similar way to the mouse, and allows the user to select the place he wishes to make an adjustment, for example, opening a file or changing part of a word in a document. The updated version of touch screen software is known as 'multi-touch'. This technology is used in tablets and smart phones; it allows the user to use their own hands instead of a stylus.

Modems

One of the methods of computer input is the use of a modem. With a modem attached to a computer as well as a telephone line it is possible to obtain data from other computer users anywhere in the world. Because telephone lines are used information is transferred quickly and therefore relatively cheaply. The fastest computer modems in 1996 transferred about 14,400 pieces of information per second. This was surpassed in 2008, when 1,244,000 pieces of information were transferred. Battery operated modems have become popular because they can be used with portable computers which is very useful for businesspersons when travelling. Some also can receive information from fax. These days even mobile phones can be used as modems. This enables people to use the Internet and the various facilities it offers when on the move.

Scanners

Until recently, all computer input had to be typed into the machine. This of course is time consuming. It also means that computers have not been able to receive input in the form of pictures. Many modern firms would have found this facility an advantage, especially in advertising when printing brochures, etc. Therefore, scanners have been developed which can include pictures or images. Some of them print in black and white (monochrome) and these have been used for optical character recognition. These can recognise a variety of typefaces. Ones that are more modern can now use colour. In some cases, it is possible to choose whether all details of the original are used or whether a particular colour might be lost.

Most of the modern scanners like photocopiers are flatbed scanners, which can scan information such as photographs or artwork, although not generally slides. Now the quality is not always good as some give a blurred image. Another problem is excessive use of software; for example, some of them may use many megabytes of information although as the size of memory of computers increases this becomes less of a problem.

15.8: Storage

There are various sources of memory for a computer. The USB flash drive, more commonly known as a 'memory stick' is the most common and popular form of external storage that is easy to connect through the Universal Serial Bus (USB) ports on all computers. These started out storing what is now considered a low amount of data such 512 megabytes but in 2013 it was announced that a memory stick of 1 terabyte would be available. CDs and DVDs are still used as a way of storing data. To transfer the data you must 'burn' it onto the disk with a CD/DVD re-writer. There is limited space on these disks, so the more information you want to store on disk, you will need space to store them. An old form of storage which is now obsolete is the Floppy disk. In 2009 Hewlett Packard (HP) discontinued supplying the floppy drive on business desktops. Some people have their old information stored on these disks and transfer them to newer storage systems.

Standalone computers all have their own hard disk, the memory of which is typically measured in gigabytes. They have the advantage of a larger storage capacity than that of CDs, but the information may be too large to transfer to another machine via a CD. One way around this is the recent introduction of portable hard disks, which are plugged into the USB port of a computer. Data is then saved on them or retrieved from them and they can be removed and used with another machine. These differ from 'memory sticks' as they were designed to store more data on them. 'Memory sticks' nowadays start at 1GB of storage whereas a portable hard drive starts at 160GB going to 2 TB.

Drives

Drives are used to access information held on a storage device. The most basic of computers usually have a CD drive whether it is CD, DVD or DVD Rewritable and USB ports. The reason for a lot of USB ports is that it has become the standard connection for keyboards and the mouse. Floppy disks are considered obsolete; computers now come without floppy drives. Floppy disk drives are available as a separate device with a USB connection.

15.9: Printers

Laser

Laser printers have an internal memory that uses computer data to compile an image of the page. Once this image is complete, the page is printed using a laser beam directed onto a drum. This means the image is used as a template, which is how a photocopier works. The commands sent to the printer are accompanied by instructions about the typeface to be used, if it is not already familiar to the machine. Commands, which are sent to the printer, have to be accompanied by instructions about the typeface if the typeface is not already shown in the machine. The main advantages of laser printers are their speed and the quality of their output.

Inkjet

Inkjet printers, as the name implies, propels tiny amounts of ink, which are squirted onto the printed material. It was in the 1970s when the first of the modern day inkjet printers appeared. Inkjet printers are the most common type of printer. This is due to the inexpensive models and low running cost compared to laser printers. Do not believe that the laser printers are only used by businesses, it is for the same reason that businesses buy inkjet printers as do the general public; the cost. A reasonably priced laser printer toner is around £45 per colour, whereas it is around £30 for a complete set of inkjet cartridges.

15.10: The Internet and the World Wide Web

The Internet is a large network of computers that communicate with each other through use of protocols. It originated from a project called ARPA in 1969 that sent messages from one Californian University to another. The defence department carried on the research in the 1970s with the idea that if information was stored on more than one machines it was harder to lose it. The World Wide Web, e-mail and newsgroups are all applications that run on the Internet. Applications such as E-mail have changed the way many companies communicate and do business with each other. There is very little delay between an e-mail being sent and it being received so it is much more efficient than traditional mail. It is also cheaper for a company to send a large document or a small document to several people via e-mail than it is with traditional mail. The extensive uptake of e-mail however, has created its own problems; in many companies it is so popular that the staff receive hundreds of e-mails a day. This means that e-mails are sometimes more likely to be ignored than a traditional letter or a telephone call.

The World Wide Web which was invented by British computer expert Sir Timothy John "Tim" Berners-Lee, allows people to create web pages that can be viewed by anyone else with an Internet connection. Many companies and organisations have their own web pages. They can contain simple information such as who the organisation is, what it does and how to contact it or they can be more complex and allow customers to buy their products by filling out online forms. E-commerce is becoming increasingly popular as companies find it is a cheaper way to conduct business and attract a larger audience and customers find that these cost savings are passed down to them in lower prices. There are a few stores that are only online. 'Woolworths' was a store that was found on almost every high street. It sold a large variety of items: CDs, DVDs, TVs, cleaning products, toys and decorating supplies to name a few of their products. In December 2008 the administrators announced that all stores would close by early January 2009, it was later reborn as an online store.

2002 is when the modern social media began, but it was not until 2009 that it became an everyday aspect in the majority of lives. There are many different types of social media from dating sites to video sites. 'LinkedIn' took what has been called a serious approach to social media by creating a site for businesspersons to connect with other professionals. At one time the biggest social networking site was 'MySpace', it had caught the majority of attention by the fact you were, amongst other things able to upload pictures and videos. In 2004 'Facebook' was released, only a year after 'MySpace' so at the start there was not much of a competition between the two sites. 'Facebook' has overtaken 'MySpace' (which is now mainly dedicated to the music scene) to be the biggest social media site. No one knows how this has happened some believe that it was due to the marketing campaign which drew in rich investors; whereas others think that it is because of the name 'Facebook', because of reasons like it is something simple and easy to remember.

The Internet can be accessed in many ways, all of which are being dramatically reduced in price due to competition amongst the service providers. Currently, the two main connection methods are modem and broadband. Modem connection is sometimes referred to as a dial up connection because the user connects to the Internet when he wishes to use it via his telephone line and then disconnects when he is finished. Broadband connection involves having another telephone line installed. This line is then connected to the Internet all the time the computer is switched on. With modem connection, the user pays for time he is connected and with broadband; the user is charged a standard rate each month regardless of usage. A broadband connection is much faster than a modem one. This means pages can be accessed quicker, images do not take so long to load up and it is possible to download audio and video files.

Many companies and organisations have their own Intranet. An intranet is an internal network of computers, which contains private company information that the staff may find useful. The internal network also allows for quick communication between employees of the firm and the management. This ensures that messages are not distorted by being passed from one person to the next. It also ensures that information within the company is only accessible to those who should have access to it. However, the intranet is still vulnerable to problems that plague the internet; these include viruses that can spread rapidly throughout the system compromising it. Hackers are another problem especially for government offices where sensitive information may be stored.

15.11: Factors affecting the Purchase of Personal Computers

One of the primary factors in buying a computer or computer system is price. With the constant introduction of new technology, the prices of computer systems have fallen dramatically over the last few years to an extent where most households now own a computer system. As well as the price of the actual computer, it is worth taking into consideration the other bits that go with it, for example a printer or scanner. Other things like the feasibility of upgrading to a larger monitor needs to be considered. Some shops have created 'computer system packages' or 'start-up kits', which give a discounted price if you buy the computer and all the extras together.

The second most important consideration to be taken into account is what the computer is to be used for. For example, if it is to be used whilst commuting on the train, a laptop may be appropriate. If the user already has a desktop computer and wants something more mobile, a 'Tablet' may be suitable. Once the decision, as to which type of computer to buy has been made, the user needs to consider which make he wants and which features he wishes it to have. For example, Apple Macintosh makes computers that are very good for working with graphics.

Desirable features may include having an operating system and word processing packages already installed, having a CD re-writer to burn CDs or a fast processor to handle tasks involving a large amount of calculations.

Another factor affecting the purchase of a home computer is that of perceived quality. If a model has been recommended by a friend, or has received an excellent review in a magazine, the user is likely to consider that when choosing which computer to buy.

Seasonal factors are also very important: considerable proportions of home computers are bought between September and December in the UK. Sales may also be affected by promotions on certain products or end of season sales.

15.12: Essay: All Modern Firms have need for Technology, Discuss.

Suggested Feedback

Organisations invest in technology for many reasons, from preserving market share to improving the internal environment for employees and achieve greater customer satisfaction. The actual technology itself has a variety of purposes from accounting to simulation, for example. Many small firms do not use information technology in the form of computers, some probably should but for others it would not bring any benefit to the company, for example a small greengrocer.

One of the main uses of computers is to aid decision-making. The computer has the advantage of being able to evaluate a wide range of options very quickly. For example, a major industrial firm could use a spreadsheet package to look at a wide range of potential machines as well as the necessary labour, costs and the likely demand for products at different prices. The firm can then come up with the optimum solution given the objectives of the company, including how far the company is willing to take risks. A risk adverse firm may not wish to put all its eggs in one basket even if it feels that this is likely to be profitable. For example, an aircraft manufacturer may feel that a larger aircraft such as an even bigger one than the present Dreamliner might be profitable but would lead to high research and development (R&D) costs. It may also be unwilling to go ahead with this because of the long time lag between the concept being developed and a reasonable quantity of the final product being produced.

A computer could be used as a more efficient filing system. For example, a car insurance firm can classify its customer records alphabetically, by name or by type of policy. The former would be helpful in the case of a customer who had forgotten his policy number, phoning up requesting a service and the latter for calculating the costs and receipts of each section or department within the company. Cross-classification such as this would be a very difficult, complicated task to do with a traditional filing system. This information, once extracted can be saved and transferred to another computer, disk or CD. This may be useful to a sales representative who may need details of all the customers in a certain area or information on select items.

The introduction and widespread use of the Internet makes global communication between departments and companies very easy. As mentioned before, concepts such as e-commerce or even a web page with company details on it can attract a much wider customer base than was previously possible. The Internet works in real time. This means that the information contained in certain sites is always up to date. This makes it useful for companies and individuals to find out exact data for exchange rates and stock prices. The Internet also makes it easy for staff to work from home. A company can set up an Extranet, an Intranet that is accessible from outside the office, providing the user has been granted access. This allows someone working from home access to his company e-mail and certain applications and files that they may need to use.

Common applications such as word processing packages make a big difference to secretaries' work. They allow the user to make instant changes, send or printout multiple copies and even have templates to make the creation of letters, for example, easy.

15.13: Difficulties with Computers

It is important to bear in mind that the introduction of technology does not solve all problems; rather its usage makes it a help or hindrance to the organisation. One problem of introducing technology to an organisation is that all users have to be trained. This can be expensive and, if the trainees are unfamiliar with computers, could take a very long time. The users then have to be retrained every time a new piece of software or a new machine is introduced. Often, too little attention is paid to training users on new technology and as a result, it is not used to its full potential.

In organisations such as borough councils and schools and many businesses, computers have made people's jobs more time consuming. For example, managers and teachers spend lots of time typing out e-mails and letters at 12-15 words a minute when it would be much faster to use a secretary. This is because it is easier to simply click on reply and send an email than to dictate a reply to the secretary.

As mentioned before, computer calculations are 100% accurate, however, this is only true if the correct information has been entered initially. There is a common phrase: 'garbage in, garbage out' (GIGO) that is particularly relevant for this. Many sources of information have to be manually entered into the computer, for example, values of cheques to be paid into an account. As well as the pieces of data being entered, someone also has to enter the formulae to carry out the calculations. If a spreadsheet, package is being used, particular attention also needs to be paid to exactly where in the table, and each piece of data goes. This comes back to how well the users have been trained to use the packages they need for their jobs.

Another problem with computers is that of backing up information. Nearly everyone who has ever used a computer to write something has lost some of their work because they failed to make a backup. For a home computer user, backing up work means saving it in more than one place, for example, saved on another hard drive and on a USB memory stick. In an organisation, the process of backing up becomes much more complex as everything everyone has done needs to be copied. The backup copy needs to be stored in a different location so that a fire in one building would not destroy both the original and the backup. Companies are now using the internet to save data. Using 'The Cloud' to save data has the advantage of there being no reason to have another space to store backup, thus saving the company money. What is considered to be a problem with saving to 'The Cloud' is that an internet connection is needed to access the data. If there was a problem with the original hard drive stored data and the company was to lose its internet connection, then no one would be able to access the backup data. A few companies only store their data in 'The Cloud' this has the advantage of being able to access the data from anywhere but, has the downside that you must have an internet connection to get the data.

It is vital that an organisation that works with computers has the appropriate security in place to protect them and the information they contain. Actions such as ensuring users do not disclose their passwords, change them regularly and choose suitably hard codes help to protect systems from inside the office but companies also need to consider outside attacks. Connecting a computer system to the Internet can leave it open to all sorts of attack from hackers accessing private documents to viruses that can destroy information. A firewall is a piece of software that can protect a computer system from external attack. It can be programmed to detect and block e-mails with executable attachments (programs that may contain viruses) as well as blocking access into the computer system except from certain machines. It can also prevent people from inside the firewall from accessing certain sites and downloading certain files or programs. As well as these security measures, the organisation also has to guard against physical attacks, for example, theft of the machines in a break in. Computer companies that specialise in powerful, multi-million pound servers take the threat of burglary very seriously and might be protected by a moat to stop ram raiders or based in an atomic bunker. Security guards also continuously patrol their buildings. In 2012 the Minister of Education announced that he wanted to drop the current ICT curriculum and change it to Computer Science. He said "Instead of children bored out of their minds being taught how to use Word and Excel by bored teachers, we could have 11-year-olds able to write simple 2D computer animations using an MIT tool called Scratch. By 16, they could have an understanding of formal logic previously covered only in University courses and be writing their own Apps for smartphones."[6]

Another problem computer users can face is that of a lack of compatibility. Some companies deliberately create new software that is only compatible with their other products and no one else's. Some software has been written to ease these problems. As mentioned before, James Gosling wrote Java with the aim to allow programmers to write programs that will run on anything. Leading on from this is a problem that the Government is facing now. All Government documents and letters are made accessible to the public 30 years after they were written. The documents that are being made available now are all in paper format so they are easy to access and copy. Documents created today, however, are created using computers. Instead of paper memos, staff are issued with e-mail ones, documents and records are stored in a specific format on CDs, portable hard drives or on actual machines. The problem is in 30 years will this information still be accessible or will the technology used at that time be incompatible with the technology used today?

Self-examination Questions

1. How can computers change the way in which firms are organised?

2. Why could the use of computers influence decisions a firm makes on whether to have small or large branches?

3. Why might people fear computers in their organisation?

4. Why might people welcome computers into their organisation? (Hint: think of accounts)

5. What are the main forms of input into a computer? What are their advantages and disadvantages?

---

[6] https://www.gov.uk/government/news/harmful-ict-curriculum-set-to-be-dropped-to-make-way-for-rigorous-computer-science

6. What effect would having Speech Recognition Software have on a firm? What would be the obvious problems of trying to have voice input? (Think of words that are similar in sound but not in meaning.)

7. What are the main languages used in the computer and what are they used for?

8. What is meant by interactive when considering computers?

9. How might computers be used to assist in medical care?

10. How could computers be used for simulation purposes and why might they be useful for architects?

11. Why do airlines frequently use computers for reservations?

12. Why must great care be taken to consider the total cost of computerisation when compared with a conventional filing system?

Chapter 16: STATISTICS AND OPERATIONAL RESEARCH

16.1: Introduction

Most firms keep basic statistics on production and sales levels as well as inputs and expenses. There are also several ways in which these statistics can be used to aid different management tasks.

Probability: Probability is the likelihood of a certain event happening. Firms can use this method to create data to base their investment decisions on. It can also be used to aid other decisions such as location policy.

Decision-making: Decision-making teams often use decision trees. They help the team choose which form of action is the most appropriate and judge the future consequences of each choice.

Quality control: Firms may wish to test a product's dimensions against control charts. The current standard for quality control is ISO 9000.

Smoothing: Firms may see repeating patterns in their demand, these could be four or five-week periods or a seasonal pattern, for example. Smoothing is a forecasting technique that smooths out the random fluctuations that may occur at a certain time each period.

Regression: This forecasting technique is used to develop a mathematical equation that shows how variables are related to each other. Many firms use it to test for growth of population. The formula to calculate the least squares line for simple linear regressions is
$y = ax + b$ and this is the equation that will be used in this book.

Linear programming: LP is a mathematical tool that is used to determine the optimum choice when given two options within set constraints. It involves maximising or minimising a linear function subject to the constraints that limit it. An example is a factory that has to decide how many of product A and product B to make. By using information such as production times and value of the products, an optimal solution can be found that will maximise the use of the firm's resources and its profit.

Stock control: The costs of holding stock such as the warehouse space, staff, insurance and depreciation, are compared with the savings that can be made through bulk purchase. The firm can then see if it is worth keeping lots of stock of certain items. Other methods such as Pareto's ABC analysis can be used to work out which stock items need stricter control and which only need periodical review.

Projects: Projects are one off jobs that have resources dedicated to them. Project planning techniques help the project teamwork out how long each stage should take, which stages can be carried out simultaneously and what effects any changes made will have. The techniques that are typically used include network analysis and queuing theory.

Simulation: It generally, models a real life situation or product and highlights any potential problems without the costs of testing the real thing.

Simulation has a variety of uses from using computer simulation to predict queues and bottlenecks in a factory to assessing whether a new aircraft will withstand extreme weather.(Refer to 15.6.2: Aviation)

DCF: This stands for discounted cash flow and is necessary because returns in future years do not have the same value as cash now. It involves outlining the concepts of net present value and rate of return.

16.2: Presentation of Tables

When presenting tables, it is important to ensure the headings are clear and descriptive. It is also crucial that the data and calculations are dated so that a user can instantly gauge its relevance to the situation in hand. For example, a table showing the population of the UK will not be altered much over a period of five to ten years. A table showing ownership of cars for the same period, however, would rapidly be outdated.

Any qualifications about the data need to be stated. For example, which samples the data was based on, any confidence limits placed upon the figures and maybe if the information is primary or secondary and who carried out the calculations. See example table in the 'frequency distribution' section.

16.3: Graphs

There are several different types of graph. The first thing the statistician needs to decide is which one will display the data in the clearest form. Another factor to consider is the amount of information being represented in the graph. If there are too many lines, the graph will be very hard to read.

Histograms: A histogram illustrates a frequency distribution. It is made up of rectangles drawn on a continuous base. The area of each rectangle is proportional to the frequency of the class it represents

Bar charts: A bar chart is made up of parallel bars of equal width, which represent the data. The length of each bar is proportional to the frequency of the class it represents.

Component Bar Charts: This is when individual bars from a bar chart are broken down into smaller groupings. For example, a bar chart showing the population of the UK at five-year intervals could have each bar divided into male and female members to give more information on the specific breakdown of the population's demographics.

Pie Charts: The area of a circle represents the total data. This circle is divided into one sector for each category. The angle of each sector is a fraction of the total (360º) and represents the fraction of the total that the sector represents. They are easy to draw especially with computers but care must be taken to avoid too many sectors otherwise it becomes difficult to see accurately the areas of different portions in relation to each other.

These are generally used to show approximate relationships and information.

Sales breakdown by percentage

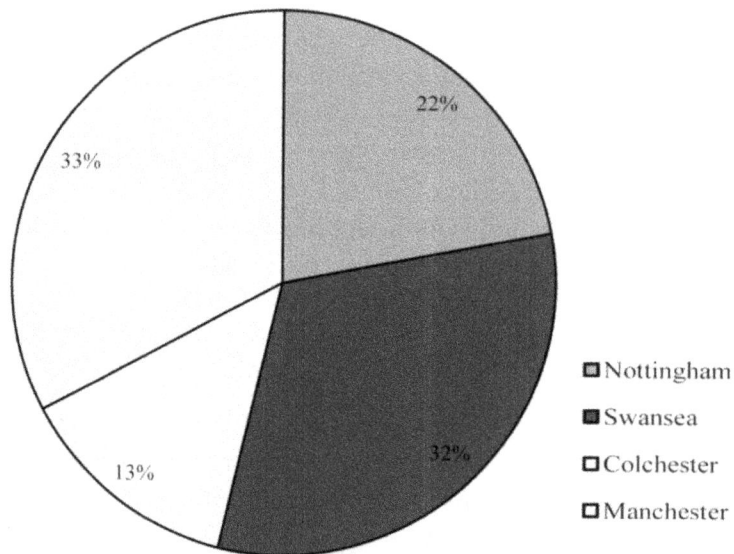

- Nottingham
- Swansea
- Colchester
- Manchester

16.4: Common Statistical Terminology

Data can be split into to two types, discrete and continuous. Discrete data is a whole number and continuous allows decimal places. In some situations, the distinction is very important, for example, the human population should be a discrete number although in certain calculations this may be ignored. Data such as weight, height or time on the other hand is continuous.

An **attribute** describes another piece of data, for example the colour of an object or nationality of a person.

Ranked data is data sorted into an order. For example, ranked exam grades may have the highest first and the lowest last. Another meaning of the term rank is to see a list of data in terms of preference, for example, to see in which order people would place their choices.

Primary data is data collected in the form the statistician requires, this means he knows the limits of the data. For example, if he/she chooses to look only at a small sample of the population of the UK, he would just collect data from those people living in London, using primary data collection. Compare this with secondary data, where in general, the statistician has no control over the quality of the data that has been collected.

The dictionary definition of the term ratio is the measure of the relative size of two classes expressed as a proportion. For example, the ratio of girls to boys in a school class is 1:2.

The practice of **rounding** usually involves turning continuous data into discrete, for example, 2.8 children would be rounded up to 3 children. In some cases a number is rounded to a number of decimal places, for example, 2.3729 to three decimal places would be 2.373. The usual method is to round up if the last digit is five or more and to round down if it is less than five.

An associated term is **spurious accuracy**. To say that the percentage of people who passed an examination is 55.56% is spurious if it means that 5 out of 9 passed.

16.5: Frequency distributions

Once collected, data usually needs to be tabulated or categorised in some way. Common problems include how to choose the right number of classes and how to organise the class limits because bias can creep in. For example, many houses are priced with a figure ending £9990, say £119,990. This means that in a class showing house prices between £110,000 and £120,000, the average is likely to be closer to £120,000 than £110,000.

House prices in town x, for year 200x, by area

Price	Number of houses
Up to but not including £70,000	100
£70,000 - £79,999	40
£ 80,000 - £89,999	300
£ 90,000 - £99,999	600
£100,000 - £109,999	160
£110,000 - £119,000	100
£120,000 and over	50

Table 1: All houses

There are many possibilities in terms of tabulation for housing data. For example, it could be tabulated by area, size of house or by the price of the house. It should be noted therefore that there is no one way in which to represent the data, as it depends on what the data is to be used. For example, from a buyer's viewpoint, the first parameter is probably that of price and therefore this is the most important variable.

The use of **bar charts** and **cumulative bar charts** has limitations. For example if we had some house location data we could show a bar for the North, a bar for the East, a bar for the South, a bar for the West and then a bar for the central area. This would probably be easier to understand than a pie chart. These bars could be split further to show the number of houses in each price range in each area thus forming a component bar chart.

Common errors can occur when using pie charts and when drawing segments of unequal size. Here, as in the bar charts, we could show the number of houses by geographical area. If we had forty houses we would divide 360 degrees by forty to determine how many degrees each house is worth. We would then multiply this value by the number of houses in each area to determine the size of each segment. We need to think about what we wish to emphasise, say, composition from one year to another. We would not show for example 80 houses in one year with all dimensions twice as big as 40 in the current year, alternatively we could show the price of houses. Whilst pie charts are often used, they are not very easy to draw manually.

16.5.1: *Median*

The median is the middle item of data. To find it, the data has to be listed first in some order either ascending or descending. Once this is done, the middle value is taken as the median. For example, if there are 20 pieces of data the 10th and 11th will be the median. If there are 21, pieces of data the median will be the 11th item.

Finding the median in grouped data is slightly more complex and the following formula is used to calculate it:

$$Median = L + \left(\frac{(0.5 \times N) - (\sum f) L}{f} \times C \right)$$

Where

L	= Lower boundary of median class
N	= Total frequency
$(\sum f)L$	= Sum of frequencies below median class
f	= median / frequency of median class
C	= width of median class

Example:

Mark	10-	20-	30-	40-	50-	60-	70-	80-90
Frequency	18	34	58	42	24	10	6	8
Cumulative frequency	18	52	110	152	176	186	192	200

$$Median = 30 + \left(\frac{(0.5 * 200) - 52}{58} \right) * 10$$

Median = 38.3

16.5.2: *Mean*

The mean x̄ is the average value of the data. The formula for the mean in ungrouped data is the sum of all the items divided by the total number of items.

Example:

Given three pieces of data: 7, 9 and 11 ;

Then: Total = 27

$$\text{Mean} = \bar{x} = \frac{27}{3}$$

$$\bar{x} = 9$$

The formula uses every piece of data which means it can be taken as representative. However, it is worth noting that an extreme piece of data can distort the data.

16.5.3: Range

The range is a way of assessing the spread of the data. It is the difference between the top and the bottom item, when they are in ascending order. It is widely used by customers and suppliers alike, but can be misleading. For example, the output of a factory in a year is 1,000-1,200 units per week but a strike meant that no production took place in one week. To say that the range was 1,300, that is 1,300 being the top production week and 0 the bottom would give a misleading impression of the firm.

16.5.4: Variance and Standard Deviation

Variance and standard deviation are also used to establish the spread of the data. Variance of a sample (S^2) is found by the following equation:

$$S^2 = \sum \frac{(x - \bar{x})^2}{n-1}$$

1. Subtract the mean $\bar{x}$ of the sample from each data item (x)
2. Square each of these new values
3. Add up the squared values
4. Divide the answer by one less than the number of items of data (n-1)

The standard deviation (s) is the square root of the variance.

Example:

x	$\bar{x}$	$(x - \bar{x})$	$(x - \bar{x})^2$
9	11	-2	4
9	11	-2	4
11	11	0	0
13	11	2	4
13	11	2	4

Total $(x - \bar{x})^2$ = 16

16 / (n-1) = 16/4 = 4

Variance S^2 = 4

Standard Deviation(s) = 2

If we do the same by grouped data, we have similar calculations.

x	$\bar{x}$	f	$(x - \bar{x})$	$(x - \bar{x})^2$	$f(x - \bar{x})^2$
9	11	2	-2	4	8
11	11	1	0	0	0
13	11	2	2	4	8

Total $f(x - \bar{x})^2$ = 16

16 / (n-1) = 16/4 = 4

Variance (S^2) = 4

Standard Deviation (s) = 2

16.6: Control Charts

The use of control charts is common in industry. They can have warning and action values set into them. This means that when the data it receives triggers one of these, the control chart either sends a warning to a manager or starts an action. For example, a control chart may specify the upper limits of pollution from a certain source. If this point is reached, the plant will be closed down.

16.7: Network Analysis

Network analysis is used to construct a critical path diagram. This diagram shows the critical path, this is the shortest amount of time the project or task can take to be completed. From this, management scientists can then see what effects making changes to any of the activities will have on the overall project time and assess if the changes are worth it. The first task involved in network analysis is to work out which activities are dependent and independent. Independent tasks can be run simultaneously whereas dependent ones are dependent on another finishing before it can start. For example, for the task of making a cup of tea, taking the milk out from the refrigerator is independent of taking the sugar from the cupboard.

However pouring the milk into the tea is dependent upon having taken the milk out of the refrigerator.

There are two types of network diagram: activity on node (AoN) and activity on arrow (AoA). The activity on arrow diagram will now be explained further.

An Activity:
An Event:

A   *activity reference*

3   *activity duration*

EST

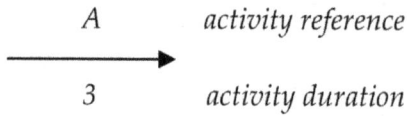

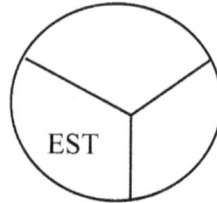

EST = Earliest Start Time

Rules for drawing the diagram

- All diagrams must have at least one start and one end node.

- Each event must have at least one preceding activity (except the start event).

- Each event must have at least one subsequent activity (except the end event).

- Any 2 events must have one activity joining them.

- In the case of two activities having the same head and tail event, a dummy activity is used.

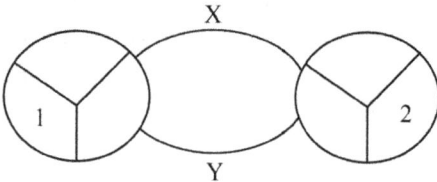

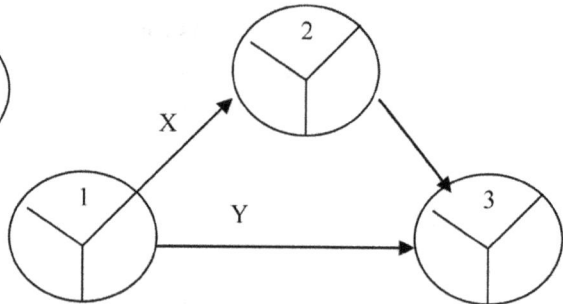

Example:

Activities for the project: 'Decorate Apartment'

Activity	Immediate Predecessors	Activity Duration (in days)
A	None	1
B	A	2
C	B	3
D	A	1
E	D	2
F	C,E	1

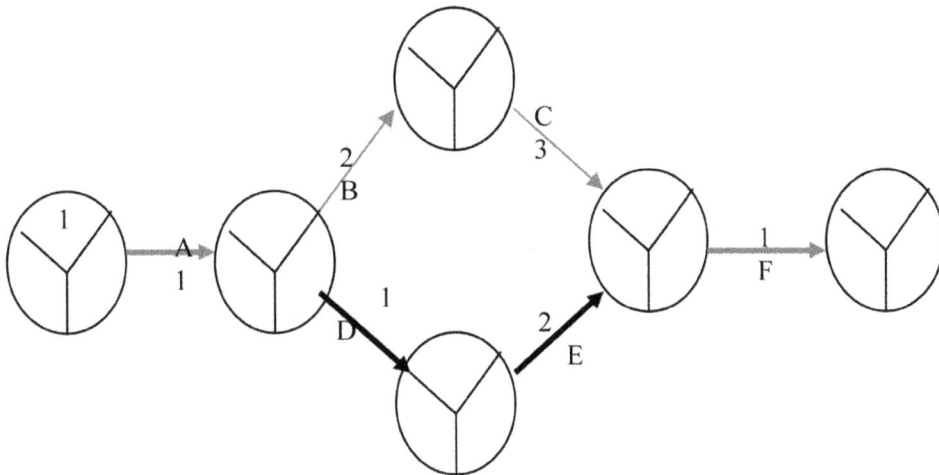

As mentioned before, the critical path is the shortest time in which the project can be completed. In the example above, the critical path is marked in bold and it can be seen that the shortest time to complete this project is 7 days. Once the critical path and shortest completion time have been calculated, it is possible to work out the earliest and latest start times and float. The earliest start time is the earliest time an activity can possibly occur if all preceding activities are completed as early as possible. Float is the difference between the earliest and latest start times for each activity. It shows where the areas of flexibility lie, that is activities that can be altered without affecting the overall time of the project.

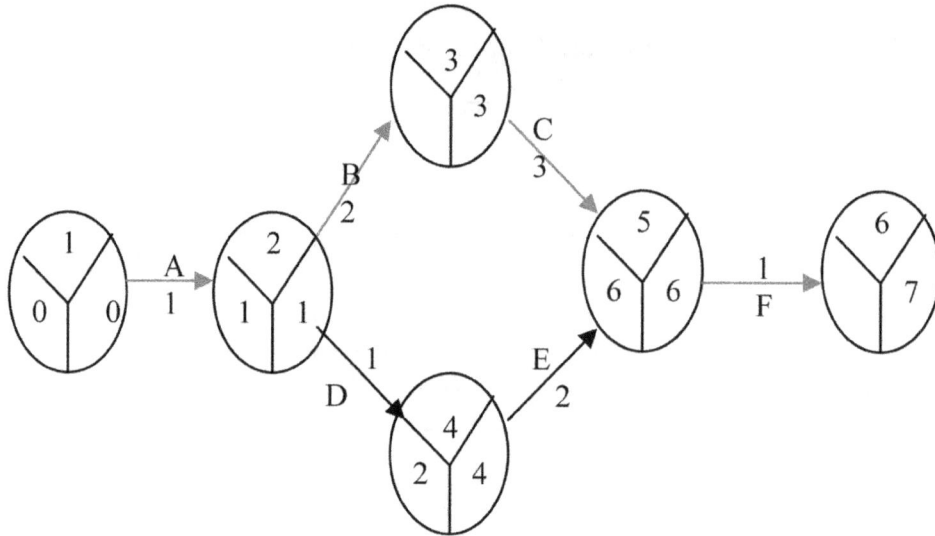

Note that for activities on the critical path, the earliest and latest start times are the same and the float is 0.

Firms can use this information to work out where changes can be made to the project. For example, if it were possible to complete activity E in 1 day as opposed to 2, it would make no difference to the total time for the project. On the other hand reducing task C from 3 days to 1/2 a day will make a difference to the project and will change the critical path to A-D-E-F

16.8: Using Surveys to Collect Data

The process of carrying out a survey consists of a number of stages:

- Establishing the objectives of the survey, that is what needs to be found out.

- How to conduct the survey, for example designing suitable questionnaires that are unambiguous and contain the correct type of questions, that is open ended or closed questions.

- Select a test sample. For example, for an opinion survey for a local shopping centre, the sample would be of local people only.

- Carry out a pilot test to identify any potential problems.

- Amend the questionnaire or sample in light of the pilot results.

- Recruit a suitable person or people as interviewers.

- Brief the interviewers on the survey objectives and methodology to be used.

- Print out the questionnaires and check that it is un-ambiguous and contains the correct sort of questions.

- Conduct the survey.

- Enter the data.

- Debrief the interviewers, record and store their comments for future reference.

- Analyse the data.

- Produce a report.

Once all the activities have been identified, the team need to decide how long each of them are going to take and identify the independent and dependant activities so that the task can be properly planned.

16.9: The Nash Equilibrium

The 'Nash Equilibrium' is a concept in game theory first described by John Nash. Nash was awarded what is effectively the Nobel Prize in economics for his work in this area. The 'Nash Equilibrium' describes an 'optimal' strategy for games where no such optimum was previously defined. If there is a set of strategies for a game with the property that no player can benefit by changing his strategy while the other players keep their strategies the same, then the resulting set of strategies and the corresponding scores form a Nash equilibrium.

Consider the following two-player game as an example:

- Both players simultaneously choose a whole number from 0 to 9.

- Both players then win an equivalent amount in pounds, of the smaller of the two numbers.

- If one player chose a larger number than the other, then he has to pay £3 to the other.

Example:

Player 2

	0	1	2	3	4	5	6	7	8	9
0	0-0	0-1	0-2	0-3	0-4	0-5	0-6	0-7	0-8	0-9
1	1-0	1-1	1-2	1-3	1-4	1-5	1-6	1-7	1-8	1-9
2	2-0	2-1	2-2	2-3	2-4	2-5	2-6	2-7	2-8	2-9
3	3-0	3-1	3-2	3-3	3-4	3-5	3-6	3-7	3-8	3-9
4	4-0	4-1	4-2	4-3	4-4	4-5	4-6	4-7	4-8	4-9
5	5-0	5-1	5-2	5-3	5-4	5-5	5-6	5-7	5-8	5-9
6	6-0	6-1	6-2	6-3	6-4	6-5	6-6	6-7	6-8	6-9
7	7-0	7-1	7-2	7-3	7-4	7-5	7-6	7-7	7-8	7-9
8	8-0	8-1	8-2	8-3	8-4	8-5	8-6	8-7	8-8	8-9
9	9-0	9-1	9-2	9-3	9-4	9-5	9-6	9-7	9-8	9-9

(Player 1 labels the rows)

So, if Player 1 chooses 9 and Player 2 chooses 5 then Player 2 wins £8
(£5 from Player 2's choice and an extra £3 for winning).

This game has a unique Nash equilibrium: both players have to choose 0. Any other choice of strategies can be improved if one of the players lowers his number. If the game is modified so that the two players win the named amount if they both choose the same number or otherwise win nothing, then there are 10 Nash equilibria (0-0, 1-1,…, 9-9).

If a game has a unique Nash equilibrium and is played among completely rational players (who also know that all players are completely rational), then the players will choose the strategies that form the equilibrium.

The standard example given in academic texts and one that is often examined on is the Prisoner's dilemma.

Two suspects are arrested by the police. The police have insufficient evidence for a conviction, and having separated them, visit each of them and offer the same deal:

- *If you confess and your accomplice remains silent, he gets the full 10-year sentence and you go free.*

- *If you both stay silent, all we can do is give you both 6 months for a minor charge.*

- *If you both confess, you each get 5 years.*

Each prisoner individually reasons like this:

- *Either my accomplice confessed or he did not.*

- *If he did, and I remain silent, I get 10 years, while if I confess I only get 5.*

- *If he remained silent, then by confessing I go free, while by remaining silent I get 6 months.*

- *Therefore in either case, it is better for me if I confess.*

Since each of them reasons in the same rational way, both confess, and get 5 years. But although each followed what seemed to be rational argument to achieve the best result, if they had instead both remained silent, they would only have served 6 months.

The Prisoner's dilemma has one Nash equilibrium: when both players confess. However, this is clearly inferior to both of the prisoners staying silent. This strategy, i.e. "both cooperate" is unstable, as a player could do better by defecting while their opponent still cooperates. This indicates one of the limitations of using the Nash equilibrium to analyse a game.

There are a number of more realistic and business based examples of the influence of the prisoners dilema. For example, if two countries are in the business of producing and exporting a product and the prices they attain for the good depends on the production level of not only their own source but that of the other country. Take the oil industry as an example. It may be that the following pay-off matrix is formed between two rival nations.

Nation 2

	High Production	Low Production
High Production	Nation 2 gets: £70 billion — Nation 1 gets: £70 billion	Nation 2 gets: £45 billion — Nation 1 gets: £100 billion
Low Production	Nation 2 gets: £100 billion — Nation 1 gets: £45 billion	Nation 2 gets: £80 billion — Nation 1 gets: £80 billion

Nation 1 (row axis)

If the table is thought through the values make sense. If both nations produce small amounts of oil, this pushes up the price per unit as supply is restricted. If both follow a 'High Production' option then price per unit decreases as supply is ample. However if the two nations choose opposing strategies then the nation that chooses to produce more oil reaps the rewards. The Nash Equilibrium in this situation is for both to choose the 'High Production' option, however if both nations worked together then the higher revenues in the bottom right section of the matrix can be achieved. This is one of the reasons for the OPEC organisation.

Self-examination Questions

1. Go back to the house prices data in Table 1 of this chapter. Produce both a bar chart and a pie diagram for this information. Which do you think is the most useful style to use?

2.   Find the critical path through the following set of activities.

Activity	Immediate Predecessors	Duration (in weeks)
A	(None)	2
B	A	2
C	A	3
D	A	3
E	B	4
F	C	2
G	D	1
H	E, F	2
I	G	4
J	H, I	1

3.   Find the Standard Deviation (s) and Variance (s^2) from the following data by filling in the blanks and using the equations stated in the chapter.

x	$\bar{x}$	$(x - \bar{x})$	$(x - \bar{x})^2$
4	11.25	-7.25	52.5625
7	11.25		18.0625
9	11.25	-2.25	
9	11.25	-2.25	
14	11.25		
14	11.25		
16	11.25	4.75	22.5625
17	11.25	5.75	

Chapter 17: EMPLOYMENT

17.1: Employment Tests

Unlike tests on machinery, which are made up of standard tasks, tests on employment are not so straightforward. For example, it is easy to test how effective a forklift truck is at carrying loads but it is much harder to test if a person will enjoy challenges. It is possible for firms to buy tests to use in recruitment from outside companies, but they need to make sure the tests are testing for the same types of people the firm are looking to recruit. One of the main problems with employment tests is that the employees can manipulate them, if they know that the management is looking for a certain type of person. Some appraisals such as aptitude tests have proved themselves useful for identifying a person's suitability for jobs such as computer programming. These tests however, are not so useful when testing whether the person has the social skills to get their ideas implemented. To overcome this problem, many graduate recruiters put their applicants through an assessment centre. This typically lasts 1-2 days and is made up of a series of tests and exercises, each designed to test some part of a person's ability. Typical tasks include aptitude tests and group decision-making exercises.

Other tests such as speeds in word processing may be thought to be more objective, although even here some care should be taken as they may show what can happen at the peak. For example, the test may show that someone has high audio typing records but does not show if that person could maintain that speed throughout the whole of the working week. They will also not show if the tests are naïve, for example, whether or not the same person can quickly adjust from one word processing package to another. This is important if, for example, the person is to be employed as a temporary worker who will be asked to work in many different offices.

Some simple tests have proved to be very effective and useful. For example, in the 1940s a test to show the level of a person's hand to eye co-ordination showed a very strong correlation with accidents involving London bus drivers. In general, performance tests such as these have been far more useful than other tests. Even if firms are convinced of the value of such tests, the important question is whether they are better than the existing methods of recruitment or promotion procedures or whether they should be used as a complementary measure.

17.2: The Management Grid - R. E. Blake and J. Moutons

R. E. Blake and J. Moutons suggest that there are various common management techniques, which managers can use when faced with problems. They published a book called the Management Grid in 1964, which explains some of these techniques. One suggested technique is to 'force the issue', that is to employ an attitude of take it or leave it. This perhaps has become more common now, as managers feel that they have more power than in an era of relatively full employment. One of the problems, this may cause is lasting bitterness among the employees, even if they accepted the decision at the time. For example, the bitterness caused by management attitudes in the 1930s lasted well into the post war era.

Another technique is 'smoothing the way', which is sometimes referred to as the country house style. The idea is that managers invite people to a country house for meals whilst trying to keep talks going. Whether this is successful or not depends partly upon the attitude of the parties. If it is thought of a sign of weakness, it may well fail since either party may strive to get more.

Another approach is to abide by the majority rule; this may mean taking the board's vote. In a trade union, there may now be little choice about this in some cases. This is because the government insists upon certain actions such as strikes being put to a vote. In many cases, however, people will use this method of approach when they think that the majority is on their side.

17.3: Compromise

This is common in many industrial disputes where both managers and workers have something to lose by holding a strike. In many cases, both sides will try to save face by giving certain concessions so that neither is seen to have lost in their dispute. The opposite approach is that of confrontation. This was perhaps seen closely in the bitter mining dispute in the UK in the mid-1980s, which lasted about a year. In some cases however, it may be a ploy. If, for example, there are several different unions in an industry, the one that is seen as most militant may be the one that attracts more members at the expense of other unions that are seen to be weak.

17.4: David McClelland (1917-1998)

In his book 'The Achievement Motive' (1953), David McClelland set out his ideas on motivation. There are three motivating factors that characterise the behaviour of managers and employees; these are need for authority, need for achievement and the need for affiliation. He suggests that some people see the need for power and get satisfaction from controlling other people. Such managers do not regard people as important in themselves but as a means to an end. Other people wish for affiliation and as such value relationships and wish to be liked. They would like to be known as someone who is easy to get on with. Other people see the need to achieve and they want to avoid being labelled a failure at all costs. Such people are frequently loners so they may take jobs that involve working as an individual. In many cases, they will take on jobs that are well within their capacities as this way they will always be successful. Mostly, people are a mixture of the three motivational aspects.

17.5: Personnel

While many firms study the assets that appear on their balance sheet, a few pay little attention to how much human capital they have. One exception to this is in professional football where a club can sell its players for a large transfer fee. There are also other exceptions to this so it is advisable for firms to look at human asset accounting.

17.5.1: Human Asset Accounting

Rensis Likert (1903 – 1981) suggested that there should be some form of human asset accounting. Some of the associates of Likert started doing this. R. G. Barry Company was one such associate, in 1968 it employed 1300 workers. It looked at its outlay costs, salary costs and others. It then looked at the costs that would be incurred, if the posts had to be refilled with staff of the same calibre. The logic of human asset resource accounting is that, in many ways, trained people can be treated like capital. For example, the costs involved in training a doctor are very high with seven years of training. From the viewpoint of the NHS, there is a choice between investing in medical training or investing in hospitals and other buildings. Human resource accounting can be used to make better use of the people currently employed as well as helping the organisation to see if human resources are a worthwhile form of investment. The same principle can be applied in many other situations; for example, the costs of running an education system in this country are very large. Human asset accounting can be used to establish if the money is being spent in the right way.

17.5.2: Job Security

Job security is important to everyone, particularly when unemployment is high. Some economically successful countries, notably Japan, started from a very low industrial base. Their success has been achieved through good management and high productivity from workers. Developing world countries should learn from Japan's example and employ managers who do not just think of workers as tools but as people who are important in their own right. The workers too will need to work hard and consider the company by not making excessive demands. This helps ensure that the employer is not priced out of markets by the intense foreign competition. For a long while, Japan was taken almost as the model economy from which other countries could learn. However, for the last few years Japan has been in a comparative recession. This may however have more to do with the Japanese culture of not wishing to spend money unnecessarily in their view on luxuries.

Many UK trade unions belong to the Trade Union Congress (TUC). They can be classified in different ways, such as the "white collar" unions, which include trained individuals such as teachers and nurses. An industrial union is made up of all the workers in a particular industry such as mining. There are also commercial unions, which deal with people in the financial sector. Sometimes trade unions find that there is a conflict between security of employment and other objectives. For example, if workers receive wages that are over and above levels of inflation and more than their productivity would suggest, it is likely that some unemployment will occur particularly if the firm is facing foreign competition. Similarly, whilst everyone wants pleasant working conditions, if too much is spent on comfort then this could also be at the expense of employment. On the other hand, pleasant and safe working conditions will help to stimulate greater productivity and this could in turn lead to greater security. It is therefore necessary to find a balance.

17.5.3: *Labour Management Relations*

All countries need skilled people. In the past, it was often claimed that productivity in the UK per head was low but this is not the case anymore. There are several possibilities, to ensure that a country attracts and keeps people that are more skilled in order to raise its productivity per head. The first is that the country must try to ensure that skilled workers are given incentives to stay in the country and not emigrate. The second is that trained people should be allowed to use their specialisms rather than to spend time on other matters. For example, doctors and nurses need to be given help so that they do not spend a great deal of time doing paper work. The same applies to other professions such as teachers, who should be able to spend their time preparing lessons and teaching rather than on other tasks. Training people is expensive but necessary and therefore, the longer people can be persuaded to work, the better it is for the country's economy. It is not only the young who need training, women returning to work after having children may need retraining, especially in a rapidly changing society. An example of this was the move in the early 1990s away from the use of typewriters to the use of word processors. An adequate system of payments, and other rewards, for qualifications help encourage people to gain them. For example, the cost of completing a degree in the UK is rising, leaving many graduates in debt. If it works out that a graduate will be little or no better off than non-graduate, university admissions may decline. Firms can also play their part by encouraging apprenticeships and giving scholarships wherever necessary.

Whilst it is impossible to list all the types of jobs that require training, it is possible to identify the training required for the different sectors: primary, secondary and service. In the primary sector agriculture is important. Most developing countries have a high proportion of their labour forces in this sector. In contrast, the percentage of workers in the UK employed in the agricultural sector is now less than 2%. Farmers need training in many areas including the use of fertilisers to ensure that they are used correctly or pollution and other side effects may result. They need advice regarding the best crops to grow, using high yielding varieties but at the same time being aware of the risks of soil erosion. There are modern management techniques such as input/output analysis that farmers may also find it useful to know about. This training could be received from agricultural advisers, who themselves will need to keep up to date with modern chemicals, pesticides and current developments, in order to give the best advice.

Forestry is another important industry in the primary sector, as it affects the whole world. Many countries have lost a great deal of their forests and there is concern regarding global warming and its effects. There are many consequences of global warming, including the flooding of low-lying areas, and a rise in temperature, leading to more deserts. Countries need to keep a balance between using wood as a fuel and ensuring future supplies. Forestry workers need to be trained to know when the ideal time for cutting down trees and replanting them is. They also need to learn to predict which types of timber they should be replaced with to ensure future supply. They may also need customary training in how to care for existing forests.

Another important industry in the primary sector is that of mining materials. Geologists are required to recognise the most likely sources of new minerals as well as being able to make the best use of existing mines. This may involve co-operation with multinational firms who employ experienced people, possibly from other countries.

Fishing and the conservation of the world's fish supplies is another primary sector industry. Fish are a natural resource but, as many countries have discovered, if too many are taken at any one time the fish will no longer be a renewable resource. Therefore, anglers need training in recognising what is best for the country as a whole. The use of fish farming is possible but it is very complex if diseases are to be avoided. There are particular problems of conservation of fish since by definition fish do not keep to national boundaries. The Common Fisheries Policy (CFP) of the EU has been fraught with bitter arguments partly for that reason. In 2013 the European Parliament voted to reform the policy to include measures to protect endangered species and ending the discards. These new CFP Rules will come into force in 2014 and there are hopes that these regulations will encourage the depleted fish stocks to recover.

One of the largest industries in the secondary sector is that of manufacturing. In order to expend a country's manufacturing base, production engineers need to be trained. These production engineers primarily need knowledge of modern management techniques including operational research. Operational research includes topics such as queuing theory, linear programming and network analysis. Queuing theory is used to establish the effects of changing the amount of machines on queues and delays in the production process. Companies have to find the correct balance, large amounts of equipment will be expensive to install but may give production that is more efficient by reducing delays. Production engineers are trained in such techniques so they can make the most economical decisions for the firm.

The manufacturing industry also needs trained economists and statisticians to predict future demand to interpret production data and other statistics. Financial expertise can also be a great asset to a company; unfortunately, many developing countries lack this financial expertise. Personnel managers are important in every industry; they ensure that the best people are hired for the job and work to reduce conflicts. They also assist others in personal development and find the best methods of training to enable the firm to get the most out of its employees.

The construction industry needs people trained in many disciplines including building, carpentry, decorating, and plumbing. This is achieved both through apprenticeships and through theoretical training to make sure old mistakes are not passed down. The construction industry needs architects to design the buildings, both to make it suitable for its intended purpose and pleasing to the eye. The latter aspect is a subjective one; it will be neither right nor wrong but will depend upon taste. Architects can also advise clients on which materials are suitable for the purpose and the climate. The architect's training also includes learning about strains and stresses on buildings. This is particularly important for a building in place prone to earthquakes or heavy storms or where there may be heavy loads imposed on floors, for example in factories or large-scale hotels.

In developed countries, the service sector is growing rapidly; it is the predominant form of employment. People trained in land-use planning are very important to the services sector, especially in developing countries where the population is growing rapidly. One of their main roles is to plan roads and transport links to ensure that there are adequate distribution patterns in the future and to improve the current infrastructure. As well as land-use planners, the services sector of developing countries needs transport specialists, in particular people trained in railway operations. Part of their job is to study the effects of different types of signalling systems and facilitate the purchasing of the most appropriate types of signals, rolling stock and locomotives. They also need to be trained to maintain the ones the country has. Likewise, countries also need bus operations specialists who can advise them on which buses to buy and how to maintain them to ensure that they will run well into the future. An example of excellent bus operations organisation is the state Transport Corporations Coach Service in Ghana.

Another important area of transport is shipping. Ports have changed drastically with the introduction and worldwide spread of containerisation and other forms of unit load, that is loading and storage as one unit. A good port system helps a country to improve its prospects for exports as well as reducing the costs of imports, which means that having a good port management system is vital. This involves technical operations, for example, training crane drivers and port administration. Shipping, in the case of ferries, is also a form of public transport. Shipping personnel need training whether they are crew or in administration. The industry also requires qualified skippers who are knowledgeable in the local shipping routes and laws.

The road systems in developing countries have improved but having well trained highway engineers to advise on suitable materials and maintenance is still a major advantage. Road haulage is another important means of transporting goods around a country. Whilst it is relatively easy to drive lorries, this is not the only pre-requisite for running a road freight business. People who understand the concept of costing of lorries and maintenance as well as having knowledge of regulations such as speed restrictions are vital. The ferry services on the short sea routes are also important. Again, people who have knowledge of shipping will be helpful here and on the international routes from the main ports. Shipping personnel need training whether as crew e.g. for masters certificates, or in administration.

The existence of a health service is important for all countries. Training doctors, nurses and ancillary staff to provide administration is essential to maintaining and improving the health of the people in a country. Not only is this an end in itself but if production also rises in consequence then the economy and the standard of living rise for the country as a whole. Other trained personnel needed to maintain an adequate health system include specialised staff that can make the best use of new and expensive drugs. At the other end of the scale, specialists are required to give advice on good diet and hygiene, for example, the drive in the UK now is to encourage people to eat five portions of fresh fruit and vegetables a day. They should be trained not only to understand the principles but also in the best ways to increase general health and in other areas such as helping to reduce infant mortality. Other people are employed to help increase the quality of life in a country, for example engineers who set up adequate water supplies to a town or village.

17.5.4: The Collective Bargaining Process

A typical collective bargaining process involves the management being able to say that because of difficulties within the last year, they are not able to offer more than X%. The trade unions will come back with X% is not enough to be considered a rise, taking into account inflation and will demand Y%. There would then follow some form of negotiation. Trade unions are usually unwilling to strike because their members will suffer as a result. Similarly, management does not normally want a strike because it means loss of production. In some cases in manufacturing, these losses can be made up after the strike, which means management and workers both have less to fear. This is less likely to be true in the service industry, where it is difficult to make up for lost production.

If the dispute is local (that is confined to one plant or factory) both management and trade unions will wish to settle the dispute locally if possible. There may be room for manoeuvre; for example, the trade unions may be able to offer management increased productivity by agreeing to the use of new machines. Alternatively, the workers may be willing to reduce their break time in return for a higher pay settlement. The management may increase the wage offer if productivity is increased by other means such as staff being willing to receive further training and perhaps gain qualifications. There may also be scope for more flexible working hours that could bring significant improvements to some industries, for example, shipping. Even in the tourist industry staff levels vary considerably throughout the year; there are peaks, which are difficult to anticipate and so staff flexibility could be an asset.

Changes in wages affect the supply of workers to different occupations. Demographic patterns show that the increasing number of older people also has an effect, for example, in 2001 there were more people over 65 than those younger than 16 for the first time ever. This has an effect on things such as the demand for carers for older people and the number of schoolchildren requiring teachers. Demographic patterns also show regional movements, usually from poorer areas to richer ones in many countries, not just in the UK. Immigration and emigration has an effect on the number of workers and the types of workers a country has. For example, many of the people working in the UK National Health Service will originally have come from overseas.

Government plans can also affect the supply of workers to different occupations. The present government wishes to have 50% of the relevant age group going to higher education. This will reduce the number of workers in the short run but it is hoped will increase the ability and skill of people in the longer term. Retirement conventions may also change, in the UK the retirement age has been 60 for women and 65 for men since 1909 but the Turner commission suggested in 2005 that this should be raised to 67 or 68. Pension schemes have a large effect on people's ability to retire early and the change in these is one of the reasons the government is considering increasing the retirement age.

The supply of workers is also dependent on the location of the firm, this in turn can be linked to the fact that house prices differ between the north and south of England. In general, it can be said that a person moving from the north to an affluent area in the south, for example London, will have difficulty finding suitable, affordable accommodation. There is a lack of teachers and nurses in the London area now because many cannot afford to live there. Social ties also affect where people choose to live and in many cases is a deterrent to moving, as most people do not wish to move away from their family and friends. Obviously, that does not apply to all, some people are quite happy to move away if it means a better job.

Many firms are moving from permanent contracts to short term ones for many of their employees. This has a major effect on the housing market as well as on the employees and the company itself. The employees are less likely to have the security of people who took their first jobs in say the 1950s or early 1960s and this makes it harder for them to get mortgages. It may also be difficult to get staff to have a long-term perspective since the future of their jobs is not guaranteed. It may have other effects on individuals such as having to arrange their own training programmes.

17.5.5: Human Resource Management

One of the key tasks of human resource management is to plan and estimate personnel needs. This includes anticipating how many employees will be required for the following year. This partly depends upon demand for the product and as demand is often difficult to predict so too are the staffing requirements. In the manufacturing industry, staffing is also dependent on how many operators are required to operate a machine. This again is difficult to determine because it changes with the introduction of new technology. Staffing levels also depend on how hard people work.

17.5.6: Recruitment

Another function of the human resource department is to create and run the company's recruitment policy. The aim of recruitment and selection can be described as identifying and attracting people who could fill positions and securing them as applicants. The first stages of this are deciding how many people are needed, in which roles and how to advertise the positions. Advertising options include word of mouth (asking existing employees), local and national newspapers and professional journals. The firm then needs to decide how it wishes its applicants to apply: by sending a CV or completing an application form or both. A well designed application form means that the recruiters can readily see the different qualities of the applicants and can compare them easily. However, more applicants tend to apply if a CV is all that is required.

17.5.7: Selection

How applicants are assessed and eventually selected depends on the type of position to be filled. Probably the most common method is that of a face-to-face interview. This may be carried out with one interviewer or a panel. The advantage of a panel interview is that several people may have a more balanced view. For example, it may consist of the head of a section, a personnel department representative and an outsider to see fair play. In some cases, there is more than one interview. For example in a large firm, the applicant will often have an interview with the human resource department and then a second interview with the section or department concerned. It is important to be fair in the selection process, for example, taking nervousness at an interview into account.

If the job requires it, it may be necessary to test the applicant's skills. For example, potential secretaries may be tested on the speed and accuracy of their typing. If the job is that of an operator in a factory, for example, it may be necessary to test the applicants' skills and prior knowledge of certain machines. Aptitude tests are frequently used to test an applicant's abilities in maths and English. In 2013 there was discussion about doctor's ability to communicate in English.

In other cases, psychological tests are used to determine the applicant's suitability. This is particularly relevant if the job requires sensitive, personal skills. Psychological tests include group tasks and role-playing exercises.

17.5.8: Promotion

Promotion is another aspect of human resource management. The firm first has to decide exactly what the job entails and what experience and/or qualifications are necessary for it. In some cases, firms advertise for people of particular age without considering why they are doing this. For internal promotion, people often take account of reports of present supervisors. In some cases however, these reports are biased according to whether the applicant is liked or disliked by his superior, especially when the applicant is more qualified.

17.5.9: Training

In some companies, the human resource department is also responsible for training. Taylor defined the following three phases of a systematic approach to training.

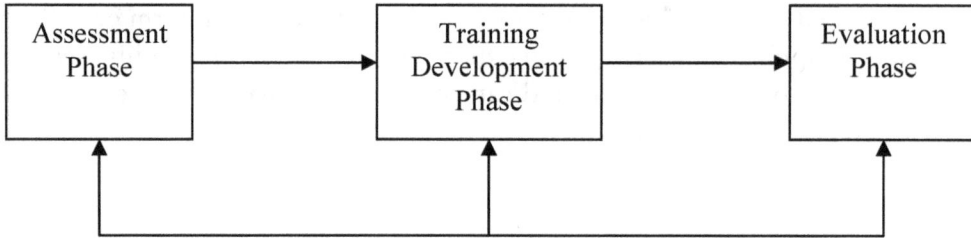

```
┌──────────────┐      ┌──────────────┐      ┌──────────────┐
│ Assessment   │─────▶│ Training     │─────▶│ Evaluation   │
│ Phase        │      │ Development  │      │ Phase        │
│              │      │ Phase        │      │              │
└──────┬───────┘      └──────┬───────┘      └──────┬───────┘
       ▲                     ▲                     ▲
       └─────────────────────┴─────────────────────┘
```

Companies spend generous amounts of time and money on training so it is important that they get it right. Once the company has decided whom it wishes to train and in what area, it then needs to decide how the training should be carried out. One option is external training, which includes distance learning. One of the advantages of outside training is that it may give a wider perspective but the trainers may not know the intricacies of the firm and its specialised needs. An advantage of distance learning is that the students can work in their own time and it is flexible. Some companies may encourage employees to undertake the training in their own time thus minimising time off to attend a course. If the student has to attend a course, the firm has to consider the loss of productivity and other costs. It then has to establish whether the benefits of having a better trained work force outweigh these initial costs before sending the employees on the course.

Internal training is an option if the firm is large enough to have its own specialist managers to act as trainers. One method of internal training is letting the trainee 'shadow' and learn from a more experienced employee. This has the advantage of being cheap but may lead to jealousies from the employees not chosen as trainers. Other problems include a lack of motivation or knowledge to train someone. In this case, it is always a risk that old mistakes are passed on.

Once the type of training has been decided upon, the next step is to choose a method of training. One such method is discussion, which is very common but needs to be managed and stimulated to produce the best results. For example, it is very easy for extrovert students to dominate the proceedings while quieter people do not get a chance to speak. The size of the room and group also need to be taken into consideration to ensure that all participants get the most out of it. Depending on the temperament of the participants, it may be useful to have someone to take notes from a group discussion that can then be shared after the event. It is advantageous if the 'secretary' is identified beforehand and imperative that he/she is capable of accurately reporting the ideas of the group.

Training may take place in the form of lectures, which is an efficient way of training many people at once. If the material is descriptive, it is good to back the lectures up with hand-outs. Having hand-outs means that the students can concentrate on what is being said without having to worry about writing it all down. A disadvantage of lectures is poor feedback, that is; the lecturer does not know if all the students understood. A good lecturer can judge the audience through other factors such as the attendance as well as their interest and concentration.

17.5.10: Sensitivity Training

Sensitivity training involves members of a group learning about their own behaviour and perceiving themselves as others see them, thus helping them to respond accordingly. It is commonly achieved through role-play exercises and has three objectives:

- To increase sensitivity, that is the ability to perceive how others will react to oneself

- To acquire diagnostic ability, that is the skill of assessing behavioural relationships between others and the reasons for them

- To gain the ability to change ones behaviour according to the requirements of the situation

Sensitivity analysis is a useful skill to have when participating in a group exercise or any face-to-face contact with another person.

17.5.11: Appraisals

A satisfactory form of appraisal is critical for a company; it helps employees understand what is expected of them and the ways in which their results are measured. A regular assessment of an employee's performance can highlight training needs, potential and improve their future performance. To conduct an appraisal, it is often customary to ask the immediate superior for a report. This can be either open ended meaning the superior just writes what he thinks about the employee, or closed meaning specific questions have been answered. One of the problems with appraisals is that they often only look at current performance not the employee's potential. For example, it may not pick up that the reason someone appears to be bad at their job is that the work is too tedious for their abilities. As mentioned before, an appraisal can identify faults that can then be rectified through training or otherwise. Similarly, if someone is very talented it may be possible to find a more suitable position for them where they can use and develop their skills further.

17.5.12: Transfers

It is important that the human resource department is involved with office transfers. Transfers occur for many different reasons, including moving to a better job, and personal ones such as wanting to move to a new area.

17.5.13: Redundancy

The human resource department may have to deal with redundancy at some point. There are many laws governing the practice of redundancy to ensure that it is fair. These laws affect how the company decides who will be made redundant. Most firms offer voluntary redundancy before they identify people who must go. Voluntary redundancy, as the name suggests, means that people volunteer to be made redundant in return for compensation. Sometimes the firm will help employees find another job if they have been made redundant.

Some firms try to manage using only 'natural wastage', meaning that they do not replace staff when they leave. This can lead to an imbalance of ages in the company; there may be more mature employees than young ones.

17.5.14: Staff Turnover

Staff recruitment and training is very expensive so it is better for a company to strive to keep the staff it has. If a company has a high staff turnover, it would be beneficial to look into the reasons for it and to try to solve them.

The first step is to work out why people choose to leave the firm. It could be because of normal reasons such as retirement, desire to get a better job, pregnancy, redundancy or dismissal although the latter two would of course be known to the management already. It may also help to look at the length of service. For example, if it is found that many people leave their jobs after only a few months, it would be worthwhile introducing a better induction scheme so new employees are not demoralised by frequent mistakes. Better safety training could also be included in the induction course, which would reduce the risk of accidents. If it were mostly long serving members of staff who are leaving, it would be a good idea to look into the pay scheme. For example, does it give any sort of reward for people who stay with the firm? Some firms pay employees a 'loyalty' bonus or have an incremental pay scale, which pays according to length of service.

17.5.15: Health and Safety

Another task assigned to the human resource department is to attempt to improve health and safety at work. Accidents at work account for a large number of days lost. A systematic study of accident prevention will involve surveying specific areas and tasks such as good handling and identifying and removing possible risks. This topic of health and safety also includes health and personal wellbeing of the employees. This can be improved by providing canteen facilities on site as well as exercise facilities on site or nearby to keep them fit and nourished.

17.5.16: Wages

The human resource department manages the various wage systems within a firm. One such wage system is job evaluation where people are divided into about five to nine main grades. People are allocated a grade using factors or a point system according to the degree of training required, the degree of responsibility taken for staff or for equipment and other factors such as responsibility for safety. A wage is then associated with each grade. Job evaluation is generally found in large firms rather than small ones. Another wage system is an incremental one where greater experience will command a higher salary. This is common in the financial institutions and is advantageous as it encourages the retention of experienced workers who add to the productivity of the firm.

As well as wages, the human resource department is also responsible for awarding bonuses. Bonuses may be paid for many reasons, some firms may pay employees an 'end of year' bonus reflecting the firm's profitability for that year. Bonuses may also be paid for safety although there is the risk then that accidents will not be reported for fear of losing the bonus. Firms may give leave allowances according to the seniority of the person and the number of years' service. This latter aspect may encourage staff to be loyal to the firm. Some firms may also give scholarships to people for training and it is now law that a firm must pay new parents maternity and paternity allowances.

It is common for white-collar workers (office staff) to have a set rate of pay per hour or per day. The advantage to the employer is that it knows the total expenditure whilst employees know how much they will receive. The disadvantage of time rates is that workers have little incentive to produce more and management has little control over total output. Piece rates, where the workers are paid according to the number of pieces they produce, give workers an incentive to produce more. However, there may be problems in paying piece rate if there are changes in technology or workers have to use different machines. Disruption in other parts of the factory can also cause productivity to fall, affecting piece-rate workers. Quality is another factor, in that a poor supervisor will permit a drop in standards in order to maintain productivity.

17.5.17: Performance-Based Pay

A common task for personnel managers is to assess the efficiency of different departments and to create a suitable system of wages. Often some employees are paid time rates and others piece rates, but they have not always been considered systematically. For example, production workers paid using piece rates may produce a high enough output to make more money than their supervisors do. Not surprisingly, supervisors resent this, especially as they tend to be older and more experienced and this may lead to people turning down the offer of a supervisor job. However, the piece rate workers may complain that when there are disruptions to the system, for example inadequate supplies of component parts, they lose money through no fault of their own.

One solution to this problem is to introduce a system of measured day work whereby a specified output is required in return for a guaranteed wage. This would overcome some of the problems mentioned by piece-workers. It would also give management an incentive to ensure that it maintains supplies. Another possibility is to have a system of job evaluation, whereby a person's salary depends on their responsibility for staff and equipment, boredom and degree of training required.

One way of establishing the efficiency of each department is to look at their productivity.

$$Productivity = \frac{Input}{Output}$$

From the above equation, it can be seen that productivity can be measured in terms of output per head. Care has to be taken here though, because a department with more modern machinery will appear to be more productive than one with older tools. Once productivity and performance has been established from the firm's departments it may be helpful to compare them with those in similar companies.

17.5.18: Flexibility

There is often conflict between having a flexible workforce and having the advantages of specialisation. In smaller firms there is always likely to be flexibility since, for example, the market stallholder will be a salesman, accountant and personnel manager at the same time. This is not usual in larger scale firms where there can be an over rigid division between workers. Sometimes there are problems in demarcation; for example, one group of workers may not be allowed to undertake routine maintenance work even if they are competent to do so. It is sometimes suggested that there should be less demarcation, for example, in a slack time on a production line some of the production workers might be able to perform routine clerical work or vice versa. Many firms use training to try to ensure that production workers' skills become wider so that if there is slack on one production line they might be moved elsewhere. From the point of view of the workers, there are many advantages of job flexibility such as job variation and being multi-skilled. Job flexibility does not just apply to production workers. A traditional train guard had the sole task of looking after the safety of the train. In recent years, however, this role has been extended to that of a conductor guard who checks and issues tickets as well as providing information to passengers and guarding the train.

As well as flexible jobs, many companies have the need for flexible hours. This is especially common in the transport and catering industries that do not just work from nine until five each day. It may also be possible to introduce flexi-time in some offices and factories so when demand is low, workers can go home, and when it is high they work longer hours. This makes sense, as there is no point having bored workers who are just sitting around twiddling their thumbs.

Job Training - Case Study

A lot of training is done 'on the job'. This works very well, especially in the case of new machinery being added to the factory or office. For example, if the company introduced word processors to replace electric typewriters, the typists will need to be retrained. This could be done through an external training company but they would not know about the existing work practices and filing systems. In-house training is cheaper and more convenient as it does not require the staff to leave the office. One problem with on the job training is that the worker required to carry it out is not usually trained to teach. This may lead to jealousy and resentment amongst his colleagues or with a manager who dislikes one of his sub-ordinates telling him how to use something.

In many cases, training on the job is neither systematically delivered nor subject to any form of appraisal. Again, this can lead to problems of resentment and inefficient training.

One way of checking the efficiency of the job training is by using a 'mystery' visitor. This is commonplace in the tourist trade where an employee, unknown to a particular office, poses as a potential customer. He or she then reports to management as to the conduct of the staff. For example, was the telephone operator efficient and courteous, was the receptionist helpful and was the office clean and tidy?

Activity:

Based on your working experience:

- Did you have a good personal relationship with your superiors? If "yes" what were the reasons for this? For example, was it that the person concerned was very helpful or that you made a special effort? If the relationship was poor, do you know why? For example, were you asked to carry out tasks that you were unsuitable for?

- Did your induction training help?

- Is there any advice you would give to the group about improving human relationships at work?

Self-examination Questions

1. Is there a conflict between a firm being both flexible and at the same time specialising in only one area?

2. What problems might arise if people had to work both on the production line and do occasional clerical duties?

3. Why might it be better to have a more flexible payment system? What would be the reactions of the trade unions?

4. What is 'on-the-job training' and why is it so common?

5. Why do few firms evaluate training?

6. How else could one evaluate on-the-job training apart from the example mentioned? (Hint: would it help if questionnaires were sent to staff?)

7. Why would firms want to evaluate their training?

8. What are the advantages and disadvantages of internal training compared to external training?

9. What qualities and qualifications might be specified in an advert to recruit workers for a large firm to fill various clerical posts?

10. Most firms carry out some form of induction training. What is the purpose of inductive training? Why is it important?

11. What is meant by the terms 'piece' rates and 'time' rates? What are the advantages and disadvantages of changing from the payment of piece rates to time rates in a manufacturing industry?

12. What makes a shop employee suitable to become a shop manager?

13. What are the problems in estimating the number of employees required in a manufacturing industry? In what ways, if any do these present different problems to those of estimating numbers of workers required in a large service industry?

14. What does 'human resource accounting' mean?

15. Why is it more difficult to measure the value of staff than the capital value of equipment? Is it different in principle?

16. Why might it be helpful for Governments to understand the concept of human resource management?

17. In what way is it possible to judge how much should be spent on training? Does the concept of human resource accounting help?

18. What is meant by performance tests? Why might they be easier to administer than personality tests?

19. What personality tests if any would be needed in the following cases?

    a. A lorry driver working almost entirely away from base.

    b. A systems analyst who spends most of his or her time listening and talking to managers about their computer needs.

    c. A personnel manager in a large electronics company.

20. i) What are the advantages and disadvantages of appointing people in the above 3 categories in the following circumstances?

    •   The firm has run into financial difficulties and if it keeps all members of staff there is the risk of going bankrupt in 2 years.

- The firm wishes to appoint a sales manager. The sales force has been successful in the last few years but some salespersons complain that other salespersons have not been passing on information, which would help them to develop the company as a whole.

- The firm wishes to appoint a new managing director and expand into new areas where it has not been successful before. So far it has concentrated on the UK market but it wishes to expand into the Swedish Market following Sweden's entry into the EU. The company with which it wishes to merge has a strong egalitarian tradition. (Treating people as of equal importance) and the managing director will need to take account of this.

ii) Do people keep to the same characteristics all the time or are most people an amalgam, of the types outlined above?

21. What are the consequences of this for managers?

22. What factors affect the supply of labour? Will the quality and quantity be different in the future?

23. Is the movement towards temporary contracts inevitable?

24. Can the UK ever return to an era of full employment?

25. What can be noticed about geographical mobility in the UK?

26. Could working from home become a major part of the employment market? What are the consequences of this?

27. Why is it very important for countries to increase the number of skilled people?

28. Why is it difficult to assess the number of trained people needed in a period of rapid change?

29. How far does the increasing use of computers mean that countries need fewer people who are numerate?

30. What are the different trade unions involved in the public sector? What are the main objectives of the trade unions?

31. What are the issues involved in the recent fire fighter strikes in the UK? Could either better management or better trade unions have avoided the dispute?

32. The number of males in full time higher education had risen from 519,000 in 2001-2 to 785,475 in 2011/12 and from 620,000 females to 935,920 in the same period. The number of people in full time postgraduate education had risen

from 86,000 males to 148,690 males and from 86,000 females to 160,735 female in the same period.

i) What would be the effect on:

a.   The quality of the supply

b.   The likely demand for labour because of this trend

ii) What further information would you require to establish your hypotheses?

33. What effect will changes in the age at which people leave school or further education in the UK have on the supply of labour?

Chapter 18: MOTIVATION

18.1: Motivation

Motivation is the study into why people behave as they do. In a human being, motivation involves both conscious and unconscious drives. Psychological theories account for a 'primary' level of motivation to satisfy basic needs, such as those for food, oxygen, and water, and for a 'secondary' level of motivation to fulfil social needs such as companionship and achievement. The primary needs must be satisfied before a person can attend to secondary drives.

18.2: Abraham Maslow's Hierarchy of Needs

In 1943, the American psychologist, Abraham Maslow published his Hierarchy of Needs. This identifies eight innate needs, divided into five categories. The idea is that once one set of needs has been met it is no longer a motivator. Maslow suggests that most people's needs follow this order but stresses that this is not true for everyone. For example, a very creative person may be driven by the need for creativity and self-actualisation without satisfaction of the lower needs. Differences in what motivates people affect the style of management needed.

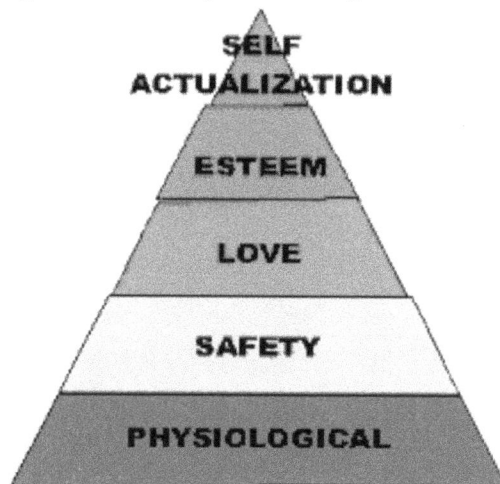

Figure 18.1: Maslow's Hierarchy of Needs

- **Physiological needs** include basic needs such as food, water, oxygen, warmth and sleep. In most developed countries, all jobs should allow for this although encouraging practices such as shorter lunch breaks, for example, can lead to people not eating properly which has the opposite effect.

- **Safety needs** include safety from attack, pain and danger and the need for orderliness and predictability. It can also mean job security and protection from the elements whilst working.

- **Love needs** include social desires such as friendship and a sense of belonging as well as the giving and receiving of love. Firms that make their employees feel like they are part of the team are more likely to retain them than firms which do not. The peer group is also important (see Elton Mayo's work)

- **Esteem needs** are made up of self-respect and the esteem of others. These include a desire for confidence, independence and freedom as well as status, appreciation and recognition.

- **Self-Actualisation needs** describe the development and realisation of ones full potential. This varies a lot from one individual to another. For example, people running kite shops are usually very interested in their hobby.

No single theory of motivation has been universally accepted, but a direction is evident. Formerly, many psychologists stressed the reduction of stimulation to its lowest possible level. An organism was thought to pursue that behaviour most likely to bring about this desired state of no stimulation. Many human physiological systems do in fact operate in this manner. Recent cognitive theories of motivation, however, portray humans seeking to optimise rather than minimise stimulation and are thus better able to account for exploratory behaviour, the need for variety, aesthetic reactions, and curiosity.

18.3: Industrial Psychology

Industrial Psychology is the application of various psychological techniques to the selection and training of industrial workers and to the promotion of efficient working conditions and techniques, as well as individual job satisfaction. This field of applied psychology first became prominent during World War II, when it became necessary to recruit and train the large number of new workers who were needed to meet the expanding demands of industry.

The selection of workers for particular jobs is essentially a problem of discovering the special aptitudes and personality characteristics needed for the job and of devising tests to determine whether candidates have such aptitudes and characteristics. The development of tests of this kind has long been a field of psychological research.

Once the worker is on the job and has been trained, the fundamental aim of the industrial psychologist is to find ways in which the job can best be accomplished with a minimum of effort and a maximum of individual satisfaction. The psychologist's function, therefore, differs from that of the so-called efficiency expert, which places primary emphasis on increased production. Psychological techniques used to lessen the effort involved in a given job include a detailed study of the motions required to do the job, the equipment used, and the conditions under which the job is performed. These conditions include ventilation, heating, lighting, noise, and anything else affecting the comfort or morale of the worker. After making such a study, the industrial psychologist often determines that the job in question may be accomplished with less effort by changing the routine motions of the work itself, changing or moving the tools, improving the working conditions, or a combination of several of these methods.

Industrial psychologists have also studied the effects of fatigue on workers to determine the length of working time that yields the greatest productivity. In some cases such studies have proven that the total production on particular jobs can be increased by reducing the number of working hours, or by increasing the number of rest periods, or 'breaks', during the day. Industrial psychologists may also suggest less direct requirements for general improvement of job performance, such as establishing a better line of communication between employees and management.

18.4: Jeremy Bentham (1748 -1832)

There are many theories of motivation. One of the first theories put forward was by Jeremy Bentham. He was best known as an 18th century philosopher and was a utilitarian, meaning he took the view that people have an enlightened self-interest and will act upon this. He believed that people would therefore look to find pleasure and to avoid pain in work as elsewhere. This leads to the stick and carrot approach, which states that people will work if the rewards are high enough or if the punishments for not working are severe enough. This can be related to the argument about Government policy in 2014 where the Government was trying to make it tougher for the unemployed not to work. In the 1950s when full employment was the norm, it could be suggested that the firms would have had to more in order to attract people or to give fringe benefits etc. We can also relate it to the disputes about high salaries particularly in the privatised industries where it is claimed that top managers such as the chairperson of BT will only work for such an organisation if the salaries are high enough.

18.5: F. W. Taylor (1856 – 1915)

F.W. Taylor is often said to be one of the main theorists of the scientific management school of thought. He was an industrial engineer. Prior to him, most people had been paid on an hourly rate but he introduced piecework as a system of motivating workers to work harder. He also emphasised work measurement as well as work simplification. He was also one of the earliest people to look at work-study. In particular, he looked at the size of shovels and discovered that people using different size of shovels achieved different rates of production. From this he and other writers have looked at the right size of machinery and equipment. Not only piecework was introduced but also other wage systems, which took account of productivity. He made the assumption that just as there were the right machines to do certain jobs so there were certain working methods, which were appropriate, jobs. He was concerned about how the constituent parts of the job could be looked at and how these tasks could best be made into a job for the workers.

18.6: Henri Fayol (1841 -1925)

Henri Fayol was one of the members of the classical school of management. He distinguished between management and supervision.

He suggested that management had 5 main functions:

1. **Planning** - examining the future, deciding what needs to be done and creating a plan of action.

2. **Organising** - providing the human and other resources and building the structure to carry out the functions of the organisation.

3. **Commanding** - maintaining activity amongst personnel and ensuring that the best performance is achieved of each of them.

4. **Co-ordinating** - unifying all activities from all departments to facilitate the smooth running of the organisation

5. **Controlling** - checking everything occurs according to plans, instructions and established principles.

Presently, planning may include a variety of different things. For example, it could mean looking at the whole cash flow over a number of months and arranging suitable methods of finance including short-term overdrafts. Organising might mean arranging a suitable method of allocating people to shifts and having adequate numbers of staff at peak times. Controlling could mean amongst other things financial control of both income and expenditure. Directing does not only mean telling people what to do but also motivating them. Co-ordinating may mean having a corporate plan so that different departments do not just do what is best for them or their department but for the organisation as a whole.

Fayol also suggested that established principles would help an organisation to concentrate on management theory. He listed 14 principles but emphasised that these must be flexible so that they could be adapted to organisation's needs. These are three of the principles suggested by Fayol.

1. Division of labour
2. Unity of command
3. The concept of span of control, which he thought should not be more than 6.

He also thought that flexibility of management was important for management and that managers could be taught to manage. This was in contrast to many people then and now who believed that managers were born not made.

There are several common assumptions made by the classical management theorists. These include the idea that people are only interested in material rewards, people are rational and that managers will act in the interest of their organisations.

18.7: Victor Vroom (1932 -)

Vroom assumed that people wanted things such as status and power. He called these things valences. If having a larger office and greater status was more important than a company car to a worker Vroom would say that he had a stronger valence.

If workers had valences and expectancies of achieving them then they would be motivated.

Vroom is perhaps best known for his expectancy equation. This says that people are motivated by how attractive an outcome is to them and how close they perceive themselves to be to achieving it. For example, if someone really wants the top position in a company but feels that he only has a 1% chance of achieving it, he will not be very motivated. However, if he wishes to become the head of department and has a 50% chance of achieving it this will motivate him more. This has been put in the form of an equation where F is the motivation to act, E is the person's expectation and V is the value of the outcome.

$$F = EV$$

18.8: Henry Ford (1863 -1947)

Henry Ford worked on ideas of specialisation, which is, training workers to work on minute tasks. He came out with the well-known phrase that customers could have any colour car they wanted as long as it was black, referring to the famous model T, and the first low priced car. To have different colour cars would have reduced the specialisation. Prior to this car making had been largely a craft occupation, with each car taking a long time. If you look at many of the early cars, they literally were horseless carriages with the same designs as in horse drawn vehicles. He persuaded large numbers of workers to come to his factories by paying $5 per day when the usual rate for similar jobs in other industries was only half this. He could afford to do this since production was so much higher.

18.9: Other Writers

Other classical school theorists include Lillian Gilbreth who developed operational research and Henry Gantt who developed the well-known Gantt charts.

18.9.1: Paternalism

The predominant management style in the 19th century was authoritarian, that is the assumption of owner managers that firms should have profits as the only motive and workers should do as they were told. Some firms, however, adopted a more paternalistic approach. For example, Rowntree the well-known confectionary manufacturer was formed partly because chocolate was thought to have some medicinal properties and partly to give employment and prevent people becoming alcoholics. Rowntree's influence can still be seen in York with the provision of parks and other leisure facilities. The conflict between the Rowntree style of management and that of Nestlé was clearly seen in the take-over battle for Rowntree in the 1990s. Similarly, another paternalistic company owner, Cadbury, built the model town of Bourneville near Birmingham for his workers. Titus Salt (a textile manufacturer and Liberal MP) built a complete town near Bradford called Saltaire which, with its well laid out streets and other features, was a model for town planning in the 19th century. Robert Owen in Lanark in Scotland owned one of the first paternalistic firms. He took the view that people who were looked after would work more efficiently. He compared them to machines, which need maintenance. He produced company housing and a company shop, which sold goods at fair prices.

18.9.2: Scientific Management

Perhaps the most important achievement of this school of thought was the introduction of trying to measure efficiency. This has traditionally been done, particularly in engineering firms, using work-study and work management. It has now been refined using management techniques such as operational research methods including queuing theory and critical path analysis. It is very much associated with F W Taylor.

This follows on in some respects from the utilitarian theory, which assumes that workers are entirely materialistic. It also assumes that workers are ill disciplined and therefore need threats. Some modern management writers query whether this is still relevant today where the bulk of jobs are white collar and increasing and the number of graduates is also becoming higher.

18.10: The Human Relations School

18.10.1: Elton Mayo (1880 -1949)

Elton Mayo was a psychologist and formed what is commonly called the human relations school. His work was carried out at the Hawthorne works in Chicago in the 1920s. At that time there were over 30,000 people employed there. The firm was concerned because productivity was low and dissatisfaction was high. This was in spite of the company being progressive for that era; for example, it had a company pension scheme. He had the theory that better working conditions would lead to greater productivity. It was therefore no surprise to him that when lighting was improved productivity increased. However, it was a surprise when lighting was worsened that productivity still improved.

There were also experiments with size and length of breaks. However, the employees (nearly all women) complained that too many breaks stopped the rhythm of work and therefore lowered productivity. When the experiment of extra breaks stopped, productivity still improved. The assumptions that were drawn at the time were that management taking an interest had led to the increase in productivity. Some later writers suggested that it was because the era was one of high unemployment and the employees feared that the management thought that they were doing something wrong and so their jobs were in danger.

18.10.2: F. Hertzberg (1923 -2000)

During the 1950s, Hertzberg followed on the work of the human relations school. He conducted surveys throughout the USA to find out what people felt most satisfied about in their jobs. He called those with the highest priority motivators and established that having a sense of achievement was a motivator for many people. A way managers can use this information is to ensure that they give people tasks that are complete rather than having very specialised work so that they never see the finished product. Whilst this has been done in factories such as Volvo, it could equally be applied in an office. For example, in some offices it is customary for people to draft out letters and then give them to a manager to sign. Occasionally this is important but in many cases, people would have more of a sense of responsibility and achievement if they type the letters, sign them and then send them out.

Another group of factors caused dissatisfaction if absent. Hertzberg called these hygiene factors as they serve to prevent dissatisfaction. Some commentators concluded that the hygiene factors were less important but this can be challenged. The 1950s in the USA was a time of full employment meaning factors such as security of employment were much less important. Hertzberg relied heavily on subjective comments that may not always have been true, for example, people may not like to be thought of as greedy causing money to have been downgraded as a factor. A further point is that ranking may not be very helpful since in extreme cases some factors may become very important. For example, if social relationships are usually good they may not be important whereas if there is complete friction between new colleagues they will suddenly become very important.

Salary
Job Security
Working Conditions
Level and Quality of Supervision
Company Policy and Administration
Interpersonal Relations

Hygiene or Maintenance Factors

↓

The Dissatisfiers

↓

Motivation and Job

↑

The Satisfiers

↑

Motivators or Growth Factors

Sense of Achievement
Recognition
Responsibility
Nature of Work
Personal Growth and Advancement

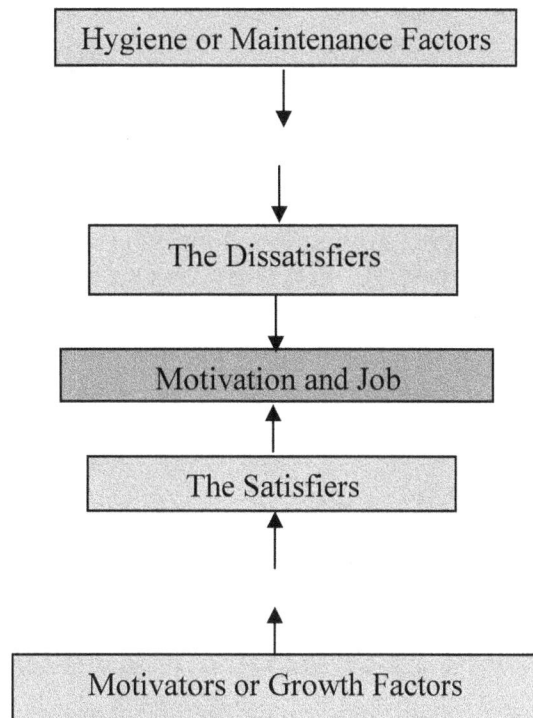

Figure 18.2: Representation of Hertzberg's two-factor theory

Gaining Recognition of Achievement
This is important because too many managers only comment if things go wrong and do not comment if anything is right. This can sometimes be an unfortunate by-

product of management by exception. Giving compliments and recognising an employee's efforts is one of the easiest ways to motivate them.

Interesting or Challenging Work

This is more difficult to achieve, it means allowing people to use their own ideas rather than imposing them. This is coupled with possessing responsibility for their ideas and the authority to execute those ideas.

Possessing Responsibility

This includes the availability of promotion, which can be hard to give. Some firms have a system of promoting only from within, which is not always helpful because of the smaller pool of available candidates. However, firms could often find training internal people or the next layer of management more beneficial than looking for someone with different skills. This is because internal people have an advantage in that they are already familiar with the procedures of the company, which would otherwise be time consuming to learn.

Growth and Development of Skills

A second group of factors, which Hertzberg called the hygiene factors, is also important. The first factor was the quality of supervision received by an employee. This is perhaps less dependent upon the management style and more to do with the quality of the supervisors. Unfortunately in the UK today it is still too common to find people supervising others who have not received any training (informal or formal) in the art of supervising.

Social Relationships

Social relationships can be helped by allowing people to choose to some extent who they wish to work with rather than imposing relationships upon them. It is also beneficial if the management realises the importance of such relationships and considers social skills when recruiting new people.

Security of Employment

This is becoming increasingly important as the early 2000s is in many ways an era of insecurity not just for blue-collar workers but also for white-collar workers.

Conditions of Employment including Holidays and Hours

Whilst many firms claim that they cannot manage with fewer hours, this is not always true. Surveys show, for example, that many of the people using computers cannot use keyboards properly, that is they cannot touch type. Training on this may well speed up processes and could reduce hours. Another way to produce more hours when needed is to run flexitime rather than a 9 to 5 day.

18.10.3: McGregor's X and Y Theories

McGregor put forward his theories of motivation in the 1960s. He suggested that there were 2 types of people;

Theory X assumes that people are lazy and try their best to avoid work at all times. From a managerial point of view, people will only work if they are coerced or threatened by punishment. This is known as the carrot and stick approach, meaning the two ways of getting a donkey to move are to bribe it with a carrot or threaten it with a stick. In full employment, money or benefits may motivate them as Theory X people tend to only be motivated at physiological and security levels. In a recession, they will be motivated by fear of unemployment. The individual will take little responsibility and will need close direction in the tasks that they do.

In contrast, Theory Y assumes that people find work inherently interesting. This may be assisted by measures such as job enrichment, enlargement or rotation. Theory Y people seek and accept responsibility and are motivated at all five levels. To take a Theory Y approach, the management has to create the conditions whereby employees can work to motivate themselves and achieve their own goals through those of the organisation. Examples of Theory Y in practice include sportsmen playing a game and the entertainment and craft industries.

In relation to the modern day it can be seen that X and Y relate partly to different types of jobs. For example, X is more likely to apply to routine jobs such as checking of invoices and the production line, which may need an authoritarian style of management. People who have more scope in their jobs and are motivated by their own or the organisation's successes are likely to work better under Theory Y practices.

The leadership style may also affect workers. Some people seem to like being told what to do and thus favour the authoritarian style. Other people favour being left to do things on their own without interference from outside that is they favour the laissez faire style.

18.10.4: Burns and Stalker

Burns and Stalker carried out a study of 20 industrial organisations in the 1950s. They concluded that there are two basic style of management, organic and mechanistic. The mechanistic style is more formal with vertical chains of command.

The jobholders are encouraged to be specialists and appointments are based on experience and knowledge. The organic style is less formal and is more appropriate to changing conditions. Jobs are more informally defined as there is a constant adjustment and redefinition of tasks. It is much more about teamwork. There is a network of control and communication, and technical and commercial knowledge is widespread throughout the organisation.

18.11: Job Grouping, Enlargement, Rotation and Enrichment

Few people now stay in one job for the whole of their working lives. There are many reasons for this. In a boom period, people move on to better jobs and in a recession they may well be out of a job. People also move for personal development. The job groupings that are used will depend partly upon common knowledge or skills. For example, to get a job in a factory, a basic knowledge of the machines used may be required. In the office world, a basic knowledge of the standard computer packages may be required. In other cases, there may be common aspects of the job, for example, many jobs may require a good telephone manner. To be effective, job grouping requires the use of job profiles.

Trade unions and professional bodies may wish to have demarcations since they fear for job security. Part of the reasons for the bitter newspaper dispute at Wapping with the Murdoch group of newspapers was that workers were expected to be more flexible which in turn lead to larger job losses.

Job Enlargement

Job enlargement makes a job bigger by increasing the scope and range of tasks that the employee carries out. For example, train guards used to be in charge solely of the safety of the train. Nowadays they are employed as conductor guards issuing tickets and giving information to passengers as well as guarding the safety of the train.

Job Rotation

Some jobs are inherently boring which means job satisfaction will only be obtained if there are a variety of tasks. For example in a perfume factory, people screwing on bottle tops used to do the job for a very short period (about 15 minutes) because it was so boring. For the rest of the time they would be doing a different task such as sticking the labels on the bottles or packing. Many people argue however that rotating every 15 minutes or so breaks the work pattern and causes disruption. Another use for job rotation is to train managers by giving them a taste for what each part of the company does.

The assumption behind job grouping, rotation and enlargement is that workers prefer variety. Obviously, this is not true in every case; workers carrying out routine tasks may not wish their jobs to be made more complicated or to be given more responsibility

Job Enrichment

Job enrichment makes the job bigger by extending it vertically by adding more authority and autonomy over the planning, execution and control of the job. It increases the complexity of the job and makes it more meaningful and challenging. Examples of job enrichment include:

- Giving employees tasks which challenge their abilities and make better use of their skills.

- Giving employees greater freedom over the scheduling and pacing of their work.

- Providing employees with the opportunity to work in self-managed teams with greater responsibility and minimum supervision.

18.12: Money as a Motivator

It is sometimes said that money will motivate people to go to work but not to work whilst they are there. This means that when people are looking for a job they will, other things being equal, look for the job with the highest wages including perks. Once they are there, however, if they become bored or demotivated they will not tend to work as hard. It can be argued that piece rates help people to work harder. Studies show, however, that workers often just set themselves a target for earnings and work only to achieve that target. It should be noted that it becomes more difficult to test this theory for top workers. This is because of the many fringe benefits they are often paid, for example, a company car, pension schemes, more holiday and cheap loans. Some of these fringe benefits may be related to Maslow's theories. For example, it can be argued that the use of pension schemes is related to the concept of security and the use of company cars (except by sales representatives) is related more to perceptions of status than need.

18.12.1: Fringe Benefits

Many firms offer canteen or restaurant facilities. In some cases, as with large factories in smaller towns there may be little choice where shift work is involved, as there are unlikely to be many places open at 2 am. In other cases, the canteen and restaurant are thought to be acceptable socially as a place where people can relax. If the canteen is subsidised, it is a good way of encouraging staff to eat adequately although many people in recent years have argued that they have the opposite effect and have caused obesity. Some firms have separate canteens or restaurants for different grades of workers. This is sometimes justified because workers do not wish to feel that they will be scrutinised by their bosses and that managers wish to have conversation about policies without being overheard by the workers. In other cases, the use of management restaurants may be used to entertain clients although the main purpose may seem to be to improve the status of managers.

18.12.2: The Use of Sports and other Recreation Facilities

Encouraging employees to keep fit has many benefits to the firm. As well as having healthier employees who take fewer sick days, exercise is a good way of stress relief so leads to happier workers as well. If the firm has a sports team, it brings people together and acts as an attraction for people to join the firm. If the sports team plays in a league, the name of the firm will often appear in local papers making it a cheap form of publicity.

18.12.3: Motivation and Promotion

Many people particularly those who are ambitious will work harder if they feel that it will lead to promotion. This has traditionally been regarded as more important to white collar rather than blue-collar workers but is not entirely true. Many people in the UK, in the days of long apprenticeships, put up with low wages at the beginning on the assumption that they would eventually get a relatively well-paid job. The phrase 'deferred gratification' means that such people are not just motivated by short term but by long-term prospects.

18.13: Cambridge University Research

This was published under the heading 'The Affluent Worker' in 1968. The researchers assumed that as workers became more affluent, they would adopt a more middle class life style. They suggested that since job satisfaction was often correlated with acceptance by a group, people would claim job satisfaction even if it were not the case. To overcome this problem they persuaded people to look at their current job compared with previous work experience. They used the terms extrinsic to refer to working conditions such as pay and intrinsic to refer to the details of the job itself. Even in 1968, earnings were the top factor followed by job security and work organisation.

When considering their evidence, it is important to look at the nature of the sample. For example, a sample comprising of the largest three firms may well be quite different from smaller firms that are often less formal and less mechanised. The Cambridge University sample would almost certainly have included car firms in which many people have tedious, boring jobs. People working in car firms will almost certainly be aware of the nature of the job before taking it on and they will not necessarily be representatives of the working class as a whole.

18.14: Management by Objectives (MBO)

MBO was developed by Drucker and Humble. It is based on two main principles:

1.   Efficiency depends upon clear objectives.

2.   Mutual agreement will help to motivate both superiors and subordinates.

Aspects of MBO

1.   Overall, corporate objectives should be created and communicated to everyone. This can be done as part of a corporate plan, for example, the former British Railways company created 5-year corporate plans, including their goals and objectives for that period. A corporate plan for IBM when it made large losses in the 1990s would have included turning the emphasis from selling mainframes to consultancy and developing other types of computers and software. Corporate plans may also specify profits, turnover and work force levels. Banks want greater security when lending money after recent debts so in these cases a corporate plan is even more vital. In the early 1990s, many commercial banks lost vast sums of money partly on lending to 3rd world countries but partly because money had been lent, for example, based on increasing property prices.

2.   Once the corporate goals and objectives have been set, the departments can create their own objectives to support the overall ones. Making sure the individual objectives support the overall ones is very important. If the subordinate objectives do not support the overall ones then the capacity of the plant, for example, would not be sufficient.

3.   Objectives may be set in numerical terms, for example, the number of patients treated by the NHS, the size of the budget, and the length of the waiting list. Within those objectives, other measures need to be taken into account; for example, hospitals need to consider recovery time in the time it takes to treat a person. From this it can be seen, that someone with a more serious condition is going to receive treatment for a longer time compared to someone with a minor injury. Other examples can be found in education; for example, a bright 15-year-old taking GCSEs would worsen the results for their year. This is because the statistics looks at the people in the relevant age group and ignores those who might take it at an earlier age.

Features of MBO

1.	The superior should assist rather than direct, meaning a positive involvement. From this, it can be seen that MBO may be hard to achieve in an authoritarian firm.

2.	Appraisal should aim to motivate not just to reward or punish. For example, if faults are found what steps can the firm or individual take to eliminate them? Likewise, if there are good points, how can the firm make the best use of them?

3.	Following the review, the objectives may need to be modified so there is a need for flexibility. In some cases, firms may have overestimated the ability of a group of workers to carry out certain task within a specified period. It will help if the firm will look at the objectives rationally and not just assume that any faults are the workers fault.

4.	MBO should be forward looking, that is looking at how the standards could be achieved in the future. This involves retraining.

5.	The emphasis should be on how the individual can help the organisation possibly leading to or following on from a promotion or transfer.

6.	It looks at the key functions of the organisation and ensures they continue to work effectively.

7.	The job description should be mutually agreed by the employee and the firm.

Self-examination Questions

1.	Is there an essential difference between supervision and managing? Does this difference apply only in the manufacturing industry or can it apply in offices as well?

2.	Would modern managers agree that there are only 5 functions of managers? If not, what other functions might they add?

3.	Should workers always be treated in a consistent way? For example, if someone was aggressive to his or her manager would it make any difference if they had been recently aggrieved or if it is their nature to be aggressive?

4.	What is meant by 'unity of command'? Is it compatible with delegation?

5.	What is meant by the term 'bureaucracy'? How far can any set of rules help to ensure that organisations are well managed?

6. In many industries little attempt has been made to teach managers how to manage. It has been assumed that if they have been good at their previous jobs, or if they have qualifications such as a degree or professional qualification they will be good managers. What are the merits and demerits of this point of view?

7. What are the basic assumptions of the scientific management theory? In which ways are they compatible with and in which ways do they differ from other theories of motivation?

8. What is meant by 'work-study'? Why has it been used more in factories than in the service industries? Does this mean that it is inappropriate for offices?

9. Are Henry Ford's ideas from the early part of the 20th century still applicable today for the car industry?

Chapter 19: COMMUNICATIONS IN ORGANISATIONS

19.1: Communications

When considering communications, the first things to think about are the objectives and goals of the organisation. For example in business, the objectives may include selling so many items during the year or achieving a particular market share. In order to achieve these objectives there are various strata of management, for example within a typical manufacturing company there is a board of directors, chief executives, senior executives, middle management, supervisors and operatives. The communications between them are often referred to as vertical. The chief executive passing on information to a senior executive would be a vertically downward communication whilst communication from middle management to senior executives would be a vertically upward communication.

Similarly, within the school structure communications from the head teacher to pupils will be vertical downwards whilst communication from pupils to the head teacher will be vertical upwards. In some cases, communication is passed on at the same level, for example from one student to another or from one teacher to another. This is referred to as horizontal communication. The same applies within a business; for example, a supervisor in the production department may need to communicate with a supervisor in the distribution department.

Some organisations are sometimes referred to as being a flat organisation if there are relatively few people at the top and middle levels in an organisation chart. The number of layers in the organisation may be referred to as the chain of command. In a school the chain of command might be from the head teacher to head of year, to another teacher, and then to the pupil. In this case the chain of command is four. The number of people reporting directly to one person is called the span of control. Therefore, organisations may choose a large span of control or a lengthy chain of command. The number of people one person can control will depend partly upon the geographical split. For example, an organisation such as Lonrho, which is spread across several different countries, may be more difficult to control than an organisation based solely in one country. The spans of control will also depend upon the nature of activities; for example, it is easier to supervise several people who are all typing or word-processing rather than if they are doing different jobs as in the general office. It may also depend upon the nature of the individuals; for example some people are much easier to supervise than others. The same features apply to a school or college where it is easier to supervise several teachers teaching similar subjects than if they are all teaching different ones.

Businesses are usually split either by function or by geography. The functional split can be clearly seen in the manufacturing sector where the various offices may be purchasing, production, marketing, accounting, personnel, distribution and general.

19.2: Functional Organisation

One of the advantages of a functional organisation is that most communication occurs within departments, for example, accounts staff will wish to communicate with other accounts staff. However, problems often arise with horizontal communication between different departments. For example, letters that are sent to an organisation, which refer to more than one department may well get lost between them.

19.3: Geographical Organisation

The geographical split of an organisation means that all functions may be controlled from one point though departments are in different geographical areas, for example, a factory manager may be in charge of all the processes within a factory. This may be sensible if communications between different branches are not for any reason difficult.

19.4: Informal Organisation

Whilst an organisation chart shows the formal organisation, in many cases there is also an informal organisation. For example in many firms, the secretary may be much more important than is shown on the organisation chart since he/she may well have access to considerable information. The secretary, in some cases will also have considerable powers of persuasion over his/her superior.

Similarly, people who are very experienced in their jobs, even if only in a junior capacity, may well have greater power than a newly appointed executive may. The advantage of the informal organisation is that it often represents the better use of talent. However, in some cases it may merely reflect the fact that older people will try to exert more power than their position or competence warrants.

19.5: Informal and Formal Methods of Communication

Within an organisation, there are both formal and informal methods of communication. In a school, for example, informal communication may well be a chat between the teacher and the student whilst leaving the school. Formal procedures may occur if a student has misbehaved in some way and has to see the head teacher. The advantage of the informal communication, which may not necessarily be recorded, is that it may well be appropriate. For example if someone has been doing something in a different way the head teacher may wish to find out the reasons for this behaviour without the student feeling threatened.

Regardless of whether communications are formal or informal they need to be effective. For example, formal procedures such as school reports or the comparable idea in business of a reference will only be effective if the person writing it has a genuine knowledge of the person concerned. Increasingly, it has become easier to record more written material using devices such as photocopying machines and computer scanners. In some cases, these communications have been written in either poor language or type of language that is not understood by the recipient. Similarly, if verbal communications have to be passed down the line there is a severe risk of distortion. This can be demonstrated by the children's game of Chinese Whispers. The players sit in a circle and whisper a message from one person to another. By the time the last person has received the message it is usually very different from the original. Whilst this may sound somewhat flippant, it is the same process in many businesses.

The appropriate method of communication has to be used. Probably the most common form of communication in offices in the UK today is E-mail. An email message, once written, can be sent to many people and/or saved for future reference. Most companies have 24-7 Internet access, so the cost of using E-mail is virtually nil even for messages being sent to different countries. Another big advantage of E-mail is that it is paperless. This saves firms money in stationary as well as in storage space. Documents can be sent as attachments in many formats such as a word-processed document, a program or an audio file. E-mail is not a perfect communication system and one of the problems associated with it is that E-mail can be used to transmit computer viruses. Virus checkers may be used but are not 100 % effective. Another problem with E-mail is that people receive so many of them a day that they do not have time to read every one properly. The danger here is that an important message may be missed. In this case, an important message is better off being followed up orally.

The advantage of oral methods of communication is that they are quick to use and instant feedback may be obtained. Oral methods include the use of formal and informal meetings both face to face and over the telephone. Committee meetings are quite common in most firms; by being able to see other delegates, it is often possible to judge their reactions even if nothing is said. These reactions are sometimes referred to as non-verbal communication or body language. The telephone has a similar advantage of speed but without face-to-face interaction, and there is more likelihood that communication failure will go unnoticed. Many firms have not only an external telephone system but also an internal one. One of the problems with a telephone service is that staff can misuse it. For example, they will use it for their own private conversations or, even on business calls, they may not be mindful of the duration, and therefore expense, of the call.

In a school, letters will not normally be used except for formal items such as appointing a new member of staff. Memos, the commonly used abbreviation for memorandums (short notes) are frequently used. The same applies in business. A memorandum will not have an address on it, but will merely say, for example, from Mr. X the head teacher to Miss Y the teacher. It would not end formally either but it should be dated. The advantage of letters and memorandums as with other written items is that a record is kept. However, the communicator does not know whether the message has been received or adequately understood and there may not necessarily be a feedback. Some letters therefore have a tear off slip, which has to be returned to the sender.

Where senior management wishes to communicate with large numbers of staff or with students, it may well use notice boards. For these to be effective they must be kept tidy and up to date. They are no good if there are personal adverts stuck over the top of important messages.

Another form of communication used for transmitting messages between different branches of a firm is facsimile copying. Facsimile copying is like having a photocopier at each end and was an improvement on telex in that it allowed the transmission of maps and other diagrams. Another advantage of facsimile copying and E-mail is that messages can be sent between countries and stored, meaning that the problem of differing time zones does not arise. This is obviously a problem when the telephone is used. However, facsimile copying can be seen as being more efficient than telex in that whole documents are transmitted and therefore there is less likelihood of transmission errors. Many modern facsimile copying machines have a delay device, which means that if they are not urgent that they can be sent in the off-peak hours when telephone charge is less. For most organisations, it is cheaper to send a page of text via a facsimile copier than to send it by letter post. Email has the advantages of fax in that different types of material may be transmitted very quickly. The material from a computer system may be transmitted without the need for printing out, which is necessary with most fax systems.

19.6: Barriers to Communication

One of the problems with many organisations is that there are barriers to the formal communication process. This could be due to a number of factors, including language where more than one is spoken in a country, and between countries. In other cases, even where people speak the same language, say English, there may be a problem of different accents and the same words may have a slightly different meaning in different parts of the country or world. For example, the word 'pavement' in the UK means the portion of the road where pedestrians walk but in the USA, it refers to the part where vehicles are driven. In some cases, messages can be distorted by jargon. If a sales representative tells a customer who is not used to computers that the speed of the computer is measured in megahertz or the memory in gigabytes it is doubtful whether this would be understood.

In some cases, status can act as a barrier. For example, employees may well be suspicious of employers and will naturally be defensive. In other cases, messages may be very vague, for example, students who have studied abroad have sometimes received a message to attend a particular college without realising that it is situated on more than one site. Confusion can also arise with firms, which have many branches.

19.7: The 'Grapevine' Effect

These barriers to communication lead to a 'grapevine' effect in an organisation. This refers to an informal line of communication, sometimes based on gossip. For example, if a firm intends to make people redundant, workers use the grapevine to pass on the message very quickly. This is obviously highly undesirable, because the information may not be 100% accurate and could cause a lot of unnecessary bad feeling. Another disadvantage of an office grapevine is that it can distort information more than the official channels. For example, details of a small argument between manager and worker may well become magnified as people tell their different sides of the story. If you have ever witnessed a road accident, you will be aware that different people seeing the same incident will have quite different opinions about what happened.

Occasionally the grapevine is helpful, for example, it can help managers and workers become aware of a possible conflict. The use of the grapevine to replace official channels can usually be minimised by better industrial relations and better formal communications.

19.8: Minutes

The term 'minutes' is used when reporting on committee meetings. Minutes report the business that has been completed during the meeting. They do not include accounts of the discussions that took place, but record any decisions such as votes taken. In some cases, they may even show the number of votes for and against the particular item. Minutes have to be signed by the chairperson and can be held as legal evidence of the proceedings although this is quite unusual. At the next meeting, it is customary for the minutes of the previous meeting to be presented and the participants have the opportunity to accept or object to them.

Textile Factory - Case study

As an expert in communications, you have been appointed to investigate communications within a large textile factory. Recently, productivity has fallen but it is felt that since nothing has changed significantly, then these changes in productivity could be attributed to poor communication. You have been asked to carry out your investigation in a systematic way.

Feedback

The first step when studying communication within an organisation is to look at the appropriate organisation chart to establish who reports to whom. In some cases, it may be instantly obvious that the span of control of certain managers is too large. For example, the managing director may have difficulties if he/she has several departmental managers reporting to him/her whilst carrying out other tasks. In other cases, it may be that the chain of command is too long and that messages from the production workers to the senior management, for example, never get through.

It is quite likely that a large textile firm works a two or three shift system. There are often communication problems with shift work because messages passed to workers on the first shift are not necessarily passed on to the second shift and third shifts. Many of the so called white collar workers, that is the office staff and top management, will not be there in the evenings. This means that if there are disruptions in supplies to the production workers, the shortage will not be noted and dealt with until the next day. It is also possible for workers and supervisors to evade responsibility if there are no top managers in the factory. Anti-social hours may also be a problem in that the evening shift may resent having to work when others are at leisure.

It might be sensible to introduce some form of joint consultation between workers and managers. If, for example, there have been rumours of redundancies or a possible take-over or merger, the workforce may be unsettled and unproductive. Under these circumstances the so-called 'grapevine' often flourishes. A good system of communications should be established to keep the workers informed. Some large firms use regular newsletters to give information to their employees. In other cases, a set of systematic notices on a notice board may help, provided it is kept up-to-date. Outdated information may give a bad impression and sometimes will lead to false information being received.

The firm also needs to investigate how well it communicates with its customers. It needs to find out whether customers are content with the products and services, and whether they have any complaints or suggestions for improvement. All this information can be very useful to a firm as it is much more expensive to attract new customers than it is to keep existing ones. Satisfied customers also provide free, positive word of mouth advertising for the firm. One way of gathering this information is to ask the sales representatives, as they have much more contact with them. The firm might also investigate whether it is communicating sensibly with potential customers, perhaps throughout the use of adequate advertising. It may also be worthwhile finding out why new customers come to the firm. For example, does it mainly happen through word of mouth or is it a result of a particular advertising campaign? Some assessment of how the customers react to advertising may also be useful.

Another communication channel to investigate is between the firm and its suppliers. Does the firm have one main supplier or several different ones? Does the firm build up strong relationships and have a few regular suppliers or does it use tendering for each order? Does it give its suppliers plenty of notice for orders or does it contact them with emergency orders that have to be delivered within a few hours?

Once the different channels of communication have been evaluated, it is important to look at the technology of the communications. For example, does the internal telephone system work adequately and are there enough lines? Are people trained in the use of telephone techniques? Do they spend a lot of time in conversation or on personal telephone calls rather than working? Likewise, do the staff members know how to send E-mails? Can they send attachments and do they have the ability to manage their received messages. Again, do they waste time sending personal messages instead of working?

Though email is increasingly popular, many firms still communicate using letters. This is especially if the documents are important and have been signed to make them official. IT is important to monitor how this mail is dealt with. For example, is it passed to the correct department and answered, if necessary, by the correct person?

Self-examination Questions

1. It is sometimes said that communication consists of stimulus and response. Is it true that all communications require a response?

2. How can management ensure that it receives feedback from information which is sent down the chain of command?

3. What problems do people on the shop floor find in trying to communicate upwards? How can management try to ensure that they get feedback to their messages?

4. Why are communications from the shop floor to managers usually much more difficult than communication the other way round?

5. It is sometimes suggested that far from having too little information, too much information is presented to most people. How, if at all, can management help to select the appropriate amount of information for the appropriate people?

6. What is meant by lateral communication? What communication problems exist between departments in a large organisation?

7. Why might the problems of lateral communication be more difficult in an authoritarian than a democratic organisation?

8. What are the major barriers to communication between managers and workers? How might these be overcome?

9. Why might communications in a Multi-national or Trans-national organisation be more difficult than in a national organisation?

10. In what ways are communications with customers more difficult than communications with workers?

11. What type of communication does a firm need to make with its suppliers?

12. What does the phrase 'selective listening' mean?

13. How far is it true to say that better communications reduces the risk of conflict within a firm?

14. How far does the setting up of committees help and how far does it hinder communications within a firm?

15. What is meant by the term 'grapevine'? Is it always unhelpful?

16. Why does the 'grapevine' arise?

17. How far does having trade union members on the board help to improve information transfer?

18. Why might annual reports be of some help to improve communication?

19. What is the advantage of having an in-house journal or magazine?

20. How far might suggestion schemes help to improve information transfer?

21. Is written information always better than oral information?

22. How far does modern technology help and how far does it hinder communication?

23. Why might the use of staff manuals help communication?

24. How far do manuals of procedure help to improve communication?

25. It is sometimes said that people are highly trained in their technical aspects, for example, accountancy, engineering and law, but are not well trained in communication. How far is this true? What are the possible solutions to these problems?

26. What is meant by the term 'span of control'? What is meant by the term 'chain of command'? Are there any preferences regarding the size of these?

27. What is meant by vertical communication? Why is vertical communication downwards often much easier than vertical communication upwards?

28. What is meant by the word 'jargon'? In what ways can it be an obstacle to communication?

29. Why are communications so poor in many firms when the availability of communication technology means that it so easy to communicate?

31. In what ways does the structure of the organisations help or hinder communications? What factors should firms take into account if it restructures itself?

Chapter 20: TRADE UNIONS

20.1: Who Joins and Who Does Not Join Trade Unions

If people are in one place, for example working in the mines, it is comparatively easy to persuade people to join a Trade Union because of peer group pressure and it is easy for officials to contact members. On the other hand, where employment is scattered as with small shops it is more difficult to recruit members.

In general, it is easier to recruit members from people in large firms rather than small ones. This may be because industrial relations are better in very small firms or that people in very small firms feel that national wage bargaining is inappropriate. Exceptions to this rule exist, for example, farm labourers who have often belonged to a relevant trade union.

Research suggests that men are more inclined to join trade unions than women. However, it is difficult to determine what affects the different membership ratios. One reason may be that in the past men were often engaged more in primary and secondary industries whilst women were more often engaged in tertiary industry. Another possible reason is that more women are involved in part-time employment and part time employees are less likely to become members of a union than full time workers are.

Blue-collar workers are more likely to join trade unions than white-collar workers are. This may be because white-collar workers feel less of a gap between themselves and the managers. It may also be because working conditions are often more unpleasant in jobs such as mining and working in the docks than working in offices.

The public sector has had a higher proportion of unionised members than the private sector. This is partly because local authorities and central government have usually been less hostile to union membership than the private sector. There have been some exceptions to this such as the ban on union membership at GCHQ (The intelligence headquarters).

20.2: Craft Unions

Craft unions cater for people with particular skills. Craft Unions have declined over the years because greater automation and improved technology has meant fewer workers are needed. An example is the case of the Associated Society of Locomotive Engineers and Firemen (ASLEF). Firemen used to work on the railways in the steam age to help the main driver. As train speeds and utilisation have improved, far fewer people are needed to carry the same number of passengers and the numbers of workers has decreased dramatically.

20.3: Industrial Unions

Industrial unions aim to represent all the workers in one industry. They make it much easier to avoid the problems of fragmentation of the trade unions when dealing with management. This fragmentation makes it difficult for the management to deal with all the trade unions representing one industry, for example, the car industry. It is also in the past when trade unions were often more militant and made leapfrogging claims more likely. This meant, as Lord Kahn (1905 -1989) pointed out, that if one union demanded 10% for its members the next union would probably demand 11% to try to impress its members that it was a better trade union.

Japanese managers often insist upon single union negotiations within their factories. Industrial unions have the problem that smaller groups within the industry, for example the managers and supervisors, are likely to feel left out. For example, supervisors in the mining industry for a long while resisted the calls to join the NUM (National Union of Mineworkers), which was until the 1980s a very powerful trade union for this reason. Similarly in the railways the NUR (National Union of Railwaymen) was by far the biggest trade union but clerical staff generally preferred to join the TSSA (Transport Salaried Staff Association). The NUR has subsequently merged with another union to become the Rail and Maritime Union.

20.4: General Unions

General unions, as the name implies, do not cater for one group of workers but for a very wide variety, they may be subdivided by functions or geographical area. Unite the Union (known as Unite) was, for a long while, the largest trade union and at its peak had about 3 million members. If a trade union such as the Unite is divided by function, for example, road haulage in one section, then trade union officials will have more expertise in that part of the industry. However, trade union officials will also have to cover a very wide area. If the Trade Union is divided by area then the officials have less expertise but have less travelling. The advantages and disadvantages of a general trade union are similar to those of a diversified firm. Communications may become more difficult because of the wide variety of workers involved. The union has the advantage that if one-occupation declines, other occupations are likely to increase and so the union will have a more stable membership.

20.5: Organisation of the Trade Unions

Unions have a president whose role is similar to that of the chairperson of the board of directors of a firm. At one stage, presidents might have been elected for life but nowadays there is legislation in the UK about elections of presidents. Other officials such as general secretaries also form part of the headquarters of the trade union. Most large trade unions also have regional branches, at this level some trade union officials may be paid whilst in smaller trade unions they will not be. Below this, there are trade union representatives in the relevant plant or office (branches). Within factories, there are 'shop stewards' who historically have had considerable power. In the 1960s, it was often thought that shop stewards had more power than supervisors and this lead to some bitterness within some factories.

20.6: Closed Shop

Closed shop means that trade unions have the power to insist that all workers must be represented by trade unions. There are two types of closed shops pre-entry and post entry. Pre-entry means that only existing members of the trade union are allowed to apply for jobs in the firm. This is in many ways comparable to professional bodies such as doctors where only doctors can carry out certain activities. Post-entry closed shops mean that once the person has been offered the job they are required to join the appropriate trade union.

20.7: Problems of Getting People to Participate

Many trade unions suffer problems in persuading people to take an active part in it. The main reason for this is that most of the posts in a trade union, including branch secretaries, branch chairperson and shop stewards are all unpaid.

There are also particular problems with persuading people on shift work to attend branch meetings. In some factories, workers are constantly on a particular shift pattern so that it is not too difficult for a shop steward working on pattern A to talk to somebody else who has the same pattern. In other cases, the pattern is haphazard which makes communications very difficult.

There are also problems of communications within large trade unions, which are similar to those of large firms.

20.8: Strikes

Strikes may be ostensibly about wages but it is often difficult to work out the original cause; pay may be a symptom rather than the problem. Trade unions may ask for higher wages because this is a relatively easy target to refer to but it may not be the main grievance of workers. Lack of motivation may be the underlying problem. Strikes in most countries have been centred in the coal, car and port industries. What are the reasons for this? For example the coal mining and port industries tend to be close knit communities whereas the car industry is renowned for boredom.

In the UK, traditionally most strikes have been short. Some have been so called wildcat meaning that they have occurred without the HQ of the trade unions being involved. An example of a wildcat strike is the strikes held in the summer of 2003 by British Airways Check-In staff over the introduction of a new automated clocking in process. In 2005, there was a strike by catering staff about the conditions of work at a former offshoot of BA. There were strikes in 2013 against the government proposal of performance-related pay for teachers.

In many cases, employees will wish to form trade unions. These will have both obligations and rights. Trade unions have an obligation not to withdraw their labour by striking or holding a picket line, if there is no moral reason for them to do so. On the other hand, the employers will also have a moral obligation towards the trade union.

20.9: Sympathy Strikes

Many trade unions have strong links with other trade unions. Historically, for example, the railwaymen and miners have been linked. This was partly because coal was a major product for the railways to carry and until the 1960s coal was used to power trains. When one union has come out on strike, they have often called on members of other trade unions to help them. In recent years, this has been outlawed.

20.10: Picketing

Picketing is another way in which trade unions try to achieve their aims. Trade union officials or other members of the trade union stand outside firms to try to prevent trade unionists and other workers working during a dispute. In some cases, they will prevent transport from getting through to the firm to deliver essential supplies or to remove finished goods. Most picketing has been peaceful but there have been occasions where violence has been used. Partly for this reason, there have been limits on the number of people who can picket factories etc at any one time.

20.11: Non-strike Measures

In many cases, trade unions do not call strikes but use overtime bans. The advantage of this from the trade union point of view is that it does not use up funds to pay to the strikers. It does however draw attention to members' grievances. Industries such as the railways, which run on overtime, will suffer losses if overtime bans continue for any length of time.

In the early 1970s, some trade unions used sit-ins. The most famous one was probably in the Upper Clyde shipyards.

20.12: Labour Disputes

Labour disputes occur from time to time, particularly in a period of either inflation or where workers feel that they are not getting a fair share for their work. They may occur for a number of different reasons and are not welcome to either trade unions or managers. Sometimes they happen because of unfair dismissal or poor working conditions or low rates of pay.

It is common tactics for trade unions to ask for a wage claim, which is above what they would hope to get whilst similarly management may offer a lower wage assessment than it could reasonably afford. Both sides may well be willing to agree on an intermediate figure. However the union will not wish to pitch a claim too high otherwise its members may feel aggrieved if the final figure is much lower than they had been led to expect. Similarly management, whilst wishing to keep down its costs will not offer a figure which is completely unrealistic if in a final analysis it can afford much more. However, much will depend upon the relative strengths of trade unions and management. For example, a very large firm dealing with a small group of workers is likely to have considerable power whereas a small firm will have relatively less power when confronted with a powerful trade union.

When a trade union cannot reach agreement with management, it may resort to a strike. These are generally more effective in a capital intensive rather than a labour intensive industry. This is because in a capital-intensive industry the firm is losing a considerable amount of money, at least in terms of opportunity cost, if the plant is not working. For example in the extreme case of an oil refinery nearly all the costs are fixed and will be payable whether employees are working or not. At the other end of the scale in a business such as a postal service nearly all costs are labour costs and therefore if there is a strike these costs will no longer have to be paid.

The cost of strikes to the community may be much greater than people calculate. For example a strike in a major industry such as post or transport may mean that other people cannot work effectively. In some cases there may be detrimental effects on the country as a whole as well as on employment, for example there could be an effect on the balance of payments. This could apply if there is a port strike and both imports and exports cannot get through.

Trade unions do not generally welcome lengthy strikes since their members will suffer hardships. This is sometimes alleviated when there are large-scale union funds although this is unlikely in some countries.

20.13: Trade Unions and Strikes

Trade union strikes are likely to arise for different reasons. For example, they may relate to the terms and conditions of employment. Therefore, both firms and trade unions might be under a moral obligation to try to work out a satisfactory compromise. The trade unions should not try to ask for more than they know that the firm could afford. Similarly, managers and trade unions might be able to get an agreement on productivity, which would be helpful to both sides.

20.14: Total Costs of Strikes to the Firms

The costs of strikes in the oil refining industry will be much higher than in the post office with its low fixed costs. Therefore, strikes in the oil industry will probably be settled more quickly since management will be aware of this. Allocation of work too can lead to problems. Deciding which workers should be allocated to what jobs can be decided amicably.

20.15: Work to Rule

Sometimes trade unions resort to a "work to rule", which may show up the ineptitude of many rules. For example, some rules may have been drawn up many years previously and will not be appropriate. If workers obey every single rule, the rate of production will slow down very considerably. Management should attempt to impose sensible rules in the first place.

20.16: Boycotting

Another example of union action is that of boycotting the product. (This is not necessarily confined to strike action, for example, sometimes people have boycotted goods from foreign countries for political reasons, notably in the past from South Africa).

20.17: Management Measures

Lock Out

The management has a number of weapons at its command. One of these is the lock out which is virtually the opposite of a strike. The management will state that if trade unions do not conform to some conditions then they will not allow the workers on the premises or, in some cases, particular trade unionists. The advantage to the management will be that it will save the costs of wages. The disadvantage will be the loss of production. Therefore, in capital-intensive industry management will tend to be reluctant to impose lockouts.

Strike Breaking

In some cases, management may break strikes by employing workers from outside the established work force. In some countries, this has included workers from other countries.

Lobbying

In other cases, the management will try to reduce the effectiveness of trade union action through intensive lobbying. For example, it may try to persuade workers that it cannot afford the wage claim by giving details of the relevant figures. Unfortunately, the figures are not always honest. In other cases, they may try to "play off" the different groups of workers.

As mentioned earlier neither responsible unions nor management wish to resort to strikes, lockouts, etc. if they can be avoided. Therefore, many firms have a series of grievance procedures. For example, conflicts often arise because of poor communication. Therefore, the firm should try to agree with the trade unions on a set of rules, which are both fair and, as far as possible, easy to understand. The agreement under collective bargaining may well specify what happens if there is a dispute about unfair dismissal for example any sanctions against individual workers. It may also, particularly if piece rates are being paid, suggest how grievances may be minimised. One of the problems with piece rates is that when new items are introduced or new machinery installed processes take longer at first. This causes a fall in production, and therefore wages, which makes workers reluctant to accept such changes. This could be covered by grievance procedures.

20.18: Discipline Problems

Discipline problems, for example, what should happen if people arrive late or do not obey orders, should be settled fairly. There is a danger that some employers may try to victimise employees. Trade unions may equally be bad and willing to strike because it seemed satisfactory at the time. Good firms, along with trade unions, will try to get disputes settled at several stages. For example, the supervisor and the trade union representative in the local factory will get together at an early stage of the dispute, to see if they can iron out any difficulties.

20.19: The Role of Mediation

Sometimes unions and management will try to find a mediator. Ideally, he or she will be acceptable to both union and management. The person concerned should be someone who is known to be fair and, if possible, has a wide view of the particular industry and, possibly, of the firm. The advantage of a mediator is that he or she may be able to see a middle course of action, which will help both sides. Sometimes this could take the course of suggesting a change in working practices. This could lead to greater productivity and therefore the firm could afford to pay more.

20.20: The Role of Arbitration

Arbitration is similar to mediation but in most cases, it means that the union and management will agree to whatever the arbitrator suggests. There seems little point in arbitration unless this is so.

In some cases, the government itself may intervene. This is likely to be the case in the public sector where the industry is of prime importance to the economy as a whole. Even where industries are no longer in the public sector, one might expect the government to take some sort of action.

20.21: Factors Affecting Wages

The price of the final product will affect potential wages. If we are selling something for £1000, then the wages cannot be greater than £1000 for any length of time. However, the price elasticity will also have an important effect. If for example wages rose by 20%, could we then sell the article for £1200? If the demand for the product is inelastic then it may be less important to hold down wages but if the demand is elastic, the firm will lose a large proportion of its sales if it cannot keep down its cost. The importance of wage demands may also depend upon whether all firms face the same increase in costs. Compare this with the arguments about the social chapter in 1996. The social chapter of the EEC laid down a number of conditions for workers and this included the maximum hours of work, minimum wage etc. If all firms have similar restrictions on hours then it will be easier to pass on costs than if only a handful has the problem.

20.21.1: Proportion

What proportion of the total costs are the wage costs? For example in the Post Office, postal workers and sorters' wages will be a high part of the total whereas in the oil refining industry it will not. This means that it may be easier for people in the oil refinery to obtain higher wages than in the Post Office.

20.21.2: Substitutes

Are there substitutes for a particular group of workers? This is not only other groups of workers but also capital e.g. the use of computers for printing as in former Fleet Street Wapping. We might note for example that multinationals may be able to substitute one country's labour for another. At the present time some call centre jobs in the UK have been transferred to other countries.

20.21.3: Level of Profits

The level of profits may affect wages. Generally, we would expect higher profits to lead to higher wages. In 2013, however there was controversy about the fact that Executives pay was increased whilst other workers pay increase was below the rate of inflation.

20.21.4: Inflation

Inflation may also affect wages since workers expect to be compensated if their cost of living increases. At one stage under a former Conservative Government the maximum wage increase allowed was index linked e.g. if inflation rose by 10% that would normally have been the maximum increase allowed.

20.22: How are Wages Paid?

20.22.1: Time Rate

Here total cost is known but not production levels or cost per unit. Time rates are common in white-collar jobs where traditionally people have been paid a salary, which is usually quoted as so many £s per year e.g. people will say that they are getting £20000 per year. From the employees' point of view, this is helpful especially where credit is needed. The importance of this may be seen in the housing market where one of the reasons for the so-called feel bad factor in the UK for the mid 1990s, was that contracts were no longer permanent. This meant that people could not easily obtain a mortgage. Even if they could obtain a mortgage, they were more reluctant to since there had been a great deal of publicity about houses being repossessed. The workers knew what their income was and this would help them to budget irrespective of the credit factor. They would not have to rush at jobs. It could also lead to reasonable flexibility since people going from one job to another would not be penalised. However, from the employer's point of view productivity is not known. In recent years however particularly in the privatised and public sectors, more emphasis has been placed on improving productivity.

20.22.2: Piece Rate

Here total costs are unknown but cost per unit is known. It has been common in many jobs especially on the production floor but it is not confined to this. For example, writers may be paid a fee for a piece of work, which is essentially piecework. Some typists working from home have offered word-processing at so much per page or 1000 words. It gives the workers the incentive to work harder and it is claimed that it is fair e.g. if someone works hard they will get more money than someone else who lazes around all day. There are however, a number of disadvantages, for example, workers may be inclined to skimp on the quality of work that they do. In the past it was not uncommon for workers to 'satisfice', that is they would hand in the same amount each week, to be paid the same amount even if the next week some of the items came back rejected. If we are working with valuable materials, it may lead to waste. More money may therefore have to be spent on supervision.

There are also problems when the management installs new machines. These will probably lead to higher productivity in the long term but in the short term, may lead to problems of lower productivity whilst the workers learn how to use the new machines. This is not necessarily a problem of the shop floor. The same problem could be faced when learning a new computer package. If the management keeps the same rate, the workers will lose in the short term but may gain in the longer term. There are also problems of payments for superiors. They may find that workers with high productivity may be earning more than them. Therefore, in these circumstances there is little incentive to become a supervisor.

20.22.3: Measured Day Rate

Here total cost and production is known and hence cost per unit. With measured day rate both sides get their wishes. The management also eliminated many of the so-called demarcation disputes whereby workers could only do a limited range of jobs. This has been common in many industries e.g. a qualified electrical engineer would not be allowed to put in a light bulb.

20.23: Dismissals

If workers are to be dismissed, then it is common for employers to give a minimum period of notice. This would generally increase according to the length of service. For example, if somebody has served their firm for about eighteen months, they might be entitled to one week's notice. If they had worked for twelve years or more they would normally be entitled to more notice. This is because people who have worked for one employer for quite a while may find it difficult to obtain suitable alternative employment. In addition, this would seem to be a moral obligation.

Employees who have invested their services for a considerable period should not just be dismissed on the whim of an employer.

Unless the person has done something drastically wrong, for example stealing from the organisation or perhaps being late every day, there seems little reason why employers should not give a satisfactory period of notice. It would generally be considered a moral, though not necessarily a legal obligation, when people are dismissed to give the reason for this in writing to the employee. There should also be a satisfactory method of trying to assess what had gone wrong long before there is a threat of dismissal.

20.24: Redundancy

Employers may also be under a moral obligation if there is likely to be redundancy or short term working to allow employees to take time off to look for alternative work. Employers may also be under a moral obligation not to dismiss people if they could find alternative work within the organisation. For example they may have too many employees in one area but may be able to find alternative work in another town or possibly even to be able to re-train people for another job.

A firm that was a major employer in the town, and was going to make a large number of people redundant, might give notice of this to the appropriate government minister. This would enable the government minister to consider whether there might be any possibility of assistance to the firm and relief from the effects of unemployment.

If the firm is likely to make people redundant, they should follow a fair system. This again may be a moral if not a legal obligation. For example, some firms would make people redundant on a last in, first out (LIFO) basis. This means that employees who have only been there a short while would be made redundant before people who have worked for the organisation for a longer time. This benefits older workers who may have family obligations as well as other commitments, compared to younger workers.

20.25: Fairness and Pay

It is important, particularly in a time of high inflation as the early 1980s, that wage systems should be seen to be fair in the following ways. Wage systems should keep pace with inflation particularly if the employees have contributed to greater profits through greater productivity then wages should rise. It may however be more difficult to convince employees of the opposite. If profits have gone down partly because of bad workmanship workers should receive less pay.

As we have seen there are different types of wage payments, payments by results, times rates and measured day work. Whatever the type of payment, there should be a degree of fairness if possible. Time rates would normally seem to be fair, but piece rates may be difficult particularly if there are differences in working conditions between one place and another. For example, if people are paid according to the number of pieces they have produced in a factory, and one factory had much better machinery than another, it would not seem fair.

20.26: Collective Bargaining

Within a firm collective bargaining is often important. Collective bargaining concerns the wages, including type of wages that might be paid for example time rates, piece rates, job evaluation, etc. For collective bargaining to be effective there must be good communication between the trade unions and management. They would need to ensure that they both mean the same thing by average earnings, for example do they mean the "take home" pay that an employee receives including overtime but after deductions of income tax or do they mean the gross pay? Collective bargaining not only discusses ordinary wages, but also overtime payments. It can also be used to discuss whether more money is given on special days, for example Sundays. It may also cover conditions for dismissal and grievance procedures. It is helpful if grievances are dealt with quickly, and at the lowest level, otherwise the grapevine may spread rumours, which may lead to greater hostility between management and workers.

Case Study

A factory situated just on the outskirts of a town decides to close because of lack of profitability, what will be the consequences?

Feedback

Many factories are noisy, cause pollution and may look rather ugly. People living near the factory but not being employed by it may at first sight, seem to gain from the closure. However a little bit of thought will show that this is not necessarily the case.

The government will probably lose, because the workers of the firm will no longer receive wages or salaries and therefore in turn will not be paying income tax. The government may also lose if there are taxes on sales such as VAT. However, this is not the full extent of the losses to the government. People who have supplied the firm with office equipment such as calculators and stationery will lose business. Therefore, the office equipment firm in turn, may employ fewer people and the government will lose their tax payments. Local market stallholders and shops that have supplied the workers with food and clothes may also lose some business and therefore they, in turn, may pay less tax. Other firms such as road haulers who have transported the material both to and from the factory may also lose business.

All of the above analysis assumes that there is no suitable employment for such workers. How difficult it is for the workers to find jobs depends upon their individual talents and upon their occupation. For example, qualified accountants within the firm may find little difficulty in obtaining suitable employment elsewhere, since there is likely to be a shortage of such people. Personnel managers have skills, which are readily transferable to other firms, though there may not be such a shortage. Production managers however, have often obtained jobs, which are highly specific to an industry and in some cases highly specific to the firm. They will often find it difficult to obtain suitable employment elsewhere. The firm, before making redundancies, will therefore feel under a moral obligation to try to find suitable vacancies, either within their organisation, or with other firms. They may feel a particular obligation to older workers, who have invested a large part of their working life to the firm. Generally, it is easier for younger people than older people to move partly because of social ties.

Social ties include the fact that people have their roots in the local town or village. Younger people are much more likely to move and in extreme cases to emigrate. The people in a town, as we have already shown, may well feel annoyed if the firm closes because their own employment prospects are lower, even if they have not worked directly for the firm. They will want to know what actions, if any, can be taken to bring in suitable employment. Many countries nowadays try to encourage large-scale manufacturing or other firms from overseas to come in. There may be disadvantages in this. For example, profits are transmitted to the country's home base. On the other hand, the firm will provide training. However, even if possible, such factories are likely to take a long time to establish. The government might also try to see whether there are alternative uses of land. For example, housing or other facilities such as shops or markets might benefit the community more than the original factory. The building of houses will give a boost to employment. In some cases, recreational facilities might be used.

Evidence from the London Business School has emphasised that irrespective of the type of ownership that productivity improved considerably in these sectors.

Case Study

In the UK, there is conflict between having a flexible workforce and having the advantages of specialisation. In some smaller firms, there is always likely to be flexibility since, for example, the market stallholder will be both a sales representative, accountant and personnel manager etc. at the same time. In larger scale firms however there may be an over rigid division between workers. Sometimes there are problems in demarcation, for example, one group of workers may not be allowed to undertake routine maintenance work even if they are competent to do so. It is sometimes suggested that there should be less demarcation, for example in a slack time on a production line some of the production workers might be able to perform routine clerical work or vice versa.

There may also be a need to vary working hours as in the transport and catering industries. It may be possible to introduce flexi-time in some offices and factories. There are sometimes suggestions that, apart from basic time rates, there is a need to have some sort of payment by results. For example in the service industries, this could include a commission on total sales to be split between the workforces.

1. What is meant by saying that there is a conflict between flexibility and specialisation?

2. What problems might arise if people had to work both on the production line and do occasional clerical duties?

3. Why might it be better to have a more flexible payment system? What would be the reactions of the trade unions?

Self-examination Questions

1. Does the classification of who is likely to join and not likely to join help to explain the decline of trade union membership in the UK from a total of about 12 million members in the 1970s to about 7 million in 2009-10?

2. How can the trade unions encourage more women workers to become involved in the trade unions?

3. Trade unions have not usually recruited unemployed people. What are the likely effects of this on trade union size and also their objectives if they continue with this policy?

4. What problems are there for the trade unions to organise in an industry where many workers are on shift work?

5. What is meant by the term "closed shop"? Why might pre-entry closed shop give a large amount of power to trade union leaders?

6.   Why is it difficult to persuade people to take an active part in trade unions, how far is it possible for trade unions to use incentives such as cheap insurance etc. to persuade people to join?

7.   What procedures should a firm follow before dismissing workers?

8.   When making people redundant some firms use a system of voluntary redundancy i.e. they pay a larger amount than the legal maximum in order to encourage people to leave. What are the advantages and disadvantages of this system from the firm's point of view?

9.   What is meant by the term "collective bargaining"?

10.   In some industries, there has been national collective bargaining to cover industries as a whole. What are the advantages and disadvantages of this?

11.   What are the different types of wage systems, and what are their merits and demerits?

12.   Trade unions may use a variety of different methods to try to influence the management. These include:

a) Overtime bans

b) Work to rule

c) Sympathetic actions (although these have now been outlawed)

d) Sit-ins

e) Picketing

f) Strikes

What are the merits and demerits of the above actions from a trade union's point of view?

Chapter 21: IMPERFECT COMPETITION AND MONOPOLIES

21.1: Market Structures

A market refers to all the individuals and firms who are willing and able to buy goods and services. Note that willingness must be complemented by ability to buy, therefore wishful firms or individuals (known as households) are not part of the market.

The market structure can be defined as the distinctive characteristics of a particular market. It is defined by four aspects:

1. Buyers and sellers who determine the demand
2. Product differentiation
3. Availability of information
4. Conditions of entry to the market and exit thereof

Buyers, Sellers and entrants: In economics, people who desire to buy or sell and have the capability to buy or sell constitute the demand. If firms and households intend to join a market then there is the possibility that the demand will change, as they may be perceived as added competition to the market. In a perfect market, no one firm or household can affect the price of products; this structure is maintained by the fact that there are many firms and households in the market.

Product differentiation: This characteristic looks at how many different goods and services are in the market. Differentiation can either be real or perceived; either way it plays a significant role in the determining the structure of the market. A market that has highly differentiated goods may have some firms charging more for the differentiated good as compared to other firms. For example, a BMW ActiveHybrid 7 is a highly differentiated good in that it has: safety, handling, comfort, environmentally friendly features etc. that make it different from other cars. The BMW is however still a car whose purpose is to transport people from place to place just as a Nissan Micra would. While a new Micra would cost less than £10,000 a new BMW ActiveHybrid 7 costs upwards of £66,000. The high product differentiation in the car market therefore produces a different market structure from say the fruit and vegetable market where an orange is an orange and prices will vary minutely from trader to trader.

Availability of Information: The market structure is highly dependent on information available about firms, households, goods and services. Take for example that you are in the village market shopping for vegetables. As you walk down the aisles you notice that the prices increase as you walk further East through the market, yet there are people buying at the most Easterly store, which has the highest prices. If you pull one of them aside and inform them that there are cheaper stalls on the western side of the market then, ceteris paribus, they are likely to walk westwards in search of the cheaper vegetables. Households and firms agree on a price based on the information available. In the case above, the people, buying at the easterly store may not have had the correct information about the prices in the market. Once the easterly-most stall realises that its buyers are leaving for cheaper stalls he or she may decide to lower the prices to compete effectively with the rest of the market. In perfect competition, we assume that we have the best information available regarding prices in the market. For perfect competition to exist, therefore, people must have the same information throughout the market. When information is unavailable, those who have the correct information tend to use the information to make profits.

Conditions of entry and exit to the market: This refers to the ease with which households and firms can enter a market. For example, it would not be easy to enter into the banking industry because there are certain minimum funds that you must have to do so. The barriers to entry refer to any requirement that gives an advantage to those already in the market over those who intend to enter the market. If there is a situation where those who intend to enter the market cannot do so because of the entry fees, patents, licences, experience or even access to a natural resource; we say that the market has high barriers to entry.

21.2: Types of Market Structures

The market structure of any market can be defined using the four characteristics discussed above. The market structures represent a continuum between a market where prices are determined by the firms and households collectively, to the other end where prices are determined by either a household or an individual.

This can be illustrated as follows; the arrows indicate the direction of increasing competition.

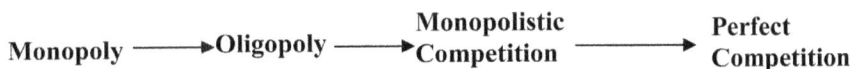

Monopoly ⟶ **Oligopoly** ⟶ **Monopolistic Competition** ⟶ **Perfect Competition**

21.2.1: Perfect Competition

In a perfectly competitive market, there are many buyers and sellers such that none of them can influence the price of the market. These buyers and sellers are known as 'price-takers'. For example, in a village market there could be 50 unrelated orange farmers and about 100 buyers. The fair price of the oranges will depend simply on the demand there is for the oranges. If the 100 buyers demand more oranges then the 50 sellers may increase the prices and vice-versa. Other things being constant (in economics 'ceteris paribus') the prices will be determined by the market rather than either the buyers or the sellers. This is known as perfect competition. Other characteristics of a perfectly competitive market are that all the buyers and the sellers have the same information regarding the market condition. For example, all the buyers know where the cheapest sellers are and what their prices are. There are no barriers to entry in a perfectly competitive market and anyone can enter or leave the market at will and can do so as many times as they please.

The product differentiation is also minimal and buyers both perceive and know that each of the products is similar to the next and therefore price variations for the same product cannot exist. A perfect competition is utopian and rarely if ever, exists. Even in markets that we would expect to have perfect competition we find that monopolistic tendencies and other inefficiencies still exist.

21.2.2: Monopolistic Competition

This market structure occurs where the barriers to entry are relatively low; anyone can join these markets. For example, one can start a plumbing business with minimal capital. In this sense, the market can be perceived as a perfect competition market where you would expect that firms and households are price-takers. However, in a monopolistic competition there is strong product differentiation. Monopolistic market structures have developed rapidly with the development of technology. Technology allows firms to differentiate their products and this differentiation offers the firm a competitive advantage over other firms in the market, such a firm can set higher prices for its goods until other firms catch up with innovation and reduce the premium they impose on their products. For example, in 2002 mobile telephone companies that included cameras with the phones enjoyed the innovation and the resultant higher prices for such phones. Today almost all mobile telephones have cameras and the prices of mobile phones has come down.

Monopolistic competition like perfect competition has many buyers and sellers and prices are more or less set by the market unless where a firm is enjoying a product differentiation.

21.2.3: Oligopoly

A large number of players, either buyers or sellers guarantee that none can force the other to take prices that they deem unfavourable. An oligopoly is characterised by a few supplier firms, which are in direct competition with one another. This means that they make pricing, and other decisions depending on the pricing decisions of their competitors or even anticipated pricing decisions. Oligopolies are common in very developed economies because they are generally very large firms that have developed dominance in a certain market, they have either forced smaller players out or have bought them up to reduce competition from them. The oil industry dominated by a few international companies is an example of an oligopoly. In this market, there are huge players such as BP/ Shell, Texaco, Esso and so on. Their pricing decisions while lately heavily influenced by Middle East politics is also influenced by the pricing decisions of oil firms.

A duopoly is a special type of oligopoly characterised by the presence of only two firms. Two dominant firms may decide to collude while still competing with each other. Oligopolies come into existence much like monopolies; the barriers to entry into an oligopolistic market are usually prohibitive. For example, the capital outlay required to set up an oil-drilling company that distributes petroleum products worldwide is out of reach for many. A second barrier is that the products are so differentiated that anyone who wishes to join the market might find that there is almost no room for innovation and he or she cannot therefore out compete the incumbent market players.

Oligopolies have been known to collude and form a cartel to control the prices that they offer to the market. This is however illegal.

21.2.4: Monopoly

On the other side of the spectrum from perfect competition is a monopoly. This is where there is only one producer or supplier of a good or service. In a monopoly, the producer may set the prices for goods in the market without regard to the buyers' intents. This is especially true where the goods are necessities and their demand does not vary with the prices (price-inelastic demand).

Monopolies arise where there are formidable barriers to entry. If you own the only oil well in the world, for example, then you would automatically have a monopoly develop from that. Monopolies can also be created through mergers and acquisitions where one firm buys up all the competition and merges with the existing firms to create a monolithic firm that dominates the whole market. Such mergers may be disallowed by the law in most countries.

Another reason why monopolies arise is patents and copyrights. A patent may stop other firms from investing in a certain innovation, as it is the property of another firm. Such a patent turns the market into a monopoly. Heavy product differentiation by a dominant firm also means that entrants find that they cannot gain innovative advantage over the incumbent.

A monopoly is said to be a price-maker if it dictates the price of its products to the market.

An imperfect competition is a situation where the sellers or the buyers rather than the market determine or significantly influence the prices in the market. An imperfect market will occur where there is few or just one producer. The few producers can collude to control the price or just simply set high prices for their products knowing that that there are no alternatives. If such a good enjoys an inelastic price demand, (this means that the quantity demanded of a commodity does not alter with changes in the prices of that commodity, usually such commodities are necessities). Then consumers will buy at whatever price is offered.

Imperfect competition therefore gives rise to monopolies. A pure monopoly is one where there is only one firm producing all the goods and therefore faces no competition. The economist's definition of a monopolist is 'the sole producer of goods or services for which there is no substitute in the eyes of the consumer'. This means that the consumer for different reasons cannot find in the market an equivalent substitute.

Water companies are a good example of monopolies, since there is no substitute for water. The monopoly held by the water companies became even more apparent in the summer of 1995 when many water companies restricted their supply because of the very hot summer. There were disputes about the efficiency of the water companies since in some cases as much as 30% of the water supply was lost through the piped system.

A pure monopoly more often than not arises because of the nature of the resources that are required to produce goods. For example, the supply of petroleum is dependent on the availability of oil wells, and unless you have an oil well, you have to buy the oil from those who have oil wells. This causes a natural monopoly due to naturally occurring resources. In defining a monopoly, care must be taken to define it within the context of its occurrence. A monopoly can be defined as such if there are no logical substitutes to its product. This means that if you were defining a monopoly a very large area of definition would mean that there are very few monopolies or in a very small geographical area, almost every trader is a monopolist.

21.2.5: *Monopsony & Oligopsony*

A monopsony is akin to a monopoly. The only difference is that instead of there being one producer or seller, there is only one buyer. For example, a single employer in a small village may be a monopsony where the villagers are looking to sell their labour for wages. In such a situation, the employer may refuse to pay the fair market wage rate. Another common monopsony has come to be with farmers who have to sell their produce to the already oligopolistic supermarkets. The supermarkets dictate the prices.

21.3: Effects of Market Imperfections

A perfect market is one where the prices are set collectively by all the players in the market rather than a few buyers or sellers. An imperfect market is characterised by prices that do not reflect the true value or cost of production of the goods or services sold.

A monopoly is characterised by the sale of a low outputs at very high prices. A monopoly therefore under produces as it does not have to increase production to break even; it simply increases the prices. A second problem posed by monopolies is lack of innovation, as the firm is not forced to modernise, differentiate or innovate to compete successfully, simply because there is no one to compete against them. A monopoly does not have to perform extremely well to survive, on the contrary, it needs to just produce something to sell, this means that the firm will be very inefficient and will tend to misallocate resources.

Another problem that may arise is deliberate misinformation that can be used to cover up the inefficiencies in the market. A perfect market is characterised by the right information being available to all the agents (buyers and sellers) at the same time. In order that a monopoly can continue to exist, it may invest in distorting the truth about availability, cost of production among other things further increasing the cost of producing the goods.

Either way the biggest problem posed by monopolies and other market imperfections is that of increased social injustice.

21.4: Dealing with Imperfect Competition

As much as we would prefer that markets were perfect and we were informed rather than confused through excessive advertising and differentiation as to the true value of a product, in reality markets are imperfect. Many solutions have been proposed and implemented. The following section discusses these solutions:

1. **Direct government intervention:**

Governments in most countries and even economic regions have created bodies that oversee the operation of oligopolies, monopsony, and monopolies. Some of these organisations have been mandated to recommend that certain monopolies be demerged or others be disallowed from merging.

In the USA, the powerful anti-trust laws that prevent monopolies and encourage competition were enacted after a series of debacles. Anti-trust laws do not target monopolies per se but the incidents where the monopoly is seen to gain unfairly at the expense of other competitors. While mergers can increase the efficiency and productivity of companies by creating economies of scale, the problem arises when merging is meant to stifle competitive innovation and lower the welfare of consumers by increasing prices without increasing the value of the products. Two statutes form the basis for the interpretation of laws governing anti-trust cases in the USA; these are Sherman's Act and Clayton's Act. Sherman's Act (1890) forbids contracts, combination, or conspiracies in restraint of trade and monopolising behaviour. Clayton's Act (1914) strengthens Sherman's Act by including problems of mergers, interlocking directorates, price discrimination and tying contracts.

In the UK, a special body has been set up to deal with anti-trust issues. The Competition Commission is an independent public body established by the Competition Act 1998. It replaced the Monopolies and Mergers Commission on 1 April 1999.

The Commission conducts in-depth inquiries into mergers, markets and the regulation of the major regulated industries. Every inquiry is undertaken in response to a reference made to it by another authority: usually by the Office of Fair Trading (OFT) but in certain circumstances the Secretary of State, or by the regulators under sector-specific legislative provisions relating to regulated industries. The Commission has no power to conduct inquiries on its own initiative.

The Enterprise Act 2002 introduces a new regime for the assessment of mergers and markets in the UK. In most merger and market references the Commission is responsible for making decisions on the competition questions and for making and implementing decisions on appropriate remedies. Under the legislation which the Act replaces, the Commission had to determine whether matters were against the public interest. The public interest test is replaced by tests focused specifically on competition issues. The new regime also differs from the previous regime where the Commission's power in relation to remedies was only to make recommendations to the Secretary of State[7].

The Competition Commission like its USA counterpart is not against monopolies per se or large organisations rather it investigates unfair trading practices.

2. Countervailing measures

These measures may be put in place by the agent who is disadvantaged. In case of a monopsony where there is abundant labour and few employers, or as in our earlier case, one employer, the employees may form Trade unions to countervail the negative effects of the monopsony.

Farmers who find that they are not receiving a fair price for their products from monopsony and oligopolistic supermarkets may decide to form a farmers' cooperative to distribute their produce.

3. Competition from abroad

Some monopolies and oligopolies can be broken by the invitation of powerful competitors from abroad. This means that suppliers will not only have few people to sell to and consumers can have a choice of other products. International firms also increase the innovation and competition between firms therefore improving the welfare of the consumers.

4. Education and Sensitization

Consumers who are targets of advertisement especially in a monopolistic competition where the differentiation is pronounced need an impartial, government or voluntary educational body that helps them make decisions and therefore avoid hyped up products that reduce their welfare.

Information is also key to improving the competition because innovatively differentiated products gain market share while poor products are discovered and lose their market shares.

5. Lowering the barriers of entry

To reduce the incidents in which monopolies and oligopolies are developed, the government can help small and medium sized businesses compete by offering funds for research and development, tax breaks and even contracts.

---

[7] Excerpt from the Competition's Commission website.

This will enable the firms to survive in markets dominated by oligopolies and monopolies.

We have looked at market imperfections, at how they reduce consumer welfare as well as human competitive innovation. The section that follows looks at the technical analyses of market imperfections.

21.5: Technical Analysis of the Effects of Competition on the Market.

As we have already seen, a market structure is determined by the number of agents in that market, the ease of entry and exit, the level of product differentiation and the amount of information available to the agents.

1. Perfect Markets Analysis

Starting with one extreme of the spectrum; perfect competition where there are many agents, agents have perfect information, product differentiation is minimal and there are minimal barriers to entry, then we can say that the agents in this market are price-takers. This information can be represented graphically as follows:

Quantity Demanded at Price P1

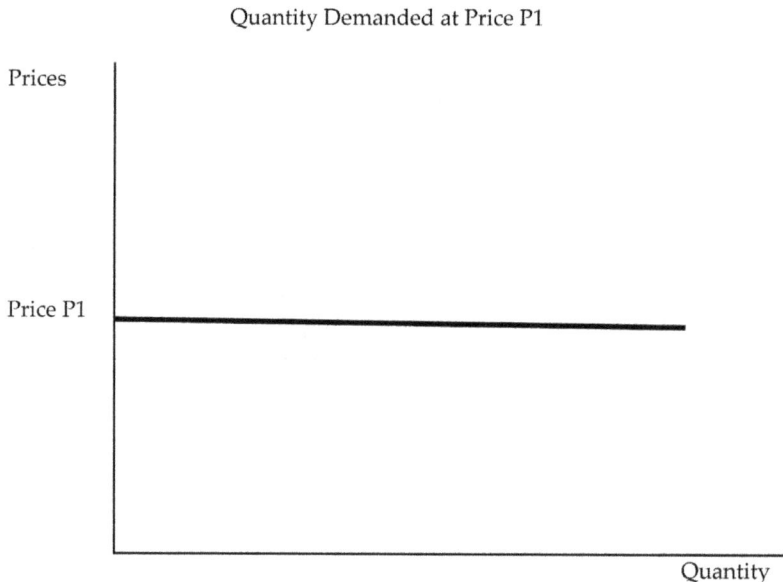

Prices

Price P1

Quantity

Figure 21.1

At price P1, the supplier can sell an unlimited quantity of goods without changing the price because this is the equilibrium price. This equilibrium price is determined by the demand and supply of goods by the agents in the market. In perfect competition, the market forces of demand and supply determine prices. The buyer will only offer the price that they are willing to offer and that which maximises their welfare.

In figure 21.2, the Pe is the equilibrium price. Any prices higher than Pe reduce the amount of goods that buyers are willing to buy therefore the quantity demanded falls to Q2. However, at price Q2 suppliers are willing to supply more so that they can enjoy the higher prices. An increase in supply means that there is more competition from the suppliers, some of the suppliers then lower their prices back to Pe, the equilibrium price, and buyers buy at equilibrium price Pe. Suppliers selling at P2 find that they can no longer sell and therefore the whole market gets back to its equilibrium point. (Qe, Pe).

This mechanism only works in perfect competition, which demands a large number of agents in the market at the same time, the same, correct and timely information, the entry barriers to the market are minimal and that the goods are sufficiently similar.

The Equilibrium Price and Quantity Demanded

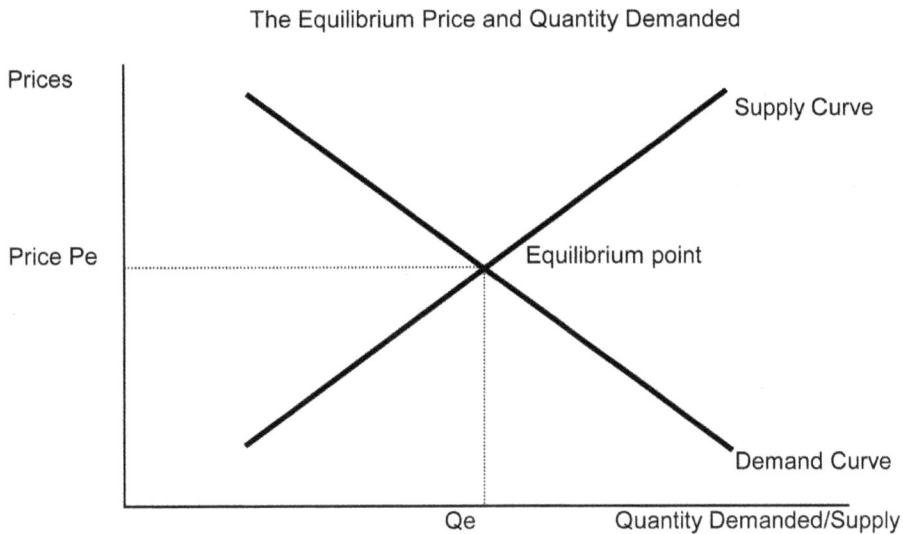

Figure 21.2

Changes in prices from the equilibrium cause disequilibrium in the market, which is corrected by the activities of the agents. Therefore, the perfect market is a self-correcting mechanism.

The Equilibrium Price and Quantity Demanded

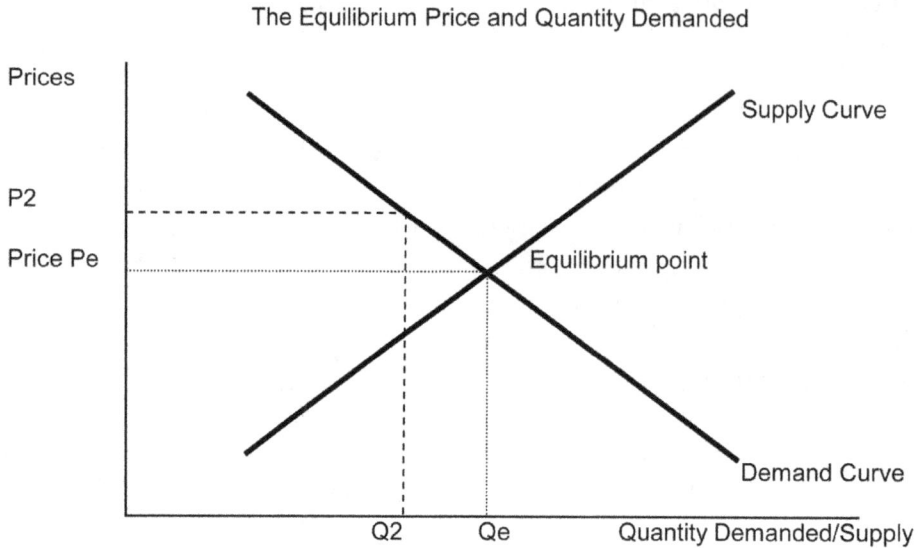

Figure 21.3

As we have already, established perfect competition is difficult to come by. The rest of this chapter discusses the effects of monopolies, monopolistic competition, monopsonies and oligopolies to the welfare of the consumer.

2. Monopolistic Competition Analysis

Monopolistic competition occurs where the barriers of entry are low and there is a firm in the market enjoying a monopoly status. As a result, other firms join the market to enjoy the supernormal profits generated by the monopoly market. This leads to many firms joining the market and becoming very innovative in that market such that they enjoy a supernormal profit when they introduce their innovation, until another firm produces a superior innovation.

Figure 21.4, depicts the market before when only one firm is operating within it and enjoying supernormal profits.

Supernormal Profits of Monopoly

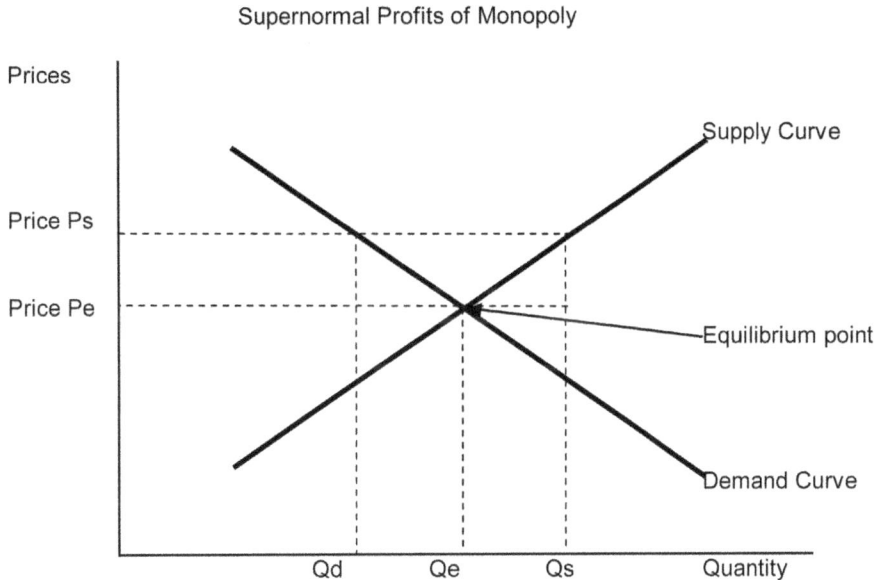

Figure 21.4

In a monopoly, the supplier is only willing to supply at price Ps, but at price Ps, the buyers are demanding the the quantity Qd. However, the markets reach an equilibrium quantity at Qe. If the good that is a monopoly is essential such that people have to purchase it regardless of the price.

The firm therefore makes a profit equivalent to difference between Ps and Pe for each unit they sell. This supernormal profit is what attracts other players to the market. When other competitors come into the market however, this extra profit is whittled away until we return to the equilibrium point as shown in figure 21.2.

Self-examination Questions

1. Explain the four aspects used to classify markets.

2. Why is it important that governments intervene to right the imperfections of the market?

3. Discuss the advantages and disadvantages of having a powerful monopoly in naturally occurring monopoly such as the supply of water.

4. Discuss four approaches you may adopt to deal with market imperfections.

5. It is difficult to analyse the behaviour of oligopolies, why is this and why might it be important?

Chapter 22: MARKETING

22.1: Introduction

The Chartered Institute of Marketing defines its subject as 'the management process responsible for identifying, anticipating and satisfying customer requirements profitably'.

The basic idea behind marketing is that to succeed an organisation needs to satisfy and please its customers. If this is achieved, they will provide the firm with additional custom. In exchange for this custom, be it payment in money, donation or trade, the customer receives a product or service that satisfies their needs. It could be said that marketing is the matching function between businesses and consumers. Unfortunately, customers' desires change all of the time so businesses must be responsive to these and adapt their approach. An example of this situation is the decline in the sales of audio tape players. Firms had to adjust to this decline by offering what the customers wanted; CD players. Marketing departments must continually reassess their approach to discern whether it is effective or not. The American management theorist Peter Drucker (1909 – 2005) may have said it best with the following statement:

'The aim of marketing is to make selling superfluous; to know and to understand the customer so well that the product or service fits him/her and sells itself!'

It is sometimes said that marketing aims to sell goods to people who will come back but with goods which will not. This means that if people are satisfied with the goods or services that they have bought then they will tend to become repeat customers. This can be very important in various markets where people have to buy items regularly, such as grocery shopping. It is also important in the clothing and footwear industry, as many people become loyal to particular brands, small shops or chain stores.

22.2: Two Different Perspectives

Traditionally most business organisations first manufactured goods or created services and then tried to find a market. In modern society however, many firms have realised that there is a need to operate the other way round. In other words, management needs to be 'market orientated' rather than 'product orientated'. A market orientated firm questions what the market wants and tries to provide it, at a reasonable profit. This not only applies to manufacturing but also to services such as transport and banking. There is no point in running an airline service from one country to another that few people wish to go to. Product orientated goods and services can still be successful in the modern market. One of the most famous in the last 20 years has been the introduction of 'Post-It Notes' by 3M. The 'not-so-sticky' glue on the back of these re-usable notepapers was created accidentally when 3M scientists were working on a new highly adhesive glue. By 1999, there were 600 different products in the Post-it range sold in over 100 countries.

It is often very difficult to find products or services that are solely market or product orientated. In the Post-it Note example above, the adhesive was discovered but they still had to find a use for it, a market need. In the same, way once an un-catered market has been identified, then a product must be designed to meet the need. Adapting an existing product in a form of diversification may solve this problem. The synthetic material Nylon has been used in hundreds of different consumer goods for this very reason. Nylon is used in carpets, hosiery, car tyres and synthetic rope amongst others.

22.3: Need for Marketing

Sometimes it is claimed that marketing goes too far in that it encourages consumers to buy products, such as tobacco, that may ultimately harm them. These are sometimes called demerit goods. Many governments, especially in the developed world, seek to control the promotion of such items for the protection of their populations. In other cases, it is argued that consumers are encouraged to buy goods that they do not want or do not need. However, even responsible firms will need to market their goods in the modern business environment. It is noticeable that many firms which have experienced rapid growth have been well aware of the need for and the power of marketing. A multinational such as Coca Cola must devote a considerable amount of time and money to this aspect of management in order to gain the market share it desires. At the other end of the scale, the shopkeeper who anticipates demand and sells products that buyers want will do better than one who ignores these trends. This is particularly important when selling goods such as clothes or shoes where tastes and fashions change rapidly.

Perhaps the most important time for a marketing department to perform is the launch of a new product. The term 'product launch' refers to the point at which a new product is released for sale by a firm. For any firms this usually involves large-scale advertising to establish the product in a market and gain a respectable market share. If the marketing of this launch is not organised correctly the results can be extremely costly. To have a product that is ready to launch takes massive research, development, production and managerial effort and so to fail to recuperate any of this money may have severe financial repercussions. To increase the chances of a successful launch, a firm will sometimes advertise in only one part of the country, in order to test whether its choices and approach may be effective when used on the wider target market. This 'test marketing' is very useful as a gauge of the likely market demand before going into full production.

How do firms know what products to produce in the first place? In some cases customers could suggest items that could be produced. For example, disabled people may make suggestions for products that would be of particular use to them. In other cases pressure groups or people with similar interests, might get together and demand that a particular product or service be manufactured or provided. In many situations there is a long time lag between the original idea and the availability of the finished product. For example, the government will quite rightly try to ensure that environmental problems will not arise from a new factory, such as waste products being discharged into rivers. Land use planning is therefore important. Before an expensive new product is produced it must pass through several stages. It would need to be tested by a pilot survey to show whether or not the public is willing to accept it. There may be a temptation for firms to bring out a new product before it is properly developed. In the 1980s, as the computer market expanded rapidly, this was often the case.

22.4: The Marketing Function

Marketing people often refer to the phrase 'marketing function'. Whilst different textbooks define this in different ways, it can be taken to include marketing research, branding, public relations, advertising, distribution and packaging. There is a need for co-ordination of these different functions, as it may be found that the advertising creates a demand, which however, cannot be met since distributing the product has not been properly organised.

The marketing function will vary between organisations of different sizes. For example, the market trader or shopkeeper will tend to know his or her customers and will therefore not need market research in the same way as a large organisation does. On the other hand, display of items may be important. Even a market stallholder will tend to display the best fruit or vegetables at the front of the stall. Clothes shops will spend a considerable amount of management effort on product display.

All firms have to identify the type of business they are in. For example, a cinema competes not only with any other cinemas in the same town but also with a wide range of other entertainment including television, pubs and restaurants. If the cinema is not aware of its competition it could make major mistakes.

Marketing is primarily the function of smoothing and aiding the sale of goods or services but it may include other functions such as distribution, standardisation and research. The marketing department will consider the purchase of goods in order to resell them at a profit, usually through the outlet of shops. Sometimes distribution is seen as another role, and in some firms this is dealt with by a separate department. However, even if the distribution department is a separate one the marketing department will still need to be aware of the problems of distributing the product. There is no point, for example, in being able to produce goods unless they can be delivered to the customer. This is particularly important where items are perishable.

Exporting firms will need to be aware of the different tastes of people in other countries. The marketing function will also need to consider standardisation. Standardisation often arises from specialisation. The marketing department will need to look at economies of scale, where costs reduce as output increases, and will need to carry out research to find out what the customers wants from the product. This can be done, as we shall see later, by looking at both the potential and the current market.

22.5: The Marketing Mix: The 4 P's

The Marketing Mix for a product is often referred to as the four P's, Product, Price, Place and Promotion. These four parts of the mix are the elements of a firms marketing strategy that are designed to meet the needs of the customer. To produce a successful product the organisation needs to provide the right product, at the correct price, available at the right place and ensure customers have the correct information on it through good promotion.

22.5.1: Product

It is essential that the product that a firm makes will meet the expectations of its target market. It is important to consider the range of different aspects of the product that help to satisfy the customer's needs.

Firms are likely to use some form of product differentiation to make their offering stand out from the competition. Common forms of differentiation in the soft drinks market include branding, offering more flavours in the range and innovative package design.

Branding refers to the use of brand names and well-known firms use their 'name' to charge a higher price for their products. Firms may also use this to relay a perceived quality in the product by the use of brand names. This is often reassuring

331

for the customer because if they have tried the product before they know what to expect. If this was a positive experience in the past then may well lead to repeat purchases of the product.

A wide product range is also beneficial if the individual brands are not competing too much with each other. Customers may be more willing to purchase a new product if it is in the same range as one that they already know and buy. For example, a wider product range often allows firms to target different flavours or style of drinks at different consumer groups. This way a larger number of customers will be able to purchase a product that they like, therefore giving the customer what they want.

The ways in which a product is presented are important and much time and money is spent on designing and producing packaging. This can be important to protect the goods but more often it is to make the product look bigger or better than its rivals.

There are also differences in packaging for industrial goods. Packaging is less important as a way of persuading industrial customers to buy items. This is mainly because industrial customers will often employ purchasing managers who are specialists in their own right. They will therefore have a much greater knowledge of say, office equipment. The purchasing managers will be looking much more at value for money rather than being influenced by the design on the package. The industrial consumer is likely to be more concerned with whether or not the package is safe in transit. If goods are sent in flimsy cardboard boxes, they might be damaged. Similarly, packaging may be necessary to keep the goods in good condition, and some packages may need to be both watertight and air resistant.

22.5.2: Price

The price that a firm charges for its goods and/ or services will be dependent upon what their customers are willing to pay. No matter how good a product a firm has developed and brought to market, they will not sell it if the price is above the point that people are willing to pay for it. For example, there is very little point in making toilet paper out of silk because very few people would buy it! On the other hand, if a product were priced too cheaply, customers may get the impression that it is of a poor quality and so buy an alternative product. The phrase 'you get what you pay for' is often used in this sense and so firms should not seek to undervalue their products.

In business, there is no one best method of pricing. The ethical aspects of pricing may be important. It is sometimes said that some firms 'profiteer', which may well occur when firms have a monopoly. This does not necessarily mean the firm is very big, it just means that there is no alternative from the consumer's point of view. Such a firm has no immediate substitutes so it can raise prices without losing too much demand. The government may try to restrict this profiteering by, for example, having a prices and incomes policy.

One of the common methods of pricing is to have a 'Cost-Plus' method. This is widely used because it is easy to calculate and simple to implement. Here the price is meant to be high enough to keep the business in production. The price is fixed by considering the costs of production, the distribution, the overheads and then adding a profit margin. For example if the total cost for an item was £10,000 and the firm wanted a 20% profit it would charge £12,000. However, it is not obvious what a satisfactory profit level should be. It also tends to ignore the fact that unless the customer is willing to pay £12,000 it will be unsatisfactory. Cost plus pricing has sometimes been used in government contracts. This is because for many items, such as defence equipment, there may be no market price by which to judge the items.

In some cases consumers may be able to pay much more than the cost plus a reasonable profit. This could apply to a very popular new item, such as the latest computer equipment or wide screen TV. A firm may wish to charge a premium to these customers by using 'Price Skimming'. This occurs with the introduction of most new electrical items. They are released with a relatively high cost, which they know some consumers will be willing to pay. Such a tactic is often used to recover the research and development costs as quickly as possible. After a period, the price is reduced to expand the number of sales to people less willing to pay the premium for the chance to be one of the first owners of the product. Firms can justify this price reduction by the fact that as production of the good increases, the cost of producing the item is reduced via economies of scale. The opposite tactic is used in different industries. Often a product is released at a special introductory level that is below the normal retail price. This is so that the new item can gain a larger market share and so that customers try the product in the hope that they will buy it in the future. This policy is known as 'Penetration Pricing'.

Where there is a considerable degree of competition however, firms will need to take note of prices set by rivals. For example in a street market, one grocer cannot set his prices at a higher rate than other market stallholders can. This is because its customers are able to see identical products on sale at a lower price, i.e. they have good information. The matching or monitoring of rivals' prices is often referred to as 'Competitive Pricing'.

An extreme case of competitive pricing is that of predatory pricing. This is where a firm will reduce its costs to very low levels to undercut their rivals. This can lead to products selling for less than a firm pays for them. Such goods are known as 'loss leaders'. Firms use loss leaders to get people into their stores. The use of such tactics is often found in supermarkets in the UK. Firms will tend to offer a few products at or below cost to tempt people into the store, safe in the knowledge that they will spend more than enough on other goods to make up the shortfall. This approach can only be used in situations where a customer will buy more than just the loss leader products otherwise the firm will make heavy losses. Imagine if a car dealer used loss leaders in their showroom, people would just buy them and nothing else and so the owner would gain no more profitable sales unlike the supermarket.

Another pricing policy that firms can use is 'Psychological Pricing'. Sometimes psychological thinking influences the price firms will charge for their products. For example, prices may be set at just below a rounded sum so goods may sell at £995 rather than at £1,000 even though there is very little monetary difference. The firm may carry out research into what customers expect to pay. As mentioned previously sometimes customers judge quality by the price charged and do not buy items if they feel they are being sold too cheaply. Conversely, they will not buy items if they appear too expensive. Packaging can also influence the price that a customer is prepared to pay for a product. The more attractive or elaborately packaged item can usually be offered at a higher price.

22.5.3: Place

This refers to the way that the customer will be able to get the product. The positioning of a firm's product in a place that the customer can get to is obviously important. If a customer has to travel a large distance to buy the product or service then they are likely to look for nearer alternatives. There are two main factors to consider when looking at the 'place' variable in the marketing mix. These are methods of transport and channels of distribution.

The product needs to be available in the right place at the right time and so the method of distribution needs to be carefully considered. Obviously, we would like products to be transported as fast as possible to where they need to go. However, this speed increases costs and so a balance must be struck that allows a firm to meet its desired price point. Bananas, for example, are not flown by aeroplane to this country but are shipped by sea. The reason for this is that the cost of the transport of these bananas would increase dramatically. Fewer people would buy this firm's products, as a reasonably comparable quality substitute, i.e. shipped bananas, would be available at a fraction of the price.

The method of transport will also depend on the location of production and the location of the product's market. If these two are close, such as a seafood restaurant in a fishing village, the problem of transportation is less of an issue. However, if large distances are involved, such as the banana trade, then transportation will take up more management effort and make up a larger proportion of the cost of the product.

The channel of distribution is important to firms that do not sell directly to the end user. Many firms seek to control their channels of distribution to get the best deal and highest sales for their own products. Some possible supply chain options from a farm to a customer are shown in Figure 22.1 below.

In practice, the producer will have a very large number of different options to choose. A firm may have in operation many different channels for different companies, regions, products or countries.

Possible Channels of Distribution for a large food producer

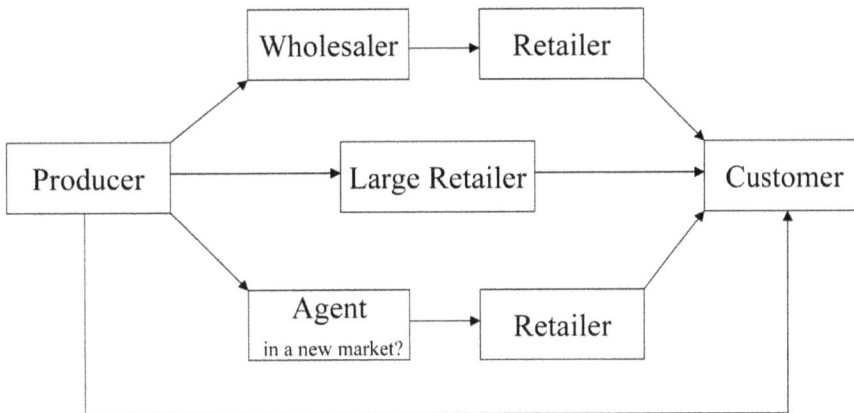

Figure 22.1

The function of the Wholesaler is to break up large deliveries of the product from the producer and sell these to a number of different retailers that require smaller consignments.

The Retailer is the shop or outlet that the end customer buys the product or service from. These may range from very large to very small. Some of the largest, such as the supermarkets, will deal directly with the producer. This is for two main reasons. The first is that they are able to sell all of the stock that the producer sends out without the need to have it broken into smaller quantities by a wholesaler. The second is that by dealing direct with the producer they can negotiate a lower price than other, smaller, retailers can.

The same principle can be seen when producers sell direct to the consumer. In this example, the farm may have a small farm shop that sells the product directly to local customers. This cuts out several layers of intermediaries and so the customer should be able to get the product cheaper and the farm should be able to receive a higher price than if they sold to Wholesalers or Retailers

The Agent in the figure 22.1 is often important to a firm if it is entering a new market abroad. These professionals often have great knowledge of the selling of similar products in different regions. To expand into these regions a firm may appoint an agent to oversee the distribution of the product. Agents usually work on a commission based on the value of sales that he/ she generates for the firm.

22.5.4: Promotion

Promotion can be thought of as the attempt to bring a product or service to the attention of new customers or to retain existing ones. Promotion of products and services often takes the form of either above or below the line promotion activities. Above the line promotion includes all of the promotion done through the media. Firms wishing to promote 'above the line' commonly use media such as television, radio, newspapers, posters and cinemas. Below the line, promotion is used if firms want slightly more control over the process. Commonly used methods include direct mail advertising, exhibitions, personal selling and merchandising. Five forms of promotion are discussed in the following paragraphs.

1. Advertising

There is a common misconception that promotion *is* advertising. As we shall see there are a number of different aspects of promotion and advertising is just one of these.

Advertising will often be used to target different groups of consumers. It will sometimes take account of different psychological reactions. People who are very conservative i.e. those who do not like change, will prefer advertising that may emphasise that the firm has been in business for a long time and is producing a conventional product. Others may be more concerned about the moral aspects of a purchase and may consider safety or environmental factors and these individuals are referred to as 'reformers'. Others, dubbed 'aspirers', will be attracted to different advertising features because they wish to be, or wish to appear to be, rich or important. They may well choose based on a brand name, or the size and styling of the product. In the case of cars, this style of advertising will show a driver who appears successful.

Advertisers need to take account of the media they plan to use. Part of the choice will depend upon cost. It may also depend upon potential demand. Advertising on television tends to be very expensive and therefore only usually available to firms selling high value or a high volume of items. Some firms may have a local market like a large shop in one particular area and therefore local advertising will be more cost effective. If a product is very complicated, it may be important to offer a considerable amount of information. Therefore, television would not be very effective since advertisements do not last very long. For this type of product, a glossy brochure might be more useful. Where there are wide varieties of choices, as in the holiday markets, brochures are regularly used. These points can be illustrated if we look at different markets, for example foods and textbooks. Everyone buys food and there is a wide national market. Therefore, the advertising for such products will be different from that of textbooks. Textbooks on specialist subjects, like criminal law, will be bought by a limited number of customers. A national advertising campaign would hardly be worthwhile. Therefore, the textbook promoters will try to sell directly to the customers, the lecturers and students studying law. This is a form of direct selling.

What different factors will influence choice of media for different firms? How might market segmentation influence this choice?

The media includes national newspapers, which comprise both weekday and Sunday newspapers. Firms wishing to advertise luxury products and services, including holidays, may well wish to advertise in the Sunday newspapers, since this appeals to people aspiring to a particular lifestyle. In addition, they may involve the 'leisure' industry and 'up market' goods. To use the psychological phrase, Sunday magazines probably appeal to the aspirers and the achievers. Achievers are similar to aspirers, who have achieved their materialistic aspiration. Different daily papers appeal to different socio-economic classes and to different psychological groups. Firms selling 'green' products will probably find that they are more likely to appeal to Guardian readers than the Daily Express. Regional newspapers are common and may be suitable for firms including retailers, where the majority of their trade is in that region.

Most magazines appeal to a particular market segment. The 'Tatler Magazine' for example, will appeal to women in the higher socio-economic groups and thus may attract advertising for more expensive fashion items. Some magazines cater for particular hobbies such as car magazines that attract vintage car users. Magazines catering exclusively for say photographers will be very useful for firms in that trade. There are a large number of magazines catering solely for the computer market. Firms wishing to sell computer games will find some of these magazines much better than others will. Firms wishing to sell business software on the other hand will find magazines catering for that segment.

Radio advertising is comparatively cheap to use when compared to other forms of media. Whilst advertising is limited to nine minutes in the hour, it often attracts the young due to playing modern music and therefore may be suitable for firms trying to attract this market segment. The advantage of radio advertising is that because there are a number of radio stations the style can be altered to the different needs of market segments in the different areas.

The cinema has benefited from increasing audiences after a long period of decline. Some small cinemas run adverts for local garages and restaurants. The visual image can be helpful to promote the idea of the atmosphere of a slightly up-market restaurant and its level of service.

2. Personal Selling

Salespeople often visit homes or businesses to sell products or services; this is known as personal selling or 'door to door'. In fact, any promotion that takes place through personal contact can be regarded as personal selling. The more complex, specialised or individual the product is, the more important personal selling becomes. Most organisations that sell to other firms rely on sales representatives to promote their goods and services. This could be done over the phone, or by setting up meetings or visiting company premises to give demonstrations. Demonstrations can be useful in giving more details to potential customers. For example, customers may not understand the uses of a computer unless it is demonstrated to them personally.

Personal selling can provide a firm with a number of advantages that may help to facilitate more sales:

- Create awareness of a good or service to those who do not yet know of its existence.

- In depth explanation of the features and uses of the product with a chance for customers to ask questions of a knowledgeable member of staff.

- Chance to take orders for the product.

- Helps firms to get a clearer image of their customers.

- Feedback from customers helps a firm to meet customer expectations better in the future.

3. Publicity

Some firms have public relations departments to handle their publicity while others hire outside agencies. The idea behind publicity is that a firm wishes to control its image in the eyes of current and potential customers. If a firm's image is good it will tend to sell more goods or services than if the public dislikes it. Publicity can be used to create an appealing image or enhance an existing one. It can be used to inform potential customers of their goods or services or existing ones of their new products.

Larger firms often use their publicity departments to lobby politicians to try and influence legislation and government opinion on matters that will affect the firm. This can be seen in US politics where people who wish to influence policy decisions often help to bankroll the presidential election campaigns of their chosen candidate.

Giving to charities or running a charitable trust can also obtain positive publicity. This creates a favourable public image, which is used to show a caring side to the often thought of inhuman large organisations.

Sponsorship has become increasingly important as a publicity tool, especially in sports such as football, cricket, tennis and rugby. In fact nearly all professional sports and participants are used to advertise goods and services. The advantage of sponsorship is well noted by the tobacco companies who can still get their name across on televised motor racing events even though cigarette advertising is banned on television in this country.

4. Sales Promotion

This consists of producing incentives that encourage new customers to buy now rather than later, or not at all. A sales promotion can be used to launch a new product, increase demand for an established line or maintain market share in a turbulent market environment. There are different types of sales promotions that a firm could implement to achieve these aims. Examples include Free Samples, Coupons, Free Gifts, New Packaging, Limited Editions, Price Reductions, Competitions or Multi-buy offers (such as Buy 1 Get 1 Free).

5. Direct Marketing

This refers to a type of promotion where a company contacts potential customers directly. While the use of above the line promotion, such as TV or radio advertising, can reach a wide number of potential customers, a better response rate may be possible through a more personal, direct approach. Promotion encompasses the following sales channels: Internet shopping, television marketing, Mail-order catalogues and direct mail.

6. Marketing Segmentation

Firms need to identify their customers. For many firms the final consumer, i.e. the household, is the customer. In other firms, however, the customer may be another business; for example, a firm may make components that are used by another organisation. The market itself is often divided into definable segments. We can see this in the vehicle market. Someone with a higher income may buy a car from the 'top end' of the range because it demonstrates his or her wealth. Others will want a car not for status but merely because they want to go from A to B. Many will not be able to afford a car at all and may have motorcycles or bikes. The market is therefore very much segmented. A firm entering the vehicle market has to consider which end of the range it wants to cater for or if it wants to cater for all sections of the car market. In the case of the vehicle market it is complicated because many firms sell to several countries.

Examples of Marketing Segmentation

The clothing and footwear industry is firstly segmented by gender i.e. man's and women's clothing. It may then be segmented by age i.e. children, teenage, etc. and then further segmented by use i.e. school, business, leisure and sportswear. A firm therefore has to consider which segment, or segments, of the market it wishes to enter. It may enter all segments but this will involve employing workers with differing skills and possibly employing different types of machinery.

In the toiletries market there is a similar segmentation between products for men and women. Firms may try to differentiate their products from others through use of branding or advertising. The advertising itself will often stress the product differentiation. This means that the differences, real or imaginary, are in the eyes of the consumer. For example, there are considerable variations in different types of cars. Car firms stress different aspects of their products' design such as speed, reliability, fuel consumption, and passenger and storage capacity.

22.6: Product Differentiation and Why is it Used

Product differentiation is defined as a conscious effort by a manufacturer to distinguish a product and sell it on the basis that it is somehow different from other products. Whether the differences are real or imagined the product is no longer a perfect substitute for another in the eyes of the consumer. For example, even if petrol comes from the same refinery consumers may believe that one brand is better than another is. Similarly, they may, or may not, buy supermarket "own" brands. What is important is what happens in the eyes of the consumer.

In many cases, as with consumer durables there may be a range, perhaps from basic to deluxe products, available on the market. The concept is not however confined to durable products. In the service sector we find theatres selling a wide range of tickets from expensive boxes to cheap seats in the gallery. Passenger shipping companies sell a wide range of tickets ranging from very expensive suites to dormitory class.

It can be argued that product differentiation helps to increase the choice for customers. If there was only one standard model available for everything then some potential customers may not be able to afford the item while other consumers would find that they were not getting the product that they required. In some cases, customer choice would be restricted as if the firm only sold the basic product the revenue would be small, although sales were high. If it sold only the deluxe product, it again would not be able to cover its costs since the market would be too small. However, critics would suggest that there are problems associated with product differentiation. In the car industry new models seem to come out every year. The changes may be merely cosmetic but the consumers are persuaded, through large-scale advertising as well as media coverage, that the changes are important.

Industries no longer have very large production runs and therefore production costs rise. Customers also suffer if they do buy the latest product since spare parts for the older models will not be kept in stock. In the case of the computer industry, newer models mean that software is no longer available for the older machines so many computers are discarded well before their technical life is finished. Some critics, including the late economist J. K. Galbraith, have therefore talked about the problems of built-in obsolescence. By reducing the commercial life to well below the technical life, the producers are making more profits but this is at the expense of consumers. It also contributes to social costs since more materials and fuel are used without comparable gains in economic welfare. This is particularly true of the 'white' goods industry, which includes washing machines, dishwashers and fridges.

On the other hand, there are defenders of product differentiation who have made the point that by slightly modifying products over time firms can often gain the advantages of economies of scale while at the same time meeting customers' needs and wants. Without product differentiation, consumers would not buy the product and it would come to the end of its product lifecycle. Defenders of product differentiation however will also argue that product differentiation has often helped the customer and in some cases the public as well. For example, the emphasis on safety by some car manufacturers, especially Volvo, has helped protect customers and reduced the risk to other road users. Where one firm has differentiated its product, other manufacturers such as Saab and Ford have eventually been forced to follow. Similarly, other car firms have differentiated their cars by improved fuel consumption. Improvements in fuel consumption are good since they reduce the costs to the consumers and can help to reduce pollution.

Car Export Marketing - Case-study

What factors should a car firm take into account when considering its export marketing?

Suggested Feedback:

The Effect of Exchange Rate Fluctuations

We would need to have some idea of the exchange rate fluctuations. For example, against the $ during the 1980's the pound fluctuated very considerably from $1.36 to $2.11. A car which costs £20,000 in the UK would, ignoring distribution costs and inflation, have cost from $27000 to $42000 during that period. The firm should have, or could easily acquire data about the price fluctuations and respond accordingly. The firm could also try, though with more difficulty, to obtain figures of cross price elasticity e.g. how far would price changes in other cars affect its market?

Comparison with Other Firms

We would wish to look at the performance of other car manufacturers. For example, did Mercedes, which did make similar models or other companies face the same difficulties?

Pricing Policies

What is the price elasticity of demand for the cars? Have they been priced too high perhaps because of a market 'skimming' policy? Should the board try a market penetration policy? What is the income elasticity? Has the firm changed its pricing policies due to fluctuations in foreign taxation policy such as changes in income tax or on the cars themselves?

Non-Price Competition

Is the quality of the car right for the different export markets with their different regulations and cultures? For example, the USA speed limits are generally lower than the UK's. In contrast, the Germans do not have a speed limit on their autobahns. Does the type of car allow for this? What would be the cost of modifying the car and what would be the benefits?

Is the marketing suitable for the different markets? We may be able to get some indications for this from the car's relevant market share in the different countries. How are we trying to sell the cars in the different countries, are we using agents or are we trying to set up dealers directly? What information do we have about the effectiveness of our dealers and agents? Do we consult with them enough about any new proposals for models or changes in marketing? Are we getting people to become repeat buyers?

Do we sell cars to individuals or to firms? The UK probably has one of the biggest fleet markets, partly because of the tax advantages of this to executives. However, in recent years the tax advantages have been reduced, such that today, cars that are more expensive generally are being more highly taxed.

Where do we currently advertise? What are the reactions of people to the advertisements? Do the advertisements reflect the differing tastes of the country?

Reactions of Past and Present Customers

The firm could try to look at customer's reactions to the present models. In the U.K, a consumers association, known as 'Which,' gives an objective view on the consumers' views on their cars. This may highlight both technical problems, like the performance of the car, as well as safety features and value for money. Recently the British Government has published a list of which cars have been involved in accidents with data taken from police records. This information is being given to potential customers in this country so that they can make a better-informed purchasing choice. The data compared cars with others in the similar range. Most countries will have some publications that show the different types of cars and compare them in some way.

The company should take note of the good features, which the publications describe and publicise them and attend to any criticisms. For example, shortage of spare parts in certain countries may be rectified with a better distribution system whereas poor fuel consumption may mean a different style of design, which will take time to rectify.

Has the firm obtained a good or bad reputation for after sales service? What feedback can the firm receive from its dealers or agents? Have the existing models deterred potential buyers? If so can these features be changed easily? Is the range of models sufficient to satisfy the customers? If the market is the USA, where people may travel long distances, do the car's features allow for this type of driving as opposed to the urban style driving?

The company will need to look at the ways in which it tries to sell its cars e.g. if the market share in one country is low but in a similar country it is much higher what are the reasons for this? Do other firms give dealers in those countries higher profit margins?

Attitudes of the Workforce

Can the firm improve on its quality of manufacturing? Would the use of quality circles help the firm? Has the firm generally consulted its workforce? One of the major British car firms advertised the number of suggestions its workforce had made in May 1994. There is no reason to believe that other employees would not do so if consulted.

Case Study One

In what ways might a computer firm attempt to compete with its rivals using marketing methods?

The answer will depend upon what market segment or segments it wishes to attract. For example, some firms compete very strongly in the higher priced computers market, whether in high specification home systems or very large business computers. The marketing methods for these will vary quite extensively from those competing for the small firm or standard home computer market, which is much larger.

Firms competing on large business computers may well decide to specialise. For example, Fujitsu competes very strongly in the market for retail applications. Due to there being relatively few large supermarket chains and large retailers, the marketing method is likely to be through personal selling rather than via commercial television advertising. Fujitsu is much more likely to concentrate on direct approaches to its existing customers and to potential large buyers. Emphasis in the marketing will be upon how quickly and efficiently computers can help business, the emphasis will not only be on the sale of the computers and relevant software, but also the way in which they supply customers with extensive after sales advice and keep them in touch with any changes in technology.

The price of software was important, as was the availability of a large number of different types of games. The computer itself was advertised in terms of its ability to handle graphics and processing speed, since this improves the representation on screen.

The computer firms will not only promote their products based on price of the hardware, but also of all the related items. For example, rational consumers in the business market will not only take account of the price of the individual computers, but also how much it costs to set up a network. They would also need to look at the price of different types of compatible printers, as well as price and availability of relevant software. Other aspects to take account of will be the cost of maintenance and repairs. Will they for example, offer these at a reasonable price to customers? Will it include a 24-hour call service? Will they offer to replace computers when they fail to function? In other cases, they may offer a 'hotline' so that not only technical faults, but also software difficulties can be solved. Certain computer firms have tried to gain dominance in the educational computer field in this way.

The computer companies may also stress in their marketing their compatibility with future products. One of the problems for many customers is that when they buy a computer system, they know that it will be outdated quickly. However, it is essential that information that has already been processed does not have to be keyed in again at a later stage. Future releases should therefore be 'backwardly compatible'.

The computer companies may also compete using the term 'user friendly' as a selling feature. Sales representatives will be able to show the computer to the consumer and demonstrate that it is easy to use. Many computer firms use business exhibitions as well as specialist computer exhibitions to demonstrate their products.

Computer manufacturers may also emphasise how well their keyboard is laid out and that it is easy to use. They may also show how the additional keys, apart from the standard 'Qwerty' keys, are very easy to use. For example, since the release of Microsoft Windows 95, nearly all keyboards come with two 'windows' buttons beside the Alt keys and also a 'menu' key to open menus within windows compatible software.

Computer companies will also need to take account of the different advertising methods and media areas. The use of highly numerate and articulate sales representatives may be helpful in the higher levels of computer systems. For example, firms trying to sell to government departments or large-scale business firms would almost certainly use personal contact in this way. The use of direct mailing is increasingly important as distrust in the level of knowledge in the high street computer shops grows. Many firms use computer exhibitions, partially in order to be able to gauge reactions of potential clients and to build up an accurate database from which to make mail shots. In computer magazines, many companies agree to a system whereby the computer journal will send them a list of potential contacts. These forms will usually contain information about the computers that the client already has, as well as when they are likely to buy future computers and the general specification that they will want.

Some 'business to business' computer firms advertise in the so-called quality press such as the Guardian, Times and Independent. This may be a cost effective way of promoting computers to consumers in socio-economic classes A and B. This is beneficial as they are likely to be the people that buy computers in small firms.

As with other products, some computer firms still sell on the computers based on their well-known name. For a long while, IBM seemed to rely heavily on this, perhaps too much so. The advantages of a well-known name from the firm's point of view is that consumers will assume that compatible software is more likely to be available than if they bought from a lesser known company. This seems to be of prime importance since many commentators suggest that firms, when buying computer systems, should really look for the software first rather than the hardware.

In other cases, computer firms sell their product partially upon the relevant package that they offer. As the price of computers and software has decreased, some firms will now produce packages that include not only the computer and screen, but also other hardware such as printers and scanners. They may also include bundles of software such as word processing, spreadsheets and media software. This may well be helpful to small firms using computers for the first time as well as to the growing number of self-employed and home workers.

Case Study Two

You are appointed as marketing manager for a large hotel that caters for the conference traffic as well as the wealthier tourist. However, there still tends to be seasonal trends, with most tourists coming in May to August. You are asked to see how the demand for the hotel could be improved.

Suggested Feedback:

The first step would be to see what existing customers think of the hotel. Are they satisfied with the accommodation, the meals and the level of service within the hotel? A second step may be to ask where they found out about the hotel. This will be particularly important for overseas visitors, without local knowledge. The third step would be to ask what has attracted them to come to the establishment. Is it the advertising that has impressed them, that other satisfied customers have told them about it, or that the prices seem reasonable compared with others?

Once this has been done, the management might try to improve the hotel. For example, if service is poor, staff training and setting them targets may be helpful. Some targets are easy to quantify e.g. the average time the telephone rings before it is answered. Other standards, by contrast, are much more difficult to quantify e.g. the courtesy or lack thereof of the staff, checkout questionnaires can be useful here. The management should try to see whether advertising has been cost effective or not. Word of mouth recommendations are always useful as can be the issuing of vouchers, perhaps in the national press.

A hotel estimates that the fixed costs, its mortgage, etc. amount to £250,000 and its food costs per day, per person amount to £10. Its pricing policy is to charge £55 per day per person in July and August and £50 in April, May, June and September with £40 in October. It closes for the remainder of the year.

The hotel has 20 double rooms and 5 single rooms. It charges £5 supplement for single occupancy at any time of the year. Looking through past records the hotel finds that it has 95% occupancy of double rooms in July and August, 85% in May, June and September, 70% in April and 75% in October. The hotel has 100% occupancy of single rooms in June, July and August, 80% in September and 60% in April and October.

A consultant suggests that it considers opening in March and November.
What further information would you need before going ahead with this advice? Are there alternative ways in which the hotel could consider boosting revenue? What types of promotions could the hotel run to increase custom? When would the use of special offers be unadvisable?

Case Study Three

You are employed as a management trainee in the marketing department of a large soft drinks company. You are asked to investigate why there has been a decline in sales.

Suggested Feedback:

The first step would be to find out the actual sales figures for the different products in different areas of a country. If they have decreased in only a few areas, is this due to lack of advertising, marketing or distribution? It may be that there has been a breakdown in supplies or some shopkeepers decided not to stock your products. If this is the case, what is the reason? The next step would be to assess the degree of competition from other drinks products and other substitutes for your goods.

You should know what age group primarily consumes your product. Is it the young, the middle aged or the elderly? If it is the young, is the current advertising geared to this market, for example, if you advertise on television or in your newspapers are your adverts in the right time slots/ sections?

How much control over your distribution channels do you have? Are your products sent to wholesalers, agents or retailers direct? What prices do you charge the channels and what prices do they usually sell the goods for? Do they receive enough to be able to make a reasonable profit? If they do not, is there any possibility of reducing your price? Do you charge all firms the same? or do you give a discount for large sales?

You might also ask customers what they think about the product, whether they have a favourable or unfavourable image, if they have tasted the product and did they enjoy it, or have they been put off the product by adverse publicity from rivals?

Case Study Four

You have been approached by an Eastern European car firm, which has not previously sold cars to a particular developed country in Western Europe. You are a senior marketing manager and they ask you for advice on whether it would be worthwhile to sell to this country.

Suggested Feedback:

The first step would be to give the firm an overview of the country such as the size of its population, its income levels and distribution. You would also need to advise them about the possibilities of distributing within the country, for example, what the distribution costs would be. You would also need to advise them about the makes of cars that are currently selling in the country and their current prices. You should also inform them about the marketing mix that the competitors use, for example, how they promote and price their cars, whether they have employed agents within the country or set up their own offices, and what type of advertising they use.

You should also be aware of the idea of market segmentation. For example, will different people use different types of vehicles? You should be aware of the price elasticity of demand and perhaps determine this by using some form of marketing survey. You should also be aware of any restrictions on imports. You must also be aware of how the firm can distribute their products, for example are there reliable retailers to sell the product?

- How far would different regulations for cars, in different countries, affect the costs of supplying cars to Western Europe?

- What environmental pressures and standards would you advise the firm to take account of in the manufacture of its cars?

- Why might you want to know the rural/urban split when looking at demographic details?

- What would you expect to find about income elasticity for cars as a whole and for individual models of cars? How would this affect your marketing?

- How could you use market segmentation in this case?

Self-examination Questions

1. Where do firms get new product ideas? Is it solely from the firm's staff?

2. Can you think of any new products that would help the standard of living in your area? If you live in an agricultural area is there a need for a different type of tractor?

3. Why might the government be wary about some new products?

4. Why might there be a long period between the start of a product idea and its availability to the public?

5. It is sometimes said that instead of firms determining the needs of society they create the need. What is meant by this and is it necessarily desirable?

6. Why is it important for modern firms to take account of changes in demand? What are the reasons for these changes?

7. What is meant when people say that marketing has to take into account the distribution, standardisation and research processes?

8. What does the term 'marketing mix' mean and why is it important? Do the 4 P's cover the marketing of services as well as products, or are there other factors that must also be considered?

9.   What is meant by 'market segmentation'? Why might it be used in the vehicle or the clothing and footwear industries?

10.   What do you notice about the packaging of cosmetics? Are the products different or does packaging just disguise the same products?

11.   What is meant by the phrase 'marketing aims to sell goods to people who come back but with goods which will not'?

12.   What choice of advertising media might a large car firm use?

13.   For what goods or services, if any, is personal selling appropriate?

14.   Why do we sometimes divide consumers into socio-economic groups? Why might firms wish to use this classification? Are there any disadvantages in doing so?

15.   Why do firms sometimes use psychological groupings to target their chosen customer segments?

16.   What does the term 'cost-plus pricing' mean? Can this method be used in all market situations?

17.   What is meant by the term 'psychological pricing'?

18.   How true is it that people will judge quality by the price charged?

19.   What are the different measures of price elasticity? Why might firms and Governments use them?

20.   Why do some small shops seem to use cost-plus pricing? Why might it be easier for them than for some other firms?

21.   Why might it be very difficult for a firm with very high fixed costs to use cost plus pricing?

22.   What does using a 'market skimming policy' actually mean?

23.   What is meant by a 'market penetration policy'? Would you expect a large or a small firm to adopt this policy?

24.   What does predatory pricing, sometimes called 'fight to kill', mean? Would you expect large or small firms to adopt this pricing policy? Why might the firm reduce prices below those of variable costs under some circumstances?

25.   Many newspapers now advertise cheaper trips to tourist destinations, what is the logic behind this?

26. What are the advantages and disadvantages of product differentiation for:

    a) The consumer

    b) The producer

    c) The public

    d) Employees

27. Why might product differentiation hinder economies of scale? Under what circumstances might it help?

Chapter 23: MARKET RESEARCH

23.1: Why do Firms need Market Research?

While discussing marketing in Chapter 22 we found that firms needed to know their target market in order to satisfy their needs. Market research is a firm's way of investigating and discovering these customers' wants and desires. Market research is often defined as the systematic collection, collation, analysis and reporting of information for the aid of marketers to solve specific marketing problems or take advantage of specific market opportunities.

The cost of product development is often so high that the risk of failure has to be reduced by making sure that a product really satisfies the requirements of the target customer. The cost, for example, of producing a new car design or a new aircraft will run in to many millions of pounds. Pre-production planning was dealt with in Chapter 8 where we learnt that many concepts never reach the production stage and so the cost of these failed products must be recouped. There are two main causes for these failures. The first is that without market research, goods and services may be produced without a market to sell to. An example of this would be the Sinclair C5, which was a battery-operated vehicle. The limited range and speed of the vehicle meant that it failed to sell in any large quantities and the project had to be abandoned. The second problem is that without market research, opportunities may be missed completely. If a firm does not know about market segments that are not currently catered for, then they will not be able to exploit them.

23.2: Methods of Researching

Firms may carry out market research, although these can be combined in two ways. The first is called 'desk' or 'secondary' research. This means using data that has already been published. Using trade association or government data, we may be able to find out total sales of a product type as well as the volume and value of both imports and exports in its market. In some cases specialised agencies, for example, the Economist Intelligence Unit, may have carried out research on particular products. Whilst their reports are expensive, it may be less expensive in the long run than to designate or employ researchers 'in house'.

For small firms secondary research may be the only viable option since the expense of the alternatives could be more than the total volume of the sales that they are likely to obtain. A small shop, for example, could not carry out a detailed analysis of likely customers, but could use data from their local authority. For example, towns may carry out research to find the volume of footfall, i.e. the number of people who walk past a particular stretch of road in an hour. If there are only 12 people an hour walking past say, a potential greengrocer's, it is unlikely to be a large enough market, given that most people spend relatively little in such a shop. This would not prove that it is an undesirable location since the shop might eventually be able to build up a clientele. It would be much more likely to succeed in a road where the footfall was say 200 people per hour.

The other type of research is called 'field' or 'primary' research. Organisations may employ either outside agencies or the firm's own staff to carry out custom research into the market for their good or service. The advantage of employing outside agencies is that they may well have specialist expertise in the field. Whilst the cost per hour may be high, they may require relatively few hours to carry out surveys etc since they may be able to adapt existing materials.

The advantage of using one's own staff is that they may have more interest in carrying out the research, and may easily spot any limitation in the survey. A problem of using one's own staff is that it may be difficult to keep them fully employed in this area. If the firm is very large or diversified this may be less of a problem but it is unlikely that, in a conglomerate, they will always have enough knowledge of the different products to be able to carry out research into all of them. In some cases however, conglomerates may find that whilst they are doing research into one product the cost of carrying out additional research into other products may well be very low.

The main advantage of primary research is that, if done properly, a firm can get the exact information that they require. With secondary research, it is unlikely that another firm or agency has produced research on the same subject. It often has to be adapted or adjusted to make it more applicable. This is obviously not ideal, but the relatively inexpensive cost may convince firms to take this approach.

23.3: Primary Research Techniques

Market research agencies often use questionnaires to gauge the public's views on particular products. However, there are a number of considerations to make before deciding what method of collecting data will be used.

23.3.1: Data Collection

Which method will be appropriate to collect the data required?

Will a questionnaire be sent in the post for people to answer themselves, or will the firm telephone or personally interview people in the street? There are a number of ways for firms to collect primary research data, each with its own strengths and weaknesses.

Postal questionnaires are cheap to set up, distribute and record data from. If the questionnaire is constructed well, then a firm will just have to send it out to a suitable sample of the public and wait for the responses to be returned. The downside to this method of gathering answers is that the response rate is often very low. The oft-quoted statistic is that less than 10% of people return the form completed. In order to increase this, firms often give incentives to return the completed survey such as entry into prize draws or promising to send out free samples or vouchers for the firm's goods. The use of long or difficult questions must be avoided when using this approach. Respondents are likely to be put off answering if there are too many open ended or complex questions. Postal surveys are therefore most useful for asking short questions to many people. The collation of answers once they have been returned can be simplified using Optical Mark Recognition (OMR) systems. This scanning technique uses a piece of computer software to process the answers on a standardised form and record them into a computer document such as a database or spreadsheet program. The collated answers can then be easily analysed and interpreted for use by the marketing department. The use of e-mail questionnaires has grown in recent years. The response rates to these are thought to be around that of postal surveys but the electronic nature of them means that there is no need for OMR scanning.

Telephone interviews can provide a higher level of response than postal surveys. Call centres can be used to conduct the research on another firm's behalf. There are a number of benefits to using this system of data collection. The telephone operator can be given a script into which they can type the respondent's answers. This negates the need for the answers to be processed and collated again, saving the firm time and employee effort. The drawback to this approach is that people often object to being called to answer customer surveys and it may lead to resentment from consumers towards the firm, which would not be desirable. In addition, the people employed to ask the questions may not have a thorough understanding of the product, so should any questions be asked back to them they may not be able to answer them. This can also be frustrating for the respondents.

Face to face interviews can be an important way of collecting primary research. Firms hire interviewers to get responses from the public. These interviewers are trained in the use of questionnaires and the ability to obtain the results required by their employers. For example, if a firm knew its target market for a particular product was males aged between 25-40 years old then the interviewer would be tasked with getting, say 60% of all responses from this demographic group. A possible negative aspect to this approach is the opportunity for bias to be introduced by the interviewer. Their personal views may be impressed upon the respondent and so they could influence the results. The other problem with this approach is getting a representative sample. Consider an interviewer working in a small town's high street, on a weekday afternoon. There will be a bias as to the types of people that they will be able to question. For example, it is unlikely that there will be a large number of office workers or young people as they would be at work or school respectively.

Some firms choose to use consumer panels to gather customer responses. Broadcasting bodies often use these to find out the reactions to particular programmes. A group of people are asked to give their reactions to particular product or service over a period. The advantage of consumer panels is that it is easier to detect changes in attitudes over time than with other methods. However, the consumer panel may become unrepresentative since they will know more about the product than the average consumer. It is also a difficult and expensive job keeping the panel operating over a number of years.

What does the firm want to know?

Consideration must be given to the actual questions to be included. For the results of the research to be usable by the firm, the correct questions must be asked. The designer needs to include all the topics that are needed by the firm and allow the people answering to give clear and useful responses. If a firm does not ask all of the questions that it needs to, then the project may need to be carried out again to get the required information. When carrying out research it is often helpful to conduct a pilot survey in the first place. This will enable the firm to find any faults in the first draft of the survey. For example, some words may be ambiguous or have different meanings in different parts of the country. A pilot survey may ask people in one part of the country their views before asking people on a national basis. Any problems with the test questionnaire can then be adjusted and ironed out for the final version.

How will you ask it?

A third issue to consider is that of the question format. Questionnaires may have either open or closed questions.

A closed question is one in which there is a limited range of answers, often yes, no, or do not know. The advantage of closed questions is that if we are asking large numbers of people the same question it is easy to analyse their answers. For example, we can say that before a marketing campaign X% of people had heard of the product, whilst after it Y% had. Quantitative information is more effectively dealt with by closed questions, possibly using ranged options. For example, 'Please state how many people live in your household? 1, 2-3, 4-5, 6+.

Open questions on the other hand allow people to state their views or answers more precisely. A firm may wish to find out what people like and dislike about a product. It may use a series of closed questions, such as, 'Do you like the appearance of the product, yes or no?' It may then ask an open question to find out their overall views. Open questions are more useful for gathering qualitative information. An example of this could be 'What about this product would encourage you to buy it?'

Leading questions should be avoided in any research. A leading question is one that encourages a particular answer. An example of a leading question would be 'Do you believe that Coca Cola has a better taste than Pepsi?' A better way of wording this question would be 'which soft drink do you believe tastes better, Coca Cola or Pepsi?'

23.3.2: Sampling

It would be incredibly expensive and time consuming to get responses from all possible customers of a new product, known as its population. The government conducts a census of the population to provide various statistical data for the long-term planning of various projects. This is an extremely difficult task and so is only carried out every ten years. Firms must attempt to gather information from a sample group of the population. The sample chosen for research needs to be representative of the population. This increases the credibility of the results to the firms that use the results. There are different approaches to selecting a sample that firms can choose to take.

Random Sampling

This method gives each member of the chosen population an equal chance of being selected to go into the sample group. Using a list of the population, for example from the electoral roll, a computer can be used to produce a list of random numbers. The corresponding people are then included in the sample.

The main advantage in using this technique is that no bias can enter the selection process due to the random nature. Disadvantages include the need for a very large sample to get a representative mix of individuals in cases where members of the population are generally not very similar. It is also extremely costly and time consuming to obtain or draw up such lists. In most cases, it is impossible to include all members of the population. The electoral roll suggested above is often not 100%

inclusive. One way of reducing the cost and time it takes to construct a random sample is to take every 20th or 30th etc. name on the list. This is known as systematic sampling and is not as random as using the above technique.

Stratified Sampling

Stratified sampling is another form of random sampling. Market researchers break up the population into groups that share similar characteristics. These groups are called the strata. This technique is useful if a firm wishes to gather a more representative cross section of a population, whilst using a smaller sample size than standard random sampling requires. This will only work if the researchers know the breakdown of the population to be investigated. For example, where a firm were interested in the effect of household income on consumer demand for a luxury brand of washing machine powder, researchers would attempt to segment the market into different household income brackets. A random sample would then be chosen from each of these strata, ensuring that the relative proportions were still maintained from the original population data. This means that if the population had 4% of households earning between £60,000 and £100,000 then so would the sample.

Multi-stage Sampling

This technique simply involves taking a sample from another sample. The advantages of such an approach are that it is inexpensive and simple to do at short notice. The disadvantages of such a method include the possibility of ending up with an unrepresentative final sample group to work with and the stacking of any other disadvantages inherent in the two sampling techniques used. A common example of a multi-stage sampling method is cluster sampling, discussed below.

Cluster Sampling

Researchers separate the population to be sampled into clusters. These are geographic areas, often quite small, that are assumed representative of the larger population. Once a suitable area has been located, it is then randomly sampled to provide a quick and cheap sample from which information can be gathered. This specific from of multi-stage sampling may not end up being perfectly representative but it can be used when data is needed quickly. A common situation where clustering may be appropriate is opinion polls for newspapers or other media bodies wanting to gauge the public's views on a particular subject.

Quota Sampling

This method of sample selection involves the population being divided up into groups that have certain characteristics in common. These are often based on socio-demographic categories (See Chapter 4). Interviewers are then given target numbers of responses from each of the different groups. An example of this would be if a researcher were asked to interview 26 men between the age of 16-28 or 30 women over the age of 60. Once these targets have been met, the interview process is stopped and no more respondents are sought. This is a simple way of gathering information but it does have a number of drawbacks, the first being the confidence in the results. The sample is likely to be biased in one of two ways. The first is the use of an interviewer who may introduce a personal bias to the results by expressing their own opinions. The second, as discussed in face-to-face interviews above is the choice of location for the interview. There is also a likelihood of there being a temptation for interviewers to complete their quotas as quickly as possible. This may lead to them asking people who do not quite fit the description or falsifying a response in order to speed up the process. The final drawback is that the sample will not be randomly chosen and so caution should be taken when considering any conclusions that are made from the results.

Snowballing

This is a specialised way of selecting a research sample. The term 'snowballing' is used to describe the way in which additional people are added to the sample. When a snowball starts at the top of a snow covered hill it is small, as it gradually rolls down the hill it gathers snow from the path it creates downwards and grows. A similar approach is used in this sampling method. A small number of contacts are used to provide information that a firm may need. These people then provide a small number of contacts that the firm can also consult; this continues expanding through personal contacts until enough data has been collected. It may seem like a strange way to conduct research but some industries may require it. For example, snowballing could be used when a firm does not want the public to know it is researching a particular topic. The arms trade often uses this technique to gain contacts and information on this often secretive and private market. Snowballing techniques are also used in many semi-legal 'grey' and illegal 'black' markets. The results can often be relatively representative of the population, especially where the market for such goods is small, as in the arms trade. The randomness provided by some of the other techniques is not found with this approach, this can prove problematic if the market is relatively large. Contacts in such industries often share similarities and, due to the branching method used, significant segments of the market may not be questioned and so left out of any conclusions. Information gathered in this way must be treated with extreme caution.

International Airline - Case Study

You have been appointed as a marketing research officer for an international airline. Your first task is to see how far the existing passengers are satisfied with the service and why travellers sometimes choose to use other airlines in preference to yours. You are asked to prepare a customer questionnaire. Explain what sample of people, if any, you would use and explain the purpose of your questions.

Suggested Feedback:

One of your first steps is to consider when the survey would be carried out. For example airlines will have two distinct classes of passengers, those who are on business who might well travel during the week and those who are on leisure activities, and more likely to travel on the weekends. The pricing policy is likely to be quite different for the two groups. You would also need to decide whether the questionnaire was to be filled in solely by potential passengers, or whether you would employ a researcher to ask the questions. This has the advantage that you are more likely to get a more accurate and higher response rate although it will be more expensive. Sample questions may include:

1. How often do you travel by air?

    (a) Every week

    (b) More than once a month

    (c) Less than once a month but more than once a year

    (d) Once a year or less

    (e) This is the first time

2. Why did you choose to travel by this particular airline?

    (a) Because there was no choice

    (b) The price was better

    (c) That you wanted to travel by the national airline

    (d) That the in-flight service was better than other airlines

    (e) Other reasons please specify below

3. How satisfied or dissatisfied were you with different aspects of this flight?

	Very Satisfied	Satisfied	Dissatisfied	Very Dissatisfied
Actual Flight:	☐	☐	☐	☐
Ground Staff:	☐	☐	☐	☐
In flight Service:	☐	☐	☐	☐
Baggage Return:	☐	☐	☐	☐

4. Was the timing of the flight satisfactory? Would you have preferred to have had a flight at another time, if so please specify:

5. What was the main purpose of your flight today?

    (a) Tourism only

    (b) Business only

    (c) Visiting friends or relatives

    (d) A mixture of the above

Having constructed this simple questionnaire and testing it on a small group of customers, you may see the need for changes. Do you think that there are enough questions to gather the amount of information needed? Have all of the topics been covered? What would you change about the layout, question styles, detail and possible answers etc.?

Self-examination Questions

1. If market research is so important, why do many firms not use it?

2. What is meant by 'desk' research?

3. Why it is important to investigate the sources of information used in the construction of 'secondary' data reports? Does it matter what purpose the data was originally obtained? Do the collection techniques employed matter, if so how?

4. What is meant by 'field' research? Give three ways that this can be conducted.

5. What type of question style would suit the collection of quantitative data, open or closed ended?

6. Can you think why questionnaires have simpler rather than more complex questions towards the beginning of the response section?

7. What are the advantages and disadvantages of using outside agencies when carrying out market research?

8. What are the comparative advantages and disadvantages of telephone and personal interviews? Hint: remember that not all people have phones.

9. What is the problem with conducting telephone surveys during the daytime?

10. What are the advantages, if any, of secondary research over primary research?

11. Why are samples used instead of conducting a national census?

12. What is the advantage of having a random sample from which to conduct primary research?

13. Why is important to create a sample that is representative of the population that it is drawn from?

14. Why is it best to have a large sample from which to gather information rather than a very small one?

15. Why are some local areas and towns picked as a cluster more frequently than others for cluster sampling are? What characteristics make these locations popular choices?

16. Can respondents always be trusted to answer surveys truthfully? Consider a questionnaire seeking to investigate the consumption of alcohol in teenage males.

17. Does successful market research guarantee a smooth and profitable product launch?

Chapter 24: MARKETING STRATEGY

24.1: Cost Benefit Analysis

Marketing strategy involves both market research and marketing in the conventional sense, which includes selling and promotion. The firm will need to carry out a cost benefit analysis to consider the comparative costs of marketing research, advertising and promotion against the likely benefits. This means that they have to consider the total costs of marketing including, not just financial costs but also opportunity costs of managers and staff, against the likely financial and other positive returns. Some forms of marketing may have much longer-term benefits compared to others for example; sponsoring a football club is not likely to have an immediate effect but can probably lead to the firm being better known. It is almost certain that Barclays, a multinational banking and financial services company, has become better known since it sponsored the premier league in 2001. A firm should only go ahead with the scheme if the benefits outweigh the costs.

24.1.1: Consultation with Staff

The firm will need to consult staff whether they are directly involved as sales representatives or indirectly involved in other areas. For example, in shops people on the counter will often be aware of items that customers have asked for which are not currently in stock. Similarly, in transport, a bus driver may well be aware that there are customers waiting at a stop that cannot fit onto an already full bus. This may give the idea to the bus company of which routes to alter or increase capacity. In the shop, this may give a firm ideas for new or modified products, for example, a shoe shop may discover that there is a greater demand for larger size shoes than it currently caters for.

Some of the original ideas for marketing could be developed from complaints or customers' comments to members of staff. For example, if customers comment that there is a need for a switch to transfer their fax machines to an answering machine, the firm might take account of this and buy in such items.

In some cases, pressure groups might suggest items that could be produced. A group representing its members who have a specific physical disability might, for example, suggest that there is a need for a vehicle, which could carry them safely together with a small load, such as that needed for shopping, or to go to an office or a factory. The vehicle would not necessarily need a fast top speed but would need to be able to go up steep slopes and also be able to overcome problems such as getting over kerbs, etc. In other cases, legislation regarding products or other environmental problems might lead to the development of a new product. For example, the government is considering imposing a landfill tax. If this is imposed, there are a number of possible ramifications. Incineration of products may become relatively cheaper, especially if the products can then be used to provide heat and power to local residents. The government also set a target of 25% of domestic waste to be recycled by local authorities by the year 2005 rising to 33% by 2015. This will encourage paper firms to use a wider variety of materials (reinforced by the increasing price of paper pulp in the mid 1990's). The firms themselves will then need to encourage the use of recycled paper, perhaps through a marketing campaign. The Department for Environment, Food and Rural Affairs (DEFRA) sets targets for recycling and waste recovery each year. In 2002, businesses were asked to meet targets of 59 per cent recovery and 19 per cent material-specific recycling of packaging waste under the Packaging Regulations. In 2003 the Waste Electrical and Electronical Equipment Directive (WEEE) became European law. The WEEE directive set the targets for the collection, recycling and recovery, when revised in 2012 it was set at 45% of the weight of electrical products entering the market.

24.1.2: Databases

The firm will try to build up a database of both existing and potential customers. For some firms this would be comparatively easy whilst others may find it more problematic. A computer firm that specialises in sophisticated forms of barcode scanners that give information to the managers of large supermarket chains would find this quite simple. There may be relatively few customers for these products as the prices are relatively high and the product is very task specific. These customers will be well known to the computer firm and the relationships between supplier and customer may be quite close. On the other hand, a computer firm trying to sell word processing packages that are suitable for both home and small business use would find it more difficult to find out the names and addresses of customers who might be interested. Many consumers often choose not to register their software so the supplier may not even have any information on current users. Once a suitable database has been set up, even if this only gives an approximate number of customers who might be interested, the firm can consider the types of marketing that it wishes to use to appeal to the different users.

24.1.3: Implementation Stage

Once ideas about marketing have been formulated, it will be necessary to present them to the staff involved to see whether they can be improved. For example, sales representatives in many cases may know from experience that certain items will be more likely to attract certain customers than others. They may also know that customers interested in this product are likely to consider other related offerings as well. It may also help, if there are no great problems of commercial confidentiality, to talk to potential and existing customers in a test marketing campaign.

24.1.4: Feedback from Campaigns

Many firms use advertising campaigns but do not adequately receive feedback from them. The Sun Alliance Insurance Company in 1996, for example, asked its policyholders what they had thought about its recent advertising campaign. Sometimes it is possible to obtain information about campaigns using vouchers that are coded. For example vouchers in one area might have the letter "E" to denote East, whilst others would have "S" to denote South. Advertisements in newspapers also have coding, for example, an advertisement in "The Guardian" might ask people to reply to department "GN". There will not be a separate department with this title, but it will give a quick indication as to where people saw the advertisement. Some local authorities, such as Swale Borough Council in Kent, have issued voucher schemes that can be redeemed in the local high street within the borough. From this, both shops and local authority can readily see both the individual and collective response to the promotion.

Smaller firms may more readily receive informal feedback that may be acted upon. This is because the workers are likely to deal with a limited number of customers or have a number of 'regulars'. The relationship that builds up over time allows the owner/ worker to understand better what their customers want from the firm. It is also more likely that customers will give their opinions more freely and honestly to someone that they know personally.

Whilst complaints are a sign that the business is not performing to the expectations of its customers, they should be welcomed to increase the flow of feedback. The complaints should be analysed to see how the firm could improve its marketing performance. For example, mail order firms have return forms. When a customer wants to return an item, they must fill some information as to why they want to do it. This information can be used to adjust the products offered or the way they are displayed in the catalogue. It may have been that the item looked different in the photographs than under natural light or the size descriptions were wrong. These comments could then be investigated to try to reduce the number of returns and dissatisfied customers from the next edition of the catalogue.

24.1.5: Price Discrimination

One of the most important areas of marketing strategy in recent years has been price discrimination. This is where the firm charges the consumer different prices for the same good or service, which is not accounted for by differences in costs. The reasons for differences in price here may be for social reasons. For example, the NHS allows free dental treatment for children and those on low incomes. In other cases, for commercial reasons, the firms will charge some customers less than usual, such as when the train operating companies offer discount schemes for students etc. Airlines have a somewhat bewildering number of fares. Often these are based on the amount of notice that is given between purchasing the ticket and the flight, for example, the sale of standby fares. These are offered when the airline cannot guarantee a seat on the plane and the passenger can fly only if one becomes available. The ticket would be offered at a low price since the marginal costs of an extra passenger are negligible apart from a slight increase in fuel costs. The assumption here is that it will increase total revenue and hence profit by obtaining another fare.

Airline operators often have 'Yield Management' programs to calculate the best price to offer at different times and to different customers. Yield Management is a technique to help organisations increase their turnovers, it is a process of allocating capacity efficiently to maximise revenue. The idea behind this technique is to get the maximum price for a product or service at any given time; this is achieved by eliminating consumer surplus.

Once the market has been studied in depth, an airline firm will know how much to sell a particular flight ticket at so many days before the flight is scheduled. For example, 54 days before the takeoff of a Thursday 5:30am flight to Prague the ticket may be offered for £56 one-way. The same flight 2 days before departure may cost £150. However, research may show that if the ticket is not sold 3 hours before the flight is due to takeoff, it should be reduced in price to £30 to ensure that the plane is filled. Of course, these amounts would vary depending on any number of factors such as the flights time, day of the week, distance, location, number of passengers usually using the service and even the weather.

Yield management can be used in many different industries and not just the airlines. It is most effective in situations where the following are involved:

- There are high fixed or sunk costs
- There is a highly perishable inventory
- A fixed capacity
- Advanced purchase of the service or product is possible
- Fluctuations in demand occur over time
- Consumers cannot sell on the good or service at a later date

Therefore, hotel reservations and car hire are also markets where this technique can be used. On the other hand, fast moving consumer goods and internet access providers would not be suitable for this treatment, as they do not display the above characteristics.

24.1.6: Segregation of the Market

If firms charge different prices for the identical good or service, whether for social or commercial reasons, they must be able to segregate the market in some way. This is usually easier with services such as medical treatment or entertainment because it is possible to stop the resale of such goods and services. A 25-year-old man is not likely to be able to claim that he is a child and therefore obtain a cheap rail ticket. On the other hand, if television sets were to be sold cheaply to older consumers it would be very difficult to stop their resale on to other consumers. Prices may be allowed to differ due to geography; it is possible to sell the same car at different sides of a common border if the countries concerned have a strict policy of not allowing re-exporting. Until recently, it was possible to buy some cars much more cheaply in Belgium than in the UK.

Whilst economic theory emphasises the idea of perfect information this is rarely the case for consumer products as opposed to those capital goods or commodities mainly bought by firms. Where consumers do not have perfect information, this will make segregation easier. For example, British Gas, whose prices are unlikely to be known by other consumers, has negotiated a range of different prices for large-scale consumers.

24.1.7: Differences in Price Elasticity

For commercial reasons to be the cause of price discrimination, the price elasticity of demand must be different in the different sectors. The reduction in fares for families by former British Rail will have been justified commercially if the reduction in price was generally matched more than proportionally by an increase in revenue. For example, if the reduction is 20% then they will need to increase the number of passengers by at least 25% to compensate for loss of revenue. The percentage is not the same for the decrease in price as it is for the increase in the number of units demanded. Suppose, for example, a journey cost £10 and there were 1000 passengers then the total revenue would be £10,000. If the price was reduced to £8.00 and this caused a 20% increase in customers, the total revenue would be 1200 times £8.00, which would still only be £9600. If the total number of passengers increased to 1250 (by 25%) then the total revenue would be the same as before, i.e. £10000. If extra costs are incurred because of more passengers, they will need to increase the revenue further.

24.1.8: Logic of Eliminating Consumer Surplus

Consumer surplus is the difference between what people are willing to pay and what they actually pay. It should be emphasised that if firms had perfect information they would try to eliminate the consumer surplus for each consumer.

If, to take a simplified example, three consumers were willing to pay £30, £40 and £50 respectively for a service and the current price is £30 the second consumer has a surplus of £10 and the third has £20. See figure 24.1 If the firm can eliminate the consumer surplus it can charge £120 (£30 + £40 + £50) altogether instead of £90 (3 x £30) Figure 24.2.

Figure 24.1: **Consumer surplus**

Amount willing to pay	Amount actually paid	Consumer surplus
£ 30	£ 30	£ 0
£ 40	£ 30	£ 10
£ 50	£ 30	£ 20
Total	Amount paid: £ 90	Consumer surplus: £ 30

Figure 24.2: **Price discrimination- eliminating consumer surplus**

Amount willing to pay	Amount actually paid	Consumer surplus
£ 30	£ 30	£ 0
£ 40	£ 40	£ 0
£ 50	£ 50	£ 0
Total	Amount paid: £ 120	Consumer surplus: £ 0

In some cases, this can be advantageous even for the person who pays the highest price. For example, if the cost of running the service is £100, to charge £30, £40 or £50 will not enable the firm to run the service. This can be seen in the following calculations:

If the price is £30, total revenue will be £30 + £30 + £30 = £90, not enough to run the service.

If the price is £40, total revenue will be £0 + £40 + £40 = £80, as consumer 1 is only willing to pay £30 they do not purchase the service at all.

If the price is £50, total revenue will be £0 + £0 + £50 = £50, as neither consumer 1 or 2 is willing to pay the £50 price.

A system of price discrimination will enable the firms to do so since it can charge the consumers a fee of £120. The reasons for the differences in price are that there are different points on the product or service's demand curve.

Self-examination Questions

1. What is meant by the term 'marketing strategy'?

2. What is meant by formal and informal feedback?

3. How can firms use staff and customers to improve their marketing strategy?

4. What is meant by the term 'price discrimination'?

5. Why might it be necessary if using price discrimination to be able to segregate the market? Why might it therefore be more appropriate, generally, for services rather than for goods?

6. Why would it normally be necessary for price elasticity of demand to be different in different markets for price discrimination to be possible?

7. What it meant by two-tier or multi-tier tariff pricing? Why does BT, the electricity companies and British Gas use such a system?

8. Why would you expect firms to adopt two-tier or multi-tier tariff pricing if average costs were reasonably constant?

9. Why might a firm using Yield Management outperform a competitor who does not?

Chapter 25: INTERNATIONAL TRADE

25.1: Why trade?

Trade within a country takes place if both customer and supplier consider that it is mutually beneficial. This means that both parties must feel that they will be better off because of the trade. International trade takes place for exactly the same reasons. International trade allows countries to specialise in the production of particular goods or services. Specialisation means that each country will concentrate on the goods and services that they are most efficient at producing.

The import and export of products tends to lead to economies of scale. The car manufacturers in Europe, for example, are very large since they export to a wide variety of countries.

Many developing countries tend to specialise in primary production. These include the extractive activities such as mining, agriculture and forestry. Western European countries specialise in secondary production such as manufacturing and tertiary services.

Some countries cannot produce all the raw materials they need and will therefore need to import some. Countries also import manufactured goods including textiles at lower prices than they are produced for in their own country. This has resulted in some job losses within various industries in these countries.

25.2: Cultural Factors

When trying to sell overseas it is important to understand the social and cultural behaviour of consumers in other countries. One of the problems is a broad classification of countries or regions suggesting that the cultures are virtually identical. For example, the term 'Middle East' is often treated as virtually the same as the term 'Arab'. In practice, Iran is not Arab and uses the Farsi language that is not an Arabic language but is referred to as being in the 'Middle East'. On the other hand, some African countries such as Sudan, Somalia and Somaliland have very strong Arab influences. Similarly, it is a misconception to assume that all of Europe has similar tastes.

In some cases, as in the U.S.A., there are strong ethnic differences that may well influence patterns of consumption. Therefore, some marketing opportunities should be specifically targeted to appeal to these ethnic groups. In some countries, cultural differences affect patterns of decision-making. For example, in Saudi Arabia, husbands tend to shop for many items and this may well influence the marketing of these goods. On the other hand, in some countries such as the UK, women may well shop more often and this might influence ways in which exports from a developing world country could be marketed.

Culturally there may also be linguistic differences. In Belgium, for example there has been some conflict between French and Flemish speaking people. Therefore, it would be sensible to conduct market research in the two separate languages. In the Netherlands, on the other hand almost everyone can speak English so market research could be conducted in English, which may be cheaper. It would be more desirable to conduct the research in Dutch however, so as not to cause any undue offence to the nation's population. Culture may also influence the design of a product. Sweden, for example, has a small population but a very high income per head and seems to be particularly influenced by the design of products. The Swedish people are well known for their distinctive culture and ideologies, which tend to be more concerned with the environment and durability of products rather than being influenced by advertising alone.

25.3: Hofstede's Dimensions of Culture

For success, firms must understand cultural areas; there is the corporate culture of the firm that includes the organisational structure and the beliefs and ideals system of the firm's employees and owners and there is the national culture within which the firm operates.

Culture is often defined as the shared beliefs, moral values, behaviour, knowledge and 'way of thinking' shown by members of a society.

For a long period, there was lack of an applicable model to describe the culture of different societies. In the 1970's the Dutch organisational theorist Geert Hofstede conducted research on over 100,000 IBM employees over 40 countries to see if there were any similarities and differences between different nation's cultures. He suggested that four dimensions of culture influenced organisations. These are discussed below:

- **Power Distance (PD)**

[Diagram]

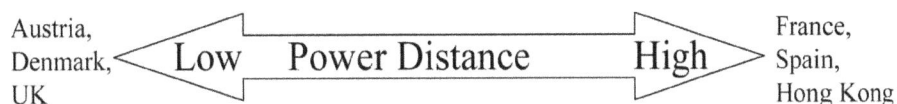

This is described as the degree of inequality between people. In organisations, Power Distance is related to the degree of centralization of authority and autocratic leadership. A high PD score means that people accept the large inequality of power within the organisation between subordinates and superiors.

- **Uncertainty Avoidance (UA)**

Uncertainty avoidance involves the acceptability or tolerance of uncertainty. High uncertainty avoidance societies socialise their members to be averse to uncertainty. The higher the UA score the less the member of a culture is likely to be comfortable with risk and ambiguous situations.

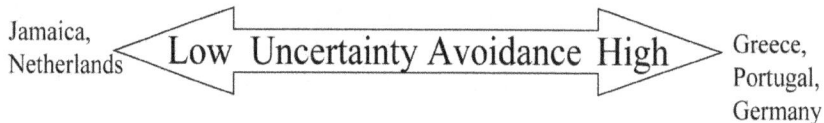

Jamaica, Netherlands ← **Low Uncertainty Avoidance High** → Greece, Portugal, Germany

- **Individualism vs. Collectivism (IDV)**

This dimension seeks to classify the relationship between an individual and his or her fellow individuals. In collectivist societies, group interests are more important than those of individuals are whereas the opposite is likely to be true in a more individualistic society. The higher the IDV score the more a culture emphasizes the right and obligations of the individual over the group.

[Diagram]

China, India ← **Low Individualism High** → UK, USA, Canada

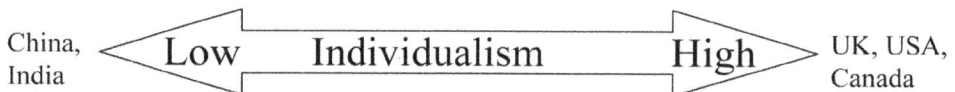

- **Masculinity vs. Femininity (MAS)**

In 'masculine' societies, masculine social values such as the importance of achieving something visible, heroism, assertiveness, or making money predominate, while more 'feminine' societies would be more oriented to cooperation, group decision making, quality of life and personal relationships. The higher the MAS score the more masculine a culture is said to be. Hofstede himself points out that this dimension is often neglected. It may be that the controversial name given to this dimension has somewhat influenced the popularity of it in recent years.

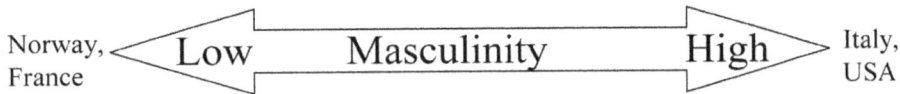

Later on, Hofstede and his colleagues suggested that a fifth dimension should also be included in the model. This used the idea of long-term versus short-termism. It was found that some cultures concentrated on short-term aims and ideals whist other preferred to be more aware and proactive in their ways of dealing with the future. These long-termist cultures are more readily found in nations such as China and other typically Eastern countries. Short-term orientation was found to be more common in Russia and many West African countries.

25.4: Possible Disadvantages of International Specialisation

A country that specialises in the production of a particular commodity may suffer diseconomies of scale. A country that over-specialises in a particular commodity may well find itself very susceptible to changes in demand, which could lead to large-scale unemployment, at least in the short-term, should there be a down turn. This could apply particularly to countries growing cotton, the demand for which is susceptible to rising demand for synthetic fibres. Specialisation puts the specialising country in a very vulnerable position if other countries take economic action, such as imposing quotas on imports.

25.5: Obstacles to International Trade

Obstacles to the international trade of goods and services include quotas, which restrict the amount of goods countries allow to be imported. Nations may also use tariffs; these are duties charged on imported goods. Governments may give 'hidden' subsidies to home industries. For example, they have often allowed firms in the shipbuilding industry to obtain 'soft loans' (cheap loans) that give them advantages over foreign organisations. The products of firms that receive these hidden subsidies can potentially be produced relatively cheaply, making them more competitive than the products of rival foreign firms that do not receive such subsidies. The cheaper domestic products then discourage imports. Governments might only purchase domestic goods; for example, the British Government might give subsidies to schools to buy British assembled computers.

Countries might impose non-tariff barriers (NTB's). Such barriers might include the imposition of regulations that tend to favour the home market rather than the overseas market. It has often been alleged that Japan uses such regulations to keep out imports. A government might impose higher taxes upon those goods its country is likely to import than on those goods it produces itself. For example, the UK had much higher taxation on wines and spirits, which it tends to import, than on beer that is generally home produced. This was brought up within the EU and led to the duties on wines being cut in the 1984 Budget.

Where information about a country is not enough as compared to another, then there may be reluctance to trade. In the UK, the Export Services Branch, the Export Credit and Guarantee Department and commercial banks are able to provide a great deal of information.

25.6: Exchange Rates

Differences in currencies can make international trade difficult. Whilst sterling is acceptable within the United Kingdom, an exporter from the United States will generally want payment to be made in dollars. Similarly, if the Rover Group is exporting cars that sell in the UK for £10,000, they will require payment in pounds from whomever they sell their cars to. This is to ensure that they receive at least £10,000 per car. If they are exported to the US then the importer will have to purchase a sterling cheque to pay the Rover Group. Assuming that each car is priced at £10,000 and that the rate of exchange is $1.20 to £1, the cheque must be worth $12,000 per car in order that Rover Group receives at least £10,000 per car. This way, if the exchange rate alters, Rover still receives the original amount and it is up to the importer to absorb the changes.

The exchange rate is the price at which transactions take place. Since 1972, British exchange rates have been floated so they respond, in theory, to changes in supply and demand.

Features of a floating exchange-rate system

Since 1972 the pound has 'floated', except for a brief period in 1990 when it joined the European Rate Mechanism (ERM). In a freely floating exchange rate system, the determination of equilibrium is made through supply and demand changes. The point of equilibrium is where the value of a particular currency neither appreciates nor depreciates. See Figure 25.1 below:

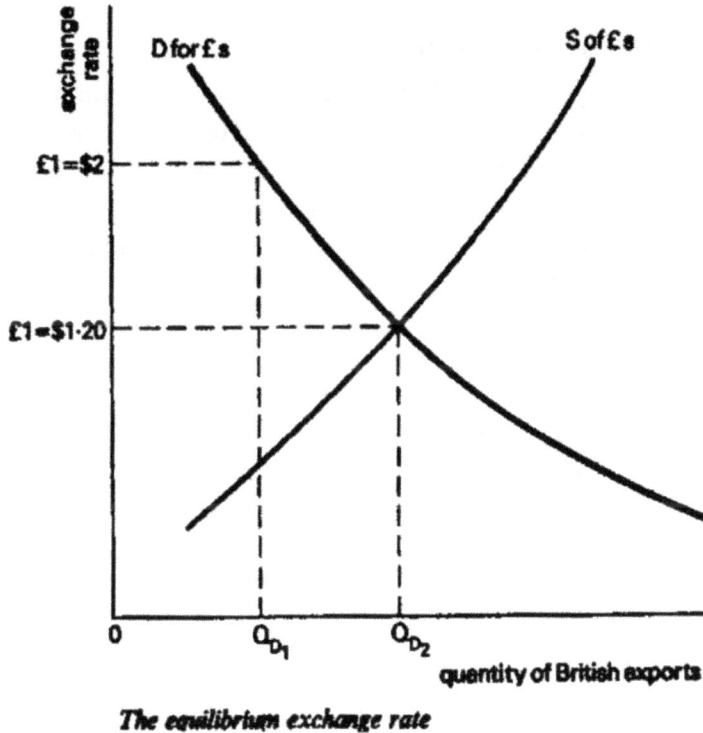

The equilibrium exchange rate

Figure 25.1:

If at a given exchange rate, say £1 = $2, the demand for dollars exceeds the supply available, the value of dollars will appreciate.

As the price of dollars rises, the price of US exports rises. Thus, the demand for US exports falls and the demand for dollars fall towards the equilibrium level.

As the value of dollars appreciates, the relative value of the pound depreciates. Thus, one pound becomes worth fewer and fewer dollars. The exchange rate, from the British point of view, falls until the equilibrium point is reached, which might be, say, £1 = $1.20.

As the value of the pound falls, British exports become more and more cheaper relative to US exports. Thus, more UK exports will be demanded until the equilibrium exchange rate is reached.

A freely floating exchange rate system is easily operated as rates under such a system fluctuate freely without the need to deflate or inflate through monetary or fiscal policy. In the UK, such deflationary policies are likely to be politically unpopular and cause resistance from trade unions.

25.7: The UK's Exchange-rate System

Whilst the exchange rate system adopted by the UK in 1972 might be thought to lead to the pound's exchange rate being determined by supply and demand, many commentators feel that the British Government has tended to push up the price of sterling above that which purchasing power parity theory might suggest to be reasonable. However, in the mid-1980s the exchange rate had been below the level that supply and demand would suggest to be reasonable.

Reluctance to allow the exchange rate to be determined solely by supply and demand might be partly due to the historical role of sterling as a reserve currency. More importantly though, seems to be the fact that the government is reluctant to let the exchange rate fall since this lowers the price at which North Sea oil can be exported. This is unfavourable since the demand for North Sea oil tends to be inelastic: a fall in its price reduces revenue.

25.8: Problems faced by the Exporter

One of the problems faced by the exporter is that different countries use different units of measurement. For example, when considering volume America uses gallons whilst most other countries use metric units such as tonnes. Voltage also varies between countries; for example, North America supplies 110-120 volts whilst in Britain the supply is 240 volts. Firms must consider this when producing electrical goods for export.

There are also storage considerations to be made, for example cocoa may sweat if not properly stored whilst on ship. Items should be carefully packaged and stacked so they are not damaged in transit, especially when there is rough weather. The use of containers, which tend to be of a standard size, 8' x 10' or 20' or another multiple of 10', has helped. In some cases, the risks can be insured against by agents or by the senders themselves. Sometimes licences and other types of documentation may be required.

The exporter will also have to ensure that the payments are clearly set out. Sometimes exports are charged on a 'free on board' (FOB) basis. This means that the price that is quoted applies only to the time that the goods go on the ship from a particular country. After that, the importer of the goods will have to pay extra costs. On the other hand sometimes the goods are sold on a 'Cost and Freight' (CFR) basis where the price applies until the goods reach their port of destination. In other cases, the agreed price will also include the insurance charges.

25.9: Visible and Invisible Trade

Exports and imports consist of visible and invisible trade. Visible trade means the exporting and importing of goods. A high percentage of some country's exports consist of food and raw materials. There are some problems in exporting goods because many countries have trade barriers, for example, the EU with its agricultural policy tends to bar any products that could be grown within the EU.

The difference between the value of visible exports and the value of visible imports is the value of the visible balance, which is more commonly referred to as the 'balance of trade'.

Invisible trade includes trading in services plus profit earned from overseas dividends and interest payments. Services include financial services such as banking, insurance, shipping, tourism and education. Tourism has become more important in invisible trade. Shipping is still important for freight although not for passengers. A great deal of world shipping takes place in ships owned by European, Asian and American companies. The United Nations Trade Conference on Aid and Development (UNCTAD) has tried to reduce the amount that developing countries spend on shipping where payment is made to other countries.

Some students especially from developing countries may still need to go overseas if they want to pursue specialist studies. Other invisibles are financial services, including banking and insurance.

If a country exports more invisible trade by value than it imports, it is said to have a favourable balance on the invisible account. However, if it imports more invisibles by value then it is referred to as a deficit. The total of visible and invisibles is the balance on current account.

25.10: The European Union

The EU consists of 28 member states (Austria, Belgium, Denmark, Finland, France, Germany, Great Britain, Greece, Ireland, Italy, Luxembourg, the Netherlands, Portugal, Spain, Sweden, Poland, Hungary, the Czech Republic, Slovenia, Estonia, Cyprus, Slovakia, Latvia, Lithuania, Malta, Romania and Bulgaria). In 2013, after successful referendums in the candidate countries Croatia became the 28th member. The European Union is more than just a customs union because its aims to go beyond liberalisation of trade. It also aims to become an economic and political confederation of European nations that are responsible for a making common foreign and security policy and for ensuring cooperation on justice and home affairs.

Multiple Choice Questions: Use figure 25.2 below to complete questions 1-4:

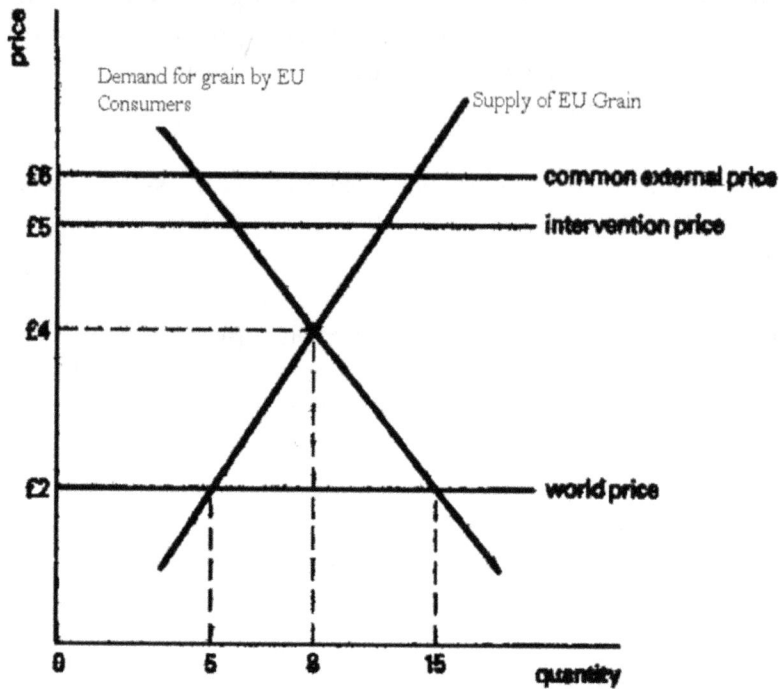

Figure 25.2

1. If EU farmers produce an output of 8 units of grain, what price would they expect to receive for each unit of grain?

   a) £2

   b) £4

   c) £5

   d) £6

2. Given this same output (i.e. 8 units) how much do EU consumers pay for EU grain?

   a) £2

   b) £4

   c) £5

   d) £6

3. If the EU imposed no intervention price and no common external tariff on imports of non-EU grain, how much non-EU grain would be imported?

    a) 3 units

    b) 7 units

    c) 10 units

    d) 15 units

4. In Figure 14a.3, what is the value of the tariff placed upon non-EU imports of grain?

    a) £2

    b) £3

    c) £4

    d) £5

    e) £6

Answers: 1 C, 2 C, 3 C, 4 C

25.11: Aims and policies of the EU

25.11.1: Competition policy

The European Union does not rule out the possibility of giving state aid to companies, but will only allow it if market conditions hinder progress towards certain economic or social objectives or if market conditions only allow these objectives to be attained with unacceptable repercussions. The EU would also allow state aid if intensified competition would be self-destructing. Therefore, aid for production should not be permitted except if it is part of a reorganisation programme or if rescue measures permit breathing spaces. In general, state aid should not expand capacity.

The EU has sometimes been concerned that research and development costs have been borne entirely by the domestic consumers of nationalised industries, which has meant that goods and services could be sold overseas at artificially reduced prices. Article 85 of the Treaty of Rome attempted to deal with this situation. This was set forth by the European Economic Community, a forerunner to the EU. It stated that, "Agreements between undertakings or decisions by associations of undertakings and concerted practices which may affect trade between member states and which have as their object prevention, restriction or distortion of competition within the Common Market, shall be regarded as incompatible with

EEC rules". The European Union is eager to limit price-fixing by firms seeking competitive advantages. There have also been moves towards uniform regulations regarding competition in an attempt to make sure that firms do not impose their own restrictions to prevent imports.

25.11.2: The Mobility of Labour

The EU aims to increase the mobility of labour. It has allowed citizens of the EU nations to take a job in any other member state without needing a work permit. There are however, some barriers to complete mobility of labour. For example, some jobs in public administration may be confined to nationals of that country.

There are obstacles to increased mobility of labour. These include such factors as language barriers and national prejudices. If complete mobility of labour is to become a reality for workers in the end, there must be some harmonisation of professional qualifications among EU members.

25.11.3: The Mobility of Capital

The European Union also aims to remove all real obstacles to medium-term and long-term movements of funds between member states. The UK has abolished the majority of foreign exchange controls since joining Europe.

In the longer term, we might expect British financial institutions such as building societies, to enter other members' national markets. Similarly, we might soon find that other members' commercial banks wish to expand their lending into the UK. Such moves could well pose problems for any country that is trying to impose a unilateral restrictive monetary policy.

25.11.4: Regional Policy

The Common Regional Policy aims to help regions of high unemployment. However, relatively little has been done about regional policy, partly because of budgetary constraints.

25.11.5: Transport Policy

The EU also has a Common Transport Policy, without which some firms might gain hidden advantages over others. Whilst progress towards harmonisation of transport systems has been slow, there has been harmonisation of restrictions on drivers' hours throughout the member states for all road haulage vehicles over three and a half tons. There has also been the introduction of tachographs, mainly for reasons of safety. Tachographs record speed, distance and time of driving.

Road haulage companies did not used to be able to carry goods solely within a foreign country. For example, whilst British firms could transport goods from France to the United Kingdom they could not transport goods solely within France. There are bilateral agreements between countries on the number of overseas vehicles that can carry goods. 'Cabotage' is now permitted; a UK road hauler can pick up goods in France and put them down in Germany. In the longer term, we would expect to see a system of multilateral agreements, so that road haulage firms can compete on the same basis as other firms.

25.11.6: The Harmonisation of Taxation

Unless there is some harmonisation of taxation, particularly value added tax (VAT), there may be a number of hidden barriers to trade. For example, Britain has imposed in the past much higher rates of taxation upon wine, which is generally imported, rather than upon beer, which is generally home-produced. This has been held to distort trade between the member states. In the long term, there should be harmonisation of tax rates, at least upon fuel and alcohol. There are currently no proposals for harmonising income tax.

25.11.7: The Common Agricultural Policy

One of the most controversial aspects of the EU has been the Common Agricultural Policy (CAP). Whilst within the EU one of the most important aims is the liberalisation of trade, CAP provides a system of protection for its agriculture in order to prevent the closure of uneconomic farms. Originally, the common agricultural policy was expected to restrict trade less than individual national protection schemes, but CAP has led to more rather than less protection. It is felt that some degree of protection for agriculture will:

- Increase efficiency by providing a better flow of agricultural products and by increasing specialisation

- Eliminate price variability

- Encourage self-sufficiency and protect members' balance of payments.

CAP uses a system of setting bureaucratic prices for various agricultural products in an attempt to keep the price of, say, grain stable.

The equilibrium price of EU produced grain tends to be well above the world price, mainly because of higher costs of production. This means that, in the absence of a very high tariff on imports of grain from non-member countries, European consumers would buy foreign grain rather than EU produced grain.

Using Figure 25.3, we can assume that the EU aims to keep the price of its own grain at P2 the bureaucratic or intervention price. If the world price is P1, at this price EU producers will only supply an output Qsi, whilst consumers in the EU will demand QD1. In order for this demand to be satisfied there must be some imports of non- EU grain. However, a common external tariff, which pushes the price of non- EU grain to P3 (above the intervention price), discourages any consumption of non- EU grain. This makes it possible for the EU to force the price of its grain up to P2. Consumers in the EU must pay this price since there are no imports flooding the market to force the price down.

Since the intervention price is P2, this means that the EU encourages its farmers to produce an output Qs2. Given that this price is above the equilibrium price (P*), then the suppliers will tend to supply more leading to a surplus. The EU, though, buys up any excess stocks, forcing the price to be P2. These stocks are released at times when the equilibrium price is higher than the intervention price (P2). Since, in the case of grain, the intervention price tends to be way above the equilibrium price, it is unlikely that any shifts in demand and/or supply will be sufficient to force the EU to release any stocks.

The prices of many agricultural products tend to be kept artificially high just about all of the time, so that a great deal of goods is wasted. This aspect of CAP has been criticised on moral grounds for the so-called 'food mountains' it produces.

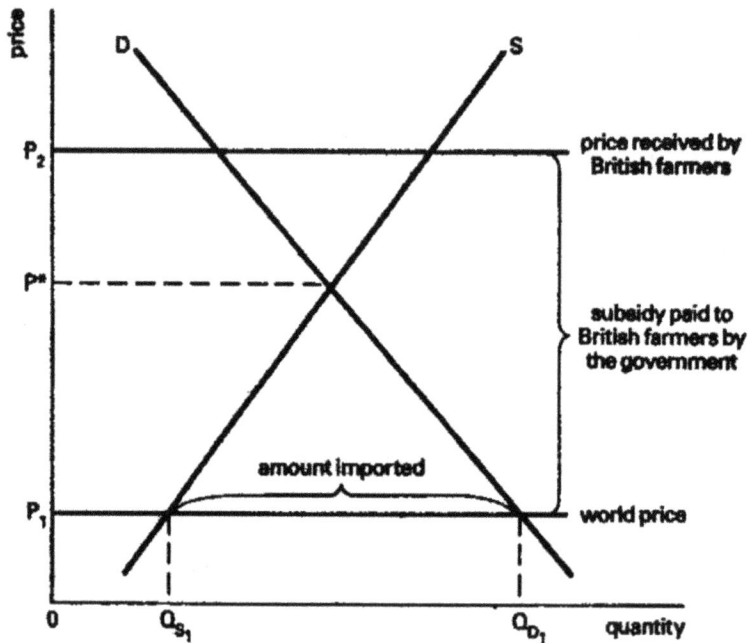

Figure 25.3: The effect of farmer-deficiency scheme on prices

The effect of CAP differs from the effect of the former British deficiency payments system, which made up the gap between the price of an agricultural product, such as grain, that the government was willing to pay to farmers and the world price. Unlike CAP, the deficiency payments system was a cheap food policy.

Working from Figure 25.3, if the government wished farmers to receive price P2 for each unit of grain supplied, whilst the market price was P1, under the deficiency payments system consumers only paid price P1. British farmers received, though, price P2, whilst supplying an output of only Qs1, since the price paid by consumers was Pi, they demand an output of QD, which meant that grain had to be imported in order to satisfy this demand.

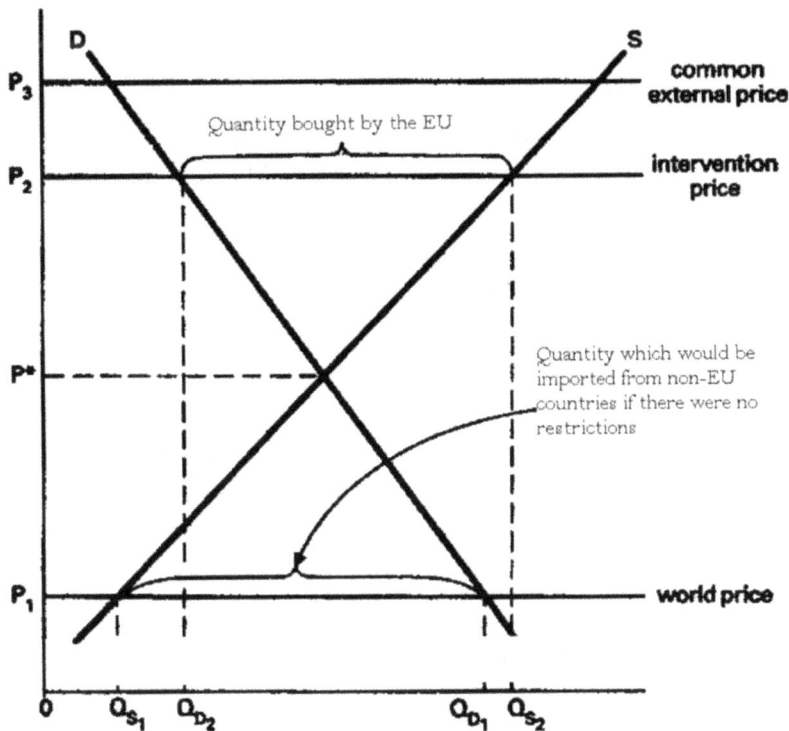

Figure 25.4: The effect of CAPs on grain prices

25.11.8: The Single Currency

In 1994, the European Monetary Institute was created as stepping stone in establishing the European Central Bank (ECB) and a common single currency for members of the EU. The ECB, established in 1998, is responsible for setting the single monetary policy and interest rate for the member states adopting the 'Euro'. Not all of the EU member nations joined at the currencies inception. Great Britain,

Denmark and Sweden chose not to enter immediately. In 2011 there were 23 countries that used the Euro but 5 of them are not part of the EU. The timetable of events leading to the full introduction of the Euro was as follows:

- **January 11, 1999-** The Euro begins to be used electronically and for foreign currency exchange.

- **January 1, 2002-** Euro notes and coins enter circulation.

- **July 1, 2002-** Local money is completely replaced by the Euro.

The Euro's introduction has been with the aim of increasing trade between the adopting nations. Without the need to pay currency exchange fees and the threat of daily changes in exchange rates gone, the barriers to open trading has been reduced.

25.12: Foreign Exchange

Foreign exchanges are the claims on another country held in the form of that country's currency or in interest-bearing bonds. In 2011 there were 23 countries that used the single currency of the Euro.

Factors affecting the supply of and demand for foreign exchange include the following:

- Changes in tastes and income may alter countries' supply of and demand for foreign exchange. As countries get richer, their tastes might change partly because of the demonstration effect. We might expect that as UK residents become richer, they will want more consumer durables. The consumption of more consumer durables might lead to the UK trading with different countries and alter the supply and demand for foreign exchange.

- Changes in tariff barriers may alter the supply and demand for foreign exchange. If the EU's Common External Tariff were abolished, the price of both British exports to and imports from countries outside the EU would fall. Therefore, the UK's demand for the currencies of these countries would be expected to rise.

- A reduction in non-tariff barriers, for example a harmonisation of regulations relating to vehicles, might be expected to have a similar effect.

A relative change in the price of one country's export prices, perhaps because of general inflation, can affect the demand for foreign exchange. If British prices rise relative to US prices, the demand for British goods will tend to fall and, therefore, the demand for sterling will fall. The effect would be shown diagrammatically as a movement along the demand curve.

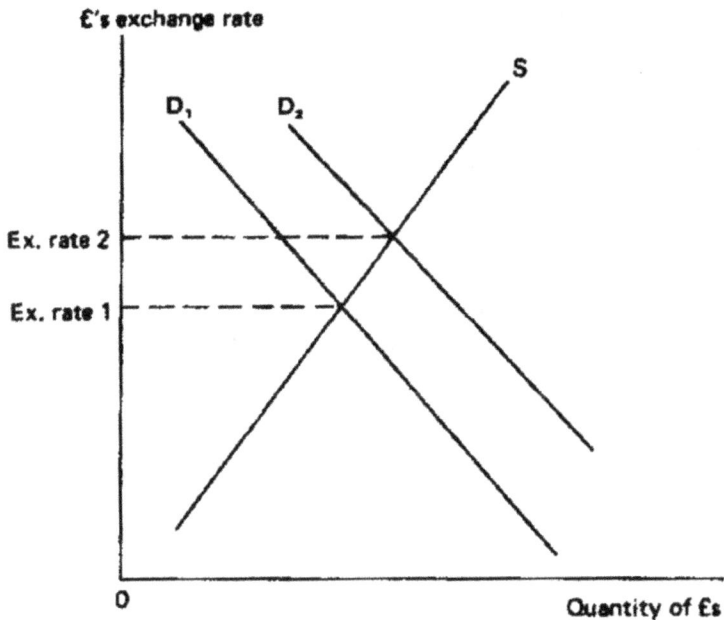

Figure 25.5: A rising exchange rate

The Capital Account

The UK's capital account is made up of the flow of money for investment purposes between the UK and other countries and of the flow of international grants. The flow of investments between the UK and other EU members should increase as the mobility of capital within the EU improves.

25.12.1: Balance Of Payments Disequilibrium

Balance of payments disequilibrium may take the form of a deficit or the form of a surplus. A payments deficit leads to a loss of reserves, whilst a payments surplus leads to a build-up of reserves.

How might a government attempt to correct a balance of payments deficit? If a government imposes restrictions on the flow of investments abroad, the balance of payments may improve, but these restrictions may prove unpopular with industrialists. There might be payments problems in the future because of restricting investment abroad because more investment abroad now often leads to a better balance of payments in the future. Restrictive fiscal and/ or restrictive monetary policy might be used to try to control the balance of payments, whereby the government tries to control the level of aggregate demand at home. 'Back-door' methods may lead to the exclusion of some imports. For example, regulations specifically designed to curb imports may be introduced. Japan has been accused, on a number of occasions, of using such regulations. Indirect subsidies, such as 'soft loans' as mentioned earlier, may be given to help gain export orders

Another method of trying to restrict imports might be with higher interest rates. These will tend to attract, in particular, more 'hot' money and, therefore, lead to some inflow of currency. American interest rates were high in 1985 partly for attracting hot money. However, high interest rates discourage firms from investing (borrowing) and so may prove to be self-defeating. A government, rather than trying to discourage imports, might try to stimulate exports in an attempt to improve the balance of payments. Exports might be encouraged if the government provides improved information. The provision of information in the UK might be improved through the Export Services Branch and the Export and Guarantee Department. A policy of devaluation (in the case of a fixed exchange-rate regime) or of allowing the exchange rate to move downwards will make exports cheaper and imports more expensive, other things being equal.

25.12.2: *The Importance of Adjusting a Payments Surplus*

A persistent balance of payments surplus for one particular country is undesirable in the context of the world economy since one country's surplus is another country's deficit. A country that maintains a surplus at the expense of a trading partner might find that this partner is reluctant to import commodities from the surplus country because of its own payments difficulties. It is possible that, in the case of the UK for example, a persistent surplus in the balance of oil trade in the early 1980s forced up the exchange rate and so made the UK uncompetitive in other fields.

25.13: Withdrawing from the EU

What would happen to British firms if Britain withdrew its membership of the EU?

One needs to consider the effect upon the balance of payments that British withdrawal from the EU may have. If tariffs were not imposed upon British goods entering the EU, we might expect there to be relatively little impact upon the balance of payments. If tariffs were imposed because of British withdrawal, British exporters would find it much more difficult to export whilst British importers would face less competition. The resulting effect upon the balance of payments would depend upon the price elasticity of both imports and exports. Since the UK exports to the EU goods and services, which are similar to those it imports from other members, we might expect relatively little change, except the imposition of a common external tariff of about 5%. The UK would presumably however wish still to be part of a free trade area with the other members of the EU. Even if the common external tariff, which amounts to about 5% on average were imposed this would have little effect upon firms except where products were very price elastic.

We need to consider the effect that CAP has upon the UK. If the UK withdrew from the EU, would we return to a deficiency payments scheme? If we were to, there may be relatively little effect upon actual agricultural prices received by farmers. If the UK has benefited from greater economies of scale because of membership of the EU, withdrawing may well cause the loss of these benefits. There may be less project co-ordination between the UK and other European countries. However, the harmonisation of regulations in some cases may have been a hindrance to the UK rather than beneficial. There has been relatively little harmonisation of taxes so far but it is being proposed within the EU at the time of writing.

British withdrawal would mean the UK losing some regional project aid and the mobility of capital and labour being restricted. The control of multi-nationals would be more difficult for a British government without the co-operation of other European agencies, but the control of national monopolies would probably be little affected by any decision to withdraw from the EU. Issues such as the Common Fisheries Policy would have to be renegotiated if the UK were to withdraw. There would seem to be little point to the UK withdrawing from the EU unless it was to embark on a radically different policy. One alternative to the UK being in the EU would be to form some sort of trade agreement either with the Commonwealth or with the USA, which would involve higher transport costs and, therefore, probably higher prices. Prior to the UK joining the EU, the UK was in EFTA (the European Free Trade Area) it would be difficult reforming such a trade agreement since almost all of the original members of EFTA are now in the EU.

The UK might decide to withdraw from the EU in order to become a 'siege economy' and impose high tariffs on various imports in an attempt to reduce unemployment. It is unlikely that such action will be successful as there would almost certainly be retaliation.

It is difficult to assess the economic advantages and disadvantages of the UK withdrawing from the EU. This is because the policy that the UK would pursue instead, would very much depend upon the internal and external politics surrounding the issue. The political consequences that would ensue mean that it could not be a purely economic decision and so complicate the matter immensely. What we can say is that it would be virtually impossible for the UK to return to patterns of trading which existed prior to its entry into the EU. Japan has warned that many of the jobs provided by Japanese firms would be at risk if the UK was to leave the EU.

25.14: Cartels

In what ways might developing countries co-operate in order to improve their economic prospects? Evaluate the likely success of such methods.

One possible method of co-operation is through the formation of a cartel, particularly for primary products. Producers could then adopt the traditional methods of restricting output in order to be able to increase price. OPEC has done this successfully since 1973. If the price of agricultural products was pushed up as the result of the formation of a cartel, countries not at present specialising in such items, might decide to invest in improving their own production.

The formation of a cartel is likely to cause problems. For example, there will need to be agreement on quotas. However, particularly those countries which have large-scale balance of payments problems or other problems, may be tempted to produce beyond their quotas, either openly or secretly. Low-cost producers will tend to have very strong incentives to go beyond their quotas.

Cartels will tend to be more successful if the demand for the products concerned is price inelastic than if it is price elastic. The demand for oil has tended to be price inelastic, but the demand for many agricultural products from developing countries has tended to be less inelastic as prices move upwards.

Co-operation can exist in manufacturing. For example, in the textile industry there are multi-fibre agreements. However, many developed countries have their own textile industries and are reluctant to import textiles from developing countries, especially where importing is likely to increase unemployment in the developed country.

Developing countries might be able to reduce their balance of payments problems through collective agreements. For example, the United Nations Conference on Trade and Development (UNCTAD) suggested a 40:40:20 roles for liner conferences, whereby 40% of the trade between two countries could take place in the importing country, 40% in the exporting country and 20% of trade would be left to so-called "cross traders". This action was suggested partly because developed countries, both in Western Europe and in Eastern Europe, have tended to have a large part of the total shipping market. Such a move would tend to be against the principles of free trade and specialisation and would possibly lead to higher charges. It would not be in the interest of potential individual importers and exporters though could be beneficial to developing countries as a whole. However, some of the poorest land-locked countries might have to pay higher charges without any offsetting benefits. Developing countries could try to develop joint projects. The "Tan-Zam" railway was the result of a joint project, built partly to reduce the cost of transportation of exports from and imports to the land-locked country of Zambia. The problem with such projects is that capital supplies tend to be very limited. In some cases, the instability of regimes means that there is little likelihood of the creation of an integrated social infrastructure between countries. The East African Federation split up in the 1970s partly because of political instability.

Co-operation would tend to be improved by the creation of institutions, comparable to the EU. Such co-operation might lead to economies of scale, particularly for small countries. However, such institutions take a long time to develop and political differences may hinder progress. There may be benefits to developing countries from forming collective agreements with existing large-scale markets in the developed world. They might try, for example, to become associate members of the EU.

25.15: International Co-operation

No nation is self-sufficient, meaning that overall most international trade is beneficial, in the sense that the countries involved will usually benefit (obvious exceptions may well include products like tobacco). Given the fact that no country is an "economic island" meaning that no country can carry out a successful economic policy without due consideration to the rest of the world, it is necessary for there to be some level of international co-operation. This would enable nations to achieve the highest prosperity possible from world trade. The absence of such international co-operation has in the past led to dire consequences. One has to only look to the inter-war period (1918-1939) in the developed world to see how protectionist, self-centred measures brought the developed world into a huge depression. The fear of this occurring again spurred the creation of a multitude of international organisations that in the last few decades have attempted to smooth out any obstacles to trade.

25.15.1: ECOWAS

One such organisation is that of ECOWAS (Economic Community of West African States). This fifteen-member organisation was set up in 1975 and it was hoped that it would promote regional growth through closer co-operation of the member states, and that eventually a customs union would be created with the ultimate goal of eliminating any trade restrictions between member states, so making trade easier. Indeed its goals are similar to those of the European Union, who by the start of 1993 had eliminated all such trade barriers between member states. Despite having similar aspirations to the EU, ECOWAS has not developed as much as it might have been hoped. Currently there are fifteen member states; Benin, Burkina Faso, Cape Verde, Côte d'Ivoire, Gambia, Ghana, Guinea, Guinea-Bissau, Liberia, Mali, Niger, Nigeria, Senegal, Sierra Leone, and Togo.

25.15.2: WTO

At the start of 2013 there were 159 members of WTO (World Trade Organisation) formerly known as GATT (General Agreement on Tariffs and Trade), which as its title suggests has the main aim of expanding world trade through reducing tariffs, subsidies and other distortions to world trade. The agreement was originally signed in 1947. In 1965 GATT introduced a new chapter, which laid particular emphasis on the development of third world nations in calling for a reduction of tariffs and quotas on developing nations.

All such international organisations provide a forum where individual nations come together and try to co-operate as much as possible. However, the existence of such organisations does not mean that all problems are sorted out. One only has to look at the Uruguay round of talks (GATT) in the early 1990s, where the EU and the USA could not agree on a reduction in agricultural subsidies, to understand that co-operation in the world is far from smooth. Given the interdependence of the world today such disputes can only have a disadvantageous effect on world trade.

25.15.3: The International Monetary Fund

The International Monetary Fund (IMF) was set up after the Bretton Woods Agreement in 1944. The main aim was to avoid the problems of protectionism and competitive devaluations, which had occurred during the 1930s and had contributed to the world recession.

The IMF aimed originally at having a system of stable exchange rates, under which each member country had to keep the parity of its currency within relatively small bounds. Most currencies are now floating rather than constrained by such a structure.

The Fund obtains money from its member countries partly according to each member's gross national product. If countries have difficulties with their balance of payments, they can withdraw some foreign currency in exchange for their own. The more money they borrow, the more stringent are the conditions the Fund tends to apply. Interest payments are made on any loans from the International Monetary Fund.

Unlike national trade, where the domestic currency is accepted in all of the country, there is no international currency for use among members. However, Special Drawing Rights, which can sometimes be obtained from the International Monetary Fund, helps to overcome this difficulty of there being no single international unit of account.

The EU believes that there should be efforts to harmonise national taxation and domestic energy prices, since otherwise there will be distortions of trade between member states and of energy consumption within states. Therefore, consumer oil prices, which are largely dominated by taxation, should reflect increases in world prices. Changes in coal prices have reflected market conditions, but EU production costs are well above world costs and, therefore, subsidies have often been introduced to keep the price to consumers and industry down. For gas, conditions vary between a free market in Germany and a nationalised system in France. Governments, generally either directly or informally controls electricity prices. The Commission has argued that the question of harmonisation of oil prices requires separate consideration. It has been suggested that the taxation burden, regarding taxation of oil, should be shifted from light to heavier products.

The harmonisation of energy prices is important if there is to be a genuine common market among the EU members because expenditure on oil represented, in 2012, about 10% of EU members' gross domestic product and a quarter of total imports.

Self-examination Questions

1. What are tariffs? How far do they affect international trade?

2. What are quotas? Why are they imposed?

3. What is meant by the balance of trade?

4. What is meant by terms of trade?

5. What is meant by a 'soft loan'?

6. In the EU, there was considerable controversy over the movement of people from new EU members to the UK. What might be the underlying reason for this?

7.   Many people suggested that when Britain joined the EU there might be the problem of the so-called "Golden Triangle" of Northern France, South East England and former West Germany forming attractive areas for industry at the centre of the market at the expense of other areas. Have these worries been justified?

8.   What factors might deter British firms from trying to locate in other parts of the EU?

9.   Why might harmonisation of regulations lead to an increase in trade? What disadvantages might there be because of the harmonisation of regulations?

10   It has sometimes been suggested that membership of the EU will lead to greater economies of scale in certain products, such as in aircraft and computers. How far is this suggestion correct?

11. In 2013 the USA Government among others, tried to persuade the Japanese Government to remove some of its non-tariff barriers to imports. What is meant by the term "non-tariff barriers" and why are they so important?

12. Most of the members of the EU have adopted the European Single Currency and so the European Central Bank governs their interest rates centrally. What are the advantages and disadvantages of such a system for:

a)   Intra-EU trade?

b)   Trade between members and non-members?

13. Why have some companies manufactured cars under licence in other countries? What are the economic consequences of such practices? How far has it been successful in achieving them?

14. Why might energy prices have fallen below their "true" levels? What does the Commission mean by the "true" level?

15. Why does the EU have a different policy towards coal than towards agriculture?

16. How has the privatisation of British Gas affected the likelihood of harmonisation of energy policy in the EU?

17. What would be the effect on British firms if VAT at 8% were imposed upon all fossil fuels but not upon energy saving products? For example, loft insulation, double-glazing, etc.

Chapter 26: THE CHANGING ENVIRONMENT

26.1: Evaluating Change

Businesses need to be constantly aware of the changes taking place in the environment around them. Managers need to consider the potential of these changes to damage the firm and the opportunities they may present. Today organisations are not just affected by their local environments but also by changes in the global market place. Interest rates in foreign countries affect the level of investment in others. Exchange rates between nations affect the balance of imports and exports. The realm of business is truly global and with it comes the need to take into account global changes, influences and trends.

There are three very useful theoretical frameworks discussed in the next section that help businesses identify these factors. The first analyses the 'macro' environment of the firm, the second its immediate industry and the final one attempts to gauge the internal influences and external pressures directly felt by the firm itself.

26.2: PESTL Framework

This framework is used to analyse the business environment of a particular firm. It is made up of five categories of influences and possible changing factors. A PESTL analysis is used for many different situations. One of the most useful of these is when a firm wants to find out about a new market or geographical region that it is considering entering into. It is a good way of researching the differing areas of a country or a regions overall business climate.

Political: This section highlights the effects of the government policies, regulation and the influence of pressure groups in the firms operating environment. When considering these it is important to recognise that not only their 'home' government, but also those in which they trade may influence a firm. Government influences can include changes in policies that may affect the profitability of a firm. For example, if the government introduces a new deposit system for sparkling canned drinks, which was done in Germany in 2003, then this will affect the sales turnover of soft drink companies. This system requires consumers to pay a small deposit on their purchase that then are returned to them when they return the drinks can. This has caused a decrease in the sales of canned drinks and an increase in those packaged in plastic bottles. A firm that had anticipated this quickly would have been able to switch production sooner and be ready for the change. It is therefore very important to make sure that a firm is aware of the current and possible future political environments that they face.

Economic: If a firm recognises current and future trends in their economic environment they will be better off than a firm that does not. Economic growth, inflation, interest rates, exchange rates and levels of unemployment have all sorts of effects on a firm. For example, if interest rates are erratic and change often then it may not be such a good idea for a firm to borrow money to invest without studying what effect this will have on their loan and investment income (Sensitivity Analysis). If unemployment in the region is very low then a firm may need to increase their wages in order to hang on to and attract new employees away from other firms. The economic environment is often closely linked to the political environment, as different political parties often have conflicting economic attitudes. If there is a change of government, then this may cause changes in fiscal and monetary policies.

Socio-demographics: Social, demographical and cultural changes will affect the way in which a firm may operate. It affects the type and availability of customers and buyers. A firm that wishes to enter a foreign market is likely to conduct market research into the demographic make-up of the country. This is especially important if the firm targets specific age or lifestyle groups. For example, if a family car manufacturer considered entering a new market they would need to know the typical make-up of the family unit; is it 2, 3, 4, or more people? The social aspect to this category includes public opinion. In the current climate, there has been a lot of public concern over Genetically Modified (GM) foodstuff and this has affected a large number of food producers and retailers. It is also important to take into consideration the cultural factors in any area a firm trades in. Religious, ethical, racial and community lifestyles need to be taken into account so that a firm does not inadvertently cause upset and distress to certain citizens. For example, it would not be advisable to set up a pork restaurant in Israel or for a Korean firm to export dog meat to the UK.

Technological: Increased availability of technology whether they are new products, processes, materials or systems will affect how a firm operates. Changes in information technology and telecommunications have changed the way many people work, shop, socialise and relax. The Internet and e-mail have changed the way in which organisations buy, sell, inform and satisfy their customers. It has also offered up new and simpler ways to increase the number of potential customers a firm has by offering products and services to overseas consumers. This has caused a number of problems for traditional 'bricks and mortar' firms that often struggle to keep up with online stores pricing and 24-hour service.

Legal: Like the economic factors, legal influences are heavily linked in with the political category of PESTL. Legislation affects all aspects of a firm from accounting rules and tax laws through to worker rights and provision of safety regulations.

Firms may be influenced by a number of legal entities. Unions, governments, consumer associations and international organisations and communities like the EU, World Trade Organisation (WTO) and the International Monetary Fund (IMF) laws, decisions and legal guidelines may affect firms either directly or indirectly.

The example of a PESTL analysis below is for a firm wishing to set up an Internet based stationery supply firm in the UK called Stationery Direct Ltd.

Political	Economic
Expansion into EU markets has been made simpler with the wide spread adoption of the Euro.	Introduction of free internet access will allow more people to use the service.
Possible to offer products globally as there are few restrictions on the movement of stationery products across borders.	Growth of internet firms has recovered since the 'Tech bust' in the early 2000's.
Industry not really affected by changes in domestic governments.	Interest rates are at their lowest for fifty years.
	Product is a necessity to most business customers so an economic slowdown will have less of an effect on us than other industries.
Socio-demographic	**Technological**
People may be unwilling to do business over the internet for a variety of reasons. i.e. Security, lack of interaction, unable to use computer software needed etc.	Improvements in speed of internet services to the home (Broadband) mean that more visual and interactive content is possible without long download times.
Future expansion will bring employment opportunities.	Security increases and developments in encryption allow safer payment over the internet.
The need to recycle has been recognised by the public and businesses. Firms may need to provide these services or be conscious of where they source their goods. i.e. recycled office paper .	Rapidly changing technology means that the firm may have to upgrade more often than thought to keep up with rivals systems.
Different countries may have different product needs such as different paper sizes etc.	There have been widespread computer virus scares during 2003. Effective protection from these is needed to ensure that the service is always available.
Legal	
Introduction of minimum wage may mean that wage structures need to be reconsidered.	
Changes in pension rules mean that advice is needed on the best option to take for the employees.	

Figure 26.1

26.3: Porters Five Forces Model

Michael E Porters 'Five Forces' model is used to depict the competitive factors in a given market or industry. The five forces involved are the threat of New Entrants, the power of Suppliers, and the power of Buyers, Competitive Rivalry and the availability of Substitutes as shown in the diagram below.

Porter's Five Forces

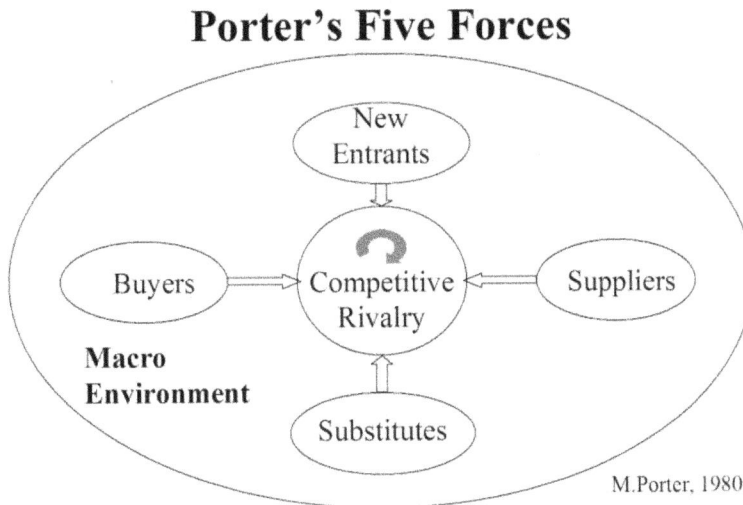

Figure 26.2

If there is a high threat of new entrants to the market then this is often bad for existing firms. Market share could be stolen away by these newcomers and profits are likely to fall. Ideally, there would be barriers to entry that prevent new firms from competing in the market. These come in a variety of forms from a wide range of sources. For example, a legal licence may be needed to operate, as in mobile telecommunications, there are often limits on the number of licences available for purchase and so once they are all bought the only way into the market is to purchase a firm that has one.

Alternatively, a firm may hold a physical barrier to entry over other firms. If there are only limited resources in the world, such as diamond mines, the firms that own these can prevent others from producing their product.

The power of suppliers has an influence on the competitive nature of the industry. If there is only one or a limited number of suppliers for a component or raw material, they will have a lot of power over their customers. This is the case in the oil industry and the influence of OPEC. If however, the number of suppliers is large, for example in the supply of milk, the purchasing firm is likely to have more power over them. This is because if the suppliers do not co-operate with the firm, they know that they can easily find a similar priced alternative elsewhere.

The converse is true when looking at the power of buyers. i.e. if there are only a small number then they will have more of an influence, as there are only limited numbers of organisations or people that will buy your product. If there are a large number of buyers then it is usually easier to sell on your own terms.

Competitive Rivalry is high if industry growth is low, fixed costs are high, product /service differentiation is low and switching costs between rival firm's products are low for buyers.

The availability of substitute products is also an important factor to consider. If you raise the price of your product and there are cheaper alternative products that will satisfy the same needs as yours, then consumers are likely to purchase these instead. An example of this could be in the butter market. If the price of butter were increased by, say 50%, while the price of alternatives such as margarine stayed constant, more people would switch away from the butter. Therefore the ideal situation is that there are few substitutes for the market, meaning that the availability of substitutes were low.

26.4: SWOT Technique

Andrew's SWOT analysis is used to assess the current and possible future market situations of a particular business. Four sections to the analysis need to be considered. The first two are Strengths and Weaknesses (S&W). These are both current and come from within the firm. The second half of the analysis focuses upon the Opportunities and Threats (O&T) that the firm may face. As such, these are future issues that need to be considered. These are also external to the firm, although there may be some internal factors.

Strengths: What is the business good at? What are its competitive advantages over its rivals? Are they well established or do they have a good reputation within the industry? Are the management the best in the market? All businesses have some form of strength otherwise, consumers would choose to purchase from another firm. The easiest way to fill in this section is to ask the question 'why do our customers purchase from us?'

Weaknesses: What areas of the production or service processes could the company improve? Do customers complain about particular areas of operations? Firms have at least one area they can improve on. Is it customer care, after sales service or delivery? It is important not to concentrate solely on customers when considering a firm's weaknesses, all areas of the organisation and all people who encounter the firm in any way should be considered. Do suppliers have a good working relationship with the firm? If not how can these, be improved? Does the firm pollute unnecessarily? Are dividend payouts fair to shareholders in a PLC?

When this half of the analysis has been satisfactorily completed, the firm should try to build on its strengths and work to reduce its weaknesses. If a firm attempts to do this it is likely to prove more attractive a proposition to work for, buy from, sell to and invest in and so on. If it seeks to minimise its weaknesses it will be able to retain valuable customers and maintain good relationships with other firms and organisations. In short, their reputation will improve if the process is successful.

Opportunities: What opportunities are available to the firm? These can often be linked to a PESTL analysis of the external environment. For example, if interest rates are low and the economy is growing it may be that it is a good time to invest in expanding the firms operations. Have new trading laws or changes in quotas or export taxes meant that it is easier to enter foreign markets? Has a competitor had financial troubles and is now primed for a takeover or can you take control of their falling market share? Has a new technology been introduced that will reduce your costs or increase your revenues?

Threats: The PESTL analysis may provide some information on possible threats to the firm's profitability or even its survival. Are new regulations to be introduced that will affect the organisations industry? What about new employment laws? May there be an influx or cheap foreign imports to the market if proposed international trade agreements are altered? Internal problems could also be threats. If the CEO is due to retire and no suitable replacement has been found, then this is a threat to the continued smooth operation of the firm.

Once this half of the analysis has been completed a firm must try to harness the opportunities that it sees as being worthwhile pursuing. It must also seek to neutralise any threats that it sees as being a problem in the future. It is quite often the case that threats that will affect the whole industry, if dealt with faster and more efficiently than a firm's rival, will provide a competitive advantage to a firm. As mentioned previously, the change in the sale of sparkling soft drinks laws in Germany has allowed some quick thinking firms to increase their market share. Whilst rivals prices increase, quick-thinking firms moved production to containers not covered by the deposit scheme. As the cans must be returned to the same shop that they were bought, with a receipt, few consumers are willing to reclaim their deposits. The firms that switched packaging early have increased market share through their lower prices whilst other firms have lost out.

An example of a SWOT analysis is shown below. Once again, the firm being analysed is Stationery Direct Ltd.

Strengths	Weaknesses
Premises need not be in expensive town site.	Many companies will have regular supplier already.
Local business so better customer relations.	
Internet is a growing medium so good expansion potential.	
Few competitors on the Internet.	Not yet able to use economies of scale to advantage.
Product sold is always required by business so market safe.	
Superior after sales service due to time saved using the Internet.	Initially only covering a small region of the country.
Opportunities	**Threats**
New Internet market is there to be taken advantage of.	More conventional established suppliers.
The Internet is a global market.	Lower priced competition.
Expansion to multi-national company.	The company relies upon the Internet connection being constantly on so it has to be reliable..
Diversification into computer systems and office furniture.	

Figure 26.3

26.5: The Accelerator and Effect on Capital Goods Industries

Capital goods industries include, for example, shipbuilding, machine tools, lorries, etc.

A definition of capital goods is that they are used in the production of other goods and services. A small change in total demand has a much greater effect proportionately on these industries. They therefore tend to be more volatile than the retailing trade in clothes or food.

High-risk industries

The high-risk industries include fashion and the music industry. Setting up a business in these markets will be risky. Managers will try to anticipate demand rather than react to it. If they do not anticipate correctly, they will be left with unused stock. Rapid changes in tastes and trends can leave many slow firms holding this unwanted stock, which is often then placed in sales. The fashion industry is very fast moving so this is why many clothing retailers have so many 'end of season' sales each year. Conversely, in the short-term pop music personalities have a form of monopoly power. They can charge almost whatever they like for a concert and customers will still buy tickets.

Energy prices

Energy prices may change because of cartels such as the Organisation of Oil Producing and Exporting Countries (OPEC) or government, with the imposition of Value Added Tax (VAT) at 8% on domestic fuel. In the short term, there may be no substitutes for the fuel whereas in the long term firms can change fuels. However, in the short-term firms may be able to use fuel more efficiently, e.g. for central heating or as motive power, etc.

Changes in the High Street

There have been a number of changes in the High Street, e.g. more building societies and financial institutions. In addition, the larger chains of shops such as Boots, Currys, etc. now dominate almost every High Street. There has been a relative demise of the independent shop. However, in recent years, some of the larger shops have moved out of town to retail parks leaving shop space for small independent retailers. Local authorities often try to compete with the retail parks by pedestrianising High streets. OECD (Organisation for Economic Cooperation and Development) reports indicate that on average pedestrianisation increases trade by about 15%. In some cases, local authorities try to encourage retailers to unite to combine their marketing campaigns. This can occur in shopping malls especially when the mall in owned by one firm.

Changes in technology

Managers have been able to exercise more control over individual workers, e.g. tachographs installed in lorries, which were known as the 'spy in the cab', record time, distance and speed. This made it more difficult for a driver to say that he or she was held up in a traffic jam if the tachograph showed differently.

Shopping from home is now possible. Catalogues have been available for some time but now the Internet is used routinely. This could have an effect on the location of shops and their size. Shops could be smaller since deliveries could be made from convenient warehouses on the outskirts of towns. It could lead to a lack of personal contact and so many people may prefer to shop at bricks and mortar stores still. There might be problems in how we describe goods. For example, people do not necessarily know the contents of washing powder, etc. but probably recognise the appropriately sized box. It might be difficult for the customers to describe the box that they would need without actually seeing it. People are more likely to buy branded goods than an unknown make if they had to state their order. It is unlikely that people would wish to look through a list containing 20,000 items, which would be a typical number of types of goods in a large supermarket.

Computerisation has had an effect on stock control. It is now possible for employees to know what products their firm has in stock, the numbers of each item and their locations in the store. This has sped up the sales process and allowed firms to serve customers more effectively.

Working from home

By the mid-1990s, only about 1 in 3 people were employed on permanent '9-5' jobs. This was caused partly by the increase in numbers of people working from home. One of the problems in working from home is the lack of human contact. The work place is often one of the employee's main social interactions outside of the family. There may also be problems in finding the space to set up a home office in many houses and the conflicts that this may cause for members of the family who will lose space where equipment has to be stored. On the other hand, there are opportunities for parents, carers and those with disabilities or lack of transport to work more efficiently. Those whose most important commitment is not work can arrange their work around their other priorities.

Changes in population of rural and urban areas

The depopulation of areas such as rural Wales and the Scottish Highlands and Islands, perhaps because of remoteness, has implications for the location of firms. For example, retailers would prefer to be in areas where the population is growing such as East Anglia. It also has implications for manufacturers who would probably prefer to be near a suitable growing labour market.

Problems with public transport in rural areas means that those on lower incomes tend to live in towns whilst the higher income families move to the more rural areas but with access to towns. This has implications for rural shops and post offices since those with cars will often use such shops only for topping up purposes rather than getting all their shopping in the local shop.

Economic considerations

These include changes in total incomes and distribution of income. As people get richer they will tend to demand more goods and services. There are a few exceptions and economists usually call these goods and services 'inferior goods'. An example of an inferior good is tinned food and bus travel could be considered as an inferior service.

Firms will form various forecasts to try to assess the likely changes and make plans accordingly. This will particularly apply when there is a large time lag between the time taken to go from the underlying concept of wishing to change and the time at which production can take place. Therefore, a car manufacturer may take a considerable amount of time to plan for car production. In some cases, as with the Pacific Rim countries, which include Singapore and Indonesia, the firm may wish to get into their markets through establishing factories in their territories. With total incomes held constant, changes in the distribution of incomes will also affect the firm. An example in the U.K was the tax cuts for higher earners from 50p to 45p in the pound in the 2012 budget.

Changes in indirect and direct taxation

Changes in indirect taxation will have an effect on firms, for example, the imposition of VAT on domestic fuel will tend to reduce the demand for fossil fuels and make people slightly more inclined to consider fuel saving measures. With demerit goods, the intervention of VAT or other sales taxes is relevant. A demerit good is a product or service available for purchase on the market that people regard as unhealthy, degrading, or socially damaging for other people to consume. Examples of these goods include tobacco, alcohol, gambling or anything else that society sees as somewhat questionable. Higher taxation on tobacco will deter some smokers particularly those in lower income brackets. However, these effects are sometimes short term as the population accepts the price rises. The government may impose lower taxation on some expenditure or even give subsidies in order to encourage investment in some goods or services. The nuclear industry, for example, has in the past been subsidised and therefore has a higher proportion of the supply than would be the case if market forces prevailed. There have often been subsidies made to public transport and even more so in many other countries. Subsidies have been given in many countries to agriculture and therefore the agricultural communities in the UK and in the USA have received much benefit.

Case Study

Until recently, most firms needed a large head office since all files needed to be in one place as people making enquiries by post, phone or personal call expected to receive an answer within a short time. An example of this is that files containing information about insurance policies are easier to access when in one place rather than when scattered among the branches. A client who had moved house several times might have to have correspondence with several different addresses otherwise. Similarly, with building societies and banks interest added to accounts was a complex calculation, which was best done by head office. With modern computers however, this information can easily be contained in a computer with a large memory. Machines that can determine signatures are also widely available. This means that clients of some building societies may use any branch for transactions. It also means that head offices of newer financial services e.g. First Direct are very footloose since all communications are by post or telephone. The National Giro, now part of Santander, has been able to exploit this possibility since the 1960s. A footloose firm is one, which does not have to locate near either their market or where their supplies of raw materials come from. This is often the case in the service sector and was one of the main reasons why financial service firms chose to locate in the South East of England. There has been a movement away from this region in recent years but the majority of international tertiary service companies still base their UK headquarters in London and the surrounding areas.

There are wider implications. With the advent of the Euro and a more open European marketplace, service industry Headquarters services, for example dealing with accounts, secretarial and printing services, no longer have to be in the same expensive buildings in the centre of a large town such as London where rents are very high. Some of the services could be sent to other places in the country or even abroad. This would be in line with manufacturing organisations where a great deal of the assembly work is done in Far Eastern countries. Some commentators have gone even further and suggested that the large firms are the business dinosaurs of the modern world and are unnecessary. Other more moderate writers have suggested that the large firms might continue to exploit their economies of scale but will divest themselves of the problems of span of control and chain of command by contracting out many of the jobs required. For example, computer programming often needs a mind that is quick to take advantage of the rapid changes in technology in both software and hardware. This is not easy to do in large firms, which are geared to slower moving bureaucratic decision-making.

Self-examination Questions

Theoretical Frameworks

1. Pick a firm that you are familiar with; it could be one that you are or have worked for or bought from. Construct a SWOT analysis matrix for the firm. What should the firm do to improve its performance? Are there any major threats to its continued existence?

2. Carry out a PESTL analysis into the current business climate in your local county. Is now a good time to start up a new firm in your area? Remember not only local influences effect the business environment but national and international factors do as well.

3. Conduct a Porters Five Forces analysis of the grocery shopping industry at present. For each of the five forces state whether the effects are strong medium or low. Give your reasons for these decisions.

Economic changes

1. Which industries suffer most in a recession?

2. Why do capital goods suffer more than consumer goods in a recession?

3. Which goods are more likely to be sold in a boom period?

4. Which businesses, if any, might gain in a recession?

5. Which goods or services are most likely to be affected by a change in interest rates?

6. How do changes in interest rates affect the ways in which firms may try to obtain finance?

7. How may an increase in VAT on domestic fuel affect firms?

8. How may significant changes in the highest rates of income tax affect firms?

Privatisation and deregulation changes

1. Which industries have been mainly affected by privatisation?

2. Why might privatised industries often want to diversify?

3. Why has the Government often imposed limits on the maximum price increases that privatised industries such as B.T. can charge?

Production life cycle

1.   Does the production life cycle affect all firms?

2.   In what ways can the production life cycle cause changes that can be predicted?

3.   How can firms cope with the changes caused by the product life cycle?

Location changes

1.   Why have more shops moved away from town centres?

2.   It is sometimes said that manufacturing firms have become more footloose. What does this mean and what are the reasons for this?

3.   Why have more service industries headquarters become more footloose?

4.   What effect do changes in location have on public transport systems?

5.   Why has the UK government said that in principle it does not favour more out of town shopping sites?

Environment pressures

1.   Which pressure groups have been most conspicuous in the green movement?

2.   Which industries have been most affected by green pressure?

3.   Have firms actually changed their total production processes or have they merely changed their image?

4.   How could firms try to improve the environment at the following levels?

     a)   The fuels that they use

     b)   Other materials that they buy

     c)   The manufacturing process

     d)   The distribution process

Chapter 27: ROLE OF GOVERNMENT

27.1: Governments

Economists often classify countries into 'command' economies, where the government makes all the major decisions and 'capitalist' economies, where individuals make all the decisions. In practice most economies are a mixture of both i.e. the government makes some of the decisions about, for example, roads, energy and transport whilst consumers have a free market in items such as clothing. The situations mentioned above where the government makes the majority of decisions are public services. In recent years, governments have sought to relinquish control over some of these areas to private firms. This is referred to as an act of privatisation. There has been a great deal of controversy about some privatisation schemes, notably the water supply and rail services within the UK.

At the macro level, the Government has a number of aims or objectives. These could include control of inflation, reduction of unemployment, ensuring a healthy balance of payments, increasing economic growth and having an equitable income distribution. There are a variety of instruments available to them with which to achieve these goals.

One approach is the use of a monetary policy as favoured by the monetarists. The monetarists, as the name implies, believe that the control of a nation's money supply is important. The instruments that the Government can use to control the money supply will include the control of interest rates. On the other hand, the 'Keynesians', who follow the ideas of John Maynard Keynes, will favour changing government expenditure and taxation to achieve their aims. There have also been vigorous debates, especially in the USA, for the need to balance the government budget. It is usually the case that right-wing governments make a virtue of balancing their budgets.

The cost of the war in Iraq throughout early 2003 and the effects of the 11th September 2001 terrorism in the USA may have slightly lowered worldwide economic growth rates. It remains to be seen whether governments will be able to go on balancing their budgets.

In 2007 the global financial crisis known in the British press as the 'credit crunch' is considered to be the worst financial situation since the 'Great Depression' in the 1930s. This resulted in the in the government having to bail out the banks, financial giants failing and the stock market falling.

27.2: Inflation

Inflation is a redistribution of income. Some people gain whilst others lose. Unanticipated inflation is the real problem for modern governments. Who gains and who loses in different situations? There are often great problems for people with or dependent upon fixed incomes and contracts. For example, property owners who let property to students on fixed student loan amounts or pensioners on a fixed annual income. This may even apply to firms who have made a long-term fixed term contract with another party. For example, if a firm quoted a price for a hydroelectricity plant but then prices raised rapidly the firm is likely to make a loss. When inflation was very high, some firms offered a "rise and fall contract", i.e. if inflation rose with the price in order to offset this potential problem. Inflation for these people will mean that their incomes are reduced in real terms. This means that, while their wages remain at a constant amount, the price of goods increases, meaning that their income can buy less goods and services than before. An extreme example of the effect of inflation was in Germany during the period after the First World War. The country experienced a bout of hyperinflation causing prices to rocket. The currency became devalued so fast it was literally not worth the paper it was written on. This caused massive economic problems such as mass unemployment within the nation.

In the UK, since at least the 1860s, there has been a trade-off between unemployment and inflation.

Norman Lamont, the former Chancellor of the Exchequer, commented that unemployment is the price that we pay for keeping down inflation. This is called the 'Phillips' curve named after the economist Alban W. Phillips. He observed the inflation and unemployment figures from the 1860s to 1958.

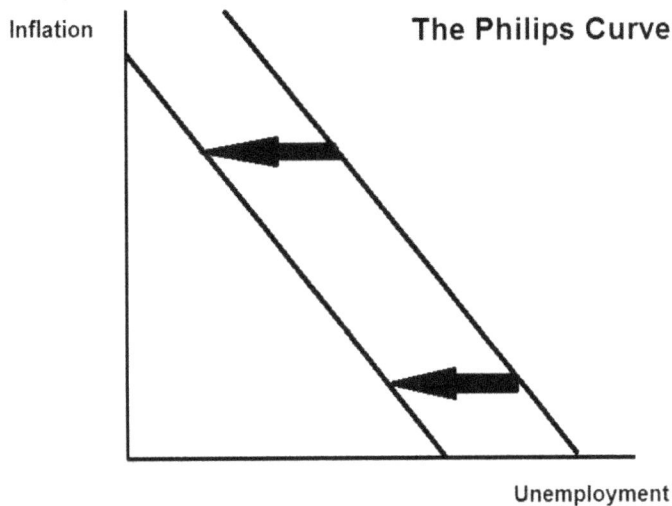

Figure 27.1

413

In almost all cases, the rate of inflation and unemployment were negatively correlated, this means that when unemployment was high, inflation was low and vice-versa. Since that time, the Phillips curve seems to have moved to the right. This means that when inflation is low it is associated with an even higher level of unemployment than before. All governments would like to move the curve to the left by using income policies, selective policies, and so on. In 2008 The Philips Curve did move slightly to the left due to the Credit Crunch.

What are the causes of inflation? The monetarists would claim that it is the money supply to an economy.

Using the formula: $\mathbf{MV = PT}$

(Where M stands for money, V for velocity, P stands for prices and T for transactions) monetarists would claim that an increase in M leads to an increase in P.

Keynesians on the other hand would suggest that inflation is caused by too much demand. This is sometimes called demand-pull. Another explanation is sometimes called cost-push. This is where a rise in costs triggers a rise in prices causing inflation to occur. An example of this can be found in the Organisation of the Petroleum Exporting Countries (OPEC) price increases in 1973. These led to inflation by pushing up the price of oil, as did the Iranian revolution in 1979.

Trade unions or monopolies can sometimes raise prices without fear of loss of demand. For example, in 2012 the last of the six energy companies raised prices of its services. In the short run, people might be able reduce their demand for gas but they cannot alter the fuel used since it would be very expensive to install another type of central heating system. However, in the long-term, such price rises may become too much of a burden and consumers may switch the fuel that they use to heat their home and provide hot water. The privatised water companies have been regulated in the amount that they can increase their domestic customer's charges since, almost by definition; they are a monopoly in their local areas.

27.3: Unemployment

Unemployment is a problem since it affects incomes. It may also have links to certain other social problems that the government should discourage such as specific types of crime. This is partly because people will have more of a need to commit such misdemeanours. It also affects the whole population due to the multiplier effect (also known as the 'vicious circle'). For example, local industry and services may suffer if people in a coal mining area are unemployed. The local shopkeepers will sell fewer goods as their customers will have less to spend without their wages. Throughout the years between 2000 and 2006 unemployment in the UK remained at around 1.5 million.

The government could spend money on public works e.g. as in the New Deal in the inter-war years in the USA or as many countries did after the Second World War. The New Deal approach was in line with Keynesian thinking. Most governments in the UK from the end of the Second World War adopted J M Keynes' policies whether they acknowledged his influence or not. The same was true of many other Western style economies.

Governments could try to protect their own industries by introducing import taxes or quotas on the amount of foreign goods entering the home market. The problem with this approach is that if everyone does it all countries may suffer. For one country, the reduction in imports will help bolster its economy. However, one country's imports are another country's exports. Therefore, the country that exported the goods or services may also try to restrict imports. The so-called 'beggar my neighbour's' policy made unemployment worse during the 1930's.

Unemployment will be affected by interest rates as many people buy goods and services on credit. Generally, the higher the interest rates the less people will be inclined to buy goods and services. This is particularly true of the housing market where almost everyone buying a house in the United Kingdom does so through a mortgage. Unemployment fell slightly in the UK when Britain left the European Monetary System in 1992 and was able to lower interest rates. In 2003 however, some economists would have claim almost the opposite. The argument is that if Britain was to adopt the Euro currency we would be able to have the lower interest rates, which prevail through the other members of the EU. In the UK, this is despite interest rates, by 2013, being at their lowest with a base rate of 0.5%.

Problems with the EMS were not confined to the UK. On 6th March 1995 Spain devalued its currency by 7% having an unemployment rate of 24%. All the different countries in the EMS had to have similar interest payments. This is because investors will tend to hold money in the country with the highest rate of interest and will borrow from the country with the lowest rate of interest. For example, in the 1990s when the UK was in the EMS it was financially worthwhile for people to take out large mortgages in Germany since the rate of interest was about 10% compared with 15% in the UK, however since that time interest rates have fallen worldwide. By 2003, the interest rates in the USA were much lower than in Europe or the UK.

27.3.1: Frictional Unemployment

There are different types of unemployment that a government must seek to control. Frictional unemployment is when people are without a job during the time it takes to move from one job to another, assuming that suitable employment is readily available. This is something that the government can do little about apart from providing a better and faster supply of information on available jobs. Frictional unemployment can be affected by big redundancy payments, which may mean that people will take longer to look for a job rather than accepting the first available job.

27.3.2: Seasonal Unemployment

Seasonal unemployment is important in the construction, tourism and agriculture sectors. There is little that the government can do about seasonal unemployment although it might try to encourage counter seasonal patterns such as building a university in a seaside resort to create a 12-month demand for local services. In 2012 University College Falmouth was recognised and given university status. Part of the University of Exeter is now located in this county. Residential accommodation would be needed in the winter periods. This might offset problems of students of finding accommodation and Cornish property owners having little demand in these months.

At the beginning of 2013 there was considerable turmoil within the EU. Unemployment is high in several European countries: A rate of 10.8% in France, 11.9% in Italy and 26.7% in Spain. In the UK this is despite the base rate of 0.5%. The European central bank in 2013 lowered the base rate to 0.250%.

27.3.3: Structural Unemployment

Structural unemployment refers to particular industries in decline. For example, in many countries there has been reduced employment in the primary sectors such as agriculture and mining and in the secondary sectors such as steel manufacturing and shipbuilding. The government can try to stop the decline of these older industries through subsidies, such as those to shipbuilding, whilst trying to ensure that newer industries take their place.

27.3.4: Regional Unemployment

Regional unemployment is often linked to structural unemployment e.g. regions have often had a high percentage of employment in one industry. In the 1970's the West Midlands had 40% of its employment linked directly or indirectly to the vehicle building industry. Not only was the then British Leyland a major employer but also Dunlop who made tyres and Lucas Girling who made car batteries.

27.4: Balance of Payments

The balance of payments is the difference between the value of imports and the value of exports traded by a country. A deficit for one country is a surplus for another. Therefore, not all countries, by definition, can have a favourable balance of payments. Some countries such as Japan have had very favourable balance of payments whilst other countries such as the USA, for a long while, had a deficit. The balance of payments will be influenced by the prices charged by the country and by the exchange rate. For example, a German consumer prior to Germany joining the Euro in 2002 would have been less likely to buy a £11,000 car than a £10,000 car but this may be offset by changes in the exchange rate. If the exchange rate were 3 marks to the pound then the £10,000 car would cost 30,000 marks whilst if the exchange rate were 2.5 marks to the pound then the £11,000 car would cost 27,500 marks. The balance of payments will also be affected by the rates of interest overseas and UK investors can obtain. For example, when interest rates were higher in Britain than in other parts of the EU, people put their money into British banks assuming that they did not expect the pound to be devalued. With a single currency throughout most of the EU, the balance of payments becomes largely a regional problem for the governments. For example, we do not talk about a balance of payments problem between New York and Texas.

27.5: Economic Growth

Gross National Product (GNP) usually measures economic growth per head although it is not a very good measure of the standard of living but rather a measure of economic activity. GNP does not consider the distribution of income. GNP also does not look at the areas where money is spent. For example, during a war, a great deal of money is spent on armaments but this does not increase what most people would think of as their standard of living. It also does not look at working conditions, pollution or non-traded goods such as the contribution that people may make to the home in unpaid work such as childcare etc. The measure also does not consider the black market for goods and services, which in some countries is substantial.

27.6: Fiscal Policy

Fiscal policy refers to both taxation and subsidies. Taxation is divided into indirect taxes, which are levied on expenditure, and direct taxes, which are paid by taxpayers either out of their own income or out of that of their organisation.

27.6.1: Direct Taxes

Direct taxes are taxes on income and wealth. In the UK it includes income tax, which in 2013, was 10% at the lowest level of up to £2,790 of taxable income, 20% up to £23,010, 40% up to £150,000 and 45% on higher income brackets. Most wage earners will fall within the middle section. The difference between the marginal rate of tax and the average rate of tax is caused by the various tax allowances the government gives. If, for example, the tax allowance is £4,615 and the person has an income of £10,000 then the income tax at 20% is levied on the remainder making the average rate of tax 9.543%. See Figure 27.2.

Tax paid on £ 10,000 (simplified version) as at March 2013

Income	Tax Rate	Tax Amount
£ 4,615	0 %	£0
Next £2790	10 %	£279.00
Next £ 3,465	20.00%	£693.00
Total: £ 10,000	Various	£ 954.30

Figure 27.2

The national insurance tax, which was originally meant, as its name implies, to be an insurance that paid for the nation's pensions, social security and other liabilities. It is now, for all practical purposes, another part of income tax. It is currently about 9% for most taxpayers.

Income tax is likely to change according to the economic needs of the country. This is only levied on larger incomes since income tax rates increase with income. Below a certain threshold, which will vary generally from one year to another, no tax is payable (the tax allowance mentioned above).

The main advantage in direct taxation is that income tax is usually a progressive tax. It reduces purchasing power rather than increasing prices. Tax liability is easily calculated although it may be complicated by tax allowances.

It is sometimes claimed that if income tax is too high it will reduce the incentive to work. There is little evidence one way or the other to prove this claim. A very high rate of income tax may deter people from working longer hours rather than avoiding work itself. This situation can occur when employees are offered overtime that will take them up into the next tax bracket. The hourly rate that they get for the work may not then seem worthwhile for them to work. Taxpayers may consult accountants on how to minimise their tax payments, usually known as 'tax avoidance'. This is legal although it may be seen as being unethical. Tax evasion, where an individual or firm seek to deceive the government, on the other hand is illegal and the punishments can be severe.

27.6.2: *Profits of Public Enterprises*

Another source of income to the government may be the profits of public enterprises. These organisations are often given targets for profit making. In the past, some enterprises have made losses. If this is due to inefficiency it not only increases the tax burden upon citizens of the country but also leads to an attitude that the government will merely subsidise the loses. In recent years however many of the public utilities have made a great effort to improve productivity. In some cases, the government may face a dilemma. For example if an enterprise raises its prices, because it has monopoly power it will increase profits. However, this may be thought of as unfair to the poorer citizens. On the other, hand greater investment in the service may be a necessity if countries are to develop not only a satisfactory standard of living for its citizens but also to provide for industry. There is, of course, no easy solution to this problem. In recent years, there has been much interest in Public Private Partnerships (PPP's) where the government works with industry to improve services. The worry is that the opposite will happen, as the firms, naturally wanting to make a profit, will not have the same priorities as the public expect from their government.

27.6.3: *Corporation Tax*

Corporation tax is a tax on companies' profits. It is evaded by some of the large firms by registering in countries with low or non-existent corporation tax. One of the problems is that if company tax is too high, owner managers might prefer to spend money within the firm for their own benefit, for example, on improving premises, rather than trying to make more profits. This is possible as taxation is only charged on profits and not before expenditure of this type. Multinationals may also be deterred from investing in countries where company tax is high. At the end of 2012 it was found that many companies were avoiding or paying little corporation tax. Included in this list of companies are several big names. In 2011 'Google' only paid £6 million despite having an annual revenue of £2.5 billion. The coffee giant 'Starbucks' in 2011 made £398 million that year and did not pay any UK Tax. 'Amazon' the large online retailer bought in £3.35 billion in UK sales in 2011 and paid £1.8 million in tax, claiming that they only made £74 million in profit. The British telecoms group 'Vodafone' made a profit of £9.5 billion in 2011 and only paid £4 million pounds in tax. 'Npower' has admitted that between 2009 and 2011 it paid no corporation tax in the UK.

27.6.4: Capital Gains Tax

Capital gains tax applies to many types of investment but not to Personal Equity Plans (PEPS), which were the forerunner of Individual Savings Accounts (ISA). It is also not levied on a person's primary residence. This was because in periods of rising house prices, such as the late 1980's or the early 2000's, people often bought a house with a view to making capital gains rather than simply as a place to live.

27.6.5: Value Added Tax

The most important indirect tax in the EU is VAT, which now is set at a rate of 20% in the UK. It is not levied on fares, newspapers, books, children's clothes or basic foods at present. The European Parliament is however, discussing the expansion of this tax range to include some of these items. VAT on fuel in the UK is currently levied at a rate of 8%, the higher amount of 17.5% having been defeated in the House of Commons in 1995.

27.6.6: Proportional or Specific Taxes

Indirect taxes may be either proportional or specific. Specific means that the same amount is charged irrespective of the value. For example, in many countries the same annual tax is charged for a vehicle licence irrespective of the value of the car. This may be thought to be regressive since a larger car will usually belong to a wealthier person. It may also be considered unsatisfactory because larger cars cause more wear and tear on the roads. In general, a proportional tax would seem fairer because it imposes more heavily on the rich than the poor. To some extent, this has been introduced in the UK with the new categories of road tax.

Taxes are said to be 'progressive' if they take proportionately more from the rich and 'regressive' if they take proportionately more from the poor. For example, a £1 levy on a bottle of alcohol would probably penalise someone on a lower income rather than a higher one whereas a proportional tax would penalise those drinking champagne. The person with the lower income is more likely to buy a more inexpensive wine at say £4 a bottle. The £1 tax means that the wine now costs £5, an increase of 25%. A wealthier person may well be able to, or choose to spend more. If their wine costs £20 a bottle before the tax and £21 afterwards then they are only paying a 5% increase in the form of tax.

27.6.7: Levying of Fines

The government will obtain extra income through the levying of fines. An example of levying on a firm was seen in September 1995 when a heavy fine was imposed on the Nuclear Industry. Fines may be imposed on individuals in order to deter anti-social behaviour such as theft and noise pollution. Businesses may be fined if they impose external costs upon the community such as contraventions of safety or pollution legislation. In 2012 a banking scandal which involved changing the 'Libor' (London Interbank Offered Rate) which is the average interest rate estimated by the leading banks. This is the interest rate that banks are charged when borrowing from other banks. A fine was levied against Barclays of £59.5 million and UBS was fined £160 million for their involvement.

27.6.8: Excise Duties

The government will also impose excise duties. These are commonly levied on vehicles and petrol because they are luxury goods rather than necessities.

27.6.9: Customs Duties

Many countries have imposed customs duties on some imports, though partly through the influence of the International Monetary Fund, these have tended to be reduced in recent years in order to have a more open global economy. The effect of custom duties is to raise the price of imported goods. If the demand for such goods' price elasticity is greater than 1, the result of revenue effect is nearly always negative, i.e.

$$\frac{\% \text{ change of demand}}{\% \text{ change in price}} > 1$$

As prices go up demand goes down but as it is customary to ignore the minus sign then a relatively small increase in import duties will probably improve the countries balance of payments. If, on the other hand, demand is inelastic then the government will merely raise revenue through import duties. One of the effects of customs duties, as with excise duties, is that it may be inflationary in the short-term as it alters prices and not peoples ability to spend.

27.6.10: Local Taxes

The taxes discussed so far have all been national or used to affect the national economy. There is a need to gather money for use within the local areas to pay for services used by residents.

27.6.11: Rates

Rates were based on rateable value. This is a hypothetical value of rent in the free market. If the rateable value for a house was £400 and the rate in the £1 was 75p then the ratepayer would pay £300 per year. This applied irrespective of the number of inhabitants living in the house or their incomes. There were some problems in valuation although administrative costs were low since valuations were done infrequently. Central heating installation was seen to raise rateable value and therefore was a slight disincentive to improve housing. There is some relationship between the ability to pay tax and standards of housing although during a lifetime this could vary. A newly married couple with no children would be better off than a one-parent family. In a family where both parents were working then the household would be better off than that of a lone single unemployed person. Administrative costs were low since all dwelling places would receive a rate demand. It was a tax on housing so it gave a slight incentive to share housing since the rate payable was the same irrespective of the number of inhabitants.

27.6.12: Community Charge

The community charge, also known as 'Poll Tax', was a tax per capita and as with rates, the amount levied varied between different local authorities. An authority with a large number of elderly or unemployment persons would need more money for social services than a richer borough with a younger working population.

The poll tax levied was the same for all people with the exception of the unemployed and students. Administrative costs were high especially where mobility was high because many did not register on the electoral roll to avoid paying. The poll tax was regressive and was evaded widely. The Council Tax in April 1993 superseded the community charge via the Local Government Finance Act 1992.

27.6.13: Council Tax

Local authorities now impose a 'Council Tax' that is based on the value of houses. Values are divided into bands that indicate the amount of local tax the householder will be charged. This replaced the community charge, which charged all those over 18 the same amount irrespective of the value of the house.

The new tax is in many ways similar to rates but there is a 25% reduction for single person households. The bands are based on a 1990 estimation of house market values. This posed a problem in the early 1990s when house values declined. Householders with large houses and therefore usually larger incomes will pay a lot less than with the previous rating system since the highest band covers a very wide range.

In 2009 the Liberal Democrats proposed a tax on properties valued at over £2 million; this became known as the 'Mansion Tax'. The Labour party agreed to this policy in 2013 saying that if in power they would introduce it. A criticism against this is that almost half of the properties valued over the £2 million mark are owned by people who no longer work and they would therefore struggle to pay this new tax rate.

27.7: Alternatives

Local Income Tax

Some people have suggested a local income tax. This would be more progressive than the other measures. It would bring in little revenue where there were high rates of unemployment. The administrative costs would be quite low if the data was linked to a computerised Inland Revenue system, although this is disputed by some politicians. There are problems in determining whether it should be based on where people live or where they work. The City of London, for example, would gain considerably if the tax were based on the place of work.

Sales Tax

This has been used in other countries such as the USA. It is like a local version of VAT that is added to certain items purchased in a region. It would be difficult to impose in a country where the size of local authorities is small unless it was a standard rate. This is because people would cease to buy most goods that could be obtained more cheaply within another local authority borders. With VAT currently at 20%, it is unlikely that the Government would wish to have a higher rate of tax on consumer goods and services.

27.8: Why are Taxes Imposed?

The government needs to provide public goods. These are goods and services whose consumption by one person does not affect the consumption by another person. The extent of usage cannot be measured per individual and therefore individual charges cannot be levied. In most countries, the Government owns firms that provide a large proportion of these goods and services.

1. **Provision of Essential Goods and Services**

   In many countries, goods and services in the fuel, transport and communication industries are also provided by the state. For example, in the UK the Government had nationalised bus, road freight, rail and airline companies as well as a shipping company owned by British Rail. It also had companies in the fuel, gas, coal and electricity sectors. The majority of shares in BP were owned by the state. The nationalised industries, as a whole, tended to break even for many years, although some, such as British Rail were major loss makers. It is noticeable however that, in spite of claims of increased efficiency and independence at the time of privatisation, there are still large subsidies paid to most of the privatised rail companies. In the non-commercial sector, health, education and social services have been provided by the state.

2. **Merit Goods**

   A merit good is one that people think should be provided irrespective of income e.g. health is regarded as a merit good in most nations, although in the USA most health care is paid for from private health schemes. The government in all countries provides education, although in the UK and some other countries it is possible to pay for private education.

   A demerit good is one that the Government does not consider essential for Society such as tobacco, alcohol and gambling. These are usually highly taxed, or occasionally banned.

3. **Government Borrowing**

   The monetarists would suggest, as did the classical economists, that a public sector borrowing requirement is bad. Hence, in the USA in 2013 the President sought to have a balanced budget. His proposals which included a tax increase angered the Republicans. Republican Martha Roby said "The president says he has to have tax increases to head off the sequester. Well, he already got his tax increase,"*. Keynesians, on the other hand, would argue that a balanced budget is not necessarily helpful and that in a recession it is sensible for the Government to inject money into the economy. Injections (J) into the economy include Government (G) Exports (X) and Investment (I). An alternative would be to reduce withdrawals (W), which are tax (T) imports (M) or savings (S). The letters in brackets denote the Keynesian convention.

4. **Redistribution of Income**

   Another reason to borrow money is to redistribute income. Generally, in the developing world, the taxation policy of countries will be progressive i.e. more will be taken from the rich than from the poor. This will also discourage consumption of certain goods or services or influence the location of industry.

5. **Influencing the Market**

   Another reason might be to influence the market itself. For example, if there are undesirable external effects such as noise pollution or accidents then the government may impose such taxes on the firms or the users. The tax on leaded petrol is higher than on unleaded petrol for this reason.

6. **Macro Reasons**

   Government borrowing may also be to influence macro-economic factors. For example, unemployment, inflation, economic growth and balance of payments will be affected by taxation. If the Chancellor wishes to deter demand then he will raise taxation whereas if he wishes to increase demand then he will reduce taxation.

27.9: Principles of Taxation

There are several principles of taxation. In the 18th Century Adam Smith, who was one of the earliest economists, first suggested the following:

Taxes should be economical. The cost of collecting should not be more than the revenue. The dog ownership tax was abandoned in the UK in 1987, as the charge per dog per year was only 37.5p.

Taxes should be convenient. This means that a tax like PAYE (pay as you earn) can be said to be convenient since it is deducted from earnings before they are paid to employees, usually on a monthly basis. VAT is less convenient since it is levied on a large number of items and thus the administrative costs of levying it are much higher.

There should be certainty. It should be obvious how much people should pay. Taxes should be equitable by taking account of the ability to pay. Smith suggested that taxation should be proportional to income and it should be certain, so that everyone knows what he or she has to pay.

Other principles have now arisen, for example, that taxpayers should be treated impartially. This may be difficult if taxes are imposed only on certain goods such as cars as it will only affect car purchasers. Many now think that a proportional tax was not in fact equitable since 10% of a low income would be harder to pay than 10% of a high one. Therefore, many now accept the idea of progressive taxation.

Another major principle is that taxation should not deter people from working, whether they are high or low wage earners.

27.10: Time Lags in Policy

One of the problems with Government policy is that almost any measure to achieve anything takes time to take effect. Keynesian economics would suggest that the Government should have a deficit in a recession and a surplus in a boom in order to tackle the problems of inflation. Unfortunately, Governments do not always have sufficient information. In addition, an improvement in economy may lead to a boom in one part of a country and little effect on employment elsewhere.

27.11: Legal Aspects of Business

Law is a set of rules that guide human beings and is imposed by governments upon the citizens of each country. We now live in a world of nation states and therefore the laws of one country will generally apply to that country alone. However, problems can arise between countries. For example, if citizens of one country have contracts with other countries it must be decided which laws will apply should there be a dispute. Where trading takes place between one country and another it is not immediately obvious whose laws apply, for example, a ship may trade between one country and the United Kingdom but may be registered in Liberia. Ships are often registered in Liberia or Panama, so called 'flags of convenience' countries, since these reduce costs for the shipping company. Apart from governmental laws, there also exist what called common laws. This consists of conventions, which have grown up over time.

27.12: Contract Law

A contract is a legally enforceable agreement between two or more individuals or companies, whereby each person will gain from some act of the other. For example, if person A agrees to give goods to person B on a particular date, for a particular sum of money, both A and B have acquired rights against each other. There are a number of rules about binding contracts. Both parties must have the 'capacity to contract'. This rather odd phrase means that the individuals have to be adults. Generally, it is not possible for minors, i.e. people below 18, to make contracts except for necessities and for the young persons' benefit, for example as in employment or job seekers allowance. It should be noted that whilst limited companies are not people they are corporate bodies. In law, corporate bodies are allowed to do most things which ordinary people are allowed to do. However, the powers given are stated in the objects clause of the company and if the companies try to do anything outside those powers it would be considered 'ultra vires' or outside the powers. For example, if a textile factory had in its objects clause a statement that it was allowed to manufacture textiles only then a contract that said that it was also going to supply electrical components would not be valid.

There must be a clear offer. Binding agreements have to be clear since courts will not generally uphold vague arrangements. Many firms therefore will have a standard contract entitled "conditions of sale". Standard contracts will particularly apply to industrial concerns selling only to other businesspersons rather than directly to the public. For example, the conditions of sale may specify how quickly items will be delivered and what will happen if they are not delivered within that period. It will also include the type and number of articles to be traded.

There must also be a clear acceptance. For example if someone offered to sell some goods for £100 and the other person said, "Yes, thank you very much that seems acceptable", this would be a clear acceptance. On the other hand, if they said that £100 was too expensive and they offered £90 instead this would be regarded as a counter offer and would not have been a clear acceptance.

There must be valuable consideration. This means that in law each party has to get some benefit from the performance of the other person or company's part of the bargain. The word 'valuable' does not mean that it has to be adequate. For example, if someone were to sell a house for £1,000 this would obviously be ridiculously cheap, but the courts could still uphold it. On the other hand, if a person offered to give his son a house for nothing this would not be a valid contract since there is no consideration on the son's part.

Contracts have to be freely made without pressure of any sort. If bargains are made under duress, they cannot be upheld. An extreme example of this would be that if a person were to hold up someone at gunpoint and demand money, which was then offered, this would clearly not be a valid contract since it was made under duress. A more likely type of duress would be if a solicitor tried to influence a client by claiming that he had superior knowledge of a situation.

Contracts have to be able to be performed. This may sound obvious but, for example, if a firm offered to sell goods from its shop that in the meanwhile, unbeknownst to both people making the contract, the goods had been destroyed in a fire, there could be no claim for damages since there was no possibility of performing the bargain.

Contracts have to be legal. For example if a company tried to have a contract, which would contravene the Company Acts then clearly this contract is not valid.

Void and Voidable Contracts

Contracts can be voidable. This means that if the aggrieved party does not wish to carry on with the contract it can say so and the contract is then at an end. However if it wishes to carry on then the contract is valid. A contract can also be void, which means that the contract does not exist.

27.13: Agency Law

Agency occurs where one person or firm authorises another person or firm to act on their behalf in making necessary arrangements with a third person or firm. The person or firm is often referred to in law as a party. The parties to the contract are called principals whilst the intermediaries are called agents.

27.13.1: Agents Authority

Often an agent will have express authority, which might have been given orally or in writing or in a deed that has been prepared by a lawyer. For example, in many countries people will not sell their houses directly but through an agent. The agent would therefore have express authority. Sometimes agents have implicit authority. For example, if goods are delivered to a business premises and received by an employee of the firm who happens to be in the reception area then the employer has held him or her out as having authority. If he or she then steals the parcel, the employer cannot deny authority to have given a signature for delivery. There can also be, under special circumstances, an agency of necessity.

Agency of necessity is part of common law. If, for example, there was an accident in a firm and a person moved some articles for fear that, they would explode then the person moving the articles is regarded as an agent of necessity. Even if the movement of these goods caused another accident it would not be possible to say that it was that particular person's fault provided he or she has done their best at the time.

27.13.2: The Rights and Duties of Principals and Agents

If a principal appoints an agent, the main obligation is that the agent will be paid an agreed commission or charge and expenses, which have been properly incurred. The principal has the right to expect their agent to act properly. Both principal and agent have the right to trust one another. The agent must give proper accounts and must not take secret commissions, for example to sell goods or services at a lower price than the principal could have had otherwise. However, even if the agent acts improperly the principal is still liable. Of course, at a later stage the principal may sue the agent for the wrongful act. For example, if the agent had agreed to sell an item for £5,000 instead of £10,000 then the contract would still be valid but the principal could sue for the difference.

27.14: Employment Law

27.14.1: Background

The number of days lost to industry through accidents is immense. It is even more significant than the worker hours lost through striking. For this, as well as other reasons, successive governments have introduced a range of health and safety at work legislative acts. The main act in operation is still the Health & Safety at Work

Act 1974. It should be noted that employees and employers are bound by the terms of the Act.

The employers are allowed to adopt a cost-benefit-analysis approach, i.e. they have to do what is reasonably practicable.

Accidents such as the Piper-Alpha oilrig accident, the Zeebrugge ferry disaster (a shipping accident in which many people lost their lives), and the Kings Cross Underground disaster have hit the headlines. Often disasters are followed by enquiries, which investigate the causes and suggest further remedies, which usually include more legislation. However, in many cases they also highlight the problems of communication and supervision as well as the technical aspects. The problems of communication have been dealt with in Chapter 19.

Partly because of the problems in communication, the Health & Safety at Work Act specifies that there should be an organisation to back up the safety procedures. There are considerable detailed provisions about physical equipment and its use. A great deal of this is common sense, for example, about hand guards on dangerous equipment, testing of firefighting aids and the use of fire doors and so on.

However, in practice common sense is not always used. Whilst fire drills are common in schools they are rarely used in firms. Loading and handling causes many problems and accidents that can result in fatalities or cause long-term injury to not only staff but also the public. Many accidents are caused by pressure to get work completed within time schedules.

The handling of dangerous substances causes many problems. This seems to be acute when handling everyday substances such as aerosols. For obvious reasons the labelling of dangerous goods for transport purposes has been done on a worldwide basis whether for air, rail, road or sea carriage. Safety representatives have to be appointed with at least two years' relevant experience. They are allowed to have time off to train if necessary. They are required to investigate potential hazards with a view to reducing the number of avoidable accidents. Under the Regulatory Reform (Fire Safety) Order 2005, which became law in 2006, regarding the training of staff in fire safety, the use of firefighting equipment and that there is a means of escape with emergency lighting.

For the benefit of improving legislation, accidents need to be reported if they are fatal, or if a person is incapacitated and off work for more than three days, or if there are serious injuries. An accident report book has to be completed with details recorded as a legal case may ensue.

All firms need to have employers' liability insurance at a sum of £5 million. This covers accidents committed by employees that may result in a lawsuit. The compensation culture has begun to drift over to the UK from the USA and the cost of this insurance is on the increase. Organisations cannot afford to not be covered though as one accident could mean the end of a firm.

Noise regulations were introduced for the first time by the 'Noise at Work Regulations 1989'. This requires tests to be carried out because noise may cause deafness or affect a person's capacity to work. Exposure to sustained loud noise can be detrimental to health and so employers should not expose their workers to such risks

27.14.2: Training

Until 1964, firms were responsible for their own training. Some firms carried out intensive training whilst the subject was ignored by others.. There were complaints from the firms who carried out good training that in many cases they had provided expensive training only to have their employees poached by other firms. The consequence of this was that the Government set up a series of industrial training boards that covered most of the major industries. One of the criticisms of this system was that certain types of employment e.g. coal miners, could work only in one industry whilst others, such as secretaries could work in any number of different areas. The same would also have been true of accounts clerks and road haulage drivers.

Under the Industrial Training Act 1964 a levy was made on employers towards training. They could recover fees if they either sent employees for training or carried out their own training subject to agreement with the relevant training board.

27.14.3: Trade Union Law

Before the 1960's there was comparatively little Trade Union law in force within the UK. The first major part of legislation was the 1971 Industrial Relations Act that was brought in, as there was concern about the number of strikes, especially unofficial ones that interrupted industry. These were often called 'wildcat strikes' as their effectiveness was in their unpredictability and instant nature. The majority of strikes were very short, usually less than three days. How much effect strikes have on production will depend partly upon the industry in which they are taking place. A rail strike in the London area may have significant effects not only upon rail users but also upon other forms of transport as people have to find alternative ways of getting to work, such as: using the bus, getting a taxi or hiring a car if able to drive.

Some commentators pointed out that strikes often acted as a catharsis, i.e. that production often rose after a strike since both management and trade unions had sorted out the grievances.

Self-examination Questions

1. What is meant by the free market, mixed and command economies? Why are most economies in practice some combination of a mixed economy?

2. What are the main economic objectives of government? How far do these objectives conflict and how far are they reconcilable?

3. What is meant by inflation? Why do governments tend to believe that it is a problem?

4. How may government try to tackle inflation?

5. What are the different types of unemployment? How may Government try to influence them?

6. What is meant by indirect and direct taxation? What are the characteristics of a good tax?

7. How far does the gross national product of UK help to show the standard of living? In your answer, refer to a warmer country such as in East Africa. (Hint-think of how much they might need to spend on heating compared with UK.)

8. Why has the UK in the past had lower economic growth rates than the newly industrialised countries such as Singapore?

9. How far will increases in savings, which leads to more investment, help to improve the UK's standard of living?

10. What do the letters GNP stand for?

11. Why might it be difficult to compare GNP of a developed and developing country?

12. Discuss the ways in which the level of savings could be increased in the UK.

13. Carry out a survey of savings amongst people that you know. Ask what factors determine how much they save, is it, for example, always influenced by their income.

14. What is meant by the term 'a legally enforceable agreement'?

15. At what age is it usually possible for people to make contracts in the UK?

16. What does the statement that limited companies are 'corporate bodies' mean and what the implications for this in contract law are?

17. What does stating that there must be a clear 'offer and acceptance' when considering a contract actually mean?

18. What is meant by the term 'valuable consideration'? Does this mean that it has to be adequate?

19. What does stating that contracts are freely made without pressure mean?

20. What is the difference between void and voidable contracts?

21. What do the terms 'principal' and 'agent' mean? What is the difference?

22. What is meant by the term 'agent of necessity'?

23. How far do days lost by strikes in the UK reflect their importance to the economy? (Hint: why might a dock strike with relatively few days lost be important?)

24. Why did governments intervene, from 1964 onwards, in training rather than allowing each individual firm to carry out training?

25. What would be the advantages and disadvantages of having industrial training boards for each industry?

26. Why was the Health & Safety at Work Act 1974 set up?

27. Do major accidents tend to have anything in common? Are they all investigated in the same way?

28. How would you expect an organisation to set out its main requirements in a safety plan?

29. Why might it be very important for a firm engaged in shift work to pay particular attention to fire hazards? (Hint: think of problems in communication)

30. What is the role of the Health & Safety Executive?

Chapter 28: PRESSURE GROUPS

28.1: Definition and classification of Pressure Groups

There is no precise definition for the term pressure group. A general description would be *'organisations that put pressure on other organisations usually central or local government or possibly the EC in order to change either taxation or regulations.'* A more specific definition of a pressure group is;

'a group of people who come together with a common objective to change a prevailing condition or restriction imposed by a powerful body or organisation'.

Such a group aims to influence the decision making of the more powerful organisation. Depending on the type of issue and the influence that the pressure group has on body it aims to influence, the pressure group can apply a variety of tactics to influence the targeted body. For example, Greenpeace, the world famous organisation, is concerned with environmental issues. Greenpeace champions the need for a more sustainable exploitation of natural resource. It has to face down huge organisations such as governments and multi-national corporations. Pressure groups 'apply pressure' to nudge decision makers to make the right decisions and in the direction that the pressure group would prefer. An example of such a 'nudge' was the Live 8 concert held in London and eight other cities of the world to coincide with the opening meeting of the world's most powerful leaders. The aim of the concerts, apart from sensitising the rich countries to the plight of the poor countries, was to appeal to the collective conscience of the world leaders to make decisions that would be in favour of the poor.

There are various ways of classifying pressure groups. These are discussed in the following section:

28.1.1: Single Issue or Multi Issue

Pressure groups can be either single or multi-issue, single issue, as the name implies, are focused on one campaign, multi issue groups focus on many. For example, the pressure group Action on Smoking and Health (ASH) is a single-issue group, focused on one thing only - anti-smoking campaigns. Greenpeace and the Trade Union Congress (TUC) are examples of multi-issue pressure groups because they both focus their attention on many different subjects. In the USA, there are far more pressure groups than there are in the UK, for example, the National Rifle Association that resists arms control for citizens.

28.1.2: Temporary or Permanent

The second way of classifying a pressure group is whether it is temporary or permanent. A temporary pressure group is one which comes about to respond to a new proposal. For example, in 2003, many pressure groups had been formed to protest against the plans to build a new airport at Cliffe in Kent or alternative plans to expand any of the three London airports. They felt that an international airport at Cliffe would degrade the environment by increasing fumes and amount of noise. No pressure groups existed before to fight for this cause because there was no need for them. Permanent pressure groups work on ongoing campaigns, for example the National Society for the Prevention of Cruelty to Children (NSPCC) and various trade unions. Such pressure groups remain in place because the issues they address are also permanent and pervasive; such problems also tend to be ubiquitous causing a lot of distress yet not easily visible unless someone points them out.

28.1.3: Altruistic and Self Interest Groups

Pressure groups can be classed either as being altruistic or for self-interest. Altruistic groups include such bodies as Oxfam, Christian Aid and the Red Cross. The pro-smoking pressure group, FOREST and other groups who protest about projects affecting themselves are examples of self-interest groups. The term 'Not in my Backyard', (NIMBY) is used to refer to such people. It is possible for a pressure group to be a mixture of altruistic and self-interest beliefs. For example, the groups fighting against the plans for a new airport at Cliffe have their own interests at heart in terms of noise pollution and increased traffic as well as concerns about the worsening of the local environment in particular the destruction of the marshlands in the area. As a matter of self-interest the Cliffe pressure groups stand to lose both their sleep and the value of their properties as the noise levels, road traffic and air pollution increases. However altruistically we can argue that such a group is concerned with the environmental degradation that results from the increased air-traffic.

28.2: Why do Pressure Groups Exist?

Pressure groups exist both within political parties and outside them. They may exist for solely self-interest reasons. These would include groups such as the employer's organisations for example the Confederation of British Industry, Institute of Directors and trade associations such as SMMT (Society of Motor Manufacturers and Traders). Other groups such as the professional associations for example BMA, (British Medical Association) and the trade unions may exist partly for self-interest reasons and partly for altruistic reasons.

There are some other altruistic pressure groups such as those dealing with the developing world including Oxfam, Christian Aid and Traidcraft. These will exist in order to help poorer people who they know are not getting fair treatment from either government, international organisations such as the World Bank or the multinationals in many cases. There are also environmental pressure groups such as Greenpeace and Friends of the Earth.

Whatever the type of pressure groups it will try to ensure that the interests whether selfish or altruistic are considered when major decisions are being made, whether by central or local government, or by large or small firms.

They may try to get their way by lobbying directly the people concerned with the decision making process. For example in July 2005, many people took part in the 'Make Poverty History' campaign when campaigners assembled at the Gleneagles summit of many of the world leaders.

The 2013 meeting of the Group of eight (G8) Summit that took place in Lough Erne, Northern Ireland on the 17-18 June gathered leaders from eight of the most powerful countries - the United States, Canada, Britain, Germany, France, Italy, Japan and Russia. The meeting was chosen by the host Britain, to discuss items like, advancing trade and tax compliance.

The 'Make Poverty History' campaign - the UK version of GCAP (Global Call for Action against Poverty) - used the pop stars such as Bob Geldof, who led massive concerts (Live 8) around the world, which aimed at increasing political pressure on world leaders. Live 8 called for international aid, debt relief and trade justice but focused exclusively on Africa.

Sometimes pressure groups may use other more imaginative methods for example the popular BBC TV programme "The Vicar of Dibley" had at the end of the Christmas time programme partly along these lines of supporting the campaign 'Make Poverty History' in December 2004 .

Sometimes the lobbying is less conspicuous. People may approach Members of Parliament or political parties generally. These meetings are for informal purposes of proposing amendments to legislation or even initiate legislation.

In some cases, government may ask pressure groups look at proposals. For example, in the case of dangerous goods legislation where there is general agreement that we want safety to be improved the government department may ask representatives of the chemical industry as well as shipping pressure groups and trade unions for advice. In some cases, this may go further than this with people sitting on an advisory committee before a UK delegation discusses these matters at international level such as the International Maritime Organisation.

Sometimes as with the rail, freight sector the industry has taken the initiative. They have placed information increasingly on the internet about ideas, which are being discussed. Currently, the rail freight industry has drawn attention to what it regards as the defects of the proposed Cross Rail link, which will serve as the name suggests through services using a new line   between Paddington to the West of London and Liverpool Street to the East of London. This is because it fears that having 24 trains per hour and with passenger trains having priority that too many passenger trains will have an adverse effect on its member's interests.

Trade unions have sometimes used picketing to try to get their message across. This has usually been peaceful but there were comments about both the miners and the police behaviour in the bitter miner's dispute in the 1980s. There are now restrictions on the number of people allowed on pickets in the UK and secondary picketing is not allowed. Secondary picketing is defined as a situation where a trade union does not have a direct dispute with the employer in question but may join in as an ally of the trade union involved, historically the miners and the rail unions were linked in this way. Sometimes secondary picketing has been used for other reasons for example to try to stop immoral trading. In the UK, you cannot picket at the Docks for the reason of immoral arms sales to dictators as the Dock authorities are not in dispute over the sales of arms. The alleged transport of people to be tortured in other countries would be an example where secondary picketing would not be allowed at the airports in the middle of the scandal.

Sometimes there have been demonstrations. An example of this was with the campaign about the transport of live animals to and from the continent when the protests made forcibly pointed at the docks where the animals were going and that the carrying conditions were cruel to the animals.

Sometimes there have been boycotts of the products or services. For example, Barclays faced boycotts of its services during the 1960s because of its involvement in lending large sums of money to the pro-apartheid South African government. Middle class pressure groups have often written letters to their local newspapers about particular issues. This was the case with 'The Make Poverty History' campaign.

In 2012 the new High Speed 2 (HS2) rail network was given the go ahead by the British government. The phrase that follows the HS2 project is "bring the UK's Victorian railways structure into the 21st Century"[8]. As with most projects concerning construction, arguments about the environment have turned up. The

---

[8] http://www.hs2.org.uk/about-hs2

biggest one is concerning the track going through woodland that has always been there.

Case Study 1

Imagine you are a leader of the construction industry concerned about its decline in 2013. Consider the following:

(a) What data you would use in your campaign?

(b) What methods would use, for example, leaflets or lobbying?

(c) Whom would you approach?

(d) How much finance would you require for your campaign?

(e) How would you try to arrange this finance?

Suggested Feedback

In 2013, the construction industry faced major problems. A projected increase of 3% in the construction of private houses, but there was a projected fall of 23% in the construction of public properties. The governments 'Green Deal' which removed the upfront costs of improving a house to help cut carbon emissions and reduce energy bills will have little affect concerning the private house in regards to maintenance and improvement. There was a fall of 2% in the construction of office buildings in 2012. Improvements in the construction would be the 55% increase in the creation of railways and the 115% rise in energy construction.

Self-examination Questions 1

1   What data, for example, about number of houses sold, prices paid and areas would you expect the construction industry to give to the Chancellor of the Exchequer?

2   Why might different branches of the construction industry and the building societies have different views on what could be done? Is there any way to reach a consensus?

3   What would be the advantages of local building firms approaching MPs and local councillors about new projects?

4   Why might the industry wish to commission opinion polls showing local views on potential projects? Why is this less likely to be done at a national level?

5   What groups, apart from politicians, would you expect a local building firm to approach about the idea of a major sports centre in the centre of a town?

Case study 2:

You commute by train to London from Kent each day. You have heard rumours in the press that fares are going to rise by an average of 3.9%.

You are concerned that evening services and weekend services will be reduced. Already Southeastern has tried to reduce the hours that booking offices are open.

You are perturbed about this since you work in London during the week and visit London on Saturdays to watch sport and attend theatres.

You wish to join a pressure group to fight against the anticipated hike in prices as well as reduced services. You find out that there is a Rail Development Association known as Railfuture.

Self-examination Questions 2

a) What data would you expect Railfuture to use in its submissions to relevant bodies?

b) Since the budget of Railfuture is about £50,000 per year what methods would you expect it to use to pass on its message?

c) What other pressure groups might Railfuture approach?

d) How could Railfuture try to obtain new members?

Chapter 29: THE PAST AND THE PRESENT

29.1: Introduction

In the 18th Century, there was a move from cottage industry to working in factories. This had a number of consequences such as people not being able to choose the hours they work. Today, there is a move from people working in an office to working from home. This is cheaper for a company because money for expensive office space can be used for other things and it benefits the workers by allowing them more free time. The Trade Union Congress (TUC) and Confederation of British Industry (CBI) produced independent reports, in the early 1990s, which suggested that by the year 2000 about 6 million people would be working from home. It is difficult to get accurate figures since some people working at home may not declare their income for tax reasons or may simply be below the earnings limit for National Insurance or income tax.

The use of computers with facilities such as the Internet that can be used to access the firm's intranet or for remote access and E-mail has made it much easier to work from home. However, there is the problem of motivation. Is it socially desirable for people to work all day with machines and not to meet anyone?

As mentioned before, people who work at home have minimal personal contact with colleagues and obviously do not have factory machinery available. This means that working at home suits those jobs that do not involve lots of contact with colleagues and customers and machinery. Many workers who take Open University or other remote college courses do their coursework from home. It has been suggested that people should work in small offices as opposed to at home to help them have some group dynamism. Some firms have a 'work from anywhere' policy, which means employees can work from virtually every computer in an office or in any other office in the world. Their staff have no fixed desks, which mean that there is always workspace available for visitors. They also have 'drop-in' centres, which are offices just for people visiting the area.

29.2: Timing of Work

Up until the 18th Century, the timing of work was mainly up to the individual employer or employee. Farmers and agricultural workers would have worked longer hours in the summer and harvest time and fewer hours at other times of the year. The coming of large factories meant that because of the interdependence of workers, people had to be in the factories at the same time. In a typical production line, for example, workers on one part of the line have to wait for workers on a preceding part of the line to complete their tasks. Countries such as the UK have far fewer people engaged in manufacturing than in services, so the interdependence is often less. Even where there is still interdependence, the need for people to follow on from one task to another is less important in some situations. For example in an office, a particular course of action may go through 5 or 6 hands but it is the total time that is most important, not when each individual piece of work is done. This means that, in some situations, there is more scope for flexitime. Flexitime working means that that employees stay in the office and work more hours if there is more work to do and have the option of leaving early if there is less work to do.

Office work is often done on a flexitime basis, around a core time, say 9 to 5. Flexitime is easier to implement in situations that do not require much personal contact. It is also used in fast food restaurants. For example, a magazine editor will not usually care whether someone writes the article at 2 am or 2 p.m. so long as they meet the deadline. It is more difficult on production lines where one activity depends upon previous activities. Flexitime and job sharing have become more common and tend to be helpful for parents with young children.

29.3: Urban Drift

In the 18th Century, there was urban drift (people moving nearer to towns to work). Today, there is often a drift to the suburbs and in some cases rural areas, to live, for example, East Anglia. Most large cities have had a fall in population particularly in the inner city areas. This is partly because housing is more pleasant and cheaper in the suburbs and rural areas and partly because of improvements in transport. For example, with fast rail links, many people now commute the 70 miles from Peterborough to London because it is fast. Advances in communications, especially the introduction of the Internet and E-mail have made it easier for commercial firms to move out of the Central Business District (CBD). Motorways and car ownership mean that it is easier for many firms to be on the outskirts of a city. Coventry, which was heavily bombed during the war, rebuilt most of its factories on the outskirts of the town.

Retired people, of whom there is an increasing number, tend to move to seaside towns, especially along the south coast.

In developing countries, there is still very much an urban drift with the associated problems of shantytowns. This is where there is little social infrastructure such as water supply or drainage and no town planning. Housing is usually poor and there is scope for disease to spread rapidly.

The British Government has tried to discourage the urban sprawl, which is common in other countries such as in the USA, especially in cities such as Los

Angeles. It has done this with the introduction of restrictions in green belt areas and projects such as those for new housing development.

Successive governments in Britain have used new towns in two ways. The first is to avoid London growing, by investing money into towns such as Basildon and Stevenage, which are situated 30-50 miles out of London. The second reason is to provide a focal point in the so-called development areas such as Cwmbran and Washington in Tyne and Wear. The Government has also provided enterprise zones such as the Isle of Dogs (in East London), to try to prevent inner city dereliction. Other measures it has taken in the last few years to minimise dereliction include projects such as the Thames Gateway. This, as its name implies, is trying to make use of the derelict land along both sides of the river Thames. There is little controversy about building on and using derelict land, but there is conflict when the proposals include using previously unused land. For example, the proposal by the Government in 2003, to build a large airport in Kent, has been met with a lot of controversy and conflict.

29.4: Can newer Transport forms reduce Monopoly Power?

The canal system in the 18th Century and later periods destroyed local monopolies since the lower cost of transport meant that it was not possible to charge much higher prices in one area than another.

Today, improved transport systems such as motorways and railways have helped to destroy some local monopolies, such as the local breweries, but may have created larger national and international monopolies. This is because it is feasible for a large company to deliver goods to the other end of the country or to another company. An example of such a company is in the computer industry with companies such as Microsoft.

The Channel tunnel, which opened in 1994, coupled with the single market of 1992 with its reduction of trade barriers, helped to reduce local monopoly power in the 1990s. It gave people the opportunity to go to France to buy goods that cost less there than in England such as alcohol. The constant enlargement of the EU is making travel and carrying back of goods for personal use even easier.

29.5: Development of Tourism

Thomas Cook had one of the first excursions from Leicester to Loughborough (a distance of about 15 miles) in the 1850s. The modern equivalent is the continual growth of the airline industry, offering more flights to more destinations in a shorter time and for less money. This encourages people to go further for their holidays and on business trips. The Channel Tunnel has made travelling to France and Belgium easier and consequently has boosted trade and travel between the countries.

29.6: Changes in Management Style

In the early 20th Century, many businesses employed a system of scientific management. One of the main beliefs behind scientific management is that workers are an extension of machines, that is, the aim is to get as much out of them as possible without much regard for their needs. The carrot and stick approach to motivation was popular. People were motivated by higher wages and threatened with losing their job.

Whilst some people still do believe this, most people now agree that people are motivated by a variety of different approaches. McGregor 's theory is used to describe the different motivational approaches that can be employed to two groups of people. There is a different way of motivating people who are usually proactive (i.e. have the initiative and drive to work and achieve) while there is a different approach to motivating those who are reactive (opposite of proactive).Theory X people have an inherent dislike for work and are therefore motivated by the stick and carrot approach. Theory Y people regard work as natural and are motivated by gaining more responsibility and more challenging work. Different jobs may lend themselves to different approaches; for example, it is difficult to imagine the inherent interest in some factory jobs whereas for other jobs like professional sportsmen it is much easier.

29.7: Changes in Life Expectancy

In the early part of the Victorian era, the life expectancy of many workers was very low. In Manchester, it was about 18 whereas for middle class people in Lincolnshire it was about 45. Even in 1901, the average life expectancy for men was 45.5 and for women it was 49.0. By the year 2021, it is estimated that life expectancy for men will be 76.6 and for women 82.6. What are the consequences of people living longer, for businesses, and how far do modern changes, in life expectancy, affect business?

The consequences of short life expectancy were that training and education were almost totally disregarded for the manual classes. Since labour was cheap, health and safety were largely ignored.

The present life expectancy of about 78 for women and about 74 for men means that training and education can provide a return for the Government or employers.

Increased longevity in the developed countries has meant that more care and nursing homes are needed to cater for the elderly. This in turn has contributed marginally to the rise in house prices.

29.8: Changes in the Working Week and Educational Patterns

In the 19th century, working hours were very long, for example, a typical steam engine driver on the railways, would have worked an average of 66 hours per week. In contrast, in 2011, UK men worked an average of 42.7 hours per week and the EC average was 41.6. Denmark had the lowest average number of working hours per week, in the EC, of 39.1. The recent social charter, which is under discussion in the UK, suggests a maximum working week of 48 hours and a typical week of 39 hours. The UK Government argues that this goes against different national traditions. The original concept in the Butler education Act 1944, which stated that there should be day release training for people up to the age of 18, has never been implemented. The number of males in full time higher education had risen from 519,000 in 2001-2 to 785,475 in 2011/12 and from 620,000 females to 935,920 in the same period[9].

29.9: Hostility towards Technology

In the 18th Century, the Luddites destroyed machines because they believed that they were responsible for destroying jobs. Are there any modern parallels?

Pessimistic View

Some trade unionists, the late Clive Jenkins (1926 -1999), for example, suggested that the introduction of computers and mechanisation would destroy many jobs. The case of Tilbury Docks goes some way to proving this. In the late 1960s, Tilbury Port (it was a port then and a dock now) employed about 25,000 workers whereas today, because of containerisation, there are only 1,000. Similarly, in the newspaper industry, the bitterness with the Wapping (in East London) dispute, in the mid-1980s, was partly because many well paid but specialist workers had lost their jobs because of the introduction of new technology. The recession in the late 1980s and early 1990s made white-collar workers redundant in many industries for perhaps the first time. For example, in 1991 the Law Society laid off people, as did the commercial banks including cashiers. The current economy is leading to more redundancies in the city especially in investment banking and the IT industry.

---

[9] http://www.hesa.ac.uk/content/view/1897/239/

Optimistic View

Optimists say that since the 18th century, people's standard of living has increased because of the introduction of new technologies. This, in turn, has lead to more demand for technology and created more jobs. Two examples of this are the introduction and now widespread of mobile phones and computers for personal use. 25 years ago, to own a huge portable phone or have a computer at home was very rare. Today the majority of people in the UK own both. The technology for these items has evolved over the last few years to make them more powerful, much faster and much smaller. The increase in demand for these products as well as the demand to improve them has created many jobs.

Conclusion:

What is reasonably certain is that people will find it difficult to retain the same jobs for the whole of their careers. This means some form of retraining will be necessary. Unfortunately, the present educational system is not geared to this.

29.10: Concentration of Wealth, Income and Power

In the 18th Century, power and money was concentrated in very few hands; is this still true and what are the consequences?

Wealth is still unevenly distributed. Between 2004 and 2005, the percentage of wealth (marketable wealth less value of dwellings) that was owned by the top 1% was 21%. Inheritance tax (formerly called Estate duties) has done little to alter this. However, income tax has altered the distribution of income as has other factors such as social security and pensions.

The consequences of a more even distribution of income have been that there is often more scope for mass markets. For example, in the 19th Century, the market for carriages was only relevant for a limited proportion of the population. Today the market for cars is much bigger. In the last quarter of 2009 around 70% of UK workers drove to work. For many items, such as television ownership, almost everyone has one. In 2012 93% of households had televisions. Increases in income can be linked to the idea of the product life cycle. For example, poorer people will usually buy consumer durables towards the latter stages of the product life cycle whereas richer people will buy it towards the start.

For example, Social Trends 2011[10] shows at the end of 2009 over 110,00 hybrid powered cars were licensed in Great Britain. That number may seem impressive but, it only counts as less than half of one per cent of all licensed cars. This shows

---

[10] http://ons.gov.uk/ons/rel/social-trends-rd/social-trends/social-trends-41/index.html

that the move towards alternate power vehicles has not been taken up by the majority of the population.

29.11: What are the Consequences of Moving from Extended Family Systems to Nuclear Ones?

One of the consequences can be seen in the housing market. The 3 or 4 bed-roomed house has largely replaced large Victorian houses, which housed all the relations. However, there have been a few moves towards the provision of so-called 'granny flats', which are not that common. The name 'granny flat' has come about due to women living longer than men, meaning there are far more widows than widowers. Research carried out in 2011, showed that in the UK, 16.6% of the population were 65 or over. As well as the introduction of granny flats, there has also been an increase in special homes for the elderly. As well as residential 'nursing homes', there are managed apartments, which are blocks of apartments that are manned 24 hours a day by a porter. The apartments usually have 'panic buttons' positioned around them and security regarding visitors is tight.

The reduction in typical house size has led to the need for more houses being required for the same population. This, in turn, has consequences for washing machines, refrigerators, freezers and cookers because most households will have one of each of these articles irrespective of their size. The move from extended families to nuclear families also has had consequences for the travel market. Airlines often use the term VFR meaning visiting friends and relatives and a considerable proportion of travel to and from such places such as Australia consists of people doing just that.

Self-examination Questions

1. What were the original reasons for the cottage industry? How far does technology help people to work effectively at home?

2. It is often suggested that the people who work at home are very much exploited. Why is this likely to be the case?

3. The end of the conventional work practices have been frequently prophesied, but have not come about. Why is this and it has ever come to pass?

4. What have been the past trends in the travel industry? Will the trend continue in the future?

5. What are the effects increased inequality of wealth and incomes have on firms? (Hint: think of firms in the consumer durable markets.)

Chapter 30: MANAGEMENT ROLE: DECISION-MAKING I

Theoretical Approach to Strategic Decision making

30.1: Introduction

Decision-making is an everyday activity. Decisions range from complex multi-faceted decisions to simpler decisions such as where to have lunch or dinner today. The amount of time that goes into decision making usually reflects the amount of resources that are involved. That is why a committee may be appointed to deliberate on the installation of a new computer system in a government department, as this may involve millions of pounds and it is important that the right decision be made at the first instance. On the other hand, it takes a minute or so for you and your friends to decide where you will have a cup of coffee. This is because there is little to be lost if you end up having a bad cup of coffee.

Decision-making is the process that is used to arrive at a decision. A decision is a passing of judgement on a certain issue under consideration. It usually involves the consideration of various alternative judgements and choosing the most appropriate judgement of those available. More often than not, a business decision will be made to increase profits or enhance future chances of increased profitability.

In management, most decisions tend to be rational. Rational in this context means that the decision is based on a consistent, reasoned and factual process. On the other hand, day-to-day decisions may be based on emotions, part factual reason and part emotion and sometimes on a factual reason. For example, visits to a favourite café may be based on an emotional reason like the friendly waiters, rather than lower prices, which is a rational basis. In other cases, both rational and emotional factors may be incorporated in arriving at a decision.

Though the management is expected to make rational decisions, emotions do play an important role. Decisions made in teams for example could be based on various emotional factors such as a team member trying to prove a point. However, decisions in management will often be based on reasons and facts. Decisions made in the business world follow a clear sequence of events. This sequence ensures that all the important factors are taken into consideration. These are the decisions that we will study in this chapter.

30.2: Theoretical Model of Decision-making

Usually the management team will adopt the following sequence of events to arrive at a decision:

1.   Define the problem:

The parameters of the problem must be established using the basic characteristics or the nature of the problem. A poorly defined problem may lead to solutions that do not address the problem and hence lead to a waste of resources.

2.   Collect the relevant data:

Once a problem has been defined, then data that appertains to the problem is collected. The collection of data ensures that decisions made are based on facts and can be shown to be true. This is known as empirical evidence. Data is processed using various statistical methods to yield information. Information is data that has been organised to yield knowledge. Information must be relevant to the question. Data has thus to be organised into information to yield the knowledge requisite to good decision-making.

3.   Develop alternative solutions:

Having processed data into information then the management is in a position to create alternative solutions to the problem.

4.   Evaluate the alternative solutions:

The advantages and the disadvantages of each alternative solution are evaluated. The time and resources available are then matched to each solution. The solution must be realistic.

5.   Selection of the optimum solution:

Given the pros and cons of each solution, the best solution must be taken by the management. This may be contentious and where a team is used to arrive at a solution then the decision may be put to the vote.

6.   Implement Solution:

More often than not, this is the most delicate part of the decision making process, poor implementation or failure to adhere to the definitions of the problem may even result in other problems or worsening of the original idea.

7.   Measure results:

Once a solution has been implemented then it is important to ascertain that the anticipated outcome has been achieved. The implementation may lead to unanticipated results, which may be either positive or negative. These outcomes define the next problem.

```
                          ┌─────────────────────┐
                          │   Define Problem     │
                          └─────────────────────┘

┌──────────────────────────┐
│ Measure & Evaluate results │
└──────────────────────────┘                    ┌──────────────────────────────┐
                                                  │ Collect data, create information & │
                                                  │ knowledge                     │
┌──────────────────────────┐                     └──────────────────────────────┘
│ Implement the solution    │
└──────────────────────────┘
                                                  ┌──────────────────────────────┐
┌──────────────────────────┐                     │ Formulate alternative solutions │
│ Choose one of the decisions for │              └──────────────────────────────┘
│ implementation             │
└──────────────────────────┘
                          ┌──────────────────────────────┐
                          │ Evaluate all proposed alternative │
                          │ solutions                     │
                          └──────────────────────────────┘
```

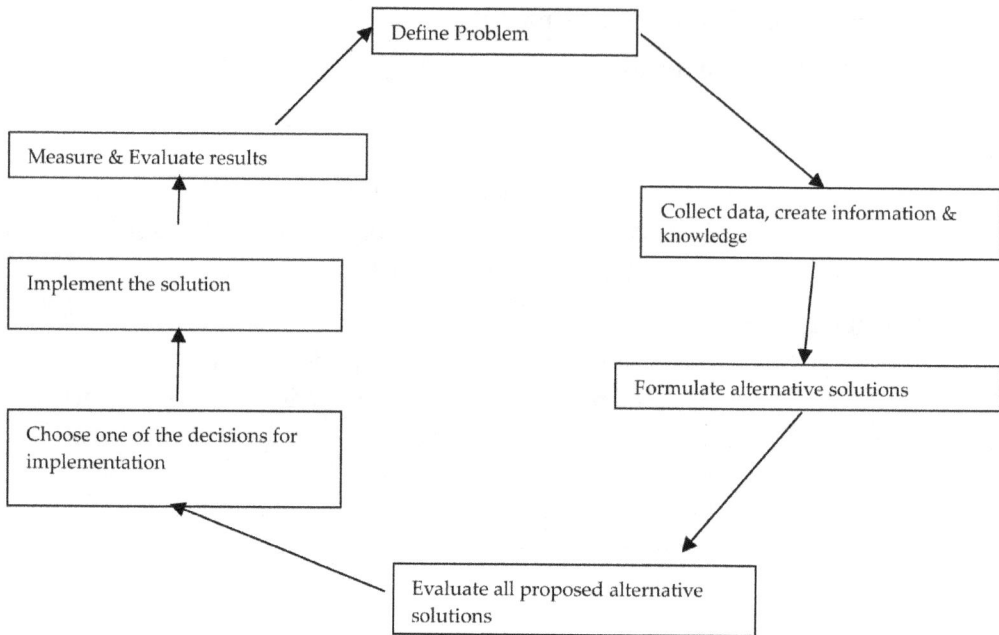

The seven steps outlined above form a cyclical process where step seven leads to step one. The outcomes of the implementation may: solve the original problem, cause more problems or yield positive outcomes that may need to be pursued. These unexpected results are known as externalities. Decision makers will seek to enhance the positive outcomes while trying to minimise the negative outcomes.

This seven-step model oversimplifies the issues that go into actual decision-making process. It assumes that the decision made out of this process is rational and based on empirical facts. However, decision makers may have to consider other factors such as personal prejudices. A strongly religious management may not choose the most rational alternative because it may involve what they may consider to be against their faith. The quality of the final decision may then be compromised due its unacceptability to the management.

A second issue could be the availability of resources an adequate time to implement a decision. This model may take a long time to complete a cycle especially due to the collection and processing of data. As a result, it may not be very suitable for short-term decisions.

This process leads us the different types of decisions that a management may need to make in a business.

30.3: Types of Decisions

Decisions can be classified according to the nature of their content, and the time needed to implement them.

A. Nature:

The nature of the decision process yields three types of decisions:

1. **Structured/programmable decisions**: these are usually repetitive, and adhere to certain procedures. The variables in such decisions are quantifiable and the decision rules are clearly stated. They often follow the format: 'if...then' for example, if Event A happens the decision to be made is B. These decisions are also called programmable as computers can be programmed to make such decisions without human intervention for example, streetlights that are switched on automatically with the approaching darkness. In this case, the machine has a precise rule to follow: 'IF darkness approaches, THEN switch on the streetlights.

2. **Semi-structured decisions**: these are decisions which require both human intervention and automated decision-making. This may be for example a computer task that is performed by the continuous data entry by a human being, however the computer does the processing of such data and the output is interpreted by the human being.

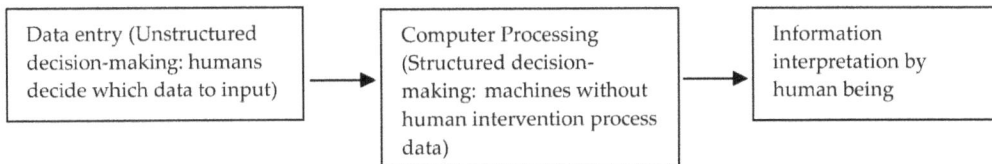

Data entry (Unstructured decision-making: humans decide which data to input)	→	Computer Processing (Structured decision-making: machines without human intervention process data)	→	Information interpretation by human being

The diagram above shows an example of a semi-structured decision process.

3. **Unstructured decisions/non-programmable decisions**: these are decisions that have to be made through human intervention. They are usually highly technical and may be generally long-term. Such decisions are made using variables that are neither quantifiable nor subject to clear decisions rules. More often than not, the outcomes of the variables are alternative decisions. For example: To increase the market share of our business's product we can:

    a)   Be innovative

    b)   Reduce our prices

    c)   Provide incentives to use our product

    d)   Break into new markets in different countries

e) Produce differentiated products

f) Advertise more aggressively

g) Target a different market segment

In this case, there are many decisions that can arise from our problem. Each of these decisions contain unquantifiable variables, if we took the first decision of making our products more innovative then we have other indeterminate variables to consider, for example, what if we are innovative and consumers do not like our direction of innovation? At each stage in the above problem, human intervention is important. Such a multi-faceted decision is said to be unstructured.

B. Time needed to implement the decision:

Here decisions are classified according to the length of time that they would take to be implemented.

1. **Administrative decisions** are often mechanistic and have very a short-term effect. They are concerned with the day-to-day running of the business. These are more often than not mechanistic and can be computerised. For example, stock-control decisions that depend on a pre-set reorder level (clear decision rule); the reordering is done at certain stock level by making a call to the suppliers. This can be computerised such that the computer monitors the stock levels and at reorder level alerts the suppliers of the impending replenishment.

2. **Operating decisions** contain more variables some of them unquantifiable and indeterminate. It is concerned with short-term goals that are used to achieve the longer-term strategy. They may involve ensuring that the longer-term strategy is adhered to and negative deviations are minimised while positive ones are enhanced. These often tend to be semi-structured, with the quantifiable problems being mechanistically resolved through pre-set decisions rules and unquantifiable decisions being made through human intervention. Examples include managing the increase in output of a product.

3. **Strategic Decisions**: these are often long-term decisions that may involve many indeterminate variables. Such variables may be indeterminate because they are in the future and are hence dependent on the future outcomes of the business's activity and the dynamics of the environment. In making strategic decisions, the management would have to consider external influences. For example interest rates, income increase, inflation, legislation, and market

preferences and so on; all these variables would have effects on the business that are unquantifiable. Strategic decisions are more often than not long-term covering between five and ten years and aimed at positioning the business in its environment. Such decisions also tend to be strongly unstructured.

The next section looks at various theoretical models that are used in strategic decision-making. These theoretical models have been developed due to the many indeterminate variables that everyday strategic decision makers have to deal with.

30.4: Strategic Decision-making

Strategy refers to a sequence of events that is used to arrive at a predetermined objective or goal. Business strategies are often long term and dependent on indeterminate variables. In order that managers can deal with such variables, models have been developed to account for as many variables as possible.

Strategy in business refers to plan that is used to direct the whole organisation towards the overall goal. It ties in various aspects of the organisation to produce a cohesive whole. Often organisations come up with visions. A vision in business, as in common parlance, is a mental image of what the business will be like in future. This refers to what the business intends to have achieved at some time in the future: They answer the question: "What will success look like?" Their main purpose is to articulate the "dream" state of the business. If your business could be everything you dreamed, how would it be?

For example, one of the world's top car manufacturers, Honda, has the following environmental mission statement: "Honda has endeavoured to solve environmental problems since the 1960s. We introduced the Compound Vortex Controlled Combustion (CVCC) engine, becoming the world's first automaker to comply with the 1970 U.S. Clean Air Act—a challenge thought by many at the time to be insurmountable. In 1992, we released the Honda Environment Statement to articulate the basic stance we had developed until that time to reduce environmental impacts at every stage in the life cycles of our products. Today, this Honda Environment Statement is the foundation upon which we carry out all our environmental efforts."

Honda Environment Statement

As a responsible member of society whose task lies in the preservation of the global environment, the company will make every effort to contribute to human health and the preservation of the global environment in each phase of its corporate activity. Only in this way will we be able to count on a successful future not only for our company, but for the entire world.

We should pursue our daily business interests under the following principles:

1 We will make efforts to recycle materials and conserve resources and energy at every stage of our products' life cycle from research, design, production and sales, to services and disposal.

2 We will make every effort to minimize and find appropriate methods to dispose of waste and contaminants that are produced through the use of our products, and in every stage of the life cycle of these products.

3 As both a member of the company and of society, each associate will focus on the importance of making efforts to preserve human health and the global environment, and will do his or her part to ensure that the company as a whole acts responsibly.

4 We will consider the influence that our corporate activities have on the local environment and society, and endeavor to improve the social standing of the company.

Established and announced in June 1992

Activity:

1. How important is Honda's Vision in achieving their success?

2. What would happen if they did not have a vision or a mission statement?

3. Create two other visions that Honda could choose to pursue.

Modelling Strategic Decisions:

A model refers to a preliminary work or construction that serves as a plan from which a final product is to be made. In decision making for a business, a model would refer to a simulation of the outcome of business decision.

A model seeks to quantify the indeterminate variables of the problem to enable consideration. This is achieved through taking reasonable assumptions; an assumption is a statement taken to be true without evidence. For example, in making a decision that a journey between London and Canterbury will take one hour we may have to assume that there will be no traffic jams on the motorway. This is a reasonable assumption, as more often than not there are no traffic jams on that motorway. However, if a traffic jam were to occur then the model that we used to determine the length of the journey will not be true for our journey.

This section looks at some of the most common management models.

30.4.1: The Rational Choice Model

This model is strongly based on the assumption that managers will arrive at their decisions by using the most rational and empirical method. All the factors used in arriving at the decision can be verified using the available information.

Rationality is defined as the ability to arrive at a decision using a logical sequence of relationships between empirical variables. In a rational decision making process, there will be both logical sequences as well as sensible deductions, which are derived from experience knowledge, probability and expectations rather than facts that can be verified. Hence, rationality is both logical and sensible, given the circumstances. For example, in marketing a product to women only, it is logical to place an advertisement in a women's magazine, and the sensible deduction is that women will see that advertisement and be interested enough to read it and buy our product.

The rational choice model is based on the important assumption that human beings are generally rational and will tend to go along with a decision that they deem rational. This is an important thought when it comes to business decision making because a business makes products for human beings. Innovation in products is often expensive and if the consumer at which it is aimed are rational, and then we can make reasonable assumptions in our innovation as to what our consumers would like and hence create products to meet those needs.

However, what we assume to be a rational decision may not be rational to many other people, because in deciding that our decision is rational we assume that:

1. We have all the information that we need to make the decision. In this, we are assuming that at the time of making the decision we have the correct information about all the variables we are using to make the decision.

2. That the variables will not change during the time when the decision is being made and implemented

3. That the goals and objectives are clearly defined by the management

4. That what is considered rational is that which maximises the aims of the business, or maximises the benefits to the business.

5.   That the information can be gathered within the time that it is required and made available and that the decision makers have enough time to let the information are gathered.

The rational choice theory has been criticised especially on the assumption that the decision makers have all the information that appertains to a decision, and that they have adequate time and ability to consider all the alternatives that have been made available to them. However, it remains as the most consistent decision-making process since the assumption that human beings are rational and will choose the option that maximises their benefits holds true more often than not. Rationality being a shared characteristic of human beings means that even the decision maker will rationally be able to make the most desirable decision.

30.4.2: Bounded Rationality Model

Applying the rational theory and its assumptions is more an ideal to aspire to than a reality. Due to the assumptions, other theorists have come up with different formulation for the rationality theory. This is known as the Bounded Rationality Model. A bounded rationality theory takes into consideration that it is not possible for decision makers to have all the information and at times, some decision makers will have information that other decision makers will not have.

Another serious limitation is that decision makers are assumed to have the ability to use the information that has been presented to them to make rational decisions. However, this might not be the case; the information available may for various reasons be misinterpreted or due to personal prejudices and inability to accept change unacceptable to the decision-makers. For example, on the advent of computers, many decision makers resisted the computerisation process as it represented a completely new way of doing the jobs that they had been used to doing manually.

Bounded rationality also recognises that the decision making process may be undertaken in uncertainty, urgently and without enough time to consider all the options. As a result, more often than not the decision might not be optimal. In fact, in most cases decisions are made to meet the minimum requirements of the problem at hand.

The bounded rationality model states that decisions need to be made within the constraints and pressures of organisational life, and so managers have to make the decision 'that will do'. The term used to describe this is 'satisficing', the practice of choosing an option that may not be the optimal solution, but one that does satisfy the minimum requirements to achieve a goal or solve a problem.

This concept was proposed by Herbert Simon (1992), in *Models of My Life*, points out that most people are only partly rational, and are in fact emotional or irrational in the remaining part of their actions. This is seen to be a constraint in rational decision-making.

30.4.3: Garbage Can Model

This model was developed to deal with ambiguous behaviour that does not conform to the rational theory. The behaviour may appear contradictory to what is considered rational. Instead of the rational systematic deliberation and decision-making, rather it is a result of several relatively independent streams of events within the organisation. Four of these streams were identified in Cohen, March & Olsen's (1972) original conceptualization: These streams are:

1. Problems

This is the first stream; it is assumed that problems lead organisations to seek solutions, which involve going through the 'garbage can' to come up with a solution that is befitting of the problem. Problems arise inside or outside the organisation but they all require attention.

2. Solutions

This is the second stream. These exist independently of the problem. These solutions had been formulated for other problems but were discarded because they were inappropriate for the problem for which they were formulated so they were discarded into the 'garbage can'. By looking into the garbage can a solution for the problem may be discovered in the form of a previously inappropriate solution.

3. Choice opportunities

Refer to occasions during which organisations are called upon to make a decision. This is usually when a problem arises; it could also be when the organisation becomes aware that a problem has occurred or for some reason expect a problem to occur.

4. Participants are random

Individuals called upon to seek a solution for a problem are also indeterminate. They may depend on time constraints, their interests in solving the particular problems, managerial preferences and so on. Thus, participants in decision-making are seen to come and go.

The model is an attempt at the study of 'organisational anarchy' where decision makers are not expected to be aware of all the facts and communication between the players is not very clear. There are also no boundaries in the decision-making and it is the work of the management to match the four streams together in time of need. Decisions are made through trial and error. Many solutions can be formulated without any problems and problems exist independent of solutions, participants and choice opportunities. Thus, a decision will be made when the four streams are matched.

30.4.4: *Game Theory Model*

This decision making process is applied in a particular case where there are two players. The theory was proposed in 1947 by John von Neumann in collaboration with Oskar Morgenstern in their book *The Theory of Games and Economic Behaviour*. This model assumes two scenarios. Firstly, that there are two players in decision-making where the gain of one player is the loss of the other player. This is known as zero-sum game. Therefore, the first player can only gain if the second player loses. In the second scenario, two players can increase their gains through cooperation.

The game theory is based on the ability of various players to make decisions by anticipating the action of the others with whom they share a restrictive decision space. A classic example is the Prisoner's dilemma explained in chapter 16.9.

Game theory is most applicable where there is a conflict between the players. In this case, one player can only gain at the expense of the other player. A good example would be the market share of two businesses. If during the game the market size does not change then one of the players can only gain what the others lose.

Situation 1   Situation 2

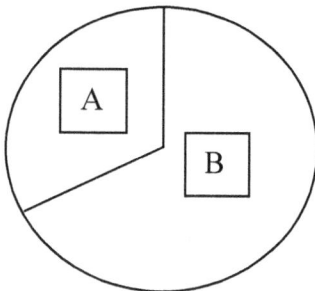   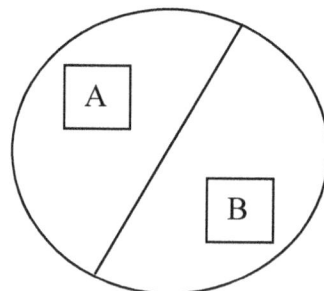

In situation 1, player A has less than half of the market, whereas in situation 2, he has gained half of the market. His gains have wholly come from losses incurred by player B.

The game theory assumes that player cannot act independently to change his share of the market without affecting or cooperating with B. For example, if player A became more innovative then he would take away B's market share.

However, if players A and B cooperated with each other then they can produce more innovative goods or services and hence attract more people to their market. In the example above the size of the circles would increase to indicate a larger market is now available.

A game consists of a set of rules governing a competitive situation. Von Neumann and Morgenstern restricted their attention to zero-sum games, in which no player can gain except at another's expense. Each of the players or player groups choose strategies designed to maximise their own winnings or to minimize their opponent's winnings; the rules specify the possible actions for each player, the amount of information received by each as play progresses, and the amounts won or lost in various situations.

These restrictive requirements of the original game theory are difficult to maintain, especially the assumption that all the players will stick to predetermined rules. In 1950, John Nash made the distinction between cooperative and non-cooperative games. In the non-cooperative games, no outside authority exists to ensure that players stick to the predetermined rules of the game. The assumption that the players have binding agreements to behave in a certain manner is also not feasible. Nash also recognised a set of optimal strategies and no one player can benefit by acting unilaterally and changing his/her strategy, without the cooperation of the other players. These set of optimal decisions are known as **Nash' Equilibria**.

Nash further tried to approximate reality in the game theory by introducing the concept of bargaining. This is where the players collude and produce a situation that is mutually more beneficial than if they had persisted in competition.

Activity:

1. Think of other examples of Nash's Equilibria.

2. Investigate the relationship between Boeing, the American Aircraft builder, and its European counterpart Airbus in the light of the Game Theory. How does it apply to these two aircraft giants?

30.5: Other aids to Decision-making

30.5.1: The SWOT Analysis:

Many other techniques have been developed to assist in decision-making. One of the most popular is the SWOT Analysis (Strengths, Weaknesses, Opportunities and Threats). SWOT is used either at the start of a business project or as a continuous process aimed at evaluating the performance of a business at various points in time.

The swot analysis is used for evaluating the internal and the external environments. The internal influences in a business are the strengths and weaknesses whereas the external influences are classed as threats and opportunities.

The external environment

In SWOT analyses, the threats are seen to be a result of the environment that is outside the control of the business and the business can at best mitigate their effects rather than prevent their existence or control their occurrence. Various management pundits classify the threats as coming from competitors and government actions. However, threats to a business may be from many other sources. The effects of September the 11th attack against the United States did affect businesses. The aftermath of this attack led to widespread fear in the United States and the world as a whole that a similar attack might happen, thus consumers reduced their spending in anticipation of another attack. In turn, reduced spending by households led to less profit and reduced business growth. A business in this situation would not have prevented the attack or in any way boosted consumer confidence; however, it could reduce production costs to ensure that profitability was maintained.

Competitors also pose a threat to the business, apart from direct competition that can easily erode the customer base of a business; competitors can become more innovative or invent a new product that will make your businesses produce obsolete.

The government could also be a source of threats. For example, after the Enron scandal the government imposed stricter controls over the accounting profession. It also placed more responsibility on the management of the businesses in ensuring that the statements of accounts reflected the true and fair picture of the businesses financial performance and position. Accountants also came under stricter scrutiny and they have more regulations to comply with in their business. This has translated to higher costs of operation. All these are external threats that a business may have no control over but should be prepared to reduce their negative effects.

On the other hand, risks that entrepreneurs undertake are motivated by the opportunities they have identified in the businesses that they choose. Opportunities are external to businesses, so they have no control over them. They can however seize these opportunities and use them. Presently, the drive for more fuel-efficient vehicles that emit less dangerous gases into the atmosphere presents an opportunity for innovation of the existing models and invention of new ones that meet these specifications.

For example, Toyota took the lead in producing a gas/electric hybrid car that is capable of switching between electric power and hydrocarbon fuels and thus reducing polluting emissions while reducing the overall cost of running the vehicle. The opportunity that exists in this case is the production of an environmentally friendly vehicle. Successful businesses are those that correctly identify and exploit opportunities.

The internal environment

These are influences, which are inherent to the business. Every business has characteristics that are unique to its nature. These can be either strengths or weaknesses; strengths are the resources and capabilities that can be translated into competitive advantage. Strengths answer the question: 'What can our business offer the market that other businesses cannot offer that market?'
Examples of such strengths would include patents, copyrights (in fact during the tech boom of the late 1990s whole businesses were based on patents and copyrights) and access to exclusive natural resources, which can give a competitive advantage.

Weaknesses can be the absence of strengths that your competitors have, if you start an oil refining business and your competitors have oil wells as well as refineries then you have a serious weakness. Some weaknesses are so severe that it is impossible to compete in the target market.

The SWOT matrix

SWOT is a relatively simple but important tool in analysing the viability of a business and helping in decision-making. Strengths and opportunities are used to mitigate the threats and deal with the weaknesses inside the business. This is done by matching the four factors each other in a matrix. This is known as the SWOT matrix.

*   The strengths are matched to the opportunities where they can be used to create a competitive advantage.

- The strengths are matched to the threats to help mitigate the effects of the threats to the business. At the same time, strengths are matched to the weaknesses to counterbalance their effect on the business. For example, the weakness of business A could be that they do not have a patent for any invention but they have resources to invest in research and development. To deal with the weakness of no patents this business can invest in R & D and patent a product if they are successful.

- Threats may at times translate into opportunities; for example, a sudden shift in the market's preference for your business' product may mean that there are opportunities in the new preferences that the market has over the products that you are presently producing.

The matrix below shows the four different strategies that a business can adopt using the SWOT analysis:

	Strengths	Weaknesses
Opportunities	S-O	W-O
Threats	S-T	W-T

Strategy 1: Strengths – opportunities

Under this strategy, the business is optimistic and aggressive and it is going out to get the opportunities by using its resources and competencies. This is usually useful in a stable growth industry.

Strategy 2: Strengths – threats

These are usually remedial strategies where the business is using its resources either to mitigate the threats that have materialised or to prevent the effects inflicting too much damage to their business if the threats were to materialise.

Strategy 3: Weaknesses and opportunities

Here the business has identified opportunities that can be used to reduce the effects of its internal weaknesses. This is a risky strategy as the business is taking on more risks hoping that the strategy will be used to eliminate the weaknesses inside the business.

Strategy 4: Weaknesses – Threats

This is a cautious and pessimistic strategy where the business is more intent on dealing with the weaknesses and reducing the effects of the threats, they face. The strategy concentrates on reducing the weaknesses internally to prepare for threats that materialise. The strategy is useful in cases where the external environment is unpredictable or highly volatile.

30.5.2: PEST Analysis

PEST, like SWOT is an acronym. PEST stands for Political, Economic, Social and Technological analysis and is an analysis of the external and internal environment of a business before any marketing is carried out.

1. The internal factors, for example the technology that is available for marketing and the availability of the requisite expertise.

2. Macro-environmental factors, these overall external factors are usually on a national or international scale, for example national politics or economics, socio-cultural factors.

3. Micro-environmental factors are external factors that constitute the overall environment. These are the components of the overall aspects of the economy for example consumers, competitors, suppliers, manufacturers, activist groups and so on.

Political factors

One of the major macro environment factors is politics. Politics refer to the governance of a national entity; it involves the regulation of resources and other factors that affect the performance of an economy. When a business considers its marketing options, it must consider the prevailing political climate in the market that it intends to market in.

The key political factor is the stability of the government. Unstable governments make businesses and households sceptical about spending their incomes, as they are not sure that they will be able to continue with the stream of income that they have been enjoying. Such firms and households tend to increase their savings. They spend less and even borrow less to spend, as they are uncertain about the future. At times of great uncertainty, a business may need to advertise more aggressively. Sometimes, the advertising may not be successful as businesses and households cut their expenditure in anticipation of worse times ahead.

Another political factor is the government regulations on the advertising ethics. In a drive to reduce cigarette smoking, most governments have laws against advertising cigarettes on prime time TV. Strongly religious governments may object to nudity being used for advertisements. Government policies on the economy may also affect the nature and timing of your businesses advertisement.

In the developed countries, the mounting level of household debts and the housing bubble may lead the governments to warning households about burying themselves in debt. This might lead to a business that is advertising credit cards to fail in a campaign to increase the number of cardholders.

Economic Factors

There are key indicators of the economy in which a business intends to advertise in. These key indicators include inflation, interest rates, and levels of unemployment and so on. The inflation is indicative of rising incomes and therefore this could represent a market that is growing and hence worth marketing in. However, inflation must be put in context of the political factors; rising inflation could also be because of political instability and low productivity. These two are not ideal conditions in which to advertise. The indicators should also be viewed in terms of the long-term prospects of the economy. A high interest rate may mean that the returns on investments in the economy are very high. However, it may not be sustainable if the high interest rates are caused by the government trying to mop up excessive money supplies in the economy.

Social Factors

The socio-cultural factors affect the preferences of a target market. Attitudes towards the products that your business is marketing could be affected by the economies' views on foreign products if your business is foreign. In certain markets, contraceptive products may be frowned at, as it may be perceived to increase promiscuity. Dominant religions have profound effects on the cultural attitudes; the strong Christian Right in the United States may make it difficult to market abortion clinics for example. Strongly religious Muslim countries may not be receptive to strong depictions of human sexuality.

Language differences and the meaning of certain symbols in different countries may pass on a different message. A good example is how HSBC, an international bank, has depicted these differences in its advertisement under the slogan '**HSBC, the worlds' local bank**'. In the United Kingdom, it is polite to finish a meal, whereas in other cultures, you must show your satiation by leaving a bit of your meal on the plate, indicating that you have eaten to your fill. Hence, marketers must be keen not to offend local sensibilities of their target market.

Other socio cultural factors include the levels of wealth and information available to the market. Rich markets tend to be more aware of environmental factors; their tastes are more discriminative. For example, in a market where the consumers are strongly aware of the environmental degradation that is incurred by the products your business is offering may not be very receptive to your marketing campaign.

Technology

Availability of technology has changed the amount of information available to consumers. Consumers can now quickly compare prices between various vendors. They can also express their opinions freely and share them across the globe. Technology has also changed the manner of distribution. A good example is Dell Computers, a computer hardware manufacturer, that have cut out the intermediaries in the distribution of their computers. They have taken their marketing a step further by allowing consumers to customise the computers that they would like to buy. The simplicity of the transaction is already a powerful marketing tool for Dell. Most consumers are put off shopping by the travel involved and unhelpful shop attendants. Hectic lifestyles also mean that the time taken to walk from store to store looking for the product of choice is no longer available. By being able to customise a computer, pay for it and wait for its delivery without listening to the endless drivel of technicians is certainly more attractive to most consumers. Identifying this need in the market and acting upon it has increased Dell's sales considerably. The four factors analysed in the PEST approach can be classed in the SWOT analyses as opportunities and threats.

30.5.3: *The Boston Consulting Group (BCG) Growth - Share Matrix*

This is a portfolio-planning matrix developed in the 1970s by BCG, a leading consultancy firm in the USA. It is based on the product lifecycle theory. It is particularly used to track the market share and the market growth of products in a business. A wider use is the tracking of a business' units as opposed to products. A business portfolio can be defined as a collection of products and business units that form the whole business entity. The BCG matrix is used in planning the operations of the business portfolio as follows:

- The business unit or product which will receive the more or less investment.

- Developing growth strategies for products or business units, or preparing to withdraw or close down a product or business unit respectively.

The BCG matrix analysis is based on two aspects; the first aspect is the market growth, which in new products, as in business units, tend to follow the product lifecycle. The second aspect is the market share of that product as it goes through its lifecycle. The lifecycle is indicative of the competitive advantage of that product over other products in the same market. As the product is introduced to the market and as it becomes widely consumed the market shares may rise considerably. However, this is not always the case.

The Product Lifecycle

The product lifecycle theory follows a product from its introduction to its growth and final acceptance in a market. A business unit may also follow the same lifecycle. At the introduction stage, a new product is brought into the market. It is backed up with aggressive marketing; this is aimed at creating a brand image for the product. At this stage, there will be few customers for the product and most of them will sample the new product. The initial users may like the new product and inform other people of its benefits. They also tend to become repeat buyers if they do like the product. Once the market is more aware of the new product, more customers will buy the product. This stage is known as the growth stage. The growth stage is also characterised by the entry of competitors to the products market. The consumers and the suppliers increase gradually to a point where growth plateaus off and there is no more growth. This is the maturity stage. The maturity stage may last for long or be short lived depending on the volatility of the market in terms of technology, innovation or rapidly changing tastes and preferences.

Product lifecycle

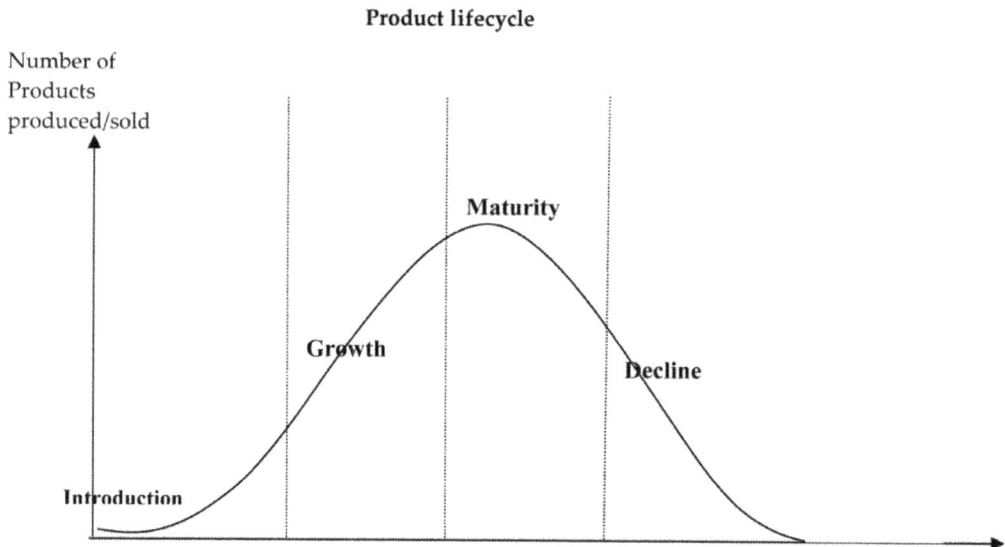

After the maturity stage, the popularity of the product may start to fall off as new products are adopted and tastes and preferences change to new products. This is the decline stage of the products' lifecycle.

The market shares

Once a product has been successfully introduced into a market, and if there is demand for it then more competitors will enter the market and try to supply the product. This will split the market into market shares according to the popularity of the differentiated products.

Each of these factors measure different market characteristics of the product. The market growth measures the attractiveness of the industry. For example, an increase in the number of subscribers to the Internet over various service providers in the UK indicates that this is a popular growth industry. Each service provider has a market share, and an increase in one of the service providers Internet connections market share indicates that there is a competitive advantage of that service provider over the other providers. Competitive advantage in this industry could be the reliability of the service, the ability of the technical support team to resolve the customers' problems or the comparative costs to the consumer among others.

When the two aspects of a product are combined, a decision can be made on which product needs more investment and which product will be expected to have the highest return. A product with a high market share in a rapidly growing market will need more investment to ensure that it grows with the rest of the market, while at the same time; we expect more returns from the increased returns.

Below is a BCG matrix:

Market Growth	Market Share	
	High	Low
High	Stars	Question Marks
Low	Cash Cows	Dogs

Stars

A star is a business unit or a product that has a large market share in a high growth market. This product or unit has a lead position in the market. To ensure that it sustains this position, it is important that there is increased investment in the product. Depending on the product lifecycle position, the investment in the unit or product may be reduced to turn it into a cash cow. This is known as a 'Harvest' decision. A harvest decision increases short-term returns, if the industry has become saturated and the rate of growth has reduced then unit or product will turn into a cash cow.

Question marks

These have low market shares in high growth markets. They also require more investment as it means that there is potential of increasing the market share. Some of the question marks may not be pursued because the other competitors may enjoy a substantial competitive advantage. This is known as a 'build share' decision, the aim of this decision is to turn a question mark into a star.

Cash cows

Cash cows are units or products that are in the low market growth industries but have a substantial market share. This means that the products already enjoy a substantial competitive advantage but since their industry is not growing then there is no need for large investments to maintain this market position. This decision is known as 'Hold' it means investing just enough to keep the status quo.

Dogs

These are units or products in low growth markets and have low market shares in these low growth markets. Since the industry is unattractive and the market share is low then it is often not worth investing in a dog. This is a 'divest' decision, which means that the unit should be closed or the product withdrawn from the market, as dogs cannot be turned into stars or cash cows.

The market share/market growth approach is an important growth oriented approach to big enterprises that produce a number of products for different markets.

30.5.4: Qualitative Decision-making Processes

Instead of elaborate statistical modelling, the management may resort to qualitative methods of decision-making these include:

Brainstorming

Relying on the knowledge and expertise of your members of staff may be a simpler way of making decisions. Brainstorming is a popular method of making decisions. A group is usually constituted, and the larger the better, and presented with a problem. They are given a limited amount of time to come up with possible solutions.

It is important that at the start of the brainstorming session the problem is clearly defined. Then everyone is given some time to come up with a solution off the top of his or her head. There should be no criticism, as this will reduce creativity. All ideas are to be noted down however strange they might be. The brainstorming session should not be too long as it will not be effective. Each of the ideas and its merits and demerits are discussed and the best five or so are chosen. Those chosen should be accepted by the whole group, as it will encourage them to participate in future sessions.

These five ideas are then measured against a criterion that could be time-related, cost-related or revenue related. The one idea that meets the criterion should be chosen while the other four should be kept for future reference.

Focus groups

These are in-depth interviews carried out on a small select group with homogenous members. It is not a sample but a group of carefully selected individuals. These individuals often have common characteristics like a similar background. Instead of a normal one on one interview, the people in a focus group are involved in discussions about various issues, they are then observed and their views noted. This way we can collect both their views and why they hold such views. This approach is used in many cases:

1. Organisational researchers: they use focus groups to learn how the management and the employees feel about the organisation.

2. Political pollsters use focus groups to collect the voters opinions about candidates.

3. Market researchers use the same approach to test the market and the reception of their products.

4. Public services may use focus groups to improve their services.

5. Survey designers may use this approach to test their ideas before they carry out a survey.

In choosing focus groups, we include homogenous individuals who share certain characteristics in one focus group. We are trying to find out what each focus group feels about a certain issue without them getting into an argument due to differences between them. For example, in finding out the employees' feelings about an organisation, it may be counterproductive to include members of the management as this may impede free discussion and vice versa. There can be as many focus groups as possible in researching the same problem.

Focus groups are very important in learning about opinions and attitudes in an organisation or towards a product.

Simulations

A simulation is a re-enactment of reality in a controlled system. It is an imitation of what would happen in reality. Dangerous or expensive activities are first simulated before they are implemented. This offers an insight on to what we can expect in reality. For example, pilots are trained in a simulator as in real life; there is no chance for mistakes. In business, a simulation is important where we cannot afford to lose the resources in the real activity.

An example of simulation is the **queuing theory**; a queuing simulation is used to plot the allocation of a scarce resource such as machinery or human resource to various activities that the business needs to carry out. The queuing theory is formally defined as the study of how systems with limited resources distribute those resources to elements waiting in line, and how those elements waiting in line respond. An example is that of a car pool business. Resources will be allocated to suit the needs of a business as the day progresses, also it is important that the vehicles be allocated optimally to minimise costs.

Decision trees are graphical representations of all the alternatives in a decision making process. A decision tree is used to evaluate each alternative by writing down all the anticipated decision outcomes and further outcomes under those new alternatives. The decision tree maps the alternative decisions to the final anticipated outcomes of those alternatives. For example, a business may make decisions on whether or not to invest in a new product.

```
YES, reception is good ────────────────► Go into mass production

                         ──────────────► Sell patent to another
                                          business to develop

YES, evaluate its reception in the market

                                                    Sell in new markets

                    NO, reception is not good

Introduce new product                               Market is saturated, no new market

                    NO, terminate the product runs
```

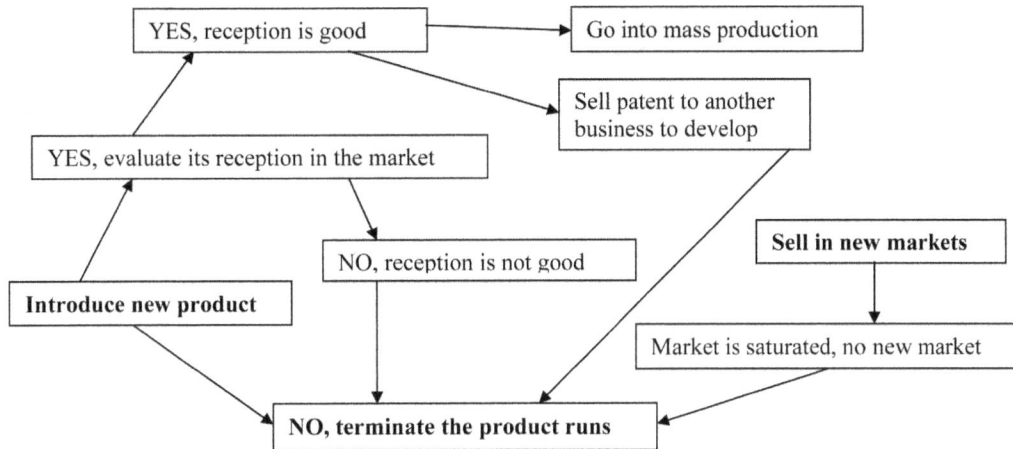

In the above decision tree simulation, each alternative is followed to its logical conclusion. There are at least two logical conclusions for this decision one is to terminate the product while the other is to continue production and movement into new markets.

Self-examination Questions

1. Carry out the following tests on your life plans, a SWOT analysis, PEST analysis and a decision tree.

2. Identify at least two cash cows in a market familiar to you. Recommend what you think the business that produces these cash cows should do.

3. Discuss to what extent decision making models help the management to make complex decisions in a climate of uncertainty.

4. Explain the following decision making models: a). Game theory, b). Garbage can theory, c). Rational Choice Model, d). Bounded rationality model

5. Compare and contrast the effectiveness of the models you have discussed in question 4 above, in decision-making.

Chapter 31: MANAGEMENT ROLE: DECISION-MAKING II

31.1: Organisational Change

Change is defined as becoming different or undergoing transformation. Planned changes are those implemented in the business with a view to improving its performance. In this case, the change is usually initiated by the management and is not forced upon them.

On the other hand, unplanned change is forced upon the management due to changes in the circumstances of the environment within or outside the organisation. Forced change is often referred to as reactive change because it forces the organisation and the management to react to the changes caused by inevitable circumstances.

The planned change is referred to as proactive change as this not induced by changes in the environment rather by the drive of the management to improve the business.

Depending on the size of change in an organisation, change can be transformational changing the whole organisation as well as the structure on which the organisation rests. This is because the structure on which the organisation rests can no longer sustain the transformations. Change can also be gradual or incremental such that their business' decision-makers have to adapt the business to the needs that arise from the gradual change.

Change is triggered by internal or external factors: External factors include:

1. Competitors: these may increase prices, reduce their prices and/or produce better products. Competitors may join the market whereas others move out of the market. All these changes will then require a rethink of the business's strategies and hence change.

2. The government is another powerful external trigger for change in a business. New laws about a particular industry may come into play, for example, the maximum car emission standards in most of the developed countries may force car producers to concentrate on more fuel efficient and environmentally friendly cars.

3. Suppliers of raw materials may be unable to fulfil the needs of the business or they may change the type of supplies they have triggering the business to change the manner in which they receive supplies or even the final products.

4. Consumer tastes and preferences can also trigger change in a business.

5. Political or economic instability can cause changes in business.

6. Changes in technology mean that the business will need to adopt new methods of production without which they might not be able to compete in the market.

7. Change in the labour force, this includes the availability of employees and the requisite skill levels.

The internal triggers, which should be more predictable, include:

1. Strategic plans to change the organisation.

2. Research and development which may lead to innovations that will in turn require an organisational change.

3. Drive for a more efficient organisation, which might require the reorganisation of the internal structure of the business.

4. In addition, a reorganisation may be triggered by a need to develop more efficient structures to deal with outside influences, such as, the government, suppliers, customers et cetera.

Changes in an organisation can be classified into four depending on whether they are proactive or reactive and depending on whether they are incremental (gradual) or transformation (sudden and far-reaching). This has been illustrated in the table below:

Type of Change

	Incremental	Transformational
Proactive	Tuning	Planned transformation
Reactive	Adapting	Forced transformation

Incremental changes from within the organisation are said to be proactive that is the management initiates them in an attempt to make the organisation more efficient and productive. This is referred to as tuning. The changes are gradual and are imbued into the day-to-day operations of the business from within .The management may also decide to change suddenly the way the business operates and this would be a planned transformation.

Outside influences may be so profound that the business is forced into a transformation. In this case, the business is reactive, as it has to deal with the sudden environmental changes to survive. Changes from the environment may be slow and may come in small instalments so that the business has to adapt to these changes.

In this book, we are concerned with how businesses proactively change their organisations over time. This is known as organisational development. In the next section we will closely examine this concept.

31.2: Organisational Development

An organisation is defined as a group of people brought together by one or more common objectives. Organisational development (OD) is defined as the conscious process of adapting to change. A better working definition would be:

OD is the strategy aimed at improving organisational effectiveness by means of behavioural science approaches involving the application of diagnostic and problem-solving skills by an external consultant in collaboration with the organisations management. (Cole, 2004)

From this definition key issues that emerge these are:

1. That OD is aimed at improving organisational efficiency. The management usually realises that there is need for change of an organisation to improve the performance of the organisation and hence initiate change.

2. It involves behavioural studies. Many disciplines are involved in making the change successful this may include: social psychology, human resource management, sociology and so on.

3. That the change is organisation-wide rather than parts of the organisation, it may involve a complete overhaul of the organisation or a change in one section that affects all the other parts of the organisation.

4. That it involves a 'change agent', change agents might be from without the organisation for example consultants or from within the organisation. Change agents from within the organisation must be proactive and able to appreciate the need for change. More often than not organisations will use change agents from outside as they have a fresh look into the organisation. People within the organisation might not be as objective.

Initiating change in the organisation

An organisation will need some impetus to change; internally the management who recognise that there is a need for change may generate this impetus. Organisations are formed to achieve certain objectives, as they grow bigger and more complex, these overriding goals may be lost in the day-to-day activities of that organisation. Organisational development is an important turnaround point that can be used to refocus the organisation to these key goals for which it was formed.

Organisational change may also be caused by external influences. Competitors, the government, politics or any other external force may change substantially leading to the organisation having to change to adapt to its environment. . However, it must be noted that organisational change rarely occurs because of external influences. This is because an OD is a result of a well-thought proactive approach to changing the organisation.

Who is involved?

Organisational development is a sweeping change to the whole organisation initiated from within. It involves everyone in the organisation led by the management. It also involves a change agent, some one or a group of people who have the vision, energy and skill to turn the vision into reality through a workable plan.

31.2.1: Implementing Organisational Changes

OD is a process that involves an overhaul of the whole organisation and it is essential that this be successful in its first implementation. This is because no organisation can afford an unsuccessful OD. As a result, a systematic approach has been developed to ensure that success of an OD.

Step 1: The preliminary Stage

This stage precedes any commitment to an OD. It involves the senior management and an external change agent. A proactive management realizing that there is something that is need of change can call in a change agent to discuss the possibilities that are available to the organisation. If the management and the change agent come to a decision to implement an OD then they will have to agree on the scope and extent of the changes that they can implement. They will also agree on the relationship between the change agent and the management.

Step 2: Analysis and Diagnoses stage

This is the stage where the change agent and the management collect all the information they need to implement a successful change strategy. They design methods of collecting the data that can later be processed into the useful information on the needs of the organisation.

This stage must be carried out swiftly as a long delay between the collection of data and its implementation will make the data obsolete. It is at this early stage that the management and the change agent should strive to involve the other members of the organisation. This is because the participation of the employees who have to live with the changes reduces the resistance to change as well as increasing the feeling of ownership of the changes.

Step 3: Setting common aims and objectives

Once all the important information is collected then aims and objectives of the OD must be set and explained to in the organisation. This ensures that the members of the organisation understand the changes that are due to happen and support those aims and objectives. Changes that are well explained and supported by a common consensus tend to succeed more than those that are forced on the organisation.

The aims should be few and simple. Preferably they should be stated in short sentences thus ensuring that they are easy to understand. For example, the aim will be to 'to increase profitability'

The objectives usually explain how the aims will be achieved. To this end, objectives must be Simple, measurable, attainable, realistic and time-related (acronym SMART). For example under the aim, a company that has been making £1,200,000 in profits for the last two years can state the following objectives under the aim of increasing profitability:

1.   To increase our profits to £2million by the end of the next financial year

2.   To reduce costs by £0.5million by the end of next year

3.   To make efficiency savings in the delivery of our services of £0.2million

4.   To replace the production line with a more advanced version which will save us a further £0.1million

The objectives are simply stated, they are realistic as they take into account that the profits cannot increase suddenly to £20 million as much as this sounds very favourable. Each of them is measurable as clear figures and time lines are stated.

Once these aims and objectives have been agreed on then the business is ready for the next stage

Step 4: Action planning

Action planning is the process of allocating time, resources and expertise to various tasks in the OD process. In step 3 above the intended outcome has been clearly stated in the aims and objectives. The action planning matches the individual tasks under each objective to the resources required to fulfil the task as well as the expertise. It is important that the action plan is sequential and allocation of resources is optimal.

Step 5: Implementation

Using the action plan the process of organisational change can start. It is important that the implementation be according to plan and there is control over excessive deviations. . Where positive deviations should be encouraged and enhanced, excessive deviation could throw the whole process into chaos. It is better that the implementation proceeds according to the plan as closely as possible and after its completion the areas where a deviation is recommended be evaluated. This is the next stage of the OD

Step 6: Evaluation and review

The evaluation and review process is both on going at the end of the implementation. Monitoring the implementation could highlight areas where the initial ideas may need a review. If these changes can be implemented without jeopardising the whole OD then they should be incorporated. A more sweeping review is however carried out at the end. This review is aimed at creating future improvements of the new organisation. It is also important in evaluating the success of the 'change agent'.

It is also from this step that new aims and objectives can be set.

Change is a pervasive and complex aspect of social life; as a result, many theories have been developed to aid in a successful change process. In the section that follows we are going to discuss how to manage change in an organisation.

31.3: Managing Organisational Change

Change is a social phenomenon: organisations change as a result of human intervention and in changing they affect human beings. Therefore, in managing change we are actually managing the interaction between individuals and organisations. Since organisations are groups of two or more people with a shared purpose, we are in essence managing the interaction of human beings in the pursuit of their common goals. Change in an organisation demands that the relationships between the human beings and the common goals that they share also change. This is a very scary prospect for humans who belong to an organisation. An organisation breeds security as the interaction between the humans therein is governed by the rules of that organisation. Any changes to the organisation, therefore, may be interpreted as interfering with these rules and may be resisted.

However, there may be obvious benefits to changing an organisation such as: releasing latent energy and skills in the organisation, better use of resources, efficiency gains and/or employees involved in the change process may better understand the aims and objectives of the organisation. For these advantages to be realised then change must be carefully managed.

31.3.1: Dealing with Resistance to Change

One model that has been proposed to deal with resistance to change is the Kotter and Schlesinger (1979) Model. They start by explaining the four reasons for which there may be resistance to change in an organisation. These are:

1. **Misunderstanding:** persons in the organisation may not understand why the change is necessary and may even perceive it as aimed at them. This is usually as a result of inadequate information or other communication problems within the organisation. Inadequate information through the formal channels is supplemented by rumours and misinformation from the informal channels. This may lead to a lot of resistance against the proposed changes.

2. **Parochial Self-interest:** this is where some individuals do feel that their interests will be jeopardised by the proposed changes in the organisation, rather than appreciate the greater good that will come from an overhaul of the organisation.

3. **Low tolerance to change:** some individuals in the organisation may find it difficult to adapt to change and may thus resist change as it represents a threat to their security and stability and hence vigorously resist change.

4. **Different assessment of the situation:** Some of the individuals in the organisation may hold different views as to the reason for change and as such may resist change since they do not agree with the reasons for it, or they do not agree with the touted advantages or disadvantages. They may agree with the need for change but not the direction the change is taking or the aims of the change.

Some solutions to these problems are also proposed in the model. These solutions are aimed at gaining the support and cooperation of the employees of the organisation. These include:

1. **Education and communication:** clear communication that leaves no doubt as to the direction and purpose of change will have a profound effect on the employees. It also reduces the undercurrents caused by informal channels of communication that may lead to misunderstanding. Where adequate

knowledge or education is lacking then this should be provided. Knowledge not only increases the participation of the people that the change will be affecting but also helps them understand the logic behind the proposed changes.

2. **Collaboration and participation:** to enlist the support of people it is important to include them in the planning process. Involvement increases identification of the people to the project of change. They feel that their input is valuable and hence support the change, rather than merely going along with the plans.

3. **Facilitation and support:** where there are people in the organisation who are anxious about the change it is important that the support they need be provided. The management can hold a one to one session with most of the employees and discuss their views on the changes that are happening. Support groups can also be constituted to provide a peer support system for the employees.

4. **Agreements and negotiation:** in a case where some parties lose out then there is need to negotiate and come to concessions. The concessions could include schemes of early buy-outs or retirements for those who do not want to experience the change. Concessions in the types of change and in this reduce losses to the losers of the planned changes.

5. **Co-option and Manipulation:** where the resistance cannot be dealt with through the four methods above then the management can try including the resisters to the changes in the planning process. Their inclusion would not be based on their substantive contribution, but rather for appearances' sake. This approach may backfire if the resisters realize that they are being manipulated. Resorting to this approach may be indicative of underlying problems in the communication. Resisters may feel excluded and unappreciated by the organisation and may rebel against any changes especially if they feel excluded from the process of change.

6. **Implicit and Explicit coercion:** this method may be employed where the change has to be implemented quickly. This is also a last resort tactic as it may have long-lasting and far-reaching effects on the employees' morale. The employees may be explicitly or implicitly threatened with the termination of their employment, transfer to undesirable locations and so on, if they fail to participate in the change process.

Activity:

Look at the following scenarios and suggest the best solutions to the problems highlighted:

Scenario 1:

Arthur is a very dedicated employee who is rarely ever late and does all the work allocated to him. He has a family of three, his wife and child. He works at a backend office doing a routine job that ensures stability and security. A backend office is an office where all the routine administrative work is carried out for example the processing of wages. He also has an outstanding mortgage of £60,000 and his young child has just joined a local private primary school that costs £7,000 a term. His wife is not in employment yet.

Arthur is vigorously resisting changes to the back end office. These changes include a more integrated computer system that will cut down work in the back end office.

Suggest approaches that could be effective in dealing with Arthur's resistance to change.

Scenario 2:

Angela is a senior manager; she has worked for ABC Company for the last 6 years and has risen gradually through the ranks. She does not think that the proposed changes are important and does not even agree with aims and objectives. She has mobilised other senior managers to reject the changes. However, there is a need for change; this is a fact that everyone in the organisation agrees on.

Suggest ways in which Angela can be brought on board to accept the proposed changes.

31.4: Beckhards Model of Change

This model deals with the push that leads to change in an organisation. Since resistance to change is an inherent characteristic of organisations then for change to be effective there are factors that must be present. These factors are represented in an equation proposed by Gleicher Beckhard Harris.

Dissatisfaction X Vision X First Step > Resistance to Change

The above equation refers to the three factors that are necessary to overcome resistance to change.

This can further be explained under the various headings:

Dissatisfaction

Dissatisfaction is the key to change. If an organisation evaluates its present situation and finds that they are not at the position where they wish to be then they are dissatisfied. They then need to make a change.

It is necessary to be clear on what the desired organisational condition is after the change has taken place, which includes having defined goals. The present situation of the company in relation to this desired state and goals needs to be clear. This difference in situations is known as dissatisfaction and so long as it persists then a push for change will be there.

Vision

An organisation must have a vision of where they would wish to be. This is the vision; a vision is contrasted to the reality in which the business exists. The difference between the vision and the present situation of an organisation provides the drive for change. If the organisation does not recognise this difference then they will not move to make a difference.

First step

An organisation must then make the first step to make the change that is required to make the change from the situation that the business is at to the situation that is decided upon in the vision.

These three factors must work in concert to overcome the resistance to change in the organisation. All of these factors must work for the resistance to change to be overcome. Any weakness in any of the factors outlined may lead to problems in an effort to change the organisation.

Practical example

In the temporary employment business, employers call the recruitment business when their regular employees fail to show up.

ABC limited is a successful Recruitment business; however, there is a general feeling amongst the employees that there is a need for a change to offer clients a better service. This is borne out by the fact that there are better services offered in the same market. As a result the employees have put together a document in which they have explained to the management of changes that they need to implement to make the business more successful. These are as follows:

ABC ltd: needs to make a phone call to cover for a staff shortage in one of the clients' business.

Dissatisfaction: the notice may be too short for the recruitment agency to cover the shortage.

Vision: Employers can provide a monthly forecast for periods when they anticipate shortages. This would allow the business some time to prepare all the workers that will be needed to cover the shortage.

First step: The document prepared by the employees recommending changes to communication between the business and its clients.

If any of these three elements is missing then the business might not be able to overcome the resistance to change.

31.5: Lewin's Freeze Phases

Lewin (1951) a physicist-cum-social scientist came up with the freeze phases.

The unfreeze stage: An organisation in a freeze state is one which has established behaviours and norms. Individuals in such an organisation are not ready to change and do not see the need for any change. Such an organisation offers the individuals security and stability. For change to occur this frozen state must be overcome. Thus the first stage of change is known as the unfrozen stage. It is during this stage that the norms of the organisation are questioned and new ideas about what should be done to develop the organisation are discussed. However, the discussion and the awareness for need to change are inadequate drivers for change. For change to occur the people in the organisation must make a real effort, there must be action that leads to change.

The transition: Lewin sees change as a process rather than a sudden move from one state to another. He warns managers of what is known as a 'Transition trap', this is where managers take time to adapt to the changes and then expect the employees to make those changes in a single step. This often produces resentment and resistance to change. Transition is also a period when no one is accountable to the norms of work and therefore a lot of what is normally done and the accountabilities that come with it may be abandoned for the transitional hype.

Refreeze Stage: This is the other end of transition; at this stage the organisation establishes new systems and norms within which to operate in the changed organisation. The refreeze stage need not be rigid; as this would make it difficult for future changes unfreeze stage. However, failure to freeze may have its own negative effect of not imbuing the organisation with the stability and security that breeds commitment from the employees, as they will be working anticipating the next change.

31.6: Total Quality Management (TQM)

TQM is defined as the continuous process of improving the quality of the goods and services offered by a business. The concept of TQM holds that everyone is involved in the management of the process of maintaining and improving quality. Quality management is carried out on all activities of the business. TQM encompasses all the influences external and internal that is deemed to affect the business as a whole.

The concept of TQM is embodied in Dr Edward Deming's fourteen points of management. The areas of improvement vary from business to business. These are:

Conscious planning of resources to maintain the quality: A business that implements TQM needs to make a conscious and consistent effort to allocate resources to maintaining the quality of their goods and services. Other resources should be allocated to ensuring that the products are continually being improved. Innovation and inventiveness needs to be supported with the appropriate financial and human resources

Adopt the new philosophy: The government needs to adopt the new philosophy that supports and allows for total quality management. The government should be ready to encourage this transformation. This is a view of the external environment that affects the business. Though it is beyond the business to ensure that the government removes regulations that are obstacles to the adoption of TQM, bodies that represent businesses may be used to pressure the government into making such changes.

Cease dependence on mass inspections: In order that quality of the business' products can be guaranteed, the business must inspect the product through the various stages of its production. Rather than ensuring that the final product meets the standards, each stage of production should be inspected to ensure that the product would meet those standards of production. The stage-by-stage inspection is a preventive measure as products with defects or below the expected quality can be corrected at the earliest stage, preventing excessive loss. For example, in a car assembly plant, a car will be assembled from the chassis up, a faulty chassis if not detected at the start of the production process can have a good body placed on it, the interior designed, engine and even expensive in-car accessories. If the defect of the chassis were to be detected at the end of the car production, the car would have to be removed as production waste, or stripped down to the chassis again, which would be expensive and time-consuming. Another problem would be if that the car was sold on to the market without the defect being detected, this could be dangerous to the consumer, and the government may censure the company.

End the practice of awarding business based on price tags alone: This practice is directed at the relationship between suppliers and the business. The business should establish relationships with suppliers known to supply quality goods. Every business is both a supplier and a consumer of another business. If each business will only choose suppliers who provide high quality products then the products in the whole sector would improve drastically.

Institute continuous training on concepts of TQM: Due to the total involvement of all the employees and all the resources available, then training programs should be instituted throughout the organisation. This will ensure the participation of all the employees up to and including the management. Various studies on TQM found that increased knowledge in the business not only made the implementation of TQM easier, but also provided a basis for invention and innovation of the procedures. Training empowers the employees to participate in the TQM.

Adopt the institute of leadership: This is aimed at the management; the management should lead rather than supervise. This means that they should provide direction and influence rather than order the employees to implement the TQM measures. The reason for this that TQM is dependent on continuous improvement, such improvement can only be achieved through innovation, failure to lead stifles innovation and hence the best approach is leadership.

Drive out fear: Employees should be secure so that they can contribute to the business without fearing repercussions from their employers. The freedom to express ideas not only increases motivation for the employees to build their careers, but also for the business aims and objectives. It also provides more ideas that can be tried out and hence higher chances for success.

Breakdown barriers between working groups: More often than not teams created to achieve a certain objective may be carried away by the achievement of that objective to the point that they forget the overriding goal of the business. All the different teams use the businesses resources to compete against each other and produce results. Sometimes, this competition can be so fierce that some of the teams may resort to dirty tricks just to emerge the best. Such competition should be discouraged. Teams should be in constant communication and should be made to understand that the real objective is to promote the business as a whole.

Eliminate slogans, exhortations and targets for workforce: While slogans and exhortations may be used to motivate the workers in a business, they can also stifle individuality and motivation. Slogans tend to ask for conformity from the workers, conformity reduces the individuality of the employees and hence self-motivation and innovation. For TQM to be successful employees must be encouraged to be unorthodox in finding better ways of carrying out their task.

Targets on the other hand are useful in ensuring that tasks allocate are achieved in the time and within the resources allocated for those tasks. However, an extreme system that is bent on meeting targets at the expense of quality should be discouraged. Targets should support the continuous improvement of quality of the products.

Eliminate numerical quotas: Quotas are stringent targets that have number values attached to them. Sometimes business may set unachievable quotas or may overemphasis the importance of quotas to the detriment of quality. Quotas may be useful in measuring the achievement of goals however; they must not be the overriding outcomes.

Remove barriers that rob people of the pride of workmanship: While individual reviews may be used to evaluate the workmanship of workers and highlight areas of improvement, it may also result in individuals being overly concerned with their own output to the detriment of the rest of the organisation. The total quality of the final product should be the main concern of the business as a whole rather than individual performance.

Encourage education and self-improvement: Self-motivation and self-improvement of the employees can improve the quality of final products, especially if this is a continuous process.

Take action to accomplish the transformation: Changing to TQM requires the commitment and the will to follow through. This may be obvious but it is what is obvious that is required.

TQM is therefore a process that involves the continuous improvement of the quality of products through ensuring that each of the processes and inputs that go into production.

Chapter 32: BUSINESS AND ITS ENVIRONMENT

32.1: Approaches to understanding the Business Organisation

Business and management can be viewed from a multi-disciplinary perspective. An organisation can be defined as a group of people who share a common objective. In studying organisations, we are studying human beings, their origin, their development to date and their present day interactions. This study encompasses different disciplines: such as, Sociology, Anthropology, Psychology, and Economics. This chapter will investigate the different thoughts on business and management in each of the disciplines mentioned above.

32.2: The Anthropology of Organisations

Anthropology is defined as the scientific study of the origin, the behaviour, and the physical, social, and cultural development of humans. Organisations have been an important aspect of the origin of human society. A whole area of study has developed under anthropology of business organisations; this is known as Organisational Anthropology. In this field, anthropologists use the theories and methods used in anthropology such as participant observation, ethnography, interviewing and semiotic interaction analysis; to conduct inquiries that focus on such issues as, work practices and cultures of occupational communities and culturally based patterns of consumer behaviour amongst others.

As businesses become more complex, organisations that are more elaborate are hatched and these are supported by increasingly complex management structures. Cultural anthropology studies how the interaction between human beings has changed over thousands of years. This can give us an insight into the nature of human beings and the expected directions in which they will change. Modern businesses are based on corporate cultures; the change and evolution of those cultures can make or break an organisation. Corporate structures define whether a business entity will succeed.

Ethnography, a branch of anthropology, is the study of a small group of people in their environment with large numbers of variables, as opposed to ordinary sociological enquiry where there is a large group of people and hence relatively fewer variables can be studied. This is especially important in business organisation; they can be used to understand employee groups and group dynamics.

Another common method of anthropological research is the participant observation approach, this is important in a business context in that it allows business researchers to enter the world of their research subjects and feel how it feels to be the subject. For example, if a business were undergoing rapid change, an anthropologist would be invited to participate in the change experience with the employees and experience first-hand what they are going through.

Semiotic interaction analysis is an even more interesting area of anthropological study. It refers to the interpretation of signs within the organisation. The key to success is efficient and effective communication in an organisation. Semiotic analysis studies the signs and symbols in a business organisation, what those signs and symbols stand for and how their interpretations. While humans have evolved very advanced speech capabilities, the effectiveness of speech is dependent on the signs that accompany the speech. Without these signs then we would have to speak out all our meanings, and explain our feelings, convictions and so on. This would not be efficient, as a smile can indicate happiness, as we speak, or a pleasant thought. Semiotic analysis in a business communication will hence be useful in enabling efficient communication.

Anthropology is hence a useful area of study understanding and developing the corporate organisation.

32.3: The Sociology of Organisations

As we have already seen, individuals with common goals form organisations. Sociology is the study of the interactions of human beings in their day-to-day lives; it encompasses studies of human behaviour, organisations, institutions, and development. The sociology of business organisations is studied from the three broad perspectives of sociology. These are the functionalist perspective, which holds that society is akin to a living person, each part of society has a role to play, and each part must work together in harmony for success of society. Failure of one part of society will lead to the failure of the whole society. Everything in society thus has a function. This functional approach would seem to be the best representative of the business organisations; however, it fails to take into account self-development and wealth motivation of social classes.

The **conflict perspective** holds that the society is in a continuous state of conflict. The conflict is caused by the existence of class differences defined by disposable wealth. The upper class or ruling class consists of people with great wealth who own factories, companies and so on. They also have control over vast productive resources. The middle class consisting of professionals such as lawyers, doctors, accountants and so on, these generally achieve their position through educational qualifications. A working or a lower class, which consists of people with relatively less qualifications than the middle class, usually do the manual work in society. The existence of classes lead to conflicts in society as people try to move into the classes above their own and those at the top of the classes try to stay there and prevent movement by imposing their beliefs and ideals to those below them. The ensuing conflicts then lead to alliances and competition between groups. This is the key to explaining business organisations today, as the owners and the upper class employ the professionals and the working classes to increase their wealth and dominance. The professionals try to break into the upper class and this brings conflicts between the professionals and the upper class. To protect the investments of the upper class, elaborate ownership laws and procedures have been invented to ensure that the ruling class cannot lose their businesses easily. In this case thus, a more elaborate organisation is needed to deal with class conflicts and hence the modern business organisation.

A third sociological perspective is that of **interactionism**. This perspective is a relatively new area of sociological study. It focuses on the individual and holds that rather than the individual being a product of the society, the society is a product of the individual interactions. The society is a fictitious creation of these individuals trying to impose order and predictability in their interactions with one another. Business organisations could be such an example of fictitious creation that is imbued with order and predictability. The interactions within a business organisation of the employees and the management can be said to create an organisation and a society that is predictable.

An important contribution to Business organisation thoughts is the Weberian postulation on the origin of capitalism. Max Weber was a German political economist and sociologist who wrote the book 'The *Protestant Ethic and the Spirit of Capitalism*'. In this book, he showed how the puritanical Protestant ethic influenced people to form their own enterprises, engage in trade and gather wealth. To Weber, the Protestant ethic led to the unplanned and uncoordinated mass action that led to capitalism. Belief in the rewards of hard work and self-improvement led to the Protestants applying themselves to enterprise. He drew a comparison in Europe between the strongly Protestant ethic in England, Germany and Holland which at the time were experiencing a strong capitalistic growth, and contrasted this with the slow growth in the rest of Catholicism dominated countries in Europe

It may appear as though human beings are in control of businesses because they create them, but business organisations seem to acquire a life of their own. The interactions in a business are dictated by laid down rules and procedures, this could also indicate that human beings are formed by the society in which they live, therefore human beings could be slaves to business organisations. Either way sociology is very important in understanding business organisations.

32.4: The Psychology of Business Organisations

Psychology is the science or study of the thought processes and behaviour of humans and other animals in their interaction with the environment. The study of psychology sees clear relationship between the thought process and the behaviour of human beings. One such behaviour is the formation of business organisations. Hence, to understand human organisation it is important to investigate the thought process behind the behaviour.

Psychology in businesses is applied to a wide range of areas these include:

- Management and leadership.
- Job satisfaction and motivation.
- Communication and counselling and development.
- Stress and stress management.
- Psychology of Training needs and learning patterns in businesses.
- Business organisation.
- Consumer and marketing strategies.

All these areas are very important to the management of the human resources in a business organisation.

Motivation: Influencing employees to carry out the work allocated to them is a complex and multi-faceted undertaking. A.H Maslow's Hierarchy of Motivation is an important contribution to businesses seeking to motivate their employees. As we have already seen in page 182, he used the diagram below to illustrate the hierarchy of needs:

Increased satisfaction

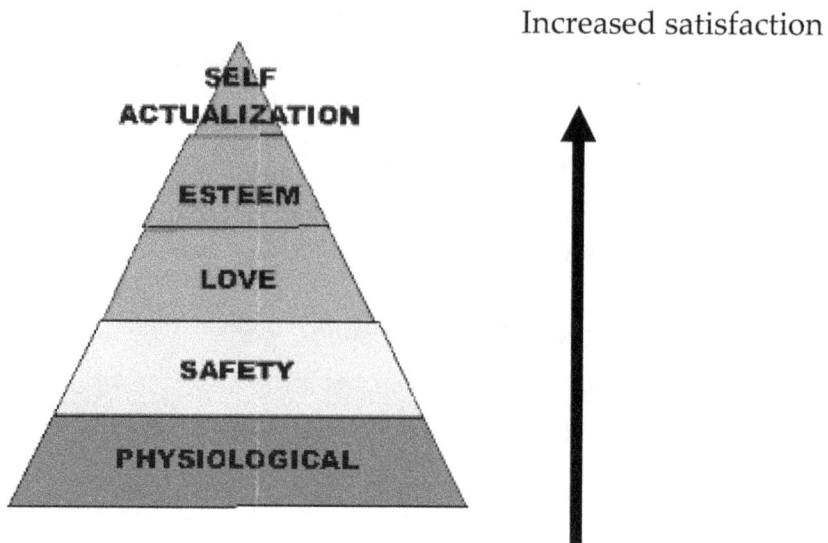

Maslow proposed that different people need different forms of motivation depending on their position in the hierarchy of needs. He proposed that all human beings tend to seek self-actualisation but before they arrive at this highest level of satisfaction, they must first satisfy lower needs.

The most basic of needs is the physiological needs; these are physical needs such as food, shelter, clothing, education, and access to health services and such other basic needs. Failure to meet these needs may lead to discomfort, pain or even death; these consequences motivate people to pursue the satisfaction of these needs.

The second stage is the security stage; once the physiological needs have been met then human beings seek for their physical security and stability in the chaotic society. Security could include moving to a residential area, job security at their place of work and so on.

Once security is attained, the next stage is acquiring love and a sense of belonging. People tend to join groups and clubs to attain this sense of belonging. The love here is non-sexual and more to do with companionship and friendship. This stage is closely connected to the love stage, this is the Self-Esteem stage, instead of craving for belongingness, and individuals crave for recognition. People want to master skills and gain recognition for those skills. People at this level of the hierarchy buy prestige cars and live in prestigious addresses.

The last and the highest level in the hierarchy of needs, is the desire to become more and more of what one is capable of becoming. This is known as self-actualisation. Such people have the resources to maximise their potential.

In reality, the levels are not as distinct as they are in the pyramid. People may fulfil two or three levels at the same time. A person who graduates from a medical school will get a high paying job and fulfil his physiological needs, as well as security and love needs. By identifying the level at which an employee is at, the management can create incentives for that employee to work hard. Employees who are on the lowest level will work harder if their wages are increased. Increase in salaries of highly paid individuals at the levels of self-esteem may not have this effect. However, a plaque at the door of the highly paid individual showing his/her credentials may be more motivating as it is recognising his/her achievements.

Learning: Various theories on learning are important to the business organisation. The best method of training and developing the employees should be used. They need those learning and teaching methods that best suit them. Some of the theories include:

Constructivism: this is where an individual reflects on his experiences to construct an understanding of his environment and how to interact with it. In a business setting, the employees who are able to learn very fast using their experiences in the work place are rewarded with promotions and increased responsibility. The business organisation hence encourages experiential learning. This encourages hands-on problem solving and teamwork as employees seek to find solutions. This method of developing employees is especially important in the middle and senior management levels where the decisions are more unstructured than in the lower levels.

Behaviourism: this theory holds that animals and human beings learn by acquiring new behaviour. Individuals acquire new behaviour by being stimulated either positively or negatively. This is known as conditioning, there are two types of conditioning. The first is **Classic** conditioning is where natural reflexes such as salivating is a response to certain stimuli like food. The second is **Behavioural** or **Operant** conditioning, where a certain response to stimuli is rewarded thus reinforcing that response to that stimuli. In a business organisation, behaviourism can be useful in ensuring conformity, where failure to conform is discouraged and certain responses to stimuli for example failure to respond to a fire alarm is dealt with by a severe reprimand from the management.

Psychology is also useful in many other business areas such as marketing. As more studies are done into psychology, then psychology will become increasingly useful to business organisations.

32.5: The Economics of Business Organisation

Economics is concerned with understanding the mechanism for allocation of limited resources to achieve unlimited wants. Economics addresses the question of choice of the best way to allocate the limited resources to the unlimited wants of the economy.

Classic economic dilemmas include the game theory, which has been covered elsewhere in this book. Under game theory, some business decisions cannot be made unless other decisions are abandoned due to the limited resources available.

Economic optimisation in business is the process of establishing the most efficient and effective way of ensuring that the business utilizes its resources for the most productive purpose.

Economic rationality holds that firms or businesses strive to maximise profitability while consumers work to maximise the utility of the goods and services that they consume. Consumers like firms have limited resources with which to acquire goods and services that confer utility. Consumers, if offered two products with the same utility but different prices, will consume the products with the lower price. Low prices on the other hand conflict with the firms' goal of maximising profitability. The market must hence set a price that is optimal for both the firms and the consumer. A low price will discourage the firms from producing a certain product, while a price that is too high for the consumers will discourage its consumption. Therefore, economic rationality is an important determinant in pricing a firm's products.

Economics is an important area of study for businesses especially due to the importance of matching unlimited needs to limited resources and making the right choice in the modern day business environment, which allows for very few mistakes.

32.6: The Stakeholder Model of the Firm

The stakeholders' model of the firm departs from the theory of economic rationality. Economic rationality postulates that the firm's overriding goal is maximising profitability for shareholders. However, the stakeholders' model shows that there are other parties affected by the decisions and the objectives that the firms set. These are known as stakeholders. Stakeholders refer to anyone who is affected by or who affects the decisions of a firm. There is a two-way relationship between the stakeholders and the firm.

Stakeholders thus include:

1. **Consumers**: the decision to continue or discontinue the production of a certain good or service, or even alterations to that product will affect the consumer. The firm depends on the loyalty of the consumers to their products.

2. **Government**: the government collects taxes from the firms as well as ensuring that the firm's legal rights and obligations are protected.

3. **Suppliers**: if the business makes a decision to discontinue sourcing products from the supplier then the supplier has lost a market.

4. **Employees**: have a big stake in the business, a business that is prospering assures the employees of their own security and hence increases their commitment to the business.

5. **Communities**: apart from the direct action of businesses in their communities, businesses create employment in the community and hence improve the standards of living of those communities. On the other hand, they provide a market where the products of the firm can be sold.

6. **Investors**: investors support firms. Without investment in a business idea then businesses would not survive. They provide the needed capital for the firm to start and continue. Investors gain profits from their investments and interest for the risks they undertake

7. **Trade associations**: employee trade associations are used to safeguard the rights of the employee in the businesses as well as create a forum where the company and employees can negotiate terms and conditions of their employment. Trade associations can also represent the businesses interests to the government. Businesses join trade associations to represent their interests to the government as well as have access to legal advice and representation should the need arise.

8. **Political Groups**: where a business operates in a sensitive industry such as energy may attract a lot of political attention. One such industry is the oil industry.

The following diagram can represent these relationships:

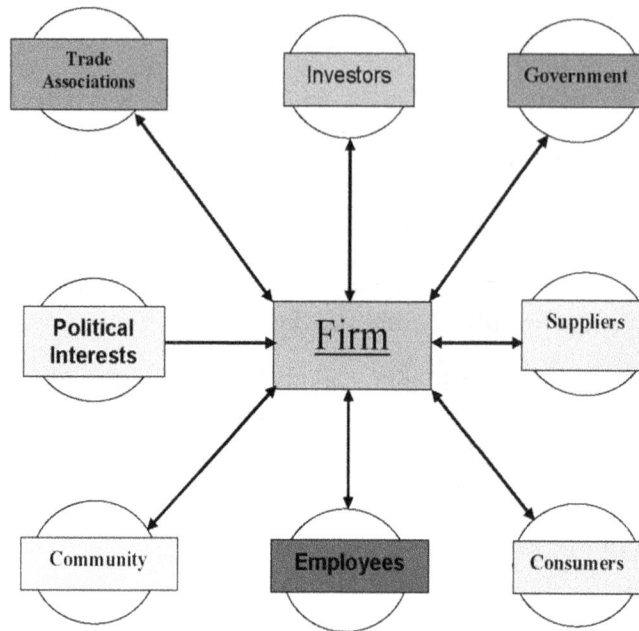

There is a two-way interrelationship between these stakeholders and the firm. Each of the stakeholders confers benefits to the firm as well as gains from the decisions and activities of the business. The model recognises that profits are not the only reason that a firm exists and seeks to create a decision-making framework that includes all the aims and objectives of the various stakeholders.

The stakeholder model ensures that there are no predefined priorities of one set of interests over the others, the management is charged with the responsibility of ensuring that there is a balance of goals and the use of resources effectively.

Complex business organisations in an endeavour to satisfy the investors may make decisions that will jeopardise the welfare of other stakeholders. This must be minimised by involving as many stakeholders as possible in decisions. Where the stakeholders cannot be directly included in the decision-making internal representation can be made available. For example, to safeguard the community, an oil-drilling company may have a committee that is responsible for the environmental issues that may affect the community. Their role is to ensure that in the profit making and value-maximisation (investors' objective) the community's objectives of a cleaner environment and employment are not jeopardised. Some of the stakeholder's objectives may be in conflict. In the example above, profit maximisation and environmentally friendly methods of production may be in conflict. More often than not, the cleaning up necessary after a production activity may lead to higher costs and hence lower returns and profits.

The stakeholder model advocates for a balanced decision making approach that meets all the stakeholders needs.

Activity:

BERNOL is huge international extractive firm with offices in a developing country. The company's annual turnover worldwide exceeds the GDP of the developing country. Discuss how the company can jeopardise the welfare of the stakeholders in this host country.

Suggest ways in which the stakeholders' model can be used in decision making to safeguard these interests.

Self-examination Questions

1. 'The study of businesses is multi-disciplinary'. Discuss this statement using examples.

2. Discuss the learning theories in psychology in relation to employee training and development in a business organisation.

3. Economic rationality is an important assumption in resource allocation; however, economists still observe seemingly irrational behaviour by consumers. Discuss how these irrational behaviours affect decision-making in a business organisation.

4. Anthropology is the study of the origin of man, his physical, cultural and philosophical development. Discuss the importance of anthropology in developing the corporate culture of a complex organisation.

5. Motivation is an important responsibility of the management; discuss how Maslow's hierarchy of needs can be used to motivate various employees.

Chapter 33: INTERNAL ELEMENTS OF BUSINESSES

33.1: Internal Elements of a Firm

The internal environment of an organisation is determined by factors that are particular to that firm for example its employees, available resources, unique ideas, the skill of the management, the firm's culture and so on.

The internal environment of an organisation refers to the interrelations that exist between the various elements within the control of the business. These elements reside in the very nature of the organisation and define the organisation. The organisation may seek to consciously modify some of these elements or find that the interrelationships between the elements, by themselves, define each other. Organisational elements are constantly changing because organisations are made up of people who are also constantly changing and surrounded by an ever-changing environment without the organisation. These elements include the size of the firm, the type of business that the firm does, the strategies it adopts and the type of ownership.

Organisational dynamics are the socio-cultural forces within the organisation that lead to and govern change. Organisational change is a continuous process. Organisations are groups of people who come together with a common goal of achieving certain pre-set objectives that they have agreed. Fierce competition besets today's firms, this, together with rapidly changing external environments, means that the firms must also change rapidly to cope with these changes.

Rapid change also means that the firm must establish norms and cultures that govern its day-to-day operations as well as its overall strategy. These values, norms, beliefs, attitudes and assumptions are known as the organisational culture. The organisational culture of a firm ensures the cohesion of the internal environment of a firm. Probably, the most destabilising change within a firm is technological change, in the past three decades technological changes have accelerated in pace. Computerisation, the internet, availability of information both on 24-hour breaking news channels and the internet has led to a need in every organisation to take on board the changes while maintaining its organisational structure and overriding goals.

The rest of this chapter discusses how the internal elements interact and the important roles of organisational structure and culture in dealing with change as well as the effects of technological change to these elements.

33.2: Organisational Change, Behaviour and Structure

As already discussed in earlier chapters in this book, **organisational change** refers to alterations and modifications made to the internal elements. Change is inevitable since the inherent nature of organisations is that they are constituted of human beings. Human beings are constantly changing; they learn and develop. This means that the organisation acquires the same change characteristics of human beings. The organisation's objectives may also change; this will lead to modifications of the whole organisation. While the external environment is beyond the firm to change and the firm has to react to it, the internal environment is presided over by the management of a firm; they can implement changes to all the elements of the organisation.

Nadler and Tushman (1980) define **organisational behaviour** as how people within organisations act individually or in groups, and how organisations function in terms of their structure and processes. They further state that all managers are in the business of influencing behaviour in directions that will meet business needs. Both the management and the external environment define business needs. This influences behaviour within the organisation. Other factors that influence behaviour are the personality traits of the individuals in the firm and the internal environment in which they are working. For example, poor working conditions may lead to an otherwise competent employee underperforming, while an employee with personality problems may be very productive in an enabling environment.

Lastly, Professor John Child (1977) has defined **organisational structure** as all the tangible and regularly occurring features, which help to shape an organisation's members behaviour.

Organisations are systems that depend on the clarity and commonality of objectives as well as a consensus on how to achieve those objectives. Organisational structures not only allocate the resources of the business efficiently but also ensure that all its members act in synergy to create a greater good than they would create as individuals. Organisations' structures are also important in ensuring that there is specialisation based on the skill and experience of employees. Delegation of duties makes for lighter work done to higher standards; this is an important function of an organisation. Importantly, structures ensure the continuity of organisation even if some of the individuals leave, die or become incapacitated. The formalised structure also serves as a conduit for values norms and methods of carrying out certain functions. Without these structures then the learning achieved over a certain period would be lost. For example, if no formal structure existed at Ford

Motors then new versions of Ford cars would not be developed, as each generation would die with its expertise leaving the new generation to start from scratch. Organisational structures have been one of the most important innovations in the business world, the more business becomes complex the more elaborate the organisations become.

There are many types of organisational structures including:

1. **Line and Staff organisational structure**: In this structure, the focus is on the personnel who directly produce and provide the goods and services required by the customers. They are known as the 'Line personnel'. The line personnel are supported in their work by the 'Staff'. For example, in a company that produces tinned vegetables, the line personnel would be the people who put the vegetables in the cans, seal and label them. They are directly involved in the production of the final product. The staff would refer to the departments that support the production of the vegetables; these include the finance department that does the wages, the marketing department that sells the canned vegetables, the purchasing department that buys the cans, the vegetables and the paper or paint with which to attach the label. The line and staff structure is prevalent in the manufacturing businesses due to the highly specialised skills required for the line personnel.

2. **Divisionalised structure**: Here the business is divided into the divisions that operate in near autonomy to achieve their goals. Each of the departments has a distinctive role to play, targets are set for each and their performance evaluated at the end of the relevant period. The interrelationships are usually within the divisions and a final product or service comes out of it. A division is headed by a divisional manager who reports to the board of managers on the performance of his/her division. Each division operates in full autonomy and may have its own finance, personnel, and manufacturing functions. The criteria of creating divisions may be the type of product they produce, their proximity to the market and so on. For example, an electronics firm may produce three different types of electronics say, home appliances, entertainment gadgets and industrial electronics. Such a firm may be divided into the three divisions, each fully functional on its own, but with a shared business ethic or basic technology. The home appliances division will then be expected to report to the board of division managers at the end of year how the division fared and so on. Within the home appliance division, there will be an accounting function, sales and marketing function, purchases function and planning and development function.

3. **Decentralised structures**: Where the divisions are very different in the services or products they produce then firms tend to decentralise completely leaving only a skeleton umbrella firm. In this age of mergers and diversifications firms will have distinctively different businesses. As a result, complete autonomy may be required to improve efficiency. For example, a mobile phone company, which also owns an airline may need to decentralise its business as the two may have very little in common.

4. **Matrix structures**: are best suited to a firm which runs projects. Since projects are transient, the main structure of the firm supports the projects by 'lending' certain members of its staff to the project. These members of staff remain under the long-term supervision of their departments but also for the period of the project under the project manager. The dual supervision could result in a conflict of interest, but it is also very effective in ensuring that projects are carried out by people who understand the main aims of the whole organisation.

5. **Flexible organisations**: are usually found in environments that are rapidly changing Mintzberg (1983) called such organisations Ad hocracies. In these organisations, decisions and roles of the people change rapidly; the environments are usually complex and dynamic. Rather than doing the work as it has always been done, a flexible organisation does what works. Industries in their infancy need this kind of flexibility. As we have witnessed during the internet boom of the late 1990s, the businesses in the this industry could not adhere to any preset norm of the industry as none existed and also new opportunities kept presenting themselves to the industry which required unorthodox and flexible approaches to exploit.

6. **Process-based organisations**: These organisations focus on quality rather than some overall firm ethos. In the last decade of the 20th Century many companies turned to concepts of total quality management and process reengineering. These concepts demand that quality be integrated in every process of the firm. This requires that there is a flow of the products and services from the purchasing of the raw materials to the sale of the final product. The communication between departments needs to be flawless and efficient to ensure that quality is maintained throughout the organisation. This is an important departure from the traditional hierarchical structure where each department is clearly separated from all the other departments. Its output is not governed by quality rather by the efficiency and the profit turning that is often the goal of many firms.

All these structures affect the behaviour of the people working within the organisations as well as the manner in which change can be effected.

Organisational behaviour, its change and structure interact to create an environment that is unique to the organisation. These organisational characteristics also affect the elements that govern the internal functioning of the organisation. Elements include the type of firm according to the type of business it engages in, the type of ownership as defined by its legal structure, the strategy of the firm and the size of the firm. The next section discusses in detail the internal elements of a firm.

33.3: The Internal Elements of a Firm

The internal elements of the firm are the characteristics within and unique to a firm that define that firm. These include the size, the type of business and the ownership of the firm, and the strategies the firm adapts to meet its aims and objectives.

33.3.1: *The Ownership of the Firm*

The legal structure defines the ownership of a firm, and refers to the number of people who own a business and how they own that business. A *sole proprietorship* (*sole trader*) is not usually regarded as a firm as it is a business owned by one person. Such a person makes all the decisions regarding the business and gains all the profits as well as shouldering any losses that may occur. This legal structure has a number of advantages not least amongst them; not sharing profits and quicker decision-making. A sole proprietor need not find consensus to make a decision and implement it. In the conventional sense thus, a sole-proprietorship is not a firm and does not require the elaborate organisation of firms owned and operated by a larger number of people.

A *partnership* on the other hand is a business owned and operated by at least two people. In a partnership, all the owners are personally and equally liable to any outstanding debts. This may reduce the burden that the sole trader may face all alone. However, in a partnership as with a sole trader there is no limitation to the liability. This means that in both legal structures the owners are expected to pay all the outstanding debts regardless of their contributions to the businesses. Their personal property may be attached if the business resources cannot be used to satisfy those debts.

The non-limitation of debts in the two preceding legal structures makes them very unattractive especially to very young business that has not yet established itself. To encourage small-business formation the United Kingdom introduced the idea of companies in 1844. *A company* is a business owned through shares, those who own the shares are known as shareholders. The shareholders may be directly involved in the day-to-day management of the business or may appoint other people to manage the business for them. The company is known in legal terms as an artificial person with its legal rights and responsibilities. A company can therefore sue or be sued, own property and insure the said property just like every other natural person. The shareholders are liable to the debts of the company as far as they have invested in the company. If for some reason the company is required to repay debt and is unable to do so then the shareholders' personal property cannot be attached to repay the debts.

The legal structure therefore has a profound effect on the firm's organisational behaviour, structure and change. Usually professional businesses such as accountants and law firms are partnerships; this is because people depend on their judgement and advice to make important decisions that could result in huge losses. Each member of the professional firm hence needs to be held personally liable in case of negligence, fraud or poor services. A partnership is usually dissolved if one of the partners leaves the partnership and a consensus must be reached between all the partners to admit additional partners. A partnership agreement is also written out stating the share of profits and losses to be borne by each partner. In a company on the other hand, the liability is limited to the shareholders contribution known as share-capital. The shareholders may not be directly involved in the day-to-day running of the business. Day to day running of the business is delegated to a management team and as a result, a different organisational structure exists for a company that is different to a partnership.

33.3.2: The Type of Business

The type of business a firm engages in may also define its organisational structure. A car-manufacturing firm will be different from a law firm. In the car-manufacturing firm, there could be an assembly line with workers being highly specialised, work may be repetitive and no one person makes a whole car by himself or herself. In a law firm, a lawyer may be allocated a case to research and represent in a court of law. The work in a law firm changes rapidly because lawyers may be asked to represent different cases at the same time. These two scenarios demand different organisational structures.

The registrar of companies in the UK has come up with a business classification code known as the Standard Industrial Classification (SIC). The SIC describes all the business activities that companies can engage in. For a full list, you can visit the Companies house website.

What business a firm does dictates the type of people and the general organisation of the firm. A highly specialised manufacturing business may prefer a Line and Staff organisation to an adhocracy that may be required for a budding e-business.

The type of business will also dictate the type of ownership. Professional firms will often be partnerships as holding companies will be limited companies. Holding Firms will tend to be limited companies due to the need to raise additional capital. A very big company may float its shares in the market to attract new capital. To ensure that the shareholders funds are safeguarded the company will be required to make its accounts available for public scrutiny. Due to the great number of shareholders, a public limited company will have a management team that is separate from the shareholders. This means that the organisation will be different from that of a partnership.

33.3.3: Size of the Business

Most big firms nowadays are formed through mergers and acquisitions. Others grow in their industries and come to dominate those industries. Innovative organisations have managed to grow in the rapidly changing environment of the last 50 years of the 20th century. The size of the firm may be geographical or financial. British Airways flies to different destinations all over the world so has a huge geographical presence as it has offices in every city where it goes. On the other hand, Wal-Mart is one of the richest companies in the world with a smaller geographical presence.

The financial size of a business requires organisational change and structures that are different from smaller firms. Dominant firms in a certain industry are subject to scrutiny by the government and industry regulators, as they tend to out compete smaller firms through either price wars or owning the basic technology and the funds to carry out an extensive research and development. They are also more often than not listed on the stock market thus the government may require that their operations be disclosed to the public.

Larger firms also employ a lot more people than smaller firms and interact with labour unions. Such firms have dedicated human resource departments to deal with the needs of their employees. Elaborate transition plans must be put in place for organisational change to be successful. The decision-making process will also tend to be longer as all the stakeholders with a say in the decision must reach a consensus. Once a decision has been made then it has to be communicated correctly throughout the organisation. Huge organisations are prone to change problems as some people may misunderstand the purpose and methods of change. Organisational culture is very important in huge organisations. Without it, there would be no common goals and it would result in sub-optimality. Sub-optimality occurs in an organisation when a certain function operates so efficiently that it jeopardises the operations of the whole organisation. For example, a firm that assembles vehicles may have an overenthusiastic purchasing department. Without proper communication, the purchasing department may order more material than is needed for production. This could result in resources that can be used elsewhere being tied up in purchasing, reducing the overall efficiency of the organisation. An organisational structure and culture maintains the organisation's overall goals and coherence. The larger the firm the clearer the organisational structure and culture needs to be.

33.3.4: *The Strategies*

A strategy is defined as a method of doing something. The success or failure of organisations in today's highly competitive market is dependent on the suitability of the strategies. Innovative strategies that exploit upcoming technologies such as the internet have proven to be very successful. EBay and Amazon are very successful businesses based on the internet. Their strategies have made them reach an ever-increasing number of internet subscribers. Dell Computers has launched a new strategy of only selling their computers over the internet and then delivering them to the doorstep of the buyer.

Firms employ strategies in dealing with different facets of their business. These facets include the market, the employees, production methods, products and services on offer, and the supply side for their production. In creating a strategy, a firm will both be interested in securing its long-term growth as well as maximising its short-term returns. Strategies are important in ensuring that the optimal allocation of the business resources is achieved.

The market refers to those with the need and the means to acquire the products of a firm. A strategy must be adopted to ensure that the products or services reach the market on time and conveniently. The marketing strategies include advertising, free sampling, free shipping, attachment to other goods; the list being endless as it is innovative. It is the firm's responsibility to ensure that they recruit and retain skilled and capable employees. This means that there is a need to put in place strategies to deal with the employees. The production methods have often defined industrial successes from failures. Rapid adoption of more advanced techniques does not necessarily result in better and more efficient production and may at times be detrimental to the organisation. A careful adoption of technology and reaping maximum benefits from such is an important strategy that goes hand in hand with strategies for the employees. Another important strategy area is the supply –side. The suppliers of a firms input must maintain the high standards that the firm requires to produce high quality product or service. The firm must also ensure that such a supplier is reasonable compared to other suppliers. The products and services offered by the firm are also an important strategy area. Firms must also anticipate the future product and service demands and prepare to offer those products. This strategy has led to many firms succeeding while those which fail to anticipate future needs find that they are left behind. Anticipating and producing goods for a future market can also lead to consumer demanding those future products. Huge firms today can actually influence the demand of the market by aggressive advertising and meeting the needs in the market.

Strategies of different firms differentiate the internal elements of different firms. A firm that is determined to lead in technological innovation will hire and retain technologically skilled personnel and highlight this fact to the market. Anticipating future products for example the current push by car manufacturers to produce environmentally friendly vehicles is an anticipation that as petroleum becomes more expensive people will demand more fuel-efficient transport.

Strategy also dictates the culture of the firm, to make a strategy work then certain norms and values must be imbued in the organisation that explain and justify the strategy and provide a framework in which the strategy can work. Organisational change should also be consistent with the strategy set. The strategy is prepared to include the future growth of the firm. Changes within the firm will therefore be within the strategic plans. The strategy is also central to other management functions such as planning, organising, staffing, directing and controlling. The strategy can thus be said to define the character of the organisation and its uniqueness.

The interaction of the four elements discussed above and the organisational structure and culture define the character of the organisation. They also define the differences from other firms as well as the changes that can be made to the firm to make it more successful. Probably, the greatest need for change comes from technological changes and their effects on the methods of production, administration, communication, service delivery, access to expertise and support. The following section discusses the importance and the effects of technology to the internal environment of businesses today.

33.4: Technology and the Firm

In the 20th century, age-old production methods were taken over by technologically advanced methods. Technology has grown over the years hand in hand with the changes in the organisational structures and business approaches. Probably, the most telling changes have been the organisation adaptation to technological changes. From a negative backlash to the computer, to its being embraced as the most important tool in business today. The rapid growth of the internet and its functions has completely changed the rules of the business world.

Today, firms based in Shanghai can reach customers in London within seconds, internet products such as VOIP (Voice over internet protocols) have made it possible for people to communicate as if they are sitting in the same room. Internet web log (popularly known as 'blogs') are used by firms such as Microsoft to collect candid response from their customers and identify future needs. Technology has extended markets beyond national borders. Technological development has also changed data processing and storage making vast amounts of information available to a larger number of people. The market is better informed and the consumers can compare products by a click of the button on their products. Sales persons in car-showrooms find that people already know the specification of the car they want to buy and its price. It is with this in mind that Dell has chosen to cut-off the intermediary and speaks directly to the now empowered consumer. Technology has had a profound effect on business strategies therefore. Being hired in firms is now dependent on your computer skills and expertise.

Computers are however not the only innovations of technology though they have been a big part of it. More efficient and safe industrial processes have been introduced to safeguard the employee as well as provide precision and cut down on labour costs. New industries have emerged because of technological change. Space travel is even tipped to be a leisure activity in the future. Governments are working with entrepreneurs to make fuel-efficient technology available to as many people as possible. Hybrid cars are the vogue in developed countries as people become more aware of the dangers of emissions from petroleum based engines.

All these technological changes and many more have had profound effects on the firm in many ways, some of which include:

1. **Communication**: firms today have a greater variety of means of communication; apart from the conventional meetings, written memos and letters. Firms can now discuss issues in chat rooms which have video-linked teleconferences with counterparts halfway across the globe and use powerful

mobile phones to hold a conference. The interconnectivity of communication technology has also increased the possibilities for the firms. An employee can send a fax message using his/her mobile telephone. This has also allowed workers to work from home changing the very culture of organisations by reducing the interaction between employees.

2. **Production technology**: changes to more efficient methods of production has reduced wastage, increased production levels while reducing production costs. This has led to firms making ever increasing profits and allowing for further investment and expansion. This in turn has led to an increase in wages and general demand for more of the firms' products as their employees have more money with which to buy what they need. Technology has also led to the release of human intellect in general into tasks that require more skill. This in turn has increased labour productivity.

3. **Information**: information is now readily available. 24-hour news channels and the huge storage capacity of computers have made information quickly and easily available. Availability of information has made it easier to take advantage of opportunities that present themselves. Consumers who are more informed also demand higher quality and this has had a strong effect on the firm as they search to satisfy the consumer more. The focus of most firms has changed to speed of delivery and quality management.

4. **Administrative Technology**: the computer has made filing, ordering and retrieving information an easier human occupation. Efficiencies gained from administrative technology have not only released personnel to do more challenging work hence increasing productivity, it has also reduced costs of operation by making available to the firm superior processing power and virtual storage that would occupy acres of land.

5. **Self-service and support**: The internet has brought products to the consumer homes. Consumers no longer need to walk the high street in search of a certain good. They can book airline tickets and buy furniture on the internet. This has reduced the costs of maintaining premises everywhere where your customer is likely to be and has increased consumer satisfaction. These are also important efficiency gains. Consumers can also access support easily over the internet. The National Health Service (NHS), in the United Kingdom provides a self-diagnosis on the internet; this increases the chances of saving lives before medical assistance while releasing doctors from routine chores of ailments that can be easily diagnosed and treated. There are many other examples of how the internet and other technologies have changed the landscape of the business world.

However, on rare occasions technology can be detrimental to the firm. The obvious problem that is presented to most firms is failure to access new technology quickly and efficiently which could result in the loss of market share. Adopting new technology without proper planning can lead to profound employee problems especially if the employees have not been trained to use the new technology or do not understand the efficiency gains that come from technology.

The associated costs of buying new technology and installing it could also prove to be counterproductive especially if there is no real need for it.

It is important that a firm understands the uses of technology: Before investing in it, a firm should:

1. Consider whether the benefits gained are worth the costs incurred. In effect do a cost-benefit analysis.

2. Identify the training needs for the new technology, workers with top-end technology but who do not know how to use the technology are in danger of getting frustrated.

3. Identify the need for which the technology has been acquired. A specific need helps in the training regimen that will be prepared for the employees. It also makes it easier to identify the cost-benefit relationship.

4. Assess the technology market to ensure that the firm purchases the best technology available.

5. Ensure that the technology acquired can be upgraded and is compatible to the other technologies generally used in the same industry.

6. Ensure that there is both support for the technology from the manufacturers of such technology and that there is support for the end-users.

7. Ensure that there are back-up systems in case the new system has any problems. If installing a new computer system throughout a firm: set-up a backup filing system in either removable storage or paper or in case of changing an old production method into a technologically advanced one.

33.5: Organisational Culture

A culture is a system of norms and values that characterise an organisation or a society. A culture must be agreed upon for it to be effective. It is increasingly important that complex organisations have a culture. A culture dictates what is and what is not acceptable within the organisation, it forms the basis for expectations. When people interact, they do so based on a consensus of what to expect from the other person. When we meet someone new, we extend our hand expecting the other person to clasp and shake it vigorously. This eases communication within the organisation.

An organisational culture is based on values and norms. Values are defined as the beliefs or the principles that govern an organisation or society. Values influence the way people behave in the organisation and the stronger the values the more they influence behaviour. Generally, the organisation will encourage positive values such as competence, innovativeness, dedication, development and so on. Norms on the other hand are the informal ways of behaving. These are derived from the values. They are unwritten since if they were written then they would be policies rather than norms. The norms reflect the values held by the organisation. Norms can also be expressed as artefacts these are symbols of the values held within an organisation. A norm of respect for all can be seen in the way memos are written, or the way the receptionists welcome visitors or even in the tone of telephone conversations.

A culture can be developed in an organisation consciously or unconsciously. Some of the sources of a culture include:

1. Charismatic leadership: a culture can develop around an individual with strong leadership qualities. The people working under and around him/her would emulate what he/she does, thus developing a culture.

2. Events: an organisational culture may develop from an occurrence in the organisation that served as a turning point. For example, mineworkers who endured a cave-in may form a habit of carrying flashlights and supplies down into the mines or looking out for each other.

3. Effective working relationships: sometimes a culture develops around what seems to work. Seemingly effective methods of communication and cooperation can become entrenched in the organisation for the simple fact that they seem effective compared to other methods.

4. External environment: the nature of the environment in which the business operates may influence the internal culture. A rapidly changing environment may require that the firm change rapidly and with it the culture. Relative stable industries may foster firm cultures within the firms.

Organisational cultures were categorised by Harrison (1979):

1. Power-orientated culture: this is the culture of competitiveness, and has more to do with playing politics and personality cults rather than expertise or competence.

2. People-orientated is focused more on meeting the needs of the individuals rather than the tasks. The management is consensual rather than controlling.

3. Task-oriented; this approach is about getting the job done, it centres on competence and innovativeness.

4. Role oriented: focuses on the 'properness' of the organisation; it is a culture usually found in slow bureaucratic organisation, things have to be done in a certain order and the chain of command is followed strictly. Legality and legitimacy is also very important.

Many factors affect the development of culture in an organisation. They include:

1. **History**: all organisations have history; huge worldwide organisations such as Toyota have very rich histories from which a culture develops. For example, in 1954 Toyota introduced the 'Just in Time' system, which revolutionised car manufacturing. Taiichi One fine-tuned the process and the system began in the 1960s. This was later renamed Toyota Production System. Toyota has used this method to date improving and perfecting As a result it has become an important component of the culture in Toyota.

2. **Primary function and technology**: the culture in most firms develops around its main function. As we saw earlier, the relationships and work methods that seem to work are developed into an organisational culture. Those that do not are discarded, which results in a culture that is unique to the organisation. This culture is closely related to the main functions and methods of production. For example, after an accident the warehouse operatives may develop a culture of shouting 'Clear!' and expecting shouts of 'Clear!' from everyone before they start a machine that runs throughout the building.

3. **Goals and objectives**: Sometimes the management of an organisation may decide to set goals and objectives, which can only accomplished by certain norms that develop in term over the goals and objectives. A regular weekly meeting may lead to a culture of department heads conferring to ensure that they are up to date before the meeting.

4. **Size**: smaller firms have a more discernible culture. This is because there are fewer people and they probably spend more time together, if the culture is developed around the main function then it is also easier to maintain, as there

is a likelihood of there being one or two main functions only. Small firms also have a close-knit community feeling, most relations are personal. It is also more likely that all the offices are located in the same environment again fostering the same internal environment and hence a similar culture throughout the organisations. However, larger organisations like Sony might have different sub-cultures in the organisation due to the different primary functions, geographical presence in almost every continent. Different political, economic, technological environments also mean that the culture within the organisation alters to suit these aspects of its external environment.

5. **Location**: The locality of the firm if urban will tend to take on the more metropolitan culture as opposed to the quiet conservatism of a rural location.

6. **National culture**: the multinational companies operate in different countries and often employ the people of those countries. These people bring with them the national culture. As HSBC articulates very well in its promotion campaign dubbed 'HSBC, the world's local bank'. Every country has a different culture and for a firm the size of HSBC to succeed then it needs to understand and inculcate those cultures into its business dealings.

7. **Management and staffing**: the people who work within that organisation can consciously cultivate culture. The type of management also dictates how the organisational culture will develop; a person-orientated management style will develop a culture of concern for the employee over and above the achievement of the tasks laid down for the firm.

8. **The External environment**: an unstable external environment leads to an unstable internal environment; the same applies to the stable environment. A rapidly changing environment would mean that the firm has to change rapidly as well to keep up with the industry.

Self-examination Questions

1. Discuss how the size of a firm affects the strategies that the firm would use to enter a new market.

2. 'Computers and the internet have given consumers more power to choose'. Discuss.

3. Define organisational culture, how does organisational culture ensure that the aims and objectives of a business are met?

4. 'A task orientated culture is more effective than a people orientated culture' discuss.

5. Define the following terms:

    - Size of the firm

    - Ownership of the firm

    - Strategies of the firm

    - Type of main activity

6. Describe how each of the four factors above influence the organisational structure of a firm. Explain using examples.

Chapter 34: EXTERNAL ELEMENTS OF BUSINESS

34.1: The External Elements of a Firm

The firm exists in the environment made up of the economy, the political atmosphere, households, the sociological and cultural aspects of the community in which it operates. To understand the operations within a firm it is important to consider its external environment. This chapter explores the effects that the environment has on the firm and the manner in which the firm responds to these effects. Some firms may have an effect on the external environment, especially currently where some firms contribute a significant part of the Gross Domestic Product of an economy.

Competitors are an important part of the external environment. They shape the firm's policy on issues such as marketing and the type of products. For example in 1992, IBM created the first 'Smartphone', which in 2012 had become almost the replacement for the standard mobile phone. In 2012 IBM did not have a market share in Smartphones. The top competitor in shares was Samsung, with Apple close behind. The majority of the market share was made up of several companies. The relationship between competitors is the market share. In cases where there is a dominant competitor, smaller firms may be forced to identify niches that are not being covered by the dominant firm rather than compete directly with the larger firm. Competitors also affect pricing decisions; the price wars waged by British supermarkets can testify to the importance of competition-driven pricing decisions.

The economy of the country in which a firm is situated plays a crucial role in influencing the decisions of the firm. For example, a pricing decision in a low-income country will be based on whether or not the target consumers can afford the prices that have been set. Interest rate levels affect the availability of cash, the persistent low interest rates in the developed countries has fuelled consumer spending. Firms benefit from low interest rates as they can borrow money cheaply and increase their investments, at the same time cash is available in its target market, which means that consumers will continue to purchase their products. Sometimes, extremely low interest rates may be detrimental to the firm, as they will fuel inflation pushing many goods out of reach of the consumer hence reducing the demand for those goods. A well-managed economy is consequently important for the firm.

The political climate of the country in which a firm is situated also affects its operations. One of the most important factors that led to the growth of the large firms in the developed world is the political and legal stability. Firms can operate in relative certainty of the government's actions. The legal frameworks of the business also help the business claim redress where a wrong has been committed.

The government must also enforce the provisions of the legal system. At the same time, the judicial system must be fair expedient in dealing with cases brought to it for redress.

Maybe the most important of all these factors is the sociological and cultural characteristics of the society in which the firm is situated. A culture of innovation and hard work fosters a strong basis on which the firms can set root and prosper. The competitive society of the USA has made the country a world super-power as they relentlessly work and reinvent themselves. The Japanese society seeks and applauds excellence. This is reflected in the success stories of Toyota, Honda, Sony, to mention but a few excellent Japanese firms.

This chapter discusses in detail the effects of the external elements on the firm and its internal elements.

34.2: The Economy

The system or range of economic activity in a country, region, or community is known as the economy. It refers to all the activities that go into the allocation of the scarce resources in the country, region or community to the unlimited wants. It refers to what needs that region, or in our case country, prioritises in making a choice on how to use their scarce resources. The government is in charge of all the resources, the firm is in the private sector and operates within the framework set by the government of the country. In economies where capitalism and market economies are prevalent, the firm is left to the devices of the market to help it determine what needs to meet with its resources. In a controlled economy for example the former Soviet Union the government decided how best to use the resources available to them. This led to the Soviet Union producing a large amount of capital goods and fewer consumer goods. The collapse of the Union partly goes to show that the system was unworkable, as the goods produced were not needed and this lead to a reluctance to produce more.

A firm in a market economy on the other hand has to look at the market to decide what to produce. This means that some firms may choose to misallocate resources and this could have negative outcomes to the society. In this case, the government must intervene to ensure that production does not harm the country. For example, while the sale of heroin pays well; its effects on the users have led to governments all over the world banning the use, carriage or sale of heroin. Apart from direct intervention by the government, there are indirect effects of the economy on the firm. Some of these may be aimed directly at controlling the performance of the firm or at the wider economy.

One key tool of controlling the performance of an economy is the use of interest rates. An interest rate is defined as the cost of borrowing money. If you take a loan from a bank, they will usually quote an interest rate for the loan. This interest rate is the cost of taking the loan. The Central Banks of most countries set interest rates for the economies. The interest rates of the central banks are used as the benchmark for lending money by the firms and the households in the economy. If these are set too high, then households will not be able to borrow money to spend on their needs. As a result, firms will not have a market for their goods either. This means that the firm will have to cut down on production and maybe lay off some workers who become unemployed and therefore reducing the market for goods produced by the firm. Another problem of high interest rates is that the firms may also be unable to borrow money to expand their businesses. It is therefore very important that the economy have the optimal interest rate.

Very low interest rates on the other hand could lead to inflation. Inflation is the persistent rise in prices of commodities. This may have positive short-term effects on the firm as they reap increased profits. The wages of worker remain constant as the prices increase, which means that eventually the workers will be unable to buy products from the firms leading to a rapid fall in prices and the inability of the firm to produce more. In the long-run inflation could therefore be a problem. Another aspect of the economy is the exchange rates, especially for firms that have international trade. An exchange rate is the price of one currency in another currency for example; £1 is equal to $1.89. This means that if you want one pound then you will need to give $1.89. If the exchange rates fluctuate widely then it is difficult for a firm to determine the actual cost of international transactions, as they cannot conclusively establish the price of a currency using another. Firms also run the risk of losing considerable amounts of money if the exchange rate fluctuates widely during a transaction. For example if a truck making company exported ten long-haul trucks to the USA today at the agreed price of $1.89million, overnight before the trucks arrive, the exchange rate becomes £1 for $5 which would immediately change the price to $5million. The person in the USA who had ordered the trucks would have to pay $5million for trucks he had originally bought at $1.89million. Such wild fluctuations do happen to less stable currency. This means that the firm must enter into agreements to ensure that the price remains constant. Government implements policies that ensure that the exchange rates remain constant. The interest rates, inflation rates and the exchange rates are interrelated and a change in one of them leads to changes in the other two. The United Kingdom policy is said to be 'inflation-targeting'. By changing the interest rates, the amount of money circulating in the economy can be increased or reduced. People tend to borrow less if the interest rates are high and they spend less, as they cannot borrow to spend. To reduce the level of inflation in the economy, which is caused by a larger circulation of money, the central bank simply raises the interest rates.

Inflation has an effect on the exchange rates too. If the cost of goods in a country increase, several things are likely to happen. One is that the demand of those goods and services might fall. Another effect is that people will want to import what they cannot buy locally. If the local prices are too high then more people might opt to import. Importation of goods from Germany into the UK requires that you change your Pounds into Euros. This creates a demand for the Euros increasing their value in relation to the pound. As more people ask to change their money into Euros so that they can purchase more German goods, the value of the pound will begin to fall. This way the exchange rates change.

What does all this mean to the firm? The firm must carefully consider these three economic indicators. If it is in the export or import business, it must also consider the performance of other economies and make wise predictions.

Activity:

Jacques International, an international commodity firm, has received information that the Central Bank is set to increase the interest rates to 'cool down' the housing market. 'Cooling down' the market refers to reducing the rate of the persistent rise in prices. Discuss what possible effects this could have on Jacques' International import and export of cars.

34.3: The Political Factors

The political elements of the environment and the economic factors are very closely related. This is because the political government is in charge of the economy. The political sphere influences, significantly, the operations of the economy. Laws that are enacted and enforced have direct effects on the economy. The firm interacts with the political sphere in many ways. One of the most significant is the taxation of the firm. Taxation is another tool that is used to control the performance of the economy. Taxation can also be used for political reasons, for example a stepped taxation system where people who earn more are taxed more than those who earn less. To discourage cigarette smoking, the government can impose heavier taxes on the production and distribution of cigarettes. Tax breaks can be used to encourage investment in certain industries, for example, a government may offer tax breaks to innovators and scientific businesses to encourage their establishment.

The legal system that safeguards the rights of firms and households or imposes obligations on the same is also affected by the parliament. The parliament discusses and enacts laws that are used to determine cases brought before the judiciary. Any firm operating within a country must carry out its functions in accordance to the law. For example, in the Sales of Goods act a sale is defined as the exchange of goods or services for a monetary consideration. Consideration here refers to the money that you give in exchange for the goods or services. If you buy a car for £1 then that is a sale. Therefore, a sale in law only occurs with this exchange. Failure to exchange anything for goods and services means that there was no sale. This distinction is important as it safeguards the rights of the buyer; the seller of a £1 car cannot later claim that the car was not sold because someone is now offering him £3000 for it. It also safeguards the seller because a buyer cannot return a good on the basis that there is a cheaper one elsewhere. The political sphere hence influences the firm through the legal system and the taxation system.

A more profound effect is however, the quality of governance by the political system. The suitability of the political system, the stability and the political will to maintain law and order in the country. Firm's employees live in the political system; their safety must be safeguarded at all if they are to give their best to the firm. Countries with poor governance are also prone to corruption and bribe seeking behaviour. When a firm or person with resources lobby the government to enforce activities that have no benefit to the society and are designed to safeguard their ownership of the resources they are said to be rent seeking. Corruption and rent seeking makes it difficult for businesses to operate as the costs of operation is very high. It also fosters unfair competition and firms are unable to operate optimally.

The prevalent political ideology, whether liberal or conservative, also affects the operations of a firm. A liberal political system that believes in free-markets and liberal economic policies will foster competition between firms and develop a strong market led economy with minimal interference in the operations of the firm. A conservative ideology may interfere more with the firm and its allocation of resources. An extremely conservative ideology such as communism will dictate where resources are used and by who.

Probably, the stability of the political sphere is the most important. The political stability of Western Europe and North America after the Second World War has led to rapid economic growth. This can be contrasted with the African dilemma of politically unstable governments that have eroded the confidence of investors and failed to lay the infrastructural foundation for vibrant economies. Political instability could lead to wars and loss of life. A firm cannot operate in a politically unstable environment because not only is there no market to which they can sell their products but their employees can be killed in war. Buildings may be bombed.

Decisions made by the firm therefore will be influenced by the political factors ranging from peace and security to the enactment and enforcement of the legal structures.

Activity:

The government closely monitors large firms that have a monopoly on naturally occurring resources. Discuss whether direct intervention by the government is good for the firm; do you think that firms should be left to the forces of demand and supply?

34.4: The Cultural and Sociological Factors

A culture is defined as the totality of socially transmitted behaviour patterns, arts, beliefs, institutions, and all other products of human work and thought. A culture is unique to a society; it distinguishes that community from other communities. A culture is transmitted through the society through communication. This uniqueness of cultures is an important external influence to the firm's workforce and market. Since firms operate in communities they must understand the people derived from the community and work in the firm for them. At the same time, they provide goods and services to the external culture. Since the firm cannot succeed without either employees or its market then it needs to understand the various aspect of the culture of its target community.

A community is a market for products and services. The following cultural aspects are very important:

Firstly, the tastes and preferences which are derived from the culture, in a community where health is a very important issue, selling fast food that is soaked in oil might not be a very successful venture. On a larger scale, developed countries are heavily consumerist compared to emerging economies such as China. A firm investing in producing capital goods in a developed economy may not be as successful as one investing in consumer goods.

A second cultural factor is religion, in a Muslim state a pork firm might run into serious problems as the religion prohibits eating pork. Another factor in the market that is affected by culture in the market is the general population age. In a country where the population is aging rapidly, medical services may be more important than flashy cars.

Certain community values may also affect the market. For example, India has the highest propensity to save in the world. This means that the community saves a higher proportion of their income than any other community worldwide does. This society will thus tend to be less consumerist and may not borrow as much. In 2012 the UK debt as a proportion of income stood at 212%. The spending culture in the UK is different therefore as we borrow more than we earn to sustain the consumerism culture.

Culture will also affect the employees of a firm. Practices that go against the culture may not be well received. Muslim employees asked to slaughter and package pigs will refuse this job, as it is a violation of their religious beliefs. There are many examples where the firm must be more sensitive to the culture in which they operate.

Dr. Geert Hofstede conducted perhaps the most comprehensive study of how values in the workplace are influenced by culture. From 1967 to 1973, while working at IBM as a psychologist, he collected and analyzed data from over 116,000 individuals from forty countries. From those results, and later additions, Hofstede developed a model that identifies four primary dimensions to differentiate cultures. He later added a fifth dimension, Long-term Outlook. These cultural dimensions have already been discussed in chapter 25.

Self-examination Questions

1.   Briefly describe and assess Hofstede's dimensions of culture (refer to Chapter 25).

Classification of cultures by dimensions

	Country A	Country B	Country C	Country D
Power Distance Index	Medium	High	Medium	High
Masculinity	High	Low	High	Medium
Uncertainty Avoidance Index	High	Low-to-Medium	High	High
Long-Term Orientation	Medium	Low	High	Medium
Individualism	Medium	High	Medium	Medium

Given the above cultural difference, how might you advise a Country 'A' firm acquiring an established company in each of the other three companies?

2. Discuss how globalisation may reduce or increase cultural problems in the firm.

3. *"Culture is more often a source of conflict than of synergy. Cultural differences are a nuisance at best and often a disaster."* (Prof. Geert Hofstede, Emeritus Professor, Maastricht University) Discuss this statement giving examples.

4. The persistent rise in prices could be advantageous to the firm. Discuss how a fall in prices could be advantageous to the firm.

5. Country X is in rapid political and cultural transition, discuss how this can affect the internal elements of a firm.

Chapter 35: CASE STUDIES & REVISION QUESTIONS

35.1: Introduction

This chapter on case studies is designed to give the learner a feel of the practical issues that businesses and their managers have to deal with. It is designed to test your creativity and ability to appreciate the larger picture. While there are rationally 'correct' answers to most questions, you can propose a solution or insight so long as you can argue your point of view and defend it using examples. The case studies chapter is therefore supposed to stimulate you and prepare you for the real world of business.

This topic also aims to revise several basic business and management concepts including factors influencing location, demand, social costs and finance. The aim of case studies is to give students a feel of business and management.

35.2: Fictional Football Club

A fictional football club is located in a densely populated city. The football club stadium is approximately 400 yards from the main railway station. It is also located about 100 yards from the city's large shopping centre. The club has ambitions to gain promotion from a regional non-league division into the Football League. The club currently attracts around 700 people per match to its home games. Larger crowds would be expected if the opposing teams improved through promotion. The clubs stadium currently has a capacity of 800 seats. According to the latest balance sheet the stadium and the surrounding land is worth approximately £4 Million. Most football clubs aspire to join the national league as this increases their status and the number of people who come to watch the games.

This case study needs you to think seriously about land use in relation to the cost and the opportunity costs (the good foregone by using the land for the purpose of a football stadium). You should also bear in mind that land is very expensive in the United Kingdom due to the both the high population and the high cost of living.

Self-examination Questions

1. It recently received an offer of just over £6 million for the stadium. Why would a firm consider offering an amount so much higher than the clubs estimate? This offer was tabled in 1989. Would the amount have been higher or lower in the mid 1990s? Would it be higher or lower now?

2. What alternative use is there for a ground in a town centre?

3. Supposing the ground was to be converted into a car park by the town council. The council would have to consider the following questions: What is the approximate size of a football pitch plus surrounding area? How many cars

would it therefore hold? What would be the likely interest charges on such a purchase if it were financed by a loan? How much would it therefore have to charge just to break even on this? Would there be advantages in having a multi-storey car park instead?

4. What would be the advantages and disadvantages of postponing the decision on whether to sell?

5. What are the other possibilities that the football club could pursue instead of selling their ground? e.g. could the club try to convert the stadium itself into a sports and fitness club?

6. How might it finance the money for the extra seating needed to meet league entry requirements? Why might the method of finance be different if it stays as opposed to if it moves?

7. Why might it be difficult to expand facilities if it remains in the town centre?

8. One possibility is that it can move to the suburbs outside of the main city centre. What would be the advantages and disadvantages of doing this for the home and away supporters?

9. What would you think about the cost of land? Which area of town is usually cheaper?

Another possibility is to move to the countryside. What would be the advantages and disadvantages of this?

Demand factors

1. What factors influence demand for football grounds? Hint: Think of price elasticity.

2. Can the club use any form of price discrimination in regards to its ticket pricing?

3. What differences in price occur e.g. for different parts of the ground, for different age groups?

4. What are the advantages and disadvantages of offering season tickets (tickets for the whole football season)?

5. Would there be advantages in offering a family ticket?

6. What other types of revenue can it obtain? How much money can a small football club obtain from programmes, car parking charges, sponsorship etc?

7. Is it possible to forecast demand for the future accurately?

8.   Why might it be important to do this?

Cost factors

1.   What number of seats should it cater for? Does it cater for the maximum it could ever get or the typical numbers of supporters who come, with a few more for insurance?

2.   Is it likely that there would be economies of scale if the capacity of the ground were increased?

3.   What other facilities should it provide e.g. sports facilities for the community?

Finance

1.   Why might the club find it difficult to get an overdraft if it remains where it is? Would it make any difference if there were a recession or property boom?

2.   What type of organisation is a small football club likely to be: Sole trader, partnership, private company or public company? Why does this influence the types of finance it can obtain?

3.   Why might it find it difficult to get sponsorship compared with a larger club in the Premier League?

Additional Questions

1.   Why might the local authority have views about the possibility of the club selling their ground to another firm? Think of any private and social costs that could be involved.

2.   Are there other possibilities e.g. close the club or ground share (allow another football club to use the stadium when the football club that owns it is not practicing or playing)?

3.   What are the problems with ground sharing e.g., what happens to the attendances of both clubs? Most ground shares take place between two clubs that are close to each other, what problems could this cause? What are the solutions to problems arising from ground sharing?

4.   Supposing it ground shares with another small club? Will this prevent it from achieving further ambitions? Supposing it shares with a league club. What would be the disadvantages and advantages of this?

5.   What happens to costs with ground sharing?

6.   Why might the directors of the club be reluctant to shut the club? Would they make more or less money as a result?

35.3: Channel Tunnel

In November 1984, the British and French Government announced their intention to seek private financiers for the construction and operation of a fixed link between their two countries without public funding. A rail design using two separate tunnels connected via a smaller service tunnel was chosen on 20th January 1986 by the then Prime Minister of Britain, Margaret Thatcher (1925-2013), and the then President of France, François Mitterrand.

On 12th February, the foreign ministers of both countries signed the Franco-British Treaty in the city of Canterbury. On 14th March that same year, the Concession was awarded, granting the two countries "jointly and severally...the right and the obligation to carry out the development, financing, construction and operation' of the 'Eurotunnel'."

The following questions may require you to conduct some of your own research into the channel tunnel; it is a useful skill to develop and is one of the main reasons for the inclusion of this case in the course.

Self-examination Questions

Demand

1. How did the promoters know that there was going to be a demand for the project? Why is it so important to try to estimate demand? Why is it more difficult for a new rather than an existing good or service?

2. Can we use questionnaires to determine the demand?

3. What type of sample could they use for the questionnaires e.g. quota or random? What is the problem of trying to obtain a random sample of

   a. Existing cross channel users?

   b. Potential users?

4. What are the advantages and disadvantages of both methods? If quota, what type of quota could they use e.g. road haulers, business travellers or social travellers. Would we just want to sample existing users? If not, how do we want to sample potential users? Would we want a sample of people from different parts of the country?

5. What type of questions would you ask if you were designing the questionnaire? Would your questions differ between nationalities?

6. Does knowing the total market of those who currently use the short sea routes help to determine the demand? Would it help to know the past numbers in order to find a trend?

7. What are the problems of trying to determine the demand in fifty years time? (Hint: Try to imagine that you made the forecast in 1963. What would you then have forecast for 2013?)

8. What has happened to incomes, leisure time, holiday patterns and trade patterns in the last 50 years? Is this necessarily a guide to the future?

9. What might we expect to find out about income elasticity of demand for

   a. Passengers?

   b. Freight?

10. Would we expect the channel tunnel to be a normal or an inferior good? Will this apply to all incomes?

11. How far will the single market of 1992 have affected demand for freight? Will the enlargement of the EU to 28 members in 2013 affect demand?

12. Will the introduction of the Euro have affected demand?

13. Why is the demand for cross channel services very much influenced by EU developments? Will it be influenced by changes elsewhere such as the rapid changes in Eastern Europe?

14. How far does a boom or recession affect the various types of demand?

15. What factors would induce long distance freight to move by rail rather than by road? Would a computerised system of international rail freight movements help? Would a different system of vehicle taxation make a difference?

16. How do we know what would happen if the channel tunnel was not built e.g. what types of transport development might occur during the period of lease of the tunnel?

17. What is meant by saying that we should judge a project on a with or without basis rather than a before and after?

18. Which journeys will the channel tunnel be competing with other services for?

19. What can we say about the price elasticity of demand for these different groups?

20. Why do they give different rates to different groups of passengers e.g. large groups etc.?

21. Why might price discrimination and price differentiation be important in this market? Why might it be less important for the channel tunnel than for some of its rivals?

22. How far do the rivals compete on other factors e.g. overall speed, comfort and other facilities including those at terminals?

23. How far will the 'open skies' policies in 1992, i.e. more open competition of airlines, have affected the demand? What is likely to happen to the price and supply of air travel as a result of these policies?

24. Will the rapid rise of the so-called budget airlines have affected demand?

25. What will be the overall journey times for the different modes? Why might this be important?

26. What is meant by accessibility time, waiting time and in vehicle time? Which of these are under the control of transport operators?

27. Why might it be important for the success of the tunnel if long distance passengers could have Customs checks and passport controls carried out on the train?

28. How important will the time be for:

    a. Social traveller?

    b. Business travellers?

    c. Freight transport?

    In your answer to 'a': would it make any difference if the trip is a long one with many connections or a short direct one?

29. Given that the EU imposes limits on the amount of time that road haulage drivers can drive without a break, why may some drivers and their employers prefer the ferry service?

30. Some economists have suggested a quality elasticity of demand, measured as the percentage increase in demand against the percentage decrease in lapsed time. Why might this vary between different traffic categories?

31. Does the channel tunnel merely divert traffic from one mode of transport to another or does it generate traffic? Will this vary between the short and the long-term?

32. What pricing policies should the channel tunnel adopt e.g. should it have different prices at different times of the day or week or season? Is this price differentiation or price discrimination?

33. In 1993, P&O approached Euro tunnel for a joint fares system whereby travellers could travel out through the tunnel and come back on P&O ferries. What would be the advantages of this?

The Joint Governments (British and French)

In this section, you are being asked to relate the questions to political, social, technological, economic and environmental factors:

1. What factors may have influenced the timing about the decision in 1984? (Hint: Were the two Governments popular at the time? Was the image of doing something about unemployment helpful?)

2. The tunnel was originally for a lease of 55 years after which ownership would be handed over to the two governments. The franchise has now been extended though. There is also a provision for a road tunnel to be built if it is thought necessary. What are the advantages and disadvantages of these measures?

The EU

1. Why might the EU be interested in the tunnel as well as other transport links such as those across the Baltic Sea? Why might they also be interested in the links to and from the tunnel?

2. Why might the EU be concerned about a possible monopoly? What might it recommend about the number of operators who could run trains using the tunnel?

The British Government

1. Is it possible to look at the channel tunnel as a precedent for other transport developments?

2. The British Government said about subsidisation of rail routes linking to the tunnel? Why was this reversed in 1994? What has it done about road routes? What has happened to demand since the improvements to the system means that journey have decreased by about 35 minutes?

3. Would it be sensible to use a financial basis for both rail and road? Would it be sensible to do a cost benefit analysis?

4. What has the Government decided about the timing of the rail route? What effect do the delays in the link to and from the tunnel have on the demand for and the financial viability of the tunnel?

5. Why does the rail route cater for both freight and passengers?

6. Do road haulers pay their full social costs? If not does this affect the demand for the channel tunnel and why?

7. Should the gainers from the scheme compensate the losers?

8. How can we quantify the gains and the losses?

9. Does the use of different house prices give us an approximate value of the effects of the tunnel terminals noise on property values?

10. Why is it difficult to put a monetary value on pollution?

11. Are there dangers of creating a monopoly form of transport? Will a monopoly create excessive profits or management slack? What can the Government do about this? (Hint: Can the Government do anything about possible predatory pricing or pitching prices too high?)

12. Are there any problems of safety with the tunnel? Are these problems worse than with rival modes of transport?

13. What environmental effects will road or rail terminals have? What effects will road or rail links have?

14. Is it possible to think of the tunnel as purely a matter for the private sector?

15. It is sometimes said that the tunnel has added to the prosperity of the South East England whilst not helping the rest of the country. Is this true and if so how can the Government do anything about it?

Government (French)

1. Has the French Government done more about the Tunnel than the British Government?

2. What has been the reaction of French local authorities to the tunnel and rail links?

3. Does the difference in regional prosperity between the Southeast of England and the North of France affect Government attitudes?

4. Has the high rate of unemployment in France had an effect of the channel tunnel?

Cost aspects

1. What was the approximate cost of the tunnel?

2. What can we say about the fixed and variable costs of the channel tunnel? How does this differ from its rivals such as the cross channel ferries?

3. What proportion of average cost is likely to be fixed costs? Why therefore would a doubling of numbers of people using the tunnel from 20 million per year to 40 million a year make a lot of difference to the price that can be charged?

4. What is the opportunity cost of the tunnel before it is built and once it is built? Why might it differ?

5. What is the marginal cost in the off-peak of the channel tunnel and its rivals? Why might it be important?

Reactions and effects on various groups

1. Why might the reactions of different Trade Unions differ to the construction and running of the tunnel?

2. What would you expect to be the view of Unite the common name for Unite the Union? Why might it be difficult to get a consensus in this union? What will be the reaction of the merchant seamen in the The National Union of Rail, Maritime and Transport Workers (RMT) ? What will be the reactions of the rail unions?

3. What particular problems arise for trade unions in this case?

4. Has all the opposition to the various links been of the 'Not in my backyard' variety?

5. What were the short-term effects on the construction industry in the Kent area and elsewhere?

6. What would be the short-term effects on the hotel and guesthouse trade whilst it is being built? What would be the long-term effects?

7. What would be the long-term effects on the port industry?

8. How did the various rival shipping companies react?

9. What would the advantages and disadvantages of the shipping companies, having a common timetable?

10. Would there be any advantages of the two firms merging

    a. To them?

    b. To customers?

Pressure groups

1. Why might it be difficult for the Trade Union Congress (TUC) as a whole to have a view on the channel tunnel?

2. Why might the Confederation of British Industry (CBI) be in favour?

3. What reactions might you expect from the two Road haulage lobbies i.e. the Road Haulage Association and the Freight Transport Association? The RHA are the road haulers who carry freight for other firms whilst the FTA is the organisation of the main freight senders.

4. Why might people and firms around St Pancras and Stratford also have views on the HS1 (High Speed 1) Route? What type of pressure groups could they form?

5. What is meant by an 'ad-hoc' pressure group?

6. Why is it more difficult for a larger body such as the TUC or CBI to have a policy towards the tunnel than an individual firm or trade union?

Finance

1. Does the cost of the tunnel and any other features make the method of financing different from most other projects?

2. Why would it be difficult to issue enough equities to cover the whole of the costs of construction? How could you give benefits to shareholders?

3. What would be the problems of issuing fixed interest loans e.g. debentures?

4. At what period might the group try to issue preference shares or debentures?

5. Why would changes in interest rates have more effect on the channel tunnel than most other projects?

6. Why would it be difficult to obtain a conventional loan from the banks? (Hint: Think of collateral)

7. What type of investors might be interested in putting into the Channel tunnel? Would it be the type of private investor who has bought shares in the privatised undertakings?

8. Why has most of the money come from institutional investors?

Investment appraisal

1. Why would the payback period method of appraisal be wholly inappropriate in this example?

2. Why therefore would you expect the promoters to use the Discounted Cash Flow method?

3. What is meant by the Net Present Value method and the Internal Rate of Return method? Do they give the same results? How do managers using the NPV know what rate of discount to use?

4. How far will capital gearing influence the rate of return?

5. What is meant by the term incremental rate of return? How could you apply this to:

   a. The concept of a single bore tunnel suggested in 1980 compared with the present project (the single bore means that there would be one tunnel which could be used in flights i.e. there would be a series of trains going England to France and then afterwards a series of trains going from France to England.)

   b. The idea that a larger loading gauge (the maximum height and width that the wagons or carriages can be) would allow more traffic to pass?

   c. The idea that a road tunnel could be built as well in the future?

   d. The idea that the link should have more tracks for both freight and passengers?

6. Would a cost benefit analysis be a more sensible basis for judging the project?

7. It is often said that it is easier to judge costs than revenue. Is it true in this case?

8. Why might it be important to carry out a sensitivity analysis? Which of the following changes might you include in your sensitivity analysis and why?

   a. Interest rates

   b. Changes in demand

   c. Changes in fares or price charged for freight

   d. Changes in costs

9. Which of those factors in the above question are easy to forecast in the short and the long-term?

10. In your answer to question 8, why might changes in interest rates have much more effect on the value of the long-term revenue than the short term? Why is this project much more sensitive to changes in the test rate used than many other projects?

35.4: Ling Spur

Ling Spur is a hypothetical firm that is located on an industrial estate on the outskirts of the Medway towns. The Medway towns, which are in Kent, comprise Gillingham, Chatham, Rochester and Strood. They are located approximately 35 miles southeast of London. Chatham was a dockyard town but has broadened its base in recent years. Rochester is well known as a tourist town with its cathedral and castle ruins. The Medway towns are near the newly widened M2 and are also served by rail routes to London.

Ling Spur was formed in 2006 by two brothers, aged 28 and 35 respectively. They had both obtained degrees in Electrical Engineering and had then gone on to work for one of the giant electronics firms. Whilst they had both done very well within the firm they felt frustrated at not being able to develop their own ideas. They felt the firm they were working for, whilst good, could run into problems later because it was not developing new ideas quickly enough. The year 2006 was somewhat of a boom period with house prices rising very rapidly. Firms as a whole were doing very well. Credit was easy to obtain and therefore the brothers managed to raise a loan on the parental home. They started on a very small scale on the local industrial estate paying relatively low rent on an unexpired lease. They subsequently had various premises on the industrial estate since they finally made a move in 2010. The firm is presently located in some very large buildings and employs approximately 600 people.

Location

The advantage of the industrial estate to the brothers was that it was near enough to the quarter of a million people from the Medway towns, as well as other potential staff from Maidstone. At the same time, they could live in Rochester, which was a pleasant town. They felt they had the best of both worlds rather than moving to the industrial parts of the Midlands.

Legal status of Ling Spur

The brothers had originally formed the organisation as a limited company. They set up the company by buying it off the shelf (an off the shelf company is one which has been pre-formed with a memorandum of association and articles of associations but no name, if you buy the firm then the name is appended and all the legal requirements are fulfilled on your behalf by the shelved companies business). This avoided them being bogged down in legal complications which at the time they did not even pretend to understand. As the firm grew, they decided to become a public limited company (PLC). The two brothers had sufficient shares between them and some shares from their relatives to have the controlling interest.

The wage bill for 600 people is very large. However, the greatest expenditure and one of the reasons they formed the PLC, was the capital cost of machines.

Products of the Company

The firm has diversified from time to time to make a wide variety of components for musical equipment, radios, televisions, etc. However, the firm has not diversified outside the components field since the brothers want to ensure that they have the knowledge required for their markets. They feel that they have the expertise needed to operate in this particular field. Whilst they could hire in specialists to develop other possibilities they would not feel so confident about the firm's long-term skills base. It was therefore a sudden dilemma when the brothers were approached by the firm Super Sound.

Super Sound was a rapidly growing franchise chain of electrical stores that presented Ling Spur with an attractive business proposition. In their anticipation to keep costs low, they were searching for a feasible way to expand their business. They asked Ling Spur whether they would consider assembling a range of entertainment systems and sell them under their brand name, Super Sound.

Some component firms, including organisations in competition with Ling Spur, have in effect become 'satellite organisations'. However, the brothers are against this. A satellite firm is one which works almost exclusively for another firm or possibly a small number of other firms. In this case, whilst the satellite is independent in terms of its ownership in practice many of its decisions are aligned with the larger firms. The brothers are against the idea of a satellite firm for a number of reasons. The first is that to be such a firm would, in the brothers' view, mean the loss of independence that was their original impetus for setting up the firm. The second is that they have seen many companies in Super Sound's market collapse, which had previously been the 'darlings' of the stock exchange and the media. If they were associated with one of these firms then they too would find it very difficult to avoid being dragged down with them. The problems would be made even worse since much of the machinery is very specific and cannot readily be used for other purposes.

Personalities of the Two Brothers

Whilst the brothers are of an authoritarian temperament, perhaps typically for engineers, they recognise the needs for imagination in a rapidly changing market. The prices of the electronic consumer goods have fallen sharply in both money and real terms. Therefore, in real terms, the price of components has to fall rapidly if the firm is to be competitive. As the design of the final goods has changed rapidly and in many cases has become smaller so the market for component parts has also been altered.

Finance

The firm has tried to raise money as far as possible from retained profits. It has also issued ordinary shares as well as rights issues. It is trying to avoid borrowing money from the banks since after the firm was formed there were many bankruptcies involving engineering firms. These were mainly caused by over borrowing. The firm has on occasions raised money through borrowing. As with most other firms, the premises were bought on a commercial mortgage. The firm has also on occasions issued debentures, particularly when interest rates had seemed to be historically low. The brothers have so far managed to avoid problems of capital gearing which affected many other firms.

The brothers have toyed with the idea of obtaining some money from the workers possibly through special savings schemes. They also thought about issuing shares at a discount, though they are not quite sure about the legal complications that might arise from this.

The Organisational Structure

The numbers of company employees distributed under the various departments are as follows:

Department:	No: of Staff:
Sales and Marketing	40
Production	430
Legal	10
Accounts	20
Distribution	20
Personnel	10
Purchasing	10
General	60
Total	600

The following is the organisational structure breakdown within the departments of Ling Spur PLC.

Sales & Marketing	No: of Staff
Head of Department	1
Chief Salesman	4
Salesman	28
Trainee Salesman	5
Secretaries	2
Total	40

This department is commonly regarded as simply the Marketing department. The role of the Marketing Department in Ling Spur differs from firms who are producing goods for the final consumer. There is no point in mass advertising since there are relatively few buyers anyway. At present most of the Sales are repeat orders from existing customers. However, the firm is anxious to broaden its base. This is in line with the point previously mentioned that the firm does not wish to rely on a few major customers.

As competition increases following the single market 1992 and the formation of the European Economic Area in 1994, and the expansion of the EU to 28 members in 2013, the firm is looking forward to marketing in Europe and beyond. The firm has the traditional British problem of not being too aware of other cultures and languages. The Marketing department, until recently, has been fairly weak on market research although this area has now been strengthened.

The firm has considered merging with Super Sound, which is a large independent electrical stores chain. If this happened, the Marketing Departments' role would alter dramatically.

Production	No: of Staff
Head of Department	1
Head of Sections	8
Foremen	40
Operatives	371
Maintenance	9
Secretary	1
Total	430

As with most engineers the Production department is the one, with which the brothers are most attached. As mentioned before the assembly machines are extremely costly, however, the price of the assembly machines is decreasing in real terms. The technical life of the machines is much shorter than the commercial life. This reflects the rapid changes in the industry. Whilst the depreciation costs would fall if they used the existing machines for a longer period, they would probably fail to find a market for their component if they used these. The modern machines generally aid productivity considerably. In order to get the best utilisation from the machines a two-shift system is currently in use. The brothers are concerned that because the capacities of the different machines are not identical there can be bottlenecks on certain machines whilst other machines are not being completely used. They are currently trying to use more operational research methods to help overcome these problems.

The work of the Production department tends to be one of the more tedious. The brothers would like the Production and Personnel departments to work together to see if there are any methods of overcoming the problems of staff boredom.

Legal	No: Of Staff
Head of Department	1
Lawyers	2
Assistants	5
Secretaries	2
Total	10

The Legal department is unusual for this type of firm. The brothers are concerned as to the increasing volume of employee protection and consumer protection. In particular as the export markets develop the brothers have realised that they need to be aware of not only those laws, which apply to the United Kingdom, but also to other EU countries. Whilst employee relationships have generally been good the brothers are well aware of the necessity to be seen to be fair not only for legal reasons but in order to improve morale in the firm.

Accounts	No: Of Staff
Head of Department	1
Qualified Accountants	4
Trainee Accountants	5
Clerical Staff	8
Secretaries	2
Total	20

The Accounts department in common with most other industrial firms has been radically altered by the degree of automation of many routine tasks. Whilst much of the work in the Accounts department is routine, i.e., checking invoices are in and ensuring that bills are paid, there has been an increasing emphasis on Management Accounting techniques.

The brothers want a costing system, which not merely allocates overhead costs, but is also a basis for decision-making. Therefore, they are particularly interested in the concept of spreadsheets. They also like the various computer based accounting packages, which will enable them to work out investment appraisal, break-even analysis and so on.

Distribution	No: Of Staff
Head of Department	1
Fork lift truck Operators	5
Packing Staff	14
Total	20

This is often regarded as the 'Cinderella' department in many industries. Drucker, perhaps the best known of the post-war management writers, has said that distribution is the last frontier of management. At one time the firm had their own lorries. However, it was soon discovered it was difficult to obtain good utilisation from the lorries. When there were large orders urgently required the lorries seemed very inadequate. Customers tended to complain about delays. On the other hand, the lorries were often lying around empty. Due to the nature of the work, it was difficult to obtain lorry loads in both directions.

Another problem with the distribution development as far as the lorries were concerned was that maintenance facilities were not necessary so the span of control of the firm became even larger.

Personnel	No: Of Staff
Head of Department	1
Training Officers	4
Assistants	4
Secretaries	1
Total	10

The Personnel department has become ever more important as the firm has grown rapidly in size. The brothers have been impressed by the way in which Japanese firms have gained and retained the loyalty of their workers. They have tried, within limits, to follow some of the Japanese methods. In particular they have recently experimented with the idea of quality circles. This is where a group of workers, during the firms' time, meet to discuss ways of improving productivity. When the firm was originally formed, there was a high rate of labour turnover, partly because other established firms could offer higher wages. The brothers have attempted to set wages at a rate, which they consider fair, whilst keeping the firm competitive. Whereas the personnel managers make the decisions, they do take particular note of any large-scale turnover in staff.

Purchasing	No: Of Staff
Head of Department	1
Purchasing Officers	4
Clerks	5
Total	10

General	No: Of Staff
Head of Department	1
Typist/Operators	15
Clerks	14
Secretaries	2
Canteen Manager	1
Other Canteen Staff	14
Caretaker	1
Cleaning Staff	12
Total	60

The General office, as in many other firms, often feels itself to be a bit of a dog's body. This means it performs tasks that do not logically fall into other departments' jurisdiction. It originally contained a typing pool, but this of course was changed with the advent of word processing. It is also responsible for the staff canteen. The brothers being somewhat paternalistic regard the staff canteen as important. This is partly because they recognise the importance of nutrition for their workers. Therefore, there is a subsidy from the firm towards the canteen expenses. They also regard the canteen as being important in helping develop relationships between fellow staff as well as management. However, because of the shift system there are problems in maintaining the canteen over a large number of hours. There is also somewhat of a split between the blue-collar workers in the Production department and the white-collar workers in the General office and elsewhere.

The changing nature of the market

The demand for components is a derived one i.e. few people apart from some retailers who do repairs and specialist repairs people wish to buy components. The demand for final products in the electronics market is rapidly changing. Similarly, in the field of entertainment, CD's and DVD's vie for their share of the market. This is important to Ling Spur because they need, to some extent, to anticipate the market changes rather than react. There is a lead-time between seeing these changes and being able to get the right sort of capital goods, the problems of installing and removing old machines, as well as any necessary retraining.

The demand for consumer durables has risen generally in line with real incomes. It has also been helped by the fact that prices of electronic goods have fallen in both money and real terms. The age of the population is important as different age groups tend to have different needs from electronic goods. This has some effect on the demand for components. The export market is an important one. The freer movement of goods following the single market in the EU and the expansion of the EU. Discussions between the American government and the EU in 2013 may also make imports and exports easier.

Self-examination Questions

Changing nature

1. In what ways does a firm having a derived demand differ from one with a direct demand?

2. It is often said that management should be proactive rather than reactive. What is meant by this and why might it be important in this firm?

Staff

1. Draw up an appropriate organisation chart of Ling Spur PLC with reference to the staffing tables in the case study.

2. What is meant by vertical communication? Illustrate it in relation to the organisation chart. What obstacles are there to vertical communications upwards? What obstacles are there to vertical communications downwards?

3. What is meant by horizontal communication? Why should the marketing department and the production department communicate?

4. If the firm is currently working a two-shift system, what problems might you expect to arise with communication between groups?

5. Would the use of joint consultation be helpful? (There have been rumours of either redundancies or a possible take-over or merger).

6. What is meant by the phrase 'heard it on the grapevine'? Why does the grapevine flourish? Is it necessarily bad?

7. Would the use of an in-house employee newsletter be helpful?

Customers

1. Why should the firm try to communicate with existing customers?

2. What types of information does the firm want from them?

3. Who would you expect the main customers to be?

4. What methods of communication would you want the firm to use?

Suppliers

1. What communication would the firm have with suppliers?

Technology

1. What features would you want on the internal phone system? Why would you want these features?

2. What problems can arise with telephone use? How can the firm try to reduce phone bills?

3. Would you expect the firm to have a facsimile system? For what purposes would you expect it to be used?

4. Why might you expect the brothers to be eager to get into e-commerce? Would it be less important for them than many other firms and if so why?

Marketing department

Market Research

1. Why is the demand for the product a derived one?

2. Will the demand for the Hi-fi range follow the product same life cycle?

3. What implications does the above answer have for the firm?

4. What market research if any would you do? Would it be mainly field or desk research?

5. Would a firm such as this carry out its own research or employ an agency?

Pricing policy

1. How far will Ling Spur's pricing have to reflect competitor's prices?

2. Why might such a firm not be able to use either a market penetration or a market skimming policy?

3. Will price be based on cost plus a percentage profit?

4. Will there be discounts for large quantities?

Export marketing

1. Now the export market is small; will the Single Market in 1992 have offered any new opportunities?

2. Will the enlargement of the EU to 28 members in 2013 offer any new opportunities?

3. What data would you want about other countries?

4. Where would you obtain this data?

5. How far has the UK's decision not to enter the Euro been likely to have helped or hindered the firm?

6. If Ling Spur wished to expand abroad would it be best to do this:

   A) Through agents who were exclusive to the firm

   B) Through general agents

   C) Through a system of granting a franchise to an overseas firm i.e. manufacturing under licence

Production Department

1. How can the production department use network analysis?

2. How can it use queuing theory?

3. How can it use computer simulation?

4. How can it assess the number of machines required?

5. Why does it need to communicate with the Marketing department?

6. Why might production not always be within its control? Hint: What disruptions could cause problems?

7. What is meant by the term 'lead-time'?

8. Why might different payment systems cause different problems in this Department?

Legal Contracts

1. What are the main requirements for a contract to be valid?

2. Would you expect the firm to have a standard contract with customers?

3. What does 'caveat emptor' mean? Has it been modified by legislation?

Employment

1. What are the main provisions of the Equality Act 2010

2. What are the main provisions about contracts of employment?

3. What are the main provisions about unfair dismissal?

4. What are the provisions for women returning to work after pregnancy?

5.   What are the main provisions of the acts governing redundancy?

6.   What are the provisions of the Health and Safety at Work Act 1974?

Company law

1.   The firm originally started as a private limited company with the two brothers owning all the shares. What are the advantages of forming a private limited company?

2.   As it expanded it became a PLC. What does PLC mean?

3.   What is the minimum capital required in a PLC?

4.   What are the main duties of directors?

Accounts Department

1.   What routine information will the department get?

2.   What is meant by cash flow?

3.   How can the department try to improve cash flow?

Balance sheet

1.   What are the main assets likely to be in such an organisation?

2.   What different methods are there of valuing stocks?

3.   What is in a balance sheet? What is the conventional order?

4.   What are the main ratios that can be derived? Are they of much use?

Investment

1.   What does the payback period technique of investment appraisal involve?

2.   What does DCF stand for? Why is it often used?

3.   What is sensitivity analysis?

4.   The firm's financial structure is as follows:

   •   Mortgage £1,000, 000 at a fixed rate of 10% - This will mature in 2014.

   •   Equities £2,000,000

   •   Preference shares £1,000,000. These are cumulative and pay 12%. What might a financial adviser be likely to say now?

   •   Debentures £1,000, 000 at 12% these mature in 2015.

- Overdrafts can be obtained currently at around 7% APR, press reports differ about whether these will come down soon. The maximum overdraft available to the firm is £2,750,000.

A) What is the capital gearing of the company?

B) If the firm wishes to raise £2,000,000 what is the best method?

5. Show how depreciation can be calculated by the straight-line method. Assume that the assembly machines have a life of 5 years. New assembly machines will cost £100,000 and have a life of 5 years as if they are used with a two-shift system. If a three-shift system is worked, they will only last 4 years. Currently production staff works on a two-shift system, as do most of the distribution department. Calculate the straight line depreciation for both shift options

Distribution Department

1. The distribution manager has suggested that the firm could distribute its products with its own fleet of vehicles rather than relying on outside contractor's vehicles. What would be the advantages and disadvantages of this?

2. The total distribution costs include packaging insurance, costs of holding stocks and freight charges. How might air transport to Scandinavia help to reduce other costs?

3. Why might packaging costs be quite high in such a firm?

4. The distribution manager suggests that most customers would be satisfied with a guaranteed 7-day delivery rather than trying to keep to 3 days and not always succeeding. What would be the advantage of this? What effect might it have on the production department?

5. A few firms have discussed the possibility of using JIT production. How will this effect the required delivery times of Ling Spur's components? Are they capable of achieving such demand?

6. Would the Channel Tunnel be helpful in delivering to Europe?

Personnel department

Recruitment and selection

1. How would you try to recruit staff? Show what information you would put into a newspaper advertisement for at least 2 jobs(Hint: What qualifications or experience would you look for)? What legislation must you comply with?

2. What selection procedures would you choose in the firm? Illustrate your answer with a range of jobs (Hint: You could think of single person interviews, panel interviews, sequential interviews, skills testing, use of sensitivity testing etc.)

3. What people would you ask to be on an interview panel?

4. What is a contract of employment? What information has to be in such a contract? What additional information might be in such a contract?

5. What is a job specification?

Motivation

1. What methods of motivation would you use in such a firm? (Hint: What type of employees would you expect to be McGregor X and which McGregor Y? Which employees would you expect to be looking for the top ends of Maslow`s hierarchy of needs?

2. Would you expect the firm to be democratic, authoritarian or laissez-faire in its management style? Might it vary between different departments?

3. What would you include in an induction programme?

4. The firm is anxious to comply with the health and safety at work act. What measures can it takes? Draw up an outline of a suitable safety-training programme.

Training

1. Do different people in different departments require different types of retraining (Hint think of typing, computing, production department)?

2. What different types of training can you use? (Hint: Think of discussion, computer simulation, videos, etc.)

Wages

1. What different types of wages systems can be used e.g. piece rates, job evaluation, and time rates? For which jobs might these be most appropriate?

2. What statutory deductions for wages must be made?

3. What other deductions might be made?

Dismissals and redundancy

1. What steps should a firm take before considering dismissing anyone for misconduct or other cause?

2. What legislation affects redundancy pay? What are the typical rates of redundancy pay? Is there anything to stop a firm paying more?

3. What does LIFO mean in relation to redundancy?

4. The age profile of the firm's employees is as follows:

Under 20	5%
20 to 29	15%
35 to 39	25%
40 to 49	25%
50 to 59	25%
60 plus	5%

Give reasons why you would regard this as being good or bad.

Purchasing department

1. What are the advantages of a centralised purchasing department? Would it still be advantageous if the firm were split over several sites?

2. What are the advantages of bulk purchase? Are there any disadvantages? (Hint: Think of the costs of holding stocks.)

3. What are the advantages and disadvantages of having a large long-term fixed price contract with a single firm?

4. Purchasing departments sometimes ask for tenders. What are the advantages and disadvantages of these?

5. Why might the purchase of computers present more problems than most other investment purchases?

The Super Sound opportunity

1. What would be the advantage to Ling Spur of their offer? Are there any drawbacks apart from the initial cost of investment?

2. Explain what a franchise is. Why might a franchise chain do well?

3. Super Sound has vaguely hinted at a take-over or merger. What would be the merits of this?

Computers

1. Why might staff be concerned about increased use of computers? Would these fears be less or more than in an older firm?

2. What are the advantages of a network compared with stand-alone systems?

3. Why might a computer be an advantage compared with conventional filing systems? Are there any disadvantages?

4. How might the computer assist with quality control?

5. Which departments would mainly use a computer? What discussions should therefore take place before a computer system is decided upon?

6. What are the advantages of the computer for the accounts department, the personnel department and the production department?

7. Computers can sometimes help with simulation. Why might this be an advantage?

Location

1. What are the advantages and disadvantages of being located in a Medway town for:

   a. Potential European and national customers

   b. Potential national suppliers

   c. Getting good workers

   d. Attracting good managers

2. The firm even whilst suffering from the Credit Crunch are thinking long-term about expansion. There are several possibilities:

   a. Expanding on the same site, there may be problems with planning permission.

   b. Moving to the West Midlands.

   c. Moving to the North East.

   In relation to the 3 groups above what would be the advantages and disadvantages of the different locations?

3. What would be the likely costs of moving production away from the current site?

4. The firm is considering a site in the North East partly because the unit can be built there to its own specifications. What would be the advantage of this compared with acquiring existing premises?

35.5: The Chocolate Factory

David and James run a chocolate factory. Since it is near London, they have problems obtaining some of the skilled workers they require. This applies to both white collar staff and to people with good manual skills that can get very good wages elsewhere. Due to the poor public transport system, people find it difficult to fit workers into the work shifts required to utilise the expensive machinery. Another problem is that even in households where there are cars, women who need them for their shifts cannot have access at certain times of the day for example early in the morning or late in the evening. This is consistent with sociological studies by Prof Ann Oakley showing the extent to which women are often discriminated against within the family. The firm is therefore evaluating a number of options.

Option 1: To continue with the present pattern

The first option is to continue with the present production levels which mean that that they have to turn away orders. They dislike this option partly because of the immediate financial effect. They also dislike it because in spite of the rational economic model (that consumers and suppliers will make the most rational economic decision viz: they will buy at the cheapest possible price and sell at the highest possible price) which some businessmen subscribe to; they recognise the importance of habit e.g. if people have been used to buying one type of chocolate, they are unlikely to change this habit unless there are strong reasons to do so. Failure to be able to obtain the brand of choice which they are used to would be one method of breaking the habit. If they fail to give the existing customers (such as the independent retailers) the quotas which they are used to, they will lose the goodwill which has been built up over the years and it could be very difficult to return to this level of goodwill. They could try to raise the price to choke off demand but feel that they are in a ratchet i.e. If they lower prices, then they will not attract new buyers but if they raise them they could choke off demand from their existing customers. Alternatively they could try to persuade some of the existing workers to do more overtime. Some people have suggested that overtime is a morale booster but not always and given that many of the people working have youngish families that are unlikely to be willing to work overtime. If they wish to stay on the same site they could buy more equipment, but the costs of doing this are very high and a quick 'back of the envelope' calculation suggests that the rate of return on this would only give about a 10 % return. At the present time with the low inflation rate and low borrowing rates, this might be satisfactory, but they would need to carry out a more thorough investment appraisal using sensitivity analysis to see whether the case is robust.

Option 2: To build another factory

The second option is to expand by building another factory. They aim to get some funding from government grants. There are possibly some funds which might be obtained from the European Social Fund either directly or indirectly. Firms might be able to get commercial loans cheaply at the moment in any case since in October 2013 base rate is 0.5 % which is low by the standards of the last twenty years in the United Kingdom.

Option 3: To build a new factory as a substitute factory

The third possibility is to have a new factory as a substitute factory for the present one. Obviously if they do this they have to consider the likely proceeds from the present factory. The amount of the proceeds will depend partly upon whether someone will wish to purchase it as an existing business or as an asset stripper who might wish to buy it with a view to changing it into another use such as a site for housing. The local authority is keen to extend housing into Brownfield sites (the term `Brownfield site' means real estate, the expansion, redevelopment, or reuse of land which may be complicated by the presence or potential presence of a hazardous substance, pollutant, or contaminant) rather than in greenfield (uncontaminated real estate) sites. This might be an opportunity for them to allocate land for this purpose. The firm also has to consider the point that some of its loyal workers will have to be paid redundancy money and they are reluctant to do this. Apart from the financial cost there is the feeling that the members of staff were like the members of a family.

They would need to consider what happens to existing staff: will any of them be able to move to the new site and would they wish to anyway? Clearly some of the younger ones who do not have family ties might wish to move to an area where house prices are much cheaper. David and James do wish to retain some of their key workers. In the past there have been schemes which enable such firms to get grants to go to selected regions but they are not sure whether this provision still applies. The firm has to consider whether they are willing to pay the relocation expenses of workers who wish to move and perhaps to rent several houses in the short run. This would ease the pressure on people trying to adjust to a new area with the high time costs and financial costs as well as the sheer stress of moving.

David did once go on a counseling course so is well aware of the standard problems i.e. that moving house is one of the major life stress factors for most people. There would also be the question of morale at the present factory in the short run knowing that the production is coming to an end. They would have to try to motivate workers without any longer term prospects.

Option 4: to relocate to continental Europe

Another possibility is to locate elsewhere e.g. in Europe especially in one of the new entrants to the EU where the advantages of cheap labour from the firms viewpoints could be important. Recruiting staff would mean a diversification of roles since like many English people, their knowledge of foreign languages is slight so whereas they have always taken a keen interest in appointments even at a low level in the existing factory. This would be different in a factory for example in Poland or Hungary although not possibly in Cyprus or Malta as they were former colonies of Britain and there are many English speakers there. Unless they manage to buy an existing plant which is very unlikely since there are not very many chocolate factories, anyway there is a time lag with this type of expansion. If the factory is purpose built this might be cheaper in long run but they may require planning permission and their knowledge of other countries planning permission is unsurprisingly sketchy. The process will obviously take some time and will lead to cash flow problems in the short run although they have sufficient knowledge of finance to be able to overcome this. If this plant is additional to the one they have then there are problems for the chain of command and or the span of control and deciding whether they duplicate the chocolate they produce in the existing factory or whether the plant would tend to specialise. Such a plant might make it easier for them to export but their knowledge of the chocolate market whilst extensive for the UK is much less for the continental market.

Of the 13 new entrants to the EU, Malta and Cyprus would seem to be the obvious choice partly because as former British colonies they have the advantage of having many English speaking people. However, being islands they present slightly more transport problems to getting both raw material and finished products to and from them. The managers know little about Slovenia. On the other hand Hungary has a relatively small population compared with Poland but several of the towns have good links with the Danube (a river that flows through Europe connecting close to ten rivers and emptying in the Black Sea - since the Roman Empire days has been a useful means of waterway) which could be useful since carriage costs by water are low.

Since there is a common external tariff within the EU there will be no more problems with imports or exports from the EU viewpoint than locating within the UK.

Most of the basic ingredients such as cocoa are from West Africa. They assume although they have not yet done the detailed calculations which must be carried out , that if they do a serious feasibility study that the extra costs will be negligible and will be outweighed by the lower labour costs. However in general the continental countries have slightly different tastes in chocolate compared with the UK market. This is however changing as the large scale brands from companies such as Nestlé have spread as part of the globalisation process. The owners are also aware of a slight countervailing trend towards fairer play for the poorly paid workers. The growth and spread of the Fair Trade sentiment throughout the developing world has meant that they would have to be careful about the places where they source their raw material and the wages they pay their employees.

Self-examination Questions

Finance

1. What does the term back of an envelope calculation mean? Why, while there are many computer programs capable of doing sophisticated calculations do many firms still use these?

2. What alternatives to bank loans could such a firm use? What are their respective advantages and disadvantages?

3. What is meant by asset stripping? Why might this be particularly important in the case of firms with a large plant? Would your answer vary from one region to another?

Location

1. What would be the advantage of having a purpose built factory for a company such as this? Are there any disadvantages?

2. Why, if the firm is in a Brownfield site is there a problem of expanding the plant even further? What would be the advantages and disadvantages of this compared with the other options

Human Resource department

1. Why might the type of motivation vary considerably between the different groups of workers in such a factory?

2. Why might it be easier to solve personnel problems in a growing rather than a contracting plant?

3. In what ways if any might there be problems in recruiting people in an eastern European country such as Hungary or Poland?   Are there any management theories of culture which might help them to understand such problems and if so in what ways?

4. At the moment they have a two shift system which has shifts from, 6 a.m. to 2 p.m. and from 2 p.m. to 10 p.m. Why might the firm have such shifts and what are the alternatives which might be used in the U.K?

5. Why might the number of trade unionists in such a factory be fairly low?

6. In what ways are communication problems for managers easier with modern technology? How if at all can the department try to overcome any problems through better training? Does it differ partly according to the culture?

7. If they are recruiting more staff, why might it be more difficult to check they are good in another country?

8. Would induction training be different between countries and if so why?

Transport and distribution department

1. What factors might the department wish to consider if they had a new plant in an eastern European country such as Hungary or Poland?

    Why might a green transport plan be helpful to such a firm? Would it only need to consider the distribution of products or why might it be sensible to consider the employees' transport needs as well?

Marketing department

1. Why might the market for chocolate be one in which price discrimination and price differentiation is so important?

2. Chocolate firms have often spent vast sums of money including test marketing before launching a new product. Why have they done this? What does it suggest about the market for such a product?

3. Would you expect the market for chocolate to be a seasonal one and if so why? Why might this create difficulties for the production department?

4. Why might packaging be particularly important in such a market?

5.   Are there likely to be any differences between the buying habits of men and women and if so what might this suggest about the ways in which the department might approach these different markets?

6.   Are there likely to be any differences between the buying habits of different age groups and if so what might this suggest about the ways in which the department might approach these different markets?

Social responsibility

1.   What duty of care might the firm have towards customers? (Hint: think of allergies to certain products)

2.   Why might cocoa sellers often feel that they are faced with an oligopsonist market? In what ways if any does the fair trade movement offer an alternative?

3.   What effect would closure of a reasonably large factory have in such an area?

4.   Would the multiplier effect be greater or less in many other areas and if it would differ explain why?

5.   Does the factory have either a legal or moral duty to its employees?

35.6: Farmer Brown

Farmer Charles Brown along with many other farmers has been complaining about the problems of getting reasonable prices for his products. Although he sells fruits and vegetables, he is well aware that other farmers have problems during the BSE (Bovine Spongiform Encephalopathy or Mad Cow disease) crisis in the late 1990s and then the Foot and Mouth in early 2000s had caused many problems and many small farmers have left the industry. Despite the much-discussed Common Agricultural Policy farmer subsidies, Mr Brown feels that his income has decreased over the last 16 years.

The decline in farmer incomes is partly because the large supermarkets such as Tesco and ASDA have used their monopsony powers to dictate lower prices for fruit and vegetables. They have also insisted on the right shape and size because it is assumed that the British consumer is more concerned about the look of the product and the way it will last on the supermarket shelves rather than its taste. Therefore, a great deal of production is wasted. He has noted that in some other towns, there have been farmers markets and when buying his own food notices that some of it comes from farmer cooperatives.

Joining a cooperative

He is therefore considering whether to join other farmers to have some form of cooperation of producing their own food products. This is because they are producing jam, fruit juices and other farm products that are superior to the supermarket. Selling products on the high street market rather than the supermarkets may also attract more customers who may be loyal to local farmers and may be avoiding the higher prices and lower quality of supermarkets. This way they may be able to compete against the 'unfair' practices of the supermarkets

Changes in economic circumstances

Farmers have also found it more difficult to cope with the national minimum wage demands. It is difficult to obtain labour during the summer months, since the work is hard and seasonal, and therefore have often relied on people from Eastern Europe particularly since the expansion of the EU to 28 members in 2013. The Hungarian and Polish workers find wages in the UK comparatively high and are used to working hard. In some cases, they are already studying in the UK so that summer work is an additional wage, which they are pleased to have.

Outside information

Whilst farmer Brown has been used to selling his own fruit and vegetables, he is not used to working with other people apart from his family. He has however determined that a marketing cooperative might be the best form. He has approached the local economic development unit of his Borough Council and the local Chamber of Commerce. Both have been reasonably helpful but have relatively little knowledge of this form of venture since the standard industries around are the typical small industrial units on industrial estates such as plastic manufacturers and so on.

Marketing and distribution

He has looked at the idea of distribution and had an idea that if the farmers got together they could not merely sell the products on their own farms. He has also found that 'pick your own' (an arrangement that allows customers to pick fresh fruit from the farm) has been successful since many people like to know that their produce is fresh. There have been some problems though, some people trample plants when trying to get to the best fruit. He typically charges higher prices for the privilege of 'picking your own'. This charge is higher than the price of the fruits in the supermarket yet it is popular. His daughter runs the farm shop while on holiday from the university. He has shared this idea with another farmer who has been very interested; however they have not ironed out the issues of financing the venture.

Use of farmers markets

Another option is having a stall in the farmers market. As the cost is relatively low, Mr Brown and his fellow farmer have agreed on a rota for the stall. They have however not worked out how the profits should be distributed.

Who would buy the products?

They have considered their pricing policy and have tried to see who would be the likely buyers. They have come up with two categories, the reformers and the conservatives. The Reformers are people who would wish to see a greener policy applied to agriculture, and who welcome the idea of local products (particularly if they are organic). They also see that some conservatives dislike the idea of the high street becoming more and more a clone of all the other towns with the standard Boots, Marks and Spencer's, Supermarket and so on. They would agree with the New Economics Foundation survey in 2005 that many towns have become clones. They welcome shopping in the more personal atmosphere where the people selling the product have an idea of the different apples for example that they are selling rather than supermarket operatives who have no clue which apple is which.

They are also aware that the firm could grow very large if they had sufficient competence since ASDA grew out of Associated Dairies, which as its name implies was originally formed by dairy farmers. They have no intention or possibly the ability to get that far, but do see possibilities.

Self-examination Questions

1. What is meant by the term monopsony or oligopsony and why is it important for farmers?

2. Why might such an organisation want to have a market skimming policy rather than a market penetration one?

3. How easy or otherwise would it be for them to determine the price elasticity of demand?

4. Why might it be easier to set stable prices for processed foods such as jam and fruit juice rather than for fresh fruit and vegetables? What are the advantages and disadvantages of this?

5. What is meant by the term mark up? Why is it much higher for fresh fruit and vegetables than the typical mark-up in supermarkets?

6. Why might it be easier for them to sell their produce to specialised shops, which have a high mark-up rather than even an independent supermarket?

Personnel

1. Presently, the farmer merely employs his daughter on an informal basis during the summer months. What differences might it make if the cooperative as a whole decide to take on employees?

2. They have assumed that as a small organisation they are exempt from the provisions of the Equality Act 2010. Are they correct in this assumption?

3. What types of people would you expect to reply for a post in such an organisation since there seems to be little in the way of long-term prospects? How if at all could the farmers overcome this problem?

Organisation

1. What are the advantages and disadvantages of a worker cooperative compared with being either a partnership or a private limited company?

2. Why might it be relatively easy for the farmers to raise sufficient finance to set up a cooperative? How far will changes in house prices etc have affected them?

Marketing

The organisation has decided to market its products under the name Kentish Preserves.

1. What would be the advantages of such a name? (Hint: would an alternative name such as the Garden of England be preferable?)

2. They have thought about distributing leaflets to all local houses since one of the farms already has an old printing press. What would be the advantages and disadvantages of this as a method of communicating?

3. The farmers intend to put an advertisement in the local newspaper. How if at all could the farmers estimate whether this had affected their business favourably?

4. They have thought of trying to sell to some of the local cafés and restaurants, especially those that have an up market image. Are there any disadvantages of this?

5. As they have become better known they have been approached by another cooperative, "Whole foods of Maidstone Limited". This firm is willing to buy far more of their products than previously they had estimated, but would give a lower price. They have for example suggested that whereas the fruit juice is

sold by the farmers at £1.50 per litre for apple juice and £2.00 for pear juice they will offer 90p and £1.10 respectively. What further calculations if any would the farmers need to carry out before considering whether this was worthwhile?

6.   Could such an organisation advertise in the local cinema and what, if any, might be the advantages and disadvantages?

35.7: Robots

An engineering firm, which has also been concerned with plastic, is investigating the use of robots for some of its industrial tasks. This is partly because as unemployment has fallen since the late 1980s it has found it increasingly difficult to get suitable workers at a reasonable price. It has faced far more competition from other countries especially from Eastern Europe. It feels that its turnover, which has been relatively high, has made it more expensive and the advantage of robots is that unlike human beings they do not get bored with doing repetitive work.

The firm also feels that whilst the workers might feel threatened in the short run because of the introduction of robots, it can reassure them that the increases in productivity will lead to lower prices of the product therefore more sales and higher wages for them. The workers will stand a better chance of keeping their jobs and finding them more interesting. Dull jobs such as painting in unpleasant conditions in parts of the factory that the management feel cannot be improved or unsafe will be passed to the robots improving the employees' health and safety. They feel that they can point out to the workers that in most cases real wages have increased with automation. In this they can go right back to the days of Henry Ford who managed through his standardisation process to offer far more money than the existing wages rate.

They feel that robots can be re-programmed to do jobs more quickly and it would take away one of the major problems with introducing new technology which is retraining employees. Workers are on piece rate pay, so they have to renegotiate this with the workers. Robots would also take away the need to negotiate with unions, as they would not belong to any. Robots will also not attract income taxes that need accounting for nor will they require human relations management or motivation.

The management feel that they need to talk not merely with the production department but also with the human relations specialist. They would want to assess other firms how robots affected turnover. They also have the problem of how to judge which robots to use in the first place; it is easy to compare existing machines as they will have similar machinery with upgrades.

Self-examination Questions

1. Why might the firm need to carry out a discounted cash flow technique to work out whether investment in robots is worthwhile? Should it use the net present value or the internal rate of return method?

2. Why might sensitivity analysis be very important in this investment, bearing in mind that interest rates are currently much lower than they have been for 40 years in the UK?

3. Why might the firm consider issuing debentures to cover the cost of investment? Are there any disadvantages if it offers say a 20-year debenture at 7% compared with other forms of finance?

4. What type of people might want to buy debentures?

5. The firm has been used to leasing equipment when there have been changes in technology. This is because they feel that while they may pay slightly more in the short run it gives them a better chance of buying the appropriate technology. Why might this approach not be applicable in this case?

Human Resources

1. How if at all can the firm try to manage change?

2. Would the McGregor model have anything to offer the firm?

3. Why might the age profile of the workforce be relevant to the decision making process?

35.8: Triodos Bank

Following is an excerpt[11] from the Triodos Bank Website. Please read through and attempt the questions at the end of the section.

---

[11] http://www.triodos.co.uk/

Equity funds

Triodos Bank helps fund businesses or projects which bring positive social, cultural or environmental change.

Through our investment funds we raise capital from both institutional and individual investors, and make venture capital investments. Each fund has specific criteria for the types of business it will invest in.

Sustainable energy projects operating on long-term contracts

Triodos Renewables* is a public limited company looking to invest in commercially viable sustainable energy projects that minimise financial risk by adopting proven renewable energy technologies.

We consider investments in wind, hydro, biomass and solar energy projects across Europe that minimise environmental impact through sensitive siting.

Your resources and technologies should be genuinely 'clean', we would not consider municipal waste-to-energy initiatives, for example. You'll also need to show a meaningful public consultation process and follow best practice as set out by Regen SW.

In short, we will invest in suitable renewable energy projects, provide expertise and support their growth, whilst helping the business and its shareholders exploit long-term business potential.

*Triodos Renewables is the trading name of Triodos Renewables plc, Registered in England & Wales, Registered office: Triodos Bank, Deanery Road, Bristol BS1 5AS (registered number 2978651).

What are the Triodos EIS Funds?

The Triodos EIS Funds target growing companies with a strong business plan and an experienced management to deliver it.

Who are EIS Funds aimed at?

The Funds invest solely in the sustainability sector. More specifically, in high-growth businesses involved in renewable energy generation and technology, energy efficiency, sustainable living and low carbon products, and waste recycling and reduction.

The Funds will only invest in businesses that can offer shareholders an exit within three-to five years, and qualify for investment under the UK Enterprise Investment Scheme (EIS).

Like most equity investors, Triodos will normally take a Board seat and work with management teams to plug any gaps in expertise. But we bring much more to the table in terms of our shared understanding and experience of the challenges social enterprises face. And with Triodos, you'll also benefit from our extensive network of partners, who we can draw on to help your enterprise succeed.

Marilou van Golstein Brouwers' expertise

Marilou van Golstein Brouwers is Managing Director of Triodos Investment Management BV, and one of the world's leading authorities on microfinance. She started working for Triodos Bank in 1990. She was a member of the Group of Advisors for the United Nations Year of Microcredit in 2004/2005 and of the Executive Committee of CCAP from 2003-2008. She is currently on the Board of Trustees of Women's World Banking, the International Association of Microfinance Investors in Microfinance (IAMFI), BRAC Afghanistan Bank and Kashf Microfinance Bank in Pakistan

Invest in a more sustainable future, the tax-free way:

-   A flexible range of investment options offering the opportunity to invest in large listed companies or smaller pioneers

-   Invest up to £11,520 tax-free, if you haven't used your ISA allowance for this year

Self-examination Questions

Customers

1. What type of customers would you mainly expect to invest in Triodos, would it be the aspirers, achievers, reformers or conservatives? How if at all could a relatively small bank try to approach each of these groups?

2. Does the advent of modern technology make it easier or more difficult for Triodos to operate without a branch structure?

3. What might you expect to find about the default rate on loans for such a bank? For what reasons might it be bigger and for what reasons might it be smaller?

4. Will the collapse of several of the major banks and the scandals associated with some of them mean that it is easier or more difficult for Triodos to attract new customers?

5.   Will the very low rates of interest available on most bank accounts mean that people are likely to be more willing to invest in ethical equities?

Marketing

1.   What media might the bank use in order to try to make it better known?

2.   In what ways might the advertising for such a bank be different to the more commercial banks?

3.   Which newspapers would you use to advertise Triodos services?

Lending policy

1.   Some other green funds try not to invest in trades which others find repugnant e.g. tobacco, arms industry etc. Triodos by contrast has a more positive approach. What would the likely results of such a policy in terms of total lending?

2.   Some people have suggested that socially responsible companies such as the ones which Triodos tries to lend to will generally have a good rate of returns on investments. What are the reasons for this assertion? Are they true?

3.   Why might micro credit reach the parts of the developing countries, which larger organisations do not reach?

4.   A) What would you expect the lending rates to be in many developing countries compared with a country such as the UK especially to   poorer people? Are the rates of interest much different for poorer people in the UK?

     B) Why might it be particularly important to have microfinance in Pakistan and Afghanistan?

5.   It is comparatively unusual for women to have a top banking positions. Why might having women in these positions be helpful? (Hint: Think of other jobs in which women are not in top positions)

35.9: Good Energy

Good energy is a firm concerned with encouraging the use of 100% green energy. This is energy from clean, renewable and non-polluting sources. Renewable and environmentally friendly sources of energy are an important issue worldwide. The world energy needs have increased with the increase of industrial development as well as world human population. Apart from increased demands of energy, the existing sources have posed environmental problems: Nuclear power poses the risk of nuclear waste being changed into lethal nuclear weapons, or being disposed off unsuitably and destroying the environment. An even bigger risk is the radioactivity that would be released into the atmosphere if one of the nuclear power stations were to be compromised, as it did at the Chernobyl station in Ukraine and at the Fukushima power plant in Japan. The use of petroleum and other fossil fuel sources of energy such as coal pose the risk of polluting the atmosphere with the emission of highly toxic carbon monoxide and carbon dioxide that is blamed for global warming. These sources of energy are also not renewable which means that they could diminish in supply and the world economy would halt. However, there is still resistance to change of energy sources. One important reason is the amount of investment that is needed to producing the same levels of energy from renewable sources as from the non-renewable sources. Carmakers have grappled with this problem for well over a decade. Solar cars are slower and weaker than diesel or petrol cars, to be yet viable. The fluctuating winds means that wind turbines may not be reliable sources of energy as wind speed rises and falls. Biomass and biofuels pose the problem of fermentation process and the amount of biomass processing required. Due to the diffuse nature of renewable sources of energy, the investment required to make them viable sources of energy may be out of reach for most manufacturers or even end users. Electrical power consumption in Western countries averages about 600 watts per person. In cloudy Europe this would require about eight square metres of solar panels, assuming a below-average solar conversion rate of 12.5%. Due to the fluctuations of these sources of energy that are beyond human control then powerful storage systems need to be devised. However, the adverse effects of fossil fuels make the search for clean, renewable, and sustainable sources of energy to power modern economies more urgent than ever.

Solar energy has the advantage of being a clean source of energy with no greenhouse gases and it is likely that the price of solar power will come down if local and central governments encourage it. Apart from the likely high capital input required for this source of energy, solar panels require no fuel apart from exposure to the sun. This would be very important in tropics where the sun shines for 12 hours a day for most of the year with slight variations. One way of doing this would be to try to ensure that large building developments had solar panels installed at the start. Part of the high cost of solar panels is that individual firms have to have scaffolding erected which is expensive and where such scaffolding is taken from one place to another. If it could be used on new housing estates this would obviously bring the price down considerably since there would be economies of scale.

Solar energy would also be very useful in many African countries where the national grid is poorly developed, so that continuous electric energy cannot be guaranteed in most large offices in the first place. In rural areas, electricity is often quite rare and the chances of many of these areas being connected to the national grid are quite small. This is in contrast to the UK where the last area without electricity on the mainland was connected in late 2005. Solar energy also has the advantage that it does not emit any greenhouse gases, which most scientists apart from those employed by the US Government believe are responsible for global warming.

Solar energy has the advantage of requiring low capital costs compared with the costs of having a grid system although even in parts of Africa, it will be suitable for water heating but not for all electrical appliances such as televisions, computers and so on. One former UK MP, Derek Wyatt, has suggested that we need a competition to try to find if we could have solar powered computers at a low price, which could help many poorer countries to make a giant leap in technology without major costs.

There are other types of renewable energy such as wind energy. Wind energy has been met with a lot of opposition from environmental activists such as Sir Bernard Ingham, the former press secretary to the late Margaret Thatcher who claims that the huge wings of wind turbines are 'visually intrusive'. The UK has more potential wind energy than its European neighbours. The argument of visual intrusion is obviously fallacious as it can be argued that most of the alternatives, such as oil refineries, coalmines are also visually intrusive. Even worse than visual intrusion is the danger that other sources of energy such as petroleum depots pose to the environment and human life. A large-scale explosion in Hemel Hempstead, Bedfordshire UK in December 2005 sent a huge cloud of carbon heavy gases into the atmosphere, this cloud extended for hundreds of miles. Air pollution and a likely acid rain and damage to the ozone layer cannot compare to the visual intrusion that concerns campaigners such as Sir Bernard.

Some people would suggest that it would be more cost effective to reduce the demands in the first place rather than looking for new sources of energy. Simple measures such as loft insulation, cavity insulation as well as lagging of tanks could reduce electricity consumption quite considerably. Lighting is responsible for about 15% of the total electricity consumption of households and this could be reduced quite considerably using long life light bulbs. The newer light bulbs are more energy efficient. A further alternative source would be that of tidal power. This can obviously only be used in areas that have access to the oceans and seas.

Domestic waste can also be used to power stations. This has been successful in countries such as Sweden. However, care has to be taken that domestic waste is not transported too far, since this of itself requires energy.

Governments through incentives have encouraged the private sector to spearhead the search for efficient and renewable sources of energy. One such company is Good Energy and its home generation project that is discussed below.

Home Generation Project

Good Energy launched Home Generation Scheme in the spring of 2004. It was launched to fill a gap in the market place to take the output from micro generators on a standardised tariff, valid across the country. The micro-generators will now be included in a grid so that surplus power can be sold to other consumers and the producers can be rewarded by payment through the standardised tariff system. At the same time, such generators on a scale that is less than 35kW will be rewarded for reducing the carbon emission. They have identified a niche in the UK market where people and organisations that invested in alternative sources of energy were not rewarded because their contribution to the national grid was insignificant. Some of the generators are also not connected to the national power grid. Good Energy supports a growing community of over 52,000 generators across Britain. They're all harnessing natural power from either: the wind, water and sun or through sustainable biogeneration.

Good Energy pioneered incentives for renewable energy generators almost a decade ago and continue to do through the Government's Feed-in Tariff and their Power Purchase agreement for commercial generators. Whatever the size of a generator, they have a product to suit it:

Good Energy HomeGen

Award-winning HomeGen scheme is designed for home generators under 30kW who have no export metering.

Good Energy SmartGen

Larger generators between 10 – 100kW with export metering can benefit from Good Energy SmartGen.

Power Purchase Agreements

Bespoke PPA service offers a tailored service.

Good Energy pays the generators of renewable energy in terms of all the units they produce and may or may not export. In a departure from the conventional way of thinking, small generators are encouraged to use the energy they produce on site. There is only one meter reading that gives the net reading for the year of operation.

Fixed estimates of the energy produced or the energy consumed over and above that produced are credited to the account of the customer quarterly and the one yearly metre reading is used to reconcile these fixed amounts with the actual amounts produced.

An important measure for clean renewable sources of energy is the amount of Carbon-dioxide emission that is saved by using the renewable energy.

Good Energy aims to encourage more people to switch to using renewable energy sources. They have identified a niche in the market where the small-scale producers of renewable energy are have not been catered for by the government. Using this technique Good Energy is able to attract more consumers to using 100% energy from renewable sources.

A different kind of energy company

Good Energy strongly believes that we have the opportunity to use the footprint of their business as a force for good, promoting best practice and holding themselves to the high standards that are to be expected.

Good Energy is a UK owned company, based in Chippenham in the South West. It was founded in response to climate change, to be a catalyst for transforming the UK's energy market by giving everyone the opportunity to choose renewable energy.

They don't think the energy market needs to be complex and mysterious. They believe simplicity and transparency should not only be at the heart of how every energy supplier treats its customers, but in the way it does business too.

Self-examination Questions

1. What are the advantages of solar power for lighting purposes? Are there any disadvantages?

2. Why do many electricity companies in the UK have different rates at different times of day? How far can domestic and industrial users take advantage of these cheaper rates?

3. What are the advantages of wind power?

4. What are the advantages of having individual generators in people's houses? Why do some large organisations have an energy generating system rather than relying on the national grid?

5. Why is it that we find considerable differences in energy consumption for buildings, which cannot be explained by either the age of the building or the climate?

6. Why does energy efficiency seem to be unimportant to car owners, even though there have been fuel protests in the U.K and in other European countries?

7. If energy prices rise, does this mean that people have a greater incentive to be more fuel-efficient?

8. Why might small business and homes wish to generate their own electricity?

9. What type of person is this likely to appeal to, would it be the achievers, aspirers' conservatives or reformers?

10. Why might it be difficult for micro generators to export electricity?

11. What is likely to happen to long-term energy prices? What would you expect to happen to the rate of return from such schemes?

12. Why is it important that governments support initiatives that encourage usage of alternative sources of energy that are clean and renewable?

13. Why are firms and households reluctant to switch to renewable sources of energy?

14. Why does Good Energy have 3 different types of tariffs according to the volume of demand?

15. The government has pledged that there should be simpler to understand energy prices for both gas and electricity. Has this occurred?

35.10: South Africa Tourism

To increase the number of foreign tourists, the South Africans might adapt their holiday patterns to the times at which people with children can travel. The exchange rate will be an important factor when travelling to South Africa and trends in the Dollar or the Euro or the Pound Sterling may well be important. Countries which are fast growing are more likely to have the potential to send tourist than countries which have a sluggish economy for example Germany which has had a more sluggish economy in recent years. Some basic knowledge of the different climates of other countries might be important for example, Sweden and Norway have very dark winters that are extremely cold and therefore some people might be tempted to visit the sunny South Africa and get away from the gloom. Reports about different countries can be obtained very easily from the internet.

Sales representatives from other countries can be useful in describing the profiles of customers in those countries. The types of holidays which people take in South Africa would also need to be analysed in terms of whether people take packaged holidays, or come individually. The package holiday market in one way is easier since it means that South African authorities can concentrate on the few main travel agents and tourist operators who are responsible for sending these people and therefore use direct mailing and other forms of targeted marketing. In some cases, it might be sensible to give some tourists' free holidays if they do not already send people to South Africa to show them what is going on.

One of the features, which unite countries such as South Africa with the UK, is that of sports. Test matches in South Africa will often attract large audiences and therefore it would be sensible for the South African authorities to target the countries, which are playing test matches in South Africa be they India, Pakistan, or England. Rugby is a sport confined to relatively few countries, but again will attract people to specific destinations and it may be possible, in conjunction with travel agents and tour operators, to take greater care of these people. The authorities will need to consider where to advertise.

In other cases, the wild life of South Africa might well be important. It is not too difficult to find out when programmes about wildlife are being broadcast on ITV or some of the other commercial channels in the UK and this would be in many cases the ideal time to have advertisements which would go alongside the programmes.

It may be important as well to judge from existing tourists about what features they like, which they dislike, and why they would recommend or not recommend other people to visit the country.

Media advertisement is also important, as all the target countries have developed media services. Cable News Network (CNN) a world-renowned news channel is watched in almost every country in the world. Other international news agencies such as the BBC, Discovery Channels and National Geographic channels could appeal to different social classes. Print media such as newspapers and magazines are also useful if they are international for example the Time magazine or the Economist and the Fortune. Local newspapers in the United Kingdom appeal to different socio-economic groups for example, the Daily Telegraph may be read by the older generation, this is obviously a rough profile of the kind of readers. The Saturday papers will often have more sections than usual, and as they contain supplements, which are more devoted to holidays. Sunday newspapers in the UK are often very large and will be read by more members of the family in many cases than the weekdays papers will. They often appeal to people who want a particular lifestyle and therefore advertisements, which have pictures of South Africa and its attractions, might well be useful.

In the UK, there are a number of free local newspapers, although within the London area the Metro is circulated at each of the London main train stations and often on trains and buses. Local and regional newspapers have a higher readership as they are free. The Metro, which is found in every train station in London, is a useful place to advertise as a wider cross-section of people is bound to see it.

Specialist and gender specific magazines can be considered for advertisement. Women's magazines are popular in the UK and here perhaps a more homely image might be appropriate for some of them as opposed to a cosmopolitan. An advertisement selling water sports, rugby and cricket games could be used in the men's' magazines. Specialist magazines may not have as much impact as other magazines as they appeal to a specific set of people and professionals. For example, a new unbreakable test-tube would be advertised in the New Scientist with greater success than a holiday in South Africa.

There are now a large number of independent local radio stations, although the amount of advertising per hour is limited on these. The radio advertising however being local, it is more difficult to see how the South African authorities could target this.

Cinemas particularly multiplex cinemas on out of towns sites have become more popular after many years of decline and the advantage of cinema is that it is easy to portray an image on a screen. However, it would be more difficult to give many details therefore the message might need to be confined to a few words and perhaps an easy recognisable phone number or website address might be appropriate.

Posters could be useful and are frequently used on buses and the underground trains in the London area and elsewhere. One of the advantages of posters on the underground is that whilst some people are reading newspapers, other people are not doing anything and so they are more likely to notice them than if they were on the roads. An advertisement depicting the open air and freedom of South Africa as opposed to crowded and stuffy underground train is sure to elicit some interest.

Television advertising though expensive could be one of the best ways of reaching audiences in the United Kingdom. This is especially because there is at least one television set for each household. Advertising at prime time may be more expensive than at other times, but daytime TV that may be watched by homemakers which may be useful for decisions about holidays. Another problem is the ability of easily recording TV programmes and fast-forward through the advert breaks.

Self-examination Questions

1. In what ways do natural catastrophes affect the tourism industry, for example the Tsunami in 2004? How do governments help alleviate adverse effects?

2. In what ways would the tourism industry and the education industry overlap? Why might rural areas welcome the development of a new college?

3. What were the effects of the introduction of the common Euro currency in 2002 on the tourism industry? What effects have been felt in the UK which stayed out of the common currency both in terms of tourists coming to the UK and those travelling abroad? (consider the relative exchange rates of tourist destinations such as the USA, Italy or Kenya)

4. There have been many examples where safety of ships, (recent attacks of cruise ships off the coast of Somalia by pirates) particularly small ferries has not been very good. What, if anything, can the Government in the developing countries do about this? What if they do not do this would be the effect on the tourism industry?

5. What effects, if any, will a period of low interest rates have upon the tourist industry? Explain your answer with reference to both direct and indirect effects.

6. What effects, if any, are the advantages of having a separate Government department responsible for tourism in a country?

7. What effects, if any, will the freedom of movement of labour within the EU have on the tourism industry as a whole? In particular, what effects will this have in countries such as Malta and Cyprus (popular British tourist destinations)?

8. Since the marginal cost of providing for extra people, within a hotel room is often low or negligible, what effect may this have on the pricing policy for hotels and guesthouses?

35.11: Ethical Property

Investing in Social Change

The Ethical Property Company is a unique initiative in ethical investment. The company buys properties and develops them as centres that bring charities, co-operatives, campaign groups and community together under one roof where they can share skills and ideas. Groups in their centres benefit from reasonable rents, flexible tenancy terms and office space and facilities designed to meet their needs.

Ethical Property currently own and manage 23 centres in England and Scotland and part-owned centres in Belgium and France, all of which are managed to minimise energy use, waste, car travel and the use of harmful materials.

Whilst their social and environmental values drive everything that they do, they are also unashamedly a profit-making business. In fact, making a profit is an essential element of their model. Paying a dividend regularly and managing their properties so as to increase the long-term value of their shareholders' investment is necessary to attract the capital they need to put their principles into practice. In addition, by making a profit they have the flexibility and resources to expand their activities, to invest in environmental improvements and to try out new ideas, without being tied to the agendas of grant-giving bodies or other donors.

They also encourage their shareholders to use their share of the profits creatively – They have a long-standing dividend waiver scheme offering shareholders the opportunity to give their dividend back to the company to invest in new projects and to provide grants to tenants who are starting up or facing short-term funding difficulties. This year the dividend waiver fund is being used to support development of the international Ethical Property family and the Ethical Property Foundation, in addition to the £15,000 earmarked for grants to tenants.

More detailed information regarding their financial performance can be found in their Annual Reports[12].

Under the second element of their Triple Bottom Line their aim is to reduce the negative impacts of the company's activities on the environment and to encourage positive environmental practices. They do this by:

- Minimising their carbon emissions
- Minimising use of nuclear power

---

[12] For Annual Reports http://www.ethicalproperty.co.uk/annualreports.php

- Reducing water consumption

- Promoting sustainable transport

- Reducing waste

More information about their work in each of these areas and the targets they have set themselves can be found in their Annual Reports and their 2011/12 Performance Supplement[13].

They believe that their business activities should have a positive social impact. They try to achieve this by:

- Providing effective support to a wide range of social change organisations through the buildings they own and manage.

- Using some of the capital they raise from shareholders and bank loans to invest in areas of deprivation.

- Being an ethical employer.

- Being honest and transparent to all stakeholders in all areas of the business.

More information about their Social Performance can be found in their Annual Reports and their 2011/12 Performance Supplement.

The company has grown rapidly since its launch in 1999. They are now looking to continue and solidify that growth and are planning their development strategy over the next five years.

They continue to enjoy support from another ethical organisation 'Triodos Bank' (Case Study 35.8) which in 2004 offered it one of its largest ever loans to a single borrower, £7.25 million. Ethical Property established in 1982 by Andrew King; was incorporated in 1999 and underwritten by Triodos Bank, it had its first share issue, which raised £1.31 million. A second share issue was carried out in 2003 again sponsored by Triodos Bank. This issue was fully subscribed.

---

[13] For the Performance Supplement http://www.ethicalproperty.co.uk/annualreports.php

Self-examination Questions

1. How can socially sensitive organisations benefit from sharing premises?

2. How can Ethical Property differentiate their services from those of other land and office space owners?

3. What are the advantages of turning the business into a public limited company?

4. In 2003 the company had a second share issue, which was fully subscribed, what does this say about the company?

5. What are the advantages and disadvantages of quoting the company in the stock market?

6. The company has six long-term objectives. Why is it important that businesses have short, medium and long-term objectives?

7. The company intends to develop a joint venture structure that will allow the tenants to buy part of the properties. What do you think are the advantages of enabling tenants to buy part of the property?

8. Why is it important for the company to set up centres in inner-city areas of Glasgow and Manchester?

9. Why do you think that ethical investments have become so popular[14] in the United Kingdom?

10. Should all large organisations have environmental performance tests?

11. Why might social performance checks be helpful to both potential shareholders and other stakeholders?

35.12: Traidcraft

An operation which started in the heart of urban Tyneside 25 years ago, has grown into the UK's leading fair trade organisation, with a turnover of around £15 million and an international reputation for delivering practical help to small businesses across the developing world.

Traidcraft was launched in 1979 from a Victorian warehouse in the centre of Newcastle with a hand-drawn catalogue featuring a small selection of jute products from Bangladesh.

---

[14] Ethical investment is a popular concern, according to new research by Friends Provident, founder of Stewardship, Britain's first ethical investment fund. The study claims that 62 per cent of the people questioned wanted their money to go into socially responsible and ethical investments.

Now based across the River Tyne on Gateshead's Team Valley trading estate, Traidcrafts trading company deals in hundreds of fair trade food, craft and textile products from tens of thousands of producers in almost 35 developing countries, and lists Britain's leading supermarkets among its customers.

At the same time, its charity, Traidcraft Exchange, has won prestigious contracts from the British Government, the Community Fund and the EU to deliver vital, small-business development in some of the poorest countries in the world.

As the first plc in the UK to publish a fully audited set of Social Accounts, Traidcraft has pioneered the principles of corporate social responsibility and much of its policy and advocacy work continues to focus on influencing government and business in this direction.

Traidcraft has been recognised for its work through a number of awards both as a social enterprise and for Traidcraft Exchange's development work.

Traidcraft has awards for its development work, social accounting and its mail order catalogue. Traidcraft's innovative approach helped launch Cafedirect the Newcastle-based co-operative lending society Shared Interest, the Fairtrade Foundation and built its own status as a leading national social enterprise.

Although it is a Christian-based organisation, Traidcraft works with people of all faiths and none in a common struggle to use trade as a means of fighting poverty.

Traidcraft plc, as the UK's leading fair trade organisation, works with more than 100 producer groups in over 35 countries around the world, helping them build sustainable livelihoods for the future.

Traidcraft Exchange, our charity arm, develops projects and offers training and consultancy services to promote pro-poor business development. We also engage in policy work and campaigning to influence UK and EU policy-makers and raise public awareness of poverty and trade issues.

All our work is dependent on the collaborative efforts of our partners around the world with Traidcraft staff and with a growing community of supporters and activists in the UK. Together we believe we can build a better and fairer world.

How does Traidcraft fight poverty?

- Sell fairly traded products

- Build better businesses

- Influence others

- Raise funds

- Raise awareness

Traidcraft is concerned with making markets available for developing countries farmers so that they are competitively priced to those in developed countries. The heavy subsidies for farmers in the EU and the USA amongst other developed countries mean that farmers in the developing countries where there are no subsidies cannot compete. Fair trade can be ensured by either removing the subsidies or lowering the trade barriers imposed on developing country farm products.

Traidcraft is an internationally recognised leader in small business development. We work with a network of overseas partners to help poor producer groups to trade more effectively at local, national and international levels. By helping businesses to trade more effectively, we can help poor producers to get more benefits from trade, and to improve the conditions in which they live and work.

In the UK, we work with businesses on issues such as corporate social responsibility (CSR) and social accounts. We encourage businesses to change their practices so they have a positive impact on their marginalised suppliers.

Traidcraft is also committed to making itself a better business. Our programmes are based on the specific needs of poor people in each country and product sector in which we work. However, they also provide the means of co-ordinating all of Traidcraft's development work in these areas ensuring that we are as effective and efficient as possible.

In order to maximise the benefits of trade to producers Traidcraft seeks to work outside of the scope of its own producers and contacts to influence a wider collection of organisations, businesses and institutions to adopt trading practices, which maximise benefits to the poor.

We raise funds to provide the income needed to fund Traidcraft's work of fighting poverty through trade. 1.4 billion people live on less than $1 a day. For these, income barely covers the basics of food, clothing, healthcare and accommodation. Many of these people are poor because they lack the power to change their lives.

Traidcraft is funded by various donor organisations including Comic Relief, EU, Trusts and Foundations, etc. With this support Traidcraft is able to help communities in the third world to increase their income and improve their standard of living and build a better future.

Following are three focus areas of Traidcraft Plc

- **Increasing our direct impact on poverty** – by achieving steady growth in sales of fair trade products in the UK, by making the capacity building services of Traidcraft Exchange available to a wider group of organisations and by developing a more strategic approach to the projects we undertake overseas. A key element of this is the setting of Producer plans in conjunction with each producer group with whom we work – a "road-map" of how the relationship should work, for how long and what benefits are being sought.

- **Increasing our influence on others** – recognising that our own efforts will always be relatively small in the context of global poverty, we place emphasis on mobilising public opinion behind fair trade and on influencing the ways that private sector companies and governmental bodies think about trade and its impact on the developing world.

- **Enhancing sustainability** – not only making more sustainable livelihoods for our producers, but also making sure that Traidcraft as an organisation is stronger and more resilient and increasingly professional in its approach[15].

Self-examination Questions

1. Why is it important that organisations such as Traidcraft build sustainability into their aid to poor farmers in the developing countries?

2. What business services can Traidcraft offer to businesses in the developing countries?

3. Why is it important for Traidcraft to influence others in pursuing fairer trade and empowering the poor?

4. Increased awareness is one of the approaches that Traidcraft uses to meet its objectives. Explain how raising awareness helps meet these objectives.

35.13: Television and Radio

Television is an unusual industry in that there are obvious barriers to entry, which cannot easily be overcome by the purchasing power of an individual firm. BBC1

---

[15] Excerpt: reproduced with permission from Traidcraft from their website www.traidcraft.co.uk

and BBC2 are financed through a licencing system. This puts constraints on the amount of money they have to spend. Channel 4 is intended specifically to cater for minority interests. Minority interests might include sports, which are not popular, non-pop music, and other types of information and entertainment that may interest only a minority. Whilst satellite television originally lost money, the range of Sky services has increased. This, like ITV, is partly financed by advertising. Unlike ITV, it is also financed by the sale of suitable equipment. In 2013 there was considerable coverage given to the dominant ownership of Rupert Murdoch and his firm News International in the media industry. ITV itself is run through giving a series of franchises to individual firms in different regions. The term franchise is not used in its conventional sense. The franchises are allocated to the firms after they bid. The highest bid is not necessarily acceptable. There has to be some guarantee of the quality of the programmes which they produce. It would not be acceptable, for example, for them to broadcast light entertainment. In many cases, the newspapers are part shareholders in the ITV companies although there are constraints on this.

Radio was developed in pre-war years although reception of most sets was not very good. There were many comedy programmes which developed although the general tone of the BBC (sometimes unkindly referred to as Aunty BBC) was that most of them were middle class. Television coverage was by no means widespread throughout the UK, programmes were confined to the evenings. Until 1955 the BBC had a monopoly of both radio and television programmes. In 1955 after a battle within the Conservative party, ITV introduced its first programmes. There had been considerable middle class resistance to the introduction of television. Many of the middle class feeling that it would lead to a lowering generally of standards and therefore whilst to some extent the growth of the TV market reflected the typical production life cycle there were other factors as well. In some cases there were external factors such as the Coronation in 1953, which meant that far more television sets were brought in that year, although whether this merely brought the purchases forward or were a constant factor remains unclear.

It is difficult to get accurate figures since there was wide evasion of the television licence. The TV licencing authority in the UK has lists of addresses and whether there is a licence connected to that household. They have to go to the addresses that do not have a licence associated with them and do a physical check.

BBC Two was introduced in the 1960s, as was colour television. At the start of the coloured television market prices was typically around £200 (about £4,000 at today's values) for a typical set, whereas the price for a typical black and white (monochrome) was around £60. The forecast in the market was extremely difficult for example; one trade association whilst having 10 months figures in still managed to have an error of 35% for the year.

Again, there was a boost to buying television with the success of the English team in the World Cup in 1966. Presumably, this was partly because men rather than women often wanted to watch programmes, in other cases this may have been the purchase of a second set.

Self-examination Questions

1. What events might cause the number of television sets to be altered very quickly? (Hint: think of the effects of HD-TV and the development of 3D TV.)

2. The middle class in the 1950s felt that Television would 'dumb-down' the populations of Britain, has this fear been realised or has television served to enlighten the masses?

3. Why might it have been difficult to forecast the growth of the TV markets in the 1950s and 1960s, is it any easier now?

4. What effects would changes in the way computers can receive TV and Radio have on the total market for programmes?

5. If the BBC were to be financed by advertising rather than through a licencing system what effect would it have on the ;

   a. BBC?

   b. ITV?

   c. Licensing system?

6. Why might firms have been reluctant to put in bids for a sports channel, which should not be available for a large part of the UK population?

7. Why have there been restrictions on newspapers owning television stations?

8. From your answer to question 3 is there any logic in restrictions on terrestrial television but not on satellite ownership or control of digital channels?

9. What difference, if any, would it make to the types of programs if television were to be financed on a pay as you view basis rather than through financing?

10. Why has there been provision for Channel 4 to provide minority interest programs rather than allowing it discretion in the same way that newspapers compete?

11. What problems occur in trying to judge the quality of a firm bidding for the ITV market if it is a newcomer to the ITV network? Why might there be problems about gauging the length of time that franchises should be issued for.

12. In many countries there has either been a state of monopoly or the Government has at least been partially responsible for any of the TV and radio programmes. What are the advantages and disadvantages of this?

13. Since BBC programmes from the UK can often be received in other countries and for example in The Netherlands, the BBC programmes are sometimes listed in the Press. Does this mean that viewers and listeners in those countries should contribute to the cost of such programmes?

14. It has sometimes been suggested that the BBC licence should be scrapped. In what other ways, if any, could the BBC be financed?

15. There has been considerable debate about the showing of major sporting events being confined to commercial channels, which are not free at the point of the use. This has applied to the test matches, which are played in cricket between England and other commonwealth countries. What are the arguments for and against such sporting events being shown on the free-to-use channels such as BBC and ITV1 or channel 4? In January 2006, there were complaints that the cricket test matches between England and Australia, which had been shown on channel 4, would no longer be seen largely on terrestrial television etc. but only on satellite televisions. Why might some people consider this important? Are they right?

35.14: Taxi Cab Services

In the taxi business as with most others there are fixed and variable costs although how these are classified would depend partly upon the time period which we take. The following table shows how someone in the UK might try to classify some of the different costs, clearly the actual amounts will vary over time and according to the country where the taxi operation is.

Some costs are variable such as petrol although even here if we are looking at the marginal cost of picking up passengers on return run, the cost of more passengers, if the taxi was otherwise running empty back to its base is virtually a fixed cost. Depreciation is to some extent a fixed cost. If we were trying to sell a taxi, which was bought on the 1st January for £20,000 at the end of the year the car would have incurred a depreciation charge of regardless of whether it was used or not. We would probably get 35% depreciation charge of this vehicle simply because it was 1 year older than a new car i.e. £6,000 so the residual value would be £14,000. On the other hand if the driver were to have done 35,000 miles (48,000km), we would get less than £14,000 if the car was resold, because of the high mileage registered.

Some taxi firms have owner-drivers who pay commission to the taxi-firm owners for all trips made whilst others provide the taxis in the first place. Some firms would lease vehicles so that the maintenance was carried out by the leasing firm whilst others would have maintenance done as and when it was required. Some local authorities will make a charge for the taxi-route knowledge drivers' test.

Insurance is a fixed cost for the year but if there are many claims then almost certainly the insurance company will raise the premium in the next year. Taxis which are kept in a garage overnight would have a lower premium than those which are outside. However taxis in garages at night would be unusual as they are usually out working.

Fixed Costs	Variable Costs	Difficult to Classify
	Petrol	
Depreciation, even if no mileage £ 2000	Depreciation, with lots of mileage £ 2500	Depreciation
VED road tax £150		
Insurance		Premiums could go up with more mileage
Drivers Wages Time Rate	Drivers Wages Commission	Drivers Wages Commission or Time Rate
Maintenance Contract	Without Contract	Maintenance
Garage		

The Vehicle Excise Duty (VED) is a tax levied on all vehicles in the U.K, payable yearly depending on the theoretical CO_2 emission rates per kilometre.

There are 13 emission bands for cars ranging from £0 - £490 after the first year. Prices for the first year range from £0 - £1065.

Using the table above why do you think it would be difficult to calculate the break-even point?

Self-examination Questions

Pricing

1. Why would a taxi driver prefer to have a contract with a school to do school trips at 80p per mile rather than at 120p per mile and a guaranteed £2.00 for the first 1320 yards (1200metres) elsewhere?

2. What further information would you require before accepting or rejecting such an offer from the local education authority? The normal educational trip is around (6miles) 10 kilometres whereas the modal trip in this area is around 3 km

Type of business

3. What would be the advantages and disadvantages of being;

    (a) A Sole trader?

    (b) A Partnership?

    Why might this depend upon how the drivers are paid?

4. Why might it be important to have a partnership rather than a sole trader, for example, the taxi would cost altogether £100,000? How easy would it be to get a profit-sharing agreement with four partners?

5. Why might it be difficult to get agreement with the legal maximum of 20 partners?

6. What would be the advantages and disadvantages of being a private limited company?

7. What are the administrative costs of setting up a taxi business for a non-owner-driver?

8. How far is limited liability important for a non-owner-driver?

9. How far is limited liability important for an owner-driver?

10. How could such an organisation try to develop its pricing policy assuming that it was allowed to charge its own rates?

Local authorities

11. Why in many towns in the UK is there a maximum charge often imposed by the local authority?

12. In some countries such as the USA, the New York State imposes a quota on the number of taxis that are allowed to operate. What would be the

consequences of this in terms of fares and the likelihood of getting return passengers if the taxi goes outside the authority's boundaries?

13. What is meant by a two-tier tariff system? Why might this be appropriate?

14. Why do many taxi firms have in effect a boarding charge, plus a mileage charge ?

15. Why on the other hand is there often a negotiable rate for long distance? Would you expect this to be at a lower or higher rate proportionately than for short distances?

The taxi firm makes some note for a standard SWOT analysis

Strengths

- The market seems to be a steady one

- There are no major barriers to entry

- If the firm has to exit there is no great loss

- Fixed costs are low compared with a long lease on a shop

- Expansion is easy compared again with a shop where a long lease might be required and cost of stock might be very great

Weakness

- There is some trade during day but far more in the peaks

- Going home time after the pubs can be risky

- Late evening Station traffic is useful but clients have no loyalty

Opportunities

- Expansion easy compared with leasing another shop

- The local Bus companies seem very weak especially those going out of town.

Threats

- Fierce competition from other taxi companies

- Some costs not easily predictable e.g. petrol, if fuel prices go might higher then there may be reactions from some of the poorer customers

- The bus fares for Old Age Pensioners from April 2006 after the morning peak might remove at least in one direction the older customers who use the taxis for shopping

- The use of internet either shopping or possibly free deliveries by some of the supermarkets removes those customers who cannot carry large loads.

  1. Would the same SWOT analysis be useful in an area, which you know? Are there other factors which should be considered?

Insurance

1. Why might the firms need to have consequential loss insurance for vehicles which are out of action?

2. Why might it be more difficult to assess where the breakeven point is than with some other businesses?

Marketing

1. How easy is it to make the name of the firm memorable and why might it be important?

2. Why might taxi firms want to use a local phone directory, Yellow Pages or Thomsons?

3. Why might firms wish to have a Freephone in the local superstore such as Sainsbury's?

4. Why are many taxi firms and drivers willing to pay to have a station taxi site?

5. Why might firms when trying to assess demand likely to make out a pattern of demand over a day?

6. Make out a pattern for your own neighbourhood using the pattern below?

    - 7 am to 8 .35am: Business to station + children shops

    - From 10 am to 3 pm Shopping trips are probably predominant as well as medical centres, so would it be useful to advertise there

    - From 7 pm Onwards young going out seem to be important facet of demand

    - 10 0 on home and night clubs

Costs and pricing

1. What is the marginal cost of a second, third or fourth passenger if the taxi has 4 passenger seats?

2. There have been suggestions that a shared taxi service such as the one from Paddington to Liverpool Street (two London termini) is one, which could be usefully copied elsewhere? How far is this likely to be true?

3. What would be the cost of providing larger taxis e.g. a seven-seater? Who would want to have such vehicles?

4. In some countries such as the Netherlands, there have been combined fares for trains and taxi in mid-size population cities. Why might prospective passengers like this rather than to hire taxis separately? (Hint: why in particular might foreign visitors like this arrangement?)

5. Why might the disabled be a disproportionately large service for taxi firms? (Hint: help with shopping)

6. Under what circumstances might it be worthwhile for commercial reasons to have cheaper fares for such people?

7. What measures of efficiency can a taxi firm use?

8. Why might the return on capital be quite high for taxi firms?

9. Why might there be problems in trying to determine Gross profit?

10. Why might there be fewer problems in trying to determine Net profit?

35.15: Investment in the Public Sector

It has generally been accepted that investment in the public sector should take place only if it yields overall greater benefits than in the private sector. This does not necessarily mean looking solely at financial returns since in many cases for example in transport, they may well be external benefits or costs and these should be taken into account. If there are no externalities, which would be unusual, then investment could be assessed purely on financial criteria. If we look back a long while, then government could use discounted cash flow techniques to assess this. For example, the 1961 and 1967 white papers on public sector investment suggested that an 8% return on public sector investment would be comparable to a low risk pre-tax return of 15 to 16% before tax in the private sector. It might be noted that this was an age of relative financial stability although inflation was rising towards the end of the 1960s. This figure was intended to be in real rates of return i.e. if inflation was running at approximately 15% as it was in the 1976 to 1977 period then a 8% rate would have implied a monetary rate of return of 23%.

Should investment be counter cyclical?

Keynes in his book 'The General Theory' which was published in the 1930s at a time of the great depression when unemployment was very high not merely in the UK but also in most of the western countries, showed clearly that the private sector alone could not guarantee that there would be full employment. This would have been in contrast to the so-called classical economist who assumed that full employment was the norm. Therefore, it has sometimes been suggested that investment in the public sector should be used in a period of recession to bring the economy nearer to full employment. However part of the problem of this approach is that there are usually time lags between the time that the government gets hold of information. It might be noted however that there was the appointment of a national (chief) statistician in 2009 who was Jil Matheson. The national statistician is reasonably independent from government and helps to ensure that data which is processed quickly and impartially. Even if we allow for this, there are still the time lags between the time that the government takes to access the information and make any arrangements. Then there is the problem that many public sector projects take a while to implement. It should be noted that the time involved in transport investments such as the Concorde project was well over 10 years. In the private sector, the original tendering process for the Channel Tunnel took place in 1987 but it was not until 1994 when the project (which was vastly over budget) was implemented. The Channel Tunnel Link to St Pancras which was completed in 2007. Whether in the public or private sector, government backing will not be a very sensitive instrument for reliving unemployment if the project is very capital intensive and likely to take a long time.

In other countries labour intensive projects such as the Tanzam project where the Chinese were involved in the setting up of a railway between Tanzania and Zambia was more likely to be successful if the aim was to reduce unemployment.

Should transport investment be linked to a national plan?

This has been done in some countries for example, Botswana in the 1960s incorporated transport and communications in one sector of its national plan.

There are two advantages of linking the transport investment to the national plan. The first is that transport investment in many countries is a large percentage of the total gross capital formation. This is the economists' jargon for new investment in the sense of a project. Secondly that an increase in transport facilities may form part of a project to reduce bottle-necks either during the course of production or in obtaining raw materials or in selling the final product.

The only published national plan in the UK was supposed to give a national plan from 1964 to 1970 but it failed to give the higher economic growth rates, which it was aimed at mainly because of the difficulties in predicting imports and exports. Indicative planning refers to where the government indicates but does not control all the economic variables in the economy. Before the privatisation programme, which was implemented by Lady Thatcher (1925-2013) when she was Prime Minister of the United Kingdom from 1979 to 1990, a large proportion of the economy was directly controlled by the government. In spite of this about, 35% to 40% of GNP (Gross National Product) is imported or exported; a large percentage of imports and exports cannot be controlled directly by the government. Generally, the more complex the economy the more difficult and costly it is likely to be to try to accurately forecast the economy. Even here, exogenous events can make forecasting very difficult. For example, this happened in 1973 to 1974 when OPEC (the Organisation of Petroleum Exporting Countries) vastly increased the price of oil, which set back economic growth not merely in the UK but in many western as well as in developing countries.

In Western Europe, the optimal approach to the Channel Tunnel might well have been to have a multi-national basis for the project to not look merely at the tunnel itself, which whilst very expensive in engineering terms is relatively easy to build, but on the overall effect on the countries affected by the project. The assumption here is that the Channel Tunnel is as the name implies beneath the sea. However, it would have been helpful if it could have been viewed as a venture for the EU as a whole. This is because it linked for example London, Paris and Brussels but could have linked into other high-speed links such as those from Germany or Holland then it would have made more sense. Even in the UK, the failure to consider where the terminal should be reasonably located i.e. originally at Waterloo but subsequently at Kings Cross/St Pancras would have been helpful. The Channel Tunnel of course did also have an effect on both the French and British ferry services.

The Concorde project whilst romantically viewed by newspapers such as the Daily Express failed to look at future demands for transport. The main thrust of air travel has been away from being almost entirely for business travel to much greater demand for social travel whether for holidays or visiting friends or relatives etc.

There have been no subsequent developments from Concorde and the major investment in aircraft has been towards larger aircraft whether it is the European Airbus or the Boeing Dreamliner.

Investment in UK ports was piecemeal even before the split up of the ports industry. Clearly, investment in UK ports cannot be divorced entirely from what is happening in other EU countries. For road projects, there has been a need to link even at a low level the idea of marking of routes from the UK to the continent under the AGR convention. Generally, however the UK is much more independent of its road system than for example a country such as Austria or Switzerland, which has a large volume of traffic flowing through it, even though much of it is not concerned directly with either starting or finishing in those countries.

Self-examination Questions

1. What problems apply in trying to ensure that we get greater benefits from investment in the public sector than in the private sector? Illustrate your answer with reference to investment in education, the health sector and in the transport sector.

2. What would be a reasonable rate of return on private sector investment now in terms of a pre-tax return?

3. What is meant by saying that the investment should have a positive return in real terms? Would this be more difficult or less difficult to achieve in a period of recession or in a period where there was a high rate of inflation?

4. What is meant by suggesting that public sector investment should be counter cyclical?

5. Some economic commentators have suggested that public sector investment crowds out private sector investment, i.e. if we invest in the public sector this is at the expensive of investment in the private sector. Is this more applicable in time of recession, than in time of full-employment? Even if it were true, would this necessarily prove that public sector investment was not worthwhile for example in the health sector or transport sector?

6. The effects of Hurricane Katrina in 2005 were exacerbated by the failure of the government to invest in the safety features for an area under the sea. Why is it important that certain forms of investment be carried out by the government? (Hint: nature of public goods)

7. Why might it be easier for a command economy to look at the overall effects of investment than a mixed economy country?

8. Why governments might be concerned about port facilities in their country, what problems arise if we get larger and larger ships to older ports?

9. It is usually suggested that when considering investments that governments need to compare alternatives and whether projects are complementary or

competitive. Why might this be so and what problems arise is we are looking at two investments that are complementary?

35.16: Investment in the Transport Sector

In the transport sector, different reasons lead to investment. One of these is that an increase in capacity may be thought to be desirable to meet increased demand or because it will increase profitability. A great deal of investment also takes place to replace existing assets, for example on the railways, a considerable degree of investment is necessary to maintain bridges and viaducts. The third reason for investment is to improve quality of service and/or reduce costs. Most of the investment in handling equipment such as that used to handle containers will fall into this category. Containers are standard size boxes which can easily be transported from one mode of transport to another e.g. from a ship to a lorry.

A number of these reasons may govern any individual investment. For example, improvements in railway signalling such as automatic signal boxes covering large areas may be desirable to reduce the railways costs but may also have the effect of increasing capacity. A new computer, which replaces an existing one, may also have a much greater memory and facility for handling a wider range of calculations and therefore may improve the capacity of the transport system. There are a number of different methods of investment appraisal.

The concept of net present value

If we had £100 on the 1 January this year we could put it into a safe place such as a Building Society at a rate of interest of perhaps 5% and it would then be worth £105 in one year's time. If the money were to be left in the Building Society, it would be worth £110.25p in two years time because of compound interest. It could be left for a further year and it would be getting 5% interest on £110.25p and not just on the original capital. However, we will be assuming that at the end of the year we will be in a position to enjoy the money, that we will not be sick, incapacitated or even dead. We simply do not know what will happen in the future. Therefore most people would prefer to have money now rather than money at a later time, this is known as the 'time-preference of money'. If you would prefer to have £100 now rather than in the future, we will have to give you more than £100 in the future for you to take the risk to receive the same money in the future. The same idea applies to lenders of money, for example banks, when a bank lends a customer some money they are taking the risk that in the period they have agreed to have the customers repay them, such a customer will be alive and capable of paying. To account for this risk therefore they charge an interest rate. In the same way, if you were entitled to receive £100 today then those who owe you money will have to offer you more so that you may accept the same amount in future. The longer they take to give you the money the more they will need to pay you over and above the £100, so that you may accept the arrangement. This is known as a discounted cash flow, formally defined as a stream of cash flow with an attached time element as illustrated above.

The logic of discounted cash flow is to express all the different values of money in year one, two and three etc., now. The phrase, which the economist uses for this, is the word discounting which is the opposite of compound interest. On the example above if you have had money in the Building Society we would say that other things being equal that £105 in one year's time would be worth £100 at the present time whilst £110.25p in two years time would be worth £100 at the present time.

With the net present value method we look at the cost of the investment now and look at the flow of net benefits over the period. We would generally only invest if the net benefits whether savings or additional net revenue in total are greater than the cost of the investment. The Net Present Value (NPV) is the value of a cash flow discounted to the present year.

Discounting is an iterative process: using the example above:

Net Present Value at 'Year 0' is £100
Year 1 = £100 + 5% of £100 = £105
Year 2 = £105 + 5% of £105 = £110.25
Year 3 = £110.25 + 5% of 110.25 = £115.76

This iterative process yields a pattern that can be reduced to a simple formula:
$A_n = P (1+i)^n$
Where A_n is the NPV at year n
P is the original amount of money
n is the number of years since year 0
i is the interest rate applied to the stream of cash flow

If we wish to discount £100 in one year's time to the present day you have to do it by a factor $(1 + i)$ in other words if the rate of interest is 5% we are saying that we will discount it by $1 + 5\%$ or in other words 1.05. This is as you will see is the converse of the compound interest approach. If we want to discount something in two years time we have to discount it by $(1 + i)^2$.

This approach of determining the NPV of future cash flows can be used to decide whether an investment is worthwhile or not. This is achieved using the discounted cash flow method which the opposite of the compound interest above. Where in the above example the money was being offered to you, when considering whether to start a business, you will be borrowing money or using your money to invest. The value of subsequent cash flows will therefore diminish rather than increase because those whom you owe money will demand more as time goes.

With the net present value method, we then add up all the sums of the future benefits or profits and compare them with the present level of investment. In general, we would choose the investment with the highest net present value. If we have unlimited amount of capital which would be unlikely then we would choose all investments which have a positive net present value. If however we had limited amount of capital, which is more likely, then we would have to choose the ones with the highest.

The alternative approach is the rate of return where we use the same formula virtually as above but equate it. In this case, we have to find out the value of i which will equate both sides of the equation. This is slightly more difficult but can be done easily with modern calculators and computers.

Practical problems with using discounted cash flow

In our original example, we chose a rate of discount, which was equal to the rate in the Building Society. In practice, interest rates vary considerably. It is therefore somewhat difficult to know what rate of discount to use. In practice, there will also be some administrative costs involved, which would mean that any firm would wish to have at least the opportunity cost of capital plus the administrative costs. Also very few investments are completely without risk and therefore in practice a firm involved in private investment would need rate of interest which would cover both the duty cost of safe investment plus administrative costs plus an element of risk. In large firms, the board would lay down almost certainly some minimum criteria. In some cases, the firm might have to borrow the money in which case the rate of discount would need to allow for this. If for example as in 2013 a firm might be able to borrow at say 8% then the rate of discount would need to be greater than this.

When investments are alternatives, you may need to look at the incremental net present value. For example if the railways were considering whether to improve rail services on existing track as with the East Coast line or whether to have a new route as with the TGV in France you would need to know what extra costs are incurred. In practice it is often difficult to assess the net benefits or profit. Similarly, in 2013, some people have suggested that it might be better to build a completely new route to Scotland, like the HS2 route costing £70 million at the moment, than to upgrade the existing West Coast route, which would have cost £2 billion. Generally, it is easier to assess cost savings rather than increases in revenue. For this reason therefore it might be easier to apply NPV (net present value) techniques with some degree of accuracy, for example to the installation of a computer where the main aim is saving costs. It will be extremely difficult however to assess the revenue from a major new undertaking such as the Channel Tunnel. In fact the flow of freight has been vastly overestimated for long distance freight and the actual cost estimates were vastly understated with the total cost of about £11 billion. Even the more conventional investment such as the electrification of the East Coast line was difficult in the 1980s to assess. In general we can say that the longer the period the more difficult it is to forecast demand and hence revenue. For example with the Channel Tunnel, the operators had originally fifty-five years of operation although this has subsequently been extended. It is possible to imagine the problems of forecasting fifty-five years ahead if one tries to do the opposite i.e. looking back fifty-five years and trying to see whether it would have been possible to forecast transport demand now. Another problem with DCF as with any other investment technique is to distinguish between the commercial life and the technical life of the asset. It is quite possible to find a marked difference between the two, for example, steam trains were built by British Railways up to 1960, the last steam train being Evening Star. These would have had a technical life of at least forty or fifty years but in practice, British Rail had eliminated all steam trains with the minor exception of a narrow gauge line from Aberystwyth by 1968. Similarly, it is possible to find examples of aircraft where the commercial life is far less than the technical life. This means that investment appraisal is perhaps more difficult for longer life investment, for example with airports improvements to the waterways such as the South Yorkshire navigation or improvements to the track rather than in road haulage where the life of the vehicle is generally only about five years.

Because of uncertainty, it is sometimes sensible to use sensitivity testing i.e. seeing what would happen if the rate of discount or changes in demand etc. were to occur and whether these would alter the investment decision. If for example, we choose a pessimistic and an optimistic figure and this does not change our decision then there is little point in further studies. If however the investment is sensitive then it may be worthwhile carrying out further market research.

Whilst the economist usually uses the term discount in the public sector the phrase test rate is often used. The government has often used this figure net of inflation for example if the rate of inflation was 4% and the government insisted on test rate of 5% this would mean that the investment must yield at least 9% in money terms.

The payback period

One of the most common methods of investment appraisal though not necessarily a sensible one is that of the payback period i.e. how quickly will an investment pay for itself.

One of the reasons why the payback period is commonly used is that it is fairly easy to calculate. It is perhaps particularly helpful to firms if they have liquidity problems. For such firms in many cases the quicker the payback period the more likely they are to be able to survive.

The payback period however is not a very sensible method of appraisal for most firms. For example, if we consider two potential investments for a road haulage firm. A lorry costing £10,000, may give net benefits, additional revenue minus additional costs, of £2,000 a year for 5 years. At the end of which it is scrapped and a computer costing £10,000 and giving us net benefits of £1,800 for 10 years then investment in the lorry will give us a quicker payback period even though if the lorry is chosen it will not give any profits. The payback period assumes that net benefits in any year up to the time of the payback have equal weighting. This will not necessarily be the case as for example when inflation runs very high as in 1974 to 1975 when it was approximately 25%. It would also tend to bias investment towards short term rather than to long term consideration. It would therefore be unwise to use this in the case of shipping where almost by definition the majority of assets held are long term ones. Similarly, almost any transport undertaking which is responsible for infrastructure. If the British Airports Authority used such a method they would rule out longer-term investments such as terminal 5 at Heathrow. Similarly, the railways would have ruled out the electrification of the East Coast line in the 1980s or the West Coast line now, which will mean costs for several years before any returns are made. An alternative method of investment appraisal is that of discounted cash flow. The NPV is therefore the better method compared to the payback period approach.

Self-examination Questions

1. What are the reasons for investment in the transport sector? Are these reasons different to those in other commercial sectors?

2. What difficulties occur in trying to assess an appropriate rate of discount?

3. Why, even if a long-term project was givin a favourable rate of return might a firm not wish to go ahead with it?

4. Why might some individuals be more interested in long-term investments than others might?

5. Why might some firms be more interested in long-term investments than others might?

6. Can the above analysis be applied to students considering taking a long-term educational course?

7. Why might problems of forecasting demand be crucial in investment appraisal? Why is it so difficult in many cases to do this accurately?

8. Is it easier to carry out investment appraisal for road haulers than for other modes of transport?

35.17: UNCTAD: The United Nations Conference on Trade and Development

UNCTAD has been in existence for many years and in the 1970s tried to intervene in the shipping market by suggesting that developing countries should be able to gain a share of the market, which at that stage was dominated by liner conferences. Conferences in this context meant what would normally be regarded as a cartel i.e. that shipping companies usually from the major developed countries had a large proportion of the total shipping market and can specify the price and in effect the quality of service.

UNCTAD has a Trade and Development Board, which met in Geneva in October 2005 and had a number of ideas.

Amongst the conclusions, which they reached, was that there was no one method of developing a country. Any aid given should take into account both the national, social and economic characteristics.

As one might expect UNCTAD also looked at the moves towards globalisation and recognised there are aspects of interdependence.

The meeting heard from the World Trade Organisation director general who stressed that there should be cooperation between the WTO and UNCTAD. He thought that if there were moves to get rid of trade barriers then there might be a need to overcome the problems for developing countries by giving aid for trade.

It was recognised at the meeting that any gains from free trade could lead to problems for small vulnerable economies.

It might be noted here that whilst the USA has often suggested the importance of free trade, its own farming policies have often had very large-scale subsidies to the agricultural sector. Within the EU, there have been some moves to getting rid of subsidies to farmers.

UNCTAD, apart from these conferences has also published reports on the digital divide, which shows how there are major differences as one might expect between countries with ready access to ICT, and the many others, which do not have such access.

UNCTAD is also trying to see how far there could be freer access to newer software.

Self-examination Questions

1. Since the time of Ricardo in the 18th century many economists have suggested that free trade works to give optimum solutions. Why have so many countries whether rich or poor in practice not taken advantage of the system?

2. Some people have suggested that use of modern technology might help developing countries to be able to skip a generation with mobile phones avoiding the need for a costly infrastructure. How far is this a valid point of view? What would happen if a cheap wind-up or solar powered computer could be developed?

3. Does greater information about prices work in the interest of both developed and developing countries?

4. Why might tourism in particular for poor countries be a method of overcoming the many trade barriers which in practice exist in international trade? Are there however, any problems with developing the tourist industry for the rest of the community?

35.18: Information Technology and Changes in Society

One of the features of modern years has been that the predicted number of people working at home which the CBI and the TUC suggested in the 1990s would grow to around 6 million by the year 2000 has not come about. However, there have been more people working at home although it is difficult to find the precise number, partly because some of the poorer people may not be in the income tax bracket. Other changes are that some people go to work fewer days in the week but work at home for some of the time.

Whilst fax machines have been in existence for many years, they have largely been superseded by electronic mail usually referred to as e-mail. This is probably because whereas fax was very good for sending information which had already been produced such as diagrams, plans and so on, email is more instant and the costs of transmitting the information especially with the advent of broadband has been very small and in some cases the marginal cost is zero. However, fax can still be useful where people receive hand written information, with letters, which can be quickly sent from one form to another. In some cases, email can be used in conjunction with scanners, with the use of optical character recognition (OCR) which reads and interprets the handwriting. This is quite helpful.

Companies would prefer people to work from home in some respects, i.e. that they then save the costs of the office. In some cases, firms have tried to use the prestige of having London phone numbers, which can then readily be sent on to offices not merely in the UK but throughout the world. This change in prices of telecommunications has meant that in many cases, call centres can be developed overseas and this is noticeable with some of the rail enquiries, which are now transmitted to and from India. India has well-educated people who speak English but at a far lower wage than they would get within the UK.

Video conferencing or similar systems have been talked about since the early 1980s. The advantages are that it reduces the cost of travel or in some cases may eliminate it. On the other hand, at many conferences people pick up non-verbal communication, which is more difficult to obtain when people are apart. The informal atmosphere after conferences may be helpful although in other cases it could be argued as EJ Mishan argued in the past that some conferences are there to prove that people are important.

Part of the problem of working from home is that there is no interaction and there is anecdotal evidence that people do not regard working at home as having the same social status.

There has been a strong decline in the number of secretaries in many organisations. Although it could be argued that the need for transcription machines and use of secretaries might well make many businesses more efficient rather than having people who are untrained using word processing, sitting in front of computers on their desks. This has two major disadvantages. The first is that many people cannot word process very efficiently and the second is that the opportunity cost of such low speeds in word processing is a major problem. There is also the point that many managers' command of language is relatively limited whereas a good executive secretary will often be able to sort these matters out.

Some people have talked about the growth of the virtual organisation i.e. that in practice people do not need to reach each other very often and so large scale offices might well become a thing of the past except where there is a need for people to meet customers directly.

Simulation can be readily seen in most computer games and can be helpful for architects and planners to be able to look at new buildings and to see what problems, if any, might arise.

The Buchanan report Traffic in Towns, indicated that whilst there is a lot of information about travel between cities and within cities relatively little had been looked at in terms of access between and within a building. In some cases, as with the former steel plant in South Wales the building that housed the plant was over four miles (7 kilometres) long so that internal travel could be a major problem.

Computer aided design is used in many different industries; it can be used in the case of car assembly plants. It helps businesses since they no longer have to employ people whose main ability was to provide good drawings and computer aided design can give the appearance of three dimensions. Clients can quickly have their different needs catered for if they find that the original design is not to their liking.

Computer aided design may also help to reduce the number of faults which can be tested using basic statistical techniques such as the Poisson distribution. It can also test that there is compatibility between different units of production. If this is the case, the standard container size tends to be 9ft 6″ by 8ft by a multiple of 10ft then ideally, packages do not want to be 2ft 1in since this would mean there is a considerable amount of open and empty space within the containers.

There have also been cases of what is sometimes called CNC (Computer Numerically Controlled) machines. Again using computers can help in terms of quality control since the firms can specify that any components or other parts, which are beyond certain range such as greater than two standard deviations from the mean, could be rejected.

Computer aided design is meant to be able to reduce lead times i.e. the time between the original design and the production. This would well be important in industries such as vehicle assembly, where there is a considerable time lag between the original concept and that of production. This may be very useful when firms are planning to launch new products.

Perhaps paradoxically this can be important in the computer industry, when clearly computer firms face a trade-off between having a product, which is good and having a product, which is slightly in the ahead of its rivals.

Computer aided design can be used in such fields as clothes and shoes when people can have a scanner showing the foot size and then pairs of shoes which are made to the individual specification. To some extent, this can give mass customisation. In the past, we have either had the advantages of mass production, which gives low prices but not necessarily, what the consumer really wants. On the other hand one off production, which happens in clothes and shoes, can be helpful to people such as, those who have very large feet. Made to measure items like shoes are can be very expensive.

Self-examination Questions

1. How far can Computer Aided Design help to individualise products and thus give the advantage of mass productions with the individuality, which does not normally occur?

2. What is meant by the virtual organisation? Is it likely to become more important in the future?

3. How far is it possible to avoid poor product launches using computers?

4. How has improved communication systems increased the possibility for firms to obtain people from different locations?

5. How far does technology enable people to work either in smaller offices or at home? What are the social implications of this for both firms and societies?

35.19: The Soap Industry

The soap industry is an unusual one. This is because it is possible to produce soap with relatively little machinery and historically many small firms and chemists did this. However, the soap industry has been dominated by marketing and therefore most of the soap industry is produced by large firms. Amongst the large firms are those of Unilever, which is a multinational. Unilever produces not only soaps but also detergents, ice-creams and at one stage through Walls produced meats, etc.

The soap industry is also one in which there is both price differentiation and price discrimination. This can readily be seen at Christmas time when heavily packaged soaps will be sold at a much higher price than can be accounted for by differences in costs between these and the basic market.

There is also another major firm in the industry i.e. Colgate Palmolive which was originally formed in 1912. The other major competitor is Procter & Gamble. Marketing soaps can take place through television and often through journals. In recent years there has been an increase in own brands of major supermarkets as well as from Boots the Chemist. Whilst there have been some alternatives to soap, using pump action containers, the soap market is still a very large one. The soap market is one in which price discrimination is very important as is easily seen at Christmas time when similar soaps will sell for a higher price because of the packaging such as those in baskets.

Firms such as The Body Shop International PLC have introduced a new concept into the skin, and body care market. The Body Shop now has 2400 stores in over 61 countries. It claims that none of their products are tested on animals. It also tries to have natural ingredients, which are produced by small producer communities. It also claims that because of information gathered in 2010 the company is going to try helping the environment.

Self-examination Questions

1. Why if it is easy to make soap is the market dominated by a few main firms?

2. Why is advertising so important in this industry? Where does the advertising take place and what does this imply about who buys the soap products?

3. Why do some people buy liquid hand wash as an alternative to soap?

4. Why has a firm such as Body Shop managed to be very successful in selling items including soaps?

35.20: The EU and Central Government

The EU failed in its attempt to have a new constitution in 2005. One of the reasons why it needed this was because ten new countries had entered the EU in 2004 (the biggest enlargement so far in terms of number of countries and population). It has also changed numbers again with 3 new entrants bringing the total in 2013 to 28. Generally, the EU favours competition between member states as long as they are on a level footing. However, the EU also recognises that there should be social legislation to ensure that the worst aspects of capitalism are remedied. One of the problems of the free market is that there can be large-scale unemployment as was shown in the 1930s. If firms are monopsony ones, they may be able to pay very low wages since workers will have little choice about where they work. One of the features of the EU has been the social charter which the UK has been reluctant to bring in to force in this country. There is a working hours directive, which tries to ensure that no workers work excessive hours. This concept is nothing new, back in the 19th century there were restrictions on the numbers of hours that most men and women could work.

Where taxation is different between different countries the EU may have a view if it means that trade seems to be impaired. There have been problems with the so-called booze cruise where people take advantage of lower taxation on items such as cigarettes and drink especially wines and spirits. Different governments take different views on so-called demerit goods (demerit goods are those which the government thinks are bad for society as a whole).

The EU was meant to have a fuel policy. This is partly because the EU does not wish to have different fuel costs in different countries, which could help artificially some countries to be able to export goods using these fuels more cheaply than others. Fuel is in many cases a large part of the total costs of production so that a lower fuel cost to one firm is likely to give it a competitive advantage over others. The move to have new fuel policies has been recognised by the EU, as most other countries do not wish to be reliant on unstable regimes. This could mean that if fuel flows were not forthcoming that it could lead to major problems for industry as well as great hardship for individuals.

The EU as well is concerned about the environmental consequences of fossil fuels and all the members have signed the Kyoto agreement. One of the features of this environmental concern has also been that the EU is concerned that the problems of waste cause several different problems including use of more land and problems of pollution.

In 2002, the majority of members agreed to have the Euro as a common currency. This has the advantage to ordinary people that they do not have to worry about transaction costs. Typically, in the UK the high street banks have about a 10% margin between the price at which they offer currency and the price at which they are willing to buy it. It also has the advantage to firms that they can have a common price for all the countries which take the Euro, rather than having to be concerned about fluctuations in currency of those member states. It also makes it much easier for firms to be able to invest in factories and plants since the total costs of the project will not vary because of changes in the price of currency. However, this does mean that the control of interest rates has to be determined centrally by the European central bank.

The EU as a whole has an increasing number of women working both full and part time. The EU has tried to have legislation which ensures that men and women are employed on a similar basis, and that people are not discriminated against on the ground of gender.

In the UK, the Government has tried to encourage mothers to return to work when the children are young by providing more nursery places. There have been some concerns in Germany in particular, that because more women work that the birth rate has fallen quite dramatically.

Because of trying to give equality of treatment, fathers have been encouraged to be able to take time off work (paternity leave). It is hoped that this might give a better family structure.

The government in the UK has been concerned about energy use and in early 2006; a review suggested that the government might consider building new nuclear plants. In 2013 the government announced that it would go ahead with a nuclear plant renewal. One of the ways of trying to reduce energy would be to have fewer out of town shopping sites, such as Lakeside in Essex, and Bluewater in Kent. The government has gone further than this and local authorities are now meant to look at planning as a whole and taking into account the environmental consequences.

Self-examination Questions

1. Why has the EU imposed a working hours directive? Will the increased costs of complying with this necessarily be passed on to consumers?

2. What effect would there be if the EU managed to have a common taxation policy on items such as fuel, alcohol and tobacco. What, if any, would be the advantages and disadvantages of such a move?

3. Why might it be important for consumers to be aware of energy costs when buying electrical goods? What are the total costs in many cases of electricity for refrigerators, freezers, compared with the initial costs of purchase? Are consumers aware of the total costs? What might this suggest about rationality of consumers?

4. Why might the EU as a whole be concerned about the ways in which some white goods such as refrigerators are disposed of?

5. If the EU zone as a whole has low interest rates, what effects, if any, does this have on UK firms and farms?

6. What effects, if any, does the increase in the number of women working both full time and part time have on the typical EU firm? How should such firms try to react to the changes?

7. In the UK, the Government has tried to encourage more women to work providing better facilities for nursery education. This has still not gone as far as in countries such as Sweden. What will be the social consequences if the Government succeeds in getting more women to go to work?

8. Government proposals meant that fathers could take up some of the women's rights if the women agreed within the first six months after a baby was born. What are the reasons for such a move and what effect would it have on British firms?

9. What have been the effects of out-of-town shopping centres? If the Government wishes to try to keep to energy targets, does the use of out of town shopping centres help or hinder this move?

10. Local authorities are meant to look at environmental consequences of new and present developments across the board whether they are in the private sector or public sector. In what ways could energy be reduced if they succeed in this task?

Revision Questions

The following section looks at a sample of questions that you may encounter in your management and business examinations or course work. The answers provided are not necessarily exhaustive but try to cover the main pertinent issues in each question.

Question 1:

How does political stability of a country affect business?

One might need to distinguish between the stability of government i.e. whether governments change hands frequently and the overall instability of the country. For example during the 1950s, both France and Italy had many governments, and in the case of Italy, this has often continued. This does not however seem to have affected economic performance very much, partly because in France the civil servants who tend to be from one main institution have had considerable ability in managing the economy.

On the other hand the instability of some other countries has not been reflected in the change at the top, since in many cases the same dictator has remained there, but the country has had a reputation for not repaying debts. This happened for example during the 1990s when the commercial banks in the UK thought they could make large sums of money from lending overseas. In many cases of this the debt has remained even when a new more democratic government has taken over.

If a country has a reputation for instability this may well affect the foreign exchange market and countries in this situation will often find that imports become extremely expensive compared to the rest of the goods and services, which the country provided. This is particularly a problem for many non-oil-producing countries. These countries have to import fuel, and therefore because fuel costs are often a significant part of other products further costs will rise considerably.

In some countries there has been a prevailing black market. This has arisen not just in capitalist countries but also for example in much of Eastern Europe. In the 1980's, tourists were often asked to sell clothes which were better than the clothes which were make under the Gosplan aegis. Gosplan was the name of the committee under the Soviet Union, which was responsible for the economic coordination of plans from 1921 onwards.

Governments, which are very weak, will often be unable to control their borders and therefore smuggling is often rife. This means that if the government tries to impose high taxes, which are not there in neighbouring countries, they are unlikely to obtain much revenue from this.

Restrictions on foreign currency may be there but are often widely evaded.

A country, which has a reputation for being unstable, is unlikely to be able to issue gilts or the equivalent, except at very high rates of interest because investors outside perceive the government to be a high-risk area.

In some cases where there has been civil war etc., then this will have many detrimental effects apart from loss of life and injury. Firms within the country may find it difficult to get supplies to and from other parts of the country.

In 2013/14 following the 'Arab spring' and revolutions in a number of different countries including Tunisia, Egypt and Libya, many overseas people may be more reluctant to trade with these countries because of fears about the stability.

The economic instability in Cyprus has meant that it is more difficult to withdraw money from the banks in that country which may cause major problems. In Greece there has been a major problem which has caused high rates of unemployment, particularly amongst the young and therefore this in turn will cause problems with businesses whose target market includes this. On the other hand, since many young people may wish to emigrate this could mean opportunities to obtain good quality staff.

There may also be a shortage of skilled labour, since these people will be engaged elsewhere.

Question 2:

To what extent does the size of an organisation alter the way in which it is managed?

The very small organisation will have a short chain of command, and usually a small span of control for the individual manager.

The short span of control should make it easier for the manager to know the staff that he or she is working with, and therefore to know their talents and their limitations. There should be little problem of feedback to managers with the short chain of command, but there is a risk that an authoritarian manager who can make quick decisions may ignore this feedback.

Whilst most textbooks suggest that quick decision-making is good it may lead to impulsive decisions, which are unchecked, and therefore this is one of the many reasons why it is estimated that 7 out of 10 new firms in the UK do not last 5 years. There are of course other reasons as well, e.g. lack of expertise in certain fields such as marketing and costing.

Larger organisations tend to be more impersonal and more in line with Weber's comments about bureaucracy. Weber identified a number of features of bureaucratic organisations, which he assumed would prevail whether they were in the private or public sectors. Some of these features are that there will be a set of written rules, which have to be obeyed, and that decision-making is impersonal. By this, he meant that rules are not altered merely because the people making the decision know the person.

This has occasionally been referred to as red tape, but does have some advantages.

Larger organisations will tend to have more specialists in most cases. This will be especially true if the departmental system is the main one and particularly if the head of departments have to have their own specialisation e.g. the accounts department will be headed by someone who has professional accounting qualifications. The supply manager will almost certainly be a member of the Chartered Institute of Purchasing and Supply and the head of human resources as it is often now known although sometimes still referred to as the personnel department will also be qualified in that sphere. Part of the problem with this system is that lateral communication often becomes very difficult since each of the departments will have its own jargon.

C S Lewis the well-known children's writer as well as being a theologian referred in one of his books to the concept of the insider and the outsider with the insiders protecting their territory to some extent with language, which was designed to keep out outsiders. This is quite common in many business organisations.

The larger organisation will often have written rules not only applying to employees but it is much more likely to rely on a series of written contracts. Sometimes this can reach great proportions as for example Christian Wolmar demonstrates in his book entitled 'On the wrong line' which shows the sheer bureaucracy which applied with the privatisation of British Rail and the setting up of the former Railtrack. Smaller organisations by contrast will often not have a set of contracts when dealing with suppliers but will rely much more on their personal expertise in judging whether firms are reliable or not.

The allocation of tasks in larger firms will reflect the specialist nature of the organisation, for example in a large life assurance office the actuarial department may have people who are solely devoted to looking at surrender values of life assurance policies or to pension schemes and so on.

However, we might note that the concept of size applies to branches or depots in some cases as well as to the overall size of the organisation. We can readily see this, for example, in the education sector where the Department of Education and county councils or unitary councils in the UK have overall control of education. The differences between schools can be quite considerable, the small village school with a few teachers will have a quite different atmosphere to those of the larger comprehensive or even grammar schools.

Question 3:

How far does technology help or hinder communications within an organisation?

Technology makes communications much easier with the use of emails and fax. Organisations should be able to communication more easily with a wide variety of stakeholders. However, this tends to make modern organisations impersonal.

If we look at any organisation, there are the formal channels, which will often be shown on an organisation chart. What is very noticeable in most organisations is that information flows more easily down the chain of command than it does upwards. Many managers and workers complain that there seems to be an invisible barrier, which prevents communications going from the bottom to the top. People can send emails very quickly to a wide variety of people, and there is a danger that people at the bottom become overwhelmed with information without in many cases any indication of what the priorities should be. Whilst originally many people talked about the paperless office which, in practice does not work for some organisations. The example of the Audit Commission which looks at expenditure, tells its employees that all emails have to be transformed into a hard copy.

Horizontal communications i.e. between different departments or even at the same level within the department may be awkward and it has been suggested that people suffered from lack of exercise because they sent emails to other colleagues rather than walking round. The lack of exercise may not be important but the lack of face-to-face communication could be. In many cases, non-verbal communication may indicate the tone of the communication much better than written communication. One of the problems with emails is that, whilst they are efficient and provide a written record, they do not have the advantage of verbal communication i.e. that a lot of the time we recognise by the sound of someone's voice or the way in which they look whether people understand or not.

In many cases, because few people are taught word processing skills workers may well key in information at a slow rate. In many cases this would be much quicker in terms of speech and possibly telephones using voice mail especially since important messages are kept and this might well be more efficient.

Informal communications tend to become less frequent especially with tall structures where there are several layers within the organisation. In many cases, the technology is irrelevant since if managers do not wish to get feedback they will not get it whatever the type of technology employed.

There is the great danger that people do not know what was going on and this can apply whether it is the Fukushima Daicchi Nuclear Power Plant where it was very inefficient in terms of protection from natural disasters or within private sector firms such as Railtrack. There seemed to be severe difficulties between Railtrack and the vast number of sub-contractors which in many cases lead to both cost rising rapidly as well as insufficient scrutiny of safety. One might assume that a nuclear power station would have efficient technology. People do not wish to communicate since then the outside managers can be kept misinformed, it could be argued further that with less technology managers would wish to see for themselves what was going on. This could equally apply to the railways

There are a number of barriers to effective communication. One of these is that in many cases people use inappropriate language for example jargon which people do not understand. This has often been seen in railway communications where railway employees will use the phrase 'down line and up line' which is meaningful to most railway employees but not to the typical passenger. Pompous language is often used and there seems little point in calling something a strategy when it might as well be called a plan. Face to face communication does not entirely remove these barriers but a good communicator should notice from the recipient if something is not understood where technology such as emails or faxes does not have this advantage.

In some cases especially with multi nationals there may be little awareness of time differences, it is usual for firms to be unaware of this and therefore messages will be sent which are meant to be urgent without taking account of this. People may well choose an inappropriate form of medium. For example, many years ago when the author worked as an advisor on dangerous goods, firms could use the telephone to ask detailed questions about chemicals as well as the technical plans. This was almost impossible to understand and write down. A letter would have been preferable so that the information could be accurately recorded. In this case, email nowadays would be more appropriate.

Too often, the idea that the recipient has received and understood the message is taken for granted. This is very noticeable for example with sending messages to Companies House where no acknowledgement was made, and loss of messages seems to be frequent. In some cases, people may simply ignore messages, which they do not want to hear.

One of the problems with technology is that there is a danger that it is over reliant on one single source, so that if there is a power cut, which is common in many poorer countries that it may be difficult to communicate with the organisation.

One possibility in the very short term is that if laptops are available, providing they are fully charged they can be used if the problem is likely to be resolved quickly. Some larger firms may have emergency electricity supplies which can help overcome the problem. Some firms such as 'The Bunker' have their own emergency power supplies.

There is also the danger, which is being highlighted in 2013, that people can hack into information, whether it is commercially confidential or affecting government security means that privacy cannot be taken for granted. WikiLeaks and Edward Snowden (a former employee of a security firm) highlighted the problems. Apart from deliberate leaks, because information can be stored on memory sticks which can be easily mislaid, large scale information may be found by people who see a commercial advantage in gaining the information. Industrial espionage is fairly common. Fraud using computers is quite common. In June 2013 it was estimated that fraud as a whole cost the United Kingdom around £73 billion and a good deal of this was computer generated.

Question 4:

What factors cause changes and how can firms respond to these changes?

Some firms have had to respond to their rivals. For example, IBM for a long while had a near monopoly on mainframe computers. Mainframe computers were used by a relatively small number of large firms. For example, as late as the early 1970s the Civil Service did not own all its own computers but hired in the capacity on other peoples. However, with the rise of the personal computers and small computers from the early 1980s more firms entered the market. For a long while IBM were able to resist this, but eventually as the computers got cheaper IBM were forced to realise that they needed to do something and therefore itself moved into the what is sometimes called the personal computer market, but in many cases is used by small firms.

In other cases firms have got to the saturation or decline stage of the product life cycle, and therefore have a choice. They can be faced with a declining market for either their product or alternatively they try to find new uses for their existing products or alternatively they try to find a new product. For example, we can say that in the case of bicycles, which the economist would regard as an inferior good i.e. meaning that, as incomes rise sales are likely to fall, so cycle manufacturers move into BMX or the equivalent bikes whilst others introduced all terrain cycles more often known as mountain bikes.

People have become more aware of the environment in the UK since the 1970s and 1980s, partly because of the pressure groups such as Friends of the Earth and Greenpeace. It might also be thought to be an income elastic concept i.e. that as people become richer and have more goods and services they also want to live in an area, which is freer from pollution. Some people have suggested that there is a trade off between jobs and green pressures, but other people such as the founders of the Body Shop realise that they could make and sell products, which were more environmentally friendly. It is noticeable that by this period there are some dedicated green shops whilst other firms will claim that their products are environmentally friendly. People might resist changes due to social and technical factors.

We might need to look at the people who make changes within the organisation. The managers within the organisation that may make changes possible include computer programmers who have a considerable degree of technical expertise and will want the firm to take advantage of the latest results of the chip revolution. Accountants too may wish to change the firm to take advantage of different taxation laws as well as changes in which information has to be presented especially in the light of financial scandals such as that of Enron the biggest bankruptcy so far. Lawyers too may wish to make changes partly to comply with different legislation for example about personnel since the Equality Act 2010. Lawyers will almost certainly be advising firms about how to comply with the disability acts for example how people can approach and gain entry to shops and other premises.

However, the people who make changes with the organisation may well not be professional in their approach to how workers in the organisation will react to changes. People when faced with changes will tend to ask firstly how it will affect them and secondly how it will affect their colleagues. Pro-active firms will try to work out the answers to this rather than waiting for the reactions of the workers or the Trade Unions. In the transport industry a great deal of attention was paid to technology during the so-called 'container revolution'. This was wider than just merely the use of multi modal transport, but also had an impact upon other methods of loading including the use of roll on roll off ferries, palletisation and packaged timber. All of these were aimed at reducing the time taken to load and unload ships and vehicles, but insufficient attention was often paid to how workers would feel about these changess. If managers used role-play, they might have dealt with matters better.

Firms can help to overcome problems by inviting people to participate in the decision process. In some cases there will be adverse effects on individuals, but if people are not informed that it is likely that all of the people will tend to resist change, where as if there is participation the numbers of people resisting it may well fall. It is not merely within the private sector that decision-making should be better, for example the government has made frequent changes to the way which classroom teaching and management with very little reference to the needs of staff, whether they be head teachers or other teachers. In 2005 the education secretary Ruth Kelly suggested that schools should be open all day, which would help working parents. It was not obvious that the implications for either the working families or the children were considered.

Firms when making changes should use open language i.e. language which people understand rather than pompous jargon. People may well not use open language because in some cases those in authority are themselves insecure and feel threatened. In other cases jargon may be used because people are too much preoccupied with the technical details rather than the effects upon people.

The use of role-playing can be helpful since then firms and other organisations might be able to anticipate problems more easily and then try to see how the problems could be overcome.

This could be as simple as testing new computer software with ordinary people rather than computer specialists. There have been many examples where new websites have been used but have not been adequately tested to see whether ordinary people can use them effectively. It could be tested using the equivalent of mystery shoppers in the same way that some large supermarket chains have done to check whether it is easy to understand instructions to workers if new equipment is being used or if new legislation requires a different approach to safety.

The EU has wanted a different type of fishing policy so that this will offer new opportunities to the fishing fleet since at the moment a great deal of dead fish has to be thrown in to the sea. The EU also wishes to have a more environmental approach to agriculture which should mean that smaller farms gain.

In the United Kingdom there has been a ban on smoking in public places and offices. This should help to avoid the risks in passive smoking as well as reducing the number of fires caused by cigarettes starting fires. Public houses may lose some of their existing customers but may diversify into selling more meals to families who appreciate a smoke-free atmosphere.

Question 5:

Explain, with relevant examples, how organisations might carry out research surveys?

One of the first steps is to consider why the survey should be carried out is to establish the purpose of the survey. There is little point for example in asking whether people would buy a book on a subject without also specifying the price. Similarly, a firm wishing to put on a new bus service will generally find that more people will claim they will use it even if fares are specified than is actually the case. It nevertheless gives some indication of potential demand. The firm, which wishes the survey to be carried out, will need to consider how much money it can afford to spend and what degree of accuracy it needs. For example generally the accuracy of a sample depends partly upon the number of people who take part, but the relationship is not as people expect i.e. one would need to have a sample four times the size in order to improve accuracy by a factor of two.

When carrying out a survey ideally we would want to have a random sample, which is representative of the whole and where statistical analysis can be carried out. However, to get a random survey of the population may be more difficult than at first sight. We can for example get hold of the electoral register relatively easily and several websites will help us to find out details of where people live. However, some people may choose not to be registered in the first place and this applied particularly in the UK when the community charge more often called the poll tax was enforced. This will matter for some products rather than for others. For example if we were selling house insurance then the people who have not registered probably do not matter. On the other hand since the people who are not registered will tend to be disproportionately the poor and the young then if we were selling CDs or DVDs then this might be more important.

In some cases where we know what the likely population is going to be of a particular age group, ethnic group etc we might want to have a quota sample where more people are asked from those particular groups. This could apply to selling pop music. At the other end of the age scale, it may be that, more people of an older age will prefer certain types of music such as classical music or films.

Many firms will then carry out a survey in order to iron out any ambiguities. For example, it is quite common to have a question which cannot be easily answered. In travel surveys sometimes people will ask how people got to the particular shopping centre and will list rail, bus, taxi, car, walking but in some cases people might have got both a bus and a train. Which one are they then meant to answer? The question would therefore need to be re-phrased. People in the UK are often reluctant to give their incomes even when in some cases it is quite easy to obtain the information particularly for people in the public sector where the salary scales are published. Therefore, we might well find that whilst we would like to have exact incomes people are more likely to respond to asking for a broad income band rather than a specific answer. In some cases, as for example with high street interviews, people may not know their precise income and even less the total family income without further research and people are unlikely to do this in a survey.

We also need to think how we are going to amend the questionnaires because of the pilot survey. We might find as well that more difficult questions or possibly embarrassing questions i.e. about income will be at the end of the survey. We also may find that in some cases that it is sensible to amend it so that some sections are skipped. For example if people are not car owners then asking them about when their car insurance is running out and what factors determine their choice of this would be irrelevant and so it might be sensible to say for non-car owners skip to question 16 rather than ploughing through questions 12 – 15.

If we are going to use interviewers, we need to ensure that interviewers are of the right type and that they are properly briefed. If they are carrying out door-to-door surveys then they will need to be reasonably resilient but also need to be observant. For example, people who have on their door 'We are happy to stay with British Gas' may well be very rude to people on the doorstep who ask them about whether they wish to change their gas supplier. Similarly, other people will have notices saying they do not want such people calling. Interviewers will need to have the purpose of the survey explained to them and also to try to make sure they are neither too easily intimidated nor too persistent when they might annoy potential customers. If they are interviewing within peoples' houses then they will be reminded that if for example if they belong to a reputable organisation that they have the necessary identity with them. They will also been told about being discrete with information i.e. they do not pass it on to unauthorised people.

Questions should have been checked to ensure that they are unambiguous before being printed. If the people conducting the survey want to get fast results, then closed questions should be used. On the other hand, if they are trying to find out why people may not be buying an existing product there may need to be some open ended questions. For example a rail company might be proud of its services but trying to find out why some car owners would not use them. Therefore they might need to ask what other factors deter people from using such services. The answers to this might however been picked up earlier in a pilot survey in September 2005. One speaker identified perception of safety at stations as being a problem, even though the reality was that stations themselves are usually safe. However, the places around the station may be less safe. The interviewers will need to be aware of whether they are carrying out a random sample or a quota sample for example some companies will specify that they want a number of people within a particular age group 40 – 59. Clearly again here tact will be necessary since women in particular may be reluctant to admit that they are over 40. Once the survey has been finished, there may be a need to debrief the interviewers. This is to find out if there were any other factors, such as: problems with questions, if people were reluctant to answer or whether biased people were answering. It is quite likely that high street interviews will give more prominence to people who are not working since people working even if they are in the high street at their lunchtime may well have less time to answer questions.

The data will then be analysed but even nowadays when most surveys are analysed using computers a manual sort might be helpful particularly if there are inconsistencies. For example if for one question a person says they do not have a television but later on in another section says they watch so many hours per week, one might need to wonder why this is so. Even before the survey has been taken out some draft tables might have been inserted although once the results are there any unexpected results may need to be tabulated. A report will usually go alongside the tables. For example a report on tourism might indicate not only how many people travelled, but also the characteristics of passengers.

The government and businesses often use surveys of purchasing managers as a guide to future economic behaviour.

Question 6:

What have been the main external changes facing organisations in the last 20 years, how can firms react to these?

In 2013 it was reported that 1 million people over retirement age were currently employed in the United Kingdom. Whilst the healthy living age has increased, it has not done this to the same extent as the change in life expectancy, so there may need to be modifications of premises, partly to conform with disability acts, and partly because this might help to retain existing workers who may have a wealth of knowledge and skills. There is no automatic retirement default age now in the United Kingdom and some old people can be dynamic and learn new skills. At the other end of the age spectrum many young people are unemployed. The idea that they are all immature is an unhelpful stereotype.

In 2013 the European Union is under pressure to create more jobs for both young and old.

At the other end of the age scale, there has been an increase, not just within the United Kingdom but in many parts of the European Union of younger people who are Not in Employment, Education or Training (NEETs) and both governments and business organisations need to consider the implications of this. This could include fewer people in this age group buying houses and related purchases such as furniture. They will also have less money to spend on leisure activities.

One of the major changes has been that of demographic factors. In the UK for example there has been a decline in the number of young people, but as people live longer for the first time the UK has more over 65 year olds than under 16 year olds. This will affect firms in terms of both demand and employment. A cause of the 2007 'Credit Crunch' was that unemployment rose. We might therefore expect firms to concentrate less comparatively on the demands of the young, for example for toys and more for the elderly for example for leisure travel. It also means that in the longer term depending partly on recessions that firms may need to try to keep these older people within the firms since they have experience.

There has been generally a concept that the government should intervene less at the micro level although this does not mean that the need for consumer protection is not there. The type of consumer protection however may need to be altered for example 20 years ago people would not have brought goods and services over the Internet and now it is more difficult to see how the government can intervene to prevent false claims for goods, which are sold through this medium.

The motivation of employees may well have changed, as there has been a massive rise in unemployment until the early 1990s and a subsequent decline. However, security of employment may have become more important to many members. Generally, the trade unions have also reacted to the insecurity and would be more concerned about this rather than about wage claims, which would have been a feature of the 1970s.

There have also been changes in the ethnic mix of the population, which may need to be catered for, such as in the food market, whether raw foods or processed ones. There have long been Chinese and Indian restaurants and also specialist food shops in Chinatown in London. More recently, there have been specialist Polish food shops in many areas. It may alter as well the demand for entertainment, which could mean that large-scale organisations might consider different types of films or plays. It can also offer opportunities to smaller organisations which may be able to find a niche market.

Firms and governments have become more aware of climate change, and this has meant that organisations have become aware of the phrase carbon footprint and some organisations such as Marks & Spencer have advertised widely that they are reacting to this, since there is no plan B.

There has been an increase in size of the European union from 15 countries to 28, and this has meant that it is easier to recruit workers from a wider pool of labour than in the past, and also easier generally to sell to countries within the European Union.

It also means however that there is more competition from these countries and organisations will need to consider whether they cooperate with possible competitors, or in some cases to consider relocation of branches or possibly the whole organisation.

The price of both the computer software and hardware has fallen rapidly so that information about sales can be conveyed almost immediately from the electronic point of sale (EPOS) to managers so that they should be able to react more quickly to changes in demand and to alter stocks or sometimes production much more quickly. The transport industry can now use computers plus social networking to convey information to actual and potential customers about any delays to the system.

The rapid increase in economic growth in countries such as China means that imports from China are very important especially for solar panels; although in 2013 there have been complaints about dumping (the selling of a product at a lower cost than its own production cost or home market cost) which has caused international tensions between China and other countries including the United States. There has been a rapid increase in solar power in countries such as Australia and Kenya. There have also been grants to solar power in the United Kingdom and the price of solar energy has fallen rapidly. As the price of oil has increased more emphasis has been placed on renewable resources.

China is now a major export target for many countries including the United Kingdom, and organisations such as link to China, have become important.

Whilst China and India have hit the headlines for the economic growth other countries such as Qatar now has perhaps the highest gross national product per head of any country, and therefore this has been a major target for many construction industries, especially when it is due to have major sporting events such as the football World Cup in 2022.

Question 7:

Show how the different functions of management can be applied to an organisation?

Henri Fayol suggested that there were several main elements of management, although according to him many businesses engaged so much time in administration that the idea that management embraced the others was all too often forgotten. He wrote this in 1930 but the same problems can still be identified in the early part of the 21st century. The elements that he suggested include administration, planning, staffing, organising, co-ordinating and controlling. If we look at each of these in turn, we could take for example what happened within British Railways before it was privatised. Now because of privatisation, not all the functions would be carried out within the same organisation and it would probably be easier therefore to see it within a large-scale organisation, which carries out these functions.

We can see that administration is required, to ensure that passengers and freight customers know where to obtain details of fares or for freight charges. This is quite complicated especially given that the railways control over 2000 stations. It is also complicated, as the railways will charge different fares at different periods since the price elasticity of demand will vary between these periods. In many cases, therefore there are many different fares between different stations for both price differentiation and price discrimination reasons.

British railways management often complained that they could not plan for the future because of government lack of long term planning. They said that they could cope with almost any government decisions as long as they had a stable environment in which to operate. They needed long planning since projects such as electrification of routes took a long while to come to fruition. Ideally what should have happened both then and now, is that there should have been long term plans for electrification to avoid the over reliance on one source of fuel. It should have also taken place because electrification has long term benefits such as longer life of the motive power, and because it is not reliant on one source of fuel. This gives the opportunities to take advantage of future developments whether they are off shore turbines using wind power, wave power and so on.

It would also give the flexibility of routes for existing electric stock, even allowing for the fact that in the UK the South Eastern corner of the UK has a different system of third rail electrification whereas all the other parts of the UK have a system of overhead wires. Planning for electrification takes quite a while because bridges have to be altered if there are overhead wires and this in turn may mean a disruption both to the railways and possibly to road users. Planning is particularly important on the railways because of the length of life of assets, which is much longer than some other modes of transport such as road freight where typically road haulage vehicles have a life of only 5 years. There is also a need for planning to ensure that staff is adequately trained in the right numbers. One of the poor features in the immediate privatisation process was that some operators such as South West trains tried to reduce costs by cutting down on drivers, only to find out that they had a longer-term problem.

There is a need for organisation to ensure that the activities take place in the interest of both the business and its customers. Ideally, the organisation should have been given objectives so that the external effects of the railways were taken into account. This was not done in the 1960s when, as a result of the Beeching report (unofficially entitled 'The reshaping of British railways'), railways cut down on the number of stations and routes very considerably, often based on very faulty data. For example, they looked at revenue at stations where in many cases seaside resorts have very little revenue but might have been worthwhile keeping since people travelled to the seaside resorts.

Commanding is important, particularly in terms of safety. There are risks, which were shown inherently in the original private companies, but which unfortunately continued under both nationalisation and subsequent privatisation that safety has not always been sufficiently thorough. Although in fairness to the railways, they have a much better safety record than almost any other mode of transport.

Commanding however needs to take account of feedback since otherwise risks, which drivers are aware off, might need to be taken into account.

Co-ordination of activities is quite difficult especially when historically the railways often had different objectives under different managers, which continued long after they were a nationalised concern in 1947.

The problems of coordination can still be seen when there are adverse weather conditions so that information from the train operating companies does not always get passed on to Network Rail and vice versa.

Question 8:

Show with reference to specific industries how management can try to define what is the effective demand for their products or services?

If using the previous example of the railways, designing a questionnaire would be a useful way finding out about customer's requirements. The first step would be to think what the railways want to find out in the first place. A simple vague answer such as trying to find out what customers want is obviously not sufficiently helpful to give rise to any meaningful information, which the operators can use. They therefore need to put these ideas into a format, which is in some ways able to give more information about the services which they provide. If they wish to carry out a survey then they will need to think what sample size they require; are they thinking about having a census of all passengers or a smaller sample. A census is helpful because it involves a very large number of passengers, but on the other hand, the time taken to process the information may make it less helpful although computers should help to speed up the process. The major problem is likely to be one of costs. The accuracy of answers will be more difficult to test. It could be argued that however with modern computer techniques, that the business of analysis results is much faster. Almost any business will be faced with the concept of what accuracy they require, since there will almost certainly be a trade-off between cost and accuracy. A complete census with detailed information might be the most accurate but clearly pursuing the last few passengers to give information might well be very expensive and there would still be the problem anyway of non-responses.

If the organisation decides upon a sample, it needs to try to work out what is the best form of sampling e.g. quota sampling, random sampling, cluster sampling and so on.

If the railways wish to hand out questionnaires, this has the advantage of being quite cheap to do. It may mean that some questions will not be adequately answered and there is a problem that perhaps only those who have strong views which are probably negative about the survey will tend to fill them in, whereas other people will not bother to hand in replies. The problem of non-response is one which is not adequately dealt with in standard statistical techniques. If the organisation wishes to find information through a series of interviews then the railways would need to obtain suitable people to be interviewers.

If however it just the use of questionnaires then it will be almost certainly worthwhile having a pilot survey to check that the questions are adequate and unambiguous. Pilot surveys may show which of these questions do not conform to these criteria. For example a question which asks about the scheduled departure time of the train, may not mean much to passengers joining trains at Clapham Junction where for many destinations the trains are so frequent that people may well not know which train they are intending to catch. On the other hand if the train service was on the Heart of Wales line where there are one or two trains per day then clearly this information is more likely to be adequately answered. If a pilot survey has been carried out then any alterations to the questions will need to be considered and the questionnaire amended. If interviewers are to be used, then they need to be briefed about the precise meaning of the questions and will need to have sufficiently good personality to be able to answer any questions by passengers in a courteous manner.

Once the questionnaires have been returned, an initial vetting process might ensure that any answers are consistent. For example, if people say that they have no complaints about the railway journey, but then in another question complain bitterly about the service, then clearly this is not consistent.

In some cases, passengers on these surveys amongst many others may have no opinions about certain issues since they are non-applicable. For example, people who do not have a car are unlikely to have strong feelings about the adequacy or inadequacies of car parking arrangements. This may sound obvious but it is quite common on many questionnaires to be asked about car related items, which is clearly inapplicable to non-car owners.

After this, the results need to be tabulated in a way, which is helpful to the people, which have commissioned the people in the first place.

The fuel firms in the United Kingdom came under considerable scrutiny in 2013 about the adequacy of fuel supply with suggestions that larger customers might have to forego some of their supply between certain hours.

Fuel firms are meant to help their customers become more fuel efficient and this could be done by improving insulation, use of solar panels etc.

Question 9:

How far do managers in practice tend to use management and economic theory?

Frank Taylor 1868 – 1915 is very much associated with scientific management and in particular looked at the ways in which different size shovel could be used. He is however not the only member of scientific management and Lillian Gilbreth 1878 – 1972 tried to demonstrate that not merely could business methods be used within business organisations but also within the family since she wrote a book "Cheaper by the dozen", which suggested how large families could be brought up.

In modern management there are often what are called flat organisations, which have tried to reduce the chain of command and in some cases have reduced the number of layers of management. The usual assumption is that people at the senior level will make what is called strategic decisions. Middle management which includes, in most cases the managers of different departments such as the transport and distribution department or the personnel department will carry out operational level management. Junior level management, which would include supervisors, will carry out tactical management. In the past there has often been an assumption that the different genders have different qualities. It is assumed that male managers are more rational, more competitive and more assertive, whilst women are better at caring, emotional needs and tend to be more co-operative. It is never clear how far there are different attributes to men and women, and how much of it is conditioning. Women have often used the phrase glass ceiling, by which they can see the top management above them, but are unable to rise to this level. How far this is true would depend to some extent upon the society, although even here matters are changing. For example Lady Margaret Thatcher (1925-2013) famously said that she would not expect to see a women Prime Minister within her lifetime and yet she was the first and so far the only women Prime Minister of the UK from 1979 to 1990. It is sometimes assumed that women will not rise to the top for example within a Muslim culture until Benazir Bhutto became the leader of Pakistan.

One of the features that some writers such as Henry Mintzberg have looked at is the difference between what is thought to be the facts about management, and what in fact happens.

The assumption in most management textbooks is that the managers at the top should know the concept of strategic management. This implies that they should have an overall view of what is going on within the firm and then to make decisions about operational duties. In practise as Mintzberg points out if we look at many firms and also at the practise within the public sector we will find that in many cases that this is not true.

It is sometimes been suggested that British management in particularly has been characterised by anti-intelligence i.e. that managers often despise or say they despise theories even though they are strongly influenced by media projections of what management should be. This is nothing new; Lord Keynes suggested many years ago that most businesspersons were influenced by theories, which were out of date.

Whilst Weber stressed very strongly that there would be a series of written rules within the bureaucracy, in practise many managers strongly prefer to have oral forms of communication such as face to face with other members of staff and during meetings. John Cleese, actor and comedian has made a training video showing the effect of too many meetings entitled 'Meetings, Bloody Meetings'.

Scientific managers such as Henry L. Gantt (1861-1919) or Frank (1869-1924) and Lillian (1878-1972) Gilbreth looked at time and motion studies and assumed that as time went on these techniques would become more important to firms. In many cases, firms do not carry out operational research techniques as the rational theory suggests, but in fact make very pragmatic decisions.

The Mini was a major selling car although most competitors could not understand how it could be produced at such a low price. The answer was eventually discovered, was that it could not be made at that price and in fact had been loss making for many years.

One of the features found was that Japanese managers were much more likely to be technically qualified than those in the British ship building industry and that the Japanese were much more likely to use the management techniques which might be associated with scientific management.

Whilst anecdotal evidence is not conclusive, if we ask typical managers how much work they do, most of them would suggest that they suffer from overwork. Certainly, evidence to some extent from Social Trends and other government publications would suggest that the length of working hours in the UK is longer than in many of its competitor countries, which have remained competitive.

Delegation is frequently talked about in management textbooks, although many managers fail to delegate. This may be partly because the organisation does not allow this to happen, or it can be a feature of something i.e. an inferiority complex, meaning that they do not wish to delegate tasks to people who they might see as a threat.

One of the features, which have been prominent both under the previous Labour administration and under the present Coalition government, is how effective managers are within the public sector. This has led in many cases to the idea of the internal market within the National Health Service, which is supposed to ensure that managers become more effective. Part of the problem is how we measure effectiveness in both the private and the public sector. There has been little research done on the correlation between the high salaries which many managing directors achieve in the so-called Footsie firms, and the level of profitability. It is very noticeable that Ministers very rarely to have set targets for themselves. Jo Grimond the Liberal party leader from 1957 to 1967 suggested that there should be ways in which Ministers could be judged on their effectiveness, but this has never been carried out. In theory, managers should be able to set goals which can be quantified, and perhaps more importantly add to the value of the organisation. This may be more difficult since whilst some firms have moved towards the concept of cost centres in many cases there are interdependences between different activities. It could be argued for example within the Health Centre that the National Health Service is too often operated as a national sickness service and it might be better to concentrate on improving health. This does not necessarily have to be done within the National Health Service. Clearly better nutritional standards, which have been highlighted by Jamie Oliver, might help children to develop better diets. Many people were horrified at the very limited amount of money which was spent within the educational sector on school meals. Clearly, both adequate diet and adequate sleep patterns might well be beneficial.

For the nation as a whole people within local government, might well claim justifiably that improvements in sanitation following from the Chadwick reforms from the 19th century probably did more to help improve health than the activities of doctors and nurses even though these are of obvious importance.

In order to plan properly it is essential to have information which is helpful in the decision making process. This was clearly not the case for example in the Beeching reports in the 1960s, when the reshaping of British Rail closed seaside stations. This was because the revenue from those seaside stations was looked at which was often quite low because most people were going to those stations rather than buying tickets at those stations. In 2005, the BBC suggested that some of the educational improvements, which were claimed, were invalid. An example is schools wishing to improve in the league tables would use GNVQs which were counted as the equivalent of 4 GCSEs but which were not in fact of the same standard. Whether or not this criticism is right it is less important than the idea that we have to gather information, which is valid.

After this the information needs to be looked at to see how firms or organisations in the public sector can achieve these goals. In the case of the Health Service, for example it would be better to take an overall look at health education to determine what actions could be taken. For example if we look at the risks to individuals in the UK society clearly the major cause of preventable death is smoking with around 100 to 120 thousand deaths being attributable to this single cause. Therefore the government might need to see how this could be reduced. For example, they could produce more effective anti-smoking propaganda, or take measures to insure that shops do not sell to 'under 18s'. Drinking is more difficult to quantify. Apart from the deaths directly caused alcohol, it also causes deaths in terms of dangerous driving and violence. Clearly, not enough people were informed on this subject, as in 2005 when it seemed that many people were unaware that they were not supposed to buy alcohol for people under the 18. In practise alcohol abuse can start at a very early age.

Within commercial firms much the same concept are necessary. If a firm wants to achieve higher sales, it has to consider giving commission to people who will make more sales in the short term, but at the expense at the long term, since they sell products which are unsuitable and whereby people will not come back to buy such products in the future. The firm also needs to be able to measure whether it has achieved its aims. Clearly the concept of profit maximisation is not helpful, since how does a firm know whether it is actually achieving this. Therefore most firms would set out the concept that they will achieve so many sales with a total value of X million and with a number of staff which might be specified.

At a later stage perhaps at the end of the year, or sometimes with budgetary control at shorter intervals there will need to be devaluation of these plans. An analysis of variance may be helpful to judge by how far targets have not been reached because of external or internal factors.

There are many different types of leaders; one of these is the charismatic leader David Lloyd George (1863 to 1945) who was Prime Minister of Great Britain from 1916 to 1922. He came from quite humble beginnings whereas Sir Winston Churchill (1874 to 1965) who was Prime Minister in the war years from 1940 to 1945 and then again in peacetime from 1951 to 1955 is well known as an orator and perhaps particularly for his speech about fighting on the beaches. Perhaps his best known phrase which is used was in August 1940 when he commented "Never in the field of human conflict was so much owed by so many to so few" as a tribute to Royal Air Force. In other countries Mao Tse-Tung (1893 to 1976) and chairperson of the Communist party of the Peoples Republic of China from 1949 to 1976 was head of state from 1949 to 1959 is another example from history. He was extremely well known in the late 1960s for his so-called little red book. In the business field it could be argued that somebody such as Richard Branson who formed the Virgin Empire is charismatic and certainly he is much better known than most other businesspersons. It could be argued that charismatic leaders are born rather than made and they have this ability to persuade other people to follow them. There are also what might be called traditional leaders, which is usual hereditary position. This would include the Monarchy in the UK and could include tribal chiefs in other countries. Whilst it could be argued as with the charismatic leaders that the leadership cannot be learned, it could also be argued that their ability can be improved through training. Most business leaders are probably functional leaders. They have to lead because of the type of job they do. Training can be given to help them carry out these roles more effectively. For example, since Ancient Greece to the present day, it has been possible to train people to become better public speakers. There are a number of different styles however in carrying out functions and some will be democratic and encourage participate leadership whilst others are much more authoritarian. If we look at the political spectrum, for example it could be argued that somebody such as John Major Prime Minster of the UK from 1990 to 1997 would have engaged more in participative style of leadership, whereas both the late Lady Thatcher and Tony Blair would tend to be more autocratic. This was perhaps shown in the reaction and the events leading to up to the defeat on the terror motion in November 2005. There may also be bureaucratic leaders where the person holds a position of power because of a structure, for example the chief executive officer of a business or the head teacher of a school could be in this category. In the case of business, the chief executive might well be good at analysis problems but would not necessarily be at all charismatic. Within education, the role of the manager has changed from being as the name suggests the head teacher to being much more involved with budgeting, making personnel decisions and so on. The same is true of many other parts of the public sector.

Different jobs may require different types of management, although it is very noticeable with football managers that Arsène Wenger (the Arsenal manager) is much less prone to hysterical comments than many other football managers. The same is true of the current manager of England. When considering management styles managers will need to be aware of the different types of workers and what is likely to motivate them. Clearly, workers in the 21st century will be different in many ways to those of the start of the 20th century. The nature of jobs has changed with more workers being involved in white-collar jobs, compared with the predominance of the primary and secondary sectors in the early part of the 20th century. Whereas graduate education was very much a minority even amongst the richer members of society the previous Labour government aimed for 50% of people within the relevant age group to go to university or other equivalent education.

There are likely therefore to be more professional workers than in a previous era. In many cases these people may have motivation in terms of the positions which they hold. In some cases the names of the positions may be important to them. For example the author remembers interviewing one person for a job in local government and asking why they wanted to become the Borough Solicitor, one of the answers was that they thought that the title sounded good.

There is also what might be called the affluent workers, which are influence by the prospect of money. However, some people would dispute how far this would be true of the industry as a whole. The third category would be what might be regarded as some people in the political spectrum as Old Labour i.e. people who particularly in the coal mining, docks and other close knit communities would feel strongly that they wish to co-operate with each other and are motivated by this. They are much more likely to belong to trade unions than professional workers are, and will do this out of a sense of loyalty to the other members of the work force. Therefore, what would motivate these different categories is important.

It is very noticeable that ministers very rarely have set targets for themselves.
The assumption in the National Health Service has been that money will be the main motivator for both National Health Service trusts as well as general practitioners. One of the problems as the mid Staffordshire crisis showed in 2013 was that people were too obsessed with keeping targets, rather than checking whether the targets were sensible in the first place. The organisation was shown as being too autocratic where whistleblowers were often regarded as its sneaks. Too often there have been too many targets.

The government under both Labour and Conservatives has adopted what is called Neo-Liberalism; this means that the Private Sector is assumed to be more cost-effective than the Public Sector. The performance of G4S at the 2012 Olympics when over 2,000 soldiers had to replace security guards which G4S had not obtained put this theory under considerable scrutiny. The performance of the banks leading to the credit crunch 2008-9 onwards also meant that many independent commentators suggested that we needed to look at the individual organisations, rather than deciding that one sector was automatically better than the other. Although the Northern Rock building society failed, the performance of the building societies and other mutual organisations was generally better than the privately owned banks.

Question 10:

Why are commentators interested in definitions of size of organisations?

The size of a firm is not easily defined as the Bolton committee in 1971 discovered when it tried to look at small firms but failed to find a satisfactory definition. There are a number of different possibilities. We can look at the size measured by the number of employees. On this basis the Post Office, which has large numbers of workers will be a very large-scale organisation whereas an oil refinery, such as that of Fawley near Southampton will be relatively small.

We can define size in terms of the amount of assets, which the firm has. Clearly here, the oil refinery already mentioned will have very large-scale assets whereas another organisation such as the Post Office will have far less in the way of assets. Again, we could look at this within the context of the retail sector. A firm such as Harrods will have a large-scale building but also a high rate of turnover. Modern shops that sometimes looking more like warehouses will have relatively little in the way of assets but will rely on a high rate of stock turn for sales.

A third possibility, therefore, is to look at the volume of the sales of different firms. In some respects, this is helpful, since we can then more readily compare Harrods with other departmental stores and even the stores on the retail park, which tend to house firms such as Currys, Halfords etc.

However looking at the volume of sales will tend to exaggerate the differences between firms, which buy in items and the original producers. For example bread farmers get the total value of 20p for the wheat, whereas the miller perhaps buying in at 20p and selling at 30p will have higher sales. Therefore, we might want to modify this to look at the value, which has been added by the particular organisation. In many ways, this is more helpful. However, multi-nationals may have problems since they can alter their transfer prices between different countries to reduce the amount of taxation which they pay.

A firm which is vertically integrated may still only have the same volume of sales as one in which most of the processes are carried out by other firms (now often called 'outsourcing').

A third different method of measuring is that of looking at the gross or net profits. Net profit means after allowing for expenses and will usually be a better measure of size. Even if we look at net profit, this may vary between one year and another in industries which are subject to either the multiplier or the accelerator effect. The oil industry is one in which there are likely to be major changes in profits from one year to another, although this clearly does not necessarily reflect on the efficiency in which the firms have been managed. A firm, which relies on one major raw material such as copper, will find that its size varies considerably between one year and another. A firm such as Lonrho Africa will therefore find that the measures of turnover and profit may vary considerably. We also need to be careful, because if we are trying to make international comparisons the sudden change in the price, as with devaluation in the UK in 1949 and 1967, will make sales and profits look quite different if measured in terms of another currency.

The structure of the firm or industry may also be important. Structure can also refer to the type of market competition, whether the firm is in a monopoly market, an oligopoly or a competitive market.

It is sometimes difficult to look at the size of organisations since in the schools and Academy sector some schools have joined a confederation rather than being individually managed. The University of London is a federation so that with attention recently about the Russell Universities there have been fears expressed that it could split with some of the major parts such as London School of Economics being able to manage on their own.

Different commentators have different ideas on what is the ideal structure of organisations. Many commentators have suggested that the flat organisation where there are few layers of management is more helpful than when the chain of command is too long.

However, this will partly depend upon the geographical spread, and the functions within the organisation.

An organisation which is geographically concentrated in location is generally easier to manage than one which is widely dispersed. The more homogeneous the product, the easier it will be to manage than with a very diversified organisation. There have been concerns that larger organisations have a momentum of their own which makes it difficult for them to change direction. There have also been worries about monopoly and abuse.

Question 11:

How are size and strategy interrelated?

If we look at size and strategy, strategy means the overall way in which the firm is managed. A firm may well look to increase its size, through either organic growth or by takeovers and mergers. Some firms have grown rapidly through takeovers and mergers especially if they involve asset stripping, i.e., looking at the profitable components of a firm and discarding others. Hanson developed rapidly in this way.

Strategy may involve looking at which goods or services are normal goods as opposed to inferior goods (again to use the economists jargon). If there is an expectation of incomes rising, then the firm may well try to move out of basic goods, which appeal more to the poor and into ones in which both prices and profit margins are likely to be higher. On the other hand, in some cases the firm may simply try to alter the image of the product, so that it no longer is an inferior good. Inferior here means that as incomes rise the people buy less of the product. We can see this in the margarine industry, in which the giant multinational Unilever operates through its Stork brands, that the margarine industry has changed from one on which the emphasis has been price, to one on which the emphasis is on taste as well as on perceived nutritional values.

Firms may also try to grow through vertical or horizontal integration.

After some of the building societies became banks in 1986, whilst others remained building societies, they had greater scope. Then some of them tried to have a system of vertical integration by taking over estate agents. Part of the logic of this was that they could make some profit out of being estate agents but also that by owning groups of individual estate agents that the business was more likely to go through the building society or bank in the first place. However, this was not always successful. Whereas banks and building societies are in many ways akin to that of mass production with one customer's demands being very similar to another, this is much less true of estate agents where one house or flat could well appeal to one customer whilst the next customer with a similar income might think of it as completely unsuitable. Therefore in many ways estate agents is more akin to that of unit or one off production.

The structure of the industry and strategy may also be related. When for a long while IBM for many people was almost the trade name for large-scale computers, IBM could concentrate essentially on being able to produce better computers without being over concerned about rivals' reactions. However, as personal and small business computers became more common, IBM had to adapt to this demand partly by moving, after it made very heavy losses, into the consultancy field as well as moving to a more limited extent into the realm of business and personal computers.

Microsoft has often been accused by its rivals of being a monopolist and has faced court cases about how it tries to retain monopoly power through its strategy of ensuring that existing programmes are not always compatible with past ones. Usually it is possible to use a later programme but this may mean that existing data cannot readily be utilised.

The phrase too big to fail has been widely used of the banks, since the credit crunch 2008 onwards.

Part of the problem has been lack of good governance, whether it has been in the private or in the public sectors.

The bonus culture and short termism has been confirmed for the ways in which managers often work too optimistic about their ability to manage rapidly developing organisations. Part of the paradox which is not widely understood is that if we assume that money is the only motivator why should people work for the benefit of an organisation rather than for themselves.

In a small organisation the same problems still arise but it would be generally easier for one person to see what is happening overall and should be able to control the organisation, whereas with a larger organisation this is untrue.

Question 12:

Using examples discuss the factors that you would have to consider when deciding on the marketing mix for different countries?

Some of the factors will be the same, almost irrespective of the industry. The firm would need to consider the demographic features including not merely the size and gender of the relevant population but also the incomes. Average incomes may well be less important in South Africa or the USA than the number of people within the relevant income limits. This is partly because both South Africa and the USA have a very skewed income distribution compared with the Scandinavian countries.

In some cases, the firm will be able to overcome problems of income distribution by having a set of different prices, which may be either price discrimination or price differentiation. Price discrimination is different prices, which are not related to differences in cost. Price differentiation occurs when in many cases firms have the basic, standard and deluxe product. In some cases, it may be able to be possible to segregate markets by the income of the users to some extent. This would occur on the railways when Connex, the French company that formally ran services in the UK, would have adopted the common rail pricing system of having different fares for children and adults, which is clearly an example of price discrimination. It also wanted to continue with the Network South East Card being available at all times of the day and was the only operator to do so.

If we look at the book market then if a publisher who previously only sold books to the UK wanted to sell books to Kenya, they would have to think not only of price but also of promotion methods. In Kenya, would the people see advertisements on TV, or would they see them mainly in local newspapers, or through word of mouth? If it was mainly through word of mouth, then it might be sensible to approach agents in that country or in some cases to give the books free or at a reduced rate to people who they thought were decision makers.

One of the differences may be the different age structure for example whereas in the European Union, including the United Kingdom We often have an age structure where older people outnumber the young this is untrue in countries where the birth rate is much higher.

This might be important when thinking of the types of policies, which would appeal to people in the different sectors.

Sometimes the different geographical features would influence the demand. For example in landlocked countries the opportunity to go to the sea or ocean can have a novelty appeal. Similarly, winter holidays coming to the snow or mountains will have different appeals to people from different climatic conditions or people who simply want to go to an area with sunshine they be willing to their incomes are sufficient to travel long distances, mainly because of this.

Question 13:

Explain the difference between cooperative and non-cooperative games?

A cooperative game is one in which the firms or countries involved in production either explicitly or implicitly agree on tactics which will maximise the profit or sales of production for firms or countries as a whole. An example of this would be OPEC, which in 1973 to 1974 raised oil prices vary considerably through being able to restrict supply and thus being able to put up prices.

A non-cooperative game, on the other hand, is one in which the firms will fight for their own individual profits or sales irrespective of what happens to the other firms, and in some cases, as with predatory pricing, may even try to deliberately get rid of other firms.

> (i) Using examples discuss why and how businesses can wish to cooperate and why in some cases they may not be able to cooperate.

If we look at a cooperative features we could well find that the ideal is in many ways a product which is clearly homogenous in the eyes of the consumer. This would apply to oil, since the standards of oil can be clearly defined. This has also applied for a long while to airfares although in this case, because the products can clearly be different, bearing in mind the standards of service, the type of aircraft, there is a clearly defined formula to try to ensure that no one firm or national airline etc. could gain at the expense of the others.

Cooperation will arise when firms realise that they can make more money if they enforce either price collusion or preferably from their point of view price and quality of product collusion. This is likely to occur if the demand for the product is inelastic i.e. that they can raise the price for the good or service as a whole, without corresponding loss of sales. It would also be more likely to apply if there is a barrier to entry. Clearly this is the case, in the case of the oil industry. It will also apply if the governments favour cooperation rather than competition.

It will be easier to have cooperation if the shares of the market are reasonably constant.

Clearly if the governments themselves are the producers as in the case of oil production, then collusion is more likely and the same can be true of the airline market. Cooperation may also depend upon how honest or dishonest the government officials are. Clearly if government officials are dishonest and willing to take bribes then either one firm or a group of firms may find it relatively easy to sell goods or services at inflated prices, to the government sector.

Governments have sometimes tried to ensure that competition takes place for example by trying to insist that a genuine tendering process takes place rather than one in which the conditions are not transparent. For example within local authorities there are supposed to tenders, in many cases where the tenders have to be in writing and enclosed in plain envelopes so that there is no indication on the outside where the tender comes from and so that people could not favour one contract firm rather than another.

However, firms could get round the tendering process and have done in the past by agreeing beforehand that they will all tender for the same amount of money. Clearly, however, if all the contracts were exactly at the same amount then this might well arouse suspicion. Few people would think that it was an example of perfect competition, if for example all the contracts for a feasibility study or even more if all the contracts for a major building works came out to exactly 4 million and 1 thousand pound. Not just sellers can agree to cooperate. In the auction market, there has sometimes been what is called the ring i.e. the main buyers agree to bid low before the   auction and then will agree to pay a higher price between them at a later stage.

In the case of oil, the market is relatively straightforward to enforce since oil is readily transportable and the transport costs are only a relatively small part of another if one firm sold oil at a cheaper price to one customer, then that customer could clearly make a profit by reselling it. How far firms can engage in cooperative games will depend partly upon Government attitudes.

If the Government are very strongly in favour of competition, and this is rigorously enforced, then the firms may try to find ways around this. This could happen through instead of giving one price when it came to tendering for a contract, which would be clearly easily seen if all contracts were £44,731 then whilst this could be construed as an example of perfect competition?, most people would readily see it as a sign of collusion.

However, firms seeking ways around this will often counter any government moves. They might do this for example forming a cartel. A cartel means where a group of firms get together to agree on a price or supply for the market as a whole. The 'phases of the moon' collusion process is more difficult to detect than others are.

Firms therefore sometimes have got round this by having a "Phases of the Moon" collusion process. If there were four firms involved in a cartel, Firm A would be allowed to tender and obtain all the contracts in the first phase. Firm B in the second phase, etc. they may therefore have an agreement such as the phases of the moon to agree if say there were four sellers that one would get all the contracts in the first phase the next in the second phase and so on.

The airline agreement worked quite well for many years because most airlines were state airlines, and because airlines were run often for prestige as much as for other purposes The Governments were more concerned that they had a national airline than being over concerned about the exact amount of profitability.

There was also some need for cooperation since in many cases people could not go directly by one airline from one country to another, so that a ticket, which was valid for the entire journey, was clearly helpful. Even where airlines did serve one country to another, passengers, particularly business passengers, often wanted to be able to have, in effect, a more frequent service and so therefore, a ticket, which was valid on different airlines, was clearly helpful to those firms.

On the other hand, because the prices were artificially high, there was an incentive for the airlines to undercut this, but secretly. They could do this as they often did, through what was known as bucket shops, i.e., that if the price of a journey was say £400, then if the airlines knew they were not going to be able to fill up their aircraft, almost any revenue which they could obtain was going to be worthwhile for the empty seats. They therefore did not advertise these directly to the public, because this would have been seen by the rivals, but instead sold them on to people who could advertise them discretely.

An example, of a non-cooperative game could be found where firms adopt a system of predatory pricing. This is likely to occur where one firm has a much greater share of the market than another does. This is even more likely to occur if the dominant firm also has access to much greater resources than the firm with which it is trying to compete. After the breakdown of the IATA agreement, which has been described earlier, some newer firms such as Laker Airways (named after Freddie Laker) tried to get into the business. He claimed that the major airlines would then concentrate on having lower fares only on the routes on which he tried to operate, and that they could do this on the basis that once he was out of business on those routes, they could then go back and reinstate higher fares.

The same has been claimed about the bus industry, both in the 1920s before there was a great deal of legislation and in some cases after the 1980 and 1985 Transport Acts.

In this case, the emphasis on the bus industry was not so much on cheaper fares but on running buses, sometimes called "pirate buses". These buses are scheduled immediately ahead of their rivals so that, by concentrating on a few major bus stops they could pick up the majority of customers leaving the rival service only a few.

In the case of British Oxygen, then the tactics were simply to have the fighting companies often under a different name, which would get rid of the rival charging lower prices and then promptly disappear once the rival had gone out of the business.

Question 14:

Business and management is both multi-disciplinary and interrelated with many other disciplines. Using examples describe why it might be important for a manager to understand the psychology of business and management?

Business people might need to understand psychology when dealing with employees. They might think of Maslow and his hierarchy of needs, which ranges at the bottom from basic physiological factors, which include enough to eat, etc. to at the top self-actualisation, which means where people are able to develop their own talents to the greatest ability. Whilst it is usually regarded as a hierarchy, and indeed Maslow gave it this name, it could be argued that in many cases, firms need to be looking at several levels at the same time, since in many cases people will be operating on this basis.

The basic levels might be important for companies dealing with poorer people in Third World countries and even what is sometimes called the Fourth World i.e. poorer people in First World countries. If people do not have enough adequate food etc. then they are unlikely to be of much use to the firm anyway.

Marxists, whilst often critical of capitalist firms, will recognise that it is in the interest of management to do this.

Firms may need to know what motivates people to work in the first place. They might look at the McGregor X and McGregor Y theories. McGregor Y refers to people who inherently find work interesting, and this could include artisans in many jobs where the work might be regarded as inherently interesting. It could also apply to some jobs in the social scene such as teaching or social work where the job itself may provide some satisfaction. This is much less likely to be true, however, of the production line.

Businesspersons might also be aware of Elton Mayo and the Human Relations School. This experiment at the Hawthorne factory in the USA suggested that if managers took an interest in workers, then they are more likely to be motivated. Some later psychologists, however, have disputed these findings.

Whilst many managers, at least implicitly, seem to have assumed that the only psychology is either stick or carrot (i.e., threaten people or offer to give them better conditions) this does not always work, and the system of satisficing is often applied; i.e. that workers even with bonus schemes, will set themselves a series of targets. They will resent both chisellers (i.e. people who do not do enough) and rate breakers (i.e. people who they perceive as having done more work than they regard as desirable).

Business people too will look at psychology when considering the marketing of their products. They may look at the psychological grouping of the different consumers, which might be sub divided into reformers, i.e. those who would like to change society and might be more interested in green products and in ethical issues concerning employees and the environment. In recent years, there has been an increase in the volume of "Fair Trade", and organisations such as Traidcraft and Tearfund whilst still small have become more important. Even Nestlé has become more aware of this, and at least with some of its products has joined the fair trade movement. The green movement has gained some pace with countries signing up to the Kyoto agreement and because of natural disasters, which many people attribute to lack of interest in the environment. Businesspersons may either try to alter their advertising image or in some cases to alter their production methods to take account of this. Another group is the aspirers - clearly, the car market is often geared in its male image to producing cars, which have great acceleration. Advertising how quickly a car can accelerate from 0 – 60mph seems to not make sense, as it is difficult to see when the car owner would need to do this. The marketing image here will almost certainly denote somebody in a more unusual environment of relatively open roads, rather than the more common use of cars in the urban environment.

Firms may also look at the achievers, i.e. people who have already achieved their aims in material terms, and clearly, the upper end of the car market such as the Rolls-Royce, the Daimler, and some of the Mercedes cars will appeal to these people.

Another psychological grouping is that of conservatives and these people will often like things to remain as they have been. If we argued that particularly in the UK, there is often a nostalgia market which would almost certainly find that most of the people shopping in their shops would be part of this market, whereas people shopping in the body shop will probably belong to the former group. The housing market is another market in which it is possible to see the different groups being catered for. The use of "exclusive" in much of the advertising (although it is never quite clear who it is meant to exclude) is common place. The image, whether on television or in newspapers, is one which tries to reinforce the image which they feel is going to appeal most to the potential buyers.

Firms may well use what is sometimes called "psychological pricing", with prices of £999 rather than £1000. It is possible to see this on much advertising where the major electrical chains will advertise a particular product as being under £100; under £1000 etc. At the same time, they may be appealing to other aspects by advertising how quickly the computer processes information, even though in many cases the consumers are very unlikely to be aware of what these terms mean.

Clearly if one was advertising a high price product such as a Rolls Royce, this is much more likely to be brought in the richer areas rather than the poorer ones. Therefore, if the firm were doing any local advertising it would advertise these in high-income areas such as that of Tunbridge Wells in Kent rather than in the poorer areas. Census data might also indicate as it does with cars that there are differences in car ownership between the rural areas where car ownership is much higher per thousand populations than it is in the urban areas.

The firms particularly in the electronics industry may be able to sell more to their existing customers, for example by in the television sector, by offering a wider range of channels, which can be viewed than with the existing package. Recently most of the firms will have tried to persuade their customers to move away from standard cable television to a digital package. This is cheaper for the companies concerned. In the case of the computer industry, they may offer to expand the amount of information, which can be available through the Internet and the speed at which information can be processed.

The pilot survey might reveal that the answers particularly on a tick list do not include all those which the customers might want to use. For example, a rail survey might show where customers can write in some answers as their main concern may be about carrying heavy luggage or shopping up and down stairs. It might be noted here that in Germany in most cases stations have in effect a conveyor belt running alongside the stairs, so that it is much easier for passengers to carry such items. In many cases, as well the problem might be avoided by having the station platforms at one level and perhaps longer platforms so that people do not have to use stairs, lifts or even escalators to go from one train to another. A pilot survey might help to show that this is something which needs to be investigated further.

In the case of the clothing industry, feminists have often complained about the portrayal of models (sometimes called supermodels) as the image which people should aspire to.

The concept of "new" to mean "good" is very common in both the fashion industry and in the CD and DVD industry.

Environmentalists would often criticise firms for being environmentally irresponsible by trying to ensure that computer printers become outdated within a year and in 2005 estimated that one of the major computer printer manufacturers tried to ensure that their product had a life of not more than one year. John Kenneth Galbraith, the veteran American economist, has called this Built-in Obsolescence.

Businesspersons might also wish to employ psychology to try to ensure that where there would otherwise be hostility, that this does not take place. Some of the large supermarkets have tried to ensure that there is less hostility to their projects by putting in a new park, road or other feature which is considered desirable by local residents (which they are able to do under Section 106 Agreements). Major developers may also use this approach, although in some cases they try to get away with the minimum possible, by leaving 10% of the space but with only very small plots of land, which cannot be used by the community.

Tesco, who enjoyed a bad reputation when part of their building work on a new store in Buckinghamshire fell down in 2005 and blocked a mainline railway for many weeks. They tried to make some amends by providing some contribution to a replacement bus service.

Question 15:

Discuss the different forms of pressure groups that exist, and their possible influence on businesses to act responsibly.

There are different types of pressure group; some are permanent, whilst others are ad-hoc. Permanent pressure groups include Greenpeace, and Friends of The Earth, who are, as their name implies, interested in environmental issues. They do, however, tend to adopt quite different methods. Friends of The Earth have a magazine, which is available to its supporters on a regular basis, and will frequently appear on the media to argue about particular items. This has been particularly true since the Kyoto Agreement. Greenpeace, on the other hand, is more aggressive in its approach, and may use methods such as sailing in the Pacific to protest about certain features. It came unfortunately to prominence when the French Government was responsible for the death of an individual on the Rainbow Warrior, which was sunk in 1985 by the French intelligence services.

Friends of The Earth, by constant pressure on local authorities and central government, may have been partially responsible for the setting up of so-called LA21 Agreements, which in many cases means that local authorities have appointed people under this heading to look at the environment. In 2014, it could be argued that, partly because of pressure by such groups, those local authorities were required to look at environmental issues across the whole range of planning, and not just with new developments of housing. This would include the energy consumption by firms or factories directly, but also indirectly to take account of the green transport plans, which might mean that they provide a bus service or encourage people to commute to and from work in shared cars or by public transport.

In 2014, Friends of the Earth were opposing the use of fracking, saying that it could harm water supplies. Local residents in some areas were also forming their own pressure groups to fight the concept anyway.

The oil and other fossil fuel suppliers have also in both the UK and USA often acted as a pressure group. Sharon Beder of the University of Wollongong has shown how the fuel producers have tried to manipulate public opinion. This may include sponsoring University chairs as well as local projects.

In 2014, Pussy Riot have used a variety of methods including music videos and staging an unauthorised performance in a cathedral in Moscow to highlight the problems in Russia and have been harassed as a result. The problems include undemocratic approaches of the Putin government. More details about them can be found on the internet.

Question 16:

Discuss what is meant by knowledge management. What are the advantages and disadvantages of using technology to manage knowledge?

Knowledge management means the knowledge which is available to both managers and workers within a business. It has become increasingly important as websites and Internet material has become much more widely available to people not just within the developing world but also the developed world. The range of material on websites and the introduction of large-scale search engines, which connect millions of websites such as Google and Yahoo, have meant that information can be found very readily on a whole range of subjects. Part of the problem however, is that whilst it is possible for example with the Internet to find information, it is often more difficult to classify it than for example within the library system.

If for example we want to look up about South Africa or Uganda we can quickly do so. However, because the information on the Internet has frequently not been vetted this may lead to many problems. The authenticity and accuracy of information collected on the internet is still not reliable. However, authenticated websites such as the School of African Studies in Oxford may, by the virtue of the reputation of Oxford University, be relied on.

For example, we can compare it with a conventional textbook within a library; we can look at the authors, publishers and decide how far we find these people will have confidence for the tasks, which they have set themselves. The Dewey system, which is widely found in British libraries, means that as well as the ISBN numbers means that it is easy to get information very quickly about what books are available within the library system.

Most people as well find that hard copies are much easier to read than to try to get information from a screen. The internet has the advantage that it can be much more up to date taking account of developments which have occurred for example for European managers the enlargement of the EU in 2013 which would not be available in most textbooks. However, the internet frequently can be misused for example, people may spend a considerable time within the firms searching the internet for items, which they find of interest rather than being beneficial to the firm. It is also unfortunately being used in terms of emails etc. to send pornography as well as rude messages to other people.

The knowledge management can be very helpful for example within the UK, the Office of National Statistics has made available information such as Social Trends which before had to be brought in expensive book form and also the internet makes it much easier to refer quickly to the relevant tables. This has been very useful for example to the authors when producing their books.

The government have found it more difficult to control information, which has led in some cases to problems, but also makes it more difficult for authoritarian governments to censor information about what is going on outside the borders.

Question 17:

If an organisation wishes to introduce changes, what reactions might it anticipate and how does it overcome them? Explain using relevant organisations.

When an organisation wishes to introduce changes, the first reaction is often one of denial. Many staff will deny that there is any need for change. Staff may go further than this and say that "we have always done things this way and therefore there is no reason to change." This reaction is not confined to one class of employees. There were very strong reactions from senior medical staff before the introduction of the National Health Service in 1948 and there are some parallels to this in 2013. There are also similar reactions to changes in the way that police forces are managed in 2013. This reaction is sometimes known as a conservative viewpoint, although it can be equally argued that some managers want continuous change without thinking whether the changes will actually improve the organisation's performance. Therefore, an organisation may set out the evidence for what it wishes to do unless this will contravene commercial confidentiality. This could apply to public sector organisations such as the NHS or to private sector organisations such as car manufacturers. Tony Blair (the former Prime Minister) referred to the forces of conservatism. One of the problems particularly in large scale organisations is that the grapevine will often come into operation and there will be often exaggerated fears of the number of redundancies or other effects. This could include the number of people who might have to relocate. It is therefore generally better to consult workers for several different reasons. The first reason is that if people are not consulted, all people will feel that they will be worse off. A smaller group of workers who may be adversely affected may well be outnumbered by the larger number who are not. The second is that employees may have better ideas than the management of how to improve the organisation. This is particularly likely where the organisation is geographically dispersed or when there are a wide variety of activities which means that it is difficult for a single manager or even a small group to have an overall feel of the whole organisation.

NHS Example

In the public sector, the National Health Service is a major employer and it is difficult for either ministers or senior health officials to have data which is very clear. If the objective of the NHS is to reduce the number of deaths in particular areas, traditional approaches of waiting for illnesses to occur and then to treat them may be inappropriate. Listening to Doctors and other medical staff within the NHS may be helpful since causes of ill health will differ partly according to locality and partly according to social class and ethnic origin. There is often a need for joined up thinking. Sometimes, as in 2013, the same number of hospital beds could be used more affectively if social services had an adequate number of places for post-operative patients to go to.

Attempts to reduce the number of workers within the National Health Service might be popular with certain sections of the media. However for many people the NHS is the only provider. Whilst it has been assumed that competition will bring down costs, the evidence for this and whether it helps to improve health is less clear-cut. Pressure to reduce the number of immigrants including state education for overseas people outside the European Union could be counter-productive since the NHS relies to a very large extent on people outside the European Union for most medical staff below the rank of consultant.

In 2013 there was immense pressure upon NHS expenditure. Many doctors and other medical staff suggested that one way of reducing NHS costs would be by reducing the volume of smoking in the first place.

It is estimated that around 100,000 people die in the United Kingdom each year from smoking. Of particular concern in the NHS was that around 15% of pregnant women smoked which could cause harm therefore to future generations it was estimated that around 15% of 15-year-olds also smoked. Therefore campaigners wish to reduce these percentages and set up as a set of targets which would confirm whether or not these targets had achieved.

One way of achieving this would be to reduce the attractiveness of cigarette packets by having plain paper packets since it was assumed following the Australian example that this would be effective. Other people might have wished to deter smoking by making much more graphic images about what happens to smokers. Research seems to indicate that telling people that smoking might lead to amputation of a certain limbs was more effective than saying smoking kills. Other causes of NHS expenditure would be many things which are caused by poor diet such as diabetes. It has been suggested that therefore that not allowing fast food firms to be within a limited range of schools and also ensuring that healthy school meals were available at reasonable costs to pupils and that lunch boxes would be scrutinised to check that bought in snacks were healthy would result in better health overall. The professionals therefore were trying to move to a state where the NHS was as it says a national health service rather than a national sick service.

Poor air quality was also a major killer and a cross party report chaired by Tim Yeo MP has suggested that in 2010 around 45,000 people died from road pollution. This was generally held to be regressive since the poorer people lived in areas subject to worse air quality whereas they had not caused it in the first place. The government could try to reduce this by encouraging more people to use alternative to the car as well as encouraging organisations to have green plans. Additionally we could try to encourage individuals and firms to use cars for several people rather than one if it was not possible to transfer to public transport or cycling following the success of British cyclists in the Olympics in 2012 many people were hoping that the government might encourage cycling still further.

Alcoholism kills around 8000 people in the United Kingdom each year directly; it will also kill people indirectly for example through drink driving. There have been suggestions for a minimum price of alcohol which has been introduced in Scotland but the United Kingdom government has ruled this out for England and Wales, whilst people under the age of 18 cannot legally buy alcohol in the UK. This checking of age is relatively small in most countries including the UK. There are certain drugs that are banned. How far this is evaded is not necessarily clear.

In the private sector, following the Bangladesh factory tragedy which killed over 1,000 people in 2013, better systems of management and safety procedures from the large clothing buyers would help both the workers and in the longer term management.

Many of the major retailers including the supermarkets bought items from Bangladesh. In the long term, the amount of money which is needed to be spent to improve safety would be relatively negligible compared to the amount going to the actual producers.

There was scope for pressure groups to put pressure on the major firms. This would be nothing new in the 18th century the boycott of sugar took place to put pressure on slave owners to give up the trade.

Question 18:

How can firms use the Ansoff matrix?

Market Penetration

Many organisations may use the Ansoff growth matrix to see how they can attempt to improve their business through growth. One of the phrases which is used is market penetration. This means where the business looks at existing customers and existing products and to see how it could sell more.

One method of trying to do this might be to reduce the price of the product. This may be applicable where the marginal cost of the product is very low as for example with off peak travel or with music where producing more CD's or enabling people to download material. Another might be to combine this with market segmentation and using price discrimination and price differentiation. For example this can be used in the travel trade where very low prices can be charged on certain ships with dormitory class. Price discrimination can be used to segregate the young people with less money and possibly poorer old-age pensioners. Price discrimination may apply in a similar way to entertainment where stand-by sales are fairly common.

Sometimes greater sales promotion may mean that more people become aware of the product. This will apply with electronic products.
Sometimes firms use loyalty cards to try to sell more of particular products to their existing customers. They may use these to sell complimentary products for example petrol to people who are already coming to the stores. They may also advertise that if people spend more than a particular amount for 3 consecutive weeks that they will give a suitable discount.

Market Development

Market development applies where the organisation tries to sell existing products into new markets. In 2013 this could have applied to selling more goods and services to Croatia as it became the 28th member of the European Union. It could also apply as more organisations try to export to the Chinese market which is still rapidly growing and organisations could use link to China as a method of doing this.

New transport facilities for example the proposed opening of a direct rail passenger route between London and Germany in 2015 might help in the tourist trade especially as some people have a fear of flying.

In the clothes trade it could be selling different types of clothes to different groups e.g. possibly to different ethnic groups, to different income groups, or to different religious groups.

Product Development

Organisations might also aim to introduce new products into existing markets. This could apply to more healthy foods especially where there have been problems of mislabelling of meat in particular.

It could also apply to the phone market where the major organisations are trying very hard to bring in even more features to the market.

As more organisations deliver products online the cost of delivering more products to the same people is often negligible and therefore organisations will try many methods to try to persuade people to buy more items at the same time. They may use the information "cookies" store to suggest similar items to previously viewed or purchased items..

The supermarkets have diversified into the financial sector partly because many people are buying on credit cards and debit cards and therefore may be willing to bank with the supermarket especially if the supermarket will give a low rate of interest on its own credit card.

Diversification

This is where an organisation sells new products in new markets. Organisations such as Virgin may do this partly because the name is a very strong one, and the brand well established. It is however, a risky course of action. There have been several examples where organisations have attempted to sell products to countries to which they have not previously exported and not always realised that cultural problems can arise.

Question 19:

Can we use the stakeholder model for the privatisation of the Royal Mail announced in October 2013?

Employees

The employees were going to gain immediately because they were each given 725 free shares. However, in spite of this the workers in the Communication Workers Union voted by a majority of 4 to 1 to go on strike because they feared that their conditions of work and possibility of redundancy was a greater threat than the opportunity to have these shares.

Sub-Post Masters

In the UK there are many Post Offices run by sub-post masters/mistresses who are self-employed and in many cases also sell.

Shareholders (Private and Institutional)

The private shareholders were allocated shares in full if they had asked for either £750 of shares or less. There was an immediate rise in the share price once the launch was underway so that those shareholders that wanted a quick gain were rewarded. Other potential shareholders were not allocated any shares. The institutional shareholders gained especially those who gave advice to the government about the share issue. They might also gain in the long run, if the company was run successfully in financial terms.

Customers

It is uncertain particularly in rural areas whether the customers would gain. There were concerns that the price of postage might be increased in order to improve profitability for shareholders. Because of the peculiarities of the way that the public borrowing requirement is calculated, the government could welcome a reduction in the debt. The Post Offices had closed many branches in both urban and rural areas and there were fears that this trend might be accelerated. Business customers in particular might also be concerned if the trend to have a longer time for delivery meant that they received post later in the day which would not necessarily be very helpful.

There were also concerns that the government might wish to reduce costs by telling customers in rural areas to pick up letters and parcels from a central point rather than having the post delivered. This has applied in some other countries.

Overseas customers might also be concerned if there were delays in either deliveries to the UK or from the UK.

Environmentalists

Environmentalists might be concerned since whilst the Post Office had signed up to a greener agenda that the Post Office might not keep to this if it got in the way of profits. It would usually be greener to send post as far as possible by rail rather than by road haulage but this would not necessarily be the financially cheapest method. In towns, deliveries by bike or foot would be greener than by van but again this would not necessarily be the cheapest. Similarly, electric or hybrid vans would often be very suitable since with constant stop go driving conditions the emissions would be quite high with conventional vans.

Competitors

Competitors had already gained from the reduction in restrictions on competition to the Royal Mail. This had resulted in more competition from parcel firms. There are also concerns that organisations such as WH Smith (the newsagents) might be able to have more Post Offices within their premises. The workers fear this since they thought that this might lead to poorer conditions for their members.

Bibliography

These books and reports have been chosen due to their readability and interest.

Chapter 1:

Business and Enterprise Studies- Geoffrey Whitehead (9780434922086)

Chapter 2:

Finance Information and Business (Business Explained) - Malcolm Surridge , Tony Bushell, Philip Gunn (9780003223132)

Organizational Behaviour - David A. Buchanan, Andrzej A. Huczynski (9780273728221)

Chapter 3:

Business and Enterprise Studies - Geoffrey Whitehead (9780434922086)

Lean Manufacturing at Volvo Truck Production Australia - http://epubl.ltu.se/1402-1617/2005/222/LTU-EX-05222-SE.pdf

The Machine That Changed the World: The Story of Lean Production-- Toyota's Secret Weapon in the Global Car Wars That Is Now Revolutionizing World Industry - James P Womack, Daniel T Jones, Daniel Roos (9780743299794)

Chapter 4:

Who Profits? - Richard Adams (9780745916064)

Spedan's Partnership: The Story of John Lewis and Waitrose - Peter Cox (9780955187728)

Small Is Beautiful: A Study of Economics as if People Mattered - E F Schumacher (9780099225614)

Chapter 5:

The Mid Staffordshire NHS Foundation Trust Public Inquiry - Chaired by Robert Francis QC -http://www.midstaffspublicinquiry.com/report

Realising the Potential of GB Rail – Report of the Rail Value for Money Study - https://www.gov.uk/government/uploads/system/uploads/attachment_data/file/4203/realising-the-potential-of-gb-rail-summary.pdf

I Tried to Run a Railway - Gerard Fiennes (9780711004474)

Chapter 6:

Business Stripped Bare: Adventures of a Global Entrepreneur - Sir Richard Branson (9780753515037)

Small Is Beautiful: A Study of Economics as if People Mattered - E F Schumacher (9780099225614)

Organizational Behaviour - David A. Buchanan, Andrzej A. Huczynski (9780273728221)

Chapter 7:

The Frontiers of Management: Where Tomorrow's Decisions Are Being Shaped Today - Peter F. Drucker (9781422131572)

Supervisory Management - David Evans (9780826457332)

The Human Side of Enterprise - Douglas Mcgregor (9780071462228)

Chapter 8:

The Frontiers of Management: Where Tomorrow's Decisions Are Being Shaped Today - Peter F. Drucker (9781422131572)

Chapter 9:

Introduction to Transport Economics: Demand, Cost, Pricing, and Adoption - David J Spurling (9781599428987)

Public Accounts Committee - Twenty-Second Report High Speed 2: a review of early programme preparation - http://www.publications.parliament.uk/pa/cm201314/cmselect/cmpubacc/478/4780 2.htm

Cost-Benefit Analysis - Richard Layard, Stephen Glaister (9780521466745)

Transport Problem - C.D. Foster (9780856641770)

Chapter 10:

An Introduction to Accounting – Gachihi James, Spurling David (9781845491437)

Success in Principles of Accounting: Student's Book - Geoffrey Whitehead (9780719572128)

Chapter 11:

Finance Information and Business (Business Explained) - Malcolm Surridge, Tony Bushell , Philip Gunn (9780003223132)

Introduction to Transport Economics: Demand, Cost, Pricing, and Adoption - David J Spurling (9781599428987)

An Introduction to Accounting - Gachihi James, Spurling David (9781845491437)

Chapter 12:

Success in Principles of Accounting: Student's Book - Geoffrey Whitehead (9780719572128)

An Introduction to Accounting - Gachihi James, Spurling David (9781845491437)

Chapter 13:

An Introduction to Accounting - Gachihi James, Spurling David (9781845491437)

Chapter 14:

Back to Front: Efficiency of back office functions in local government – http://archive.audit-commission.gov.uk/auditcommission/sitecollectiondocuments/AuditCommissionReports/NationalStudies/BackToFront8Oct08REP.pdf

Introduction to Transport Economics: Demand, Cost, Pricing, and Adoption - David J Spurling (9781599428987)

Chapter 15:

PCs For Dummies - Dan Gookin (9780470465424)

The Hutchinson Dictionary of Computing, Multimedia and the Internet - Helicon Books (9781859862872)

Chapter 16:

Survey Methods in Social Investigation - Sir Claus Moser, Graham Kalton (9781855214729)

Experimental Statistics Using MINITAB - Colin Weatherup, Arima Publishing (9781845492083)

Business Statistics For Dummies - Alan Anderson (9781118630693)

Journal of the Royal Statistical Society: Statistics and Society - Wiley –Blackwell Volume 176 part 1 January 2013 - http://www.rss.org.uk/site/cms/contentChapterView.asp?chapter=1

Chapter 17:

People in Organisations – Norman Smith,Hilary Vigor (9780198327523)

The Managerial Grid Paperback - Robert Rogers Blake, Jane Srygley Mouton (9780884152521)

Chapter 18:

How to win friends and influence people- Dale Carnegie (9780091906818)

Elton Mayo: the Hawthorne experiments - An article from Thinkers

Selected Writings on Utilitarianism - Jeremy Bentham (9781840221114)

Motivation for Dummies - Gillian Burn (9780470760352)

Chapter 19:

The Uses of Literacy: Aspects of Working-Class Life - Richard Hoggart (9780141191584)

Harvard Business Review on Communicating Effectively - Harvard Business Review (9781422162514)

Chapter 20:

The Frontiers of Management: Where Tomorrow's Decisions Are Being Shaped Today - Peter F. Drucker (9781422131572)

Chapter 21:

Captive State: The Corporate Takeover of Britain - George Monbiot (9780330369435)

Competition Commission Private Healthcare market investigation - http://www.competition-commission.org.uk/our-work/directory-of-all-inquiries/private-healthcare-market-investigation

Competition Commission Report on Airports 2008 - http://www.competition-commission.org.uk/assets/competitioncommission/docs/pdf/non-inquiry/press_rel/2008/aug/pdf/24-08

Chapter 22:

Positioning: The Battle for Your Mind - Al Ries, Jack Trout (9780071373586)

The Hidden Persuaders - Vance Packard (9780978843106)

Marketing Made Simple - Geoff Lancaster, Paul Reynolds (9780750647717)

Marketing For Dummies - Ruth Mortimer, Gregory Brooks, Craig Smith, Alexander Hiam (9781119965169)

Chapter 23:

Teach Yourself Successful Market Research in a Week - Judy Bartkowiak (9781444159646)

Positioning: The Battle for Your Mind - Al Ries, Jack Trout (9780071373586)

The Hidden Persuaders - Vance Packard (9780978843106)

Marketing Made Simple - Geoff Lancaster, Paul Reynolds (9780750647717)

Marketing For Dummies - Ruth Mortimer, Gregory Brooks, Craig Smith , Alexander Hiam (9781119965169)

Chapter 24:

Positioning: The Battle for Your Mind - Al Ries, Jack Trout (9780071373586)

The Hidden Persuaders - Vance Packard (9780978843106)

Marketing Made Simple - Geoff Lancaster, Paul Reynolds (9780750647717)

Marketing For Dummies - Ruth Mortimer, Gregory Brooks, Craig Smith ,Alexander Hiam (9781119965169)

Chapter 25:

The Frontiers of Management: Where Tomorrow's Decisions Are Being Shaped Today - Peter F. Drucker (9781422131572)

2013 International Trade Survey - http://www.britishchambers.org.uk/policy-maker/policy-reports-and-publications/2013-international-trade-survey.html

The European Union Readings on the Theory of European Integration - Lynne Rienner Publishers(9781588262318)

Towards One Europe - Stuart De La Mahotiere (9780140212020)

The Arms Bazaar - Anthony Sampson (9780340225943)

The Seven Sisters - Anthony Sampson (9780553242379)

The European Imperative: Economic and Social Cohesion in the 1990s - Stuart Holland (9780851245577)

Both Sides Of The Coin: The Arguments for the Euro and European Monetary Union - James Forder And Christopher Huhne (9781861973214)

UNA - U.K. Global development goals leaving no one behind - http://www.una.org.uk/news/13/10/leaving-no-one-behind-una-uk-releases-major-development-publication

Chapter 26:

The Changing anatomy of Britain - Anthony Sampson (9780394531434)

The State We're In - Will Hutton (9781446483442)

After Leveson? - The Future for British Journalism - John Mair, Arima publishing (9781845495763)

2010 A Blueprint For Change - Malcolm Blair-Robinson, Arima publishing (9781845493912)

Bring on the Apocalypse: Six Arguments for Global Justice - George Monbiot (9781843546566)

The Spirit Level: Why Equality is Better for Everyone - Richard Wilkinson, Kate Pickett (9780241954294)

100 Ways to Save the World - Johann Tell (9781905825400)

23 Things They Don't Tell You About Capitalism - Ha-Joon Chang (9780141047973)

Happiness: Lessons from a New Science - Richard Layard (9780241952795)

Living in a Low Carbon World Dr Mayer Hillman - http://www.mayerhillman.com/portals/0/PSI%20UKERC%20Low%20Carbon%20Conference.pdf

Kyoto Protocol United Nations framework convention on climate change - http://unfccc.int/resource/docs/convkp/kpeng.pdf

Unburnable carbon 2013: Wasted capital and Stranded assets - http://carbontracker.live.kiln.it/Unburnable-Carbon-2-Web-Version.pdf

Chapter 27:

Economics explained - Peter Maunder, Danny Myers, Nancy Wall, Rodger LeRoy, Miller Collins (9780003277586)

Business Law - Dennis Keenan, Sarah Riches (978-1408254196)

Who Runs This Place? The Anatomy of Britain in the 21st Century – Anthony Sampson (9780719565663)

Friends in High Places: Who Runs Britain? - Jeremy Paxman (9780140156003)

Land Value Taxation - www.parliament.uk/briefing-papers/SN06558.pdf

DHL/BCC Trade Confidence Index Q4 12 - http://www.britishchambers.org.uk/policy-maker/policy-reports-and-publications/dhl/bcc-trade-confidence-index-q4-12.html

Chapter 28:

Suffer the Children: The Story of Thalidomide - Knightley, Phillip; Evans, Harold; Potter, Elaine; Wallace, Marjorie (9780233968735)

Greenpeace: How a Group of Ecologists, Journalists, and Visionaries Changed the World - Rex Weyler (9781551925295)

Chapter 29:

Work in the Future - John Osmond Thorsons (9780722512456)

Religion and the rise of capitalism - R.H Tawney (9781406724189)

The Condition of the Working Class in England - Friedrich Engels (9780199555888)

Chapter 30:

Personal Practice - Malcolm Martin and Tricia Jackson (9781843981022)

Business As Unusual: The Journey of Anita Roddick and the Body Shop - Anita Roddick (9780722539873)

Making It Happen: Reflections on Leadership - Sir John Harvey-Jones and John H Jones (9781861976918)

Models of My Life - Herbert Simon (9780262691857)

Chapter 31:

Managing change - Colin Carnall (9780273704140)

The organization man - William H Whyte (9780812218190)

Chapter 32:

The Future of Europe: Towards a Two-Speed EU? - Jean-Claude Piris (9781107662568)

Chapter 33:

EasyJet: The Story of Britain's Biggest Low-cost Airline - Lois Jones (9781845130930)

Chapter 34:

The Crisis of Global Capitalism: Open Society Endangered - George Soros (9781891620270)

A Contemporary Guide to Economics, Peace, and Laughter - John Kenneth Galbraith (9780395120958)

Interdependence and Survival: Population Policies and Environmental Control - Baroness Beatrice Nancy Seear (9780951204719)

No-Nonsense Guide to Climate Change - Danny Chivers (9781906523855)

No-Nonsense Guide to Green Politics - Derek Wall (9781906523398)

No-Nonsense Guide to World Food - Wayne Roberts (9781780261317)

Chapter 35:

What they don't teach you at Harvard Business school - Mark McCormack, John Boswell Associations (9780553345834)

Soft Energy Paths: Towards a Durable Peace - Amory B. Lovins (9780060906535)

Poverty: A Study of Town Life - Benjamin S Rowntree (9781145153288)

Index